Introduction to Ansible Network Automation

A Practical Primer

Brendan Choi
Erwin Medina

Apress®

Introduction to Ansible Network Automation: A Practical Primer

Brendan Choi
Sydney, NSW, Australia

Erwin Medina
Sydney, NSW, Australia

ISBN-13 (pbk): 978-1-4842-9623-3
https://doi.org/10.1007/978-1-4842-9624-0

ISBN-13 (electronic): 978-1-4842-9624-0

Managing Director, Apress Media LLC: Welmoed Spahr
Acquisitions Editor: Divya Modi
Development Editor: James Markham
Editorial Assistant: Divya Modi

Cover designed by eStudioCalamar

Cover image by Freepik (www.freepik.com)

Distributed to the book trade worldwide by Springer Science+Business Media New York, 1 New York Plaza, Suite 4600, New York, NY 10004-1562, USA. Phone 1-800-SPRINGER, fax (201) 348-4505, e-mail orders-ny@springer-sbm.com, or visit www.springeronline.com. Apress Media, LLC is a California LLC and the sole member (owner) is Springer Science + Business Media Finance Inc (SSBM Finance Inc). SSBM Finance Inc is a **Delaware** corporation.

For information on translations, please e-mail booktranslations@springernature.com; for reprint, paperback, or audio rights, please e-mail bookpermissions@springernature.com.

Apress titles may be purchased in bulk for academic, corporate, or promotional use. eBook versions and licenses are also available for most titles. For more information, reference our Print and eBook Bulk Sales web page at http://www.apress.com/bulk-sales.

Any source code or other supplementary material referenced by the author in this book is available to readers on GitHub at https://github.com/Apress/Introduction-to-Ansible-Network-Automation-by-Brendan-Choi-and-Erwin-Medina. For more detailed information, please visit https://www.apress.com/gp/services/source-code.

Paper in this product is recyclable

Table of Contents

About the Authors

 **Brendan Choi** is a highly accomplished tech lead at Secure Agility, with over 19 years of hands-on experience in the ICT industry. He is a certified Cisco, VMware, and Fortinet Engineer and has worked for renowned enterprises such as Cisco Systems, NTT (Dimension Data), and Fujitsu, as well as reputable Australian IT integrators like Telstra and Secure Agility. Brendan specializes in optimizing enterprise IT infrastructure management and enterprise business process optimization, utilizing both open and proprietary tools. He is the author of *Python Network Automation: By Building an Integrated Virtual Lab* as well as *Introduction to Python Network Automation: The First Journey*. Through these publications, Brendan shared his knowledge with the IT community. He has trained over 200 network and systems engineers on Python and Ansible Network Automation and enjoys sharing industry-acquired knowledge through social media, blogging, and his YouTube channel. Brendan's current interests revolve around private cloud, enterprise networking, security, virtualization, Linux, and automation technologies. His dedication and passion for enterprise infrastructure management are evident in his commitment to continuous learning, knowledge sharing, and contributing to the ICT industry as a whole.

Erwin Medina is an experienced Senior Network and Security Engineer in the ICT industry with over 12 years of experience. He holds certifications in Cisco, Palo Alto, Fortinet, and Juniper technologies. Currently employed at CSIRO, Erwin contributes to the organization's network and security operations and optimization, utilizing both open and proprietary tools. Erwin began his career as a field engineer in telecommunications before transitioning to ICT as a network engineer, working with diverse networks in customers' production environments, network, and security challenges. Embracing Ansible as his primary IT tool, Erwin has successfully transitioned away from manual-driven tasks. During his time at Telstra, Erwin had the privilege of being mentored by Brendan for over two years, gaining invaluable experience in leveraging Ansible for enterprise network and security device management. Currently, Erwin applies Ansible in real production scenarios to drive efficiency and productivity wherever possible. He thrives on technical challenges and eagerly adapts to the ever-evolving ICT landscape, actively contributing to his organization's success. Erwin's commitment, expertise, and passion for sharing his knowledge with others make him a valuable asset in the ICT industry.

About the Technical Reviewer

Nikhil Jain is an Ansible expert with over 12 years of DevOps experience. He has been using Ansible and contributing to it from its inception. He currently works closely with Ansible Engineering.

He is an open source enthusiast and is part of the Ansible Pune Meetup organizing team. He has presented multiple Ansible sessions at various global and local events. Apart from sitting in front of his computer automating things using Ansible, he loves watching sports and is a regular part of the local cricket team.

Acknowledgments

I would like to express my heartfelt gratitude to Ty Starr at Telstra Purple and Kai Schweisfurth at Ethan Group, my previous team managers, for providing me with the opportunities to work with my former teams. Under Ty's stewardship, I was able to teach myself how to use Ansible for automation and knowledge share. Similarly, under Kai's guidance, I developed a passion for network automation using Python and eagerly shared my learnings with my colleagues. I would also like to extend my thanks to my former colleague, Justin Cheong at Mastercard, who consistently encouraged me to write my first book and gave me the courage to become a published author. My deepest appreciation goes to my coauthor, Erwin Medina, for his unwavering dedication, hard work, and expertise, which greatly contributed to the completion of this book. I am also grateful to my wife, Sue, and our children, Hugh, Leah, and Caitlin, for their unwavering support throughout the process of creating this book. Their love and understanding have been my pillars of strength. To my extended family, friends, and colleagues, I would like to express my sincere thanks for your constant support. Lastly, I want to thank our readers for embarking on their incredible network automation journey with us.

—Brendan Choi

I cannot express enough thanks to Brendan Choi for continuously mentoring me and taking me under his wings to go through this journey. His passion, dedication, and drive to accomplish this book to primarily teach and inspire serve to be the greatest part for me. He taught me the valuable lesson of learning, sharing, and inspiring. I would like to thank my wife, Jenny, and my son, Deon, for their support and prayers throughout this process. To my friends and colleagues who have become like family, I extend my heartfelt gratitude. To the readers, I sincerely thank you, and I hope that this book will provide help and inspiration as you embark on your journey, just as I was inspired by Brendan.

—Erwin Medina

Introduction

The use of Ansible in enterprise network administration has gained significant popularity among leading IT organizations. It is recognized as the most effective tool for automating network devices within a short time frame, revolutionizing the way network administrators manage their infrastructure. In response to this growing demand, we present *Introduction to Ansible Network Automation: A Practical Primer*, a book that offers readers a structured learning path to build a solid foundation in Ansible.

Written by real ICT professionals for true ICT professionals, this book cuts through the fluff and delivers practical knowledge without false assumptions. We have written this book based on the assumption that all our readers enjoy working in the ICT industry and prefer a hands-on learning approach over a purely theoretical one. This book is not for the faint-hearted but is designed for individuals with an unwavering "never-say-die" attitude who refuse to give up at work and in their lives. We aim to provide an authentic experience, taking readers on the actual journey of acquiring network automation skills using Ansible from the ground up.

While there are numerous Linux and network Ansible automation resources available, most of them assume that readers have already reached an adequate skill level to start writing working YAML code from day one. These resources rarely show what it takes to reach that level and often focus solely on selling the dream of Ansible without discussing the effort and challenges involved. Our book offers a truthful approach, immersing readers in the journey and allowing them to feel what it's like to acquire network automation skills using Ansible. They will install and configure everything themselves, follow along with the book, make mistakes, stumble, and ultimately push themselves to learn the necessary skills to become comfortable with using Ansible playbooks and YAML scripts.

As you can tell from the title, this book serves as a sequel to *Introduction to Python Network Automation: The First Journey* by Brendan Choi. Both titles are indispensable resources for IT professionals and students seeking to enhance their automation skills and apply them in real-world scenarios in enterprise production networks. This book provides a comprehensive learning journey, guiding readers to master Ansible and utilize it for automating enterprise network devices such as routers, switches, firewalls,

Wireless LAN Controllers (WLCs), and Linux servers. What sets this book apart is its laser-focused emphasis on Linux, Ansible, and network automation; really, we have squeezed three basic books into one! It is specifically designed for IT engineers and students who want to get hands-on experience and build an Ansible Network Automation lab from scratch. Real-life examples of Ansible playbooks developed from actual enterprise infrastructure are provided, giving readers a thorough understanding of how Ansible can be effectively utilized in the real world.

By engaging with this book, readers will acquire valuable knowledge and skills in network automation using Ansible. The book takes readers on a structured learning path, gradually building their understanding and proficiency in Ansible. **Firstly, readers will develop a comprehensive understanding of Ansible and its essential concepts for automating network devices.** They will learn how to apply these concepts to real-world scenarios, gaining the skills required to automate enterprise network devices effectively. **Secondly, readers will master the basics of Ansible operations within Linux automation and progress to applying Ansible concepts to network devices.** They will establish a solid foundation for network automation tasks by navigating and utilizing Ansible within the Linux environment. **Thirdly, readers will learn to develop and execute Ansible ad hoc commands and playbooks for various network operations, including configuration management, software updates, and system monitoring.** Through practical examples and exercises, readers will gain hands-on experience in crafting Ansible playbooks to automate critical network tasks. **Next, readers will work with real-life examples of Ansible playbooks developed from enterprise infrastructure.** This practical experience will enable them to write Ansible YAML scripts confidently, ensuring they are well prepared to tackle network automation challenges in real-world environments. **Lastly, readers will acquire the skills necessary to automate network operations using Ansible in selective scenarios for enterprise production environments.** They will gain insights into streamlining network management processes and transitioning from manual tasks to full automation, enhancing efficiency and productivity. Through the content and exercises provided in this book, readers will be equipped with the knowledge and skills to effectively apply Ansible in network automation, empowering them to navigate the ever-evolving world of network administration with confidence and proficiency.

We designed this book for diverse readers seeking to enhance their network automation skills using Ansible. It caters to IT students, network engineers, and developers managing IP services, networking devices, servers, cloud, and data centers. Technical leaders implementing network automation, mentors training team members, instructors teaching network automation, and Cisco Networking Academy students pursuing certifications in network administration will find value in this book. It targets those interested in integrating network automation into their development process and offers practical knowledge for a wide readership. By leveraging Ansible, readers can learn and apply network automation techniques effectively. Join us on this journey to expand your network automation capabilities and unlock new possibilities in your work.

PART I

The Intros

CHAPTER 1

Is Ansible Good for Network Automation?

This chapter offers a brief overview of the current trends in the networking industry and the reasons why Ansible has become a popular tool for enterprise IT configuration and orchestration. The authors introduce Ansible, explaining its workings at a high level and its relevance to working IT engineers, operations managers, as well as to business stakeholders from a commercial stance. The chapter also lays out a comprehensive study plan that will guide readers through the technologies and help them improve their skills. Moreover, the chapter delves into the basic hardware and software required to embark on an Ansible automation journey. It provides information on the minimum PC/laptop requirements needed to build a fully working Ansible/Linux/network automation lab on a single laptop, along with a recommended software set for installing virtual devices such as Linux servers, routers, switches, and firewalls. By the end of this chapter, readers will have a solid understanding of why Ansible is important to the Information and Communication Technology (ICT) industry, what they need to know to become proficient in it, and what resources they require to build their own Ansible lab. This chapter will serve as the foundation for the subsequent chapters in the book, allowing readers to develop their skills and knowledge in a structured and organized manner.

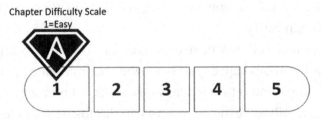

© Brendan Choi and Erwin Medina 2023
B. Choi and E. Medina, *Introduction to Ansible Network Automation*,
https://doi.org/10.1007/978-1-4842-9624-0_1

1.1 Laying the Foundation

Figure 1-1. *Super Ansible*

In recent years, network programmability has become a vital topic for CTOs and network operations managers, leading to a significant transformation in the enterprise networking industry. Python for network automation and a range of network configuration and orchestration tools have surged in popularity, driving enterprise network automation forward. As a result, organizations that once spent large amounts of resources on traditional IT life-cycle management are now looking for new frameworks that provide faster deployment and more reliable and predictable network operations. Ansible is one of the top contenders in this space, and many enterprise network engineers are eager to become experts in both Ansible and Python. Although Ansible is a super tool as depicted in Figure 1-1, mastering Ansible for network deployment and operations can be a daunting task, particularly for engineers who lack programming experience or are new to software-defined networks. It can feel like trying to board a moving train without knowing where to begin. But with the right guidance and resources, engineers can overcome these challenges and acquire the skills necessary to excel in Ansible Network Automation, ensuring that they do not become another victim of the rapidly evolving industry.

As a network engineer, you may have been comfortable with traditional work methods, but now your bosses expect you to upskill and automate some or all your manual tasks with code. If you refuse to learn new skills or embrace new ways of working, someone else will write the code, and you risk losing your credibility and job in the midterm. To succeed in network programmability, you must step out of your comfort zone, reset your knowledge base, and embrace the learning journey from scratch. While it may seem like uncharted territory, with the right resources and determination, you can master the skills needed to excel in automating a large percentage of your work using tools like Ansible and Python. IT industry insiders often recommend entrusting Ansible with routine and mundane tasks so that your team can focus on more complex and strategic initiatives. By allowing Ansible to handle the low-hanging fruit and heavy lifting, you and your team can achieve greater efficiency, productivity, and effectiveness in your daily work.

Programming languages such as Python, Shell Scripting, JavaScript, and Perl come to mind and have the potential to replace your manual tasks with lines of code. However, you may feel overwhelmed at the prospect of tackling a programming language. Perhaps your first experience learning a programming language, like Python in a classroom setting, was not so pleasant and left a bad taste in your mouth. You are hoping that you do not have to revisit that experience, but there's now an answer to your prayers, and that answer is Ansible.

Learning Ansible and applying it in a real production environment can be daunting, particularly for engineers without prior programming experience or new to software-defined networks. It can feel like climbing a mountain, and even after reaching the first peak, you realize that even bigger challenges await. Ansible is often referred to as a "code-free" tool because it relies on declarative configuration files written in YAML (YAML Ain't Markup Language), which are easier to read and write than traditional programming languages. This makes it accessible to people with limited coding experience. However, Ansible also supports writing custom modules and plug-ins in programming languages like Python, which can extend its functionality beyond what is available out of the box. So while Ansible does not require coding knowledge to get started, it can be customized and extended with programming skills. Don't let fear hold you back; the ticket to the automation bandwagon is on the other side of the mountain. No one can force you to embrace the journey, but extending your career in this cutting-edge industry requires the willingness to explore unfamiliar territory and learn new skills. It may be a challenging journey, but the reward of mastering Ansible and automation is worth the effort.

In this opening chapter, we aim to guide you through your first steps into Ansible Network Automation. If you're already on your network automation journey but feel like you're not making much progress, this book is for you. We'll start your journey by discussing what basic skills are required to be successful in network automation using Ansible as your de facto tool of choice. Discuss Ansible as an enterprise network automation tool compared to other tools. Our primary objective is to provide network students like you with a comprehensive and practical learning strategy that will help you close any skill gaps while learning Ansible Network Automation. Our long-term goal is to transform you into a cross-functional engineer, proficient in networking, Linux operating systems, and Ansible YAML code development and management. This knowledge will equip you with the necessary skills to explore other automation technologies in your career. Even if you do not secure a full-time job as an automation or DevOps engineer, learning Ansible can still significantly enhance your professional profile and give you a competitive edge over your colleagues at work.

Throughout this book, we offer a flexible approach that allows you to learn anytime, anywhere, at your own pace and convenience. You will have the opportunity to install, configure, practice, and work with YAML and JSON (JavaScript Object Notation) data serialization formats on your laptop, which is vital for your success in learning Ansible Network Automation. We aim to develop you into a hybrid engineer, a cross-functional professional who is in high demand in the current and future IT job market. To help you get started, we provide all the necessary resource information, including minimum system requirements for your PC, software used for completing the tasks outlined in this book, and download links for all the necessary software, source codes, and files. We will start from the basics and guide you through a comprehensive learning journey that includes mastering Linux, understanding various Ansible concepts, and hands-on practice with enterprise-level virtual machines such as Linux servers, routers, switches, and firewalls. Along the way, you will learn how to build a simple PoC (Proof-of-Concept) lab that can serve as a springboard for your future learning.

By the end of this chapter, you will have a better understanding of Ansible's strengths and weaknesses as a network automation tool, the underlying technologies required for success, and how to build your lab on the go. We hope that this book will provide you with a solid foundation to become a successful network automation engineer.

1.2 What Is Ansible?

Ansible is a powerful open source automation tool that helps manage infrastructure, software deployments, and application configuration across numerous servers and IP devices. System administrators can define and automate workflows, called playbooks, that can perform various tasks such as installing software, managing services, configuring settings, and deploying applications. Network engineers can use Ansible to automate configuration management, patch management, deployment, and troubleshooting tasks. Its agentless architecture, easy-to-learn language, cross-platform support, idempotent playbooks, and troubleshooting capabilities make it an ideal automation tool for enterprise network management. It also supports dynamic inventory for automatic server discovery and management in dynamic environments like cloud environments.

Ansible uses SSH and other remote management protocols to connect to servers and execute required tasks, without the need for agents or additional software on managed nodes. It also supports dynamic inventory for automatic server discovery and management in dynamic environments like cloud environments. Although Ansible may not be the current market leader in Windows automation, it is capable of managing Windows servers and desktops when integrated with Windows Remote Management (WinRM). Furthermore, Ansible can be used to manage network devices by leveraging APIs. Most modern network devices, including routers, switches, and firewalls, offer several APIs that enable their configuration and management to be automated. By utilizing APIs, Ansible provides a powerful and flexible solution to automate network device management, reducing manual configuration errors and streamlining network operations.

Ansible is known for its simplicity, ease of use, and extensibility, with a large and active community providing support, documentation, plug-ins, and modules to extend its capabilities. Ansible is widely used in IT automation, DevOps, and cloud computing.

Key points to remember about Ansible are as follows:

- Ansible is an open source automation tool for managing IT infrastructure.

- It allows for the automation of repetitive tasks, deploying applications, and managing configurations.

- It uses YAML syntax to describe tasks and workflows.

- Ansible uses SSH to communicate with remote systems and does not require any agent software to be installed on managed nodes.

- While Ansible can be used for Windows environments via the WinRM protocol, it's worth noting that there are alternative tools better suited for managing Windows systems.

- If API interfaces are available, certain network devices can be managed through API calls.

- Ansible modules are the building blocks for tasks and can be extended with custom modules.

- Ansible Galaxy serves as a repository for pre-built roles, modules, and Ansible Collections that can be utilized with Ansible.

- Ansible Automation Platform (AAP) (formerly known as Automation Tower before version 3.8) is the enterprise version of Ansible that provides additional features such as job scheduling, access controls, and a web-based user interface.

- The AWX Project is an open source community project that provides upstream code for Automation Controller and serves as a development environment for new features and improvements.

Expand your knowledge:

What is the relationship between Ansible, Ansible Automation Platform, and the AWX Project?

Ansible, Ansible Automation Platform (Automation Tower), and the AWX Project are related products developed by Red Hat. Ansible is an open source automation tool that allows you to automate repetitive tasks, deploy applications, and manage configurations. Ansible Galaxy and Ansible Collections are public libraries of Ansible roles that you can use to accelerate your automation projects.

Ansible Automation Platform (AAP) is a web-based user interface and dashboard for Ansible that provides enterprise features such as job scheduling, access controls, audit logging, and role-based access control (RBAC). It simplifies the use of Ansible by providing a central management point and a graphical user interface.

The AWX Project is an open source community project that provides the upstream code for Ansible Automation Platform. It is essentially the same product as Automation Controller but is free and open source. The AWX Project also serves as a development environment for new features and improvements to Automation Controller. Red Hat supports the AWX Project community and contributes to its development.

In summary, Ansible is the core automation engine, Ansible Galaxy is the public library of Ansible roles, Ansible Automation Platform is the enterprise version of Ansible with additional features and a web-based user interface, and the AWX Project is the open source community project that provides the upstream code for Ansible Automation Platform.

You can find more information on Ansible, Ansible Automation Platform, and the AWX Project at the following links:

Ansible documentation: `https://docs.ansible.com/`

Ansible Galaxy: `https://galaxy.ansible.com`

Ansible Automation Platform: `www.ansible.com/products/automation-platform`

AWX Project GitHub repository: `https://github.com/ansible/awx`

1.3 What Is Ansible Not?

While Ansible is a powerful automation tool, there are some things it is not:

- Ansible is not a programming language: While Ansible uses a declarative language to define playbooks, it is not a general-purpose programming language. It is designed to automate system administration tasks, not to build complex applications.

- Ansible is not a monitoring tool: Ansible can be used to configure monitoring tools, but it is not a monitoring tool itself. It does not provide real-time monitoring or alerting capabilities.

- Ansible is not a configuration management database (CMDB): Ansible does not store or manage the configuration state of servers. It only runs tasks and scripts defined in playbooks.

- Ansible is not a security tool: While Ansible can help enforce security policies and configurations, it is not a security tool itself. It does not provide security monitoring or vulnerability scanning.

Overall, Ansible is designed to be a simple and powerful automation tool that can be used to manage and automate infrastructure and application deployments, but it is not a one-size-fits-all solution for all IT automation needs.

1.4 Why Ansible?

In this section, we will take a closer look at Ansible and compare it to alternative configuration and orchestration tools. By examining the strengths and weaknesses of each tool in comparison to Ansible, we can gain a better understanding of why many organizations prefer Ansible as their tool of choice for configuration and orchestration for network automation.

Ansible is a popular configuration management tool that uses YAML for defining tasks and configurations. While there are several competitor tools to Ansible in the market, it stands out for its simplicity, agentless architecture, and idempotent playbooks. Ansible's YAML-based syntax is easy to read, write, and version control, and the active community provides many pre-built modules and roles on Ansible Galaxy. However, compared to Chef, Ansible provides less fine-grained control over configurations and has limited testing and logging capabilities, which makes it less suitable for complex and highly regulated infrastructures.

Chef is a configuration management tool that uses a client-server architecture and requires agents to be installed on each managed node. Unlike Ansible, Chef uses a domain-specific language called Chef DSL (Ruby based) to define infrastructure configurations. Chef is more complex to set up and use than Ansible but offers more flexibility and fine-grained control over configurations. It allows users to write custom resources and cookbooks to meet specific requirements, promotes a test-driven development approach, and has a large and active community with many pre-built cookbooks available on Chef Supermarket. However, its client-server architecture and DSL-based configurations can make it more complex and harder to learn than Ansible.

Puppet is a configuration management tool that, like Chef, uses a client-server architecture and agents installed on each managed node to define infrastructure configurations using a declarative language. It offers more advanced features such as role-based access control and compliance management and has a larger library of modules compared to Ansible. Puppet uses a declarative language called Puppet DSL (Ruby based) for defining configurations and provides more flexibility and fine-grained control over infrastructure configurations. It allows users to write custom modules and manifests to meet specific requirements, promotes a test-driven development approach, and has a large and active community with many pre-built modules available on Puppet Forge. However, Puppet's complexity, client-server architecture, and DSL-based configurations can make it harder to set up and maintain than Ansible.

SaltStack is a configuration management and automation tool that uses a client-server architecture similar to Chef and Puppet. It offers more fine-grained control over configurations and a powerful event-driven automation system, making it more suited to large and complex infrastructures. SaltStack uses its configuration language called YAML + Jinja2, allowing users to write dynamic configurations in YAML files. It uses Salt State Domain Specific Language (DSL) for defining configurations, which makes it highly scalable and suitable for very large infrastructures. Additionally, it is event driven, enabling it to react to events in real time and perform actions automatically. SaltStack has a large and active community with many pre-built formulas and modules available on SaltStack Exchange. However, SaltStack's powerful features come at the cost of complexity, making it harder to set up and maintain than Ansible. Its DSL can also be difficult to learn and understand for users who are not familiar with Python, and its agent-based architecture introduces security risks.

Terraform is a tool for managing infrastructure as code, specifically designed for infrastructure provisioning and management of cloud resources. It uses a declarative language called HashiCorp Configuration Language (HCL) and supports a wide variety of cloud providers, making it easy to manage hybrid and multi-cloud infrastructures. Terraform can integrate with Ansible or other configuration management tools to manage the software configuration of those resources. Its plan and apply workflow allows changes to be previewed and reviewed before being applied to infrastructure, reducing the risk of unexpected changes. However, Terraform can be more complex to set up and use than Ansible due to its dedicated focus on infrastructure provisioning, and its declarative approach can limit the flexibility of infrastructure configurations, making it harder to achieve highly customized infrastructures.

For a novice automation engineer, the amount of information presented can be overwhelming. To make it easier to compare the tools, we have compiled the information in a table format in Table 1-1.

Expand your knowledge:

Why are Ansible Automation Platform and Ansible Engine both referred to as "Ansible"?

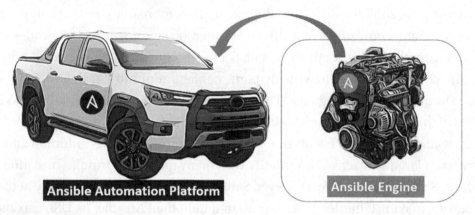

Figure 1-2. Ansible Automation Platform and Ansible Engine analogy

Many individuals who are discovering Ansible as an automation tool often find themselves perplexed by the distinction between the Ansible Automation Platform and Ansible Engine, both referred to as "Ansible" by Red Hat. While the Ansible Engine serves as the fundamental component of the Ansible Automation Platform's architecture, it is crucial to exercise caution when using the term "Ansible" because they do not denote the same entity. For example, the Ansible Automation Platform is a commercial product developed by Red Hat, whereas Ansible (Engine) is an open source tool generously shared by Red Hat with the IT community.

To help with further explanation, we will use a pick-up truck analogy to explain the relationship between the Ansible Engine, which is the focus of this book, and the Ansible Automation Platform (previously known as Ansible Tower). A pick-up truck is a versatile utility vehicle used for transporting goods from one place to another. In this analogy, Ansible Engine is like the engine of the pick-up truck (Figure 1-2), providing the power and functionality necessary to move the truck forward. Similarly, Ansible Engine is the core automation technology that drives Ansible's ability to automate IT tasks and processes. In contrast, the Ansible Automation Platform is like the cargo area of the pick-up truck, serving as a centralized location where you can store and organize your goods. This allows for easy access and transport, just as the platform provides a centralized location where you can manage and orchestrate your automation workflows, making it easier to automate complex IT tasks and processes.

Like a pick-up truck, Ansible consists of many major and minor components, with Ansible Engine at the heart of the system. Other major components include Red Hat Linux, OpenShift, and others, making Ansible a comprehensive automation solution. Ultimately, the combination of Ansible Engine and Ansible Automation Platform provides a powerful tool for automating IT tasks and processes at scale, much like a pick-up truck with a powerful engine and a well-organized cargo area is a valuable tool for transporting goods.

Table 1-1. *Network automation tools strengths and weaknesses comparison*

Features		Automation tools				
		Ansible	Chef	Puppet	SaltStack	Terraform
Key features	Agentless	✓	✗	✗	✗	✓
	Cross-cloud support	✓	✓	✓	✓	✓
	Event driven	✓	✓	✓	✓	✗
	Flexibility	✓	✓	✓	✓	✓
	Granularity (customizable)	✓	✓	✓	✓	✓
	Idempotent	✓	✓	✓	✓	✗
	Infrastructure as code	✓	✓	✓	✓	✓
	Large community and ecosystem	✓	✓	✓	✓	✓
	Logging and auditing capabilities	✓	✓	✓	✓	✓
	Resource dependencies	✓	✓	✓	✓	✓
	Scalability	✓	✓	✓	✓	✓
	Security	✓	✓	✓	✓	✓
	Test-driven development	✓	✓	✓	✓	✓
Language	DSL based (domain-specific language)	✗	✓	✓	✓	✗
	HashiCorp Configuration Language (HCL)	✗	✗	✗	✗	✓
	Ruby-based DSL	✗	✓	✓	✗	✗
	SaltStack-based DSL	✗	✗	✗	✓	✗
	YAML-based syntax	✓	✗	✗	✗	✓
Data	JSON data format support	✓	✓	✓	✓	✓
	TOML data format support	✗	✗	✗	✓	✗
	YAML data format support	✓	✓	✓	✓	✓
Learnability	**Easy to set up (less complexity)**	✓	✗	✗	✓	✓
	Simplicity (easy to learn, readability)	✓	✗	✗	✗	✓

The selection of a configuration management tool depends on the specific requirements and preferences of an organization. While Ansible is well known for its simplicity, flexibility, and ease of use, making it a preferred choice for small to medium-sized infrastructures, other tools like Chef, Puppet, SaltStack, and Terraform may be more suitable for larger and more complex infrastructures. It is also essential to consider the programming languages used by these tools, as this can provide valuable insights into their working and customization.

In enterprise network environments, proprietary operating systems or appliance-based OS are commonly used to run network devices, whether hardware-based or virtual machines. This is done to protect the system from cyber-attacks, as well as to safeguard against untested or unproven agents used by other tools. Therefore, **an agentless automation tool is a key factor that can influence the selection of a network automation tool**.

Upon reviewing the aforementioned table, it becomes clear why many organizations are opting for Ansible as their preferred network configuration and automation tool. **One of the most significant advantages of Ansible's agentless architecture is that it removes the need to install agents on target systems, making it a safe and secure option for network automation in enterprise environments. Moreover, Ansible's straightforward and intuitive YAML syntax, low learning curve, and ease of use make it a favorite among both novice and experienced automation engineers.** When choosing a tool from a network operations perspective, **learnability**, or the ease of learning and using the tool, is a crucial factor. This term is commonly used in education, psychology, and user experience design, and in the context of IT tools like Ansible, it refers to the tool's ease or difficulty of learning and mastering. Therefore, when selecting the appropriate configuration management tool for an organization, in addition to functionality, ease of use, and flexibility, learnability should also be considered as a crucial factor.

In summary, Ansible's main strengths are its simplicity, agentless architecture, idempotency, YAML-based syntax, and large community and ecosystem. However, it has weaknesses in terms of limited granularity, testing support, and logging and auditing capabilities. Chef is known for its flexibility, customizability, test-driven development approach, and large community and ecosystem, but its weaknesses include complexity, DSL-based configurations, and a steep learning curve. Similarly, Puppet shares many of Chef's strengths and weaknesses, including flexibility, customizability, and test-driven development, but also has a steep learning curve and requires more setup and configuration. SaltStack is excellent in fine-grained control, scalability, and event-driven architecture and has a large community and ecosystem but is complex to set up and use, with a steep learning curve and security risks. Finally, Terraform's strengths are infrastructure as code (IaC), cross-cloud support, resource dependencies, and a plan and apply workflow, while its weaknesses include complexity, a steep learning curve, and limited flexibility in highly customized infrastructures. **Ultimately, the tool chosen depends on the organization's specific needs, infrastructure size, and technical capabilities.**

Expand your knowledge:

Who created Ansible and why?

Figure 1-3. *Michael De Haan*

Michael De Haan (Figure 1-3) created Ansible because he encountered problems while working as a systems administrator. He found that existing configuration management tools were either too complex, required a lot of infrastructure to run, or were not flexible enough to meet his needs. He wanted a tool that was easy to use, didn't require a lot of overhead, and could be used for a wide range of tasks, from simple server provisioning to complex application deployment. These requirements led him to develop Ansible, which has become one of the most popular open source automation tools in use today. Red Hat acquired Ansible in October 2015 for approximately U$150 million. Since the acquisition, Ansible has continued to be developed and maintained as an open source project, with Red Hat providing commercial support and services to enterprise customers through its Ansible Automation Platform product, previously known as Ansible Tower. Since Ansible 3.8, the name Ansible Tower has been replaced with a new name, Automation Controller. The acquisition of Ansible helped Red Hat strengthen its position in the rapidly growing automation and orchestration market. Ansible aligned well with Red Hat's strategy of providing open source solutions for enterprise customers. Ansible's agentless architecture and focus on simplicity and ease of use made it a popular choice for organizations looking to automate their IT operations. Ansible also had a strong presence in the DevOps and cloud-native communities, which were becoming increasingly important in the enterprise market. Overall, the acquisition of Ansible provided a valuable addition to Red Hat's open source product portfolio. De Haan was working as the co-founder and CTO of a startup called Cleafy, which provides cyber-security solutions. After creating Ansible, De Haan continued to be involved in the development of the project for several years but eventually left Red Hat to pursue other interests. In addition to his work with Cleafy, he has also been involved in other open source projects, such as Cobbler and Func, and has spoken at numerous conferences and events on topics related to automation and DevOps (*source: https://techcrunch.com/*).

1.4.1 1000-Foot View of How Ansible Works

At a high level, Ansible works by connecting to remote devices and executing tasks defined in playbooks. Here are the main steps involved in the Ansible workflow:

Inventory: Ansible starts by reading an inventory file, which lists the servers or devices that it will manage. The inventory can be a static file or a dynamic inventory script that generates the list of servers based on various criteria, such as tags or metadata.

SSH: Ansible connects to the servers using SSH or other remote management protocols. It authenticates using SSH keys or passwords and then creates a temporary connection to execute the tasks defined in the playbooks.

Playbooks: Playbooks are the heart of Ansible. They define a set of tasks that Ansible will execute on the managed servers. Playbooks use a declarative YAML syntax to define the tasks, which can include installing packages, configuring settings, copying files, and more. Playbooks can also include variables, loops, and conditionals to make them more flexible.

Modules: Ansible uses modules to execute tasks on the managed servers. Modules are small scripts or programs that implement specific tasks, such as installing a package, restarting a service, or copying a file. Ansible comes with a large library of modules, and users can also write their modules if needed.

Idempotence: Ansible is designed to be idempotent, which means that running the same playbook multiple times will not change the state of the system. Ansible achieves idempotence by checking the current state of the system before executing each task and only executing the task if it needs to be changed.

Reporting: Ansible provides detailed reporting on the status of each task and playbook run. It logs the output of each task and provides a summary of the changes made to the system.

Overall, Ansible provides a simple and powerful way to automate infrastructure and application deployments, using a declarative and idempotent approach that makes it easy to manage and maintain systems over time.

1.5 Why Does Ansible Matter to You?

Ansible is an important tool for network students, engineers, operations managers, and business owners for several reasons:

Automation: Ansible allows you to automate repetitive tasks and workflows, such as configuring network devices, deploying applications, and managing infrastructure. This saves time and reduces the risk of human error, improving productivity and reliability.

Efficiency: Ansible provides a standardized way to manage and configure network devices, reducing the complexity and variability of network configurations. This makes it easier to troubleshoot and maintain networks, improving efficiency and reducing downtime.

Scalability: Ansible can manage large and complex networks with ease, allowing you to scale your network operations as your business grows. Ansible's inventory and playbook management features make it easy to manage a large number of devices, even in dynamic and heterogeneous environments.

Collaboration: Ansible provides a collaborative platform for network teams, allowing them to share and reuse playbooks and modules and to collaborate on workflows and configurations. This promotes knowledge sharing and reduces silos in network operations.

Cost savings: By automating network operations and reducing downtime, Ansible can help you save money on staffing and infrastructure costs. Ansible is also an open source tool, which means there are no licensing fees or vendor lock-in.

Ansible's effectiveness as a network automation tool is demonstrated by successful case studies from Red Hat, LinkedIn, and NTT Communications. These companies turned to Ansible to automate their network infrastructure management tasks, resulting in greater efficiency, consistency, and scalability.

Red Hat, a global software company, reduced manual configuration time by 50%, improved consistency, and increased overall network reliability by using Ansible to automate their switches, routers, and firewalls.

LinkedIn, a professional social networking platform, adopted Ansible to automate tasks such as deploying new servers, configuring load balancers, and managing network security. They reduced manual configuration time by 75% and improved overall network efficiency and uptime.

NTT Communications, a global telecommunications company, faced challenges in managing its network infrastructure across multiple countries and regions. They turned to Ansible to automate server provisioning, load balancer configuration, and firewall management. As a result, they achieved greater consistency and reliability across their global network, improved network agility, and reduced manual configuration time by 80%.

These case studies demonstrate the importance of learning Ansible as a network automation tool in the modern IT environment. IT professionals can benefit from Ansible's ability to automate repetitive tasks, improve efficiency and reliability, and save costs. The case studies of Red Hat and LinkedIn demonstrate the significant benefits of utilizing Ansible as an automation tool in an enterprise network. With Ansible, businesses can efficiently and consistently manage their network infrastructure at scale, resulting in increased productivity and reliability. Automation of network configuration tasks with Ansible reduces the time and effort required for manual configuration, leading to improved network uptime. Therefore, learning Ansible as a network automation tool is critical for IT professionals to remain competitive and address the demands of the modern IT environment. Ansible is a flexible and powerful tool that can help network engineers, operations managers, business owners, and students streamline their network operations, improve efficiency and reliability, and ultimately reduce costs.

1.6 Starting on the Right Foot, Learning Ansible Effectively

Given that you see the value in Ansible as an automation tool in the enterprise network automation environment, you want to start your study. Automation has become an essential skill in today's fast-paced IT environment, and Ansible is one of the most popular tools used for this purpose. With Ansible, you can automate a wide range of tasks, including server configuration, application deployment, and network management. However, to make the most of this powerful tool, it's important to establish clear goals and objectives before embarking on your study journey. By defining what you want to achieve, you can stay motivated and focused throughout your learning experience. Additionally, you should assess your strengths and limitations, as well as your available time, to create a realistic study schedule that you can commit to consistently. By doing so, you can ensure that your efforts are well directed and ultimately lead to a successful outcome.

When learning Ansible, it's important to have a structured study path to ensure that you cover all the necessary concepts and skills. The following steps are suggested for learning Ansible and achieving success in your automation tasks. Each step will be discussed in its chapter, providing a comprehensive guide to learning Ansible. While it's possible to skip chapters if you already have strong skills in certain areas, it's highly recommended that you follow the entire study path to get the most out of this book's format. By doing so, you can gain a deeper understanding of Ansible and learn how all the components work together to automate tasks in an efficient and scalable manner. Additionally, following along with the entire book can help you identify areas where you may need to improve your skills, even if you have existing knowledge or expertise.

This book assumes that all readers have completed Cisco CCNA or CompTIA Network+ studies and have a solid grasp of common networking concepts. However, if you're new to networking, don't worry; you can still follow along step by step. But to ensure you understand the concepts presented, we recommend studying basic networking concepts separately as you progress through the book. This will give you a better understanding of the technologies and concepts used in Ansible for enterprise network automation.

Technically, this book is subdivided into three parts. Now, let's look at the topics covered in this book to help you deep dive into Ansible.

1.6.1 Part 1: Ansible Primer

This first part provides an overview of Ansible and a discussion on its suitability as a network automation tool. Chapter 1 explains what Ansible is, what it is not, and why it matters. It also provides a 1000-foot view of how Ansible works and explains the hardware and software requirements for effective learning.

Chapters 2 and 3 are Linux Beginner's Quick Guides that introduce essential Linux commands and tools necessary for using Ansible.

Chapter 4 guides users on how to set up an Ansible learning environment, including planning the topology, creating virtual machines, installing Ansible, and creating a new Ansible testing account with sudo access.

Overall, Part 1 provides a solid foundation for learning Ansible and network automation, emphasizing the importance of Linux skills and setting up an appropriate learning environment.

1.6.2 Part 2: Ansible Concepts

Part 2 delves deeper into Ansible concepts, including data types and file formats, SSH configuration and usage, ad hoc commands, and playbook creation.

In Chapter 5, you will learn about different file formats and data types used in Ansible. These include INI format, YAML, JSON, and Jinja2. The chapter will also cover the priority of Ansible inventory. Understanding these data types and file formats is important for creating effective Ansible playbooks.

Chapter 6 is an introduction to some of the basic concepts in Ansible. It starts with an overview of SSH and how to set it up for Ansible. The chapter also covers how to run ad hoc commands on Linux devices with Ansible. It also explains how to run elevated ad hoc commands.

In Chapter 7, you will learn how to use Ansible ad hoc commands. The chapter provides examples of common ad hoc commands used by administrators and gets you ready for Ansible playbooks.

Chapter 8 covers how to write your first Ansible playbook, use the "when" conditional, and improve your playbook. It also explains how to target specific nodes with Ansible.

Chapter 9 looks at basic documentation version controlling using GitHub and follows through with explanations and examples of Ansible tags, managing files with Ansible, adding users, and bootstrapping Linux servers. Understanding these concepts is important for creating efficient and effective Ansible playbooks.

Chapter 10 covers Ansible roles, host variables, handles, and templates. This chapter also shows you how to configure working FTP and SFTP servers for file transfers using Ansible playbooks.

In Chapter 11, you will learn how to build an Ansible learning environment for network automation. It covers creating a base virtual router, cloning the virtual router, adding a GNS3 VM, and adding routers and switches on GNS3. Creating this environment is essential for practicing network automation with Ansible.

1.6.3 Part 3: Ansible Practical

Part 3 is divided into ten parts, focusing on the practical applications of Ansible in network automation.

In Chapter 12, readers will learn how to use Ansible to automate the configuration of Cisco routers and switches. The chapter covers topics such as creating playbooks, defining inventory, and executing tasks to configure network devices. Practical examples and step-by-step instructions will guide readers through the process.

Chapter 13 focuses on automating the backup of configurations for Cisco network devices using Ansible. Readers will discover how to create playbooks to schedule and perform regular backups, ensuring that critical network configurations are securely stored. The chapter provides insights into best practices for backup strategies and demonstrates how Ansible simplifies this process.

In Chapter 14, readers will explore how Ansible can be utilized to develop a network configuration comparison tool. The chapter outlines the steps involved in building a playbook that enables users to compare configurations between different network devices, facilitating efficient troubleshooting and identifying configuration inconsistencies.

Chapter 15 focuses on using Ansible to automate the process of upgrading Cisco IOS-XE routers. Readers will learn how to create playbooks that handle the complete upgrade workflow, including tasks such as downloading the new software image, verifying compatibility, and performing the actual upgrade. Practical examples and guidance will help readers implement this automation effectively.

In Chapter 16, readers will explore how to leverage Ansible for upgrading Cisco Wireless LAN Controllers (WLC). The chapter provides step-by-step instructions on creating playbooks that automate the upgrade process, ensuring minimal downtime and efficient management of WLC devices. Practical examples and considerations for successful upgrades are also included.

Chapter 17 focuses on automating the creation of user accounts on Palo Alto and Fortinet firewalls using Ansible. Readers will gain insights into writing playbooks that define user account configurations and execute the necessary tasks to provide user access. The chapter includes practical examples and considerations for managing user accounts effectively.

Chapter 18 explores how to use Ansible to automate the creation of security policies on Palo Alto and Fortinet firewalls. Readers will learn how to develop playbooks that define policy rules, configure firewall settings, and enforce security measures across network devices. Practical examples and best practices for managing security policies will be provided.

In Chapter 19, readers will discover how Ansible can automate the creation of IPsec tunnels on Palo Alto firewalls. The chapter covers the necessary steps to define tunnel configurations, establish secure communication channels, and manage IPsec settings efficiently. Practical examples and considerations for successful IPsec tunnel management are included.

Chapter 20 focuses on leveraging Ansible for automating the creation of object addresses on Palo Alto firewalls. Readers will learn how to write playbooks that define object address configurations, allowing for efficient management of IP addresses and associated objects. Practical examples and insights into managing object addresses effectively will be provided.

Chapter 21 explores how Ansible can be used to automate the process of upgrading Palo Alto firewalls. Readers will learn how to develop playbooks that handle the complete upgrade workflow, including tasks such as verifying compatibility, downloading firmware images, and executing the upgrade process. Practical examples and considerations for successful upgrades will be discussed. This chapter uses a hardware firewall for demonstration due to software licensing restrictions while performing a PAN-OS upgrade.

By quickly reading through the concise summaries of each chapter, you now have a comprehensive overview of the book's content and the authors' intended direction for taking readers on their Ansible automation journey. By following the chapters step by step, you can promptly begin your exploration of Linux, Ansible concepts, and Ansible Network Automation. This will allow you to develop proficiency in utilizing Ansible for managing enterprise devices such as routers, switches, firewalls, and Linux servers. Now, let's examine the hardware specifications of your laptop to configure your learning environment effectively, enabling you to follow along and acquire the necessary Ansible skills.

1.7 Hardware Requirements

To learn Ansible and complete the exercises and labs in this book, your computer must meet the minimum specifications listed in Table 1-2. We will use Windows 11 as the base operating system for building our Integrated Development Environment (IDE) Lab environment. If you are using macOS or Linux, you will need to find the compatible and suitable software on your own. It is highly recommended to upgrade to Windows 11 if your system is still running an older version. If you have a powerful desktop PC, it will run better than a laptop. Make sure your system meets the minimum requirements specified in Table 1-2 to avoid system performance issues.

Table 1-2. *Laptop or PC – minimum specifications*

PC components	Minimum specification
CPU (Central Processing Unit)	Intel: CPU i7 Gen6 (64-bit) or above AMD: Ryzen 5 or above
RAM – Random Access Memory	16 GB or more for DDR4/DDR5 (32 GB recommended)
SSD	240 GB or more (with 15% or free space for system paging)
Host OS – Operating System	Microsoft Windows 11 (64-bit) or newer

As a reference, you can find the specifications of the laptop used in this book in the screenshot shown in Figure 1-4.

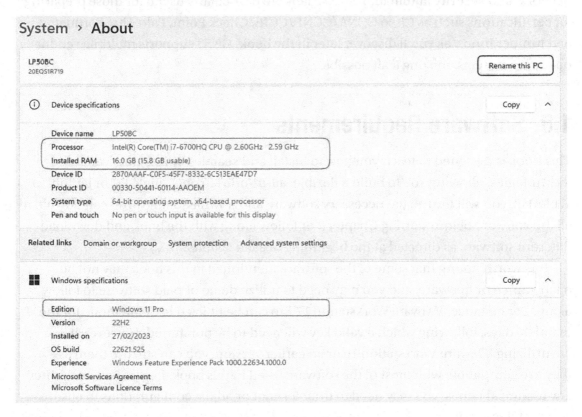

Figure 1-4. *Laptop specifications used in this book*

For optimal performance and smooth functioning of all labs, it's recommended that your CPU performance is either on par with or better than the Intel i6-6700HQ (as shown in Figure 1-4), with at least 16 GB DDR4 memory. Of course, your labs will run even better with the newer generation of CPUs and 32 GB of total physical memory. However, even if your laptop has an older CPU that falls below the minimum requirements, many of the labs should run smoothly, although performance may suffer when running multiple virtual machines. System delays may also occur due to a sluggish Windows OS caused by a slower CPU, lack of memory, or running several programs concurrently. For optimal performance, we recommend setting up the lab on external servers using a dedicated ESXi/Proxmox/Cloud environment. Additionally, opting for an SSD is preferable to an HDD, and choosing an NVMe connection over a STAT 2 connection is recommended to mitigate potential performance issuess.

The primary objective of this book is to help you set up a practical laboratory on your personal computer or laptop, enabling you to explore the world of Linux, Ansible, network, and security automation. These labs are particularly useful for those preparing for certifications such as Cisco CCNA/CCNP/CCIE, Check Point, Palo Alto, Fortinet, and Juniper Junos, as you'll discover later in the book. GNS3 supports multiple vendor operating systems, making it all possible.

1.8 Software Requirements

This book is designed to teach you how to install and seamlessly integrate various technologies, allowing you to build a flexible, all-in-one lab on a single PC or laptop. In Table 1-3, you will find all the necessary software and download links. You can download all the software before starting Chapter 2 or follow along with the book and download different software as directed at the beginning of each chapter.

It is worth noting that some of the software mentioned in this book may not be open source or freeware, and you may need to utilize demo or paid software to follow along. For instance, VMware Workstation 17 Pro can be utilized in demo mode for the initial 30 days, following which a valid key will need to be purchased. However, if you are utilizing VMware Workstation 16 or an earlier version, you can still use them as they are compatible with most of the software listed in this book. In case you encounter any technical issues, you may need to troubleshoot or adjust configurations to ensure successful integration.

Similarly, the Cisco Modeling Labs-Personal Edition (CML-PE) requires a yearly subscription of $199 (as of 2023). However, for our lab, you will only need the three files specified in the following table. This book will continue to use these older files, as we do not require new IOS-XE features provided by the newer IOS-XE software. Nevertheless, if you have the latest CML-PE images, you can use the new files to incorporate Cisco CML-PE images into VMware Workstation.

It is important to be aware that Palo Alto labs require the utilization of hardware-based firewalls like PA-220, PA-820, PA-850, PA-3220, or PA-5220. However, if you don't have a hardware-based firewall, you can still follow this book by substituting it with a PA-VM for educational and testing purposes. In this scenario, you will need to obtain the virtual image and run it in your lab. Please keep in mind that the authors or publisher of this book does not provide any software used in this book, and it is the reader's responsibility to download and obtain the suggested software for your learning. It is worth noting that all other software used in this book is open source or freeware. The same use condition applies for FortiGate's FortiOS usage; you can use hardware or the virtual machine with a 14-day trial period.

Table 1-3. *Software and download links (at the time of writing this book)*

Required software	Usage	License type
VMware-workstation-full-17.0.1-21139696.exe [607.72 MB] (or 16/15) or newer URL 1: `https://customerconnect.vmware.com/ downloads/info/slug/desktop_end_user_ computing/vmwareworkstation_pro/17_0` URL 2: `https://customerconnect.vmware.com/ downloads/info/slug/desktop_end_user_ computing/`	Desktop virtualization	Licensed
GNS3-2.2.39-all-in-one.exe [94.9 MB] or newer URL: `https://github.com/GNS3/gns3-gui/releases`	Network device emulator	Open source
GNS3.VM.VMware.Workstation.2.2.39.zip [1.53 GB] or newer URL: `https://github.com/GNS3/gns3-gui/releases`	VMware Workstation GNS3 VM ova image	Open source

(continued)

Table 1-3. (*continued*)

Required software	Usage	License type
IOSv-L3-15.6(2)T.qcow2 or newer	Cisco CML L3 image	Licensed
IOSv_startup_config.img	CML L3 booting file	
IOSvL215.2.4055.qcow2 or newer	Cisco CML L2 image	
URL: `https://learningnetworkstore.cisco.com/cisco-modeling-labs-personal/cisco-cml-personal`		
Ansible 2.14.3 or newer	Device configuration and orchestration mgt	Open source
Python 3.11.2 or newer	Programming language	Open source
npp.8.4.9.Installer.x64.exe [4.5 MB] or newer URL: `https://notepad-plus-plus.org/downloads/`	Text editor for Windows	Freeware
putty-64bit-0.78-installer.msi [3.6 MB] or newer URL: `www.putty.org/`	SSH/Telnet client	Freeware
Ubuntu-22.04.2-live-server-amd64.iso [952.1MB] or newer URL: `www.ubuntu.com/download/server` *This book uses Ubuntu Server 23.04 (Lunar Lobster) release*	Ubuntu Server image – bootable	Open source
Fedora-Server-dvd-x86_64-38-1.6.iso [2.3 GB] or newer URL: `https://fedoraproject.org/en/server/download/` *This book uses Fedora Linux 38 (Server Edition Prerelease)*	Fedora Server image – bootable	Open source
WinSCP-5.21.7-Setup.exe [11 MB] or newer URL: `https://winscp.net/eng/download.php`	Secure File Transfer for Windows-Linux	Freeware

(*continued*)

Table 1-3. (*continued*)

Required software	Usage	License type
FileZilla_3.63.2_win64-setup.exe (64-bit, for Windows) or newer URL 1: `https://filezilla-project.org/download.php?show_all=1` URL 2: `https://filezilla-project.org/`	Secure File Transfer for Windows-Linux	Freeware
PA-VM version 10.0.1	Firewall appliance	Proprietary
Fortinet version 7.1.03	Firewall appliance	Proprietary

1.9 Downloading Source Codes

Throughout this book, you will need to have certain software installed and integrated to complete the labs. Installing the necessary software is generally straightforward and may not require detailed guidance for many readers, as it often involves clicking a few "Next" or "Yes" buttons. However, if you would like to refer to our installation settings in detail, complimentary installation guides are available for download on the author's GitHub page, which we recommend you check out.

To ensure that you have everything you need before moving on to Chapter 2, please download all pre-installation guides and source codes from the following URLs:

Complementary pre-installation guides available from

URL: `https://github.com/ansnetauto/appress_ansnetauto` *or*

`https://github.com/orgs/Apress/repositories`

Source code available from

URL: `https://github.com/ansnetauto/appress_ansnetauto` *or*

`https://github.com/orgs/Apress/repositories`

You have reached the end of the first chapter! It's great to see that you are excited and eager to dive into the next chapters. We hope you've enjoyed this initial chapter and are ready to explore the amazing world of Ansible and network automation further. Keep up the enthusiasm, and we are sure you'll make the most of what's ahead!

1.10 Summary

This chapter provided a general introduction to Ansible, a widely used open source automation tool for managing IT infrastructure. The authors presented a comprehensive overview of Ansible's features, highlighting its advantages over other automation tools such as Chef, Puppet, SaltStack, and Terraform. The chapter delved into the basic architecture of Ansible and its communication mechanisms with remote systems, explaining how it can simplify complex IT tasks, increase efficiency, and reduce errors in IT configuration management and orchestration. The authors also discussed the importance of effective Ansible learning strategies, from downloading software to their installations, and provided the download links for all the source codes and files from the author's GitHub page. Overall, the chapter served as a starting point for readers who are new to Ansible, providing them with essential knowledge before embarking on their Ansible Network Automation journey. By the end of the chapter, readers should have gained a solid understanding of Ansible's significance in IT configuration and orchestration and how various organizations could benefit from Ansible during infrastructure management.

CHAPTER 2

Shall We Linux? (Part 1: The Linux Command Line)

This book contains two dedicated chapters on Linux, with this being Part 1, which is solely focused on introducing Linux command line and helping new users get started while reinforcing the knowledge of experienced users with essential Linux commands. This is the longest chapter of the book for good reason, as Ansible, a Red Hat product, runs on Linux hosts. To succeed in network automation using Ansible, one must first master the basics of Linux. The first step toward mastery is becoming proficient with essential Linux commands that experienced users rely on every day. Without this foundational knowledge, mastering topics such as Ansible, YAML, or any other advanced topics is unattainable. This chapter provides readers with an overview of Linux and its benefits, as well as a step-by-step guide on how to install Windows Subsystem for Linux (WSL) for first-time Linux users. Additionally, the chapter covers a selection of essential Linux commands, such as pwd, touch, ls, mkdir, cd, rm, rmdir, cp, mv, and grep, and provides hands-on exercises to practice them. By the end of the chapter, readers will have a solid understanding of why Linux is so important in network automation and how to work effectively with various Linux commands.

31

© Brendan Choi and Erwin Medina 2023
B. Choi and E. Medina, *Introduction to Ansible Network Automation*,
https://doi.org/10.1007/978-1-4842-9624-0_2

2.1 A Good Reason to Learn Linux

Acquiring proficiency in Linux can provide IT engineers with a wealth of opportunities. Presently, there is a scarcity of network engineers who have a solid grasp of Linux. Trying to hire network engineers with good Linux skills is even more difficult than finding a colony of penguins around the world (Figure 2-1).

Figure 2-1. *A colony of penguins*

Thus, possessing knowledge of Linux and networking administration can provide significant advantages and opportunities. A large number of enterprise-level application servers are hosted on Linux-based server operating systems. Additionally, an increasing number of Linux machines are being utilized in both private and public clouds, such as Amazon Web Services (AWS), Microsoft Azure and Google Cloud Platform (GCP). By developing Linux skills, IT engineers can position themselves to take advantage of these growing opportunities.

Over the past two decades, the use of Linux has grown significantly, leading to more and more enterprise systems making the switch from Windows to Linux in the IT and data center environments. Linux offers a better return on investment, enhanced reliability, security, scalability, and high availability, along with flexibility that is not typically seen in Windows Server environments. Linux is also a key player in the many behind-the-scenes systems that make up our daily lives. Even Microsoft has embraced Linux, as evidenced by the inclusion of Linux kernel support in a Windows 10 patch and the availability of Windows Subsystem for Linux (WSL), which allows users to run Linux VMs on Windows. In this book, we will take advantage of this feature to begin our Linux journey, eliminating the need for a stand-alone Linux system to practice Linux commands.

If you are already familiar with Linux, that's fantastic! You have a head start while following this book. However, if you have been a Microsoft Windows user all this time, this is an opportunity for you to start exploring Linux.

2.2 Linux for Ansible and Network Automation

Linux is a crucial component of network automation and configuration management with tools like Ansible. Here are some compelling reasons why learning Linux is important for becoming proficient in Ansible and network automation.

Although Ansible is built on Python, it was primarily and originally designed to be used for managing Linux systems. Hence, to use Ansible effectively, one must have a solid foundation in Linux. Understanding Linux is also critical for debugging issues that might arise in Ansible playbooks and troubleshooting both system and application-related issues.

Automation necessitates scripting and programming: automation with Ansible involves writing playbooks and some scripts in programming languages that interact with various parts of the Linux system. Being proficient in Linux allows you to write efficient and effective playbooks that automate tasks more easily and with less effort. Being able to access various Linux distributions provides numerous open source tools and the freedom to drive the automation that you dream about.

As mentioned in Chapter 1, Linux was built on robust and proven UNIX technology and overtook UNIX's popularity in the mid-to-late 1990s. Since its creation, Linux has grown in popularity and has become a widely used operating system in a variety of settings. Linux can be found on desktop computers, servers, embedded systems, and mobile devices. With all Android devices and other Linux-based systems combined, Linux currently holds an estimated 45–50% market share of operating systems. In addition to its widespread use, Linux has become the go-to operating system for many public cloud infrastructures. Both AWS Cloud and Google Cloud Platform (GCP) use Linux as the primary operating system for their infrastructure servers. These cloud services support a wide range of Linux distributions, such as Ubuntu, CentOS, Red Hat Enterprise Linux (RHEL), Debian, and SUSE Linux Enterprise Server (SLES), and even vendor-specific distributions like Amazon Linux, which is based on RHEL. Furthermore, GCP has developed its own "Google Container-Optimized OS" based on the Gentoo Linux distribution. This lightweight and container-optimized OS is specifically designed to run Docker containers and includes support for Kubernetes.

In today's enterprise network environments, Linux-based operating systems are commonly used in a significant number of network devices, such as routers and switches. To interact with these devices and automate their configurations, it is essential to have a fundamental understanding of Linux. Several major network hardware vendors, including Juniper, Arista Networks, Cumulus Networks, Extreme Networks, and Cisco, have chosen Linux as the base operating system for their products. They customize it to meet their specific needs and requirements, which enables them to take advantage of Linux's stability, security, and open source nature. By using Linux as the base operating system, these vendors can provide a robust and flexible operating system for their products.

For network administrators and engineers, having a solid foundation in Linux is critical for efficiently managing and configuring these network devices. Understanding Linux is a prerequisite for becoming proficient in network automation and configuration management, including tools like Ansible. Troubleshooting skills are also essential for identifying and resolving issues with the system, and understanding Linux allows you to diagnose issues more effectively and efficiently.

Overall, acquiring knowledge in Linux is a valuable asset that can significantly enhance career prospects, particularly for those pursuing a career in networking. Linux is the foundation for automation in many organizations and equips network administrators and engineers with the necessary skills to effectively manage and configure network devices, which can increase productivity and minimize downtime. In other words, proficiency in Linux can help organizations improve their service levels while also reducing their cost of IT infrastructure ownership, by having highly skilled engineers proficient in hardware, operating systems, and automation tools such as Ansible.

Expand your knowledge:

Who invented the Linux kernel and why?

Linux was not invented by a single person but rather created by a community of developers and contributors around the world. The original kernel was created by Linus Torvalds, a Finnish computer science student, in 1991. Torvalds initially created Linux as a hobby project, seeking to create a free and open source alternative to proprietary UNIX operating systems. He released the first version of the Linux kernel, version 0.01, in September 1991. Over time, the Linux operating system grew and evolved with the help of a large community of developers and contributors who contributed their improvements and features. Today, Linux is used widely across a range of applications and industries and has become a major force in the world of open source software.

2.3 What Is Linux?

Linux is a versatile open source operating system (OS) that can be installed on physical or virtual machines for personal or commercial use. One significant difference between Linux desktop and Linux server is the graphical user interface (GUI). Linux servers are typically installed to provide specific services to users or businesses and are usually managed by Linux administrators who are familiar with Linux commands via OS's command-line interface (CLI) or terminal console over SSH. They are often installed with only the necessary software for optimal performance, stability, and security.

Linux is an operating system that has a wide variety of distributions, commonly referred to as "distros," each of which is purpose-built to meet different needs and use cases. The different Linux distributions are designed with a specific focus, such as server use, desktop use, gaming, security, scientific computing, and education, among others. They vary in terms of default software packages, configuration options, and user interfaces, among other things. Some of the most popular Linux distributions include Ubuntu, Debian, Fedora, Red Hat Enterprise Linux, CentOS, Arch Linux, and openSUSE. All Linux systems have a strong root in UNIX because Linus Torvalds wanted to create a Unix-like operating system. He modeled Linux's design and functionality after UNIX.

Although there are hundreds of different Linux distributions available, some of the major distributions appeared between 1993 and 2004, as shown in Figure 2-2. However, new distributions are still being developed to target specific user needs. Surprisingly, even the North Korean government has its Linux-based operating system called "Red Star," which is widely used in North Korea. Red Star has a graphical user interface that mimics Apple's macOS and is reportedly used by North Korean hackers to earn foreign currency through illegal activities. Despite this, Linux users have a plethora of options to choose from and can further customize their chosen distribution by adding or removing software packages, changing settings, or installing different desktop environments. With so many options available, Linux users can select the distribution that best suits their individual needs and preferences.

Source: https://en.wikipedia.org/wiki/Red_Star_OS

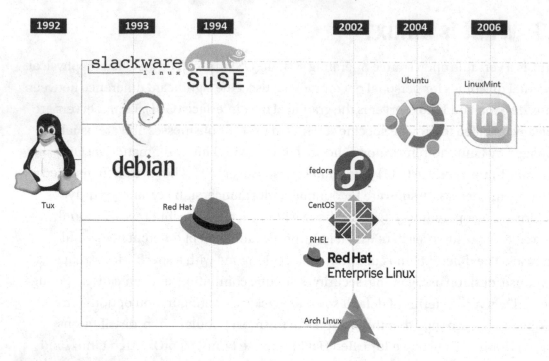

Figure 2-2. *Appearance of major Linux distributions (source:* `https://upload.wikimedia.org/wikipedia/commons/b/b5/Linux_Distribution_Timeline_21_10_2021.svg`*)*

Linux desktop and server versions typically use the same kernel for each release version of the operating system. While it is possible to install a GUI on Linux servers, many administrators prefer to use the command-line interface (CLI) for server administration, as it can be faster and more flexible. However, this may vary depending on the specific use case and the preferences of the administrator.

Unlike a GUI or CLI, which is primarily a user interface, APIs (Application Programming Interfaces) are designed for machine-to-machine communication and can be used by developers to build more complex applications. APIs have become increasingly important in enterprise IT, as they allow different applications to communicate with each other in a standardized and efficient way. APIs can use various protocols, such as HTTP or REST, to exchange data between applications. While the CLI may still be necessary for some tasks, many system administration tasks can be automated using scripting languages like Python or Bash. Automation can improve efficiency, reduce errors, and allow administrators to manage larger and more complex systems.

Overall, it is important for administrators to evaluate the most appropriate interface or tool for each task and to keep up to date with developments in the IT industry. The rise of APIs has provided a powerful new way to build and integrate applications, but the CLI and GUI remain important tools for system administration and user interaction.

In Linux, everything is organized into files and directories, making it an incredibly flexible and customizable operating system. In this chapter, we will cover only the basics of the Linux file structure so that you can progress to Chapter 4 where we will discuss the directory structure in more detail. This will enable you to develop the essential Linux command-line skills necessary to run and operate your labs and ultimately embark on your Ansible Network Automation projects. Understanding the Linux directory structure is critical for system administration and management, as it allows for efficient organization and navigation of the system. Through practice and familiarity with the command-line interface, you will become more comfortable working with Linux and be able to leverage its power to accomplish your objectives.

If you have experience administering general enterprise networking devices using the command-line interface (CLI), you may find it easier to transition to using Linux command lines. However, even if you don't have prior experience, don't worry – in this book, we will guide you through the fundamentals of Linux and its basic commands. This will help you learn at your own pace and feel confident using the command-line interface throughout the book. Understanding the Linux command-line interface is essential for effective system administration and management and can help you accomplish tasks more efficiently and with greater flexibility. Through practice and familiarity with Linux command-line tools, you can develop your skills and become a proficient Linux administrator.

To make learning Linux less daunting, we will be using WSL (Windows Subsystem for Linux) on Windows 11 and practicing various commands through hands-on exercises. These exercises will help you become familiar with the Linux environment and prepare you for the world of Ansible and network automation. Mastering basic Linux commands is essential to your success in network infrastructure automation, as they form the building blocks of the operating system and allow you to perform critical tasks efficiently. Without a strong foundation in these skills, you may struggle to progress in your studies. Therefore, acquiring fundamental Linux administration skills is crucial for your success in the IT industry. By installing WSL on your Windows system and working through these exercises, you will gain valuable experience and knowledge that will set you on the path to success in your Linux and Ansible journey.

Fun Fact:

How did the Linux Penguin get the name Tux?

The name of the Linux Penguin is officially Tux. The name "Tux" was coined by James Hughes, who was part of a Linux user group called LUG at that time. In 1996, Linus Torvalds, the creator of Linux, was looking for a mascot for the Linux operating system, and a discussion about a penguin being a good fit took place on the LUG mailing list. James Hughes suggested the name "Tux" as a play on the words "Torvalds' Unix," which was later modified to "Tux" as it fits the penguin character better. Linus Torvalds liked the idea, and Tux became the official mascot of Linux. The black and white color scheme of Tux represents the standard Unix coloring for terminals, and the penguin symbolizes the reliability, practicality, and friendliness of Linux.

Source: https://en.wikipedia.org/wiki/History_of_Linux

2.4 Install WSL on Windows 11 to Learn Linux

While this book uses WSL version 5.10.102.1, we recommend that you install the latest version of WSL available for your Windows PC to ensure the best experience. However, if you would like to refer to the WSL installation and troubleshooting processes used in this book, you can find the installation guide at the following URL: https://github.com/ansnetauto/appress_ansnetauto or https://github.com/orgs/Apress/repositories.

Warning!

WSL installation errors

Please note that when installing WSL on your Windows PC, you may encounter several issues depending on your operating system and build version. In such cases, we suggest referring to Microsoft's official documentation or Microsoft Community site to troubleshoot and complete the installation of your chosen version of WSL. Begin your troubleshooting at the following URL: `https://answers.microsoft.com/en-us/`.

Although this book presents the essential steps for installing WSL on Windows 11 to learn Linux, using Linux on WSL is not obligatory. If you currently have a functional Linux PC, or virtual machine, or access Linux on the Web, you can opt to substitute Ubuntu on WSL with your preferred method of Linux machine. Nevertheless, it is recommended that you use a Debian-based Linux operating system with the most recent kernels if you intend to follow the exercises presented in Chapters 2 and 3.

Now let's get started. To install WSL on Windows 11, follow these steps:

1. Open the Start menu and search for **"Turn Windows features on or off"**.

2. Click on **"Turn Windows features on or off"** in the search results to open the Windows Features dialog box.

3. To ensure the proper functioning of WSL, you must follow these steps: First, scroll down until you locate **"Hyper-V"** and verify that **"Hyper-V Platform"** is selected. If it is not already selected, check the box to enable it. Then, scroll down to the bottom of the list and select the **"Windows Subsystem for Linux"** option. This step is critical (refer to Figure 2-3) and should not be skipped.

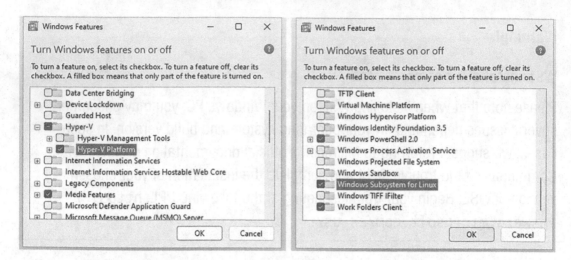

Figure 2-3. *Turn Windows features on or off to make Windows Subsystem for Linux work*

4. Click OK to install the selected feature(s). You may need to restart your computer to complete the installation.

5. After restarting your computer, open the Microsoft Store and search for "**Ubuntu**" to find and install the recommended Ubuntu WSL image. It is important to choose the version with the exact name "**Ubuntu**", as selecting other versions could cause issues that may require additional troubleshooting (see Figure 2-4).

Figure 2-4. *Get Ubuntu from Microsoft Store*

6.   Click the "Install" button to download and install the Linux distribution.

7.   After completing the installation process, you can launch the Linux distribution on your Windows machine by accessing the Start menu and selecting "**Ubuntu**" or by clicking on the "**Open**" button on the Microsoft Store screen. Alternatively, you can search for "Ubuntu" in the Windows search bar. However, it's important to note that if you start WSL by typing "wsl" in the start search bar, you'll begin in the host PC's system32 mounted folder. This may not be the desired location, so it's best to use the Start menu or Microsoft Store to launch Ubuntu, for example, jdoe@LP50BC:/mnt/c/Windows/system32$.

To create a new user account and set a password for your Linux environment, simply follow the prompts that appear after launching Ubuntu. In Figure 2-5, we have used the test username "jdoe" along with a strong password.

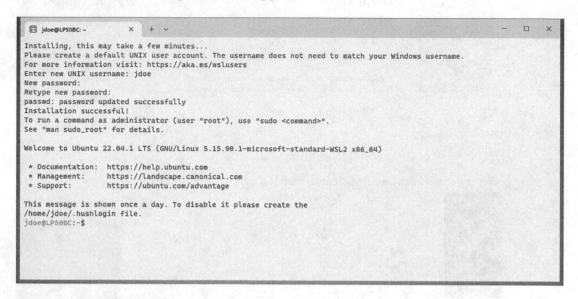

Figure 2-5. *Ubuntu on WSL – create your username and password*

As we Aussies say, "Good on you, Mate!" You have successfully set up Ubuntu Linux on your Windows 11 machine using the Windows Subsystem for Linux (WSL). Now that you have the Linux terminal ready, you are all set to dive into the world of Linux. We recommend that you follow along with the exercises in this chapter and the next chapter to get started with Linux. Don't hesitate to experiment and explore further as you learn. The more you use the terminal, the more comfortable you will become with it. Enjoy your journey with Linux!

If you are interested in mastering the world of Linux, there is no better place to start than with the command line. Although Linux does offer a great desktop GUI, most enterprise production environments will run without one, and as an administrator, it is essential to know how to navigate Linux without the assistance of a GUI.

That's where our comprehensive guide to the top Linux commands comes in. By learning and mastering each of these commands, you'll gain a deep understanding of how to navigate and manage Linux systems. But do not just read about the commands; to truly master them, you will need to type them out on the Linux console.

And fortunately, getting started is easy. Simply open your computer and launch Ubuntu on WSL, and you're ready to start typing away. As you become more familiar with these commands, you will gain a level of confidence and proficiency that will serve you well in any Linux-based environment. So why wait? Let's dive into the wonderful world of Linux commands and start mastering the commands today.

2.5 vi: The Default Text Editor

vi is a text editor commonly used in Linux operating systems, with its roots tracing back to UNIX. Despite its name, there is little about vi that could be considered visually appealing by today's standards. However, when it was first created in 1976 by Bill Joy, it may have been considered cutting edge for its time (source: https://en.wikipedia.org/wiki/Vi). Nowadays, many people are used to using graphical user interfaces (GUIs) on their computers, which makes it difficult for them to transition to using Linux's command-line interface. Learning to use vi can be particularly challenging, but it is an essential skill for IT professionals who want to master Linux. Understanding the directory structure and knowing how to use vi are critical components of learning Linux, and we will cover both in this chapter and the next one. As authors of this book, without a doubt, we can say, "By mastering vi and understanding the Linux directory structure, you have already won more than half the battle." With these skills, you will already have achieved more than half of the necessary knowledge to navigate and utilize the Linux operating system effectively.

vi employs two modes to prevent accidental edits by keeping the Command and Insert modes separately. When you open a file in vi, it starts in Command mode. In this mode, every character typed is a command to modify the text file. On the other hand, when you switch to Insert mode, you can add text to the file by typing. Pressing the <Esc> key will turn off Insert mode and return you to Command mode.

While vi has numerous useful commands in Command mode, you only need a handful to get started. Table 2-1 lists the most essential and practical vi commands. Please note that while Table 2-1 provides a comprehensive list of vi commands, not all of them will be covered in this book. If you want to learn more about each command, we highly recommend researching them further and exploring them on your own. In the upcoming chapter and this chapter, we will provide you with enough practice to get started using vi and navigating the Linux directory structure. With more practice, you will begin to develop muscle memory, allowing your fingers to work independently of conscious thought.

vi is a powerful text editor in Linux, offering many features for editing and manipulating text. Here are some of the commonly used vi commands:

Table 2-1. *vi text editor basic commands*

vi commands		Description
Basic	**vi**	Open the vi text editor or use it to open a file.
	i	Put the vi editor into Insert mode, allowing you to insert new text at the current cursor position.
	[Esc]	Exit Insert mode takes you out of Insert mode and back to Command mode.
	:x	Quit vi without saving changes; saves the file and quits the vi editor. If changes have not been saved, it prompts you to save the changes.
	:q or :q!	Quit the vi editor. If changes have been made to the file, it will prompt you to save them. Using :q! forces the editor to quit without saving changes.
	:w	Write and save the changes made to the file.
	:wq or :wq!	Save the changes made to the file and quit the vi editor. A subtle difference exists between :wq and :wq!; with :wq!, no warnings are prompted. Linux provides a security warning while changing certain files while executing commands with sudo privilege, the warning won't be displayed with the "!".

(*continued*)

Table 2-1. (*continued*)

vi commands		Description
Move	**j**	Move the cursor down one line.
	[8] key	Move the cursor down eight lines.
	[$] key	Move the cursor to the end of the line.
	k	Move the cursor up one line.
	[#] key	Move the cursor up to the line number specified in the # key.
	h	Move the cursor one character to the left.
	[backspace] key	Delete the character to the left of the cursor.
	[!] key	Repeat the last command entered.
	l (lowercase L)	Move the cursor one character to the right.
	[Space] bar	Move the cursor one character to the right.
	["] key	Specify a register to use for the next command.
	0 (zero)	Move the cursor to the beginning of the line.
	$	Move the cursor to the end of the line.
	w	Move the cursor to the beginning of the next word.
	b	Move the cursor to the beginning of the previous word.
	:0	Move the cursor to the beginning of the file.
	:n	Move the cursor to the next file.
	:$	Move the cursor to the end of the file.
Copy/paste	**dd**	Copy (cut) and delete the current line.
	p	Paste the contents of the register after the cursor.
	P	Paste the contents of the register before the cursor.
Undo	**u**	Undo the last change made to the file.

(*continued*)

Table 2-1. (*continued*)

vi commands		Description
Search text	/string	Search forward in the text for the next occurrence of the string "string".
	?string	Search backward in the text for the previous occurrence of the string "string".
	n	When used after a search command, it moves the cursor to the next occurrence of the search string.
	N	When used after a search command, it moves the cursor to the previous occurrence of the search string.

Source: Introduction to Python Network Automation: The First Journey, 2021, Apress

When using Linux servers, it is important to be proficient in the vi text editor. While other editors like nano and joe may be easier for Windows users transitioning to Linux, vi is pre-installed on almost all Linux distributions, making it a valuable skill to have. Additionally, nano is not included in many pre-installed software packages, so it may need to be manually installed by downloading the installation file or connecting to the Internet. In rare cases, a Linux system may be installed on a remote network that never connects to the Internet, or certain organizations may prohibit the installation of unapproved software. To ensure you have access to a reliable text editor, it's recommended that you become familiar with vi.

In this book, we will specifically refer to the vi editor when discussing text editors. While other text editors are available, Table 2-2 provides a quick comparison of some of the most popular Linux server text editors, including their pros and cons. While we won't provide detailed instructions for each editor, if you're interested and have time, you can explore and test them to determine which one is the best fit for your needs. However, mastering vi is essential for anyone working with all Linux server distributions.

Table 2-2. *Popular Linux server text editor features – three advantages and three disadvantages*

Editor	Advantages	Disadvantages
vi	Widely available on Linux systems Lightweight and fast Highly customizable	Challenging for beginners to learn and master due to a steep learning curve Lacks some modern features found in other text editors, such as syntax highlighting and code completion Requires memorization of keyboard shortcuts and commands to be efficient
Emacs	Versatile and customizable with multilanguage support and various features Offers a graphical user interface and different modes for different tasks to cater to all user levels Active community continuously developing and sharing new features and packages	Steep learning curve due to complexity and extensive functionality High system resource usage can be problematic on older or less powerful machines Overwhelming with many features and options, making it difficult to navigate and find specific settings or functions
vim	Powerful editing capabilities with efficient shortcuts and commands Syntax highlighting for many programming languages and file types Large user community with many customization options and plug-ins available	The steep learning curve with an extensive command set can be challenging for beginners Can be difficult to configure and customize for some users Limited graphical user interface (GUI) options, as vim is primarily used in a terminal window

(continued)

Table 2-2. (*continued*)

Editor	Advantages	Disadvantages
joe	Beginner-friendly and easy to use	Not as user-friendly as some other editors
	Lightweight and efficient for low-resource systems	Lacks some advanced features
	Offers a range of useful features, including syntax highlighting and macro recording	Steeper learning curve and limited documentation/support
nano	Simple and intuitive interface for beginners with pre-installed configuration	Limited functionality compared to more advanced editors like vi or emacs
	Supports syntax highlighting for programming languages and mouse for navigation	Not suitable for handling large files or complex tasks
	Not as versatile or customizable as other editors, lacking advanced features and extensibility	Lacks powerful features and customization options of vi and emacs

The preceding table provides an overview of various text editors available on Linux servers, highlighting only three key advantages and three disadvantages of each editor. While there are many more features and nuances to each editor, this condensed list aims to provide readers with a quick understanding of each Linux server text editor's strengths and weaknesses. This approach helps to improve readability and conserves space for the book's content. Also, gedit is a great text editor for Linux, but it is only available in a desktop-based GUI environment, so it is not included in the table. When it comes to the easiest text editors to learn and use, nano and joe with their pseudo-user interfaces are good options but have some limitations. However, hands down, the most important, powerful, and versatile text editor from the list is vi. This is an opinion shared by many Linux users.

Tip

Practicing Linux on the Web

If you are unable to install WSL on your Windows PC, don't worry; there are still plenty of ways to learn Linux using online resources. The following are some recommended websites that offer interactive Linux tutorials and exercises:

1. `https://bellard.org/jslinux/`: This website provides a virtual Linux environment that runs in your web browser. You can choose between Fedora 33 or Alpine Linux 3.12.0 and follow the instructions to get started.

2. `https://copy.sh/`: This website offers a virtual x86 machine that runs Arch Linux. Use the Esc key to escape from the terminal and access the menu. Follow the instructions provided to get started.

3. `https://replit.com/`: After logging in with your credentials, look for the "Linux shell" in the search bar; an Ubuntu 18.04 version will be available for immediate practice. Follow the instructions provided to get started.

Alternatively, if you want to install Linux on your computer, you can jump to Chapter 4 for instructions on how to do so. Once you have completed the installation, you can come back to this chapter and Chapter 3 to continue your learning journey.

2.6 Practice Linux Commands

To familiarize new Linux users with the terminal and vi editor, we'll begin with a set of essential Linux commands selected by the authors. By practicing with these commands, users can quickly adapt to working in the terminal environment and using the keyboard, with minimal reliance on the mouse.

The introductory session will be followed by a more in-depth exploration of each command, with additional practice using different examples. While users are not required to strictly follow the exercises, they must type the commands accurately to achieve the desired response from the Linux OS terminal window. Even if you are a seasoned Linux user, we recommend you follow the content and consolidate your Linux commands skills in this chapter. Regardless of your experience with Linux, we highly recommend that you review the content in this chapter to strengthen your command-line skills. Even experienced Linux users can benefit from revisiting essential commands and exploring new examples and use cases. By consolidating your skills, you can become more efficient and effective in your work with Linux.

Each exercise will include a set of commands, with new commands introduced and described if they have not been previously covered. This will help users build their skills and confidence in working with the Linux terminal and vi editor.

Warning!

Chapter 2 is the longest chapter in this book!

This is one of the longest chapters in this book, so fasten your seatbelt and get ready for a blast-off with Linux commands!

Completing all the tasks in this chapter and reading through it thoroughly will give you the necessary foundation and mindset to tackle the tasks presented throughout the entire book. By mastering the concepts and skills introduced in this chapter, you will be better equipped to approach more complex tasks with confidence and proficiency. This will set you up for success as you progress through the rest of the book.

2.6.1 The Top Ten Essential Linux Commands

To help you quickly become proficient with Linux, we have carefully chosen a list of the top ten essential Linux commands. These commands are commonly used by Linux users daily and are essential for any Linux administrator's toolkit. We highly recommend that you review the table of Linux commands (Table 2-3) carefully before beginning each exercise and then follow along with the hands-on exercises provided. Whether you are a beginner or have some experience with Linux, mastering these ten essential commands is crucial for your success.

By mastering these fundamental Linux commands, you will be well on your way to becoming a proficient Linux user. So don't hesitate, dive right in and start learning!

Table 2-3. *The top ten essential Linux commands*

#	Command	Description	Example
1	**pwd**	Display the current (present working) directory	pwd
2	**touch**	Create a new file	touch my_file.txt
3	**ls**	List all files in the current directory	ls
4	**mkdir**	Create a new directory	mkdir my_dir
5	**cd**	Change the current directory	cd /home/user/my_dir
6	**rm**	Remove a file or directory	rm my_file
7	**rmdir**	Remove an empty directory	rmdir my_dir
8	**cp**	Copy a file	cp file
9	**mv**	Move or rename a file	mv file
10	**grep**	Searches for a pattern in a file or stream of input	grep "frog" leaping.txt

Information retention is the ability to remember and recall information over time. This ability can vary depending on factors such as the complexity of the information, interest in the subject, time spent learning, and cognitive abilities. Simply reading about Linux commands may not be sufficient for retaining the information. Therefore, we recommend completing hands-on exercises to apply what you have learned and increase retention. Studies suggest that the average person can remember up to 50% of new information after one day, with the rate decreasing to around 25% after one week (source: https://en.wikipedia.org/wiki/Forgetting_curve). To improve retention, it is recommended to engage with the material by taking notes, summarizing key points, and practicing recall. Breaking down complex information into smaller chunks and taking breaks can also be helpful to avoid information overload. Consistent effort and effective learning strategies can improve information retention.

Tip

Getting most out of this chapter

To effectively learn and master Linux commands, you must engage in a hands-on approach. **When you encounter a command displayed in bold with the "$" symbol in the exercises, you are expected to input the Linux command into the Linux console.** This approach will allow you to learn by doing and experimenting with the commands to truly internalize their function and power.

It's important to note that each exercise contains a helpful explanation embedded within gray-colored fonts, indicated by the # symbol. This explanation is designed to provide you with additional context and insights into the command being discussed and will help you to better understand how the command works.

We strongly recommend that you carefully read through these explanations, as they may contain important details or tips that will help you to complete the exercise. By following this approach and engaging actively with the material, you'll be able to deepen your understanding of the Linux commands and improve your overall proficiency as a Linux user.

Active engagement with the material can help you avoid the pitfall of passively reading through the commands without truly understanding them. Therefore, take the time to complete the exercises and discover how these essential Linux commands work in practice. You can also personalize the exercise by changing the names of files, contents, and topics to relate to your personal experiences. Doing so can increase information retention, and there is a higher chance that the information will be stored in your long-term memory. So make sure to actively engage with the exercises and personalize them to your own experiences for maximum retention (source: "Fundamental Neuroscience" 5th Edition, 2021, Larry Squire Darwin Berg, etc.)

Let's begin by launching the Linux terminal on Ubuntu WSL, and then type in the commands highlighted in bold to get started.

EXERCISE 1

```
~$ pwd # print the current working directory
/home/jdoe
~$ touch my_file.txt # create an empty file named my_file.txt
~$ ls # list the files in the current directory
my_file.txt
~$ mkdir ex1 # create a directory named ex1
~$ ls # list directory content
ex1  my_file.txt
~$ ls -lh # list directory content, long listing, and human-readable
total 4.0K
drwxr-xr-x 2 jdoe jdoe 4.0K Mar 13 21:11 ex1
-rw-r--r-- 1 jdoe jdoe    0 Mar 13 21:10 my_file.txt
~$ cd ex1 # change the current working directory to ex1
~/ex1$ pwd # print the current working directory
/home/jdoe/ex1
~/ex1$ cd .. # move one directory up
~$ pwd # print the current working directory
/home/jdoe
~$ ls # list the files and directories in the current directory
ex1  my_file.txt
$ rm my_file.txt # remove the file named my_file.txt. Enter "rm my_" and the
Tab key to use the auto-completion feature.
$ ls # list the files and directories in the current directory
ex1
~$ rmdir ex1# remove the directory named ex1
~$ ls # list the files and directories in the current directory
~$     # empty
~$ touch your_file.txt # create an empty file named your_file.txt
~$ ls # list the files and directories in the current directory
your_file.txt
~$ mkdir ex1 # create a new directory named ex1 again
~$ ls # list the files and directories in the current directory
ex1  your_file.txt
~$ cp your_file.txt my_file.txt # copy the file named your_file.txt to a new
file named my_file.txt
```

```
~$ ls # list the files and directories in the current directory
ex1 my_file.txt  your_file.txt
~$ touch his_file.txt her_file.txt # create two empty files named his_file.
txt and her_file.txt
~$ ls # list the files and directories in the current directory
ex1 her_file.txt  his_file.txt  my_file.txt  your_file.txt
~$ mv her_file.txt ex1/ # move the file named her_file.txt to the directory
named ex1
~$ ls # list the files and directories in the current directory
ex1 his_file.txt  my_file.txt  your_file.txt
~$ mv his_file.txt our_file.txt # rename the file named his_file.txt to our_
file.txt
~$ ls # list the files and directories in the current directory
ex1 my_file.txt  our_file.txt your_file.txt
~$ mv our_file.txt ex1/# move the file named our_file.txt to the directory
named ex1
~$ ls # list the files and directories in the current directory
ex1 my_file.txt  your_file.txt
~$ mv *.txt ex1/# move all files ending in .txt to the directory named ex1
~$ ls # list the files and directories in the current directory
ex1
~$ ls ex1# list the files and directories in the directory named ex1
her_file.txt  my_file.txt  our_file.txt  your_file.txt
~$ mv ex1 exercise1 # rename the directory named ex1 to exercise1
~$ ls # list the files and directories in the current directory
exercise1
~$ ls exercise1/ # list the files and directories in the directory named
exercise1
her_file.txt  my_file.txt  our_file.txt  your_file.txt
~$ rmdir exercise1 # remove the directory named exercise1, directory is not
empty, so rmdir fails!
rmdir: failed to remove 'exercise1': Directory
~$ mv exercise1/* . # Move all files from exercise 1 to the current
directory. Watch out for the space between * and .
~$ ls
exercise1 her_file.txt  my_file.txt our_file.txt  your_file.txt
~$ ls exercise1/ # List the contents of exercise1 directory (should be empty)
~$   # empty
```

~$ **rm exercise1/** # Attempt to remove the exercise1 directory (fails since it is a directory and you are using the rm command)
rm: cannot remove 'exercise1': Is a directory
~$ **rm -r exercise1** # recursively remove the exercise1 directory and its contents. This should work.
~$ **ls** # List the files in the current directory (should not include .txt files)
her_file.txt my_file.txt our_file.txt your_file.txt
~$ **rm -r *.txt** # Remove all .txt files in the current directory
~$ **ls** # List the files in the current directory (should be empty)
~$ # empty
~$ **base64 /dev/urandom | head -c 100 > random.txt** # creates random.txt file with 100 bytes random data
~$ **ls** # list the content of current directory
random.txt
~$ **wc -c random.txt** # count the bytes in random.txt
100 random.txt
~$ **wc -m random.txt** # count the characters in random.txt
100 random.txt
~$ **cat random.txt** # concatenate (display) content of random.txt. Your file will contain randomly created 100-character data, so will be different from the example shown here
V55KjOubmEkg4UxHRx2oFa7i472SUcP6BPLTL6zu9TljqYwI6W2EHYPgZM+HttSXoo6BRDt4L81A
fCrSpGUT4UoAFK1DZZZO/Fi
~$ **grep -o '[[:alpha:]]' random.txt** # -o option to show only the matched patterns, '[[:alpha:]]' matches any alphabets
V
[... omitted for brevity]
~$ **grep -o '[[:digit:]]' random.txt** # -o option to show only the matched patterns, '[[:digit:]]' matches any number
5
[... omitted for brevity]
~$ **grep -o '[[:alpha:]]' random.txt | tr -d '\n'; echo** # same as above but removes the newline character to output alphabet characters to a single line, echo is used to print a newline at the end of the output
VKjOubmEkgUxHRxoFaiSUcPBPLTLzuTljqYwIWEHYPgZMHttSXooBRDtLAfCrSpGUTUoAFKDZZZFi
~$ **grep -o '[[:digit:]]' random.txt | tr -d '\n' ; echo** # same as above but only prints digits
55427472669626481410

```
~$ rm random.txt # remove random.txt file
~$ ls # list the content of the present working directory
~$ # empty
~$ clear # clears the screen, also use 'Ctrl+L' key combination to clear
the screen
~$ # empty screen
```

Wow, that was a great start, especially if you're a first-time Linux user. It is normal to feel overwhelmed by Exercise 1 at first, but do not worry – we've got you covered! Just follow along and type the commands step by step while paying special attention to the explanations that start with the "#" sign. This will help you to become more familiar and comfortable with Linux commands, which is essential for mastering the system. Remember, practice makes perfect, so don't be afraid to make mistakes or ask for help. With time and patience, you'll become a pro at using the Linux console.

Throughout the remainder of this chapter, we'll be diving deeper into various Linux commands through exercises. Our goal is to help you become proficient with these commands so that you can use them for your daily tasks. We'll not only be revisiting some of the commands we covered in Exercise 1, but we'll also introduce you to new ones. By practicing with these commands, you'll gain familiarity with the Linux command line and build confidence in your ability to use it effectively. It's normal to feel intimidated by the Linux command line at first, but don't worry – with practice and patience, you'll soon find that it's a powerful tool that can help you accomplish a wide range of tasks quickly and efficiently. So keep practicing, and don't be afraid to experiment with different commands and options. Who knows – you might just discover something new and useful that can make your life easier. Let's get started!

Tip

Viewing command options

Don't worry about memorizing every Linux command and its options. Instead, you can use the "--help" or "man" command to quickly get information about how to use a specific command. It's important to note that sometimes both commands will work, while other times only one or the other will provide the necessary help pages. For instance, to get help with the "cat" command, you can type either "cat --help" or "man cat".

~$ `cat --help`

or

~$ `man cat`

When in doubt, it's always a good idea to consult the help and man pages for guidance. These resources can provide you with valuable information on how to use specific commands, as well as their options and syntax. By using these resources, you can increase your efficiency and productivity when working in the Linux environment."

2.6.2 cat and tac

The "cat" command is a versatile tool that's often considered essential for Linux users. Although it could easily be included as one of the ten essential Linux commands in Table 2-3, we've separated it to emphasize its relationship with "tac". Its primary purpose is to display the contents of one or more files on the console. It can also be used to concatenate multiple files together or create new files by redirecting its output to a file. By default, "cat" displays the file's contents starting from the first line to the last line.

It's worth noting that "cat" and "tac" are not only palindromes but also reversed versions of each other. Palindromes are words or phrases that read the same backward as they do forward. This adds an extra layer of symmetry to this linguistic coincidence. In contrast, the "tac" command displays the contents of one or more files in reverse order, starting from the last line and ending at the first line. Essentially, "tac" is the reverse of "cat". Understanding the functionality of both commands can help you efficiently manipulate and display the contents of files in Linux.

In Table 2-4, you can find a comprehensive list of all the commands used in our exercise. These commands are designed to help you practice and improve your skills in using Linux. By familiarizing yourself with these commands and their functions, you can become more proficient in navigating and manipulating files and directories in Linux.

Table 2-4. *Linux commands in action*

#	Command	Description	Example
1	**cat**	Display the contents of one or more files on the console	cat file.txt
2	**tac**	Display the contents of one or more files in reverse order (i.e., from the last line to the first line) on the console	tac file.txt
3	**sudo**	Execute a command with administrative privileges	sudo
4	**apt-get**	A package management tool used to install, update, and remove software packages (older)	apt-get install tree
5	**apt**	A package management tool used to install, update, and remove software packages (newer)	apt install tmux
6	**cal**	Display a calendar	cal
7	**clear**	Clear the terminal screen. Alternatively use Ctrl + L keys	clear
8	**hostname**	Display or set the hostname of the system	hostname
9	**>**	Output to a file (overwrites the existing file with the same name)	cal > file.txt
10	**>>**	Appends content to the next line (does not overwrite)	hostname > file.txt

To understand the difference between "cat" and "tac" commands in Linux, it's helpful to think about how they display the contents of a file. The "cat" command displays a file in the same order that it appears in the file. For example, if you have a file that contains a list of items, "cat" would display the list from the first item to the last item. On the other hand, the "tac" command displays the file in reverse order, starting from the last line and ending at the first line. So if you use "tac" on a file that contains a list of items, it would display the list from the last item to the first item. By understanding the differences between "cat" and "tac", you can choose the appropriate command to manipulate and display the contents of files in Linux.

Keep in mind that if you use a different date or year than the ones in the following examples, your calendar outputs will naturally vary from those displayed.

EXERCISE 2.1

~$ **mkdir ex2 && cd ex2**   # creates a new directory named ex2 & navigates to the newly created ex2 directory
~/ex2$ **ls**   # lists the contents of the current directory (should be empty)
~/ex2$ **cal**   # attempts to display the current month's calendar using the 'cal' command

Command 'cal' not found, but can be installed with:

sudo apt install ncal
~/ex2$ **sudo apt-get update**   # calendar program is not installed, first updates the package list
[... omitted for brevity]
~/ex2$ **sudo apt install ncal** # now, installs the 'ncal' package which includes the 'cal' command
[... omitted for brevity]
~/ex2$ **cal**   # you can now display the current month's calendar using 'cal' command
      March 2023
Su Mo Tu We Th Fr Sa
          1 2 3 4
 5 6 7 8 9 10 11
12 13 14 15 16 17 18
19 20 21 22 23 24 25
26 27 28 29 30 31
~/ex2$ **clear**   # clears the console screen. Tip: you can also clear the screen using the 'Ctrl + L' key combination.

EXERCISE 2.2

~/ex2$ **cal** **>** **c1** # save the current month to c1 file, does not display
the output
~/ex2$ **ls** # display the content of the current working directory
c1
~/ex2$ **cat c1** # print the contents of the file c1 on the console
     March 2023
Su Mo Tu We Th Fr Sa
          1 2 3 4
 5 6 7 8 9 10 11
12 13 14 15 16 17 18
19 20 21 22 23 24 25
26 27 28 29 30 31

~/ex2$ **hostname** # display the name of the current host computer
p51-jdoe
~/ex2$ **hostname** **>** **h1** # save the name of the current host computer to a file
named h1
~/ex2$ **cat h1** # display the contents of the file h1 on the console
LB50BC
~/ex2$ **ls -lh** # list all files and directories in the current directory with
detailed information and in human-readable format
total 8.0K
-rw-r--r-- 1 jdoe jdoe 184 Mar 14 05:04 c1
-rw-r--r-- 1 jdoe jdoe 12 Mar 14 05:07 h1

EXERCISE 2.3

~/ex2$ **cat -n c1**   # display the content of the file c1 on the console with
the line number reference
```
1       March 2023
2  Su Mo Tu We Th Fr Sa
3            1  2  3  4
4   5  6  7  8  9 10 11
5  12 13 14 15 16 17 18
6  19 20 21 22 23 24 25
7  26 27 28 29 30 31
8
```
~/ex2$ **cat -b c1**   # display the content of the file c1 on the console with
line numbers, but skip over blank lines
```
1       March 2023
2  Su Mo Tu We Th Fr Sa
3            1  2  3  4
4   5  6  7  8  9 10 11
5  12 13 14 15 16 17 18
6  19 20 21 22 23 24 25
7  26 27 28 29 30 31
8
```

~/ex2$ **vi c1**   # open the file c1 in the vi text editor for editing. Add empty
lines between each lines as shown below. Save the file.
~/ex2$ **cat c1**
```
    March 2023

Su Mo Tu We Th Fr Sa

          1  2  3  4

 5  6  7  8  9 10 11

12 13 14 15 16 17 18

19 20 21 22 23 24 25

26 27 28 29 30 31
```

~/ex2$ **cat -n c1** # now run the cat command with the -n option again, and
review the output carefully.

```
     1          March 2023
     2
     3   Su Mo Tu We Th Fr Sa
     4
     5             1  2  3  4
     6
     7    5  6  7  8  9 10 11
     8
     9   12 13 14 15 16 17 18
    10
    11   19 20 21 22 23 24 25
    12
    13   26 27 28 29 30 31
    14
```

~/ex2$ **cat -b c1** # now run the cat command with the -b option again and
compare the output with the previous output above.

```
     1          March 2023

     2   Su Mo Tu We Th Fr Sa

     3             1  2  3  4

     4    5  6  7  8  9 10 11

     5   12 13 14 15 16 17 18

     6   19 20 21 22 23 24 25

     7   26 27 28 29 30 31

     8
```

EXERCISE 2.4

~/ex2$ **cal > c1** # overwrite the existing c1 file and save the current month's output to a file named 'c1'.

~/ex2$ **cat c1** # display the contents of file 'c1' on the console. Notice that the content of the previous exercise has been overwritten.

```
    March 2023
Su Mo Tu We Th Fr Sa
          1  2  3  4
 5  6  7  8  9 10 11
12 13 14 15 16 17 18
19 20 21 22 23 24 25
26 27 28 29 30 31
```

~/ex2$ **cat c1 h1** # concatenate the contents of files 'c1' and 'h1' and display the result on the console

```
    March 2023
Su Mo Tu We Th Fr Sa
          1  2  3  4
 5  6  7  8  9 10 11
12 13 14 15 16 17 18
19 20 21 22 23 24 25
26 27 28 29 30 31
```

LB50BC

~/ex2$ **cat c1 h1 > b1** # concatenate the contents of files 'c1' and 'h1' and save the result to a new file named 'b1'

~/ex2$ **ls** # list the files and directories in the current directory

b1 c1 h1

~/ex2$ **cat b1** # display the contents of file 'b1' on the console

```
    March 2023
Su Mo Tu We Th Fr Sa
          1  2  3  4
 5  6  7  8  9 10 11
12 13 14 15 16 17 18
19 20 21 22 23 24 25
26 27 28 29 30 31
```

LB5OBC
~/ex2$ **cat h1** # display the contents of file 'h1' on the console
LB5OBC
~/ex2$ **cat b1>> h1** # append the contents of file 'b1' to the end of file
'h1'. <u>Note the use of double greater signs.</u>
~/ex2$ **cat h1** # display the contents of file 'h1' on the console again,
including the contents of file 'b1'
LB5OBC
```
     March 2023
Su Mo Tu We Th Fr Sa
          1  2  3  4
 5  6  7  8  9 10 11
12 13 14 15 16 17 18
19 20 21 22 23 24 25
26 27 28 29 30 31
```

LB5OBC

EXERCISE 2.5

~/ex2$ **cat b1** # tac is a wordplay on cat and it reverses the content of
the file.
```
     March 2023
Su Mo Tu We Th Fr Sa
          1  2  3  4
 5  6  7  8  9 10 11
12 13 14 15 16 17 18
19 20 21 22 23 24 25
26 27 28 29 30 31
```

LB5OBC
~/ex2$ **tac b1** # check b1 first using 'cat b1, then use 'tac b1'. Observe the
reversed output. Just like the cat command, you can also save the tac output
to a file using the 'tac > filename' command.
LB5OBC

```
26 27 28 29 30 31
19 20 21 22 23 24 25
12 13 14 15 16 17 18
 5  6  7  8  9 10 11
             1  2  3  4
Su Mo Tu We Th Fr Sa
    March 2023
```

EXERCISE 2.6

~/ex2$ **cat** **#** What if you simply use the cat command? Use cat to print on the screen, and Ctrl+D to quit.
Tux # type this word
tux
the # type this word
the
penguin # type this word
penguin # Use Ctrl+D to quit.
~/ex2$
~/ex2$ **cat - #** You can also use "cat -", same as using "cat".
I # type this word
I
Love # type this word
Love
Tux # type this word
Tux # Use Ctrl+D to quit.

If you want to create a new file with a few lines, use cat. This could be faster than using a text editor.

~/ex2$ **cat > a4** # Create a file name a4 and opens it for writing. Type in the following using Enter keys.
I
Love
Penguin # Use Ctrl+D to quit.

```
~/ex2$ cat a4 # Display the content of a4.
I
Love
Penguin
```

Try the following exercise using the "cat" command to create your first Python script called "sayhello.py". Don't worry if you don't understand Python code; just follow along for some fun and to get started on your Python journey. You are creating a small Python program.

EXERCISE 2.7

```
~/ex2$ cat > sayhello.py # Create and open your first Python code sayhello.py
and add the lines as shown below.
name = input('What is your name? ')
print('Hello,', name) # Use Ctrl+D to quit.
~/ex2$ python3 sayhello.py # Run the Python code as shown.
What is your name? John # Enter a name to get a Hello return.
Hello, John
```

Let's create your first bash shell script called sayhello.sh using the cat command. Don't worry if you're not familiar with the syntax yet; just follow the following steps for some fun. Hopefully, this will pique your interest in shell and PowerShell scripting as well. You are creating a small bash shell program.

EXERCISE 2.8

```
~/ex2$ cat > sayhello.sh # Create and open your first bash shell code
sayhello.sh and add the lines as shown below.
#!/bin/bash
read -p "What is your name? " name
echo "Hello, $name"
~/ex2$ source ./sayhello.sh # Run the shell script using a source command.
Alternatively, use 'bash ./sayhello.sh' or '/bin/bash ./sayhello.sh'.
What is your name? Sam # Enter a name to get a Hello return
```

```
Hello, Sam
~/ex2$ chmod +x sayhello.sh # Make file sayhello.sh as an executable file.
~/ex2$ ls -lh sayhello* # List all files with sayhello. Notice the file color
change in sayhello.sh, now this file is executable.
-rw-r--r-- 1 jdoe jdoe 56 Mar 14 20:55 sayhello.py
-rwxr-xr-x 1 jdoe jdoe 67 Mar 14 20:58 sayhello.sh
~/ex2$ ./sayhello.sh # Run the executable bash shell script from the working
folder"./" denotes the current working folder.
What is your name? Jane # Enter a name to get a Hello return.
Hello, Jane
```

Well done! You have completed the exercises related to the "cat" and "tac" commands. Throughout the exercises, you have gained exposure to several other useful Linux commands and created your first Python and Shell scripts using the "cat" command. In summary, the "cat" command is a versatile tool that can display the contents of one or more files from top to bottom, concatenate multiple files together, and create new files by redirecting its output to a file. On the other hand, the "tac" command is useful for reversing the order of a file's contents by displaying them from bottom to top. Additionally, you can use the "cat" command in combination with the greater than sign (>) to create a new file quickly from the console, or even append a line to a file using two greater than signs (>>).

Keep up the good work and continue practicing and exploring more Linux commands to improve your skills. Moving on, we'll explore the "touch" command and introduce you to the vi text editor.

2.6.3 touch

In Linux, the "touch" command has two purposes. Firstly, it is used to create an empty file with a specified name or path. Secondly, it can update the access and modification timestamps of an existing file. When used to create a new file, if the specified file name does not exist, "touch" will create an empty file with that name. If the file already exists, "touch" will update its access and modification timestamps to the current time by default. However, the "-t" option can be used to set a specific timestamp. Overall, the "touch" command is a useful utility for quickly creating new files or updating file timestamps for various purposes. In Linux, there are several ways to create a new file, and two of the most commonly used methods are using the touch and vi commands as explained in Table 2-5.

Table 2-5. *Linux commands in action*

#	Command	Description	Example
1	**touch**	Creates an empty file or updates the modification time of an existing file without changing its contents	touch myfile.bak
2	**vi**	vi text editor, commands explained per Table 2-1	vi myfile.bak

The best way to become proficient with the touch command and vi is through practice. Let's get started with some hands-on exercises.

EXERCISE 3.1

```
~$ mkdir ex3 && cd ex3 / # create ex3_touch directory and changes directory
~/ex3 $
~/ex3$ touch myfile.txt # create an empty file called "myfile.txt" in the
current directory
~/ex3$ ls -lh
total 0
-rw-r--r-- 1 jdoe jdoe 0 Mar 16 00:44 myfile.txt
```

Take a break for one minute! Then run the same touch command again and observe the new time stamp.

```
~/ex3$ touch myfile.txt  # update the modification timestamp of "myfile.txt"
to the current time
~/ex3$ ls -lh
total 0
-rw-r--r-- 1 jdoe jdoe 0 Mar 16 00:45 myfile.txt # notice the time change
after the last touch command
~/ex3$ touch -t 202301241030 myfile.txt # you can use the -t option to change
the timestamp of a file. The timestamp is in the format "YYYYMMDDhhmm"
~/ex3$ ls -lh
total 0
-rw-r--r-- 1 jdoe jdoe 0 Jan 24 10:30 myfile.txt
```

EXERCISE 3.2

~/ex3$ **touch file1 file2 file3** # create three empty files in the current
directory.
~/ex3$ **ls -lh**
total 0
-rw-r--r-- 1 jdoe jdoe 0 Mar 18 20:53 file1
-rw-r--r-- 1 jdoe jdoe 0 Mar 18 20:53 file2
-rw-r--r-- 1 jdoe jdoe 0 Mar 18 20:53 file3
-rw-r--r-- 1 jdoe jdoe 0 Mar 18 20:46 myfile.txt

EXERCISE 3.3

~/ex3$ **vi myfile.txt** # vi can open the existing file "myfile.txt"

i # switch to insert mode
You can't touch this! # add some text to the file. Here I have typed in "You
can't touch this!"

Esc # switch back to command mode by pressing down on the Esc key.
:wq # save the file and exit "vi", colon followed by w for write and q
for quit.

~/ex3$ **cat myfile.txt** # use the 'cat' command to view the content of
the file.vi
You can't touch this!

~/ex3$ **vi yourfile.txt** # vi opens a new file called yourfile.txt, vi can also
be used to open a new file.
:q # simply quit without modifying the open file.
~/ex3$ **ls** # since we did not enter any data to yourfile.txt, the file was
not saved.
file1 file2 file3 myfile.txt

The touch command is a versatile tool that allows you to create one or multiple files at once. It's also useful for updating the timestamp of an existing file, as demonstrated in Exercise 3-1. However, if you need more control over the content of the file, you might prefer to use the vi editor. With vi, you can create a new file, similar to the touch command, or open an existing file, as shown in Exercise 3.3. The vi editor offers many advanced features, but for now, let's focus on using it to create and open files. By mastering these basic commands, you'll be well on your way to becoming a proficient Linux user.

2.6.4 mkdir and rmdir

mkdir and **rmdir** Linux commands are used to create and remove directories, respectively. Directories are also known as folders in Windows OS. The mkdir command takes a single argument, which is the name of the directory to be created. You can also specify a path to create a directory in a specific location. For example, to create a directory named "ex4" in the "/home/jdoe/" directory, you would use the following command:

```
~$ mkdir /home/jdoe/ex4
```

On the other hand, the rmdir command is used to remove an empty directory. It takes a single argument, which is the name of the directory to be removed. To remove an empty directory, you can use the following command:

```
~$ rmdir ex4
```

If the directory contains any files or subdirectories, rmdir will fail and return an error message. To remove a non-empty directory and all its contents, you can use the rm command with the -r (recursive) option. For example, to remove a directory named "ex4" and all its contents, you would use the following command:

```
~$ rm -r ex4
```

It's essential to use these commands carefully to avoid deleting important data or creating unnecessary directories. Always double-check the directory name and its contents before running any of these commands. Additionally, you can use the ls command to check the directory's contents before removing it. To prompt for confirmation before deleting the file "file.txt" using the "rm -r" command, you can add the "-i" option to the command. As a Linux administrator, relying too heavily on the "-i" option for prompts can hinder your efficiency in managing your system. It is crucial to have a deep understanding of the commands you're using and to exercise caution when executing commands that modify or delete files. While it's always better to err on the side of caution, a skilled administrator should be familiar enough with command behavior to execute them confidently.

```
~$ rm -ir ex4
rm: remove directory 'ex4'? y
```

Now, let's have a look at the key commands in Table 2-6, which will be used in Exercise 4.

Table 2-6. *Linux commands in action*

#	Command	Description	Example
1	**mkdir**	Used to create a new directory	mkdir ex4
2	**rmdir**	Used to remove an empty directory	rmdir ex4
3	**rm**	Remove command, removes directories and files	rm -r ex4

We've discussed the theory, and now it's time to put it into action. Let's dive in and get some practice.

EXERCISE 4.1

```
~$ mkdir ex4 && cd ex4 # create and change working directory to ex4
~/ex4$ mkdir d1 # create a new directory, d1
~/ex4$ ls -al # -a option prints all information, including hidden files and
directories, -l option display the long listing
total 12
drwxr-xr-x 3 jdoe jdoe 4096 Apr  2 17:38 .  # the . reperesents current directory
drwxr-x--- 3 jdoe jdoe 4096 Apr  2 17:37 .. # the .. represents parent directory
drwxr-xr-x 2 jdoe jdoe 4096 Apr  2 17:38 d1 # d1 is a new directory we've
just created
~/ex4$ ls -Al # if you do not want to see the all information use "-A"
option. Capped options usually carry the opposite meaning to the lower cased
option in Linux. Same applies in regular expression options.
total 4
drwxr-xr-x 2 jdoe jdoe 4096 Apr  2 17:38 d1
```

EXERCISE 4.2

~/ex4$ **mkdir d2 d3 d4 d5** # create four new directories
~/ex4$ **ls**
d1 d2 d3 d4 d5
~/ex4$ **mkdir dir{1..10}** # use range option to create ten more directories
~/ex4$ **ls**
d1 d2 d3 d4 d5 dir1 dir10 dir2 dir3 dir4 dir5 dir6 dir7 dir8 dir9
~/ex4$ **rmdir *** # for consistent directory naming let's remove all directories
in ex4 directory.
~/ex4$ **ls**
~/ex4$ **mkdir d{1..100}** # create 100 new directories starting with the
letter d
~/ex4$ **ls**
d1   d13 d18 d22 d27 d31 d36 d40 d45 d5   d54 d59 d63 d68 d72 d77 d81 d86 d90 d95
d10   d14 d19 d23 d28 d32 d37 d41 d46 d50 d55 d6   d64 d69 d73 d78 d82 d87 d91 d96
d100   d15 d2 d24 d29 d33 d38 d42 d47 d51 d56 d60 d65 d7   d74 d79 d83 d88 d92 d97
d11   d16 d20 d25 d3 d34 d39 d43 d48 d52 d57 d61 d66 d70 d75 d8   d84 d89 d93 d98
d12   d17 d21 d26 d30 d35 d4 d44 d49 d53 d58 d62 d67 d71 d76 d80 d85 d9   d94 d99
~/ex4$ **rmdir d{1..100}** # we changed our mind and no longer need these directories
~/ex4$ **ls**
~/ex4$ # emptied directory

EXERCISE 4.3

~/ex4$ **ls**
~/ex4$ **mkdir d1/d2** # try mkdir command without the -p option
mkdir: cannot create directory 'd1/d2': No such file or directory
~/ex4$ **mkdir -p d1/d2** # -p stands for parents, try to create a nested
directory with -p
~/ex4$ **ls**
d1
~/ex4$ **ls d1/** # list content in directory, d1
d2
~/ex4$ **mkdir -p d1/d2/d3/d4/d5** # create multi-nested directories at once

```
~/ex4$ ls -R # use ls with '-R' option to view sub-directories
.:
d1

./d1:
d2

./d1/d2:
d3

./d1/d2/d3:
d4

./d1/d2/d3/d4:
d5

./d1/d2/d3/d4/d5:
```

EXERCISE 4.4

```
~/ex4$ tree # check if the tree is installed on your Ubuntu
Command 'tree' not found, but can be installed with:
sudo apt install tree
~/ex4$ sudo apt install tree # install tree
[sudo] password for jdoe: *************** # enter your password
[... omitted for brevity]
~/ex4$ tree --version # check the tree version
tree v2.0.2 (c) 1996 - 2022 by Steve Baker, Thomas Moore, Francesc Rocher,
Florian Sesser, Kyosuke Tokoro
~/ex4$ tree # run tree command, you can easily see the directories and file
structure
.
└── d1
    └── d2
        └── d3
            └── d4
                └── d5

5 directories, 0 files
```

EXERCISE 4.5

~/ex4$ **rmdir -p d1/d2/d3/d4/d5** # removing nested directories are the reverse of creating them

~/ex4$ **tree**

.

0 directories, 0 files

~/ex4$ **ls**

~/ex4$ # empty

EXERCISE 4.6

~/ex4$ **mkdir d1** # make a new directory d1

~/ex4$ **cal > d1/c1** # create a file called c1

~/ex4$ **cat d1/c1** # enter this month's calendar to c1

```
     April 2023
Su Mo Tu We Th Fr Sa
                   1
 2  3  4  5  6  7  8
 9 10 11 12 13 14 15
16 17 18 19 20 21 22
23 24 25 26 27 28 29
30
```

~/ex4$ **rmdir d1**# 'rmdir' cannot delete a directory with contents inside.

rmdir: failed to remove 'd1': Directory not empty

~/ex4$ **rmdir -r d1** # 'rmdir' command is not often used to delete a directory with contents. It does not allow you to delete them.

rmdir: invalid option -- 'r'

Try 'rmdir --help' for more information.

~/ex4$ **rm -r d1** # To delete a directory with contents, use 'rm -r' command. This works!

~/ex4$ **ls**

~/ex4$ # empty

Now that you have learned the following Linux commands: mkdir, rmdir, and rm, you can create and delete directories with ease. Unlike using mouse clicks, where you can only create one folder at a time, with these commands, you can create multiple directories at once, even creating nested directories using the "-p" option. Additionally, removing nested directories or directories with items is a breeze. To check the file nesting, you can use the "ls -R" command, and if you want to see the directory structure more clearly, you can install the "tree" package and use it to visualize the directories.

2.6.5 cp and rm

Before we dive into the exercise, let's review some of the Linux commands we'll be using, including cp and rm, as well as their supplementary commands. Look at Table 2-7 and take a moment to familiarize yourself with each command and study the simple examples provided.

Table 2-7. *Linux commands in action*

#	Command	Description	Example
1	**cp**	Copy files and directories from one location to another	cp file1 file2
2	**rm**	Remove files or directories, does not prompt for confirmation before deleting files. Use with care	rm file1
3	**tee**	Redirect and duplicate the output of a command to both a file and the terminal	ls | tee file3
4	**alias**	Create a shortcut or alias for a command or series of commands	alias ll='ls -alF'
5	**>/dev/null**	Discards the duplicate output that tee writes to the standard output	cp /etc/* . 2>/dev/null
6	**ll**	Long listing command, short for "ls -l" command	ll

Now is the perfect opportunity to gain some practices and see what the preceding commands can do for you. Let's get started.

EXERCISE 5.1

```
~$ mkdir ex5 && cd ex5 # create a new directory name ex5 and change
directory to ex5
~/ex5$ pwd
/home/jdoe/ex5
~/ex5$ cp /etc/passwd .  # save /etc/passwd file here in the current working
directory with the same name
~/ex5$ ls
passwd
~/ex5$ cp /etc/passwd p1 #
~/ex5$ ls -lh
total 8.0K
-rw-r--r-- 1 jdoe jdoe 1.4K Apr  2 21:52 p1
-rw-r--r-- 1 jdoe jdoe 1.4K Apr  2 21:51 passwd
~/ex5$ cp /etc/passwd p2 # copy /etc/passwd file as p2 in current working
directory
~/ex5$ ll # long listing, shorthand for the 'ls -l'
total 20
drwxr-xr-x 2 jdoe jdoe 4096 Apr  2 21:52 ./
drwxr-x--- 3 jdoe jdoe 4096 Apr  2 21:51 ../
-rw-r--r-- 1 jdoe jdoe 1416 Apr  2 21:52 p1
-rw-r--r-- 1 jdoe jdoe 1416 Apr  2 21:52 p2
-rw-r--r-- 1 jdoe jdoe 1416 Apr  2 21:51 passwd
~/ex5$ rm p1 # remove p1 file immediately
~/ex5$ ls
p2   passwd
~/ex5$ rm -i p2 # remove p2 file interactively
rm: remove regular file 'p2'? y # yes, remove the file
~/ex5$ rm -i passwd # remove passwd file interactively
rm: remove regular file 'passwd'? n # no, keep the file
~/ex5$ ls # list current working directory content
passwd
```

EXERCISE 5.2

~/ex5$ **alias rm='rm -i'** # create an alias so each time the rm command is
used, you are prompted to confirm file/directory deletion
~/ex5$ **alias rm** # check alias has been configured properly
alias rm='rm -i'
~/ex5$ **ls**
passwd
~/ex5$ **cp passwd p3 p4 p5** # try to create three files from a single source
file passwd, this fails!
cp: target 'p5' is not a directory
~/ex5$ **cp passwd >(tee p1 p2 p3 >/dev/null)** # use cp ~ tee command with
/dev/null to make multiple copies of the same file with different names. he
>/dev/null at the end of the command discards the duplicate output that tee
writes to standard output.
~/ex5$ **ls** # list and check the new files
p1   p2   p3   passwd
~/ex5$ **rm p1** # run rm p1 command as a normal command, this will ask you for
delete confirmation
rm: remove regular file 'p1'? **y** # yes, delete file p1
~/ex5$ **\rm p2** # "\" negates the alias and deletes file p2 without
confirmation
~/ex5$ **rm -f p3** # remove p3 file forcefully (without confirmation)
~/ex5$ **ls**
passwd
~/ex5$ **rm passwd** # remove passwd
rm: remove regular file 'passwd'? **n** # no, keep passwd file
~/ex5$ **rm -f passwd** # remove passwd file forcefully
~/ex5$ **ls**
~/ex5$ # empty
~/ex5$ **unalias rm** # unalias rm
~/ex5$ **alias rm** # check that alias for rm has been un-aliased
-bash: alias: rm: not found

EXERCISE 5.3

```
~/ex5$ ls
~/ex5$ pwd # present working directory
/home/jdoe/ex5
~/ex5$ mkdir subdir1 # make a subdirectory named subdir1
~/ex5$ cp /etc/a* subdir1/ # copy any files starting with letter, a in /etc/
to subdir1 directory
~/ex5$ sudo cp -r /etc/a* subdir1 # use sudo cp to copy all files starting
with a under /etc/ to subdir1 directory
[sudo] password for jdoe: *************** # enter sudoer password
~/ex5$ ls subdir1/ # check the copied files
adduser.conf  alternatives  apparmor  apparmor.d  apport  apt  at.deny
~/ex5$ rmdir subdir1/ # rmdir cannot delete a directory with items
rmdir: failed to remove 'subdir1/': Directory not empty
~/ex5$ rm -r subdir1/ # -r, the recursive option is not enough to remove some
directories
rm: remove write-protected regular file 'subdir1/at.deny'?
rm: cannot remove 'subdir1/': Directory not empty
~/ex5$ rm -rf subdir1/ # use -r (recursive) and -f (force) options
combination to remove any directories, use with care as the directory or file
will be deleted without a prompt
~/ex5$ ls
~/ex5$ # empty
```

EXERCISE 5.4

```
~/ex5$ ls
~/ex5$ sudo cp /etc/* . 2>/dev/null # copy all files under /etc/ to the
current working directory, and append "2>/dev/null" to the end of the command
to send the console messages to the null or a black hole. This command only
copies files, but you can use '-r' option to copy the directories as well
~/ex5$ ls # you will see the copies of all whole content of /etc/ directory
adduser.conf    fstab    ld.so.cache  mime.types  protocols  sudo.conf
[...ommitted for brevity]
ethertypes      issue.net    manpath.config  profile      subuid-
```

EXERCISE 5.5

```
~/ex5$ rm -f a* # remove files starting with a certain alphabet
~/ex5$ rm -f D* G* # alphabets are case sensitive
~/ex5$ rm -f b* c* d* # you cannot remove files this way using mouse clicks
on Windows OS
~/ex5$ rm -f [g-s]* # use [g-s] range command to be more efficient
~/ex5$ ls
e2scrub.conf  ethertypes  fuse.conf  ucf.conf  wgetrc     zsh_command_
not_found
environment   fstab       timezone   vtrgb     xattr.conf
~/ex5$ rm -f [^uvwx]* # remove all files except files starting with u,
v, w or x
~/ex5$ rm -f [!x]* # remove all files except files starting with x
~/ex5$ cd ..
~/$ rm -f * # remove all files
```

During our practice with Linux, we have not only covered the basic "cp" and "rm" commands but also explored some other interesting and powerful commands. The ability to copy and remove multiple files and directories with a single command is a unique feature of Linux that sets it apart from GUI-based systems. While executing the "rm" command, it is recommended to use the "-i" option for interactive deletion, which can prevent the accidental deletion of important files. Additionally, creating aliases for frequently used commands can enhance productivity by reducing errors and saving time. It is crucial to exercise caution while removing directories by using the "-r" and "-f" options to avoid unintentional deletions, especially when working as the root user. The "cp" command makes it easy to copy files from one location to another, and the "rm" command can be used to delete files starting with a particular alphabet. Consolidating your learning through regular practice and paying attention to detail is vital to achieving proficiency in using these commands effectively.

2.6.6 rename and mv

To ensure that you're prepared for the upcoming exercise, let's take a quick look at some of the Linux commands we'll be using, including rename and mv, and their supplementary commands. Be sure to read the descriptions in Table 2-8 and study the examples to get a better understanding.

Table 2-8. *Linux commands in action*

#	Command	Description	Example
1	**rename**	Renames files and directories	rename 's/tadpole/frog/' tadpole
2	**mv**	Moves or renames files and directories	mv file1 dir1/
			mv file1.txt file3.txt
			mv -i f1.cfg f3.cfg

It's time to roll up your sleeves and start practicing what you've learned. Let's jump right in.

EXERCISE 6.1

~/$ **mkdir ex5 && cd ex6** # create a new directory ex6 and move to ex6

~/ex6$ **sudo apt install rename** # since rename is not a default application on some Linux, you have to install the software.

[sudo] password for jdoe: ******************

[...omitted for brevity]

~/ex6$ **mkdir dir1** # make a directory called 'dir1'

~/ex6$ **ls**

dir1

~/ex6$ **rename 's/dir1/directory1/' dir1** # rename dir1 directory to directory1

~/ex6$ **ls**

directory1

~/ex6$ **rm -r directory1/**

EXERCISE 6.2

~/ex6$ **mkdir dir{1..10}** # create ten directories starting from dir1 to dir10

~/ex6$ **ls**

dir1   dir10   dir2   dir3   dir4   dir5   dir6   dir7   dir8   dir9

~/ex6$ **rename 's/^dir/directory/' dir*** # rename directories starting with 'dir' to 'directory'

~/ex6$ **ls**
directory1   directory10   directory2   directory3   directory4   directory5
directory6   directory7   directory8   directory9
~/ex6$ **rmdir *** # remove all directories (empty)

EXERCISE 6.3

~/ex6$ **touch f{1..100}** # create 100 files starting with "f"
~/ex6$ **ls**
f1   f11   f14   f17   f2
f22   f25   f28   f30   f33   f36   f39   f41   f44   f47   f5
f52   f55   f58   f60   f63   f66   f69
[... *omitted for brevity*]
~/ex6$ **rename 's/^f/file/' f*** # use a regular expression to match all file
names starting with "f" (f*), and replace the first "f" with "file" using the
substitution command s/^f/file/. s/ denotes the substitution method.
~/ex6$ **ls**
file1   file12   file16   file2   file23   file27   file30   file34   file38
file41   file45   file49   file52   file56   file6
[... *omitted for brevity*]
~/ex6$ **rm -rf *** # remove all files and directories

EXERCISE 6.4

~/ex6$ **touch a{1..1000}.txt** # create 1000 files starting with 'a'
~/ex6$ **ls** # list newly created files
a1.txt   a143.txt a189.txt a233.txt a279.txt a323.txt a369.txt a413.
txt a459.txt a503.txt a549.txt [... *omitted for brevity*]
~/ex6$ **rename 's/.txt$/.bak/' a*** # rename extension .txt to .bak as these are
back-up files
~/ex6$ **ls** # check the changes
a1.bak   a143.bak a189.bak a233.bak a279.bak a323.bak a369.bak a413.
bak a459.bak a503.bak
[... *omitted for brevity*]

~/ex6$ **rename 's/^a/acorn_/' a*** # rename the file name this time, so update 'a' to 'acorn_'
~/ex6$ **ls**
acorn_1.bak   acorn_168.bak acorn_237.bak acorn_306.bak acorn_376.
bak acorn_445.bak
[... omitted for brevity]

EXERCISE 6.5

~/ex6$ **rename -v 's/acorn_/ACORN_/' a*** # use the '-v' (verbose) option to
show the changes. In Linux, '-V' normally means version, but the small '-v'
option indicates verbose.
acorn_1.bak renamed as ACORN_1.bak
acorn_10.bak renamed as ACORN_10.bak
[... omitted for brevity]
~/ex6$ **ls**
~/ex6$ ls
ACORN_1.bak   ACORN_168.bak ACORN_237.bak ACORN_306.bak ACORN_376.bak
[... omitted for brevity]
~/ex6$ **rm -rf *** # remove all files

EXERCISE 6.6

~/ex6$ mkdir dir6 # make a new directory dir6
~/ex6$ ls | grep di* #
dir6
~/ex6$ mv ACORN_* dir6
~/ex6$ ls
dir6
~/ex6$ ls dir6
ACORN_1.bak   ACORN_168.bak ACORN_237.bak ACORN_306.bak ACORN_376.bak
[... omitted for brevity]

EXERCISE 6.7

```
~/ex6$ ls
dir6
~/ex6$ cp /etc/passwd . # copy the passwd file to the current working
directory
~/ex6$ ls
dir6  passwd
~/ex6$ cp /etc/passwd pwd # copy passwd file and save it as pwd in the
current working directory
~/ex6$ ls # check the files and directory
dir6  passwd  pwd
~/ex6$ mv pwd dir6/pwd300 # use mv to move the file and change the name while
moving the file
~/ex6$ ls dir6/pw* # check that the file has move to dir6. We still have 100
.bak files in this folder, so using string specific list command.
dir6/pwd300
~/ex6$ rm -rf dir1/* # empty dir1 directory by removing all items
```

EXERCISE 6.8

```
~/ex6$ ls
dir6  passwd
~/ex6$ mv dir6 /tmp # move the directory to /tmp directory
~/ex6$ ll /tmp # long listing of /tmp directory
total 48
drwxrwxrwt  4 root root  4096 Apr  3 20:39 ./
drwxr-xr-x 19 root root  4096 Apr  3 16:35 ../
drwxrwxrwx  2 root root    60 Apr  3 16:35 .X11-unix/
drwxr-xr-x  2 jdoe jdoe 36864 Apr  3 20:28 dir6/
~/ex6$ rm -r /tmp/dir6 # remove dir6 directory
~/ex6$ ll /tmp
total 8
```

```
drwxrwxrwt  3 root root 4096 Apr  3 20:39 ./
drwxr-xr-x 19 root root 4096 Apr  3 16:35 ../
drwxrwxrwx  2 root root   60 Apr  3 16:35 .X11-unix/
~/ex6$ rm passwd
~/ex6$ # empty
```

Great work on completing your learning on the rename and mv commands in Linux! These commands offer powerful capabilities and flexibility when it comes to managing files and directories on the command line. By now, you may have experienced the true power of these commands when combined with regular expressions. This underscores the importance of studying and understanding regular expressions when it comes to searching for strings on the command line. Although you don't have to fully understand the syntax and usage of regular expressions just yet, it's an essential skill set that you'll need to acquire at some point. So keep this in mind as you continue to learn and grow your knowledge of Linux commands. It's also important to note that if you're working with a Red Hat–based Linux distribution like Fedora or CentOS, the rename command is already included in the default installation. However, it works slightly differently than in other Linux distributions, and regular expressions may not always be necessary in certain cases as you may have seen in the preceding examples.

Great job so far, and keep exploring the vast capabilities of Linux commands to enhance your workflow! Next, let's get some practice with head and tail commands.

2.6.7 head, tail, and shuf

Before we begin the exercise, it's important to review the Linux commands that we'll be using, such as head, tail, and shuf. Take a few minutes to read through the descriptions and study the examples provided in Table 2-9.

Table 2-9. *Linux commands in action*

#	Command	Description	Example
1	**head**	Views the first lines of a file, displaying the first ten lines by default. Uses the -n option to specify the number of lines	head greenfrogs.txt
2	**tail**	Views the last lines of a file, displaying the last ten lines by default. Uses the -n option to specify the number of lines	Tail -n 3 greenfrogs.txt
3	**shuf**	Generates random permutations of input lines	shuf -i 1-100

Practice makes perfect, so let's not waste any more time. Let's dive in and start honing our skills.

EXERCISE 7.1

```
~$ mkdir ex7 && cd ex7 # create ex7 directory and move to ex7
~/ex7$ cat > cities.txt # create a new file, cities.txt containing your top
10 cities around the world.
Vienna
Copenhagen
Zurich
Calgary
Vancouver
Geneva
Frankfurt
Toronto
Amsterdam
Melbourne
        # Don't forget to use Ctrl+D to save and exit!
~/ex7$ ls -lh # check the file has been saved with the data
total 4.0K
-rw-r--r-- 1 jdoe jdoe 88 Apr  3 21:15 cities.txt
```

EXERCISE 7.2

~/ex7$ **shuf cities.txt > random_cities.txt** # use shuf to copy and create new
randome_cities.txt file
~/ex7$ **shuf cities.txt >> random_cities.txt** # append the 10 more lines to the
randome_cities.txt, so now it has 20 lines of random cities.
~/ex7$ **ls -lh**
total 8.0K
-rw-r--r-- 1 jdoe jdoe 88 Apr 3 21:15 cities.txt
-rw-r--r-- 1 jdoe jdoe 176 Apr 3 21:21 random_cities.txt

EXERCISE 7.3

~/ex7$ **cat random_cities.txt** # cat command will display all lines at once
Geneva
Vancouver
Zurich
[... omitted for brevity]
~/ex7$ **head random_cities.txt** # head command displays the first 10 lines only
Geneva
Vancouver
Zurich
[... omitted for brevity]
~/ex7$ **tail random_cities.txt** # tail command displays the last 10 lines
by default
[... omitted for brevity]
Frankfurt
Melbourne
Zurich

EXERCISE 7.4

```
~/ex7$ head -n 3 random_cities.txt # use -n option to specify the number of
lines to display
Geneva
Vancouver
Zurich
~/ex7$ tail -n 3 random_cities.txt # tail works the same way but from the
last line
Frankfurt
Melbourne
Zurich
```

EXERCISE 7.5

```
~/ex7$ head -n 3 cities.txt random_cities.txt # you can display multiple
files at once for comparison
==> cities.txt <==
Vienna
Copenhagen
Zurich

==> random_cities.txt <==
Geneva
Vancouver
Zurich
~/ex7$ head -n 3 -q cities.txt random_cities.txt # use -q option to drop
the header
Vienna
Copenhagen
Zurich
Geneva
Vancouver
Zurich
```

EXERCISE 7.6

```
~/ex7$ shuf -i 1-100 > num1 # create random 100 numbers and save it as
num1 file
~/ex7$ head -n 30 num1 # display top 30 lines
56
54
64
[... omitted for brevity]
~/ex7$ rm -rf *
~$ rm -r ex7
```

In this practice run, we have gained proficiency in utilizing the head, tail, and shuf commands. Unlike the cat command, head and tail commands offer greater control over the amount of information displayed on the screen. Additionally, the shuf command allows us to shuffle information, and when combined with the ">" symbol, we can save the shuffled data to a file. Mastering these commands enables us to view and manipulate information in a more organized and manageable manner.

2.6.8 less and more

Let's take a moment to review the Linux commands that we'll be using in this exercise, particularly the less and more commands and other supplementary commands for Exercise 8. Make sure to review Table 2-10 and study the examples to prepare yourself for the exercise.

Table 2-10. *Linux commands in action*

#	Command	Description	Example
1	**less**	View and navigate through large files or outputs one page at a time in the terminal	less greenfrogs.txt
2	**more**	View large files or outputs one page at a time in the terminal, but with limited navigation options compared to the "less" command	more greenfrogs.txt
3	**apt-get install**	apt-get is an older package manager for Debian-based systems. Used to install new software	apt-get install tmux

In the case of the less command, less is indeed more when it comes to Linux commands. Now it's time to put that theory into practice and start honing our skills. Let's dive in!

EXERCISE 8.1

```
~$ mkdir ex8 && cd ex8
~/ex8$ sudo apt-get install wamerican # wamerican installs dict/words folder
which we need to create random words
[... omitted for brevity]

~/ex8$ shuf -n 300 /usr/share/dict/words > random_words.txt # creates random_
words.txt file using the dictionary words
~/ex8$ ls -lh
total 4.0K
-rw-r--r-- 1 jdoe jdoe 2.7K Apr  3 22:15 random_words.txt
```

EXERCISE 8.2

```
~/ex8$ more random_words.txt # displays content per page
Hyundai
uncorked
knowledgeable
[... omitted for brevity]
--More--(16%)
# use space bar to scroll per page or enter key to scroll down per line

~/ex8$ { shuf -n 100 /usr/share/dict/words | tr '\n' ' ' && echo; } >
random_100_words.txt # this command creates random 100 words on the same line
and saves them to a new file
~/ex8$ more random_100_words.txt # Check the content of your 100 random words
fabrication's definition recur promotion categorized inpatient garlic
sheeting toxemia savoriest sound hur
[... omitted for brevity]
itchiness impetuosity Philistine servicewoman
```

EXERCISE 8.3

~/ex8$ **less random_words.txt** # more functions than more command
'less' opens random_words.txt with above command. Now inside of less,
practice the following:

To scroll through random_words.txt:
Press the space bar to scroll down one page.
Press the 'b' key to scroll up one page.
Use arrow keys to scroll up and down, one line at a time.

To search a specific term:
Press the / key followed by the search word. Press Enter to start the search.
Press n to go to the next occurrence of the search word.
Press N to go to the previous occurrence of the search word.

To quick 'less'
Press the 'q' key.
~/ex8$ **cd ..**
~$ **rm -rf ex8** # remove ex8 directory

In Exercise 8, you gained valuable experience using powerful Linux commands
to manipulate files and install the software. By learning how to use "more" and "less"
commands, you can efficiently navigate long files with ease. Additionally, you discovered
how to use the "sudo apt-get install" command to install the necessary software, such as
a dictionary for generating 100 and 300 random words. By leveraging the shuf command,
you learned how to create random word files and save them as working files. Finally, you
gained proficiency in searching through files, a critical skill for any Linux user. These
fundamental commands should be committed to memory to help streamline your
workflow and improve your productivity.

Expand your knowledge:

What is the difference between less and more Linux commands?

In the Linux operating system, both the "less" and "more" commands are utilized as command-line utilities for displaying the contents of a file in the terminal. However, the primary difference between these two commands lies in the level of their functionality and flexibility. Specifically, "less" is considered more robust and adaptable than "more". This distinction manifests in several areas such as the following:

Scrolling: When using "more", you can only navigate forward in the file, one screen at a time. In contrast, "less" allows you to scroll both forward and backward in the file using the arrow keys or Page Up/Page Down keys.

Search: "less" facilitates the search of text within a file using the "/" command followed by the search string. On the other hand, "more" does not possess this feature.

Navigation: Apart from scrolling and searching, "less" provides additional navigation options such as the ability to jump to a specific line number or percentage of the file, as well as display the contents of multiple files concurrently.

2.6.9 ls and dir

Although we've already been introduced to the ls command, it's time to practice using it to gain a more comprehensive understanding of its functionality. Moreover, we'll be using the dir command, a ported Windows command, into our practice to further expand our command repertoire (see Table 2-11).

Table 2-11. *Linux commands in action*

#	Command	Description	Example
1	**ls**	A standard Unix command and is available in almost all Linux distributions	ls -lh
2	**dir**	A Windows command that has been ported to Linux and is available in some Linux distributions, usually as an alias to ls	dir

It's time to get our hands dirty and delve into practicing the many variants of the ls command, with dir serving as a supplementary tool. Let's not waste any more time and begin the exercise.

EXERCISE 9.1

```
~$ mkdir ex9 && cd ex9 # make a new exercise directory, ex9 and move to ex9
~/ex9$ date > date9
~/ex9$ mkdir dir9
~/ex9$ ls
date9  dir9
~/ex9$ ls -l
total 8
-rw-r--r-- 1 jdoe jdoe   30 Apr  3 23:14 date9
drwxr-xr-x 2 jdoe jdoe 4096 Apr  3 23:15 dir9
~/ex9$ ls -l -a
total 16
drwxr-xr-x 3 jdoe jdoe 4096 Apr  3 23:15 .
drwxr-x--- 3 jdoe jdoe 4096 Apr  3 22:50 ..
-rw-r--r-- 1 jdoe jdoe   30 Apr  3 23:14 date9
drwxr-xr-x 2 jdoe jdoe 4096 Apr  3 23:15 dir9
~/ex9$ touch .hidden # create a hidden file named .hidden
~/ex9$ ls
date9  dir9
~/ex9$ ls -al
total 16
drwxr-xr-x 3 jdoe jdoe 4096 Apr  3 23:16 .
drwxr-x--- 3 jdoe jdoe 4096 Apr  3 22:50 ..
```

```
-rw-r--r-- 1 jdoe jdoe    0 Apr  3 23:16 .hidden # with  the -al option, you
can see this file
-rw-r--r-- 1 jdoe jdoe   30 Apr  3 23:14 date9
drwxr-xr-x 2 jdoe jdoe 4096 Apr  3 23:15 dir9
~/ex9$ ls -Al # with the -Al option you hide the . and .. directories
total 8
-rw-r--r-- 1 jdoe jdoe    0 Apr  3 23:16 .hidden
-rw-r--r-- 1 jdoe jdoe   30 Apr  3 23:14 date9
drwxr-xr-x 2 jdoe jdoe 4096 Apr  3 23:15 dir9
```

EXERCISE 9.2

```
~/ex9$ alias ll # check what ll aliased for
alias ll='ls -alF'
~/ex9$ ll # run ll and you will see the contents with / included
total 16
drwxr-xr-x 3 jdoe jdoe 4096 Apr  3 23:16 ./
drwxr-x--- 3 jdoe jdoe 4096 Apr  3 22:50 ../
-rw-r--r-- 1 jdoe jdoe    0 Apr  3 23:16 .hidden
-rw-r--r-- 1 jdoe jdoe   30 Apr  3 23:14 date9
drwxr-xr-x 2 jdoe jdoe 4096 Apr  3 23:15 dir9/
~/ex9$ ll -h # with the -h option, the file sizes become more human readable,
i.e.) 4.0K
total 16K
drwxr-xr-x 3 jdoe jdoe 4.0K Apr  3 23:16 ./
drwxr-x--- 3 jdoe jdoe 4.0K Apr  3 22:50 ../
-rw-r--r-- 1 jdoe jdoe    0 Apr  3 23:16 .hidden
-rw-r--r-- 1 jdoe jdoe   30 Apr  3 23:14 date9
drwxr-xr-x 2 jdoe jdoe 4.0K Apr  3 23:15 dir9/
~/ex9$ alias lh='ls -Alh' # you can create your alias, but when you log off,
this is only session based
~/ex9$ lh
total 8.0K
-rw-r--r-- 1 jdoe jdoe    0 Apr  3 23:16 .hidden
-rw-r--r-- 1 jdoe jdoe   30 Apr  3 23:14 date9
drwxr-xr-x 2 jdoe jdoe 4.0K Apr  3 23:15 dir9
~/ex9$ lh -F # try your new alias lh with -F option and you see the / after dir9
```

```
total 8.0K
-rw-r--r-- 1 jdoe jdoe    0 Apr  3 23:16 .hidden
-rw-r--r-- 1 jdoe jdoe   30 Apr  3 23:14 date9
drwxr-xr-x 2 jdoe jdoe 4.0K Apr  3 23:15 dir9/
```

EXERCISE 9.3

~/ex9$ **lh -i** # -i option displays the inode of files, inodes are unique file numbers. Book has an ISBN, inode is the same concept as ISBN for books.
```
total 8.0K
29459 -rw-r--r-- 1 jdoe jdoe    0 Apr  3 23:16 .hidden
27106 -rw-r--r-- 1 jdoe jdoe   30 Apr  3 23:14 date9
29436 drwxr-xr-x 2 jdoe jdoe 4.0K Apr  3 23:15 dir9
```

EXERCISE 9.4

Try the following ls command with the -R option.
~/ex9$ **ls -R /etc/** # list the contents of the "/etc" directory and all its subdirectories
[...omitted for brevity]
~/ex9$ **tree /etc/**
[...omitted for brevity]

EXERCISE 9.5

~/ex9$ **ls -Sl** # the -S option checks the size and lists files from the largest to smallest order
```
total 8
drwxr-xr-x 2 jdoe jdoe 4096 Apr  3 23:15 dir9
-rw-r--r-- 1 jdoe jdoe   30 Apr  3 23:14 date9
```
~/ex9$ **ls -Slr** # the -r option reverses the output of the files listed
```
total 8
-rw-r--r-- 1 jdoe jdoe   30 Apr  3 23:14 date9
drwxr-xr-x 2 jdoe jdoe 4096 Apr  3 23:15 dir9
```

EXERCISE 9.6

~/ex9$ **ls --help** # Always refer to the help page

EXERCISE 9.7

~/ex9$ **ls** # ls is the original UNIX command and was carried over to Linux
date9 dir9
~/ex9$ **dir** # dir is a Windows command carried over to Linux
date9 dir9
~/ex9$ **cd ..**
~$ **rm -rf ex9** # remove ex9 directory

In Linux, ls is a standard Unix command and is available on all Linux distributions. dir, a Windows command, has been adapted for Linux and is available on some distributions, often as an alias to ls. ls offers a wider range of options and functionality compared to dir, such as displaying file permissions, file size, and file timestamps. It also provides various formatting options, including sorting, reversing, and filtering. In contrast, dir has limited functionality and options. Overall, ls is a more versatile and powerful command for listing files and directories in Linux, while dir is a simpler command that provides basic functionality and is often used as an alias to ls.

2.6.10 sort

The next command we'll be practicing is sort, which is used to sort the contents of a file or standard input in ascending or descending order. For guidance, please refer to Table 2-12 and study the commands used in Exercise 10 to begin your practice.

Table 2-12. *Linux commands in action*

#	Command	Description	Example
1	**sort**	Sorts lines of text in a file or standard input in either ascending or descending order based on various criteria such as alphanumeric, numeric, and dictionary order	sort file.txt
2	**tee**	Reads input from a pipeline and writes it to both standard output and one or more files simultaneously	cat ex10.txt | tee exercise10.txt
3	**paste**	Merges lines from multiple files or standard input and write them to standard output, separated by a delimiter	paste name age | tee userinfo

As we spend more time working with Linux commands, we'll continue to improve our skills at the keyboard. Our next exercise involves using the sort command, so let's dive right in.

EXERCISE 10.1

```
~$ mkdir ex10 && cd ex10
~/ex10$ cat > math
80
50
90
~/ex10$ cat math
80
50
90
~/ex10$ sort math
50
80
90
~/ex10$ sort math -r
90
80
50
~/ex10$ sort math -u
50
```

```
80
90
~/ex10$ cat > math
80
50
90
```

EXERCISE 10.2

```
~/ex10$ ls
math
~/ex10$ cat math
80
50
90
~/ex10$ cat > name
Lara
Peter
Bruce
~/ex10$ ls
math   name
~/ex10$ paste name math | tee nm # use tee command to display and save the
output to a file
Lara    80
Peter   50
Bruce   90
~/ex10$ cat nm
Lara    80
Peter   50
Bruce   90
~/ex10$ sort -k 1 nm # use -k option to sort using field 1
Bruce   90
Lara    80
Peter   50
```

```
~/ex10$ sort -k 2 nm # use -k option to sort using field 2
Peter     50
Lara      80
Bruce     90
```

EXERCISE 10.3

```
~/ex10$ sort nm -R # use the -R option to shuffle the items, at random.
Bruce     90
Peter     50
Lara      80
~/ex10$ sort nm -R # every time you run the command with the -R option, the
order changes
Peter     50
Bruce     90
Lara      80
~/ex10$ cd ..
~$ rm -rf ex10 # remove ex10 directory
```

You have learned the fundamental skill of using the "sort" command above, which is a critical tool for sorting data in either ascending or descending order. Sorting data is an essential aspect of computing, and it's essential to have a thorough understanding of it. During the lesson, you also demonstrated your proficiency with advanced commands such as "sort -R" and "paste name math | tee nm", which are valuable tools for working with data. However, to fully comprehend the sorting functions, we recommend exploring programming languages and the various data structures they use. For instance, in Python, you can apply to sort different data types such as strings, lists, tuples, and dictionaries. Although most data types in Python are ordered, it's crucial to note that sets of the data type are not. By exploring sorting functions across different data types, you will gain a deeper understanding of how to manipulate and sort data, which is an invaluable skill in the world of computing. Next, we will explore the Linux commands nl and tee.

2.6.11 tee and nl

The tee and nl commands are up next for us to learn, although we could have covered them earlier. As we saw in a previous exercise, tee is a crucial command that every Linux user should know by heart. So let's review Table 2-13 to familiarize ourselves with the commands used in Exercise 11 before we get started.

Table 2-13. *Linux commands in action*

#	Command	Description	Example
1	**tee**	Allows you to read input from a pipeline or file and simultaneously write it to both the terminal and a file	echo "Hi Ansible!" I tee hi.txt
2	**nl**	Used to number lines in a file or input stream. Same as using "cat -b"	nl calendar

The tee and nl commands have some exciting use cases waiting for us to discover. So without further ado, let's dive right in and get some hands-on practice with them.

EXERCISE 11.1

```
~$ mkdir ex11 && cd ex11
~/ex11$ cal > c1
~/ex11$ date > d1
~/ex11$ cat c1
      April 2023
Su Mo Tu We Th Fr Sa
                   1
 2  3  4  5  6  7  8
 9 10 11 12 13 14 15
16 17 18 19 20 21 22
23 24 25 26 27 28 29
30
~/ex11$ cat c1 > c2 # when you use > to concatenate and make another file, it
does not display the content of the file.
~/ex11$ ls
c1  c2  d1
```

```
~/ex11$ cat c2
      April 2023
Su Mo Tu We Th Fr Sa
                   1
 2  3  4  5  6  7  8
 9 10 11 12 13 14 15
16 17 18 19 20 21 22
23 24 25 26 27 28 29
30
~/ex11$ cat c1 | tee c3 # use the tee to display the content while saving the
output of the calendar to a file.
      April 2023
Su Mo Tu We Th Fr Sa
                   1
 2  3  4  5  6  7  8
 9 10 11 12 13 14 15
16 17 18 19 20 21 22
23 24 25 26 27 28 29
30
~/ex11$ ls
c1  c2  c3  d1
```

EXERCISE 11.2

```
~/ex11$ ls
c1  c2  c3  d1
~/ex11$ ls | tee -a c3 # the -a option appends the command output to the
existing file
c1
c2
c3
d1
~/ex11$ cat c3
```

```
   April 2023
Su Mo Tu We Th Fr Sa
                   1
 2  3  4  5  6  7  8
 9 10 11 12 13 14 15
16 17 18 19 20 21 22
23 24 25 26 27 28 29
30
c1
c2
c3
d1
```

EXERCISE 11.3

```
~/ex11$ nl -w6 c1
     1         April 2023
     2   Su Mo Tu We Th Fr Sa
     3                      1
     4    2  3  4  5  6  7  8
     5    9 10 11 12 13 14 15
     6   16 17 18 19 20 21 22
     7   23 24 25 26 27 28 29
     8   30
~/ex11$ nl -w10 c1 # use the nl -w10 to update the width. (Default is 6)
         1         April 2023
         2       Su Mo Tu We Th Fr Sa
         3                          1
         4        2  3  4  5  6  7  8
         5        9 10 11 12 13 14 15
         6       16 17 18 19 20 21 22
         7       23 24 25 26 27 28 29
         8       30
```

```
~/ex11$ nl -i2 c1 # use the -i option for stepping (increment)
    1        April 2023
    3  Su Mo Tu We Th Fr Sa
    5                       1
    7   2  3  4  5  6  7  8
    9   9 10 11 12 13 14 15
   11  16 17 18 19 20 21 22
   13  23 24 25 26 27 28 29
   15  30
~/ex11$ nl -i3 c1 # the number reference stepping is now 3
    1        April 2023
    4  Su Mo Tu We Th Fr Sa
    7                       1
   10   2  3  4  5  6  7  8
   13   9 10 11 12 13 14 15
   16  16 17 18 19 20 21 22
   19  23 24 25 26 27 28 29
   22  30
```

EXERCISE 11.4

```
~/ex11$ nl -i10 -v10 c1 # you can specify the beginning of the number with
the -v option
   10        April 2023
   20  Su Mo Tu We Th Fr Sa
   30                       1
   40   2  3  4  5  6  7  8
   50   9 10 11 12 13 14 15
   60  16 17 18 19 20 21 22
   70  23 24 25 26 27 28 29
   80  30
~/ex11$ nl -i2 -v0 c1 # you can start from index 0 and increment by +2
    0        April 2023
    2  Su Mo Tu We Th Fr Sa
    4                       1
    6   2  3  4  5  6  7  8
```

```
   8    9 10 11 12 13 14 15
  10   16 17 18 19 20 21 22
  12   23 24 25 26 27 28 29
  14   30
```

EXERCISE 11.5

```
~/ex11$ nl c1 # compare this output to the next command output, the nl
command is identical to the cat -b command
     1         April 2023
     2    Su Mo Tu We Th Fr Sa
     3                       1
     4     2  3  4  5  6  7  8
     5     9 10 11 12 13 14 15
     6    16 17 18 19 20 21 22
     7    23 24 25 26 27 28 29
     8    30
~/ex11$ cat -b c1 # note the two different commands but the same result
     1         April 2023
     2    Su Mo Tu We Th Fr Sa
     3                       1
     4     2  3  4  5  6  7  8
     5     9 10 11 12 13 14 15
     6    16 17 18 19 20 21 22
     7    23 24 25 26 27 28 29
     8    30
```

EXERCISE 11.6

```
~/ex11$ nl --help # always check the --help page for further clarification
and extend your knowledge
~/ex11$ cd ~ # Change to user home directory
~$ rm -rf ex11 # remove exercise 11 working folder
```

In Exercise 11, you've gained the proficiency to utilize the tee and nl commands efficiently. The tee command lets you exhibit the contents of a file while also conserving it to another file, while the nl command offers several choices to showcase the content with line references and enables the alteration of reference number behavior using options such as -i and -v. Additionally, the "tee" command can be applied in network device administration to replicate settings and instructions to another device. If you've completed a Cisco CCNA course, you may remember executing a command like "show ip interface brief | tee sh_ip_int_bri.txt" to save the "show" command's output to a file while simultaneously displaying the command information.

2.6.12 grep

We have reached the final stretch of this chapter, and it's time to learn the last essential Linux command: grep. This command is a favorite among Linux administrators and is considered a must-have tool in their arsenal. Before we start with Exercise 12, let's review Table 2-14 to get a better understanding of the command.

Table 2-14. *Linux commands in action*

#	Command	Description	Example
1	**grep**	Searches for a specific pattern or regular expression in a file or output	grep -i "needle" haystack.txt
2	**wc**	Counts the number of lines, words, and characters in a file or output	wc recipe.txt
3	**awk**	A tool used for text processing and manipulation, allowing users to specify patterns and actions to be performed on input data	awk -F',' '{print $1}' students.txt

If you're looking for a tool that can help you search for information in Linux, look no further than grep. This command is an indispensable tool for Linux users and is used extensively for searching and filtering data. With grep, you can quickly and easily find the information you need, every time.

EXERCISE 12.1

```
~$ mkdir ex12 && cd ex12 # create a new ex12 directory and change the working
directory
~/ex12$ cp /etc/services s1
~/ex12$ wc -l s1
361 s1
~/ex12$ wc s1
361  1773 12813 s1
~/ex12$ wc -l s1 # -l option prints  the newline counts
361 s1
~/ex12$ wc -w s1 # -w option prints the word counts
1773 s1
~/ex12$ wc -c s1 # -c option prints the byte counts
12813 s1
~/ex12$ wc --help # always check help for more information
```

EXERCISE 12.2

```
~/ex12$ grep http s1 # find the line containing the word "http", display them
in the terminal
# Updated from https://www.iana.org/assignments/service-names-port-numbers/
service-names-port-numbers.xhtml .
http            80/tcp          www             # WorldWideWeb HTTP
https           443/tcp                         # http protocol over TLS/SSL
https           443/udp                         # HTTP/3
http-alt        8080/tcp        webcache        # WWW caching service
~/ex12$ grep "http" s1 # the search keyword can be wrapped or unwrapped
around the double quotation marks
[...omitted for brevity]
~/ex12$ grep 'http' s1 # the search keyword can be wrapped or unwrapped
around the single quotation marks
[...omitted for brevity]
```

EXERCISE 12.3

~/ex12$ **grep ssh s1** # find a service line containing the word ssh
ssh   22/tcp   # SSH Remote Login Protocol
~/ex12$ **grep ^ssh s1** # the following three commands will give the same output
but the carrot sign (^) denotes the start of the word character in regular
expression
~/ex12$ **grep "^ssh" s1**
~/ex12$ **grep '^ssh' s1**
~/ex12$ **grep 123/udp s1** # if you know the exact format, it can be used as a
search keyword
ntp   123/udp   # Network Time Protocol
~/ex12$ **grep smtp s1** # find a service line containing the word smtp
smtp   25/tcp   mail
submissions   465/tcp   ssmtp smtps urd # Submission over TLS
                                    [RFC8314]
~/ex12$ **grep smtp s1 | nl** # use the pipe (|) to combine with another command
    1 smtp   25/tcp   mail
    2 submissions   465/tcp   ssmtp smtps urd # Submission over TLS
                                            [RFC8314]

EXERCISE 12.4

~/ex12$ **grep "^[^#;].*/tcp" s1** # using the regular expression, you can
significantly enhance the functionality of command-line tools such as grep,
awk, and sed, as well as programming languages.
tcpmux   1/tcp   # TCP port service multiplexer
echo   7/tcp
[...omitted for brevity]
tfido   60177/tcp   # fidonet EMSI over telnet
fido   60179/tcp   # fidonet EMSI over TCP
~/ex12$ **grep "^[^#;].*/udp" s1** # to identify the UDP services currently in
use, simply substitute the word udp with tcp
[...omitted for brevity]

EXERCISE 12.5

~/ex12$ **grep "^[^#;].*/tcp" s1 | awk '{if ($2<1024) print $1, $2}'** # to print the service names using port numbers smaller than 1024, combine the command with awk using the pipe (|).Combining the grep command with the awk command results in a significant increase in accuracy and efficiency.

tcpmux 1/tcp

iso-tsap 102/tcp

zabbix-agent 10050/tcp

zabbix-trapper 10051/tcp

amanda 10080/tcp

webmin 10000/tcp

kamanda 10081/tcp

amandaidx 10082/tcp

amidxtape 10083/tcp

~/ex12$ **grep "^[^#;].*/tcp" s1 | awk '{if ($2<1024) print $1}'** # remove the item reference $2 to print only the service names

[...omitted for brevity]

EXERCISE 12.6

Please try the following grep commands to see how the printed output changes. In this example, '-E' option is enabling extended regular expressions, the '\b' is the metacharacter which represents a word boundary, and the '|' represent alternation (i.e., "or").

~/ex12$ **grep -E '\b([1-9]|[1-9][0-9]|100)/tcp\b'** ss # print services using tcp ports smaller than 100

[...omitted for brevity]

~/ex12$ **grep -E '\b([1-9]|[1-9][0-9][0-9]|1000)/tcp\b'** ss # print services using tcp ports smaller than 1000

[...omitted for brevity]

~/ex12$ **grep -E '\b([1-9]|[1-9][0-9]|100)/tcp\b' /etc/services** # replace ss with the path name on the Linux to get the same result

[...omitted for brevity]

~/ex12$ **grep -E '\b([1-9]|[1-9][0-9]|100)/udp\b'** ss # print services using udp ports smaller than 100

[...omitted for brevity]

```
~/ex12$ grep -E '\b([1-9]|[1-9][0-9]|100)/(tcp|udp)\b' ss # print both tcp &
udp services between 1-100
[...omitted for brevity]
```

EXERCISE 12.7

To extract the desired information from the s1 (or /etc/services) file more accurately and efficiently, we can combine the grep command with the awk command. Using awk allows us to filter and manipulate the output of the grep command, making it easier to extract the exact information we need.

```
~/ex12$grep -E '\b([1-9]|[1-9][0-9]|100)/tcp\b' ss | awk -F/ '{print $1}'
# print the tcp services with the service name and port number in use by
combining with grep and awk commands.
[...omitted for brevity]
~/ex12$ grep -E '\b([1-9]|[1-9][0-9]|100)/tcp\b' ss | awk '{printf "%s ", $1}
END {print ""}' # print the service names on a single line with a new line
```

tcpmux echo discard systat daytime netstat qotd chargen ftp-data ftp ssh telnet smtp time whois tacacs domain gopher finger http kerberos

---

After working through the simple /etc/services file saved as s1, you've gained a solid understanding of Linux's grep command, including basic string searches as well as more advanced techniques using regular expressions. By combining grep with other Linux tools such as awk and sed, you can unlock even greater power and efficiency.

Expand your knowledge:

You want to practice more and learn even more Linux commands?

This chapter has been based on the Essential Linux Commands Guide, created to equip my colleagues at work with fundamental Linux command skills. If you are interested in delving deeper into even more Linux commands, we are providing a complementary exercise book (*Ch2_Linux_Essential_command_exercises_full.pdf*), which can be downloaded from the author's GitHub page at https://github.com/ansnetauto/appress_ansnetauto.

The suggested extra resource is designed to help readers develop a deeper understanding of these essential tools and become more proficient in their usage. It also serves as reinforcement learning for this chapter.

Congratulations on completing all the exercises related to the Linux essential commands in this chapter! As we move on to the next chapter (Chapter 3), we will explore the practical side of the Linux operating system, starting with a brief overview of its directories and file structures. We will then dive into practical Linux tools that directly apply to the IT engineer's work. By asking the relevant questions, working with real-world scenarios, and applying key concepts to solve them, you will gain a deeper understanding of how to use Linux in a professional context.

Whether you're a seasoned pro or just getting started, the next chapter will provide valuable insights and help you become more confident and efficient in your work. In addition, we will explore and share more intricate features and information about the Linux OS. So get ready to dive deeper into the Linux environment in the upcoming chapter!

2.7 Summary

In this chapter, we explored the importance of learning Linux, which served as the cornerstone for learning Ansible and network automation. We learned that Linux was an open source operating system that could be used on various devices, including servers, desktops, mobile phones, and almost any computing device. We discussed that installing WSL on Windows 11 was an easy and effective way to start learning Linux. For those who did not want to install Linux on their PC or virtual machines, there were alternative websites with 24/7 free Linux Web services. We also covered the use of vi as the default text editor and discussed the top ten essential Linux commands, including pwd, touch, ls, mkdir, cd, rm, rmdir, cp, mv, and grep. These commands were everyday commands that Linux administrators used and loved, and mastering them was necessary to become proficient in managing Linux servers. Moreover, we emphasized the importance of hands-on practice to learn Linux commands effectively. By mastering commonly used Linux commands, users could navigate through the Linux environment with ease and perform various tasks, such as creating directories, copying and moving files, and searching for specific information in files. To give readers even more practice on the Linux commands, we provided an exercise book that users could download and complete the exercises end to end.

CHAPTER 3

Shall We Linux? (Part 2)

In this chapter, we will be exploring a range of Linux utilities that will help us with Linux administration in the future and also prepare us well for the Ansible learning from the next chapter. We'll start by diving into the Linux directory system and learning how to extract system information. We'll cover how to view and read Linux processes, run disk space–related tools, and manage users on Linux. In addition, we'll take a deep dive into controlling access to files and directories in Linux, compressing files using various tools, and downloading files from the Internet in Linux. We'll also explore Linux network utilities for troubleshooting and discuss the importance of keeping your Linux system up to date. To help you start thinking about data handling, we've included a fun quiz on regular expressions. We'll show you how to convert a picture of a Jack Russell dog into ASCII using regular expressions. We'll also highlight the importance of regular expressions in Ansible and programming in general. So get ready to learn and practice your Linux administration and programming skills with us in this chapter!

Figure 3-1. *Tux, a content penguin*

© Brendan Choi and Erwin Medina 2023
B. Choi and E. Medina, *Introduction to Ansible Network Automation*,
https://doi.org/10.1007/978-1-4842-9624-0_3

Chapter 2 and this chapter are designed to work with a single Linux environment, allowing readers to focus on one server and become familiar with it. In Chapter 2, we covered essential Linux commands and history of Linux, including the naming of Tux the Linux Penguin (Figure 3-1), providing you with the skills to work confidently in a terminal environment. In this chapter, we'll delve deeper into Linux directories to help you better understand how Linux operates. We'll explore its intricacies and ask important questions about the operating system, such as how to locate system information, check processes, and troubleshoot network issues.

In Linux, many things are treated as files, including system resources such as devices, network sockets, and processes. This design allows the operating system to access and manipulate these resources using standard file system operations. For example, a hard disk is treated as a file, and Linux can read from and write to it using standard file system commands. Similarly, devices like a keyboard, a mouse, and printers are also treated as files, allowing them to be managed using the same file system commands. Even directories and symbolic links are treated as files, although they have slightly different properties and behaviors compared to regular files. This design simplifies the overall structure of the system, making it more accessible to users.

While this book is not a dedicated Linux textbook, our goal is to bring readers up to speed quickly, bypassing the novice stage, and help them embark on an enjoyable Ansible and network automation journey. We believe that mastering the fundamentals is essential to successfully navigating the world of Ansible and network automation. Therefore, we have designed this book to equip you with the skills needed to confidently tackle the tasks at hand and set you on the path to becoming a proficient Linux user.

As promised in Chapter 2, we'll begin by familiarizing ourselves with the Linux directory structure, providing you with a solid foundation for the rest of the book. We aim to make your journey into the world of Ansible and network automation as enjoyable and stress-free as possible, and we believe that a strong understanding of Linux is essential to achieving this goal.

3.1 Linux Directory

To explore the directory structure of Linux and gain a better understanding of how the OS operates, you can use the tree program that we installed in Chapter 2. Start by changing your directory to the root directory, denoted by /, using the Ubuntu terminal on your WSL. Once you're there, run the command "tree -x" to print all the immediate directories contained under the root directory.

```
~$ cd /
/$ pwd
/
/$ tree -x
.                              # Root /
├── bin -> usr/bin             # User Binaries
├── boot                       # Boot Loader Files
├── dev                        # Device files
├── etc                        # Configuration Files
├── home                       # Home Directories
├── init                       # System Initialization Files
├── lib -> usr/lib             # System Libraries
├── lib32 -> usr/lib32         # 32-bit Shared Library Files
├── lib64 -> usr/lib64         # 64-bit Shared Library Files
├── libx32 -> usr/libx32       # 32-bit Compatible Libraries
├── lost+found                 # file system checker (fsck) used to store
                                 recovered files and directories

├── media                      # Removable Devices
├── mnt                        # Mount Directory
├── opt                        # Optional Add-on Apps
├── proc                       # Process Information
├── root                       # root user home directory
├── run                        # Contains temp files created by processes
                                 during system runtime etc.

├── sbin -> usr/sbin           # System Binaries
├── snap                       # Store snap packages
├── srv                        # Service Data
├── sys                        # A virtual file system for system monitoring,
                                 diagnostics & device mgt.

├── tmp                        # Temporary Files
├── usr                        # User Programs
└── var                        # Variable Files

23 directories, 1 file
```

Most Linux operating systems will have a similar directory structure under the root directory. Take a moment to compare the output of the "tree -x" command to Figure 3-2, which shows the most used Linux directories. By studying the Linux directory structure, you can learn what each directory stands for and what services it provides for OS operations. This is an excellent starting point for your Linux extended studies and will help you gain a better understanding of how the OS works.

While it may be tempting to delve deep into each directory and provide a full explanation, we aim to equip you with the necessary knowledge to become proficient in Linux without overwhelming you with too much information. Therefore, we will focus on familiarizing you with some important directory names and their functions, which will provide you with a solid foundation for the rest of the book. This approach will allow you to quickly get up to speed with the basics of Linux and set you on the path to becoming a proficient Linux user. Take your time to carefully study the directory structure and the corresponding descriptions next to the directory names. It's important to note that the information in the preceding output and Table 3-2 may not be fully absorbed in one sitting, and there's no need to memorize everything. Instead, we recommend taking a closer look at some of the identifiable directories that are crucial for vital system operations and using the figure as a reference point for future use. By doing so, you'll be better equipped to navigate the Linux system and perform necessary tasks with ease.

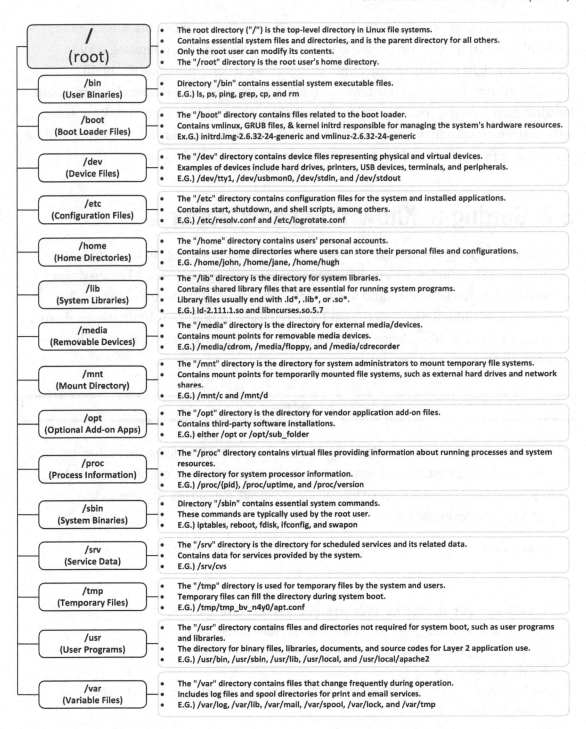

Figure 3-2. *Linux directory structure*

Currently, you're staring at the Ubuntu terminal window with a black background and white-colored fonts. However, do you know much about the operating system you're using right now? In the upcoming section, we'll delve into how to obtain valuable information about our Linux operating system, helping readers become more familiar with locating specific system information. This can be a crucial task for system administrators, who may need to gather this information manually if monitoring tools or Syslog servers aren't available or don't provide the necessary details.

3.2 Getting to Know Your Linux Better

Understanding your Linux server is essential to effectively manage it. If you're using Ubuntu on WSL, which is a virtual machine that operates on Microsoft Hyper-V, you can use the lsb_release command to check the version of Ubuntu you're using. This command is simpler than using the cat /etc/*release command to obtain comprehensive system information. lsb_release will display information such as the Ubuntu release number, codename, and description.

EXERCISE 1

---

lsb_release is a Linux command that displays distribution-specific information such as the release number, codename, and description. It may not be installed by default on your system, so you may need to install it before running the command. You can use your distribution package manager to install it.

```
~$ lsb_release -v # check the version of lsb_release program

No LSB modules are available.

~$ sudo apt-get update && sudo apt-get install lsb-core -y # update package
manager and install lsb-core (for Ubuntu, Debian)
[...omitted for brevity]
~$ lsb_release  -v
LSB Version:    core-11.1.0ubuntu4-noarch:security-11.1.0ubuntu4-noarch
~$ lsb_release -d
Description:    Ubuntu 22.04.1 LTS
~$ lsb_release -a
LSB Version:    core-11.1.0ubuntu4-noarch:security-11.1.0ubuntu4-noarch
```

```
Distributor ID: Ubuntu
Description:    Ubuntu 22.04.1 LTS
Release:        22.04
Codename:       jammy
```

EXERCISE 2

uname is a command-line utility available in Linux that allows you to retrieve information about the underlying system hardware and operating system. One of the most commonly used options is -a, which displays all information available from uname, including the kernel name, network hostname, kernel release, machine hardware name, processor type, and operating system name. In addition to -a, uname provides other useful options for querying system information. You can refer to the help page by typing uname --help or man uname in the terminal to view a list of available options and their usage. By using these options, you can easily access the information you need to diagnose issues, optimize performance, or perform other system administration tasks.

```
~$ uname -a
Linux LP50BC 5.15.90.1-microsoft-standard-WSL2 #1 SMP Fri Jan 27 02:56:13 UTC
2023 x86_64 x86_64 x86_64 GNU/Linux
```

EXERCISE 3

Now, let's try the **cat /etc/*release** command, which is a common way to check the Linux distribution and version that your system is running on.

```
~$ cat /etc/*release # run the command and this will reveal much of your
system information
[...omitted for brevity]
~$ cat /etc/*release | grep DISTRIB_* # combine with the grep command to get
specific information.
DISTRIB_ID=Ubuntu
DISTRIB_RELEASE=22.04
DISTRIB_CODENAME=jammy
DISTRIB_DESCRIPTION="Ubuntu 22.04.1 LTS"
```

```
~$ cat /etc/*release | awk -F= '/^NAME/{print $2}' | tr -d '"' # combine with
awk to pin point the info
Ubuntu
~$ cat /etc/*release | awk -F= '/^PRETTY_NAME/{print $2}' | tr -d '"'
Ubuntu 22.04.1 LTS
```

EXERCISE 4

Apart from the cat /etc/*release command, there are other commands that you can use to obtain information about your Linux system. One such command is **env**, which displays the values of all the currently defined environment variables. Running this command can help you understand the current environment of your Linux system.

```
~$ hostname # print the host name
LP50BC
~$ whoami # print logged-in username
jdoe
~$ pwd # print present working directory
/home/jdoe
~$ echo $HOME # return the path of the home directory
/home/jdoe
~$ env | grep HOME # combine env and grep commands to get specific information
HOME=/home/jdoe
~$ env # this command will display tons of environment variables
[...omitted for brevity]
```

EXERCISE 5

The following information is provided for your reference only and is specific to Fedora 38, a Red Hat–based system. You do not need to run these commands, as they are only included to provide a comprehensive understanding of the topic.

Fedora output:
```
For Fedora: Run "sudo dnf update && sudo dnf install redhat-lsb-core -y"
For CentOS and Red Hat: Run "sudo yum update && sudo yum install redhat-
lsb-core -y"
```

```
~]$ lsb_release -a
LSB Version:      :core-4.1-amd64:core-4.1-noarch
Distributor ID: Fedora
Description:      Fedora release 38 (Thirty Eight)
Release:          38
Codename:         ThirtyEight
~]$ uname -a
Linux f38s1 6.2.8-300.fc38.x86_64 #1 SMP PREEMPT_DYNAMIC Wed Mar 22 19:29:30
UTC 2023 x86_64 GNU/Linux
~]$ cat /etc/*release
[...omitted for brevity]
~]$ cat /etc/*release | grep Fedora* # notice the difference in output
and keyword
Fedora release 38 (Thirty Eight)
NAME="Fedora Linux"
PRETTY_NAME="Fedora Linux 38 (Server Edition Prerelease)"
REDHAT_BUGZILLA_PRODUCT="Fedora"
REDHAT_SUPPORT_PRODUCT="Fedora"
Fedora release 38 (Thirty Eight)
Fedora release 38 (Thirty Eight)
~]$ cat /etc/*release | awk -F= '/^PRETTY_NAME/{print $2}' | tr -d '"'
Fedora Linux 38 (Server Edition Prerelease)
```

EXERCISE 6

To find where a program is installed in Linux, use the command followed by the name of
the program. For example, running python3 will show you where the Python 3 executable is
located. It's also important to check the version of the program you are running, and you can
do so by using either the --version or -V option. However, not all programs support the -V
abbreviation, and vice versa, so it's best to check the program's documentation first. By
using these commands, you can stay up to date with your Linux system and get a better
understanding of the programs you have installed.

```
~$ which python3
/usr/bin/python3
~$ python3 --version
Python 3.10.6
```

```
~$ python3 -V
Python 3.10.6

~$ which lsb_release
/usr/bin/lsb_release
~$ lsb_release -V
Usage: lsb_release [options]

lsb_release: error: no such option: -V
~$ lsb_release --version
LSB Version:    core-11.1.0ubuntu4-noarch:security-11.1.0ubuntu4-noarch
```

Tip

Drop the number 3 from the python3 command

If you're a Linux user running Python in Windows Subsystem for Linux (WSL), you may encounter the "Command not found" error when running the Python command. To run Python in WSL, you need to use python3, which can be inconvenient if you're used to running the simpler Python command.

However, there's an easy solution to this problem. You can create an alias that allows you to use the Python command instead of python3. Here's how:

1. Open the .bashrc file using the vi ~/.bashrc command.

2. Add the following line at the end of the file: alias python=python3.

3. Save the file and exit the editor.

4. Run the source ~/.bashrc command to apply the changes.

5. Now, you can use the Python command instead of python3 to run your Python programs. For example, you can run python filename. py instead of python3 filename.py.

By creating this alias, you can save time and avoid the hassle of typing the extra 3 every time you want to run Python in WSL. This same user setting applies to other Linux operating systems too.

As a Linux user, it's important to have a clear understanding of the system you're working on. Luckily, there are several commands you can use to discover valuable information about your environment. The lsb_release command displays Linux Standard Base (LSB) and distribution-specific information, including the version number and codename. The uname command displays information about the system's kernel version and architecture. The cat /etc/*release command displays information about the Linux distribution and version you are running. The env command displays environment variables that are currently set, which can be useful for troubleshooting or debugging. The command shows the location of an executable file associated with a given command. Lastly, the --version or -V command option can be used with various programs to display their version information. By using these commands, you can gain a deeper understanding of your Linux system and confirm your running environment.

3.3 Getting Familiar with Linux Processes

Modern computers commonly support multiprocessing, which allows multiple processes to run concurrently. A process is a running instance of a program in both Linux and Windows. When you run a program, the operating system creates a new process to execute it. Each process is allocated its own memory space, resources, and stack and is managed by the kernel. As a Linux power user, it's essential to be familiar with the tools that manage processes in Linux. This knowledge is particularly important in troubleshooting issues such as resource contention or high processor utilization. In this section, we'll cover three essential tools for managing Linux processes: **top**, **free**, and **dmesg**. While this book has a focus on Ansible, it's essential to understand the use cases for each of these tools. We recommend that you take the time to expand your knowledge of the different Linux processes in use and learn from your job if you're administering Linux systems in production.

Let's take a quick look at some examples of each tool.

EXERCISE 1

The **top** command shown in Figure 3-3 is a widely used tool among Linux users for monitoring system resources in real time. It provides valuable information on CPU and memory usage, as well as a list of resources that each process is utilizing. With top, you can quickly identify any resource-intensive processes that may be causing performance issues and take appropriate action to optimize system performance. Its user-friendly interface and comprehensive feature set make it an essential tool for system administrators and power users alike.

~$ **top**

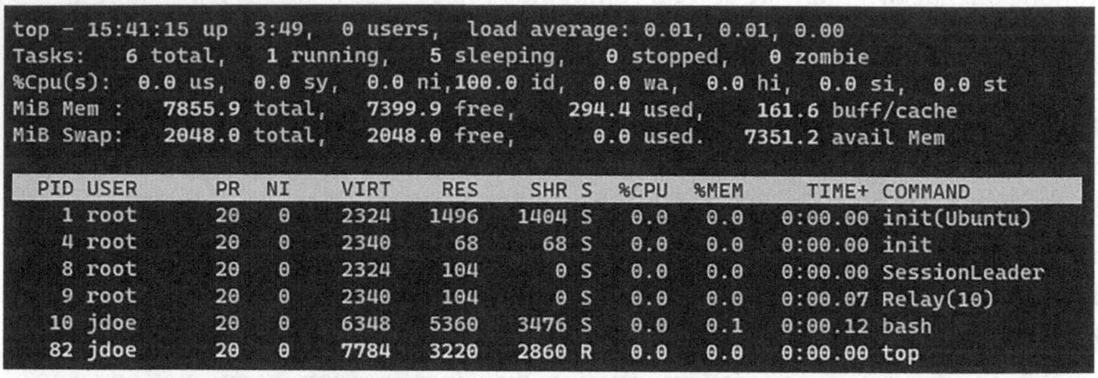

```
top - 15:41:15 up  3:49,  0 users,  load average: 0.01, 0.01, 0.00
Tasks:   6 total,   1 running,   5 sleeping,   0 stopped,   0 zombie
%Cpu(s):  0.0 us,  0.0 sy,  0.0 ni,100.0 id,  0.0 wa,  0.0 hi,  0.0 si,  0.0 st
MiB Mem :   7855.9 total,   7399.9 free,    294.4 used,    161.6 buff/cache
MiB Swap:   2048.0 total,   2048.0 free,      0.0 used.   7351.2 avail Mem

  PID USER      PR  NI    VIRT    RES    SHR S  %CPU  %MEM     TIME+ COMMAND
    1 root      20   0    2324   1496   1404 S   0.0   0.0   0:00.00 init(Ubuntu)
    4 root      20   0    2340     68     68 S   0.0   0.0   0:00.00 init
    8 root      20   0    2324    104      0 S   0.0   0.0   0:00.00 SessionLeader
    9 root      20   0    2340    104      0 S   0.0   0.0   0:00.07 Relay(10)
   10 jdoe      20   0    6348   5360   3476 S   0.0   0.1   0:00.12 bash
   82 jdoe      20   0    7784   3220   2860 R   0.0   0.0   0:00.00 top
```

Figure 3-3. *top command output (Ubuntu on WSL)*

ID: Process ID number

USER: User who started the process

PR: Priority of the process

VIRT: Virtual memory used

RES: Physical memory used

%CPU: Percentage of CPU time used

SHR: Shared memory used by the process

%MEM: Percentage of physical memory used

COMMAND: Name of the command that started the process

While the preceding output from your WSL Ubuntu server represents just a few lines of processes, it's important to note that in a production environment, there can be hundreds or thousands of processes running simultaneously. However, what matters most for you right now is to become familiar with the information presented so that you know what to look for the next time an issue arises. This will help you troubleshoot effectively and identify any problematic processes that may be causing issues. So take your time to understand the output and use it as a stepping stone to becoming more comfortable with managing server processes.

EXERCISE 2

The **free** command in Linux is a powerful tool for displaying information about memory usage and available memory on your system. By default, running the free command will display memory information in bytes. However, if you combine the command with the -h option, the output becomes more human-readable, as the sizes are expressed in units like "GB" and "MB" (see Figures 3-4 and 3-5).

~$ **free**

```
jdoe@LP50BC:~$ free
              total        used        free      shared  buff/cache   available
Mem:        8044480      302328     7576644        2292      165508     7526776
Swap:       2097152           0     2097152
```

Figure 3-4. *free command output (Ubuntu on WSL)*

~$ **free -h**

```
jdoe@LP50BC:~$ free -h
              total        used        free      shared  buff/cache   available
Mem:           7.7Gi       294Mi       7.2Gi       2.0Mi       161Mi       7.2Gi
Swap:          2.0Gi          0B       2.0Gi
```

Figure 3-5. *free -h command output (Ubuntu on WSL)*

total: Amount of memory in your system

used: Amount currently in use

free: Amount not in use

shared: Amount shared among processes

buff/cache: Amount used for file system buffering and caching

available: Amount available for new processes

EXERCISE 3

A **dmesg** command is a tool used to show the kernel ring buffer, which contains information about system events, including hardware and software events like system boot-up, device driver messages, and error messages. It is an excellent tool for troubleshooting many system issues (see Figures 3-6 and 3-7).

~$ **dmesg | less**

```
[    0.000000] Linux version 5.15.90.1-microsoft-standard-WSL2 (oe-user@oe-host) (x86_64-msft-linux-gcc
(GCC) 9.3.0, GNU ld (GNU Binutils) 2.34.0.20200220) #1 SMP Fri Jan 27 02:56:13 UTC 2023
[    0.000000] Command line: initrd=\initrd.img WSL_ROOT_INIT=1 panic=-1 nr_cpus=8 cgroup_no_v1=all swio
tlb=force console=hvc0 debug pty.legacy_count=0
[    0.000000] KERNEL supported cpus:
[    0.000000]   Intel GenuineIntel
[    0.000000]   AMD AuthenticAMD
[    0.000000]   Centaur CentaurHauls
[    0.000000] x86/fpu: Supporting XSAVE feature 0x001: 'x87 floating point registers'
[    0.000000] x86/fpu: Supporting XSAVE feature 0x002: 'SSE registers'
[    0.000000] x86/fpu: Supporting XSAVE feature 0x004: 'AVX registers'
[    0.000000] x86/fpu: xstate_offset[2]:  576, xstate_sizes[2]:  256
[    0.000000] x86/fpu: Enabled xstate features 0x7, context size is 832 bytes, using 'compacted' format
.
[    0.000000] signal: max sigframe size: 1776
[    0.000000] BIOS-provided physical RAM map:
[    0.000000] BIOS-e820: [mem 0x0000000000000000-0x000000000009ffff] usable
:
```

Figure 3-6. *The dmesg | less command pipes the output of "dmesg" to "less"*

~$ **dmesg -T**

```
jdoe@LP50BC:~$ dmesg -T
[Sat Apr  8 21:41:51 2023] Linux version 5.15.90.1-microsoft-standard-WSL2 (oe-user@oe-host) (x86_64-msf
t-linux-gcc (GCC) 9.3.0, GNU ld (GNU Binutils) 2.34.0.20200220) #1 SMP Fri Jan 27 02:56:13 UTC 2023
[Sat Apr  8 21:41:51 2023] Command line: initrd=\initrd.img WSL_ROOT_INIT=1 panic=-1 nr_cpus=8 cgroup_no
_v1=all swiotlb=force console=hvc0 debug pty.legacy_count=0
[Sat Apr  8 21:41:51 2023] KERNEL supported cpus:
[Sat Apr  8 21:41:51 2023]   Intel GenuineIntel
[Sat Apr  8 21:41:51 2023]   AMD AuthenticAMD
[Sat Apr  8 21:41:51 2023]   Centaur CentaurHauls
[Sat Apr  8 21:41:51 2023] x86/fpu: Supporting XSAVE feature 0x001: 'x87 floating point registers'
[Sat Apr  8 21:41:51 2023] x86/fpu: Supporting XSAVE feature 0x002: 'SSE registers'
[Sat Apr  8 21:41:51 2023] x86/fpu: Supporting XSAVE feature 0x004: 'AVX registers'
[Sat Apr  8 21:41:51 2023] x86/fpu: xstate_offset[2]:  576, xstate_sizes[2]:  256
[Sat Apr  8 21:41:51 2023] x86/fpu: Enabled xstate features 0x7, context size is 832 bytes, using 'compa
cted' format.
[Sat Apr  8 21:41:51 2023] signal: max sigframe size: 1776
[Sat Apr  8 21:41:51 2023] BIOS-provided physical RAM map:
[Sat Apr  8 21:41:51 2023] BIOS-e820: [mem 0x0000000000000000-0x000000000009ffff] usable
```

Figure 3-7. *dmesg -T output displays the timestamp in a human-readable format*

By piping the output of dmesg to less, you can navigate through the messages by scrolling up and down or moving one line at a time. Additionally, you can perform keyword searches within the less environment. If you prefer a more human-friendly timestamp, you can use the -T option with the dmesg command. This is a helpful starting point for troubleshooting any boot-up or hardware-related issues since it displays valuable logs related to these events and processes.

You now know where to locate critical information regarding processes, memory usage, and events and processes-related logs for troubleshooting purposes. It is not necessary to commit these commands to memory, but with frequent use, you will become more familiar with them. The essential thing to remember at this point is that these tools are widely available in almost every Linux OS, making it easier for you to access the information you need.

3.4 Getting to Know Disk Space in Linux

To help readers quickly get up to speed with Linux, we won't be covering custom disk space allocation or manual LVM configuration during installation. These topics are extensive and require separate studies beyond the scope of this book. However, we will cover the df command, which is used to check disk utilization on the current Linux OS.

EXERCISE 1

To make the output of the **df** command more easily understood, it is typically used with the -h option, which displays sizes in a human-readable format (see Figure 3-8). With this option, the output shows the size of the file system, as well as the used and available disk space, in a format that is easy to interpret. The resulting output is much more user-friendly, making it easier for even novice Linux users to understand the state of their system's disk utilization. By the way, the "df" stands for "disk free".

```
~$ df -h
```

```
jdoe@LP50BC:~$ df -h
Filesystem      Size  Used Avail Use% Mounted on
none            3.9G  4.0K  3.9G   1% /mnt/wsl
none            466G  102G  364G  22% /usr/lib/wsl/drivers
none            3.9G     0  3.9G   0% /usr/lib/wsl/lib
/dev/sdc       1007G  1.5G  955G   1% /
none            3.9G   84K  3.9G   1% /mnt/wslg
rootfs          3.9G  1.9M  3.9G   1% /init
none            3.9G     0  3.9G   0% /run
none            3.9G     0  3.9G   0% /run/lock
none            3.9G     0  3.9G   0% /run/shm
none            3.9G     0  3.9G   0% /run/user
none            3.9G   76K  3.9G   1% /mnt/wslg/versions.txt
none            3.9G   76K  3.9G   1% /mnt/wslg/doc
drvfs           466G  102G  364G  22% /mnt/c
```

Figure 3-8. *df -h output*

EXERCISE 2

The following command shown in Figure 3-9 only displays the available disk space:

```
~$ df -h --output=avail /
```

```
jdoe@LP50BC:~$ df -h --output=avail /
Avail
 955G
```

Figure 3-9. *df -h –output=avail / output*

The df command provides valuable information about disk space usage, including available and used disk space on your Linux system. By mastering this command, readers will gain insight into their system's disk usage and be better equipped to manage their Linux environment.

3.5 Getting Started with Linux User Management

Managing user accounts on a Linux server through the terminal interface can be challenging, particularly for novice Linux users and Windows users who are accustomed to user administration via a graphical user interface. While the terminal interface may not be as intuitive as user-friendly desktop GUIs, it is often the preferred method of user administration in highly secure environments where desktop GUIs and KVMs (Keyboard, Video, and Mouse) are not available. This ensures optimal system resource utilization, increased security, and fewer system bugs. As such, IT professionals who work in these environments should possess strong skills in terminal-based user management.

While APIs are becoming increasingly prevalent in machine-to-machine communication, there are still manual tasks that cannot be effectively processed and replaced by AI or ML. Until the AI can read an IT administrator's mind and the keyboard is removed from the equation, some tasks will remain manual. Despite the excellent desktop GUIs available for Linux, IT professionals should understand how to manage users through both the desktop GUI and the terminal console, with a preference for the terminal. In this way, they can ensure they are equipped with the skills needed to manage users on a Linux server effectively.

In this exercise, we will be practicing several tasks related to user management on a Linux server. These tasks include adding a new user with a home directory, adding another user without a home directory, creating a home directory for an existing user, creating a new user with a home directory and setting /bin/bash as the default shell, changing the default shell to /bin/bash for an existing user, logging in as a new user using the su – username command, setting a user's password expiry date using the **chage** command, locking a user account, removing (revoking) a user's password only, deleting a user account only using the sudo **userdel** command, and deleting a user account along with all their files and directories.

It is important to become proficient in these tasks as they are essential skills for any IT professional working with Linux servers. By mastering these skills, you can ensure that you can manage user accounts on a Linux server effectively and efficiently. These skills will be valuable throughout your career and can help you achieve success in your role as a system administrator or IT professional. So get ready and excited to practice these skills and make them a part of your long-term skill set.

EXERCISE 1

To add a new user with a home directory on Ubuntu, you can use the adduser command, which is a Perl script that acts as a user-friendly wrapper around the useradd command. This script guides you through the process of creating a new user in a wizard-like manner, automatically configuring default settings such as the user's home directory. By using the adduser command, you can quickly and easily create new users with minimal effort.

```
~$ adduser jane
```

adduser: Only root may add a user or group to the system.

~$ **sudo adduser jane**
[sudo] password for jdoe: **************** # enter jdoe's (Administrator) sudo
password
Adding user `jane' ...
Adding new group `jane' (1001) ...
Adding new user `jane' (1001) with group `jane' ...
Creating home directory `/home/jane' ...
Copying files from `/etc/skel' ...
New password: *************** # enter jane's new password
Retype new password: *************** # re-enter jane's new password
passwd: password updated successfully
Changing the user information for jane
Enter the new value, or press ENTER for the default
        Full Name []: **Jane Doe** # Optionally enter the user's full name
        Room Number []:
        Work Phone []:
        Home Phone []:
        Other []:
Is the information correct? [Y/n] **Y** # Y for yes
~$ **ls /home/** # Check /home directory to see jane's home directory
jane jdoe
~$ **tail -n 2 /etc/passwd** # run tail command to check the last 3 lines in the
passwd file
jdoe:x:1000:1000:,,,:/home/jdoe:/bin/bash
jane:x:1001:1001:Jane Doe,,,:/home/jane:/bin/bash # You can see the home
directory reference in passwd
~$ **sudo tail -n 2 /etc/shadow**
jdoe:yj9T$bSGktRfoIyAxnzrKjkuax1$vLzhNTKYGw3FKsfLnFO3J75StrwrKEt6RNjbnO5
COA5:19449:0:99999:7:::
jane:yj9T$liTOKx9tAwCF1WW4JxPgj.$v2hHIOx5SnQ2kczbLPmkS7zFnyFk6vL8Ireg
H83eAs7:19456:0:99999:7:::

You have successfully created a user with the home directory and also set the new password
for the user. Compare that to the next exercise.

EXERCISE 2

To add another user without a home directory and make this user a sudo user:

~$ **sudo useradd bob**
[sudo] password for jdoe: **************** # if you are continuing from Ex.1,
no password will be prompted
~$ **ls /home/**
jane   jdoe
~$ **tail -n 3 /etc/passwd**
jdoe:x:1000:1000:,,,:/home/jdoe:/bin/bash
jane:x:1001:1001:Jane Doe,,,:/home/jane:/bin/bash
bob:x:1002:1002::/home/bob:/bin/sh # notice that the default shell is /bin/sh
~$ **ls /home/** # the last output contains /home/bob but bob's home directory is
still missing
jane   jdoe
To create a home directory for an existing user, use the mkhomedir_helper
command.
~$ **sudo mkhomedir_helper bob** # to instate the user's home directory, run
this command
~$ **ls /home/**
bob   jane   jdoe

To create a new user with a home directory and set /bin/bash as the default shell, use
the -m option for home directory creation and the -s option to set the user's default shell to
/bin/bash.

~$ **sudo useradd -m -s /bin/bash leah**
~$ **tail -n 3 /etc/passwd**
jane:x:1001:1001:Jane Doe,,,:/home/jane:/bin/bash
bob:x:1002:1002::/home/bob:/bin/sh
leah:x:1003:1003::/home/leah:/bin/bash
~$ **ls /home/**
bob   jane   jdoe   leah

To change the default shell to /bin/bash for an existing user, bob, you must use the usermod command with the -s option.

```
~$ sudo usermod -s /bin/bash bob
~$ cat /etc/passwd | grep bob
bob:x:1002:1002::/home/bob:/bin/bash
```

With the useradd command, it does not create a password for the users as you can see from the next command. You have to use the passwd command to create a new password; you can also use the passwd command to update an existing user's password.

```
~$ sudo tail -n 3 /etc/shadow
jane:$y$j9T$liTOKx9tAwCF1WW4JxPgj.$v2hHIOx5SnQ2kczbLPmkS7zFnyFk6vL8Ireg
H83eAs7:19456:0:99999:7:::
bob::19456:0:99999:7::: # no password for the user, bob, notice the
"!" symbol
leah:!:19456:0:99999:7::: # no password for the user, leah, notice the
"!" symbol

~$ sudo passwd bob # run this command to create or update a user password
New password: *************** # enter the password
Retype new password: *************** # re-enter the password
passwd: password updated successfully
~$ sudo tail -n 3 /etc/shadow #
jane:$y$j9T$liTOKx9tAwCF1WW4JxPgj.$v2hHIOx5SnQ2kczbLPmkS7zFnyFk6vL8Ireg
H83eAs7:19456:0:99999:7:::
bob:$y$j9T$eeTek//kgFUciLGbNc4NC1$BRaA4BjO.4Jfe3EsqWU4LzOIfWOedoa.
A5tHmZFSXX8:19456:0:99999:7::: # bob's new password has been set
leah:!:19456:0:99999:7::: # user leah still does not have her password,
notice the "!" symbol
```

EXERCISE 3

Use "su – username" to log in as the new user. It is important to avoid using the command "su username" as it may result in logging into the wrong user's home directory, such as "/home/jdoe$". To ensure that you log into the correct user's home directory, it is recommended to use the "su –" command.

In this section, we will be adding the user "bob" to a sudoer group, granting him sudo privileges. However, it is important to note that the process of escalating a user to the sudoer group on Fedora is slightly different and will be covered in the next chapter, which will focus on installing and configuring both Fedora and Ubuntu virtual machines for Ansible practical. For now, we will focus on Ubuntu (Debian) user privilege escalation.

```
~$ su - bob # login as a user bob
Password: ***************
[...omitted for brevity]
~$ ls
~$ pwd # always check your working directory
/home/bob
~$ sudo ls -la /root # run this command to check that if bob has the sudo
privilege
[sudo] password for bob: ***************
bob is not in the sudoers file.  This incident will be reported. # bob does
not have the sudoer privilege
~$ exit # exit to move back into jdoe's Admin account
~$ pwd
/home/jdoe
~$ sudo usermod -aG sudo bob # add bob to the sudo group using the -aG
option. -a stands for append, -G stands for groups. Linux options are called
flags and these terms are interchangeably used.
~$ su - bob
Password: ***************
[...omitted for brevity]
$ pwd
/home/bob
$ sudo ls -la /root # if this command gives an output, bob has the sudo
privileges and "Bob's your uncle."
[sudo] password for bob: ***************
total 16
drwx------  2 root root 4096 Jan  4 08:41 .
drwxr-xr-x 19 root root 4096 Apr  9 10:12 ..
-rw-r--r--  1 root root 3106 Oct 15  2021 .bashrc
-rw-r--r--  1 root root  161 Jul  9  2019 .profile
```

```
~$ sudo cat /etc/shadow | grep bob # this command confirms that "everything
is all right" for bob
bob:$y$j9T$eeTek//kgFUciLGbNc4NC1$BRaA4BjO.4Jfe3EsqWU4LzOIfWOedoa.A5t
HmZFSXX8:19456:0:99999:7:::
~$ exit
```

EXERCISE 4

To set a user's password expiry date, you have to use the chage command. Combine
the command with a number of options to set the correct password policy for the users.
One example is shown in the following. After setting the password expiry policy for a user,
it is recommended to compare the configuration with other users such as "jane," "jdoe," or
"leah" to ensure consistency and uniformity. This comparison will provide more insight into
the password expiry policy and help to identify any discrepancies or issues that may require
further attention.

```
~$ sudo chage -M 90 -m 0 -W 14 bob # "-M 90" sets the max days between
password changes to 90 days, "-m 0" means the user can change password at any
time, "-W 14" indicate that the password warning will be sent 14 days before
the password expiry.
[sudo] password for jdoe: **************
$ sudo chage -l bob #
Last password change                               : Apr 09, 2023 # the last
                                                     password update
Password expires                                   : Jul 08, 2023 # expires
                                                     in 90 days
Password inactive                                  : never
Account expires                                    : never
Minimum number of days between password change     : 0
Maximum number of days between password change     : 90 # the days between
                                                     password change
Number of days of warning before password expires  : 14 # the password
                                                     expiry warning

~$ sudo passwd -S bob # some systems do not have chage command, then use
passwd with -S option
bob P 04/09/2023 0 90 14 -1
```

~$ **sudo passwd -S jane** # notice the 90 in bob's output to 99999 in jane's output. 99999 indicates that there is no password expiry set for the user, jane. Also, the warndays changed from the default 7 days to 14 days in bob's settings.
jane P 04/09/2023 0 99999 7 -1

EXERCISE 5

Linux housekeeping 1: **To lock a user account** in Linux, utilize the "passwd" command with the "-L" option. Conversely, to unlock the account, employ the "-U" option. This is a basic housekeeping task in Linux system administration.

~$ **sudo passwd -S bob**
bob P 04/09/2023 0 90 14 -1
~$ **sudo usermod -L bob** # lock the user account
~$ **sudo passwd -S bob**
bob L 04/09/2023 0 90 14 -1
~$ su - bob
Password: **************
su: Authentication failure
~$ **sudo usermod -U bob** # unlock the user account
~$ **su - bob** # always check the user login
Password: **************
bob@LP50BC:~$ **exit** # exit to go back to the admin account
logout

EXERCISE 6

Linux housekeeping 2: **To remove (revoke) the user password only**. **Exercise caution** when using this command as it enables users to log in without password prompts. Although the command is available, it is not advisable to use it due to security concerns.

~$ **sudo cat /etc/shadow | grep bob** # check bob's password exists
bob:yj9T$eeTek//kgFUciLGbNc4NC1$BRaA4BjO.4Jfe3EsqWU4Lz0IfWOedoa.
A5tHmZFSXX8:19456:0:99999:7:::
~$ **sudo passwd -d bob** # delete the password for user, bob
passwd: password expiry information changed.

~$ **sudo cat /etc/shadow | grep bob** # check that the password has been removed
bob::19456:0:90:14::: # bob's password has been removed
~$ **su - bob** # login as bob, no password prompt here. You got a free pass.
~$ **sudo ls -al /root** # You can still run the sudo commands even if you logged
in with no password
total 16
drwx------ 2 root root 4096 Jan 4 08:41 .
drwxr-xr-x 19 root root 4096 Apr 9 10:12 ..
-rw-r--r-- 1 root root 3106 Oct 15 2021 .bashrc
-rw-r--r-- 1 root root 161 Jul 9 2019 .profile
~$ **exit**

EXERCISE 7

Linux housekeeping 3: **To delete user accounts only. Use "sudo userdel".** By default, this command will only remove the user account but preserve the user's home directory. Remove the user's home directory separately.

~$ **ls /home/** # confirm jane's home directory
bob   jane   jdoe   leah
~$ **tail -n 3 /etc/passwd** # confirm jane's account
jane:x:1001:1001:Jane Doe,,,:/home/jane:/bin/bash
bob:x:1002:1002::/home/bob:/bin/bash
leah:x:1003:1003::/home/leah:/bin/bash
~$ **sudo userdel jane** # run userdel without options
[sudo] password for jdoe: **************
~$ **tail -n 3 /etc/passwd** # check that jane's account has been deleted
jdoe:x:1000:1000:,,,:/home/jdoe:/bin/bash
bob:x:1002:1002::/home/bob:/bin/bash
leah:x:1003:1003::/home/leah:/bin/bash
~$ **ls /home/** # check that jane's home directory is still available
bob   jane   jdoe   leah
~$ **sudo rm -rf /home/jane** # we no longer need jane's home directory, so
remove it
~$ **ls /home/** # confirm the directory deletion
bob   jdoe   leah

EXERCISE 8

Linux housekeeping 4: **To delete a user account and all files and directories** within the user's home directory

```
~$ sudo userdel -r bob # use userdel with -r option to remove bob's account
and home directory and files
userdel: bob mail spool (/var/mail/bob) not found
~$ ls /home/ # confirm the user's home directory deletion
jdoe  leah
~$ tail -n 3 /etc/passwd # confirm the account deletion
tcpdump:x:107:113::/nonexistent:/usr/sbin/nologin
jdoe:x:1000:1000:,,,:/home/jdoe:/bin/bash
leah:x:1003:1003::/home/leah:/bin/bash
```

Expand your knowledge:

/bin/sh vs. /bin/bash

Exercises 1 and 2 demonstrated that different methods of creating a new user can assign different types of shells. But what is the difference between the two types of shells – /bin/sh and /bin/bash?

/bin/sh, also known as the Bourne shell, and /bin/bash are both Unix shell interpreters that execute commands and scripts on Unix and Linux operating systems. Linux, which is designed to mimic Unix, uses both shells. However, the default shell for most Unix and Linux systems is /bin/sh, while /bin/bash is a more advanced shell with additional features, functions, and capabilities. Wikipedia explains that /bin/sh usually points to a minimal POSIX-compliant shell interpreter, meaning that it conforms to a standardized set of features that are common to all Unix-like systems, including Linux. It was designed to be simple and efficient, with fewer built-in features. In contrast, /bin/bash is a more powerful shell that supports advanced features such as command-line editing, history, tab completion, and programmable command completion. It is typically used for interactive command-line sessions and more complex scripts. To summarize, /bin/sh is a basic shell interpreter used for simple tasks, while /bin/bash is a more advanced shell used for interactive command-line sessions and more complex scripts. /bin/bash is currently more popular due to its features and usefulness. Therefore, you now have a clear understanding of the difference between /bin/sh and /bin/bash.

Source: `https://en.wikipedia.org/wiki/Bourne_shell`

Great job on completing the user account management exercise! This topic can be confusing at first, but you tackled it with focus and determination. By understanding the underlying concepts and mastering the relevant commands, you now have the skills to properly manage user accounts and enhance the security of your Linux environment. As you move on to the next topic, which is files and directory access control, you will learn how to control who can access and modify files and directories on your system. This is another important aspect of Linux security, and mastering it will make you a more effective Linux user. Keep up the good work!

3.6 Controlling Access to Files and Directories in Linux

Create a new directory called "my_data" using the command mkdir my_data. After creating this directory, use the command ls -l my_data to review the output and understand the meanings behind each character relating to the my_data directory. As you can observe, the default permissions for a new directory are drwxr-xr-x, which stands for read, write, and execute permissions for the owner and read and execute permissions for the group and others. For a regular file, the same permissions apply but with the first character being replaced with -. Understanding these permissions is crucial for managing files and directories in Unix-like systems, so take time to fully comprehend the information presented in Figure 3-10 and Table 3-1.

EXERCISE 1

```
~$ mkdir my_data
~$ ls -l | grep my_data
drwxr-xr-x 2 jdoe jdoe 4096 Apr  9 16:59 my_data
```

Let's zoom in and study each item in the output.

d	r w x	r - x	r - x	2	jdoe	jdoe	4096	Apr 9 16:59	my_data
①	②	③	④	⑤	⑥	⑦	⑧	⑨	⑩

Figure 3-10. *Breakdown of ls -l output of the my_data directory*

Table 3-1. *Breakdown of the output of "ls -l" for a directory named my_data*

#	Ref.	Explanation
①	d	"d" indicates a directory. If "-" appears, it is a regular file
②	rwx	The next three characters specify the permissions for the file's owner. "rwx" indicates that the owner jdoe has read, write, and execute permissions
③	r-x	The next three characters, "r-x", indicate that the group, jdoe, has read and execute permissions but no write permission. When a user is created, a corresponding name group is created by default
④	r-x	The last three characters, "r-x", indicate that all other users' permissions have read and execute permissions but no write permission
⑤	2	"2" indicates the number of hard links to this file
⑥	jdoe	The file's owner's name
⑦	jdoe	The file's group name
⑧	4096	The size of the file in bytes
⑨	Apr 9 16:59	The date and time when the file was last modified
⑩	my_data	The name of the file

Now that we have a clear understanding of the meaning of each character in the output of the directory (treated as a file) named "my_data", let's take a closer look and comprehend the ten characters concerning the numeric codes used for modifying file/directory modes. We can use a simple chmod command to observe the changes in the mode.

EXERCISE 2

```
~$ ls -l | grep my_data
drwxr-xr-x 2 jdoe jdoe 4096 Apr  9 18:16 my_data
~$ chmod 775 my_data
~$ ls -l | grep my_data
drwxrwxr-x 2 jdoe jdoe 4096 Apr  9 18:16 my_data
```

Figure 3-11 shows file/directory permission changes. After running the "chmod 775 my_data", you will notice that the second character in ③ or the third set has been updated from "-" to "w", meaning that this group (jdoe) has just gained write access to this file, in this case, a directory. The ② or second set remained the same as before, meaning that "rwx" is the highest permission value 7. Finally, ④ or the fourth set remained "r-x", meaning that "r-x" must be equal to numeric value 5.

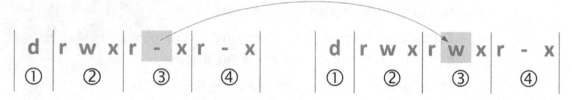

Figure 3-11. *File/directory permission change*

Using the information we gathered from our simple chmod testing and referring to Figure 3-11, we can match the numeric codes of the chmod command with the file permissions set characters. In Linux, file and directory permissions are represented by a series of three digits, with each digit indicating owner permissions, group permissions, and other permissions. These digits are calculated by assigning values to the corresponding permission types: read (4), write (2), and execute (1). Understanding the numeric code that specifies permissions for files or directories is critical, as file-related issues can arise in both lab and production environments. Troubleshooting file permission problems on Linux is a valuable skill for both novice and experienced Linux administrators. Therefore, let's examine the numeric code in Table 3-2 and the corresponding file permission characters.

Table 3-2. *File permissions numeric codes*

Numeric code	Meaning	Equivalent file permission
7	Full permissions (read, write, and execute)	rwx
6	Read and write permissions	rw-
5	Read and execute permissions	r-x
4	Read-only permissions	r--
3	Write and execute permissions	-wx
2	Write-only permissions	-w-
1	Execute-only permissions	--x
0	No permissions	---

Here are some of the commonly used Linux file/directory permissions code sets for your reference. While you don't have to memorize the values, it's helpful to be familiar with the most frequently used codes to save time. If you're unsure, you can always refer back to Table 3-3 for guidance.

Table 3-3. *Commonly used Linux file/directory permission numeric code sets*

Code set	Owner	Group	Other users	Explanation
744	rwx 7	r-- 4	r-- 4	drwxr--r-- 2 jdoe jdoe 4.0K Apr 9 18:16 my_data To give the owner of a file read, write, and execute permissions, but restrict all other users to only read access
770	rwx 7	rwx 7	--- 0	drwxrwx--- 2 jdoe jdoe 4.0K Apr 9 18:16 my_data To give the owner and group read, write, and execute permissions but no permission to other users

(*continued*)

Table 3-3. (*continued*)

Code set	Owner	Group	Other users	Explanation
777	rwx 7	rwx 7	rwx 7	drwxrwxrwx 2 jdoe jdoe 4.0K Apr 9 18:16 my_data Grants unrestricted access to everyone and is rarely used in production. Full read, write, and execute permissions to everyone. For public-facing files
755	rwx 7	r-x 5	r-x 5	drwxr-xr-x 2 jdoe jdoe 4.0K Apr 9 18:16 my_data The owner has full permissions; other users have only read and execute permissions. Commonly used for web services to allow execution but no modification to the files
644	rw- 6	r-- 4	r-- 4	drw-r--r-- 2 jdoe jdoe 4.0K Apr 9 18:16 my_data The owner has full read and write permissions; other users have only read permissions. A very common permission allows the owner to modify the file but prevents others from modifying the file. For files that are meant to be read-only for most users, such as configuration files or documentation
600	rw- 6	--- 0	--- 0	drw------- 2 jdoe jdoe 4.0K Apr 9 18:16 my_data The owner has full permissions; others have no permissions. A common setting for sensitive files, to ensure only the owner can access the file. For sensitive files that contain confidential data, such as passwords or encryption keys

Warning!

The significance of "d" and "-"

Please note that in the provided examples, the initial letter "d" signifies a directory. If the file being referred to is a regular file, the 'd' will be replaced with a "-" symbol.

It's important to note that Table 3-2 serves as a general guideline for setting file and directory permissions. However, it's essential to evaluate your specific situation and requirements to determine the appropriate permissions.

Now that you understand the meanings behind the "r", "w", "x", and chmod code sets, you may be wondering how this concept is applied in real-world scenarios. To gain a better understanding, let's explore a simple example of how file permissions can be used in practical situations. We'll use the following exercises to illustrate these concepts.

EXERCISE 3

Change the working directory to the root directory (/) and create four users. We will assign these test users to different groups with different permissions.

```
~$ pwd
/home/jdoe
~$ cd /
/$ pwd
/
/$ sudo adduser jane    # assign to no group
/$ sudo adduser bob # assign to group 1
/$ sudo adduser leah # assign to group 1 2
/$ sudo adduser tom # assign to group 1 2 3
```

EXERCISE 4

Create group1, group2, and group3 and assign users to it according to our plan.

Create three groups and assign users according to the notes in step ③.

```
/$ sudo groupadd group1
/$ sudo usermod -aG group1 bob
/$ sudo groupadd group2
/$ sudo usermod -aG group1 leah && sudo usermod -aG group2 leah
/$ sudo groupadd group3
/$ sudo usermod -aG group1 tom && sudo usermod -aG group2 tom && sudo usermod -aG group3 tom
```

Get the group's membership:

```
/$ getent group group1 group2 group3 # use 'getent group' command to check
the group membership
group1:x:1005:bob,leah,tom
group2:x:1006:leah,tom
group3:x:1007:tom
```

Check the user's group membership:

```
/$ groups jane bob leah tom # use 'groups' command to check group membership
jane : jane
bob : bob group1
leah : leah group1 group2
tom : tom group1 group2 group3
```

Another way to check the user's group membership:

```
/$ id jane bob leah tom # use 'id' command to check the user's group membership
uid=1001(jane) gid=1001(jane) groups=1001(jane)
uid=1002(bob) gid=1002(bob) groups=1002(bob),1005(group1)
uid=1003(leah) gid=1003(leah) groups=1003(leah),1005(group1),1006(group2)
uid=1004(tom) gid=1004(tom) groups=1004(tom),1005(group1),1006(group2),
1007(group3)
```

To check sudo group membership:

```
/$ getent group sudo # check sudo group membership while you are here
sudo:x:27:jdoe
```

EXERCISE 5

Now, make three separate directories and assign different permission levels exactly
shown here:

```
/$ sudo mkdir L1_data L2_data L3_data
/$ ls
L1_data  bin   etc   lib    libx32      mnt   root  snap  tmp
L2_data  boot  home  lib32  lost+found  opt   run   srv   usr
L3_data  dev   init  lib64  media       proc  sbin  sys   var
```

/$ **chmod 775 L1_data**

/$ chgrp group1 L1_data # change the group ownership to group1, all other users have read and execute permissions, but no write access.

/$ **chmod 770 L2_data**

/$ chgrp group2 L2_data # change the group ownership to group2, remove all other users permissions

/$ **chmod 770 L3_data**

/$ **chgrp group3 L3_data** # change the group ownership to group2, remove all other user permissions

/$ **sudo ls -al L*** # print the long listing of all files starting with an upper case 'L'

L1_data:

total 8

drwxrwxr-x 2 root group1 4096 Apr 9 22:13 . # group owner is group1 for L1_data directory

drwxr-xr-x 22 root root   4096 Apr 9 22:13 ..

L2_data:

total 8

drwxrwx--- 2 root group2 4096 Apr 9 22:13 . # group owner is group2 for L2_data directory

drwxr-xr-x 22 root root   4096 Apr 9 22:13 ..

L3_data:

total 8

drwxrwx--- 2 root group3 4096 Apr 9 22:13 . # group owner is group3 for L3_data directory

drwxr-xr-x 22 root root   4096 Apr 9 22:13 ..

EXERCISE 6

Since tom has access to all of the levels, we will log in as tom and create three secret files for three directories.

/$ **su - tom**

Password:

tom@LP5OBC:~$ **sudo cat > /L1_data/L1_secret** # use cat to create L1_ secret file

```
[sudo] password for tom: ***************
tom is not in the sudoers file.  This incident will be reported. # Since tom
is not part of the sudo group, he cannot use the sudo command.
tom@LP50BC:~$ cat > /L1_data/L1_secret # create L1_secret file
This is L1 secret!
tom@LP50BC:~$ cat > /L2_data/L2_secret # create L2_secret file
This is L2 secret!
tom@LP50BC:~$ cat > /L3_data/L3_secret # create L3_secret file
This is L3 secret!
tom@LP50BC:~$ exit # make sure you log out
logout
```

EXERCISE 7

Now log in as each user and test if you can open the secret files and compare the output.
If everything worked for you, you will see a similar result to the following commands and
outputs:

```
/$ su - jane # login as jane
Password: ***************
jane@LP50BC:~$ more /L1_data/L1_secret # see if you can open L1_secret file
This is L1 secret!
jane@LP50BC:~$ more /L2_data/L2_secret
more: cannot open /L2_data/L2_secret: Permission denied # see if you can open
L2_secret file
jane@LP50BC:~$ more /L3_data/L3_secret
more: cannot open /L3_data/L3_secret: Permission denied # see if you can open
L3_secret file
/$ su - bob # login as bob
Password: ***************
[...omitted for brevity]
bob@LP50BC:~$ more /L1_data/L1_secret # see if you can open L1_secret file
This is L1 secret!
bob@LP50BC:~$ more /L2_data/L2_secret
more: cannot open /L2_data/L2_secret: Permission denied # see if you can open
L2_secret file
bob@LP50BC:~$ more /L3_data/L3_secret
```

```
more: cannot open /L3_data/L3_secret: Permission denied # see if you can open
L3_secret file
bob@LP50BC:~$ su - leah # login as leah
Password: **************
[...omitted for brevity]
leah@LP50BC:~$ more /L1_data/L1_secret # see if you can open L1_secret file
This is L1 secret!
leah@LP50BC:~$ more /L2_data/L2_secret # see if you can open L2_secret file
This is L2 secret!
leah@LP50BC:~$ more /L3_data/L3_secret
more: cannot open /L3_data/L3_secret: Permission denied # see if you can open
L3_secret file
leah@LP50BC:~$ su - tom # login as tom
Password: **************
tom@LP50BC:~$ more /L1_data/L1_secret # see if you can open L1_secret file
This is L1 secret!
tom@LP50BC:~$ more /L2_data/L2_secret # see if you can open L2_secret file
This is L2 secret!
tom@LP50BC:~$ more /L3_data/L3_secret # see if you can open L3_secret file
This is L3 secret!
```

The purpose of this exercise was to demonstrate that file/directory access doesn't need to be assigned to each user. By using groups, you can assign multiple users to different groups based on their function and utilize it as a form of role-based access control. At the enterprise level, role-based access control to various resources is the preferred method over individual user-level access control due to the overhead involved in managing individual user accounts. This overhead can be costly in terms of resources and is often viewed as a waste of money, so it's not a desirable activity from a financial perspective. This is where the true power of groups in Linux comes into play. It allows for efficient management of access control for multiple users while reducing administrative overhead, making it an attractive solution for corporations.

Throughout this chapter, we have been demystifying several Linux topics, in this part, the secret codes behind the 'r's, 'w's, and 'x's of file permissions in Linux, and we have associated these characters with the chmod file permission codes. By practicing these concepts hands-on, you have been gaining a deeper understanding of Linux's file and directory permissions and access control. We believe that this section is one of the highlights of the chapter, as it will be invaluable to you when you have any questions about Linux files and directory permissions in the future. This section will serve as an excellent reference point for any future questions on Linux file/directory permissions. To help you remember these topics, we suggest practicing on the computer and using relatable examples that are relevant to your needs. If you felt that the naming conventions or examples in this chapter were not relatable, feel free to update them as you see fit and get more practice. Remember, practice makes perfect, and in this case, it will help you to retain the information in your long-term memory as well as in your muscle memory.

The last example we covered highlighted the importance of using groups for file and directory ownership, as it can significantly lower operational overheads for you and your organization. Next, we will lightly touch on compressing files, which involves zipping and unzipping files.

3.7 Working with Zip Files in Linux

Working with files in Linux often involves compressing them to save disk space, speed up file transfer, archive data, use less bandwidth, improve system performance, secure data using encryption or password protection, and organize data for easier access and management. There are several file compression utilities available in Linux, each with its strengths and weaknesses. Your choice of tools will depend on your specific needs and use cases. The most used compression tools in Linux are gzip and bzip2, which are typically used in conjunction with tar, the file archiving tool. Additionally, there are 7-Zip and zip tools that offer file compression and are an excellent choice when files need to be shared or transferred between Linux and Windows systems.

Table 3-4 provides an overview of the file extension types, features, and base algorithms used for compression in Linux. Consider the table when choosing the appropriate compression tool for your needs.

Table 3-4. *Common file compression tools for Linux*

Name	File ext.	Features	Algorithm
7-Zip	.7z	• File compression tool • Similar to zip • Often creates smaller compressed files than zip • Compresses the entire directories	LZMA (Lempel-Ziv-Markov chain algorithm)
bzip2	.bz2	• File compression tool • Often used in combination with tar to create compressed tar files • Creates smaller compressed files than gzip • Compresses the entire directories	Burrows-Wheeler block sorting algorithm
gzip	.gz	• File compression tool • Often used in combination with tar to create compressed tar files • Compresses the entire directories	LZMA (Lempel-Ziv-Markov chain algorithm)
tar	.tar	• File archiving utility • Does not compress files but is used in conjunction with the gzip or bzip2 to compress the archive	None
zip	.zip	• File compression tool • Widely used on Windows but also works on Linux • Compresses individual files • Uses a lossless data compression algorithm	DEFLATE (a combination of Huffman coding and LZ77 algorithm)

Now that we've familiarized ourselves with the various compression tools available in Linux, it's time to put theory into practice. To truly understand their capabilities, we need to get our hands dirty and learn how to use them effectively. In this section, we'll delve into practical examples of these tools in action, so you can start compressing files right away. By the end of this tutorial, you'll have the skills to compress files like a pro and take your Linux productivity to the next level.

EXERCISE 1

Exercise preparation steps. Check the current working directory. Use the dd tool to create a large file, say, 1 GB, with the file name "compress_me". And make a new directory to save the uncompressed files.

```
~$ pwd # check the current working directory
/home/jdoe
~$ dd if=/dev/urandom of=compress_me bs=1M count=1000 # create a 1GB binary
file using dd command. The content is not important here, only the size.
1000+0 records in
1000+0 records out
1048576000 bytes (1.0 GB, 1000 MiB) copied, 3.65665 s, 287 MB/s
~$ mkdir uncompressed # create a new directory for output
(uncompressed) files
$ ls -lh # check the file and directory
total 1001M
-rw-r--r-- 1 jdoe jdoe 1000M Apr 10 13:33 compress_me
drwxr-xr-x 2 jdoe jdoe  4.0K Apr 10 13:37 uncompressed
```

While a 1 GB file size may be considered large for some, we will keep the file size at 1 GB for demonstration purposes in this book. However, feel free to reduce the file size to 100 MB,10 MB, or 1 MB if you want to save time or disk space.

EXERCISE 2

To compress and uncompress the 1 GB test file named "compress_me" using the **7-Zip** software, please execute the following commands in your command prompt:

```
~$ sudo apt install p7zip-full # install 7-zip on Ubuntu
[...omitted for brevity]
~$ 7z a compress_me.7z compress_me # create compress_me.7z file in the
current directory
[...omitted for brevity]
~$ ls -l compress_me.7z
-total 2048068
-rw-r--r-- 1 jdoe jdoe 1048576000 Apr 10 13:33 compress_me
```

```
-rw-r--r-- 1 jdoe jdoe 1048631772 Apr 10 15:25 compress_me.7z # a newly
compressed file
drwxr-xr-x 2 jdoe jdoe       4096 Apr 10 13:37 uncompressed
```

~$ **7z x compress_me.7z -ouncompressed/** # extract the contents to the
uncompressed directory, you can use the -o option to specify the output
directory. Note, there is no space between the '-o' option and the directory
name 'uncompressed', so you have to use '-ouncompressed/' to specify the
directory path.
~$ **ls -l uncompressed/**
```
total 1024004
-rw-r--r-- 1 jdoe jdoe 1048576000 Apr 10 13:33 compress_me
```

(Optional)
~$ **7z x compress_me.7z** # if yo simply want to uncompress the file in the
current directory, use this simple command with the x option without the
directory path. If you already have an existing file, make an appropriate
selection from "(Y)es / (N)o / (A)lways / (S)kip all / A(u)to rename all /
(Q)uit?"

EXERCISE 3

To compress and uncompress the "compress_me" file using bzip2 software, execute
the provided commands. For faster practice, use files with smaller sizes such as 1 MB
or 10 MB. Keep in mind that bzip2 is known to be a slow software for compression and
uncompression processes.

~$ **bzip2 -k compress_me** # create compress_me.bz2 in the same directory, there
is no feedback from the program showing a percentage like 7-zip. The -k
option tells bzip2 to keep the original and make a compressed version. You
just have to wait patiently until the operation completes.
~$ **ls -lh**
```
total 3.0G
-rw-r--r-- 1 jdoe jdoe 1000M Apr 10 13:33 compress_me
-rw-r--r-- 1 jdoe jdoe 1001M Apr 10 15:25 compress_me.7z
-rw-r--r-- 1 jdoe jdoe 1005M Apr 10 13:33 compress_me.bz2
drwxr-xr-x 2 jdoe jdoe  4.0K Apr 10 15:37 uncompressed
```

```
~$ bzip2 -dc compress_me.bz2 > ./uncompressed/compress_me # extract the
contents of the compressed file to a new file named compress_me in the
directory, home/jdoe/uncompressed.
```

To decompress the file in the same directory, use the bzip2 with the -d option.

```
~$ ls -lh uncompressed/
total 1001M
-rw-r--r-- 1 jdoe jdoe 1000M Apr 10 16:20 compress_me
```

```
(Optional commands)
~$ bzip2 -d compress_me.bz2 # extract (decompress) the original file back
into the current working directory
~$ bzip2 compress_me
```

Be careful when using the "bzip2 file_name" command without the -k option. Forgetting to use the "-k" option can result in the original file being overwritten by the compressed version. For example, if you run the preceding command, the original file will be converted to "compress_me.bz2", potentially causing data loss. This is an important caveat to keep in mind, so be sure to double-check your command before running it to avoid this common mistake.

EXERCISE 4

To compress and uncompress the 1 GB test file named "compress_me" using the **gzip** software, please execute the following commands. Usually, gzip is a lot faster than bzip2, so use gzip for speed.

```
~$ gzip -k compress_me # create compress_me.gz in the same directory, with
the -k option, and keep the original file. Always use the -k option to keep
the original file intact.
~$ ls -lh
[...omitted for brevity]
~$ gzip -dc compress_me.gz > ./uncompressed/compress_me # extract the
contents of the compressed file to a new file named compress_me in the
directory specified by /path/to/uncompressed.
~$ ls -lh uncompressed/ # check the timestamp of compress_me file.
[...omitted for brevity]
~$ gzip -d compress_me.gz # extract the contents of the compressed file and
create a new file named compress_me in the same directory.
```

EXERCISE 5

To compress and uncompress the 1 GB test file named "compress_me" using the **tar with gzip** and **tar with bzip2**, please execute the following commands.

Use the tar and gzip method to compress and uncompress the test file, compress_me.

~$ **tar -czvf compress_me.tar.gz compress_me** # To create a compressed tar ball file named 'compress_me.tar.gz' in the same directory as the original file, you can use the tar command with -czvf options. The original file will remain unmodified and intact, while a compressed version will be created as a separate file.
compress_me
~$ **tar -xzvf compress_me.tar.gz -C uncompressed** # extract the contents to a specific directory, you can use the -C option to specify the output directory. For example, to extract the contents to a directory called uncompressed.
compress_me
~$ **tar -xzvf compress_me.tar.gz** # extract the files in the same directory.

Similarly use the **tar and bzip2 method** to compress and uncompress the test file.

~$ **tar -cjvf compress_me.tar.bz2 compress_me** # create a compressed tar ball file named compress_me.tar.bz2 in the same directory as the original file.
~$ **tar -xjvf compress_me.tar.bz2 -C uncompressed** # use the -C option to specify the output directory.
~$ **tar -xjvf compress_me.tar.bz2** #extract the compress_me.tar.bz2 file in the same directory.

EXERCISE 6

To compress and uncompress the 1 GB test file named "compress_me" using the **zip** software, please execute the following commands:

~$ **sudo apt install zip**
~$ **zip compress_me.zip compress_me** # reate a compressed zip file named compress_me.zip in the same directory as the original file.
adding: compress_me (deflated 0%)

```
~$ unzip compress_me.zip -d uncompressed # extract the contents to a specific
directory, you can use the -d option to specify the output directory.
Archive:  compress_me.zip
inflating: uncompressed/compress_me
~$ ls -lh uncompressed/
total 1001M
-rw-r--r-- 1 jdoe jdoe 1000M Apr 10 13:33 compress_me
~$ unzip compress_me.zip # extract the contents of the compressed file in the
same directory.
```

EXERCISE 7

To free up the disk space, delete all test files in the working directory.

```
~$ ls -lh
total 6.9G
-rw-r--r-- 1 jdoe jdoe 1000M Apr 10 13:33 compress_me
-rw-r--r-- 1 jdoe jdoe 1001M Apr 10 15:25 compress_me.7z
-rw-r--r-- 1 jdoe jdoe 1005M Apr 10 13:33 compress_me.bz2
-rw-r--r-- 1 jdoe jdoe 1001M Apr 10 13:33 compress_me.gz
-rw-r--r-- 1 jdoe jdoe 1005M Apr 10 16:54 compress_me.tar.bz2
-rw-r--r-- 1 jdoe jdoe 1001M Apr 10 17:02 compress_me.tar.gz
-rw-r--r-- 1 jdoe jdoe 1001M Apr 10 17:09 compress_me.zip
drwxr-xr-x 2 jdoe jdoe  4.0K Apr 10 17:10 uncompressed
~$ rm -rf *
~$ ls -lh
total 0
```

You have learned about various Linux file compression utilities, including tar, gzip, bzip2, zip, and 7-Zip. For each tool, you studied its features and file extensions. To test these tools, you created a 1 GB test file called "compress_me" and used each tool to compress and then uncompress the file. You discovered that tar is a file archiving method, but when combined with gzip or bzip2, it can perform file compression and decompression. Throughout your testing, you gained firsthand experience of the pros and cons of each tool and noted the speed of each compression utility. Finally, you deleted all the used files to free up disk space. In your next step, you plan to explore how to download files from the Internet using curl, wget, and git while managing your system.

3.8 Downloading Files from the Internet in Linux

Linux administration involves more than just managing the system; it also includes downloading important system files and drivers. However, the essential skills of using curl, wget, and git for file downloads are often overlooked. These tools can provide efficient management of software packages, automation of tasks, enhanced security, and accessibility to remote files, making them vital for any Linux administrator. **Make sure to keep the "jack.jpg" photo available as it will be used again in the final exercise on regular expressions.**

To truly understand the value of these tools, it's important to install them and try them out. Actions speak louder than words, after all. In the following sections, we'll explore how to install and use each of these file-downloading tools. You'll learn how to optimize their performance, take advantage of their features, and become a proficient Linux administrator. Let's get started!

EXERCISE 1

First, make three new directories to save and hold the downloaded files.

```
~$ mkdir curl_download wget_download git_download
~$ tree
.
├── curl_download
├── git_download
└── wget_download

3 directories, 0 files
```

EXERCISE 2

To download a file from the Internet, you can use the curl command. First, to download a file and save it to the current directory, use the curl command with the -O option.

```
~$ curl -O https://italchemy.files.wordpress.com/2023/04/jack.jpg
```

% Total		% Received	% Xferd	Average Speed		Time	Time	Time	Current
				Dload	Upload	Total	Spent	Left	Speed
100	164k	100	164k	0	0	393k	0 --:--:-- --:--:-- --:--:--		393k

```
~$ ls -lh jack.jpg
-rw-r--r-- 1 jdoe jdoe 165K Apr 10 21:00 jack.jpg
```

To download and save another file in a specific file location, use the curl command with the -o option. You have to specify the name of the directory along with the name you want the file to be saved as. We are renaming the original name putty_jack.png to young_jack.png and saving it under the /home/joe/curl_download directory.

```
~$ curl -o ./curl_download/young_jack.png https://italchemy.files.wordpress.
com/2023/04/puppy_jack.png
  % Total    % Received % Xferd  Average Speed   Time    Time     Time  Current
                                 Dload  Upload   Total   Spent    Left  Speed
100  435k  100  435k    0     0  1200k      0 --:--:-- --:--:-- --:--:-- 1203k
$ ls -lh curl_download/
total 436K
-rw-r--r-- 1 jdoe jdoe 436K Apr 10 21:02 young_jack.png
```

EXERCISE 3

To save a file in a specific directory, simply use the wget command with the -P option.

```
~$ wget -P ./wget_download/ https://italchemy.files.wordpress.com/2023/04/
puppy_jack.png
[...omitted for brevity]
~$ ls -lh wget_download/ # check the file
total 436K
-rw-r--r-- 1 jdoe jdoe 436K Apr 10 20:53 puppy_jack.png
```

To download the same photo and save it in the current directory, simply type in wget, followed by the URL of the file to download.

```
wget https://italchemy.files.wordpress.com/2023/04/puppy_jack.png # file will
be saved in the current directory
~$ ls -lh *.jpg *.png # check the files
-rw-r--r-- 1 jdoe jdoe 165K Apr 10 21:00 jack.jpg # a downloaded file from
the previous exercise
-rw-r--r-- 1 jdoe jdoe 436K Apr 10 20:53 puppy_jack.png # just
downloaded file
```

EXERCISE 4

To download files from the GitHub repository, "jackrussell", use the "git clone" command. If you want to save the files in a specific directory, append the path of the directory to where you want to save the files to.

```
~$ git clone https://github.com/ansnetauto/jackrussell.git ./git_download/
Cloning into './git_download'...
remote: Enumerating objects: 10, done.
remote: Counting objects: 100% (10/10), done.
remote: Compressing objects: 100% (10/10), done.
remote: Total 10 (delta 2), reused 0 (delta 0), pack-reused 0
Receiving objects: 100% (10/10), 766.08 KiB | 6.28 MiB/s, done.
Resolving deltas: 100% (2/2), done.
~$ ls -lh git_download/ # check the downloaded files
total 684K
-rw-r--r-- 1 jdoe jdoe  34K Apr 10 22:40 jack_black.jpg
-rw-r--r-- 1 jdoe jdoe 171K Apr 10 22:40 jack_cartoon.jpg
-rw-r--r-- 1 jdoe jdoe 473K Apr 10 22:40 puppy_jack_git.png
```

There are many options with even the git command; for a full list of options, please use the "git --help".

Now that you have learned three different ways to download files from the Internet, you should be able to select the most appropriate method for downloading the file you need on your Linux system, which will help you achieve your desired outcomes. Next, we will delve into managing networks in Linux and explore a range of useful network utilities that can be valuable in this regard.

Tip

Author's IT Blog, italchemy.wordpress.com

Brendan has been willingly sharing his IT expertise with the wider online community since 2014. Over the years, he has authored a total of three informative and insightful IT books, including the one you are currently reading. A lot of the content used in my books is inspired by his blog posts. The download links provided in this section are also posted in his blog. If you're interested in learning more about Brendan and staying up to date with his latest IT insights, be sure to check out his engaging and informative WordPress blog and GitHub, where he regularly posts on a wide range of IT-related topics for techies.

URL: `https://italchemy.files.wordpress.com`

`https://italchemy.files.wordpress.com/2023/04/jack.jpg`

`https://italchemy.files.wordpress.com/2023/04/puppy_jack.png`

GitHub: `https://github.com/ansnetauto/appress_ansnetauto`

`https://github.com/ansnetauto/jackrussell`

3.9 Linux Network Utilities for Troubleshooting

In this exercise, we will take a look at some of the most popular Linux network troubleshooting tools. These tools include "ip address", "ifconfig", "netstat", "ping", "traceroute", "tcpdump", "dig", "nmap", "route", and "ss". As a network or systems engineer, it is important to master the use of these tools to effectively troubleshoot network issues.

To help you get started, we have provided example commands for each tool in Table 3-5. You can access the example outputs for these commands from the following link: `https://italchemy.wordpress.com/2023/04/11/table-3-5-popular-linux-network-utilities-example-command-outputs-from-ubuntu-on-wsl/`.

We understand that going through each command output can be time-consuming and consume a lot of paper space. Therefore, we have provided the link for your convenience. You can review the outputs in your own time and at your own pace.

Please note that becoming proficient in using these tools takes time and practice. So we encourage you to start today and slowly add these tools to your skill set. To run the example commands, simply open your Ubuntu console and type in the commands as shown in Table 3-5.

Table 3-5. *Popular Linux network utilities*

Utility name	Description	Example
ip address	Display or configure IP addresses and network interfaces	ip address show
ifconfig	Configure and display network interfaces "sudo apt install net-tools" or "sudo apt install iproute2" required	sudo ifconfig eth0 up/down
netstat	Display active network connections. Has many options.	netstat -a
ping	Test network connectivity by sending ICMP packets	ping 8.8.8.8 -c 4 ping www.google.com -c 4
traceroute	Trace the route that packets travel through a network "sudo apt install inetutils-traceroute" required	traceroute www.tesla.com
tcpdump	Capture and analyze network traffic on a network interface	sudo tcpdump -i eth0
dig	Perform DNS queries and lookups	dig www.tesla.com
nmap	Scan a network and discover hosts and services running on target hosts "sudo apt install nmap" required	sudo nmap 192.168.0.83 -A
route	Manipulate and display the network routing table	sudo route -n
ss	Display information about active sockets and network connections	sudo ss -t -a

Most of the tools mentioned in this exercise are straightforward to use, but there are a couple of exceptions such as nmap and netstat. nmap is a powerful tool for remote host scanning and is an essential tool for IT engineers. To help you get started with nmap, we have provided syntax examples in Table 3-6. We encourage you to run each command provided at your own time and pace and also visit the source and reference websites for a more comprehensive understanding of the tool.

Table 3-6. *Useful nmap commands to scan remote hosts*

#	Command	Explanation
1	sudo nmap 10.10.10.1 or nmap google.com	Scan a host or scan a web site
2*	sudo nmap 192.168.30.201 –p 1-65535 sudo nmap 192.168.30.201 -p 22,69,80,443	Scan specific ports
3	sudo nmap 10.10.10.11 192.168.30.202 sudo nmap 192.168.30.11,201,202	Scan multiple Ips
4	CIDR scanning sudo nmap -p 8.8.8.0/28 IP Range nmap -p 8.8.8.1-14 Entire C class IP range (256 Ips) sudo nmap 8.8.8.* exclude an IP nmap -p 8.8.8.* --excluse 8.8.8.1 8.8.8.255	Scan IP ranges
5*	sudo nmap --top-ports 20 192.168.30.1 sudo nmap --top-ports 20 -Pn 192.168.30.201	Scan the most popular ports using -Pn option
6*	sudo nmap -iL ip_addresses.txt sudo nmap -iL ./ip_addresses.txt -A	-iL for Scan hosts in a text file -A for Operating System info
7*	sudo nmap -192.168.30.11 -oN scan_output1.txt sudo nmap -iL ./ip_addresses.txt -A -oN scan_output2.txt	#NAME?
8	sudo nmap -p 80 -n 8.8.8.8	-n Disable DNS name resolution if using only IP addresses
9	sudo nmap 192.168.30.202 -A	-A for OS scanning
10	sudo nmap -sV 192.168.30.202	-sV for Service/Daemon detection
11	sudo nmap -sT sudo nmap -sU	-sT for TCP scan -sU for UDP scan
12	sudo nmap -Pn --script vuln 192.168.30.1	NSE – full vulnerability testing
13	sudo nmap -sV --script=http-malware-host 192.168.1.105	Detecting malware infections on remote hosts

Source: https://italchemy.wordpress.com/2021/02/10/useful-nmap-port-scan-commands/

Reference: https://hackertarget.com/nmap-cheatsheet-a-quick-reference-guide/

netstat, on the other hand, is a local system tool that helps you audit, review, and troubleshoot local and remote issues. Just for fun, one of my favorite commands, 'netstat -tuna', is depicted in Figure 3-12. In this exercise, we will focus on netstat and provide some test-drive exercises. We will install OpenSSH and Nginx on our Ubuntu on WSL, which will open up some ports to help you learn about netstat commands with different options. By following these exercises, you will gain a better understanding of how to use netstat effectively.

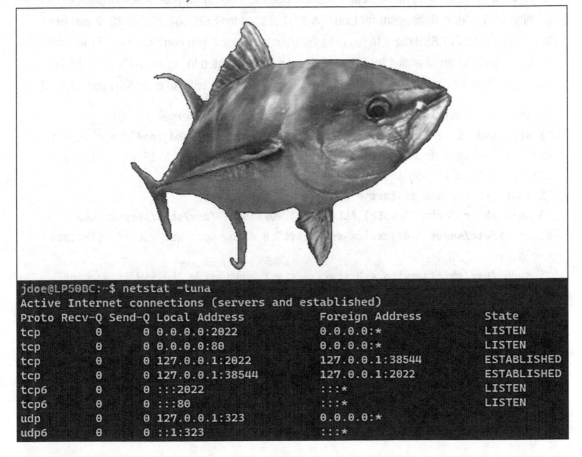

Figure 3-12. *netstat -tuna output*

It is important to note that becoming proficient in using these tools takes time and practice. So we encourage you to take the time to learn and practice using these tools regularly. As you become more comfortable with them, you will be better equipped to troubleshoot network issues and excel in your career as a network engineer.

Let's dive into some exercises using netstat and explore its various options. By practicing these exercises, you'll gain a better understanding of how to use netstat to audit, review, and troubleshoot local and remote network issues. So let's get started!

EXERCISE 1

To perform some testing, we need to install the OpenSSH server on your Ubuntu instance running in Windows Subsystem for Linux (WSL). Let's set the SSH login port to 2022 and use the Windows PuTTY SSH client to log in to the Ubuntu server. If you don't have PuTTY installed, please download and install it for this exercise. As demonstrated in Figure 3-13, from the host PC, you will be logging into WSL using the local IP of 127.0.0.1 with an open SSH port in 2022.

```
~$ sudo apt install openssh-server # install OpenSSH server on WSL
~$ sudo sed -i -E 's,^#?Port.*$,Port 2022,' /etc/ssh/sshd_config # change the
default SSH port from 22 to 2022, we will use the loopback IP of '127.0.0.1'
with port 2222 to SSH into the Ubuntu server.
~$ sudo service ssh restart # restart the ssh service
~$ sudo sh -c "echo '${USER} ALL=(root) NOPASSWD: /usr/sbin/service ssh
start' >/etc/sudoers.d/service-ssh-start" # Allow your WSL user to SSH into
the server
~$ sudo /usr/sbin/service ssh start # start and verify the SSH is working
correctly. If you get an OK, that means it is working.
~$ ip address show # check the IP and interface status.
```

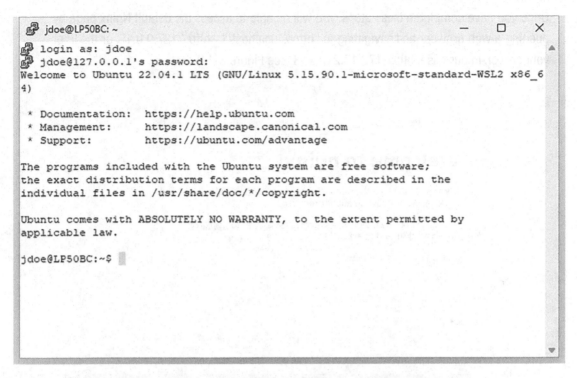

Figure 3-13. *SSH into 127.0.0.1 with port 2022 using the PuTTY client on your Windows*

EXERCISE 2

To open the standard HTTP port 80 on our Ubuntu machine, we should install a web service. Follow the the following instructions step by step to install Nginx and start its services. Please note that instead of using "sudo systemctl start Nginx", which is not supported by Ubuntu on WSL out of the box, use the command "sudo service nginx start" to manage the services.

```
~$ sudo apt install nginx -y
~$ whatis nginx
~$ whereis nginx
~$ sudo service nginx start # systemctl does not work, try to use "service
service_name start/stop/status"
 * Starting nginx ngi
nx                                                                    [ OK ]
```

Once you have completed these steps, you will be able to access the default Nginx page by opening a web browser and navigating to "http://localhost/", "http://127.0.0.1", or the IP of your server, in our case, http://172.18.213.243 (see Figure 3-14).

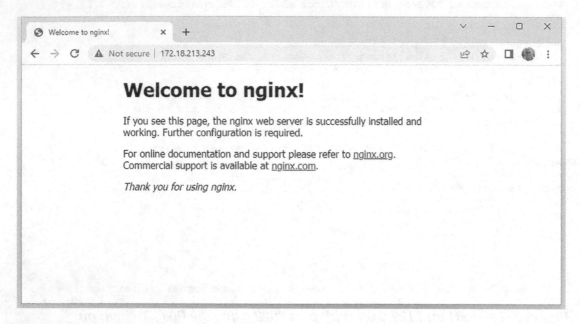

Figure 3-14. *Nginx welcome page at http://172.18.213.243*

EXERCISE 3

For interface-related information, such as IP addresses, routing tables, and other configuration details, you can use the following commands. After running them, carefully review their output and note the differences between them.

~$ **ip address show**
[...omitted for brevity]
~$ **sudo apt install net-tools** # Run this command if you have not yet installed the net-tools, alternatively, you can install the iproute2 tool as this is newer, replacing older net-tools.
[...omitted for brevity]
~$ **netstat -i**
[...omitted for brevity]

```
~$ ifconfig
```
[...omitted for brevity]

By studying the output of these commands, you can gain a better understanding of your
network configuration and troubleshoot any network-related issues that you may encounter.

EXERCISE 4

Now, execute the following netstat commands and carefully examine the different outputs
based on their options. This will help you gain a better understanding of how netstat works.

```
~$ netstat -i # display interface table
Kernel Interface table
```

Iface	MTU	RX-OK	RX-ERR	RX-DRP	RX-OVR	TX-OK	TX-ERR	TX-DRP	TX-OVR	Flg
eth0	1500	9308	0	0	0	3884	0	0	0	BMRU
lo	65536	121	0	0	0	121	0	0	0	LRU

```
~$ netstat -at # display active TCP connections
Active Internet connections (servers and established)
```

Proto	Recv-Q	Send-Q	Local Address	Foreign Address	State
tcp	0	0	0.0.0.0:2022	0.0.0.0:*	LISTEN

[...omitted for brevity]

```
~$ netstat -au # display active UDP connections
Active Internet connections (servers and established)
```

Proto	Recv-Q	Send-Q	Local Address	Foreign Address	State
udp	0	0	localhost:323	0.0.0.0:*	
udp6	0	0	ip6-localhost:323	[::]:*	

```
~$ netstat -l # display all listening connections
Active Internet connections (only servers)
```

Proto	Recv-Q	Send-Q	Local Address	Foreign Address	State
tcp	0	0	0.0.0.0:2022	0.0.0.0:*	LISTEN
tcp	0	0	0.0.0.0:http	0.0.0.0:*	LISTEN

[...omitted for brevity]

unix 2	[ACC]	STREAM	LISTENING	19699	/tmp/dbus-Qj09VNRIeA

```
~$ netstat -lt # display only TCP listening connections
Active Internet connections (only servers)
Proto Recv-Q Send-Q Local Address          Foreign Address      State
tcp       0      0 0.0.0.0:2022            0.0.0.0:*            LISTEN
[...omitted for brevity]
~$ netstat -lu # display only UDP listening connections
Active Internet connections (only servers)
Proto Recv-Q Send-Q Local Address          Foreign Address      State
udp       0      0 localhost:323           0.0.0.0:*
[...omitted for brevity]
~$ sudo netstat -ap # display IP Network port connections
[...omitted for brevity]
~$ sudo netstat -ap | grep ssh # narrow down to SSH protocol
[sudo] password for jdoe: ***************
tcp       0      0 0.0.0.0:2022            0.0.0.0:*
LISTEN      1510/sshd: /usr/sbi
[...omitted for brevity]
~$ sudo netstat -pt # for PID or Process ID, sudo must be used to see the
detailed PID
Active Internet connections (w/o servers)
Proto Recv-Q Send-Q Local Address   Foreign Address   State       PID/Program name
tcp       0      0 localhost:2022   localhost:38544   ESTABLISHED 1538/sshd: jdoe [pr
tcp       0      0 localhost:38544  localhost:2022    ESTABLISHED -
```

By carefully studying the output of these commands, you can learn more about the different network connections and the state of your network.

EXERCISE 5

For even more options and assistance with netstat, you can use the "netstat --help" command. One of the most useful commands that I've found while working on Linux is "netstat -tuna", which is represented in Figure 3-12 with a swimming tuna.

```
~$ netstat -tuna # -t for TCP, -u for UDP, -n for numeric (port number), and -a
for all connected sockets
Active Internet connections (servers and established)
Proto Recv-Q Send-Q Local Address          Foreign Address        State
tcp        0      0 0.0.0.0:2022           0.0.0.0:*              LISTEN
tcp        0      0 0.0.0.0:80             0.0.0.0:*              LISTEN
tcp        0      0 127.0.0.1:2022         127.0.0.1:38544        ESTABLISHED
tcp        0      0 127.0.0.1:38544        127.0.0.1:2022         ESTABLISHED
tcp6       0      0 :::2022                :::*                   LISTEN
tcp6       0      0 :::80                  :::*                   LISTEN
udp        0      0 127.0.0.1:323          0.0.0.0:*
udp6       0      0 ::1:323                :::*
```

This command provides detailed information about all the active network connections, including the protocol used, the state of the connection, and the IP addresses and port numbers of the source and destination. By using this command, you can quickly identify any unwanted or suspicious connections and take appropriate action.

EXERCISE 6

Take some time to read and study the netstat help page, and try combining the different options to come up with your favorite netstat commands. There are many options available that can help you obtain specific information about your network connections and troubleshoot any network-related issues.

`~$ netstat --help`

Why not experiment with some netstat commands yourself and see what results you get? You may discover some powerful tools that you can use to enhance your understanding of your network and improve its performance.

Expand your knowledge:

How do package managers differ in Red Hat, Arch Linux, Debian, SUSE, and Ubuntu?

Package managers are essential tools for managing software packages on Linux systems. While different Linux distributions may use different package managers, their primary purpose is always the same: to provide an efficient and convenient way to install, remove, and manage software packages.

Some common package managers used for popular Linux distributions include the following:

- Red Hat, Fedora, and CentOS use **DNF** (Dandified YUM), which is an evolution of the original **YUM** (Yellowdog Updater, Modified).

- Arch Linux uses **Pacman**, a simple and fast package manager that is easy to use.

- Debian and its derivatives, such as Ubuntu and Linux Mint, use **APT** (Advanced Package Tool), a powerful package manager known for its easy-to-use interface and robust dependency resolution capabilities.

- SUSE uses **Zypper**, a package manager with functionality and features similar to YUM and APT.

Regardless of which package manager you use, the primary goal remains the same: to help you efficiently manage software packages on your Linux system.

3.10 Keeping Your Linux System Up to Date

Keeping your Linux systems up to date is crucial for several reasons, including system stability, increased security, and optimal performance. When you update your Linux systems, you can ensure that all the software and packages are running the latest version, which can help to prevent crashes and improve system stability. In addition, updates often include security patches that address known vulnerabilities, making your system less vulnerable to attacks. By keeping your Linux systems up to date, you can also ensure that you are running the latest versions of software and packages, which can improve system performance and efficiency.

EXERCISE 1

To keep your Ubuntu system up to date, run the following command. This will update the package list and install any available updates for your system.

```
~$ sudo apt-get update && sudo apt-get upgrade -y
[sudo] password for jdoe: ***************
[...omitted for brevity]
```

EXERCISE 2

For future reference, to update Fedora and all its installed packages and dependencies on your system, run the following command:

```
~$ sudo dnf upgrade -y
```

Expand your knowledge:

What is the difference between "apt" and "apt-get" in Ubuntu Linux?

Both apt and apt-get are package managers commonly used in Ubuntu Linux, but they differ in their design, syntax, and features. apt-get is the older package manager that has been in use since the early days of Debian-based Linux distributions. It is a command-line tool designed for system administrators and advanced users, offering a wide range of options and features. In contrast, apt is a newer, more user-friendly package manager that was introduced in Ubuntu 16.04 LTS. It provides a simpler and more streamlined interface suitable for both system administrators and regular users. One key difference between apt and apt-get is their syntax. apt-get commands are often longer and more complex, while apt commands are generally shorter and easier to remember. Another notable difference is that apt automatically performs some operations that apt-get requires additional options for, such as resolving dependencies and cleaning up after package installations. Although both tools use the same dpkg packaging system underneath, apt provides some additional features such as managing package repositories and sources. On the other hand, apt-get offers greater control over package management tasks and is better suited for advanced users who require more flexibility and control.

Both Red Hat and Debian-based distributions offer easy ways to update and upgrade your system. Ubuntu, for example, uses the "apt" package manager, while Fedora uses the "dnf" (and "yum") package manager. These package managers allow you to easily download, install, and update software packages, as well as manage dependencies. Regularly updating your Linux system is particularly important in production environments where system uptime and stability are critical. With regular updates, you can ensure that your system is running the latest software and patches, reducing the risk of downtime and security breaches.

3.11 Jack, the Jack Russell: A Regular Expression Quiz

In Chapter 2, you were unknowingly exposed to regular expressions while using the grep and awk commands to search for strings. This section was not originally intended for inclusion in this book, as the authors assumed that readers already had a good understanding of regular expressions. However, we feel obligated to include a short section on regular expressions to keep your interest alive, as we understand their value in IT and DevOps jobs. While there are many GUI tools for data analytics, regular expressions are at the heart of all data-wrangling techniques.

Regular expressions are a complex topic that can fill entire books, so we cannot cover them in full detail in this discussion. However, we want to make learning about regular expressions engaging and enjoyable so that you'll stay interested and continue exploring the topic. To deepen your understanding, we recommend referring to a variety of resources such as ChatGPT, regular expression books, teaching websites, YouTube videos, and blogs. Push yourself to become proficient in regular expressions. You don't need to memorize or recognize all the expressions, but it's essential to become familiar with the standard set of regular expressions so you can understand what's happening in a Linux command or programming languages like PowerShell, Python, JavaScript, Perl, or others. By doing so, you'll be better equipped to read, write, and manipulate code, which is vital in today's tech-driven world.

Enhance your regular expression learning experience with a fun activity using Linux's image converter tool, "jp2a", which converts your favorite pictures into an ASCII art. Other Linux image-to-text tools for ASCII art creation include "img2txt", "caca-utils", and "aa-lib". Follow the following steps to transform an image into an ASCII art. In this example, we will use a photo of a neighbor's dog named "Jack, the Jack Russell," which has a black background and is saved in .jpg format (see Figure 3-15).

Figure 3-15. *jack.jpg and jack.txt*

We assume that you have kept the "jack.jpg" photo from Exercise 2 of section 3.8, as we will be using it to create an ASCII art of Jack. After converting the photo, we will dive into regular expressions. For a comprehensive understanding of regular expressions, we recommend referring to dedicated books, YouTube videos, blogs, and web-based regex engines. If you learn and practice the syntax of regular expressions every day, you will gradually develop proficiency in this skill.

EXERCISE 1

First, install "jp2a" using the apt-get command on your Ubuntu.

```
~$ sudo apt-get install jp2a
[sudo] password for jdoe: **************
[...omitted for brevity]
```

EXERCISE 2

To get started, locate your favorite picture and place it in the Downloads folder on your Windows PC. If you're using WSL, your Windows C drive is usually mounted on the /mnt/ drive. Navigate to the Downloads folder and make sure to replace "replace_username" with your PC user name in the folder path.

Example command to convert an image to an ASCII art using jp2a:

```
~$ ls -lh jack.jpg
-rw-r--r-- 1 jdoe jdoe 165K Apr 10 21:00 jack.jpg
~$ jp2a --width=80 jack.jpg
```

Tip   For the best effect, choose a picture that has a contrasting background to your main character.

EXERCISE 3

After testing your ASCII art and ensuring that you are satisfied with the result, you can save it to a file using the ">" symbol. Simply redirect the output to a new file by appending the ">" symbol followed by the file name you wish to create. For example:

```
~$ jp2a --width=80 jack.jpg > jack_ascii.txt # save the image to a file
~$ cat jack_ascii.txt # Check the saved art quality
```

This will save your ASCII art to a new file named "jack_ascii.txt". Remember to choose a descriptive name for your file so that you can easily identify it later.

EXERCISE 4

As shown in Figure 3-16, finally, run the cat command to check the ASCII artwork.

~$ **cat jack_ascii.txt**

Figure 3-16. *jack_ascii.txt file output*

Regular expressions are a powerful tool for manipulating text data. While we won't cover all the details in this book, we recommend that you dedicate time to studying them. Understanding how to manipulate and extract data is essential for any programmer, and regular expressions are often the go-to solution. Even Ansible and Linux rely on regular expressions for working with data.

To help you practice using regular expressions, we've included a file named "jack. jpg" for you to work on. It's important to learn regular expressions well, as they can make your Ansible playbooks and other programming language-based applications more versatile and robust. Once you master regular expressions, you can use them in a wide range of other tools. Whether you're already familiar with regular expressions or not, we encourage you to take on the challenge of solving the quiz. You can try it now or after you've completed this book, but be sure to make time for it.

If you're new to regular expressions, don't be discouraged. Learning them takes time and practice, but the effort is worth it. With dedication and a keen interest, you'll become proficient in no time. Remember, regular expressions are a vital tool in any programmer's toolkit, so start early and keep building your skills.

Quiz 1

Use the grep command to read the jack_ascii.txt file and count the total number of 0-9s and print them. Come up with the correct grep command using the -o option and regular expressions.

Quiz 2

Match any alphabetical character (upper- or lowercase) in the jack_ascii.txt file, count their occurrences, and print them out.

Quiz 3

Use Python and its regular expression module, "re", to read the jack_ascii.txt file and print the output of the following:

1. All the instances of the letter "o"

2. All the instances of the word "ll"

3. All the instances of the word "dog"

4. All the instances of the letter "l" at the end of a word

5. All the instances of the letter "o" that are not followed by the letter "l"

6. All the instances of the letter "o" or "O"

7. All the instances of a word that starts with "k" and ends with "l"

8. All the instances of a word that contains "x" followed by one or more "o"

9. All the instances of "o" with "X"

10. All the instances of a word that starts with "d" and ends with "d" with "***"

172

Answers to Quizzes 1–3

You can find the answers to the quiz questions at the following URL: `https://github.com/ansnetauto/jackrussell`. To view the answers, click on the "3.11 Jack Russell Quiz Answers.txt" file.

Expand your knowledge:

Regular expressions used in computing

Learning regular expressions can be a challenging and time-consuming process that may take weeks or even months to master. This can cause many individuals to struggle to push past the initial difficulties (pain barrier) and give up on this important skill which so many technological domains rely on, such as programming, system security, and networking administration. However, it is important to recognize that the world of technology and computing is constantly evolving with new buzzwords and innovations emerging all the time. From cloud computing to networking, server administration, virtualization, security, UC (Unified Communications and Collaboration), data centers, SD-WAN, Software-Defined Networks (SDN), Application Centric Infrastructure (ACI), Application Programming Interface (API), and, of course, the Internet as a whole, all of these technologies involve the processing of digitized data using various programming languages and interface standards.

The very concept of computers has come a long way since Charles Babbage created the first computer in 1822. Alan Turing, a pivotal figure in the history of computing, is widely credited with inventing modern computer science between the 1930s and 1940s. Today, two of the most powerful supercomputers such as Frontier and Fugaku can perform incredibly complex calculations in the blink of an eye, often using AI (artificial intelligence) and ML (machine learning) to mimic the human brain. Even the latest AI chatbots, such as ChatGPT, Bing Chat, and Google Bard, rely on these data processing machines to function and provide services to millions of users worldwide. Despite the hype and complexity involved in modern computing, the basics of chopping and cutting data using regular expressions remain at the heart of it all. **Regular expressions play a critical role in every computer's decision-making process that follows certain data analytic algorithms, no matter how complex the program or which computer language is used to process the data.** Whether you're utilizing a handheld device like an iPhone, a personal computer, powerful supercomputers like Frontier or Fugaku, or leveraging cloud-based platforms, the fundamental purpose of all computing is to process data. Data processing is computing's core strength and remains the driving force behind technological innovation.

If you're interested in learning about the history of computing, you can explore the following Wikipedia articles about notable pioneers and cutting-edge supercomputers:

Charles Babbage, who is widely regarded as the father of computing: `https://en.wikipedia.org/wiki/Charles_Babbage`

Alan Turing, a key figure in developing the first electronic computers: `https://en.wikipedia.org/wiki/Alan_Turing`

Frontier, a supercomputer developed by the US Department of Energy: `https://en.wikipedia.org/wiki/Frontier_(supercomputer)`

Fugaku, a Japanese supercomputer renowned for its high-performance computing capabilities: `https://en.wikipedia.org/wiki/Fugaku_(supercomputer)`

Each article provides fascinating insights into the evolution of computing, from its origins to the present day.

3.12 Summary

This chapter has provided a comprehensive introduction to a range of Linux utilities that are essential for efficient administration and programming. We've explored the Linux directory system and learned how to extract system information, view and read Linux processes, and run disk space-related tools. Additionally, we've covered managing users on Linux and controlling access to files and directories. We've also delved into file compression using various tools such as tar, gzip, bzip2, zip, and 7-Zip, and downloading files from the Internet in Linux using curl, wget, and git. Linux network utilities for troubleshooting have been covered, including ping, ifconfig, nmap, netstat, and more. Keeping Linux systems up to date was also discussed, as well as the importance of regular expressions in Ansible and programming in general. To help you practice your skills, we included a fun quiz on regular expressions that involved converting a Jack Russell dog picture into ASCII using regular expressions. Overall, this chapter has equipped you with essential Linux administration and programming skills that will come in handy for a wide range of tasks.

## CHAPTER 4

Setting Up an Ansible Learning Environment

This chapter of the book is all about creating an effective learning environment for Ansible. It begins by emphasizing the importance of proper planning before setting up an Ansible lab and guides how to plan the lab topology to ensure the best results. The chapter then offers detailed instructions on how to install VMware Workstation on a PC and create Fedora and Ubuntu virtual machines on the Workstation. These virtual machines will be customized by changing the hostname and assigning static IP addresses, and the chapter provides a guide on updating them for lab use. The chapter also presents two options for installing Ansible on the control node, and the reader is taken through each option in detail, with step-by-step instructions provided. Lastly, the chapter provides instructions on creating a new Ansible test account with sudoer privileges, which will be used throughout the book. With these instructions, readers can create an Ansible test account quickly and easily, allowing them to focus on learning the intricacies of Linux sudo accounts and Ansible concepts without any distractions.

4.1 Planning the Ansible Lab Topology

Using an all-in-one Ansible learning environment on a single PC without any physical hardware has several advantages. Firstly, it allows for hassle-free experimentation and testing of Ansible playbooks and tasks, without the need for complex network setups or

© Brendan Choi and Erwin Medina 2023
B. Choi and E. Medina, *Introduction to Ansible Network Automation*,
https://doi.org/10.1007/978-1-4842-9624-0_4

physical hardware. This approach can help learners save both time and money while also providing a safe environment for exploring concepts and testing scenarios.

Furthermore, consolidating all the virtual machines (VMs) on a single PC makes it a convenient and easily accessible platform for practicing network configuration and automation. This setup also enables easy scalability and customization, as new VMs can be created and configured as needed. The topology of such a lab setup is illustrated in Figure 4-1. Please note that for our initial Ansible learning purposes, we will be using four Linux virtual machines. However, we may add virtualized network devices at a later time for our Ansible Network Automation tasks.

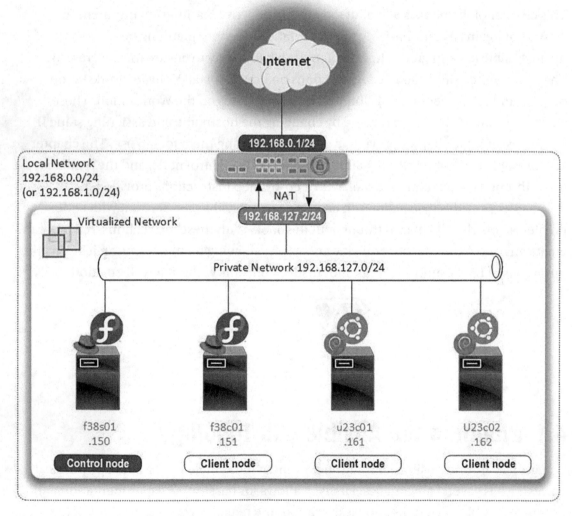

Figure 4-1. *A simple Ansible lab topology*

To build this simple lab environment, you can use Desktop Virtualization (Type 2 hypervisor) software like VMware Workstation 17 or Oracle VirtualBox, which allows you to run multiple virtual machines on a single physical machine. In this guide, we will be using VMware Workstation 17 as it offers more features and better supports virtualized network devices. To get started, install VMware Workstation 17 on your PC and create a new virtual machine by selecting the "New Virtual Machine" option from the File menu and choosing "Custom" as the type of configuration. Follow the prompts to configure the virtual machine settings, allocating at least 2 GB of RAM and 20 GB of minimum disk space for the base Fedora 38 and Ubuntu 23.04 virtual machines.

While writing this chapter, the official versions of Fedora and Ubuntu were 37 and 22.04.2 LTS, respectively. However, since Fedora 38 and Ubuntu 23.04 beta versions are available for testing purposes, we will be using them in this guide. Keep in mind that if you're deploying Linux servers in a production environment, it's recommended to use stable versions. But if you want to test the latest software releases, following this book and using the latest beta versions should suffice. Regardless of which version you choose, as long as you use Fedora 37 or newer and Ubuntu 22.04.01 or newer, you should be able to complete all exercises and tasks outlined in this guide.

Once both Fedora and Ubuntu VMs are created, you can clone them by selecting the VM and choosing "Clone" from the menu. Give the cloned VM a new name and select the option to create a full clone. This will create an exact copy of the original VM, including its configuration settings and network connectivity.

To configure the network, you can select the "Virtual Network Editor" from the Edit menu and choose "NAT" as the type of network connection for VMnet8. Set the subnet IP address to 192.168.127.0/24 and the default gateway to 192.168.127.2 to allow all the VMs to communicate with each other and access the Internet.

After configuring the network, power on each VM and assign a static IP address to each VM within the 192.168.127.0/24 subnet, set the default gateway to 192.168.127.2, and use the primary DNS address of 192.168.127.2, the secondary DNS address of 192.168.0.1, and the tertiary DNS address of Google's public DNS, 8.8.8.8, where possible for smooth lab operations. Once we add all the network devices later, our lab topology will resemble the one shown in Figure 4-2.

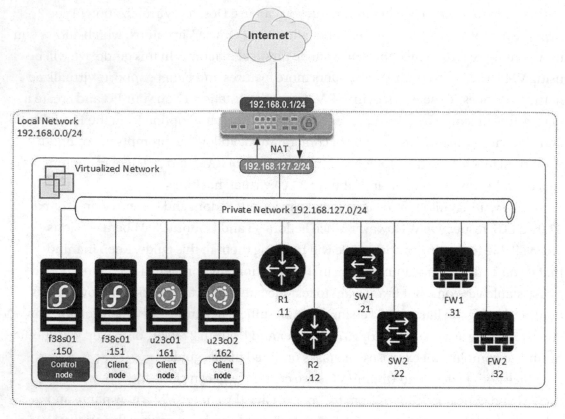

Figure 4-2. *A development lab topology example*

Finally, you can install Ansible on the control node, which is the base Fedora 38 VM. Ansible can be installed using the package manager by running the command "sudo yum install ansible". Once installed, you can run Ansible ad hoc commands and start creating and testing Ansible playbooks and tasks to automate various IT tasks on different platforms. By following these steps, you can create a powerful and flexible learning environment that can be used for a wide variety of IT tasks and projects.

Let's proceed with the steps to create our four Linux VM lab topologies and configure and update the servers for the subsequent chapters and the rest of the book. While the installation process is simple for experienced Linux users, novices might require a detailed step-by-step guide. Therefore, the installation guides are not included in this book but are provided separately as downloadable PDFs. This approach helps to save valuable book space, maintain readability, and ensure that the book is portable.

Expand your knowledge:

Upstream vs. Downstream Linux

The terms "upstream" and "downstream" are used in the Linux community to describe the flow of software from its original source to the end users. In this context, upstream refers to the original developers of a software package who create and maintain the source code. Downstream, on the other hand, refers to the distributors who take that package and package it in a specific form for end users. For example, Red Hat Enterprise Linux (RHEL) is a downstream distribution of the upstream Linux distribution Fedora. As the downstream distributor, Red Hat takes the source code from Fedora, adds its proprietary code and packaging, and distributes it to users as a commercial product with long-term security and maintenance updates. Red Hat also contributes heavily to the development of Fedora, which acts as the upstream source for RHEL. This means that Red Hat not only distributes a downstream product but also contributes to the upstream development of Fedora, making it an upstream contributor as well. The upstream-downstream relationship is crucial for the development and distribution of Linux operating systems as it enables collaboration and sharing of open source software efficiently and collaboratively. It helps ensure that software is developed and maintained in a way that benefits the entire community.

4.2 Installing VMware Workstation on Your PC

Installing VMware Workstation is a simple process and can be done by clicking next and finishing. Therefore, we won't be covering it in detail in this book. However, if you prefer following detailed steps, you can download the installation guide from our GitHub page. Once you have successfully installed VMware Workstation 17, you can create virtual machines to build your learning environment. Although VirtualBox is another option, VMware Workstation provides better features on Windows PC. If a newer version of VMware Workstation is available, you can install it and build the Linux virtual machines in the same manner as described in the guide.

URL: `https://github.com/ansnetauto/appress_ansnetauto/blob/main/4.2_`
`Install_VMware_Workstation_v1.0.pdf`

or

Apress: `https://github.com/orgs/Apress/repositories`

4.3 Creating Fedora Virtual Machines

At the time of authoring this book, the latest Fedora version was version 38, and we are using Fedora to replicate the inner workings of Red Hat Enterprise Linux version 9. Fedora 38 was the latest version of the Fedora operating system, which is a community-driven and free Linux distribution that serves as a testing ground for technologies that may eventually be integrated into Red Hat Enterprise Linux (RHEL). On the other hand, Red Hat Enterprise Linux (RHEL) is a commercial enterprise operating system that is based on the Fedora project but is intended for use in production environments and is supported by Red Hat. For lab building and testing, Fedora will always offer the latest features and can be used freely on any machine. For a production environment, RHEL is always the recommended Linux of choice by many organizations for its great support and service.

To create a Fedora virtual machine and duplicate it to create additional VMs, you can follow the user installation guide available at the specified URL. However, if you have experience with Linux, you can build the VMs without the guide.

URL: `https://github.com/ansnetauto/appress_ansnetauto/blob/main/4.3_`
`Create_Fedora_VMs_v1.0.pdf`

or

Apress: `https://github.com/orgs/Apress/repositories`

By the time you finish this task, you will have successfully created two Fedora virtual machines: f38s1, which will serve as the Ansible control node, and f38c1, which will act as the client node.

Expand your knowledge:

RHEL, Fedora, CentOS, AlmaLinux, and Rocky Linux relationships

explained

Red Hat Enterprise Linux (RHEL) is a commercially supported enterprise Linux distribution based on open source **Fedora**, which is a community-driven distribution sponsored by Red Hat. **CentOS**, a popular community-driven distribution, was once a downstream version of RHEL but is now upstream of RHEL development. **AlmaLinux** and **Rocky Linux** are community-driven distributions created as a replacement for CentOS after its shift in focus. These distributions aim to provide a free, stable, and reliable alternative to RHEL, with AlmaLinux being led by CloudLinux and Rocky Linux by the original CentOS co-founder. All of these distributions share a common ancestry and many similarities in terms of package management and compatibility with enterprise software.

4.4 Creating Ubuntu Virtual Machines

As of the time of writing this book, the latest version of Ubuntu server available was 23.04. Ubuntu is an open source Linux distribution based on Debian, which is also a community-driven and free Linux distribution. However, unlike Ubuntu, Debian is not a downstream operating system; rather, it serves as an upstream source for other Linux distributions, including Ubuntu. While other Debian-based Linux operating systems can be used to replicate the inner workings of Debian, we recommend using Ubuntu, as it provides the most features and system stability in our labs. You can use the latest version of Ubuntu if available or stick with the same version mentioned in this book if you want to follow it precisely.

If you want to create an Ubuntu virtual machine and duplicate it to create additional VMs, you can follow the user installation guide available at the specified URL. However, if you're experienced with Linux, you can build the VMs without the guide.

URL: `https://github.com/ansnetauto/appress_ansnetauto/blob/main/4.4_ Create_Ubuntu_VMs_v1.0.pdf`

or

Apress: `https://github.com/orgs/Apress/repositories`

By the time you finish this task, you will have successfully created two Ubuntu virtual machines: u23c1 and u23c2, which will also act as the client nodes.

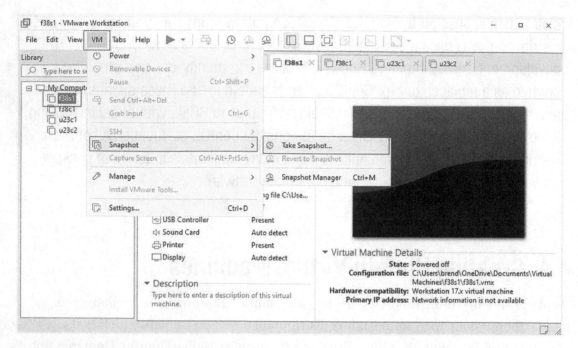

Figure 4-3. *Take a snapshot*

To ensure a smooth and seamless server management process, we highly recommend taking the first snapshot for each machine before making any changes. This precautionary step will allow us to easily revert to this point in time should we run into any issues. Additionally, we advise taking snapshots regularly at each milestone to avoid unnecessary time wastage and inconvenience. (See Figure 4-3.)

After taking the necessary snapshots, we can proceed with customizing the Linux server, which involves fixing the hostnames, and IP addresses, and installing VMware tools for optimal performance. These steps are crucial to ensure that the servers run smoothly and efficiently, without any technical glitches. By following these procedures, we can avoid any potential downtime and ensure that the servers operate at their best capacity.

Expand your knowledge:

Debian, Ubuntu, Linux Mint, elementary OS, PoP!_OS, and Kali Linux relationships explained

Debian is a well-known and widely used free and open source Linux distribution that serves as the upstream source for many other popular Linux distributions.

Ubuntu, Linux Mint, elementary OS, and many others are all based on Debian. **Ubuntu** is one of the most popular Linux distributions in use today, based on Debian. It is user-friendly and has a wide range of pre-installed software, making it an excellent choice for beginners who are new to Linux. **Linux Mint** is another Debian-based distribution that has a more traditional desktop environment and includes a set of pre-installed software, codecs, and drivers to make it easier for users to get started. **elementary OS** is a beautiful and user-friendly distribution based on Ubuntu, designed to be intuitive and easy to use, with a set of custom-built applications. **PoP!_OS** is another Ubuntu-based distribution specifically optimized for System76 hardware, which provides customizations and tweaks to enhance user experience on their hardware. **Kali Linux**, a Debian-based distribution, is designed for advanced penetration testing and security auditing, equipped with pre-installed tools that are frequently used by security professionals and hackers. Also, **MX Linux**, **Deepin**, **Devuan**, **Tails**, **Parrot OS,** and **Raspbian** are systems based on Debian.

4.5 Customizing and Updating Virtual Machines

To get started with learning Ansible and its concepts, we will need to power on each machine in a specific order and customize our virtual machines accordingly. We'll begin with the Fedora VMs and then move on to the Ubuntu VMs. While you could perform these steps as part of the 4.3 and 4.4 tasks on the base VMs first and then clone the servers to create second copies, we want you to gain more hands-on experience. Therefore, we recommend that you carry out these tasks individually on each machine. This way, you can observe and learn firsthand what happens to each machine as you perform these tasks, which will help you understand the inner workings of the Linux OS and their behaviors better.

4.6 Changing Hostname on Fedora VMs

There are two ways to manage the Linux VM running on VMware Workstation: either use the VMware Workstation terminal console within VMware or connect through an SSH client such as PuTTY. However, if you are connecting via SSH from your host PC, be aware that shutting down or bringing up the interface will result in a lost connection. In such cases, you will need to recover the interface by using the Workstation terminal. It's worth noting that the SSH server is already installed and enabled by default during Fedora installation.

To set the hostname, use the following command in the VMware Workstation terminal. If prompted for a sudo password, enter it to proceed. After configuring the server, we will use SSH to log in to the server(s).

```
[brendan@localhost ~]$ hostnamectl set-hostname f38s1
==== AUTHENTICATING FOR org.freedesktop.hostname1.set-hostname ====
Authentication is required to set the local hostname.
Authenticating as: Brendan Choi (brendan)
Password: ****************
==== AUTHENTICATION COMPLETE ====
[brendan@localhost ~]$ logout
```

After completing the hostname change, it's important to verify that the changes have taken effect. To do this, log out from the f38s1 server and quickly log back in. You should see the updated hostname reflected immediately upon logging in. Once you've verified that the change has taken effect, you can proceed with the next task of assigning a static IP address.

```
[brendan@f38s1 ~]$
```

After completing the IP assignment task, you can power on the second Fedora server and update its hostname using the same command used for the first server.

4.7 Assigning Static IP on Fedora VMs

Assigning a static IP address to enterprise servers provides several benefits. One of the main advantages is increased stability and reliability. A static IP address ensures that the server's network address remains consistent, preventing any interruption in connectivity that can occur when IP addresses change dynamically. In addition, it simplifies the process of network administration, allowing network administrators to easily identify and manage servers on the network. This can help to streamline maintenance tasks, troubleshooting, and network management as a whole. Finally, static IP addresses are generally more secure than dynamic ones, as they are less vulnerable to attacks that attempt to hijack or impersonate network devices.

Before assigning a static IP address, you will need to check which interface is currently being used. In the following output, we can see that the connected interface is ens160, which is the one we will modify. Follow the following steps to assign a static IP address to the ens160 interface of f38s1.

```
# Display network interfaces
$ nmcli device
DEVICE  TYPE      STATE                  CONNECTION
ens160  ethernet  connected              ens160
lo      loopback  connected (externally) lo

# Set IPv4 Address to ens160
$ sudo nmcli connection modify ens160 ipv4.addresses 192.168.127.150/24
# Set default gateway
$ sudo nmcli connection modify ens160 ipv4.gateway 192.168.127.2
# Set DNS
$ sudo nmcli connection modify ens160 ipv4.dns 192.168.127.2,192.168.
0.1,8.8.8.8
# Optionally configures DNS configuration of your domain, here we will skip
this configuration
$ nmcli connection modify ens160 ipv4.dns-search ansnetauto.net
# Disable DHCP and set to static (manual) IP configuration
$ sudo nmcli connection modify ens160 ipv4.method manual
# reset the interface, bring down the interface and then bring it up.
$ sudo nmcli connection down ens160; nmcli connection up ens160
```

After bouncing the ens160 interface, all the configuration changes should have been committed and applied to the server's network settings. To confirm that the changes have been successfully implemented, check the configuration settings and validate them.

```
# Check the new configuration for the network interface ens160
$ nmcli device show ens160
GENERAL.DEVICE:           ens160
GENERAL.TYPE:             ethernet
GENERAL.HWADDR:           00:0C:29:CF:39:E0
```

```
GENERAL.MTU:                    1500
GENERAL.STATE:                  100 (connected)
GENERAL.CONNECTION:             ens160
GENERAL.CON-PATH:               /org/freedesktop/NetworkManager/
                                ActiveConnection/3
WIRED-PROPERTIES.CARRIER:       on
IP4.ADDRESS[1]:                 192.168.127.150/24
IP4.GATEWAY:                    192.168.127.2
IP4.ROUTE[1]:                   dst = 192.168.127.0/24, nh = 0.0.0.0, mt = 100
IP4.ROUTE[2]:                   dst = 0.0.0.0/0, nh = 192.168.127.2, mt = 100
IP4.DNS[1]:                     192.168.127.2
IP4.DNS[2]:                     192.168.0.1
IP4.DNS[3]:                     8.8.8.8
IP6.ADDRESS[1]:                 fe80::20c:29ff:fecf:39e0/64
IP6.GATEWAY:                    --
IP6.ROUTE[1]:                   dst = fe80::/64, nh = ::, mt = 1024
```

```
# Check the IP address and interface status
$ ip address show
1: lo: <LOOPBACK,UP,LOWER_UP> mtu 65536 qdisc noqueue state UNKNOWN group
default qlen 1000
    link/loopback 00:00:00:00:00:00 brd 00:00:00:00:00:00
    inet 127.0.0.1/8 scope host lo
       valid_lft forever preferred_lft forever
    inet6 ::1/128 scope host
       valid_lft forever preferred_lft forever
2: ens160: <BROADCAST,MULTICAST,UP,LOWER_UP> mtu 1500 qdisc fq_codel state
UP group default qlen 1000
    link/ether 00:0c:29:cf:39:e0 brd ff:ff:ff:ff:ff:ff
    altname enp3s0
    inet 192.168.127.150/24 brd 192.168.127.255 scope global
noprefixroute ens160
       valid_lft forever preferred_lft forever
    inet6 fe80::20c:29ff:fecf:39e0/64 scope link noprefixroute
       valid_lft forever preferred_lft forever
```

SSH and PuTTY provide a robust and secure communication channel that guarantees the privacy and authenticity of sensitive data during remote access. The user-friendly interface of these protocols simplifies server management and remote task execution, ultimately enhancing productivity and efficiency. By utilizing PuTTY and SSH, accessing the f38s1 server from your Windows host PC is seamless and secure, as demonstrated in Figure 4-4. Notably, SSH offers a streamlined server management process, which not only improves security but also improves the overall efficiency of server operations.

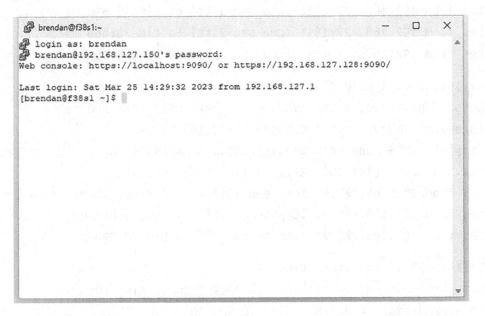

Figure 4-4. *SSH login using PuTTY*

To ensure that both Fedora VMs are correctly configured and can communicate with each other, follow these steps:

1. Turn on the second Fedora VM, which has the hostname f38c1 and an IP address of 192.168.127.151/24.

2. Verify that the default gateway and DNS settings are the same as before.

3. Repeat tasks 4.5.1 and 4.5.2 to configure the second Fedora VM.

4. Once you have completed the configuration of the second Fedora VM, proceed to step 4.5.3 as directed.

By following these steps, you will be able to confirm that both Fedora VMs are properly configured and can communicate with each other. This is an essential step in ensuring that your system is set up correctly and functioning as intended.

From any Fedora VM, quickly perform the network connectivity test shown here:

```
[brendan@f38s1 ~]$ ping -c 3 192.168.127.151 # validate connection to
f38c1
PING 192.168.127.151 (192.168.127.151) 56(84) bytes of data.
64 bytes from 192.168.127.151: icmp_seq=1 ttl=64 time=0.650 ms
64 bytes from 192.168.127.151: icmp_seq=2 ttl=64 time=0.866 ms
64 bytes from 192.168.127.151: icmp_seq=3 ttl=64 time=1.06 ms

--- 192.168.127.151 ping statistics ---
3 packets transmitted, 3 received, 0% packet loss, time 2003ms
rtt min/avg/max/mdev = 0.650/0.859/1.063/0.168 ms
[brendan@f38s1 ~]$ ping -c 3 192.168.127.2 # validate connection to gateway
PING 192.168.127.2 (192.168.127.2) 56(84) bytes of data.
64 bytes from 192.168.127.2: icmp_seq=1 ttl=128 time=0.428 ms
64 bytes from 192.168.127.2: icmp_seq=2 ttl=128 time=0.686 ms
64 bytes from 192.168.127.2: icmp_seq=3 ttl=128 time=0.594 ms

--- 192.168.127.2 ping statistics ---
3 packets transmitted, 3 received, 0% packet loss, time 2065ms
rtt min/avg/max/mdev = 0.428/0.569/0.686/0.106 ms
[brendan@f38s1 ~]$ ping -c 3 192.168.0.1 # validate connection to local
router gateway interface
PING 192.168.0.1 (192.168.0.1) 56(84) bytes of data.
64 bytes from 192.168.0.1: icmp_seq=1 ttl=128 time=1.70 ms
64 bytes from 192.168.0.1: icmp_seq=2 ttl=128 time=1.93 ms
64 bytes from 192.168.0.1: icmp_seq=3 ttl=128 time=2.11 ms

--- 192.168.0.1 ping statistics ---
3 packets transmitted, 3 received, 0% packet loss, time 2003ms
rtt min/avg/max/mdev = 1.695/1.913/2.111/0.170 ms
[brendan@f38s1 ~]$ ping -c 3 8.8.8.8 # validate connection to google DNS
(internet)
PING 8.8.8.8 (8.8.8.8) 56(84) bytes of data.
```

```
64 bytes from 8.8.8.8: icmp_seq=1 ttl=128 time=13.4 ms
64 bytes from 8.8.8.8: icmp_seq=2 ttl=128 time=11.5 ms
64 bytes from 8.8.8.8: icmp_seq=3 ttl=128 time=12.3 ms

--- 8.8.8.8 ping statistics ---
3 packets transmitted, 3 received, 0% packet loss, time 2003ms
rtt min/avg/max/mdev = 11.540/12.405/13.374/0.752 ms
[brendan@f38s1 ~]$ ping -c 3 www.google.com # validate that DNS is working
properly
PING www.google.com (142.250.204.4) 56(84) bytes of data.
64 bytes from syd09s25-in-f4.1e100.net (142.250.204.4): icmp_seq=1 ttl=128
time=14.1 ms
64 bytes from syd09s25-in-f4.1e100.net (142.250.204.4): icmp_seq=2 ttl=128
time=12.8 ms
64 bytes from syd09s25-in-f4.1e100.net (142.250.204.4): icmp_seq=3 ttl=128
time=12.6 ms

--- www.google.com ping statistics ---
3 packets transmitted, 3 received, 0% packet loss, time 2004ms
rtt min/avg/max/mdev = 12.575/13.160/14.144/0.699 ms
```

If you've received identical ICMP responses, it's a good indication that your server is ready for the next task. Perform the same ICMP test from f38c1. For now, we'll hold off on installing Ansible on f38s1 until a later time.

4.8 Updating Fedora Virtual Machines

Regularly updating your Fedora system is crucial for maintaining optimal security and functionality, especially for production machines. To keep your Fedora installation up to date with the latest software updates and security patches, follow these steps:

1. Open the terminal window in your VMware Workstation console.

2. Update the package manager responsible for downloading and installing software packages by entering the following command:

```
$ sudo dnf update -y
```

This command will not only update the package manager but will also download and install the latest software updates and security patches for your system, ensuring that it is secure and running smoothly. Optionally, to automate this process, you can configure your server with automatic updates, install third-party repositories, or install/ update VMware tools as required.

After updating the package manager, you should power on the second Fedora VM, f38c1, and run the same command to bring it up to date. This will ensure that both VMs are running on the latest software versions and that they are secure and functioning optimally.

4.9 Assigning Static IP on the First Ubuntu VM

When you installed the first Ubuntu server, you specified a hostname for it, which means there is no need to change the hostname of that server, named u23c1. However, if you have cloned that machine to create the second Ubuntu VM, named u23c2, then you will need to update the hostname on the second VM. For now, let's focus on u23c1 and configure a static IP address on this server

To check the IP address of the interface currently in use on VMware Workstation's u23c1 terminal console, you can run the command for displaying network settings. By doing this, you will see that the virtual network's DHCP server has assigned the IP address 192.168.127.129 to the ens33 interface.

```
brendan@u23c1:~$ ip addr show
```

```
1: lo: <LOOPBACK,UP,LOWER_UP> mtu 65536 qdisc noqueue state UNKNOWN group
default qlen 1000
    link/loopback 00:00:00:00:00:00 brd 00:00:00:00:00:00
    inet 127.0.0.1/8 scope host lo
      valid_lft forever preferred_lft forever
    inet6 ::1/128 scope host
      valid_lft forever preferred_lft forever
2: ens33: <BROADCAST,MULTICAST,UP,LOWER_UP> mtu 1500 qdisc pfifo_fast state
UP group default qlen 1000
    link/ether 00:0c:29:ec:47:6e brd ff:ff:ff:ff:ff:ff
    altname enp2s1
```

```
inet 192.168.127.129/24 metric 100 brd 192.168.127.255 scope global
dynamic ens33
    valid_lft 1523sec preferred_lft 1523sec
inet6 fe80::20c:29ff:feec:476e/64 scope link
    valid_lft forever preferred_lft forever
```

Before making any modifications to the network configuration file located in the /etc/netplan directory, it is important to create a backup copy of the original file.

```
brendan@u23c1:~$ ls /etc/netplan/
00-installer-config.yaml
brendan@u23c1:~$ sudo cp /etc/netplan/00-installer-config.yaml /etc/netplan/00-installer-config.yaml.org
[sudo] password for brendan: ****************
brendan@u23c1:~$ ls /etc/netplan/
00-installer-config.yaml  00-installer-config.yaml.org
```

After creating a backup of the network configuration file, use the vi editor to modify the 00-installer-config.yaml file to configure a static IP address for your first Ubuntu client, u23c1. Follow the instructions carefully, and make sure that the modified file matches the desired configuration, which should look like this:

```
brendan@u23c1:~$ sudo vi /etc/netplan/00-installer-config.yaml
brendan@u23c1:~$ cat /etc/netplan/00-installer-config.yaml
# This is the network config written by 'subiquity'
network:
  ethernets:
    ens33:
      dhcp4: false # Disable DHCP and make this interface static
      addresses: [192.168.127.161/24] # IP Address of this server
      routes:
        - to: default
          via: 192.168.127.2 # Default Gateway IP
          metric: 100 # Distance of this route
      nameservers:
        addresses: [192.168.127.2,192.168.0.1,8.8.8.8] # Multiple DNS
      server configuration
```

```
      # search: [ansnetauto.net] # Optional domain name configuration
    dhcp6: false # Disable IPv6 for the lab
  version: 2 # Network version
```

After modifying the 00-installer-config.yaml file as described previously, you need to apply the new configuration by running the command shown in the following. This will activate the changes you have made. Keep in mind that if you are currently connected to the server via SSH, your connection will be lost and you have to reconnect to the server.

brendan@u23c1:~$ **sudo netplan apply**

Next, proceed to Section 4.5.5 and power on the u23c2 server. Update its hostname and assign the next available IP address, which is 192.168.127.162/24, to its ens33 interface. Also, configure the default gateway and DNS addresses in the same manner as u23c1.

4.10 Changing Hostname and Static IP on the Second Ubuntu VM

Upon powering on and logging into the second Ubuntu VM, u23c2, you may notice that the server name is incorrect. In this case, you will need to update the hostname, modify the hosts file, and assign a static IP address to the server's ens33 interface. Before proceeding, make sure to check the current hostname and follow the following instructions carefully.

brendan@u23c1:~$ **hostname**
u23c1
brendan@u23c1:~$ **sudo hostname u23c2**
[sudo] password for brendan: ****************
brendan@u23c1:~$ **hostname**
u23c2
brendan@u23c1:~$ **sudo vi /etc/hosts**
brendan@u23c1:~$ **sudo cat /etc/hosts**
127.0.0.1 localhost
127.0.1.1 **u23c2**
The following lines are desirable for IPv6 capable hosts
::1   ip6-localhost ip6-loopback

```
fe00::0 ip6-localnet
ff00::0 ip6-mcastprefix
ff02::1 ip6-allnodes
ff02::2 ip6-allrouters
brendan@u23c1:~$ logout
```

After logging out and logging back in, you should notice that the hostname has been successfully updated and is now displaying the correct value, which in this case is u23c2.

```
brendan@u23c2:~$
```

The next step is to configure a static IP address for the VM's ens33 interface. The process is similar to that used for u23c1, but with one key difference: the IP address should be set to 192.168.127.162. To complete the configuration, follow these steps to assign a static IP address to the ens33 interface:

```
brendan@u23c2:~$ sudo cp /etc/netplan/00-installer-config.yaml /etc/
netplan/00-installer-config.yaml.org
brendan@u23c2:~$ sudo vi /etc/netplan/00-installer-config.yaml
brendan@u23c2:~$ sudo cat /etc/netplan/00-installer-config.yaml
# This is the network config written by 'subiquity'
network:
  ethernets:
    ens33:
      dhcp4: false
      addresses: [192.168.127.162/24]
      routes:
        - to: default
          via: 192.168.127.2
          metric: 100
      nameservers:
        addresses: [192.168.127.2,192.168.0.1,8.8.8.8]
        # search: [ansnetauto.net]
      dhcp6: false
  version: 2
brendan@u23c2:~$ sudo netplan apply
```

Congratulations on successfully updating the hostnames and assigning static IP addresses to all of the VMs that will be used to learn Ansible fundamentals! Before diving into Ansible, it is important to ensure that your Ubuntu VMs are fully up to date with the latest packages and that they can communicate properly with other nodes, your local host PC, and the Internet using their new IP addresses and DNS settings.

Before proceeding with the update and upgrade process described in Section 4.5.6, it is important to test the network communication on your Ubuntu VMs. You can use the following ping tests to check connectivity between the VMs, as well as with other nodes, your local host PC, and the Internet. Once you have confirmed that network communication is working properly, you can proceed with the update and upgrade process.

```
brendan@u23c1:~$ ping -c 2 192.168.127.162 # to u23c1
PING 192.168.127.162 (192.168.127.162) 56(84) bytes of data.
64 bytes from 192.168.127.162: icmp_seq=1 ttl=64 time=1.19 ms
64 bytes from 192.168.127.162: icmp_seq=2 ttl=64 time=0.669 ms

--- 192.168.127.162 ping statistics ---
2 packets transmitted, 2 received, 0% packet loss, time 1001ms
rtt min/avg/max/mdev = 0.669/0.930/1.192/0.261 ms
brendan@u23c1:~$ ping -c 2 192.168.127.150 # to Ansible Control node
PING 192.168.127.150 (192.168.127.150) 56(84) bytes of data.
64 bytes from 192.168.127.150: icmp_seq=1 ttl=64 time=1.20 ms
64 bytes from 192.168.127.150: icmp_seq=2 ttl=64 time=0.711 ms

--- 192.168.127.150 ping statistics ---
2 packets transmitted, 2 received, 0% packet loss, time 1002ms
rtt min/avg/max/mdev = 0.711/0.953/1.195/0.242 ms
brendan@u23c1:~$ ping -c 2 192.168.127.151 # to f38c1 client node
PING 192.168.127.151 (192.168.127.151) 56(84) bytes of data.
64 bytes from 192.168.127.151: icmp_seq=1 ttl=64 time=0.656 ms
64 bytes from 192.168.127.151: icmp_seq=2 ttl=64 time=0.705 ms

--- 192.168.127.151 ping statistics ---
2 packets transmitted, 2 received, 0% packet loss, time 1001ms
rtt min/avg/max/mdev = 0.656/0.680/0.705/0.024 ms
brendan@u23c1:~$ ping -c 2 192.168.127.2 # to default gateway
PING 192.168.127.2 (192.168.127.2) 56(84) bytes of data.
```

```
64 bytes from 192.168.127.2: icmp_seq=1 ttl=128 time=0.697 ms
64 bytes from 192.168.127.2: icmp_seq=2 ttl=128 time=0.541 ms

--- 192.168.127.2 ping statistics ---
2 packets transmitted, 2 received, 0% packet loss, time 1019ms
rtt min/avg/max/mdev = 0.541/0.619/0.697/0.078 ms
brendan@u23c1:~$ ping -c 2 192.168.0.1 # to local gateway
PING 192.168.0.1 (192.168.0.1) 56(84) bytes of data.
64 bytes from 192.168.0.1: icmp_seq=1 ttl=128 time=1.63 ms
64 bytes from 192.168.0.1: icmp_seq=2 ttl=128 time=1.77 ms

--- 192.168.0.1 ping statistics ---
2 packets transmitted, 2 received, 0% packet loss, time 1002ms
rtt min/avg/max/mdev = 1.634/1.701/1.769/0.067 ms
brendan@u23c1:~$ ping -c 2 8.8.8.8 # to Google's public DNS (internet)
PING 8.8.8.8 (8.8.8.8) 56(84) bytes of data.
64 bytes from 8.8.8.8: icmp_seq=1 ttl=128 time=13.0 ms
64 bytes from 8.8.8.8: icmp_seq=2 ttl=128 time=13.8 ms

--- 8.8.8.8 ping statistics ---
2 packets transmitted, 2 received, 0% packet loss, time 1001ms
rtt min/avg/max/mdev = 12.996/13.420/13.844/0.424 ms
brendan@u23c1:~$ ping -c 2 www.google.com # to internet
PING www.google.com (142.250.204.4) 56(84) bytes of data.
64 bytes from syd09s25-in-f4.1e100.net (142.250.204.4): icmp_seq=1 ttl=128
time=12.6 ms
64 bytes from syd09s25-in-f4.1e100.net (142.250.204.4): icmp_seq=2 ttl=128
time=29.8 ms

--- www.google.com ping statistics ---
2 packets transmitted, 2 received, 0% packet loss, time 1001ms
rtt min/avg/max/mdev = 12.552/21.157/29.762/8.605 ms
```

If all ICMP tests have passed as demonstrated previously, it indicates that your servers are in good condition. It is recommended to repeat the ICMP test from the second Ubuntu server to ensure that it also meets the requirements. Before proceeding with the installation of Ansible on the Ansible control node, f38s1, it is advised to quickly update the Ubuntu VMs.

4.11 Updating Ubuntu Virtual Machines

To ensure that your Ubuntu system stays up to date, you can use the following command
in the terminal:

```
$ sudo apt update && sudo apt upgrade -y
[sudo] password for brendan: ****************
```

This command updates the package list and upgrades any packages that have
available updates. Running this command regularly can help keep your system up to
date with the latest security patches and bug fixes.

To finish the system update and upgrades, you may be prompted with a "Package
configuration" message. In this case, select <OK> to restart the services. This will
ensure that all packages are running the latest versions on your Ubuntu servers. (See
Figure 4-5.)

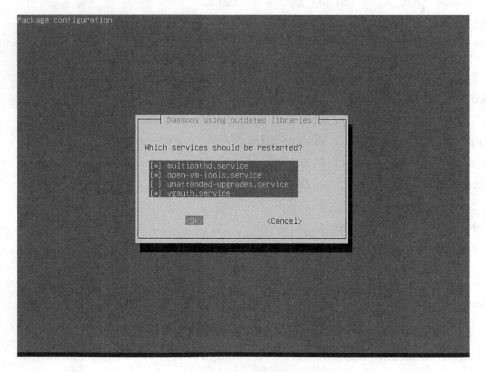

Figure 4-5. *Restarting outdated services on Fedora package configuration*

4.12 Installing Ansible on Control Node

There are two primary ways to install Ansible. The first method is to install it directly on the host virtual machine or operating system. The second method is to use Python virtualenv. For the sake of simplicity, this book will use the first method. However, we also provide detailed instructions for the second installation method in this section, should you prefer that option.

4.12.1 Option 1: Installing Ansible Directly on the Host OS

Installing Ansible directly on the host OS has some advantages. First, it is a simpler setup process, as Ansible is installed directly on the OS. Second, it can be more efficient in terms of memory usage and processing power, as it is running natively on the OS. Third, there are fewer dependencies to manage, as everything is installed system-wide.

However, there are also some disadvantages to installing Ansible directly on the host OS. First, it can lead to conflicts with other system-level software. Second, it can be harder to manage multiple versions of Ansible. Third, it may require administrator privileges to install.

```
[brendan@f38s1 ~]$ sudo dnf update -y # update the packages to the latest
version
> f38s1
[sudo] password for brendan: ***************
[brendan@f38s1 ~]$  sudo dnf install ansible -y # install ansible on OS
[brendan@f38s1 ~]$  ansible -version # check ansible version
ansible [core 2.14.3]
  config file = /etc/ansible/ansible.cfg
  configured module search path = ['/home/brendan/.ansible/plugins/
  modules', '/usr/share/ansible/plugins/modules']
  ansible python module location = /usr/lib/python3.11/site-
  packages/ansible
  ansible collection location = /home/brendan/.ansible/collections:/usr/
  share/ansible/collections
  executable location = /usr/bin/ansible
  python version = 3.11.2 (main, Feb  8 2023, 00:00:00) [GCC 13.0.1
  20230208 (Red Hat 13.0.1-0)] (/usr/bin/python3)
  jinja version = 3.0.3
  libyaml = True
```

You have successfully installed Ansible on your control node. With Ansible at your disposal, you now have the power to easily configure and automate tasks on multiple devices. Get ready to streamline your operations and achieve greater efficiency in managing your network infrastructure.

4.12.2 Option 2: Installing Ansible on Python virtualenv

Installing Ansible on Python virtualenv also has some advantages. First, it allows for multiple versions of Ansible to be installed and managed simultaneously. Second, it is isolated from the system-level software, reducing the risk of conflicts. Third, it can be installed and managed without administrator privileges.

However, there are also some disadvantages to installing Ansible on Python virtualenv. First, it requires a bit more setup as a Python virtualenv needs to be created first. Second, it can be less efficient in terms of memory usage and processing power due to the added layer of the virtualenv. Third, dependencies need to be managed separately for each virtualenv. If you want to follow along, use f38c1 to install Python virtualenv and Ansible in the virtual environment.

1. Update packages, check Python 3, and then install pip3.

    ```
    $ dnf update -y
    $ python3 -V
    Python 3.11.2
    $ sudo dnf install python3-pip
    ```

2. Install virtualenv using pip3.

    ```
    $ sudo pip3 install virtualenv
    $ pip3 freeze | grep virtualenv
    virtualenv==20.21.0
    ```

3. Create a new directory and then create a new Python virtual environment for Ansible.

    ```
    [brendan@f38c1 ~]$ mkdir ~/ansible-venv # create a new
    ```
    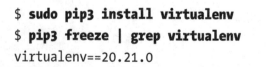
    ```
    directory
    ```

```
[brendan@f38c1 ~]$ cd ~/ansible-venv # change directory to
ansible-venv
[brendan@f38c1 ansible-venv]$ virtualenv ansible # Create
ansible virtualenv
created virtual environment
CPython3.11.2.final.0-64 in 1181ms
  creator CPython3Posix(dest=/home/brendan/ansible-venv/
  ansible, clear=False, no_vcs_ignore=False, global=False)
  seeder FromAppData(download=False, pip=bundle,
  setuptools=bundle, wheel=bundle, via=copy, app_data_
  dir=/home/brendan/.local/share/virtualenv)
    added seed packages: pip==23.0.1, setuptools==67.4.0,
    wheel==0.38.4
  activators BashActivator,CShellActivator,FishActivator,
  NushellActivator,PowerShellActivator,PythonActivator
[brendan@f38c1 ansible-venv]$
```

4. Activate the virtual environment. When you activate the virtual environment ansible, your line will start with (ansible).

```
[brendan@f38c1 ansible-venv]$ source ansible/bin/
activate
```

```
(ansible) [brendan@f38c1 ansible-venv]$
```

5. Install Ansible using the pip3 command.

```
(ansible) [brendan@f38c1 ansible-venv]$ pip3 install
ansible
```

6. Verify that Ansible is installed and working.

```
(ansible) [brendan@f38c1 ansible-venv]$ ansible -
version
```

```
(ansible) [brendan@f38c1 ansible-venv]$ pip3 freeze | grep
ansible-core
ansible-core==2.14.3
```

7. When you're done using Ansible in the virtual environment, you can deactivate it.

```
(ansible) [brendan@f38c1 ansible-venv]$ deactivate
[brendan@f38c1 ansible-venv]$
```

Installing Ansible on the Fedora 38 server using a Python virtual environment is a crucial step for anyone looking to streamline their testing process. By creating a virtual environment, you can isolate different versions of packages, manage dependencies more flexibly, and easily install and uninstall packages. To install Ansible on a virtual environment, you can follow these simple steps: create a new virtual environment using virtualenv, activate it using the source command, and install Ansible using pip. Once done, you can use Ansible to automate your server configuration and deployment tasks. With virtualenv, you can test different versions of Ansible and other software with ease.

Congratulations, you've made it this far! It's time to dive into the heart of this book: Ansible and its concepts. The next five chapters will be crucial to your success in network automation. They catalyze making a strong start in your automation journey. Once you've mastered Ansible in a Linux environment, you will be able to extend your knowledge to enterprise network device automation. So make sure to focus on Chapters 5 to 10, and you'll be on your way to achieving your automation goals.

4.13 Setting Up a New Ansible Testing Account with Sudo Access

To maximize your learning and testing experience with Ansible, we recommend creating a new test user account named jdoe (John Doe) on all virtual Linux machines. This will allow you to explore how Linux sudo accounts are created on both RHEL and Debian-based distributions while providing a fresh account to work with, free of any preexisting configurations. From this point forward in the book, we will utilize this account.

To create the new user account, jdoe, please follow these simple steps on each virtual machine.

4.13.1 Creating a Sudo Test Account on Fedora VMs

To create a new test user account, set a password, and assign sudoer privileges, please execute the subsequent commands. It's essential to create this account on both "f38s1" (192.168.127.150) and "f38c1" (192.168.127.151).

1. Create a new user and assign a new password.

```
[brendan@f38s1 ~]$ sudo adduser jdoe # add new user jdoe
[sudo] password for brendan: *************** # enter your password
[brendan@f38s1 ~]$ sudo tail -3 /etc/passwd # display the last
3 records
systemd-timesync:x:989:989:systemd Time Synchronization:/:/usr/
sbin/nologin
brendan:x:1000:1000:Brendan Choi:/home/brendan:/bin/bash
jdoe:x:1001:1001::/home/jdoe:/bin/bash # new user jdoe has
been created
[brendan@f38s1 ~]$ sudo passwd jdoe # set new password for
user jdoe
Changing password for user jdoe.
New password: *************** # enter password
Retype new password: *************** # reenter the same password
passwd: all authentication tokens updated successfully.
[brendan@f38s1 ~]$ sudo tail -3 /etc/shadow # display the last
3 records
systemd-timesync:!*:19435:::::::
brendan:$y$j9T$WB.x8Ug33pRViPwnCj9S/nE.$U.AjpyFElyNoZeBy
EJw5.BpIzWTlzsE/oMX/F4e1i6::0:99999:7::: # your password
jdoe:$y$j9T$GyGX/MwCz2iCrqoq5dwXEO$3YNSBcrcTOIA
NwSLYigEsZm4K96nzzTJ/K.g6McJlP6:19442:0:99999:7::: # user jdoe's
password
```

2. Update the user privileges by granting root access. Please refer to Figure 4-6 and add the following line: "jdoe ALL=(ALL) ALL".

[jdoe@f38s1 brendan]$ **sudo visudo #** (alternatively use "sudo vi /etc/sudoers")

[sudo] password for jdoe: ******************

[... *omitted for brevity*]

Allow root to run any commands anywhere

root   ALL=(ALL)   ALL

jdoe   ALL=(ALL)   ALL

[... *omitted for brevity*]

```
Defaults    secure_path = /usr/local/sbin:/usr/local/bin:/usr/sbin:/usr/bin:/sbin:/bin:/var/lib/
snapd/snap/bin

## Next comes the main part: which users can run what software on
## which machines (the sudoers file can be shared between multiple
## systems).
## Syntax:
##
##      user     MACHINE=COMMANDS
##
## The COMMANDS section may have other options added to it.
##
## Allow root to run any commands anywhere
root    ALL=(ALL)        ALL
jdoe    ALL=(ALL)        ALL

## Allows members of the 'sys' group to run networking, software,
## service management apps and more.
# %sys ALL = NETWORKING, SOFTWARE, SERVICES, STORAGE, DELEGATING, PROCESSES, LOCATE, DRIVERS

## Allows people in group wheel to run all commands
%wheel  ALL=(ALL)        ALL

## Same thing without a password
# %wheel       ALL=(ALL)        NOPASSWD: ALL

## Allows members of the users group to mount and unmount the
## cdrom as root
# %users  ALL=/sbin/mount /mnt/cdrom, /sbin/umount /mnt/cdrom

## Allows members of the users group to shutdown this system
# %users  localhost=/sbin/shutdown -h now

                                                   102,0-1        97%
```

Figure 4-6. Fedora – assign sudoer privileges to new user jdoe

3. To confirm the sudoer privileges, check the login status and execute sudo commands. You can use the "su – username" command to test sudo access for the user "jdoe". If both commands run without any issues, it indicates that the new user has sudoer privileges.

```
[brendan@f38s1 ~]$ su jdoe
Password: ****************
[jdoe@f38s1 brendan]$ sudo cat /etc/sudoers
[sudo] password for jdoe: ***************
## Sudoers allows particular users to run various commands as
## the root user, without needing the root password.
##
[... omitted for brevity]

[jdoe@f38s1 brendan]$ sudo ls -la /root
[sudo] password for jdoe: ***************
total 28
dr-xr-x---.  3 root root 142 Mar 26 13:14 .
dr-xr-xr-x. 18 root root 235 Mar 19 15:56 ..
[... omitted for brevity]
-rw-------.  1 root root 841 Mar 26 13:14 .viminfo
```

4.13.2 Creating a Sudo Test Account on Ubuntu VMs

The process for creating a sudo user account on Ubuntu is slightly different from that of Fedora. If you want to create identical test accounts on Ubuntu VMs like u23c1 (192.168.127.161) and u23c2 (192.168.127.162), follow the steps outlined here:

1. Add a user with details.

```
brendan@u23c1:~$ sudo adduser jdoe
[sudo] password for brendan: ************** # Enter your password
Adding user `jdoe' ...
Adding new group `jdoe' (1001) ...
Adding new user `jdoe' (1001) with group `jdoe (1001)' ...
Creating home directory `/home/jdoe' ...
```

```
Copying files from `/etc/skel' ...
New password: **************** # Enter jdoe's new password
Retype new password: **************** # re-enter jdoe's new
password
passwd: password updated successfully
Changing the user information for jdoe
Enter the new value, or press ENTER for the default
        Full Name []: John Doe
        Room Number []:
        Work Phone []:
        Home Phone []:
        Other []:
Is the information correct? [Y/n] Y
Adding new user `jdoe' to supplemental / extra groups `users' ...
Adding user `jdoe' to group `users' ...
brendan@u23c1:~$ sudo tail -3 /etc/passwd
brendan:x:1000:1000:Brendan Choi:/home/brendan:/bin/bash
lxd:x:999:100::/var/snap/lxd/common/lxd:/bin/false
jdoe:x:1001:1001:John Doe,,,:/home/jdoe:/bin/bash
brendan@u23c1:~$ sudo tail -3 /etc/shadow
brendan:$6$KZXDxIh6lwewjP8v$sdwOODIVUbdOMsbcN4F/rdYvLFjsIn
WNy8G5djQdTBTL4LBd9jYguEZiMGP1HjEHA8bXm
lxd:!:19435::::::
jdoe:$y$j9T$jqB4oyOA8hkkVA7jzPUjq.$OwSVHk/tQcbDHDBYtXRTs
JSTDtjxO3jgWTsCWST6Ou4:19442:0:99999:7:::
```

2. Modify the user account using the "usermod -ag" command.

   brendan@u23c1:~$ **sudo usermod -aG sudo jdoe**

3. To confirm that the user "jdoe" has been granted sudo privileges,
   first, log in to the system as the root user. Check if the "jdoe" user
   has been created and granted sudo privileges. Then switch to the
   "jdoe" user using the command "su jdoe" and run either of the
   root user validation commands, such as "sudo cat /etc/sudoers"
   or "sudo ls -la /root". This will help you verify if the user "jdoe" has
   been assigned the necessary sudo privileges.

```
brendan@u23c1:~$ su jdoe
Password: ***************

jdoe@u23c1:/home/brendan$ sudo cat /etc/sudoers
[sudo] password for jdoe: ***************
OR
jdoe@u23c1:/home/brendan$ sudo sudo ls -la /root
[sudo] password for jdoe: ***************
```

Remember to keep a note of the username and password you created in this section, as you will need them for the rest of the book. With these instructions, you can swiftly and effortlessly set up a new Ansible test account. This will enable you to focus on the complexities of Linux sudo accounts and Ansible concepts without any interruptions.

4.14 Summary

This chapter was dedicated to setting up a proper learning environment for Ansible. The chapter offered detailed instructions on how to plan an Ansible lab topology and create Fedora and Ubuntu virtual machines on VMware Workstation 17. It started by highlighting the importance of planning before setting up an Ansible lab and guided you on how to plan the lab topology to ensure the best results. Next, the chapter offered a step-by-step guide on installing a VMware Workstation on a Windows PC, with the reader taken through the process of downloading and installing a VMware Workstation referencing a separate complementary PDF file. Once VMware Workstation was installed, the chapter proceeded to guide the reader on creating virtual machines on Fedora and Ubuntu operating systems. The virtual machines were then customized by changing the hostname and assigning static IP addresses, with the chapter providing a guide on updating the virtual machines for lab use. Furthermore, the chapter offered two options for installing Ansible on the control node. Option 1 involved installing Ansible directly on the host OS, while option 2 involved installing Ansible on Python virtualenv. You have been taken through each option in detail, with step-by-step instructions provided. Lastly, the chapter provided instructions on creating a new Ansible test account with sudoer privileges, which will be used throughout the book.

PART II

The Concepts

## CHAPTER 5

Understanding Data Types and File Formats for Ansible

This chapter covers data and data types used in Ansible. It begins by explaining what data is and its relationship with Ansible, followed by discussing Ansible's dependency on Python data types and providing examples of basic Python data types. The chapter then delves into Ansible configuration files, including Ansible inventory in INI, JSON, and YAML formats, inventory priority, and the ansible.cfg file. It also provides YAML examples to familiarize readers with different data types. We will also talk about the preferred playbook module names. Additionally, the chapter covers Ansible data interchange and explores JSON and Jinja2 templates with simple examples. By the end of the chapter, readers will have a broader understanding of data and data types used in Ansible, how to use Ansible configuration files, and how to effectively read and understand JSON and Jinja2 templates for data interchange and rendering files.

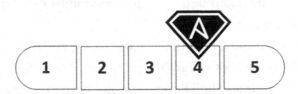

5.1 What Are Data and Data Types?

This chapter focuses on the topic of data and data types in Ansible. Data refers to any information that a program can process or manipulate. Data types, on the other hand, can vary depending on the programming language and may include numbers, strings,

© Brendan Choi and Erwin Medina 2023
B. Choi and E. Medina, *Introduction to Ansible Network Automation*,
https://doi.org/10.1007/978-1-4842-9624-0_5

Booleans, lists/arrays, dictionaries/objects/maps, tuples, and None/null. Programming languages often use casting to convert data from one format to another.

For some readers, this chapter may come as a wake-up call that Ansible is not entirely codeless or independent from other programming languages. While Ansible offers a user-friendly interface, it still requires the Ansible user to have a basic understanding of coding concepts and often integration with other programming languages to complete more complex tasks. Even if you don't plan on becoming a full-time programmer or web developer, it's important to understand programming languages and data interchange methods such as JSON, YAML, and Jinja2 to use Ansible effectively. With the emergence of artificial intelligence (AI), machine learning (ML), and ChatGPT, even non-IT workers are encouraged to learn one or more programming languages. In the IT industry, learning programming languages has become a current trend and craze.

This chapter is meant to be more of a reading and conceptual chapter than a practical, hands-on chapter. While there are some parts of the chapter that you can try in your lab environment, it's best to use this chapter as a pure reading and conceptual chapter to gain a better understanding of data and data types in Ansible and programming languages in general.

We will start by discussing Ansible's dependency on Python and its data types. To help the reader understand, we will provide a brief introduction to Python data types. Together, we will cover Ansible configuration files, inventory priority, and the ansible. cfg file, as well as various data types, including YAML examples. Furthermore, we will examine Ansible data interchange and JSON and Jinja2 templates with sample examples, discussing their usage in data interchange and rendering files. The goal of this chapter is to expose you to various data types and concepts about Ansible at its root. Overall, this chapter will provide you with a foundation for understanding data types in Ansible and programming languages in general.

There are many programming languages in use today, and each language defines and uses data types differently. For example, Python and JavaScript have built-in support for dictionaries/objects, whereas Shell Script does not have a dedicated data type for maps, and C++ requires the use of third-party libraries. Python and C++ also use tuple data types, while Shell Script and JavaScript do not. Table 5-1 shows the differences in data types defined and used in each language. This is important to consider when selecting a language for a particular task or when working with existing code bases.

For instance, Python has built-in support for tuples and dictionaries/objects, while Shell Script does not have a dedicated data type for maps. C++ requires the use of third-party libraries for some data types, such as lists/arrays.

Table 5-1. Popular programming languages and data type examples

Prog. language Data type	Python	Shell Script	JavaScript	C++
Numbers	int(5), float(3.14), complex(2+3j)	num=5; float=3.14	Number(5), Number(3.14), NaN (Not a Number)	int x = 5 ; float y = 3.14; double z = 3.14159265
Strings	"Hello, World!", 'Python', """Multiline String"""	STR="Hello, World!"; STR2='ShellScript';	"Hello, World!", 'JavaScript', 'Template Literal'	std::string str = "Hello, World!"; const char* cstr = "C++";
Booleans	True, False	true, false	true, false	bool a = true; bool b = false;
Lists/arrays	[1, 2, 3], ['a', 'b', 'c']	arr=(1 2 3); letters=('a' 'b' 'c');	[1, 2, 3], ['a', 'b', 'c']	int arr[3] = {1, 2, 3}; char letters[3] = {'a', 'b', 'c'};

(continued)

Table 5-1. (*continued*)

Prog. language Data type	Python	Shell Script	JavaScript	C++
Dictionaries /objects/maps	{'name': 'John', 'age': 40}, {'id': 1, 'status': 'active'}	declare -A my_ map=([name]="John" [age]=40); declare -A my_ map2=([id]=1 [status]="active");	{name: 'John', age: 40}, {id: 1, status: 'active'}	std::map<std::string, int> ages = {{"John", 40}, {"Jane", 30}};
Tuples	(1, 2, 3), ('a', 'b', 'c')	N/A	N/A	std::tuple<int, int, int> tpl = {1, 2, 3};
None	None	"" or 0	null	nullptr

Note   None/null is used to represent the absence of a value and is often used as a default return value for functions that do not return an explicit value.

Although data types may seem irrelevant to some, they play a crucial role in network automation. Ansible, an automation tool built using Python, relies on Python's core and libraries to perform various tasks such as SSH communication via paramiko, configuration file parsing via PyYAML and config parser libraries, and executing modules on remote hosts primarily using paramiko and pty Python libraries. Ansible also supports the WinRM library for executing commands on Windows hosts and the Docker API library for command execution in Docker containers. In network automation, data types are used to store and manipulate network-related data such as OS information, hardware information, IP addresses, network topologies, and device configurations. Ansible is advertised as codeless, but a solid understanding of Python is necessary to unlock its full potential. **Python allows for advanced use cases and customizations of tasks, modules, and plugins.** Knowing programming concepts such as data types, structures, control flow, and functions is crucial for efficient Ansible playbooks. Learning and utilizing programming languages like Python can unlock Ansible's true power, despite its simplified syntax and abstraction layer.

Ansible uses configuration file formats such as INI and YAML files and a templating language such as Jinja2 to manipulate and process data types to complete network automation tasks such as adding new users, configuring devices, and monitoring network performance. Understanding the various data types and file formats used in Ansible is essential for effective network automation.

5.2 Ansible Dependency on Python Data Types

Ansible is a powerful tool for managing and automating network infrastructure, and it utilizes a wide range of data types and formats to achieve its tasks. These data types are crucial in representing various aspects of network data and carrying out automation tasks effectively. The core of Ansible is written in Python, which means that understanding Python data types is essential for working with Ansible effectively. Although this book is not a comprehensive guide to Python, it is still important to provide a brief explanation of Python data types and a brief hands-on introduction, given the close relationship between Ansible and Python. By understanding Python data types, you can better comprehend how Ansible uses them to carry out network automation tasks. Python data types come in various forms, including numbers, strings, lists, tuples, dictionaries, and more. These data types have their unique properties, and understanding them is crucial for working with Ansible efficiently.

In Figure 5-1, you can see Python data types categories. Python has several built-in data types that allow you to store and manipulate different types of data. These data types can be broadly categorized into different groups. The first Python data type group is numeric, which includes integers, floating-point numbers, complex numbers, and Boolean values. Boolean values are a subtype of integers and can be represented as either 0 (False) or 1 (True). Numeric data types are useful for performing mathematical operations and comparisons. The second group sequences include ordered collections of items, such as strings, lists, and immutable sequences (tuples). Sequences are useful for storing and manipulating data in a specific order. The third group is mapping, which includes dictionaries, a collection of key-value pairs. Dictionaries are useful for mapping keys to values and performing lookups based on keys. The fourth data type is sets, which are unordered collections of unique elements. Sets are useful for performing set operations such as union, intersection, and difference. The final data type is None, which represents the absence of a value. None is often used to indicate that a variable has not been assigned a value yet or that a function does not return anything.

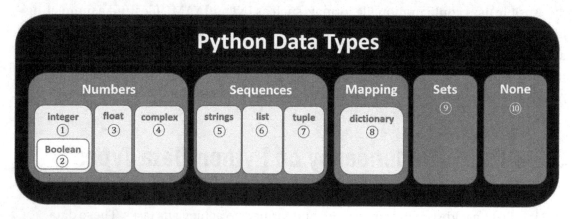

Figure 5-1. *Python Data Types*

To enhance your comprehension of the data utilized in Ansible, we recommend familiarizing yourself with the fundamental Python data types. To accomplish this, we suggest utilizing the Fedora server 1 (f38s1). To simplify the exercise, you may SSH into the device using the PuTTY tool on your Windows host PC with the IP address

192.168.127.150. While any of the Linux servers built in Chapter 4 can be used, we have chosen a Fedora server to showcase Red Hat–based distribution, and this machine will be the main machine that you will be performing most of your tasks in the second half of the book. To begin your Python interpreter session on your Linux machine after logging into the console via SSH, simply enter "python3" or "python" as demonstrated in the following. Although we will not delve deep into Python data types here, it is crucial to familiarize yourself with the various data types and their appearance. This will enable you to explore Python's built-in data types.

```
username: jdoe
jdoe@192.168.127.150's password: ***************
Last login: Sat Apr 15 11:41:39 2023 from 192.168.127.1
[jdoe@f38s1 ~]$ python3
Python 3.11.2 (main, Feb  8 2023, 00:00:00) [GCC 13.0.1 20230208 (Red Hat
13.0.1-0)] on linux
Type "help", "copyright", "credits" or "license" for more information.
>>>
```

5.2.1 Integer and Float

In Python, integers and floats are two distinct data types used to represent numeric values. An integer represents a whole number, meaning it does not have any fractional or decimal component. Integers can be both positive and negative numbers, such as 1, 2, 3, -1, -2, and -3, and are represented using the int data type. A float, on the other hand, represents a decimal or fractional number, meaning it has a fractional component. Floats can also be positive or negative numbers, such as 1.5, 2.6, 3.14, -4.2, and -5.5, and are represented using the float data type. When performing mathematical operations involving an integer and a float, the result will always be a float. This is known as implicit type conversion or coercion. If you need to convert a variable from one type to another, you can use the int() and float() functions. To work with integers and floats in Python from the Linux terminal, you can use the Python interactive shell.

```
>>> a = 5 # create a variable 'a' and assign the integer 5
>>> type(a) # check data type of variable 'a'
<class 'int'>
```

```
>>> b = 3.14 # create a variable 'b' and assign the float 3.14
>>> type(b) # check the data type of variable 'b'
<class 'float'>
>>> c = float(a) # convert integer to float
>>> print(c) # print what's assigned to variable 'c'
5.0
>>> d = int(b) # convert float to integer, this will drop .14 to bring the
number to a whole
>>> print(d) # print what's assigned to variable 'd'
3
```

5.2.2 Strings

A string in Python is simply a collection of one or more characters enclosed within single or double quotes. These characters can be letters, numbers, symbols, or any other characters that can be typed on a keyboard. For example, "John", "Hello, World!", "12345", and "!@#$%^&*()" are all examples of strings in Python because they are enclosed within either single or double quotes. To work with strings in Python from the Linux terminal, you can use the Python interactive shell as before.

```
>>> msg = "Hello, Ansible!"
>>> print(len(msg)) # prints the length of the string (15)
15
>>> print(msg.upper()) # prints the string in uppercase
HELLO, ANSIBLE!
>>> print(msg.lower()) # prints the string in lowercase
hello, ansible!
>>> print(msg.replace("Ansible", "Python")) # replaces "Ansible" with
"Python"
Hello, Python!
```

5.2.3 Booleans

In Python, a Boolean is a data type that can have one of two possible values: True or False. Booleans are used to represent the truth or falsity of a statement or condition. They are often used in conditional statements, where the program flow depends on whether a certain condition is true or false. In addition to True and False, Boolean values can also be represented as 1 or 0. However, it is important to note that these representations are not strictly Boolean and should be used with caution. Boolean values are commonly used in programming to make decisions based on certain conditions. For example, a program might check if a certain value is greater than another value and execute different codes depending on whether this condition is true or false.

```
>>> x = 1 # create a variable x and assign 1 to x
>>> y = 3 # create a variable y and assign 3 to y
>>> print(x < y) # test if x is less than y
True
>>> print(x > y) # test is x is greater than y
False
>>> z = 2 # create a variable z and assign 2 to z
>>> if z < x: # conditional, if z is less than x
...     print("z is less than 1") # print "z is less than 1"
... else: # conditional, for all other cases
...     print("z is greater than or equal to 1") # print "z is greater or
        equal to 1"
...
z is greater than or equal to 1
```

5.2.4 Lists

In Python, a list is a collection of items that are ordered and mutable (changeable). It is one of the most commonly used data structures in Python and can hold any data type, including integers, strings, lists, and dictionaries. To make data a list in Python, simply enclose the data in square brackets [] and separate each item with commas.

```
>>> list_01 = [1, 2, 3, "four", "five", [6, "seven"]] # create a new list
named list_01
>>> type(list_01) # check the data type of list_01
<class 'list'>
>>> print(list_01[0]) # print the data in index 0, index always starts at
0 in Python
1
>>> print(type(list_01[0])) # use the type and indexing to check the data
types of each indexed item.
<class 'int'>
>>> print(list_01[3])
four
>>> print(type(list_01[3]))
<class 'str'>
>>> print(list_01[5])
[6, 'seven']
>>> print(type(list_01[5])) # [6, "seven'] is a list inside another
list, list_01
<class 'list'>
```

5.2.5 Tuples

In Python, a tuple is an ordered and immutable (unchangeable) collection of items, like
a list. However, once a tuple is created, its contents cannot be modified, unlike a list. To
update an element in a tuple, you need to convert it into a list, modify the list, and then
convert it back to a tuple. To create a tuple in Python, use parentheses () and separate
the elements with commas.

```
>>> tuple_01 =(1, 2, "three", "four", [5, "six"], (7, "eight")) # create a
new tuple, tuple_01
>>> type(tuple_01) # check the data type of items
<class 'tuple'>
>>> type(tuple_01[5]) # check item data type using indexing, index always
starts at 0 in Python.
<class 'tuple'>
```

```
# Appending integer '9' to tuple_01 method 1.
>>> list_01 = list(tuple_01) # convert tuple_01 to a list
>>> list_01.append(9) # append the number 9 to the list
>>> tuple_01 = tuple(list_01) # convert the list back to a tuple
>>> print(tuple_01) # confirm the result
(1, 2, 'three', 'four', [5, 'six'], (7, 'eight'), 9)

# Appending integer '9' to tuple_01 method 2.
>>> tuple_01 =(1, 2, "three", "four", [5, "six"], (7, "eight")) # recreate
tuple_01
>>> tuple_01 = tuple_01 + (9,) # concatenate another tuple with integer '9'
as a single element
>>> print(tuple_01) # check the result
(1, 2, 'three', 'four', [5, 'six'], (7, 'eight'), 9)
```

5.2.6 Dictionaries

A dictionary is a fundamental data structure in Python that stores key-value pairs, much like a real-world dictionary where words serve as keys and their meanings serve as values. In Python, a dictionary is represented by a collection of key-value pairs enclosed in curly braces {}. Each key in a Python dictionary must be unique, immutable, and hashable, which means that it cannot be changed once it is created. The corresponding value can be of any data type and can be changed or updated as needed. You can use a dictionary to store and retrieve data efficiently, as accessing a value using its key is much faster than searching for the same value in a list or tuple. Additionally, you can add, remove, or modify key-value pairs in a dictionary dynamically using various built-in methods.

```
>>> my_dict = {'a': 'apple', 'o': 'orange', 'b': 'banana', 'm': 'mango'} #
create a new dictionary named my_dict, starting from Python 3.7,
dictionaries are guaranteed to maintain the order in which the keys were
inserted.
>>> my_dict['a'] # call out the value using the key
'apple'
>>> my_dict['o']
'orange'
```

If you are studying and using Ansible, it is essential to become familiar with Python dictionaries as YAML and JSON have many similarities to a Python dictionary. In Ansible, YAML is the primary format for writing playbooks and defining tasks, and it uses a syntax that closely resembles a Python dictionary. Therefore, understanding how to work with Python dictionaries will help you read and write Ansible playbooks more effectively.

In YAML, the same my_dict Python dictionary data will look like the following:

```
---
a: apple
o: orange
b: banana
m: mango
```

In JSON, the same Python dictionary data will look like this:

```
{
    "a": "apple",
    "o": "orange",
    "b": "banana",
    "m": "mango"
}
```

In the later second part of this chapter, we will delve deeper into YAML and JSON file types. In the meantime, take a quick look at the preceding examples to familiarize yourself with each format.

5.2.7 set

In Python, a set is a collection of unique items that are unordered and mutable (changeable). It's important to note that sets do not have a specific order, and you can add, remove, or modify items in a set after it has been created. To create a set in Python, you can enclose a list of items within curly braces {} or use the built-in set () function. Sets use the same curly braces as Python dictionaries but behave more like an unordered Python list with the condition that each item must be unique, meaning no two items can overlap each other. Sets are commonly used to remove duplicates from a list or perform set operations with built-in set methods such as add(), remove(), union(), intersection(), difference(), and symmetric_difference().

```
>>> my_set = {1, 3, 5, 7, 9}
>>> my_set.add(11)
>>> my_set
{1, 3, 5, 7, 9, 11}
>>> my_set.remove(5)
>>> my_set
{1, 3, 7, 9, 11}
>>> type(my_set)
<class 'set'>
>>> my_set2 = set([2, 4, 6, 8, 10])
>>> my_set2
{2, 4, 6, 8, 10}
```

5.2.8 None

Almost all programming languages used today have a representation for the absence of a value in output or variable. In Python, this is represented by the keyword "None", which indicates that a variable or parameter has no value or that the data has not been initialized. In Python, "None" is a singleton object, which means that only one instance of it exists in memory. It can be useful in situations where you want to assign a placeholder value that represents the absence of a meaningful value. For example, you might use "None" to indicate that a function did not return a value or that a certain condition has not been met.

```
>>> my_variable = None
>>> print(my_variable)
None
```

Now that you have gained some knowledge about Python data types, it is a good opportunity to learn about the configuration file types and data interchange file formats supported by Ansible.

5.3 Ansible Configuration Files

Ansible uses two types of configuration files for its operation: INI and YAML files. INI stands for "initialization," and INI files are configuration file format types that are commonly used on Windows operating systems but are also cross-platform supported, so they can be used on Linux. The INI files are typically used to store configuration settings for applications and system components. In Ansible, the INI file is used exactly to store configuration settings for applications. INI files are simple text files that consist of key-value pair data for the application's use. In Linux applications, the INI files are replaced by YAML, JSON, or XML files, which add more features and flexibility to applications.

5.3.1 INI Format

The INI format is a simple and widely used configuration file format that allows storing data in key-value pair format. Ansible uses the INI format as a default configuration file called inventory file to manage multiple servers or network devices and automate repetitive tasks using a simple, declarative language. The Ansible inventory file contains information about the systems or network devices that Ansible manages, grouped by different categories like geographical location, function, or environment. Each category is represented by a section heading in square brackets, followed by a list of key-value pairs in the format of key=value.

Here is an example of an INI file used in the production environment as an Ansible inventory file for an enterprise network device:

```
[all:vars]   # variables for all hosts
ansible_user=jdoe  # set "ansible_user" variable to "jdoe"

[ios_xe_routers_ny]  # "ios_xe_routers_ny" section for hosts in New York
running IOS XE routers
ny1rtr01.acme.cloud.com  # hostname or IP address of a managed device
ny1rtr02.acme.cloud.com  # hostname or IP address of a managed device
```

```
[ios_xe_routers_ca]  # "ios_xe_routers_ca" section for hosts in California
running IOS XE routers
la1rtr01.acme.cloud.com  # hostname or IP address of a managed device
la1rtr02.acme.cloud.com  # hostname or IP address of a managed device

[pa_os_firewalls_ny]  # "pa_os_firewalls_ny" section for hosts in New York
running Palo Alto firewalls
ny1pavm01.acme.cloud.com  # hostname or IP address of a managed device
ny1pavm02.acme.cloud.com  # hostname or IP address of a managed device

[pa_os_firewalls_ca]  # "pa_os_firewalls_ca" section for hosts in
California running Palo Alto firewalls
la1pavm01.acme.cloud.com  # hostname or IP address of a managed device
la1pavm02.acme.cloud.com  # hostname or IP address of a managed device

[ios_xe_routers:children]  # "ios_xe_routers:children" section to group
together the "ios_xe_routers_ny" and "ios_xe_routers_ca" devices
ios_xe_routers_ny  # Includes the "ios_xe_routers_ny" group as a
child group
ios_xe_routers_ca  # Includes the "ios_xe_routers_ca" group as a
child group

[pa_os_firewalls:children]  # "pa_os_firewalls:children" section to group
together the "pa_os_firewalls_ny" and "pa_os_firewalls_ca" sections
pa_os_firewalls_ny  # Includes the "pa_os_firewalls_ny" group as a child
group pa_os_firewalls_ca  # Includes the "pa_os_firewalls_ca" group as a
child group
```

The INI file in this example defines different sections representing various groups of network devices, such as IOS-XE routers and Palo Alto firewalls grouped by geographical location, NY, and CA. It sets the variable ansible_user to jdoe for all hosts and uses the :children syntax to group multiple sections into a parent section. Additionally, the [all:vars] section in this example defines variables that apply to all hosts in the inventory, including the ansible_user variable. Overall, the inventory file has six sections specifying the hosts that Ansible should manage: ios_xe_routers_ny, ios_xe_routers_ca, pa_os_firewalls_ny, pa_os_firewalls_ca, ios_xe_routers, and pa_os_firewalls.

To use the example shown previously, you will need a DNS-enabled environment. However, if you prefer to operate independently from DNS services, you can create a similar inventory file that specifies the IP addresses of the managed nodes. An example of such an inventory file is shown in the following. It's worth noting that the example provided here is taken from a production environment, and the inventory file is used to manage Wireless LAN Controllers (WLCs). By creating your inventory file, you can tailor your setup to meet your specific needs and requirements.

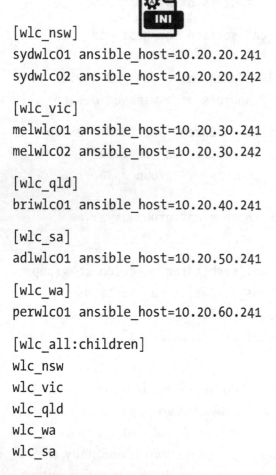

```
[wlc_nsw]
sydwlc01 ansible_host=10.20.20.241
sydwlc02 ansible_host=10.20.20.242

[wlc_vic]
melwlc01 ansible_host=10.20.30.241
melwlc02 ansible_host=10.20.30.242

[wlc_qld]
briwlc01 ansible_host=10.20.40.241

[wlc_sa]
adlwlc01 ansible_host=10.20.50.241

[wlc_wa]
perwlc01 ansible_host=10.20.60.241

[wlc_all:children]
wlc_nsw
wlc_vic
wlc_qld
wlc_wa
wlc_sa
```

To illustrate the contents of the inventory file described previously, refer to Figure 5-2.

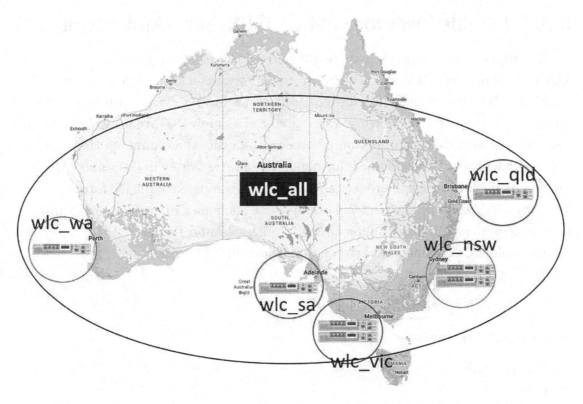

Figure 5-2. *Ansible inventory grouping uses*

Australia has six federated states, each with its state capital city. Most of the Australian population lives in cities along the southeast coast due to the harsh conditions in the outback. In Figure 5-2, seven WLCs need to be controlled and organized by state (NSW, VIC, QLD, SA, and WA). By using inventory grouping effectively, we can manage which devices we want to control. In the preceding example, we demonstrated how we could control devices by state or control all devices using the "wlc_all" inventory group name. For even more granular control, we can further subdivide states into regions or cities. If you are managing infrastructure specific to a particular country, it is recommended to apply the same inventory grouping as demonstrated in the examples to your own country and region. On the other hand, if you are managing devices globally, expand the same concept to the global level by grouping devices based on countries and international regions. This will help you to effectively manage your infrastructure and simplify the process of controlling and monitoring your devices.

5.3.2 Ansible Inventory in INI, JSON, and YAML Formats

Ansible supports the inventory in three different data formats: INI, JSON, and YAML. Although the INI format is the most straightforward, it's crucial to become familiar with the JSON and YAML formats, as the inventory file can be written in various formats. For instance, the following is an example of a simple INI inventory file for Cisco routers and switches that are commonly used in production environments. However, it's essential to note that the same information can also be written in JSON and YAML formats, which have their differences and similarities compared to the INI format. Therefore, let's examine the following example and compare it to the JSON and YAML formats to understand these differences and similarities more deeply.

Example 1: Cisco routers and switches inventory in INI format

```
[ios:vars]
ansible_network_os=ios

[ios:children]
routers
switches

[routers]
c8kv01 ansible_host=192.168.127.171 ansible_network_os=ios
c8kv02 ansible_host=192.168.127.172 ansible_network_os=ios

[switches]
c9300-sw01 ansible_host=192.168.254.241
c9300-sw02 ansible_host=192.168.254.242
```

In the case of JSON format, the preceding INI file can be converted to a JSON format and saved in the JSON-formatted inventory file by saving the file with a .json extension; for example, save the file as "inventory.json". It's important to ensure that the JSON file is properly formatted, including the use of curly braces {} to represent objects, square brackets [] to represent arrays, and commas to separate key-value pairs and array elements. Once the file is saved, its contents should be viewed and checked for accuracy; when we convert the preceding INI Example 1 to a JSON format, it will look like Example 2:

Example 2: Cisco routers and switches inventory in a JSON format

```json
{
    "ios": {
        "vars": {
            "ansible_network_os": "ios"
        },
        "children": [
            "routers",
            "switches"
        ]
    },
    "routers": {
        "hosts": {
            "c8kv01": {
                "ansible_host": "192.168.127.171",
                "ansible_network_os": "ios"
            },
            "c8kv02": {
                "ansible_host": "192.168.127.172",
                "ansible_network_os": "ios"
            }
        }
    },
    "switches": {
        "hosts": {
            "c9300-sw01": {
                "ansible_host": "192.168.254.241"
            },
            "c9300-sw02": {
                "ansible_host": "192.168.254.242"
            }
        }
    }
}
```

Ansible provides the flexibility to use the YAML format for the inventory file as well. After converting the original INI file for the Cisco routers and switches to a YAML format, the resulting file may look like Example 3. You can save this file with either a .yml or .yaml extension, for example, inventory.yml or inventory.yaml. It's important to ensure that the file is saved in a plain text format, without any extra formatting or encoding that might cause issues when using it with Ansible.

Example 3: Cisco routers and switches inventory in a YAML format

```
---
ios:
  vars:
    ansible_network_os: ios
  children:
    routers:
    switches:
  hosts:
    c8kv01:
      ansible_host: 192.168.127.171
      ansible_network_os: ios
    c8kv02:
      ansible_host: 192.168.127.172
      ansible_network_os: ios
    c9300-sw01:
      ansible_host: 192.168.254.241
    c9300-sw02:
      ansible_host: 192.168.254.242
routers:
  hosts:
    c8kv01:
    c8kv02:
switches:
  hosts:
    c9300-sw01:
    c9300-sw02:
```

Now that we have explored the various data file options available for the Ansible inventory (hosts) file, let's dive into another important INI file: the ansible.cfg file.

5.3.3 Ansible Inventory Priority

As you may have noticed from the preceding examples, an inventory in Ansible refers to a group of hosts that Ansible can manage. This inventory can be defined using various file formats, such as INI, YAML, or even JSON. When running an Ansible playbook, it uses the inventory to determine which hosts to target with the tasks defined in the playbook. Ansible searches for target hosts in multiple places, and it has a system of inventory priority in place to determine which inventory source to use when there are conflicts or overlaps in the host definitions. By default, Ansible assigns inventory priority based on the order of the inventory sources in the Ansible configuration file (ansible.cfg). The first source has the highest priority, and subsequent sources have a lower priority.

It's important to understand the order of inventory sources in Ansible, as this determines which hosts Ansible targets when running a playbook. The order of inventory sources, from highest to lowest priority, is as follows:

1. Command line: If you specify hosts or groups of hosts on the command line when running the ansible-playbook command, Ansible will prioritize these hosts, even if they are not defined in the inventory.

2. Inventory files: These files define hosts and groups of hosts that Ansible can manage. If a host or group is defined in multiple inventory files, the definition in the highest-priority inventory file takes precedence.

3. Environment variables: If you define the **ANSIBLE_INVENTORY** environment variable, Ansible will use the file specified by this variable as the inventory file. However, this source has lower priority than the inventory files themselves.

4. Configuration file defaults: If no other inventory sources are specified, Ansible will use the defaults specified in the configuration file (**ansible.cfg**).

By default, Ansible uses the inventory file located at **/etc/ansible/hosts**. However, you can change this by specifying a different inventory file on the command line or in the configuration file. Understanding Ansible's inventory priority is crucial for effectively targeting controlled nodes, so it's important to have a clear understanding of how the inventory is configured and which hosts are defined in different inventory sources.

While you don't have to perform this task, it's helpful to understand how Ansible targets inventory files based on the priorities outlined earlier. In this section, we'll walk through a demonstration of this process. To do so, we'll create some files. Note that this demonstration assumes you've already completed the private key exchange between the Ansible Control Machine and client nodes (web1, web2, and db1).

We need the following four files created and saved under a new directory path: "/home/jdoe/ch05/".

File 1: inventory.ini

```
[web_servers]
web1 ansible_host=192.168.127.161

[db_servers]
db1 ansible_host=192.168.127.162
```

File 2: production.ini

```
[web_servers]
web2 ansible_host=192.168.127.151
```

File 3: ansible.cfg

```
[defaults]
private_key_file = /home/jdoe/.ssh/ansible
```

File 4: playbook.yml

```
--- # a YAML directive that indicates the start of a new YAML document
```

```
- hosts: all

  tasks:
    - ping:
```

If we run the following command from the path, "/home/jdoe/ch05/":

$ **ansible-playbook -i inventory.ini -l web_servers playbook.yml**

```
PLAY [all] ****************************************************************

TASK [Gathering Facts] ***************************************************
ok: [web1]

TASK [ping] **************************************************************
ok: [web1]

PLAY RECAP **************************************************************
web1       : ok=2     changed=0    unreachable=0    failed=0    skipped=0
rescued=0     ignored=0
```

Ansible will target the web_servers group defined in the inventory.ini file and will run the playbook on the web1 host.

If we run the following command instead:

$ **ansible-playbook -i production.ini -l web_servers playbook.yml**

```
PLAY [all] ****************************************************************

TASK [Gathering Facts] ***************************************************
ok: [web2]
```

```
TASK [ping] *****************************************************************
ok: [web2]

PLAY RECAP ******************************************************************
Web2      : ok=2    changed=0    unreachable=0    failed=0    skipped=0
rescued=0    ignored=0
```

Ansible will target the web_servers group defined in the production.ini file and will run the playbook on the web2 host.

If we want to target both web1 and web2, we can specify both inventory files on the command line like this:

```
$ ansible-playbook -i inventory.ini -i production.ini -l web_servers
```

```
playbook.yml
PLAY [all] ******************************************************************

TASK [Gathering Facts] *****************************************************
ok: [web1]
ok: [web2]

TASK [ping] ****************************************************************
ok: [web1]
ok: [web2]

PLAY RECAP *****************************************************************
web1          : ok=2    changed=0    unreachable=0    failed=0    skipped=0
rescued=0    ignored=0
web2          : ok=2    changed=0    unreachable=0    failed=0    skipped=0
rescued=0    ignored=0
```

In this case, Ansible will use the web_servers group from both inventory files and will run the playbook on both web1 and web2.

Finally, if we define the ANSIBLE_INVENTORY environment variable in our environment variable file (in Linux) like this:

```
$ export ANSIBLE_INVENTORY=/home/jdoe/ch05/my_inventory/inventory.ini

$ pwd # check current working directory
/home/jdoe/ch05
$ mkdir test_inventory # make a new directory
$ mv inventory.ini ./test_inventory/ # move the inventory.ini file to the
newly created directory
$ ls my_inventory/ # confirm that the file exists
inventory.ini
$ export ANSIBLE_INVENTORY=/home/jdoe/ch05/test_inventory/inventory.ini #
run this command to enter the configuration to the environmental variable,
you can use 'env' to check. The default file path for the Ansible inventory
file is '/etc/ansible/hosts'.
$ echo $ANSIBLE_INVENTORY # confirm that the new Ansible inventory path
is correct
/home/jdoe/ch05/test_inventory/inventory.ini
```

And then run the command without specifying an inventory file:

```
$ ansible-playbook -l web_servers playbook.yml

PLAY [all] *********************************************************************

TASK [Gathering Facts] ********************************************************
ok: [web1]

TASK [ping] *******************************************************************
ok: [web1]

PLAY RECAP ********************************************************************
web1                       : ok=2     changed=0     unreachable=0
failed=0     skipped=0     rescued=0     ignored=0
```

Ansible relies on the inventory.ini file to manage groups of hosts, and you can specify a custom inventory file by setting the ANSIBLE_INVENTORY environment variable. In this case, Ansible will use the web_servers group defined in the specified inventory file. The inventory priority determines the order in which Ansible uses host definitions. This means that in all the examples, Ansible will use the most relevant host definitions available based on the inventory priority.

```
$ export ANSIBLE_INVENTORY=/etc/ansible/hosts

$ unset ANSIBLE_INVENTORY # To remove the default inventory from the host's
environmental variables, use the 'unset' command.
```

To verify that the system environment has been updated, you can use the env command on your Ansible Control Machine. Now that we have completed the demonstration, it's important to restore the default settings for future use.

Expand your knowledge:

Visit Ansible inventory documentation.

To learn more about Ansible inventories, visit the official Ansible documentation site at https://docs.ansible.com/ansible/latest/user_guide/intro_inventory.html.

5.3.4 ansible.cfg File

The "ansible.cfg" file is a frequently used INI file in Ansible that serves as a repository for configuration options. It utilizes the same INI file format as the inventory file and allows users to specify various options and settings to tailor the behavior of Ansible to their specific needs and preferences. This file is particularly valuable in complex environments with numerous configuration settings and options, as it consolidates all configurations into a single file. As a result, administrators do not have to manage these settings on each controlled node individually, making it simpler to manage and maintain the Ansible setup.

The following is an example of an ansible.cfg file from a production environment, formatted in INI:

```
[defaults] # defines the default options for Ansible.
inventory = inventory  # sets the path to the inventory file.
host_key_checking=False  # disables SSH host key checking.
timeout = 10  # sets the timeout for connecting to remote hosts.
nocows = 1  # disables ASCII art when running Ansible.
deprecation_warnings = False  # disables deprecation warnings.
retry_files_enabled = False  # disables retry files for failed plays
and tasks.
log_path = ./ansible.log  # sets the path for the log file.
forks = 60  # sets the maximum number of parallel processes.
interpreter_python=auto_silent  # automatically selects the Python
interpreter.
ansible_python_interpreter: /usr/bin/python3  # sets the Python interpreter
to use for modules.
```

It's not necessary to comprehend every option in the ansible.cfg file, and there are numerous options that you may not need to memorize. Instead, you can always refer to the various Ansible documentation and community forums. When you have questions regarding specific settings, it's crucial to begin your research from the official Ansible documentation. However, it's essential to ensure that you're referencing the documentation for your current version of Ansible since Ansible features and versions can evolve quickly. Ansible and its modules are continuously improving and changing based on the version of Ansible, making it crucial to keep your knowledge up to date. By doing so, you can leverage more features and automate your environment with the most up-to-date and dependable modules.

Expand your knowledge:

What is FQCN?

Throughout this book, we will strive to use Fully Qualified Collection Names (FQCNs) for module names, as it represents the updated and maintained version. The general consensus on best practices leans toward using FQCNs if you are using Ansible version 2.9 or later. However, if you are working with an older version of Ansible where the "ansible.builtin.service" module is unavailable, you may need to resort to using the "service" module with short names. While using modules with short names still functions in most cases and the use of FQCNs is not strictly required in this sense, we will adhere to industry best practices. This doesn't mean everyone has to agree with the best practices. It's important to note that there is no functional distinction between specifying "ansible.builtin." in front of the "service" and simply using "service" as in short name, as both methods will use the standard Ansible modules and plug-ins available through ansible-base/ansible-core.

There are two sides to the argument for using Fully Qualified Collection Names (FQCNs) in Ansible playbooks:

For: Namespace Clashes – In larger Ansible code bases or complex environments, multiple modules with the same name may exist in different namespaces or collections. By using FQCNs, you can precisely specify the intended module, eliminating potential namespace clashes. This helps prevent ambiguity and ensures the playbook references the desired module.

Against: Readability and Conciseness – Ansible playbooks are designed to be human-readable and easy to understand. Using FQCNs can make the playbook less readable and more verbose. The explicit specification of the entire module path can make the code harder to follow, especially for individuals unfamiliar with the specific structure of the code base. It can also result in longer lines of code, potentially affecting readability and maintainability.

It's worth noting that the concept of Fully Qualified Collection Names (FQCNs) is typically used in object-oriented programming languages to precisely specify the location of a class within a namespace or package hierarchy. YAML, being a markup language, does not directly employ FQCNs. Strictly speaking, YAML is not a programming language itself. Therefore, enforcing FQCNs in Ansible playbooks may appear unnecessary. The objective of using Ansible is to simplify tasks rather than increasing typing effort and complexity. If we are allowed to treat YAML as a programming language and adopt principles from programming languages, enforcing FQCNs contradicts the first two key beliefs and principles associated with Python concepts: "Readability Counts" and "Simplicity." Enforcing FQCNs can introduce verbosity and complexity, undermining the inherent readability and simplicity of playbooks.

The decision of whether to use FQCNs in Ansible playbooks should ultimately depend on specific requirements, the complexity of the environment, and the preferences of the team. Striking a balance between industry best practices and maintaining readability and simplicity is essential when considering FQCN usage in Ansible playbooks.

Here are some extra readings for you to decide on FQCN arguments and advocacies:

https://github.com/ansible/ansible-lint/issues/2050

https://learn.redhat.com/t5/Automation-Management-Ansible/
Why-we-need-to-put-fully-ansible-builtin-xxx-in-ansible-
playbook/td-p/27381

www.ansible.com/blog/migrating-to-ansible-collections-
webinar-qa

https://docs.ansible.com/ansible/latest/collections_guide/
collections_using_playbooks.html

5.3.5 YAML

Just like the INI file, YAML (YAML Ain't Markup Language) is often used for configuration files and data exchange between platforms and languages. YAML closely resembles JSON and XML in many ways, but it is designed to be more human-friendly and intuitive to use. It uses declarative language that reads like English sentences, requiring very little training to bring someone up to speed with reading and writing

YAML files. Simple declarative statements could include statements such as "Water freezes at 0 degrees Celsius," "I am 35 years old," and "My favorite color is blue." If we convert these declarations to system or service states on a Linux system, it would be something like "Create a new user.", "Create a directory new_dir and create a new file my_file01.txt.", "Restart OpenSSH server services.", "Install Apache web server.", "Stop the Apache service.", "Uninstall the Apache service.", "Restart ens160 interface.", "Run the "show version" command on IOS-XE Router." and so on.

Now, let's review some specific examples of tasks written in YAML that demonstrate the declarative nature of YAML files when used in Ansible. These examples will help enhance our understanding of how YAML can be used to describe the desired state of a system and how Ansible can use this information to automate complex tasks across multiple hosts in a simple, efficient, and repeatable manner.

Example 1: "Create a new user."

```
--- # a YAML directive that indicates the start of a new YAML document
- name: Create a new user with password # name for the task
  hosts: all # perform the task on hosts
  become: true # elevated privileges to root user
  tasks:
    - name: Add user # task name
      ansible.builtin.user: # Ansible's builtin module called 'user'
        name: sean # the user to be created
        password:   {{ 'Super5ecret9assword' | password_hash('sha512') }}"
        # generate a secure hashed password
        shell: /bin/bash # specify the user's default shell, /bin/bash is
        newer and better than /bin/sh
        state: present # the user should be created if it does not exist
```

In the preceding example, the YAML code defines an Ansible playbook task that creates a new user with a specified password using the latest Ansible Collection, ansible. builtin.user module, and default shell on all hosts, with elevated privileges to the root user. The password is securely hashed using the SHA-512 algorithm to ensure the user's credentials are protected. The task also specifies that the user should be created only if it does not already exist.

Example 2: "Create a directory new_dir & create a new file test_file01.txt."

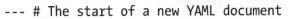

```
--- # The start of a new YAML document
- name: Create a directory and a file # main task name
hosts: all # perform the task on hosts
become: true  # the task runs with elevated privileges (e.g. root/jdoe)

  tasks:
    - name: Create a directory # task name
      ansible.builtin.file: # Ansible's builtin module called 'file'
        path: /home/jdoe/new_dir  # the path to the new directory
        state: directory        # ensure this is a directory

    - name: Create a file # task name
      ansible.builtin.copy: # Ansible's builtin module called 'copy'
        content: "This is Ansible file creation test only!\n"      # the
        content of the file
        dest: /hme/jdoe/new_dir/test_file01.txt  # the path to the new file
        mode: '0644'  # Specify the file permissions (in this case,
        rw-r--r--) # you already learned  about file permissions in
        Chapter 3.
```

In Example 2, the YAML code defines an Ansible playbook task that creates a new directory and file with specified content and permissions on all hosts, with elevated privileges to the root/jdoe user. The task uses the latest Ansible's builtin modules "file" and "copy" to create the directory and file and set the permissions. The task also specifies the path and content of the file to be created.

Example 3a: "Install Apache web server."

```
--- # The start of a new YAML document
- name: Install Apache web server
  hosts: f38c1
  become: true    # Run the task with elevated privileges (e.g. root/jdoe)
```

```
tasks:
  - name: Install Apache web server
    ansible.builtin.dnf:
      name: httpd      # Apache web server package on Fedora
      state: present   # Ensure that the package is installed and
      up-to-date
```

This YAML playbook installs the Apache web server on the Fedora host with the name "f38c1" by using the latest "ansible.builtin.dnf" module in Ansible. The task is run with elevated privileges using "become: true". The "state: present" parameter ensures that the package is installed and up to date.

Example 3b: "Start Apache web server."

```
--- # The start of a new YAML document
- name: Start Apache web server
  hosts: f38c1
  become: true    # Run the task with elevated privileges (e.g. root/jdoe)

  tasks:
    - name: Start Apache web server
      ansible.builtin.service:
        name: httpd    # Apache web server service on Fedora
        state: started # Ensure that the service is started
```

This YAML code starts the Apache web server on the host f38c1. It uses the ansible.builtin.service module from the collection to start the httpd service and runs the task with elevated privileges as root using the become option.

Example 3c: "Check if the Apache web server is started."

```
--- # The start of a new YAML document
- name: Check Apache web server status
  hosts: f38c1
  become: true    # Run the task with elevated privileges (e.g. root/jdoe)

  tasks:
```

```
- name: Check Apache web server status
  ansible.builtin.service:
    name: httpd    # Apache web server service on Fedora
    state: started  # Ensure that the service is started
    register: apache_status  # Register the service status to a
    variable

- name: Print Apache web server status
  ansible.builtin.debug:
    msg: "httpd {{ 'started' if apache_status.changed else
    'stopped' }}"  # Print a message based on the service status
```

This YAML file checks the status of the Apache web server on a Fedora host with the name "f38c1". It runs with elevated privileges and registers the status of the service to a variable called "apache_status". Then it prints a message stating whether the service is started or stopped using the "debug" module.

Example 3d: "Stop the Apache service."

```
--- # The start of a new YAML document
- name: Stop Apache web server
  hosts: f38c1
  become: true    # Run the task with elevated privileges (e.g. root/jdoe)

  tasks:
    - name: Stop Apache web server
      ansible.builtin.service:
        name: httpd    # Apache web server service on Fedora
        state: stopped  # Ensure that the service is stopped
```

This YAML script stops the Apache web server by running the ansible.builtin.service module with the name parameter set to "httpd" and the state parameter set to "stopped". It is executed on hosts specified in the hosts field with elevated privileges as specified in the become field. The task name is "Stop Apache web server".

Example 3e: "Uninstall the Apache service."

```
x--- # The start of a new YAML document
- name: Uninstall Apache web server
  hosts: f38c1
  become: true    # Run the task with elevated privileges (e.g. root/jdoe)

  tasks:
    - name: Uninstall Apache web server
      ansible.builtin.dnf:
        name: httpd    # Apache web server package on Fedora
        state: absent  # Ensure that the package is not installed
```

This YAML file describes an Ansible playbook that uninstalls the Apache web server package from the hosts listed under the "hosts" directive. The "become" directive allows the task to run with elevated privileges as root, and the "tasks" section includes a single task named "Uninstall Apache web server," which uses the ansible.builtin collection module "dnf" to remove the "httpd" package from the target hosts.

Example 4: "Restart the ens160 interface."

```
x--- # The start of a new YAML document
- name: Restart ens160 interface on f38c1
  hosts: f38c1
  become: true    # Run the task with elevated privileges (e.g. root/jdoe)

  tasks:
    - name: Restart ens160 interface
      ansible.builtin.service:
        name: network    # network service on Fedora
        state: restarted # Ensure that the service is restarted
      vars:
        iface_name: ens160  # target interface to be restarted
      shell: |
        ifdown {{ iface_name }} && ifup {{ iface_name }}
```

This YAML playbook will restart the network interface named "ens160" on the host "f38c1". It uses the "service" module to restart the "network" service and then runs a shell command that uses the "ifdown" and "ifup" commands to bring down and bring up the "ens160" interface, respectively. The "become" parameter is set to true, which means the task will be run with elevated privileges.

Example 5: "Restart OpenSSH server services."

```
x--- # the start of a new YAML document
- name: Restart OpenSSH server services on all hosts
  hosts: all
  become: true   # Run the task with elevated privileges (e.g. root/jdoe)

  tasks:
    - name: Restart OpenSSH server
      ansible.builtin.service:
        name: sshd   # the OpenSSH server service on Fedora
        state: restarted  # Ensure that the service is restarted
```

This YAML playbook restarts the OpenSSH server service on all hosts in the inventory using Ansible. The playbook uses the "service" module to manage the service and sets the "state" parameter to "restarted" to ensure that the service is restarted. The playbook also sets "become" to true, which allows the task to run with elevated privileges as root.

Example 6: "Attention all users, please be advised that system maintenance will begin in 30 minutes. Please save any unsaved work and log out of the system to avoid any potential data loss. We apologize for any inconvenience caused." to all logged-in users.

```
---
- name: Send a message to logged-in users and log them out from the
  SSH session
  hosts: all
```

```
# become: true    # Disable this as we are using private keys; this is
  needed to run commands with elevated privileges (e.g. root/jdoe)

tasks:
  - name: Send a message to all users
    ansible.builtin.command: >   # '>' helps to enter multiple lines of
    text; you can also use line separator '\'
        wall "Attention all users, please be advised that system
        maintenance will begin in 30 minutes.
        Please save any unsaved work and log out of the system to avoid any
        potential data loss.
        We apologize for any inconvenience caused."

    ignore_errors: yes # Ignore errors if there are no logged-in users
```

This YAML script sends a message to all logged-in users using the wall command, notifying them of a maintenance event.

"Broadcast message from jdoe@u23c1 (somewhere) (Sun Apr 16 12:32:36 2023):

Attention all users, please be advised that system maintenance will begin in 30 minutes. Please save any unsaved work and log out of the system to avoid any potential data loss. We apologize for any inconvenience caused."

Example 7: "Run the "show version" command on IOS-XE Router."

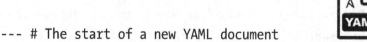

```
--- # The start of a new YAML document
- name: Run show version command on all routers and save to
individual files
  hosts: ny1rtr01,lon1rtr01,tky1rtr01,syd1rtr01,par1rtr01  # Define the
  target hosts
  gather_facts: no  # Disable facts gathering for faster execution

  tasks:
    - name: Run show version command on each router and save to file
      ansible.netcommon.ios_command:  # Use the ios_command module to
      execute the show version command
        commands:
          - show version
```

```
provider:  # Define the login credentials for the IOS devices
  username: jdoe
  password: Super5ecret8assword
register: show_version_output  # Register the output of the command
to a variable

- name: Save show version output to file
  ansible.builtin.copy:  # Use the copy module to save the output
  to a file
    content: "{{ show_version_output.stdout[0] }}"  # Use the
    registered variable to retrieve the output and save to file

    dest: "/home/jdoe/{{ inventory_hostname }}_{{ ansible_date_time.
    date }}.txt"  # Save to file with the hostname and date as part
    of the filename
```

This YAML playbook uses the ios_command module to run the "show version"
command on multiple IOS devices and saves the output to individual files using the
copy module. The register directive is used to capture the output of the command into a
variable, and then the copy module is used to save the output to a file with the hostname
and date as part of the file name. The playbook runs on a list of specified hosts, and
the login credentials are provided through the provider directive. The gather_facts
parameter is set to no to speed up the execution of the playbook.

In the final part of this chapter, we will explore Ansible's data interchange
functionality, which allows for the exchange of data between different systems. This is
achieved using JSON, Jinja2, and YAML. We have been getting familiar with YAML, so in
this section, we will delve more into the world of JSON and Jinja2, comparing them with
XML and drawing parallels to Python dictionaries. With a clear understanding of these
concepts, you will be able to work with Ansible more effectively and have greater control
over the manipulation of data structures.

5.4 Ansible Data Interchange

Ansible uses JSON and XML for data interchange with external systems, while Jinja2
is a templating engine that generates configuration files and scripts dynamically.
Ansible commonly uses three methods for data interchange: JSON, Jinja2 templating,

and YAML. YAML is typically used for configuration files and Ansible playbook scripts because it is human-readable and provides a standardized format for exchanging data between different systems. JSON, on the other hand, is a lightweight data interchange format that is easy for machines to parse.

Jinja2, however, is more of a templating engine that defines variables and templates to create reusable configuration files, enabling easy sharing and exchange of data between different systems. This approach allows for efficient management and automation of IT infrastructure. While Ansible supports both JSON and XML, they are primarily used for data interchange, whereas Jinja2 is used for dynamic templating. By leveraging these data interchange methods, Ansible can streamline infrastructure management and automation.

5.4.1 JSON (Why Not YANG?)

JSON and XML are markup languages used by Ansible for data interchange and configuration of remote systems. JSON is lightweight and easy to read, while XML is verbose and widely used in enterprise applications. Jinja2 is a templating language used by Ansible for generating dynamic configuration files with conditional logic, loops, and programming constructs. Jinja2 templates can be written in either JSON or YAML format. YANG, on the other hand, is a data modeling language designed for network configuration and management. It standardizes the configuration of network devices and is used by NETCONF and RESTCONF. Although YANG and Ansible are both used for network automation, they serve different purposes and operate at different layers of the network stack. In summary, JSON and XML are used for data interchange and dynamic templating in Ansible, while YANG is used for network configuration and management in other tools.

Reading the JSON data from a file and using it in Ansible:

1. Create a file named jack_data.json with the following contents:

```json
{
    "name": "jack",
    "age": 2,
    "sex": "male",
    "breed": "jack russell terrier",
```

```
    "a.k.a.": "Parson russell terrier",
    "origin": "Dartmouth, Devon, England",
    "first_born": 1795
}
```

2. Use the lookup plug-in to read the contents of the file and convert it into an Ansible dictionary:

```yaml
---
- name: Read data from JSON file
  vars:
    my_data: "{{ lookup('file', 'jack_data.json') | from_json }}"
  debug:
    var: dog_data
```

In this example, we use the lookup plug-in to read the contents of the jack_data.json file and convert it into an Ansible dictionary using the from_json filter. We then print out the contents of the dog_data variable using the debug module. Note that you can use the dog_data variable in subsequent tasks as needed.

To write data to a JSON file in Ansible:

1. Define a variable with the data you want to write to the file:

```yaml
---
- name: Define data to write to JSON file
  vars:
    dog_data:
      name: jack
      age: 2
      sex: male
      breed: jack russell terrier
      a.k.a.: Parson russell terrier
      origin: Dartmouth, Devon, England
      first_born: 1795
```

In this example, we define a dictionary named dog_data that contains the same data as in the original JSON file.

2. Use the copy module to write the my_data variable to a file in JSON format:

```
---

- name: Write data to JSON file
  ansible.builtin.copy:
      content: "{{ dog_data | to_json }}"
      dest: "/home/jdoe/ch05/dog_file.json"
```

In this example, we use the copy module to write the contents of the my_data variable to a file named my_file.json located at /path/to/. We convert the my_data variable to a JSON format using the to_json filter before writing it to the file. Note that the content parameter can also accept a file path to read the data from another file, and the dest parameter can be a relative or absolute path to the destination file.

Okay, we used a dog's attribute as an example, but what do the contents of a real working JSON file look like? Are there any actual working examples available? Here is a simple example from a real production environment. This is the data in JSON format returned from an API call to the IP Address Management (IPAM) application, NetBox.

```
{
    "count": 1,
    "next": null,
    "previous": null,
    "results": [
        {
            "id": 266,
            "url": "https://192.168.127.161:443/api/dcim/device-
            types/266/",
            "display": "Catalyst 9300L-24P-4G",
            "manufacturer": {
                "id": 4,
```

```
            "url": "https://192.168.127.161:443/api/dcim/
            manufacturers/4/",
            "display": "Cisco",
            "name": "Cisco",
            "slug": "cisco"
        },
        "model": "Catalyst 9300L-24P-4G",
        "slug": "c9300l-24p-4g",
        "part_number": "C9300L-24P-4G",
        "u_height": 1.0,
        "is_full_depth": true,
        "subdevice_role": null,
        "airflow": null,
        "weight": null,
        "weight_unit": null,
        "front_image": null,
        "rear_image": null,
        "description": "",
        "comments": "",
        "tags": [],
        "custom_fields": {},
        "created": "2023-03-21T04:47:28.871973Z",
        "last_updated": "2023-03-21T04:47:28.871991Z",
        "device_count": 15
        }
    ]
}
```

In the preceding example, we made an API query for information on a particular
Cisco device, the Catalyst 9300, using its slug, "c9300l-24p-4g". Slugs are human-friendly
values stored in the database and can be used as search keywords using API calls. The
returned output is in the typical JSON format, and different systems use JSON-formatted
data for data interchange.

The preceding JSON content is from a query. However, if we want to make a POST API call to add a device, the JSON format becomes a little simpler, as shown in the following example:

```json
[
    {
        "name": "SYD-RTR-01",
        "device_type": 300,
        "device_role": 16,
        "tenant": 44,
        "platform": 5,
        "site": 11,
        "location": 11,
        "rack": 38,
        "position": 20.0,
        "face": "front",
        "status": "planned",
        "airflow": "front-to-rear"
    }
]
```

The following JSON example is used to add manufacturers using POST API calls to an IPAM server.

```json
[
    {
        "name": "Palo Alto",
        "slug": "palo-alto"
    },
    {
        "name": "Fortinet",
        "slug": "fortinet"
    },
```

```
{
    "name": "Cisco",
    "slug": "cisco"
    }
]
```

If you are reading this book, you have likely chosen it to avoid programming or web development. However, **it's ironic that the same excellent tool that you are trying to master relies heavily on the same data types and file formats used by many popular programming languages and web development tools**. While Ansible attempts to detach users from the actual programming as much as possible, anyone in your position will inevitably have to bite the bullet and catch the coding bandwagon at some point in your IT career.

But don't let this discourage you! Learning a bit of programming can enhance your understanding of Ansible and make it easier for you to utilize the tool to its full potential. Even if you don't have any previous programming experience, starting with basic concepts such as data types, variables, and functions can go a long way in helping you understand Ansible playbooks and modules. By expanding your knowledge, you can take your skills to the next level and become a real asset to your team. So embrace the challenge and let your curiosity guide you!

"If you're interested in diving into network automation using Python, we highly recommend checking out the prequel to this book: *Introduction to Python Network Automation: The First Journey* by Apress. You can find it at https://link.springer. com/book/10.1007/978-1-4842-6806-3.

5.4.2 Jinja2

Jinja2 is a powerful template engine that is used by Ansible to generate dynamic content. It is written in Python and provides a simple and flexible way to create templates that can be used to generate any kind of text-based format, such as configuration files, scripts, or documentation. In Ansible, Jinja2 is used to create templates that are populated with variables and other data from Ansible playbooks or inventory files. This allows you to create highly customizable and reusable configuration files that can be tailored to the specific needs of your infrastructure. Jinja2 templates in Ansible use a combination of basic Python syntax and special template tags and filters that are specific to Jinja2. These tags and filters allow you to perform complex data manipulation and logic within your templates, making them highly flexible and powerful tools for generating dynamic content in Ansible.

5.4.2.1 Rendering JSON File Using Jinja2

Jinja2 is a template engine that Ansible uses to generate dynamic content. Let's take a closer look at how we can use it to render Jack's attribute JSON file and gain a better understanding of the rendering process.

1. First, let's review the test JSON file to understand its structure and prepare it for Jinja2 templating.

```json
{
    "name": "jack",
    "age": 2,
    "sex": "male",
    "breed": "jack russell terrier",
    "a.k.a.": "Parson russell terrier",
    "origin": "Dartmouth, Devon, England",
    "first_born": 1795
}
```

2. Now, create a new file named **dog_attributes.j2**. Open a blank file in a text editor and copy/paste the following code:

```jinja2
Here are some attributes of {{ name }}:
- Age: {{ age }}
- Sex: {{ sex }}
- Breed: {{ breed }}
- AKA: {{ a.k.a. }}
- Origin: {{ origin }}
- First born: {{ first_born }}
```

3. Save the file.

4. Now you can use this Jinja2 template in your Ansible playbook by referencing the file name with the template module as shown in the following example.

```
- name: Generate dog attributes
  ansible.builtin.template:
    src: dog_attributes.j2
    dest: /home/jdoe/ch05/dog_attributes.txt
```

This task will generate a file named dog_attributes.txt in the /home/jdoe/ch05 directory. The content of the file will be the result of rendering the Jinja2 template, where the variables (name, age, sex, etc.) will be replaced with their corresponding values.

5.4.2.2 Rendering YAML File Using Jinja2

Let's now use a YAML file containing Jack's attributes and render it using Jinja2. Understanding this process will help you use YAML data as a Jinja2 template. To do so, you can create a new Jinja2 file and use the variables defined in the YAML file.

The following process provides a guideline for creating a Jinja2 template file based on the given YAML data:

1. First, create a new file named dog_info.yaml and copy/paste the YAML data into it.

```
name: jack
age: 2
sex: male
breed: jack russell terrier
a.k.a.: Parson russell terrier
origin: Dartmouth, Devon, England
first_born: 1795
```

2. Create a new file named **dog_info.j2**. In the dog_info.j2 file, you can use the YAML data as follows:

```
{{ name }} is a {{ age }} year old {{ sex }} {{ breed }}.
The dog is also known as {{ aka }} and originated in

{{ origin }} in {{ first_born }}.
```

3. In your Ansible playbook, you can use the YAML module to read the data from the dog_info.yaml file and pass it as variables to the Jinja2 template. For example:

```
- name: Render dog info template
  hosts: localhost
  tasks:
    - name: Read YAML data
      ansible.builtin.vars:
        dog_info: "{{ lookup('file', 'dog_info.yaml') | from_
        yaml }}"
      ansible.builtin.template:
        src: dog_info.j2
        dest: /home/jdoe/ch05/output/file.txt
```

The resulting output file will contain the rendered template based on the data provided in dog_info.yaml. This approach demonstrates how to use Ansible to dynamically generate configuration files using Jinja2 templates and data stored in YAML files.

Congratulations on reaching the end of this chapter! This chapter has covered a wide range of data-related topics in Ansible, and if you're new to this area, you've covered a lot of ground. Throughout this chapter, you've been introduced to many concepts and examples, including an overview of Python data types. We discussed numerous data types and file formats, and while it's not necessary to fully grasp all of them at once, it's important to have a basic understanding of their uses.

As you continue to work with Ansible, you may find yourself returning to this chapter as a reference. We suggest reading it at least three times to gain a solid grasp of the data types used in Ansible. Keep in mind that understanding these concepts will help you write more efficient and effective code in the long run. Great job on completing this chapter, and we wish you the best of luck in your future endeavors with Ansible!

In the next chapter, we will continue exploring Ansible ad hoc and dive deeper into its concepts in subsequent chapters, which will help you further enhance your understanding and practical implementation of Ansible.

5.5 Summary

This chapter of the book focused on data and data types used in Ansible. It covered the basic concepts of data, how it is used in Ansible, and how to use data types in Ansible. The chapter also discussed the dependency of Ansible on Python data types and provided an overview of basic Python data types. The chapter went on to explore Ansible configuration files, including Ansible inventory in INI, JSON, and YAML formats, inventory priority, and the ansible.cfg file. It provided examples of YAML to illustrate and familiarize readers with different data types. We also discussed about FQCNs best practices for module names in our playbooks. The chapter also covered Ansible data interchange and explored JSON and Jinja2 templates with simple examples. It discussed why JSON is used in Ansible for data interchange and how to read and write JSON data files in Ansible. The chapter also provided examples of JSON files used in production and covered how Jinja2 can be used to render JSON and YAML files. By the end of the chapter, readers gained a broader understanding of data and data types in Ansible, how to use Ansible configuration files, and how to effectively read and understand JSON and Jinja2 templates for data interchange and rendering files.

## CHAPTER 6

Learning Ansible Basic Concepts I: SSH and Ad Hoc Commands

This chapter of our Ansible guide covers running ad hoc commands using Ansible. Ad hoc commands allow you to run a single command on multiple systems at once, without the need for a playbook. Learning Ansible ad hoc commands is a great starting point for understanding how Ansible works. It gives novice users a chance to understand how ad hoc commands can transform into a playbook. The chapter begins with an overview of SSH in Ansible, including how to set up and configure SSH connections for your Ansible environment. This is followed by sections on running ad hoc commands on Linux devices, routers, and switches. Finally, the chapter covers running elevated ad hoc commands with Ansible, which allows you to perform tasks that require elevated privileges on the target systems. This section explains how to use the --become option for privilege escalation. By the end of this chapter, you'll have a solid understanding of how to use Ansible to run ad hoc commands on a variety of systems and how to escalate privileges when necessary.

© Brendan Choi and Erwin Medina 2023
B. Choi and E. Medina, *Introduction to Ansible Network Automation*,
https://doi.org/10.1007/978-1-4842-9624-0_6

6.1 SSH Overview and Setup in Ansible

Secure Shell (SSH) is a highly secure network protocol used for remote access and management of servers and network devices. It provides an encrypted channel for communication between the client and server, making it ideal for sensitive data transmission. SSH uses TCP port number 22 by default, but in a hardened environment, the port number can be changed to something else to prevent unauthorized access attempts. The default authentication method for SSH is password based, but using SSH keys is more secure and recommended. Ansible, a popular configuration management tool, uses SSH as its default transport mechanism, requiring OpenSSH to be installed on Linux servers.

To use SSH from a PC, an SSH client such as PuTTY or SecureCRT is needed. An OpenSSH server must be installed on the controlled (client) nodes to enable secure remote access by the admin or admin machine. The OpenSSH server listens for incoming connections on port 22 by default, and by TCP nature, the connection is always connection oriented. In the context of Ansible, SSH is used as the default transport mechanism to connect to remote hosts and perform tasks securely. The use of SSH in Ansible ensures that any communication between the control machine and the remote host is protected from security threats. Ansible is an essential tool in the DevOps toolchain due to its use of SSH for secure communication between the control machine and remote hosts. Thanks to the Secure Shell (SSH) protocol, Ansible is able to operate on remote hosts without the need for an agent to be installed on them. This eliminates the additional step of agent installation and configuration, making Ansible more efficient and easier to use for remote management and configuration tasks.

6.1.1 Configuring SSH for Ansible: General Steps

To configure SSH for use with Ansible, several steps need to be completed, which include the following:

1. Install OpenSSH: Ansible requires OpenSSH to be installed on both the control machine (the machine where you run Ansible from) and the remote hosts you want to manage. Make sure that OpenSSH is installed and properly configured on both the control machine and the remote hosts.

2. Configure SSH: You will need to configure SSH on both the control machine and the remote hosts to enable password-less authentication using public and private keys. This step is essential for Ansible to function properly. You can follow the steps outlined in this section to set up password-less authentication.

3. Create SSH keys: You will need to create SSH keys on the control machine and then distribute the public key to the remote hosts you want to manage. This will allow Ansible to communicate securely with the remote hosts without the need for a password. You can create SSH keys using the ssh-keygen command and then copy the public key to the remote hosts using the ssh-copy-id command.

4. Test the SSH connection: Once SSH is configured and the keys are in place, you can test the connection between the control machine and the remote hosts using the SSH command. This step is important to ensure that the SSH connection is working properly before you start using Ansible. You can use the ssh command with the -v flag to enable verbose mode and get more detailed output. You will learn how to use the verbose mode in Chapter 8.

5. Set up Ansible to use SSH: Finally, you will need to configure Ansible to use SSH as the default transport mechanism. Ansible uses SSH by default, so you don't need to do anything extra to configure it. However, you can customize the SSH options that Ansible uses by modifying the ssh_args setting in the Ansible configuration file. You can also specify a different transport mechanism, such as paramiko or local, by using the -c option when running Ansible commands.

6.1.2 Understanding the Ansible SSH Concept

Fully grasping the SSH concept in Ansible is important because without a clear understanding of how SSH works and integrates with Ansible, users may encounter connectivity, security, and performance issues. Such issues could then adversely impact the effectiveness and reliability of their Ansible automation workflows.

1. Check the OpenSSH version: Ensure that the SSH server is configured properly on each VM. If not installed, use either the "sudo yum install openssh-server" command for RHEL distributions or the "sudo apt install openssh-server" command for Debian-based distributions.

   ```
   $ ssh -V
   ```

2. Configure SSH: To enable password-less authentication, you will need to edit the SSH configuration file (/etc/ssh/sshd_config) on the remote host to allow for public key authentication. You will also need to edit the ~/.ssh/config file on the control machine to specify the location of the private key.

3. Create SSH keys: You can create SSH keys on the control machine using the following command:

   ```
   $ ssh-keygen -t rsa -b 4096
   ```

   This will create a new SSH key pair in the ~/.ssh/ directory. You can then copy the public key to the remote host using the following command:

   ```
   $ ssh-copy-id user@remote_host
   ```

4. Test the SSH connection: You can test the SSH connection using the SSH command:

   ```
   $ ssh user@remote_host
   ```

   This should connect to the remote host without prompting for a password.

5. Set up Ansible to use SSH: Finally, you will need to configure
    Ansible to use SSH by specifying the transport method in the
    ansible.cfg file:

```
[defaults]
transport = ssh
```

6.1.3 Practical Usage of SSH in Ansible

To make sure that OpenSSH is installed and functioning on your Linux servers, you can
use a couple of commands. Firstly, to check if OpenSSH is installed and to see its version
number, you can issue the "ssh -V" command. This will output the version information
if OpenSSH is installed on the server. Secondly, to check the status of the SSH service,
you can use the appropriate command based on your Linux distribution. For Fedora
and Red Hat Enterprise Linux, use the command "sudo systemctl status sshd". If you're
using an Ubuntu or Debian-based system, use the command "sudo systemctl status ssh".
By running these commands, you will obtain the necessary information to confirm that
OpenSSH is properly installed and running on your servers. Remember to run the same
commands on the second set of servers, which are identified as f38c1 and u23c2. This
will ensure that OpenSSH is also installed and running properly on these servers and will
help ensure consistency across your entire infrastructure.

1. To check the status of the SSH server on your servers, log in to
    them using the Ansible test account "jdoe" via PuTTY, and execute
    the appropriate command based on your Linux distribution.
    It's important to note that successfully logging in to the server
    indicates that the SSH service is up and running.

```
[jdoe@f38s1 ~]$ ssh -V # check ssh version Linux                    >_ f38s1
[jdoe@f38s1 ~]$ sudo systemctl status sshd # check ssh status on
Fedora/RHEL
[jdoe@f38s1 ~]$ sudo ss -lt # check working ports on Fedora/RHEL

jdoe@u23c1:~$ ssh -V # check ssh version Linux                      >_ u23c1
jdoe@u23c1:~$ sudo systemctl status ssh # check ssh status on
Ubuntu/Debian
jdoe@u23c1:~$ sudo ss -lt # check working ports on Ubuntu/Debian
```

2. First, connect to each client node (f38c1, u23c1, and u23c2) from the Ansible control server (f38s1) and answer "yes" to the initial connection prompt. This is important as it confirms the fingerprint and ensures Ansible runs smoothly. If you don't accept the prompt initially, Ansible may encounter issues. Although there are other ways to accept the prompt, it's easier for you to take care of this step yourself to ensure a quick start.

```
[jdoe@f38s1 ~]$ ssh 192.168.127.151
The authenticity of host '192.168.127.151 (192.168.127.151)' can't
be established.
ED25519 key fingerprint is SHA256:A/eV+z5YeLFHQuzLSvXd4BUoYOoIVOnz
GENk32lsVGc.
This key is not known by any other names
Are you sure you want to continue connecting (yes/no/
[fingerprint])? yes
Warning: Permanently added '192.168.127.151' (ED25519) to the list
of known hosts.
jdoe@192.168.127.151's password: ****************
Last login: Sun Mar 26 17:33:25 2023 from 192.168.127.1
[jdoe@f38c1 ~]$ exit
logout
Connection to 192.168.127.151 closed.
[jdoe@f38s1 ~]$
```

3. **Repeat the preceding task to accept the ED25519 key fingerprint for u23c1 (192.168.127.161) and u23c2 (192.168.127.162).**

4. After answering "yes" in step 2, the server's keys were saved under the known_hosts file. To verify this, we can check the known_hosts file and confirm that the server's keys are present.

```
[jdoe@f38s1 ~]$ pwd
/home/jdoe
[jdoe@f38s1 ~]$ ls /home/jdoe/. -a
```

. .. .bash_history .bash_logout .bash_profile .bashrc .ssh
[jdoe@f38s1 ~]$ **ls /home/jdoe/.ssh**
known_hosts known_hosts.old
[jdoe@f38s1 ~]$ **cat ~/.ssh/known_hosts**
192.168.127.151 ssh-ed25519
AAAAC3NzaC1lZDI1NTE5AAAAIHDbd8q9othwdMzTmfE83WZbO5/
EzLJPBLkKizWvXOXW
192.168.127.151 ssh-rsa
AAAAB3NzaC1yc2EAAAADAQABAAABgQDeUWWtU9K3t4RT
4g8m5ZGqZnXTA3Smiol2LviBTWZD7OalEZG58oLPb45Y
kvB8+osIMyhwcy3LN6g2jl/6UUcVX6CGHKFkngbinoSX
UBtOuZxHoAvumOMLjjD1qvJPW6xZTUBgfM+c/IfwoHOZ
gJKXS+rwe2Vrw2wMDZSiK63ySnKvVxp6GbJQcGnkH2pq
pGVpNMtUm4ZIlPdj3TYvcUtjoTj7AwA5pykTrIOZB3xo
5SYPRqpYiuf+Y4nEmRW3YRnth5tQO2INGCOxlTjqVfaP
8yQB8KKbjEnOZDomY6LbjHsYawxOZaiz1yG4WVVY3sCh
KODYAmZV/JlkES9NS8X7DytN+YZVd4pqPCrByIGxk6+
6s9RA43r1KI4O1bSbTl5FHhUyrQv7xfai+zBwnMrPrEj/
LGC/2YZA89LmrSOzqcEomwOwFQwLuCp9ehv+5DonWqf
U556NgiPHgqJHqxSOD9k5QcvtNMOWOY4CAZCtJoZv7jaB2tvmyQH/8d//9d8=
192.168.127.151 ecdsa-sha2-nistp256 AAAAE2VjZHNhLXNoYTItbmlzdHAy
NTYAAAAIbmlzdHAyNTYAAABBBJeX9hLbBA7nHGDYibQSfgv224slCrxK789k8auN
J4BWZZDa8VOdU3xkMpQtpe+j+EI7ffqJRy1UjCZZ1FF1vVc=192.168.127.161
ssh-ed25519 AAAAC3NzaC1lZDI1NTE5AAAAIC4dS2kUbOQcUkD1k9MKXKGVzT
LlVFcxyI9xOjhHOb11
192.168.127.161 ssh-rsa AAAAB3NzaC1yc2EAAAADAQABAAABgQDOtEebr
OuIdDL+ZbB+RvpoGsDC89J9q60IKOnL7zJ/Elf4nagUcM1n9J1OpY+fq+7vW1Hq
F55eydkUAKfqkvcofXTzhW2LUiGmbOI9n/kkA7qNuC9EPE3WuX8BHAG9kji4Lx8or
pGi8QHApT1JyYHRRMMOn5jMn4279AgLqM2smKoLvQEjfPo+GQz2hgtcb2Y/
g6Oe81u77SDHCx1YF6LYpntw+Ja1H9fBOYkvsrDNnQJPzZF1NGd+n7eQoEbgzzd
Vu62QDPkqBjf7W9Cz3GFsPQWdhNa6XAOhu8OfJnkg/ehzfnMG6qe+lmC8+LheOeU8
scoXrULnwV7AYJbp6kp69JBffZtqxTxHj7W/9MHILOeORZmhx8AdH7jCjovWPiTmr
AX6J+1jMUV2ZgGwBr14NZgh/UF+Zh3FHBKhYJQh8MvqyOebqQElj+RyStsaCfIjRj/
uETq1ucRdSiJIHIzmCdKtcgX1cceE4ldNJRVw43ioNCL9/bi7BE6jinsrsD8=

```
192.168.127.161 ecdsa-sha2-nistp256 AAAAE2VjZHNhLXNoYTItbmlzdH
AyNTYAAAAIbmlzdHAyNTYAAABBBPvtaljn59g3gZqOrJPTpSaEZ9XfDDasaQNw
AR6uytxXMk2WvAOhTuNZNRqlTXcZy3KN1JO4L8aPW3UIX9fulvo=
192.168.127.162 ssh-ed25519 AAAAC3NzaC1lZDI1NTE5AAAAIC4dS2kUbOQcU
kD1k9MKXKGVzTLlVFcxyI9xOjhHOb11
```

5. To manage SSH keys in Ansible, it's recommended to create an SSH key pair with a passphrase for the Ansible test user account on the Ansible Control Machine, using the ed25519 public/private key pairing. While it's not mandatory, it's considered a best practice. In this case, we will create a key pair for our use. To generate the SSH key, simply follow the steps provided.

```
[jdoe@f38s1 ~]$ ls -la .ssh # check the files under .ssh
directory
total 8
drwx------. 2 jdoe jdoe   48 Mar 26 17:36 .
drwx------. 3 jdoe jdoe   95 Mar 26 17:35 ..
-rw-------. 1 jdoe jdoe 1783 Mar 26 17:36 known_hosts
-rw-------. 1 jdoe jdoe  940 Mar 26 17:36 known_hosts.old
[jdoe@f38s1 ~]$ ssh-keygen -t ed25519 -C "jdoe default" #
generate keys
Generating public/private ed25519 key pair.
Enter file in which to save the key (/home/jdoe/.ssh/id_ed25519):
Enter passphrase (empty for no passphrase): *************** #
Enter your passphrase
Enter same passphrase again: *************** # Enter your
passphrase again
Your identification has been saved in /home/jdoe/.ssh/id_ed25519
Your public key has been saved in /home/jdoe/.ssh/id_ed25519.pub
The key fingerprint is:
SHA256:bd91HcIWYqDN88HfIR3fZQ2tGhdl8jyiYpzhseYyMyU jdoe default
The key's randomart image is:
+--[ED25519 256]--+
|       ..o .o=*|
|        + o o +*B|
```

```
|   . * o * B=|
|     o.B * B =|
|     ESXoo = .+|
|       *...... ..|
|     = .  . . |
|       =       |
|               |
+----[SHA256]-----+
```
[jdoe@f38s1 ~]$ **ls -la .ssh** # check the .ssh directory again
total 16
drwx------. 2 jdoe jdoe   88 Mar 26 18:04 .
drwx------. 3 jdoe jdoe   95 Mar 26 17:35 ..
-rw-------. 1 jdoe jdoe 444 Mar 26 18:04 id_ed25519 # a private
key only for f38s1
-rw-r--r--. 1 jdoe jdoe   94 Mar 26 18:04 id_ed25519.pub # a
public key for public sharing
-rw-------. 1 jdoe jdoe 1783 Mar 26 17:36 known_hosts
-rw-------. 1 jdoe jdoe 940 Mar 26 17:36 known_hosts.old
[jdoe@f38s1 ~]$ **cat .ssh/id_ed25519.pub** # check the public key
information
ssh-ed25519 AAAAC3NzaC1lZDI1NTE5AAAAIKaBKRacKDPr5WCIpiG5ZHyyRIIue
cM7AHZYG7Au+yuU jdoe default
[jdoe@f38s1 ~]$ **cat .ssh/id_ed25519** # check the private key
information
-----BEGIN OPENSSH PRIVATE KEY-----
b3BlbnNzaC1rZXktdjEAAAAACmFlczI1Ni1jdHIAAAAGYmNyeXB0AAAAGAAAABDGnQLPV+
RRrv1l7Tb/8kQyAAAAEAAAAAEAAAAzAAAAC3NzaC1lZDI1NTE5AAAAIKaBKRacKDPr5WCI
piG5ZHyyRIIuecM7AHZYG7Au+yuUAAAAkB11w9vVyT2Jp8i9of7chGJaSQ7aYRuYhUKxct
l3KokqjV9xgvN1Ir0jo86FSeNng21R/NX6o31yOBGnofiLJC6Ef9WZ2aVQeXJXZ5PTOCNJ
tBBEXCgoI7IEUd8pqEzGsVt8jv4sH1cdlYdkUeommttZ/YFb1b1wnRr2IBDh76MfBlcuyM
AovyvkLiPQTxIhlg==
-----END OPENSSH PRIVATE KEY-----
```
```

6. To ensure that the public key is copied to all of the Ansible clients, also referred to as controlled clients, please execute the following command exactly as it is shown:

[jdoe@f38s1 ~]$ **ssh-copy-id -i ~/.ssh/id_ed25519.pub**

192.168.127.151

```
/usr/bin/ssh-copy-id: INFO: Source of key(s) to be installed: "/
home/jdoe/.ssh/id_ed25519.pub"
/usr/bin/ssh-copy-id: INFO: attempting to log in with the new
key(s), to filter out any that are already installed
/usr/bin/ssh-copy-id: INFO: 1 key(s) remain to be installed -- if
you are prompted now it is to install the new keys
jdoe@192.168.127.151's password: **************

Number of key(s) added: 1

Now try logging into the machine, with:   "ssh '192.168.127.151'"
and check to make sure that only the key(s) you wanted were added.
```

After performing the necessary actions, please navigate to 192.168.127.151 and verify the contents of the directory on the remote node. You should observe that f38s1's public key has been successfully stored in the .ssh/authorized_keys file on f38c1.

```
[jdoe@f38c1 ~]$ ls -la .ssh
total 4
drwx------. 2 jdoe jdoe 29 Mar 26 18:24 .
drwx------. 3 jdoe jdoe 95 Mar 26 18:24 ..
-rw-------. 1 jdoe jdoe 94 Mar 26 18:24 authorized_keys
[jdoe@f38c1 ~]$ cat .ssh/authorized_keys
ssh-ed25519 AAAAC3NzaC1lZDI1NTE5AAAAIKaBKRacKDPr5WCIpiG5ZHyyRIIue
cM7AHZYG7Au+yuU jdoe default # f38s1's public key has been saved
to .ssh/authorized_keys.
```

7. **Next, please repeat step 5 on the remaining clients, namely, u23c1 and u23c2.** Once the f38s1 SSH public key has been copied to these clients, execute the same set of commands to confirm that the keys are stored in the .ssh/authorized_keys directory. This

validation step ensures that the SSH keys are correctly installed on all the necessary clients.

8. To test the login, you will need to provide the passphrase for the ssh-key used in this exercise. Please enter the passphrase when prompted to ensure that the login process is successful.

```
[jdoe@f38s1 ~]$ ssh 192.168.127.151
Enter passphrase for key '/home/jdoe/.ssh/id_ed25519':
****************
Last login: Sun Mar 26 17:35:49 2023 from 192.168.127.150
[jdoe@f38c1 ~]$ logout
Connection to 192.168.127.151 closed.
[jdoe@f38s1 ~]$ ssh 192.168.127.161
jdoe@192.168.127.161's password: ***************
Welcome to Ubuntu Lunar Lobster (development branch) (GNU/Linux
6.2.0-18-generic x86_64)
[... omitted for brevity]
Last login: Sun Mar 26 06:36:25 2023 from 192.168.127.150
jdoe@u23c1:~$ logout
Connection to 192.168.127.161 closed.
[jdoe@f38s1 ~]$ ssh 192.168.127.162
jdoe@192.168.127.162's password: ***************
Welcome to Ubuntu Lunar Lobster (development branch) (GNU/Linux
6.2.0-18-generic x86_64)
[... omitted for brevity]
Last login: Sun Mar 26 06:36:42 2023 from 192.168.127.150
jdoe@u23c1:~$ logout
Connection to 192.168.127.162 closed.
```

The keys were generated under the user account jdoe, and the public key was manually added to test SSH key functionality between the Ansible control node and Ansible Client nodes. Another key will be created specifically for Ansible use.

9. To ensure seamless authentication for Ansible, it's recommended
    to create a dedicated SSH key without a passphrase. This will
    enable Ansible to authenticate without requiring a passphrase
    each time. Please proceed to create the SSH key specifically for
    Ansible.

```
[jdoe@f38s1 ~]$ ssh-keygen -t ed25519 -C "ansible"
Generating public/private ed25519 key pair.
Enter file in which to save the key (/home/jdoe/.ssh/id_ed25519):
/home/jdoe/.ssh/ansible   # Change
the file name!, Important!
Enter passphrase (empty for no passphrase):     # No passphrase! Just
                                          press <Enter> key
Enter same passphrase again:        # No passphrase! Just press
                                       <Enter> key
Your identification has been saved in /home/jdoe/.ssh/ansible
Your public key has been saved in /home/jdoe/.ssh/ansible.pub
The key fingerprint is:
SHA256:cRLllPOy5ZtfuMMvPj1FOyBOWvG/dIgOOVrVzPVXYWU ansible
The key's randomart image is:
+--[ED25519 256]--+
|        ..o.    oE|
|        +o.   ..o|
|       o ooo+ .o|
|        +.++o+ +|
|        S =B..ooo|
|         .*.o .*o|
|        o + +o.*|
|        .   + ==.|
|            o+=o|
+----[SHA256]-----+
```

10. Add the Ansible SSH key to all three Ansible clients – namely,
    f38c1, u23c1, and u23c2. Note that this task will ask for the
    passphrase of the first key to allow the addition of the new
    (second) key into the same file.

[jdoe@f38s1 ~]$ **ssh-copy-id -i ~/.ssh/ansible.pub**

192.168.127.151

/usr/bin/ssh-copy-id: INFO: Source of key(s) to be installed: "/
home/jdoe/.ssh/ansible.pub"
/usr/bin/ssh-copy-id: INFO: attempting to log in with the new
key(s), to filter out any that are already installed
/usr/bin/ssh-copy-id: INFO: 1 key(s) remain to be installed -- if
you are prompted now it is to install the new keys
Enter passphrase for key '/home/jdoe/.ssh/id_ed25519':
**************** # This is asking for the passphrase of the first
key to allow the addition of the new key to the location!!!

Number of key(s) added: 1

Now try logging into the machine, with: "ssh '192.168.127.151'"
and check to make sure that only the key(s) you wanted were added.

[jdoe@f38s1 ~]$ **ssh-copy-id -i ~/.ssh/ansible.pub 192.168.127.161**
/usr/bin/ssh-copy-id: INFO: Source of key(s) to be installed: "/
home/jdoe/.ssh/ansible.pub"
/usr/bin/ssh-copy-id: INFO: attempting to log in with the new
key(s), to filter out any that are already installed
/usr/bin/ssh-copy-id: INFO: 1 key(s) remain to be installed -- if
you are prompted now it is to install the new keys
jdoe@192.168.127.161's password: ****************

Number of key(s) added: 1

Now try logging into the machine, with: "ssh '192.168.127.161'"
and check to make sure that only the key(s) you wanted were added.

[jdoe@f38s1 ~]$ **ssh-copy-id -i ~/.ssh/ansible.pub 192.168.127.162**
/usr/bin/ssh-copy-id: INFO: Source of key(s) to be installed: "/
home/jdoe/.ssh/ansible.pub"
/usr/bin/ssh-copy-id: INFO: attempting to log in with the new
key(s), to filter out any that are already installed

```
/usr/bin/ssh-copy-id: INFO: 1 key(s) remain to be installed -- if
you are prompted now it is to install the new keys
jdoe@192.168.127.162's password: ***************

Number of key(s) added: 1

Now try logging into the machine, with:   "ssh '192.168.127.162'"
and check to make sure that only the key(s) you wanted were added.
```

11. Ensure that only the key(s) you wanted has been added to the
    .ssh/authorized_keys file on each client.

```
[jdoe@f38c1 ~]$ cat .ssh/authorized_keys
ssh-ed25519 AAAAC3NzaC1lZDI1NTE5AAAAIKaBKRacKDPr5WCIpiG5ZHyyRIIue
cM7AHZYG7Au+yuU jdoe default
ssh-ed25519 AAAAC3NzaC1lZDI1NTE5AAAAIFvayxHfA8pjZTldlXQdVPEK+fdjFe
kSPx9E4bnbPl0b ansible
```

```
jdoe@u23c1:~$ cat .ssh/authorized_keys
ssh-ed25519 AAAAC3NzaC1lZDI1NTE5AAAAIKaBKRacKDPr5WCIpiG5ZHyyRIIue
cM7AHZYG7Au+yuU jdoe default
ssh-ed25519 AAAAC3NzaC1lZDI1NTE5AAAAIFvayxHfA8pjZTldlXQdVPEK+fdjFe
kSPx9E4bnbPl0b ansible
```

```
jdoe@u23c1:~$ cat .ssh/authorized_keys
ssh-ed25519 AAAAC3NzaC1lZDI1NTE5AAAAIKaBKRacKDPr5WCIpiG5ZHyyRIIue
cM7AHZYG7Au+yuU jdoe default
ssh-ed25519 AAAAC3NzaC1lZDI1NTE5AAAAIFvayxHfA8pjZTldlXQdVPEK+fdjFe
kSPx9E4bnbPl0b ansible
```

12. Test automatic login to controlled clients using the Ansible
    SSH key.

```
[jdoe@f38s1 ~]$ ssh -i ~/.ssh/ansible 192.168.127.151
Last login: Sun Mar 26 18:37:11 2023 from 192.168.127.150
[jdoe@f38c1 ~]$ logout
Connection to 192.168.127.151 closed.
```

```
[jdoe@f38s1 ~]$ ssh -i ~/.ssh/ansible 192.168.127.161
Welcome to Ubuntu Lunar Lobster (development branch) (GNU/Linux
6.2.0-18-generic x86_64)
[... omitted for brevity]
Last login: Sun Mar 26 07:37:35 2023 from 192.168.127.150
jdoe@u23c1:~$ logout
Connection to 192.168.127.161 closed.
[jdoe@f38s1 ~]$ ssh -i ~/.ssh/ansible 192.168.127.162
Welcome to Ubuntu Lunar Lobster (development branch) (GNU/Linux
6.2.0-18-generic x86_64)
[... omitted for brevity]
Last login: Sun Mar 26 08:10:29 2023 from 192.168.127.150
jdoe@u23c1:~$ logout
Connection to 192.168.127.162 closed.
[jdoe@f383s1 ~]$
```

When logging in, if you use the default key, the system will prompt you to enter the associated passphrase. However, if you use the Ansible key, it will allow the Ansible server to gain access without prompting for the passphrase. This is because the Ansible key has been configured to allow password-less authentication, while the default key requires manual authentication by entering the associated passphrase.

```
[jdoe@f38s1 ~]$ ssh 192.168.127.161
Enter passphrase for key '/home/jdoe/.ssh/id_ed25519': **************
```

Well done! You have gained a better understanding of how SSH key sharing works between servers in the context of Ansible. Now, it's time to explore the exciting and fun world of Ansible ad hoc commands. These commands allow you to perform quick and one-time tasks on your servers, without the need to create a playbook or define a set of tasks. With ad hoc commands, you can perform tasks such as checking system status, installing packages, or running shell commands, all from the convenience of your Ansible control node. So let's dive in and explore the limitless possibilities of Ansible ad hoc commands!

6.2 Running Ad Hoc Commands on Linux Devices with Ansible

Ansible ad hoc commands are convenient, one-time commands that can be executed against one or more target hosts without the need for a playbook. These commands are especially useful for simple tasks that don't require a complete playbook or for tasks that need to be performed quickly. Becoming proficient in ad hoc commands can be a valuable skill for both system and network administrators.

Keep this in mind while learning Ansible ad hoc commands: it is essential to understand ad hoc commands and their use cases. Ad hoc commands help in performing quick tasks on a few servers, but they can become complex and hard to maintain. Therefore, it's crucial to learn how to organize these tasks into a structured format using Ansible playbooks. Ansible playbooks are text files that contain a series of instructions or declarative statements to automate tasks. The ultimate goal is to reduce the dependency on manual interventions by administrators, enabling them to focus on more critical tasks. By converting ad hoc commands into Ansible playbooks, we can achieve better control, consistency, and scalability in managing our infrastructure. In short, learning Ansible ad hoc commands is just the first step toward building efficient automation workflows. With Ansible playbooks, we can take automation to the next level by organizing tasks, minimizing errors, and allowing administrators to focus on high-value activities.

Typically, an Ansible ad hoc command follows a structure similar to the following:

```
ansible <target_host> -m <module_name> -a "<arguments>"
```

Here, <target_host> refers to the name of the host or hosts that the command will be run against, <module_name> specifies the name of the module that will be used to perform the task, and <arguments> is any necessary arguments that are passed to the module. By mastering ad hoc commands, you can take advantage of this powerful tool to perform tasks quickly and efficiently on your target hosts.

We have not yet configured any host named "webserver" in Ansible's host file. However, let's assume that we have. If you want to run the "ping" module against the target host named "webserver", you can use the following command as an example. Please note that this is only an example for explanation purposes, and you do not need to run this command.

ansible webserver -m ping

This command executes the "ping" module against the "webserver" host. At a high level, it sends an ICMP ping request to the host and returns a report on whether the host responded or not. However, the Ansible "ping" module behaves differently from the standard ICMP ping tests. We will explore these differences in greater depth later.

As another example, suppose you want to create a new file on the target host(s) and add some content to it. You can achieve this using the "file" and "lineinfile" modules, as shown here:

ansible <target_host> -m file -a "path=/path/to/file.txt state=touch"
ansible <target_host> -m lineinfile -a "path=/path/to/file.txt line='Hello, world!'"

In the first command, we use the "file" module to create an empty file at "/path/to/file.txt" on the target host. The state=touch argument ensures that the file is created even if it doesn't exist yet. In the second command, we use the "lineinfile" module to add the text "Hello, world!" to the file. The line argument specifies the text to add, and the path argument specifies the file to add it to. Note that the arguments are enclosed in quotation marks to ensure that any spaces or special characters are interpreted correctly by Ansible.

To shut down a Fedora (RHEL-based) server using an Ansible ad hoc command, you can leverage the "systemd" module with the "shutdown" command. The following is an example command:

ansible <target_host> -m systemd -a "name=shutdown state=stopped"

Replace <target_host> with the hostname or IP address of the Fedora server you want to shut down. The "systemd" module allows for the management of systemd units, including the "shutdown" unit, which can be used to initiate a system shutdown. The name argument specifies the name of the unit to manage, which, in this case, is "shutdown". The state argument specifies the desired state of the unit, which is "stopped" in this case to initiate a system shutdown. It's worth noting that this command will shut down the server without any warning or confirmation prompt. As a result, use it with caution, and if using the command on a production system, you have access to the out-of-band system management tools. Additionally, the user executing this command must have the necessary permissions to shut down the server.

To restart (reboot) a Fedora (RHEL-based) server using an Ansible ad hoc command, you can use the "systemd" module with the "systemctl" command. Here's an example command:

ansible <target_host> -m systemd -a "name=systemd-journald.service
state=restarted"

Replace <target_host> with the hostname or IP address of the Fedora server you want to restart. The "systemd" module can be used to manage systemd units, which includes the various services that make up the operating system. The name argument specifies the name of the service to manage, which, in this case, is "systemd-journald. service". The state argument specifies the desired state of the service, which is "restarted" in this case to initiate a reboot. It's worth noting that this command will restart the server without any warning or confirmation prompt, so use it with caution. Also, the user executing this command must have the necessary permissions to restart the server.

To shut down or restart an Ubuntu (Debian-based) server using an Ansible ad hoc command, you can use the "command" module with the appropriate "shutdown" command. For immediate server shutdown, you can use the following command:

ansible <target_host> -m command -a "shutdown -h now"

Replace <target_host> with the hostname or IP address of the Ubuntu server you want to shut down. The "-h" option in the "shutdown" command specifies that the server should be powered off immediately, and the "now" argument tells the command to execute the shutdown immediately. It's essential to understand ad hoc commands and syntax, which will help you write good playbooks in YAML. Please note that this command will shut down the server without any warning or confirmation prompt. Hence, you should use it with caution in the production environment. Also, ensure that the user running this command has the necessary permissions to shut down the server. In the next chapter, we'll cover ad hoc commands in more detail, which will help you become comfortable with them and prepare you for writing playbooks.

To restart (reboot) an Ubuntu (Debian-based) server using an Ansible ad hoc command, you can use the "command" module with the appropriate "shutdown" command. Here's an example command:

```
ansible <target_host> -m command -a "shutdown -r now"
```

Replace <target_host> with the hostname or IP address of the Ubuntu server you want to restart. The -r option in the "shutdown" command specifies that the server should be rebooted, and the "now" argument tells the command to execute the restart immediately. Note that this command will restart the server without any warning or confirmation prompt, so be sure to use it with caution. Also, the user running this command must have the necessary permissions to restart the server.

6.3 Running Ad Hoc Commands on Routers and Switches with Ansible

Ansible provides a wide range of vendor-specific modules that can be used to run ad hoc commands on network devices. These modules are tailored to specific operating systems and vendors. For instance, Cisco IOS/IOS XE devices are commonly used in enterprise environments. Therefore, we will use them as an example to explain this concept. The "ios_command" module in Ansible is a useful tool to execute reload operations on Cisco routers using ad hoc commands. By leveraging this module, you can easily issue commands to network devices and perform actions like reloading a router. It is worth noting that this module is specific to Cisco IOS/IOS XE devices.

For Cisco IOS/IOS XE devices, the "ios_command" module is a powerful tool that can be used to perform various actions, such as reloading a router, via ad hoc commands.

```
ansible <target_host> -m ios_command -a "commands='reload'"
ansible <target_host> -m ios_command -a "commands='shutdown'"
```

To shut down a virtual Cisco router or switch using Ansible, you can use the "ios_command" module with the "shutdown" command. For example, the command "ansible <target_host> -m ios_command -a "commands='shutdown'"" will shut down the router with the specified target host. The "commands" argument specifies the command to send to the router, and the "ios_command" module is used to send IOS-style commands to Cisco network devices. However, it's important to use this command with caution, as it will shut down the router without any warning or confirmation prompt. It's important to note that these commands will execute immediately without any warning or confirmation prompt, so use them with caution. Additionally, the user running the Ansible command must have the necessary permissions to perform the shutdown or reload operations on the router. Learning ad hoc commands well is an essential part of mastering Ansible concepts and getting ready for Ansible playbooks.

On the other hand, physical Cisco switches do not have a shutdown button and can only be reloaded. Physical Cisco switches do not have a power button or a mechanism to remotely power off the device. The only way to power off a physical Cisco switch is to unplug it or turn off its power source. Therefore, the "shutdown" command with the "ios_command" module cannot be used to physically power off a physical Cisco switch.

Similarly, you cannot shut down a physical Cisco router using the "ansible <target_host> -m ios_command -a "commands='shutdown'" command. Physical Cisco routers have an on/off switch, but as long as the power switch is in the On position, you cannot shut down the router using the "shutdown" command. The "shutdown" command is not designed to power off the device, but rather to gracefully stop the router's IOS operating system and bring the device into a standby mode. To power off a physical Cisco router, you need to physically turn off the power switch or unplug the power cable.

To clarify, Ansible elevated ad hoc commands are used when running commands or tasks that require elevated privileges or root access on the target hosts. This typically involves using the "sudo" or "become" keyword in the Ansible playbook or ad hoc command. In Chapter 7, we will dive deeper into Ansible ad hoc commands and explore best practices for using them effectively. This includes understanding the different modules available for ad hoc commands, using variables and loops, and troubleshooting common issues. By understanding the concepts of elevated ad hoc commands and how to use them effectively, you will be well equipped to take full advantage of Ansible's powerful automation capabilities.

6.4 Running Elevated Ad Hoc Commands with Ansible

When using Ansible, an ad hoc command is a single command that you can run against one or many hosts. By default, ad hoc commands are executed with the privileges of the remote user, which may not have sufficient permissions to perform some tasks on the target system. However, you can elevate the privileges of ad hoc commands by using the --become or -b option.

Here's an example of an ad hoc command that uses the --become option to run a command with elevated privileges:

```
ansible all -i inventory -m shell -a 'yum install httpd' -become
ansible all -i inventory -m shell -a 'apt install nginx' -b
```

The first command installs the Apache web server package (httpd) on all hosts defined in the inventory file using the yum package manager. The -m shell option specifies that the command should be executed using the shell module, and the -a option passes the command to be executed (yum install httpd). All parameter specifies that the command should be run against all hosts defined in the inventory file. Similarly, the apt package manager is used to install the Nginx web server.

The -b option tells Ansible to become the "root" user (or another user specified by the --become-user option) before executing the command. This allows the command to perform tasks that require elevated privileges, such as installing software packages or modifying system files.

Note that the --become option may prompt you for a password, depending on the authentication method used by Ansible. You can avoid being prompted for a password by using the --ask-become-pass option to provide the password on the command line.

```
ansible <target-host> -m shell -a "apt-get update" --ask-
become-pass
```

If you need to execute a different command, replace apt-get update with the desired command, and use the appropriate module for that command. However, keep in mind that you need sudo access on the target host to use the --ask-become-pass option. If you don't have sudo access, you won't be able to escalate your privileges and execute commands with elevated permissions. When using Ansible to run elevated ad hoc commands, you should use the --become option to escalate your privileges. This will enable you to perform tasks that require elevated privileges on the target system. We have dedicated Chapter 7 to Ansible ad hoc commands, where you can learn more about their power and flexibility.

Tip

Simplify your workflow: manage multiple SSH sessions effortlessly with

SuperPuTTY.

When working with multiple devices over SSH/Telnet, it can be challenging to manage multiple sessions at once. However, with SuperPuTTY, the tabbed version of PuTTY, users can easily manage all their SSH/Telnet sessions from a single window, as shown in Figure 6-1. You will still need to download the latest version of PuTTY before installing SuperPuTTY on your PC.

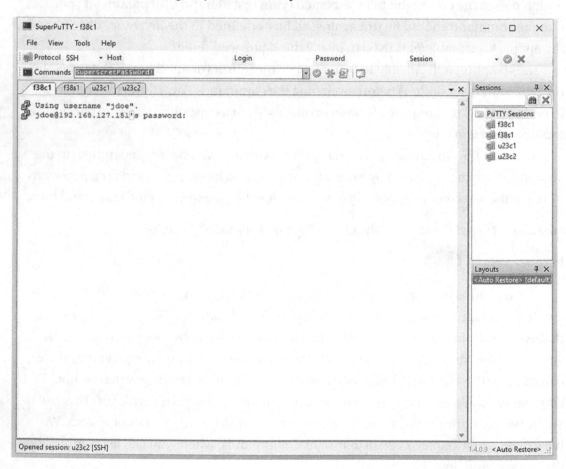

Figure 6-1. *SuperPuTTY in use*

Download PuTTY from the official website: `www.chiark.greenend.org.uk/~sgtatham/putty/latest.html`

Download the SuperPuTTY installer from the official website: `https://github.com/jimradford/superputty/releases`

SuperPuTTY is a tabbed version of PuTTY that enables users to manage multiple SSH/Telnet sessions from a single window. Its tabbed interface allows users to switch between sessions seamlessly, and it has an automatic login feature that can save time and effort. SuperPuTTY also provides users with a variety of customizable settings, including fonts, colors, and key bindings. Additionally, it can integrate with other tools like WinSCP to streamline the process of transferring files between systems. Overall, SuperPuTTY is a powerful and efficient tool for managing multiple sessions and enhancing productivity.

6.5 Summary

Chapter 6 of our Ansible guide focused on running ad hoc commands using Ansible. Ad hoc commands allow users to run a single command on single or multiple systems at once, without the need for a playbook. The chapter began with an overview of SSH in Ansible, including instructions on how to set up and configure SSH connections for the Ansible environment. Afterward, the chapter covered running ad hoc commands on Linux devices, routers, and switches. The section on running ad hoc commands on Linux devices covered the syntax for running ad hoc commands and provided examples of common ad hoc commands used for managing Linux systems. The section on routers and switches provided instructions for configuring Ansible for network devices and examples of ad hoc commands for managing them. Finally, the chapter covered running elevated ad hoc commands with Ansible, which allowed users to perform tasks requiring elevated privileges on target systems. The --become option was used for privilege escalation, and examples of elevated ad hoc commands were provided for managing systems with escalated permissions. By the end of this chapter, readers had a comprehensive understanding of how to use Ansible to run ad hoc commands on a variety of systems and how to escalate privileges when necessary.

## CHAPTER 7

Learning Ansible Basic Concepts II: Ad Hoc Commands – A Beginner's Guide

This chapter will teach you how to work with Ansible ad hoc commands on multiple machines. Throughout the chapter, you will learn the necessary steps to set up a working directory for Ansible ad hoc commands and how to run the Ansible Ping ad hoc command. You will also learn how to specify a user and prompt for their password when running an ad hoc command. This chapter covers a range of ad hoc commands, including testing the SSH connection to the managed nodes, checking the distribution of the operating system, gathering facts from all servers, and checking the system uptime of remote hosts. You will also learn how to create and delete users on Linux, create a user group and assign a user, install and remove software, and reboot and shut down Linux systems. In addition, you will learn the correct terminology for the Ansible Control Machine and Ansible Managed Nodes. You will also understand the difference between ICMP ping and Ansible ping test. By the end of the chapter, you will be able to convert Ansible ad hoc commands into a working Ansible playbook. This chapter is an essential step toward mastering Ansible, and the knowledge gained will help you automate your IT infrastructure.

© Brendan Choi and Erwin Medina 2023
B. Choi and E. Medina, *Introduction to Ansible Network Automation*,
https://doi.org/10.1007/978-1-4842-9624-0_7

In the previous chapter, we discussed the potential use cases of ad hoc commands, but we didn't have the opportunity to gain practical experience with them. In this chapter, we'll delve deeper into ad hoc commands and work with all four Linux services in operation (as shown in Figure 7-1). Our goal is to use the Ansible Control Machine to manage all Ansible Managed Nodes through Ansible ad hoc commands. All tasks will be executed from the Ansible Control Machine, simulating a scenario where you're based in your headquarters, and the nodes represent three servers in different locations. You will need Internet connection for this chapter. By the end of this chapter, you'll have hands-on experience with ad hoc commands and will be able to use them effectively in real-world scenarios.

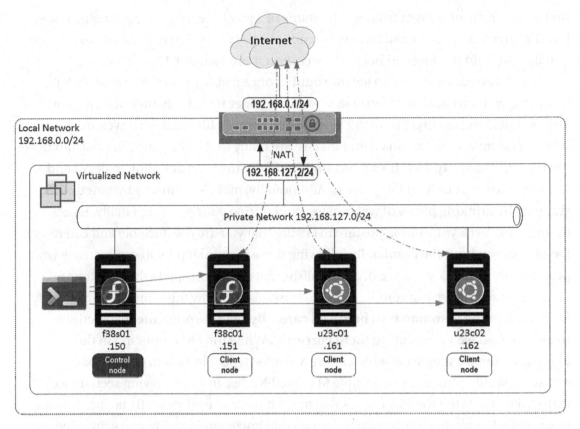

Figure 7-1. *Chapter 7 working topology*

Practicing Ansible ad hoc commands with multiple machines can provide several benefits and help you learn a lot about Ansible. Here are some of how you can benefit from this practice: Firstly, it can help you learn the concepts and syntax of Ansible. You can experiment with different modules, play with command-line arguments, and explore various use cases, which can ultimately help you build your skills and confidence with Ansible. Secondly, ad hoc commands are designed for quick and easy execution of tasks on remote machines. You can use them to perform a wide range of actions, such as installing packages, starting or stopping services, copying files, and more, without having to write a playbook. This can save you a lot of time and effort. Thirdly, ad hoc commands are ideal for testing and troubleshooting specific tasks or configurations on remote machines. You can use them to check if a particular service is running, verify the version of a package, or test connectivity to a specific port. This can help you identify issues and debug problems quickly. Lastly, ad hoc commands are a useful tool to have in your arsenal during emergencies. For instance, you can use them to quickly stop a service

that is causing problems or to check the status of a machine that is experiencing issues.
Overall, practicing Ansible ad hoc commands can provide you with valuable experience
and insights into the tool and help you become a more valuable IT professional.

To get started, we'll need to log into our Fedora Ansible Control Machine, f38s1.
Once logged in, we should create a new working folder for this chapter, such as "ch07".
This will help us stay organized and keep all our practice files in one convenient location.
With this simple step, we can ensure that we are ready to dive into the material and make
the most of our study time. It's a good study habit to maintain attention to detail and
reduce chaos in your learning process. Additionally, make sure to stay hydrated while
studying by drinking plenty of water before and during your practice. Finally, take a
moment to check your sitting posture to ensure that you are comfortable and can remain
focused throughout the chapter. By following these simple steps, you can increase your
productivity and enjoy a sense of accomplishment as you complete the chapter.

To ensure that we can complete the exercises, let's follow these instructions closely.
**We'll type in the commands in bold and carefully read through the instructions
to ensure that we're executing them correctly.** While the last command in the
following exercise may seem a bit lengthy, we must type it in as is to ensure that we
can successfully ping all three Ansible Managed Nodes. In the following section, we'll
learn how to shorten the commands and make them more efficient. By taking the time
to carefully follow these instructions, we can maximize our learning and gain a deeper
understanding of Ansible ad hoc commands.

```
ansible all --key-file /home/jdoe/.ssh/ansible -i inventory -m ping

[jdoe@f38s1 ~]$ mkdir ch07 && cd ch07 # create a new directory "ch07" and
change to ch07 directory
[jdoe@f38s1 ch07]$ cat > inventory # create a new file called inventory
192.168.127.151 # enter the IP addresses of all three managed nodes
192.168.127.161
192.168.127.162
# Use Ctrl+D to save and exit
[jdoe@f38s1 ch07]$ ansible all --list-hosts # this command lists all  nodes
  hosts (3):
    192.168.127.151
    192.168.127.161
    192.168.127.162
```

```
[jdoe@f38s1 ch07]$ ansible all --key-file /home/jdoe/.ssh/ansible -i
inventory -m ping # this command performs ping test to all  nodes
192.168.127.161 | SUCCESS => {
    "ansible_facts": {
        "discovered_interpreter_python": "/usr/bin/python3"
    },
    "changed": false,
    "ping": "pong"
}
192.168.127.162 | SUCCESS => {
    "ansible_facts": {
        "discovered_interpreter_python": "/usr/bin/python3"
    },
    "changed": false,
    "ping": "pong"
}
192.168.127.151 | SUCCESS => {
    "ansible_facts": {
        "discovered_interpreter_python": "/usr/bin/python3"
    },
    "changed": false,
    "ping": "pong"
}
```

To simplify our ad hoc commands, we can utilize the inventory (hosts) and ansible. cfg files. These files allow us to store and manage information about our nodes, making it much easier to execute commands across multiple machines. By using these files, we can significantly shorten our ad hoc commands, making them more efficient and easier to manage. Once you've set up your inventory and ansible.cfg files, you can run the shortened ad hoc command with ease. This streamlined approach not only saves time but also reduces the risk of errors and makes it easier to manage larger-scale deployments. With this powerful tool at your disposal, you can take your Ansible skills to the next level and become a more efficient and effective IT professional.

As we work through Ansible ad hoc commands, it's important to note that the responses generated by these commands can be quite large. To help keep our focus on the most relevant information, this book will only display the initial portion of each response output. Additionally, **any lengthy or repetitive information will be omitted for brevity with the comment "[… omitted for brevity]"**.

By doing this, we can keep our attention on the most important information and avoid getting bogged down by lengthy or irrelevant responses. This approach allows us to quickly identify any issues or areas of interest and move on to the next step in our learning journey. So as we work through the exercises and practice Ansible ad hoc commands, we can rest assured that we are focusing on the most important information and making the most of our study time.

Once you've created your "ansible.cfg" file, you can significantly shorten your ad hoc commands. For example, the previous command "ansible all --key-file /home/jdoe/.ssh/ansible -i inventory -m ping" can be shortened to simply "ansible all -m ping".

ansible all -m ping + inventory file + ansible.cfg file

```
[jdoe@f38s1 ch07]$ cat > ansible.cfg
[defaults]
inventory = ./inventory
private_key_file = /home/jdoe/.ssh/ansible

[jdoe@f38s1 ch07]$ ansible all -m ping
SSH password: ****************
192.168.127.161 | SUCCESS => {
    "ansible_facts": {
        "discovered_interpreter_python": "/usr/bin/python3"
    },
    "changed": false,
    "ping": "pong"
}
[... omitted for brevity]
}
```

ICMP ping is a useful tool for network admins to troubleshoot connectivity issues, diagnose latency, identify packet loss, and verify performance. It operates at a lower level than TCP and UDP, encapsulated within IP packets for network management functions. Unlike TCP and UDP, ICMP doesn't use ports as packets are addressed to a specific IP. Ansible ping is different from ICMP ping as it tests remote host connectivity via SSH, not network connectivity, so it can't substitute ICMP ping for troubleshooting network issues. Network admins should use ICMP ping in conjunction with other diagnostic techniques for more comprehensive results. More tips on this soon.

Tip

Converting the ad hoc "ansible all -m ping" command into ping.yml

playbook

```
---
- hosts: all
  tasks:
  - action: ping
```

To specify a user and prompt for their password when running an ad hoc command, you can use the "--user" and "--ask-pass" options. If you haven't already installed "sshpass" on your Fedora system, you may encounter an error when running the command. In that case, make sure to install "sshpass" on your Ansible Control Machine before executing the command.

ansible all -m ping --user=jdoe --ask-pass

```
[jdoe@f38s1 ch07]$ ansible all -m ping --user=jdoe --ask-pass
SSH password: ****************
192.168.127.151 | FAILED! => {
    "msg": "to use the 'ssh' connection type with passwords or pkcs11_
    provider, you must install the sshpass program"
}
[... omitted for brevity]

[jdoe@f38s1 ch07]$ sudo dnf install sshpass -y
[sudo] password for jdoe: ****************
Fedora 38 - x86_64                              17 kB/s |  32 kB     00:01
Fedora 38 - x86_64                             433 kB/s | 2.9 MB     00:06
[... omitted for brevity]
```

```
[jdoe@f38s1 ch07]$ ansible all -m ping --user=jdoe --ask-pass # run the
same command again, now command is successful
SSH password: ****************
192.168.127.161 | SUCCESS => {
    "ansible_facts": {
        "discovered_interpreter_python": "/usr/bin/python3"
    },
    "changed": false,
    "ping": "pong"
}
[... omitted for brevity]
}
```

When using Ansible, it's important to understand the difference between the regular ICMP ping and Ansible's ping. While the traditional ping command checks if the host is reachable, Ansible's ping tests connectivity between the Ansible Control Machine and the remote host using a specialized Ansible module. This verifies if the target host is properly configured and if Ansible can connect to the host using SSH or any other configured method.

ICMP ping is best used for troubleshooting network connectivity issues, diagnosing latency, identifying packet loss, and verifying network performance. Network admins can determine the source of the problem by sending echo requests and analyzing response time. However, it should be used alongside other diagnostic techniques for a comprehensive analysis. ICMP (Internet Control Message Protocol) operates at a lower level than TCP and UDP, which transport data between applications. ICMP packets are encapsulated within IP packets and used for network management functions, such as testing connectivity. They are addressed to a specific IP address and not to a port number, so there's no need to specify a port number when using ICMP ping.

In contrast, the Ansible Ping module tests remote host connectivity via SSH before executing Ansible modules or playbooks. It cannot substitute for ICMP ping when troubleshooting network issues. Network admins should use ICMP ping in conjunction with other diagnostic techniques for more comprehensive results.

Tip

Difference between ICMP ping, ping to IOS-XE, and Palo Alto PAN-OS

It's important to understand the differences between ICMP ping and the Ansible Ping module. While ICMP is used to test host reachability, the Ansible Ping module uses SSH to check if the remote host is reachable and has the necessary Python libraries installed. This provides more information about the host's services and applications.

Pinging different devices with Ansible may require different modules and receive varying responses. For Linux servers, the "ping" module sends an ICMP echo request and expects an ICMP echo reply response, while the "ios_ping" module for Cisco IOS-XE routers allows for more versatile testing, including TCP, UDP, and ARP packets. The "panos_ping" module for Palo Alto Firewalls sends an ICMP echo request but may receive a different response due to security measures in place. Additional parameters can be set for each module, such as source and destination IP addresses and the number of packets to send. In short, understanding the differences between ICMP and Ansible Ping module and the specific module used for pinging devices based on their type and testing requirements is essential for accurate testing and troubleshooting when using Ansible for network management.

You can **test the SSH connection to the managed nodes** by running a shell command. This will confirm that the login was successful (as indicated by a return code of zero) and that the "id" command was executed on the managed nodes as the "root" user.

ansible all -m shell -a id

```
[jdoe@f38s1 ch07]$ ansible all -m shell -a id
192.168.127.162 | CHANGED | rc=0 >>
uid=1001(jdoe) gid=1001(jdoe) groups=1001(jdoe),27(sudo),100(users)
192.168.127.161 | CHANGED | rc=0 >>
uid=1001(jdoe) gid=1001(jdoe) groups=1001(jdoe),27(sudo),100(users)
192.168.127.151 | CHANGED | rc=0 >>
```

```
uid=1001(jdoe) gid=1001(jdoe) groups=1001(jdoe) context=unconfined_u:unconf
ined_r:unconfined_t:s0-s0:c0.c1023
```

Extend your knowledge:

What if you do not explicitly define the shell in the ad hoc command?

In earlier Linux chapters, you learned that the default shell on most UNIX-based systems, including Linux, is the bash shell (/bin/bash). However, some older operating systems may use a different default shell, such as the Bourne shell (sh), the Korn shell (ksh), or the C shell (csh). To check which shell you are using, use the "echo $SHELL" or "ps -p $$" command.

For example:

```
[jdoe@f38s1 ~]$ echo $SHELL
/bin/bash
[jdoe@f38s1 ~]$ ps -p $$
PID TTY TIME CMD
1070 pts/0 00:00:00 bash
```

If you do not explicitly define the shell to use in your ad hoc commands, Ansible will use the remote user's default shell on the target host. So if the remote user's default shell is Bash, Ansible will use the bash shell by default when running the ad hoc command. If the remote user's default shell is a different shell, Ansible will use that shell by default.

However, if you want to explicitly specify the shell to use in your ad hoc command, you can use the "ansible_shell_type" variable. For example, if you want to use the Bourne shell (sh) instead of the default shell (bash), you can run

```
$ ansible all -i inventory.ini -m shell -a 'command' -e
ansible_shell_type=sh
```

To check the distribution of the operating system running on the managed nodes, you can use the Ansible setup module with the "filter" option set to "ansible_ distribution". To do this, run the following command:

ansible all -m setup -a "filter=ansible_distribution*"

```
[jdoe@f38s1 ch07]$ ansible all -m setup -a "filter=ansible_distribution*"
192.168.127.162 | SUCCESS => {
    "ansible_facts": {
        "ansible_distribution": "Ubuntu",
        "ansible_distribution_file_parsed": true,
        "ansible_distribution_file_path": "/etc/os-release",
        "ansible_distribution_file_variety": "Debian",
        "ansible_distribution_major_version": "23",
        "ansible_distribution_release": "lunar",
        "ansible_distribution_version": "23.04",
        "discovered_interpreter_python": "/usr/bin/python3"
    },
    "changed": false
}
192.168.127.161 | SUCCESS => {
    "ansible_facts": {
        "ansible_distribution": "Ubuntu",
        "ansible_distribution_file_parsed": true,
        "ansible_distribution_file_path": "/etc/os-release",
        "ansible_distribution_file_variety": "Debian",
        "ansible_distribution_major_version": "23",
        "ansible_distribution_release": "lunar",
        "ansible_distribution_version": "23.04",
        "discovered_interpreter_python": "/usr/bin/python3"
    },
    "changed": false
}
192.168.127.151 | SUCCESS => {
    "ansible_facts": {
        "ansible_distribution": "Fedora",
```

```
      "ansible_distribution_file_parsed": true,
      "ansible_distribution_file_path": "/etc/redhat-release",
      "ansible_distribution_file_variety": "RedHat",
      "ansible_distribution_major_version": "38",
      "ansible_distribution_release": "",
      "ansible_distribution_version": "38",
      "discovered_interpreter_python": "/usr/bin/python3"
    },
    "changed": false
}
```

The ansible_distribution fact is one of the many facts that Ansible collects about the managed nodes during a playbook run or an ad hoc command execution. By using the setup module with the filter option set to ansible_distribution, we can retrieve the value of this fact and use it to check the distribution of the operating system running on the managed nodes.

Gathering facts from all servers can provide valuable information about their configurations, such as hardware specifications, network settings, and installed software packages. The "gather_facts" module is a powerful tool for collecting such information and can help administrators quickly discover the ins and outs of each server.

ansible all -m gather_facts

```
[jdoe@f38s1 ch07]$ ansible all -m gather_facts
[... omitted for brevity]
```

To **gather facts from a specific server**, you can use the ansible ad hoc command with the gather_facts module and the --limit option. This allows you to limit the execution to a specific host or a group of hosts. For example, to gather facts from all Ansible Managed Nodes, you can run the command

ansible all -m gather_facts --limit 192.168.127.161

```
[jdoe@f38s1 ch07]$ ansible all -m gather_facts --limit 192.168.127.161
192.168.127.161 | SUCCESS => {
    "ansible_facts": {
        "ansible_all_ipv4_addresses": [
```

```
        "192.168.127.161"
    ],
    "ansible_all_ipv6_addresses": [
        "fe80::20c:29ff:feec:476e"
    ],
    "ansible_apparmor": {
        "status": "enabled"
[... omitted for brevity]
    "changed": false,
    "deprecations": [],
    "warnings": []
}
```

Ansible ad hoc commands provide various ways to **check the system uptime of remote hosts**. The following are three common methods to check the system uptime using Ansible ad hoc commands:

ansible all -m command -a uptime
ansible all -m shell -a uptime
ansible all -a uptime

```
[jdoe@f38s1 ch07]$ ansible all -m command -a uptime
192.168.127.161 | CHANGED | rc=0 >>
 12:59:36 up  1:15,  2 users,  load average: 0.25, 0.17, 0.11
192.168.127.162 | CHANGED | rc=0 >>
 12:59:36 up  1:15,  2 users,  load average: 0.12, 0.13, 0.13
192.168.127.151 | CHANGED | rc=0 >>
 23:59:36 up  1:15,  2 users,  load average: 0.00, 0.08, 0.14
[jdoe@f38s1 ch07]$ ansible all -a uptime
192.168.127.161 | CHANGED | rc=0 >>
 13:00:05 up  1:16,  2 users,  load average: 0.15, 0.15, 0.10
192.168.127.162 | CHANGED | rc=0 >>
 13:00:05 up  1:15,  2 users,  load average: 0.15, 0.13, 0.13
192.168.127.151 | CHANGED | rc=0 >>
 00:00:06 up  1:15,  2 users,  load average: 0.08, 0.08, 0.14
[jdoe@f38s1 ch07]$ ansible all -m shell -a uptime
```

```
192.168.127.162 | CHANGED | rc=0 >>
 12:59:52 up  1:15,  2 users,  load average: 0.09, 0.12, 0.13
192.168.127.161 | CHANGED | rc=0 >>
 12:59:52 up  1:15,  2 users,  load average: 0.20, 0.16, 0.11
192.168.127.151 | CHANGED | rc=0 >>
 23:59:53 up  1:15,  2 users,  load average: 0.00, 0.07, 0.13
```

All three Ansible ad hoc commands you provided are used to execute the "uptime" command on all hosts in the Ansible inventory. However, there is a difference in the way the commands are executed.

ansible all -m command -a uptime: This command runs the "uptime" command using the "command" module. The "command" module executes the command in a non-interactive shell, which means that any environment variables, aliases, or shell functions defined on the remote host will not be available. Also, the command's output will be returned as a string.

ansible all -a uptime: This command runs the "uptime" command using the default module, which is the "command" module. This means that it will behave similarly to the first command mentioned previously. The difference is that you do not need to specify the module explicitly.

ansible all -m shell -a uptime: This command runs the "uptime" command using the "shell" module. The "shell" module executes the command in a shell on the remote host, which means that any environment variables, aliases, or shell functions defined on the remote host will be available. Also, the command's output will be returned as a string.

Checking the free memory or memory usage of hosts is made easy with Ansible ad hoc commands. This feature can significantly simplify an administrator's workload, allowing them to quickly check memory usage on multiple nodes without having to log in to each one individually.

ansible all -a "free -m"

```
[jdoe@f38s1 ch07]$ ansible all -a "free -m"
192.168.127.162 | CHANGED | rc=0 >>
              total        used        free      shared  buff/cache   available
Mem:           3906         442        3381           1         311        3464
Swap:          3881           0        3881
192.168.127.161 | CHANGED | rc=0 >>
```

	total	used	free	shared	buff/cache	available
Mem:	3906	444	3373	1	317	3461
Swap:	3881	0	3881			

192.168.127.151 | CHANGED | rc=0 >>

	total	used	free	shared	buff/cache	available
Mem:	1953	231	1303	1	418	1575
Swap:	1952	0	1952			

In addition to the free memory, you can also check the amount of total memory allocated to the host. To target specific groups of servers with our Ansible ad hoc command, we can use inventory grouping. In this example, we will run the command twice, once for the Fedora node and another for the Ubuntu nodes. This grouping concept can also be applied to playbooks, which we will cover in upcoming chapters.

```
ansible fedora -m shell -a "cat /proc/meminfo|head -2"
ansible ubuntu -m shell -a "cat /proc/meminfo|head -2"
```

```
[jdoe@f38s1 ch07]$ vi inventory
[jdoe@f38s1 ch07]$ cat inventory
[fedora] # group server to the same OS types
192.168.127.151

[ubuntu] ] # group server to the same OS types
192.168.127.161
192.168.127.162

[jdoe@f38s1 ch07]$ ansible fedora -m shell -a "cat /proc/meminfo|head -2" #
target fedora group only
192.168.127.151 | CHANGED | rc=0 >>
MemTotal:       2000820 kB
MemFree:        1335172 kB
[jdoe@f38s1 ch07]$ ansible ubuntu -m shell -a "cat /proc/meminfo|head -2" #
target ubuntu group only
192.168.127.161 | CHANGED | rc=0 >>
MemTotal:       4000468 kB
MemFree:        3455808 kB
```

```
192.168.127.162 | CHANGED | rc=0 >>
MemTotal:         4000468 kB
MemFree:          3462208 kB
```

When managing Linux systems with Ansible, some commands require root user
privileges to execute. Ansible's --become-user option allows us to run commands with
escalated privileges by switching to the root user (using sudo) before executing the
command. This is useful for running commands that modify system files, which can only
be done as the root user. By default, Ansible connects to target hosts using the current
user's credentials, but we can use the --become or --become-user option to execute
commands as a different user (in this case, the root user).

**ansible all -m shell -a "cat /etc/passwd |grep -i jdoe" --become-user
root**

```
[jdoe@f38s1 ch07]$ ansible all -m shell -a "cat /etc/passwd |grep -i
jdoe" --become-user root
192.168.127.161 | CHANGED | rc=0 >>
jdoe:x:1001:1001:John Doe,,,:/home/jdoe:/bin/bash
192.168.127.162 | CHANGED | rc=0 >>
jdoe:x:1001:1001:John Doe,,,:/home/jdoe:/bin/bash
192.168.127.151 | CHANGED | rc=0 >>
jdoe:x:1001:1001::/home/jdoe:/bin/bash
```

Expect includes the mkpasswd command by default. mkpasswd is a utility for
generating password hashes used in Linux systems, and it is commonly installed along
with Expect. When you install Expect on a Linux system, mkpasswd should be available
as part of the installation.

To complete our next exercise, we need to install Expect on our Ansible Control
Machine named f38s1. We need Expect to use the mkpasswd command on Fedora. Once
installed, we can use mkpasswd to generate password hashes for user accounts. After
installing Expect, we can then check whether the user account "jdoe" exists on the target
nodes we are managing with Ansible.

sudo dnf install expect -y

```
[jdoe@f38s1 ch07]$ sudo dnf install expect -y
[sudo] password for jdoe: ***************
```

```
[... omitted for brevity]
[jdoe@f38s1 ch07]$ ansible all -m shell -a "cat /etc/passwd | grep -i jdoe"
192.168.127.161 | CHANGED | rc=0 >>
jdoe:x:1001:1001:John Doe,,,:/home/jdoe:/bin/bash
192.168.127.162 | CHANGED | rc=0 >>
jdoe:x:1001:1001:John Doe,,,:/home/jdoe:/bin/bash
192.168.127.151 | CHANGED | rc=0 >>
jdoe:x:1001:1001::/home/jdoe:/bin/bash
```

To ensure that the user "janedoe" exists on the Ansible Managed Nodes, check if
the user exists, and create the account without a password if it does not exist. The "-a"
argument specifies the shell command to be executed on the remote hosts, which, in
this case, is the command "cat /etc/passwd | grep -i janedoe". This command searches
for the string "janedoe" (case-insensitive) in the "/etc/passwd" file. The second ad hoc
command will add the user "janedoe" to the nodes. We can combine two commands
using the "&&" sign, but in this case, we will run two separate commands. Please note
that this command creates the user without a password.

```
ansible all -m shell -a "cat /etc/passwd | grep -i janedoe"
ansible all -m user -a "name=janedoe state=present" -b -K
```

```
[jdoe@f38s1 ch07]$ ansible all -m shell -a "cat /etc/passwd | grep -i
janedoe"
192.168.127.161 | FAILED | rc=1 >>
non-zero return code
192.168.127.162 | FAILED | rc=1 >>
non-zero return code
192.168.127.151 | FAILED | rc=1 >>
non-zero return code
```

```
[jdoe@f38s1 ch07]$ ansible all -m user -a "name=janedoe
state=present" -b -K
BECOME password: ****************
192.168.127.161 | CHANGED => {
    "ansible_facts": {
        "discovered_interpreter_python": "/usr/bin/python3"
    },
```

```
    "changed": true,
    "comment": "",
    "create_home": true,
    "group": 1002,
    "home": "/home/janedoe",
    "name": "janedoe",
    "shell": "/bin/sh",
    "state": "present",
    "system": false,
    "uid": 1002
}
[... omitted for brevity]

[jdoe@f38s1 ch07]$ ansible all -m shell -a "cat /etc/passwd | grep -i
janedoe"
192.168.127.162 | CHANGED | rc=0 >>
janedoe:x:1002:1002::/home/janedoe:/bin/sh
192.168.127.161 | CHANGED | rc=0 >>
janedoe:x:1002:1002::/home/janedoe:/bin/sh
192.168.127.151 | CHANGED | rc=0 >>
janedoe:x:1002:1002::/home/janedoe:/bin/bash

[jdoe@f38s1 ch07]$ ansible all -m shell -a "tail /etc/passwd"
[... omitted for brevity]
lxd:x:999:100::/var/snap/lxd/common/lxd:/bin/false
jdoe:x:1001:1001:John Doe,,,:/home/jdoe:/bin/bash
janedoe:x:1002:1002::/home/janedoe:/bin/sh
[... omitted for brevity]
```

To remove the user "janedoe" from all servers using Ansible, you can use the following ad hoc command:

```
ansible all -b -K -m user -a "name=janedoe state=absent"
```

```
[jdoe@f38s1 ch07]$ ansible all -b -K -m user -a "name=janedoe state=absent"
BECOME password: ***************
192.168.127.162 | CHANGED => {
```

```
    "ansible_facts": {
        "discovered_interpreter_python": "/usr/bin/python3"
    },
    "changed": true,
    "force": false,
    "name": "janedoe",
    "remove": false,
    "state": "absent"
}
[... omitted for brevity]

[jdoe@f38s1 ch07]$ ansible all -m shell -a "tail /etc/passwd"
[... omitted for brevity]
lxd:x:999:100::/var/snap/lxd/common/lxd:/bin/false
jdoe:x:1001:1001:John Doe,,,:/home/jdoe:/bin/bash
192.168.127.162 | CHANGED | rc=0 >>
[... omitted for brevity]
```

This command uses the user module to remove the user "janedoe" from all servers. The state=absent option specifies that the user should be removed. The -b and -K options are used to run the command with elevated privileges (i.e., as a superuser) and prompt for a password, if necessary.

The command "dnf whatprovides" is used to find which package provides a particular file or command. In this specific case, the command is searching for the package that provides the file or command called "mkpasswd" by using the wildcard symbol "*" before it. The asterisk matches any characters that come before "mkpasswd" in the file or command name. So when you run the command "dnf whatprovides "*/mkpasswd"", it will search for the package that provides the "mkpasswd" file or command, no matter where it is located within the file system. If a package provides the "mkpasswd" file or command, then the output will show the name of the package, its version, and the repository it is installed from. If no package provides the file or command, then the output will be empty.

We are using the Fedora server here, but if using Ubuntu, use mkpasswd to create a sha256 password.

dnf whatprovides "*/mkpasswd"

```
[jdoe@f38s1 ch07]$ sudo dnf install expect -y # expect is already
installed, so nothing to do.
[sudo] password for jdoe:
Last metadata expiration check: 0:59:50 ago on Mon 27 Mar 2023 23:49:14.
Package expect-5.45.4-18.fc38.x86_64 is already installed.
Dependencies resolved.
Nothing to do.
Complete!
[jdoe@f38s1 ch07]$ dnf whatprovides "*/mkpasswd" # search for all mkpasswd
package on your local system
Fedora 38 - x86_64                          4.9 MB/s |  83 MB    00:16
Fedora 38 openh264 (From Cisco) - x86_64    1.1 kB/s | 2.5 kB    00:02
Fedora Modular 38 - x86_64                  1.1 MB/s | 2.8 MB    00:02
Fedora 38 - x86_64 - Updates                119  B/s | 257  B    00:02
Fedora Modular 38 - x86_64 - Updates        228  B/s | 257  B    00:01
Fedora 38 - x86_64 - Test Updates           1.7 MB/s | 6.2 MB    00:03
Fedora Modular 38 - x86_64 - Test Updates   228  B/s | 257  B    00:01
cjdns-21.1-8.fc38.x86_64 : The privacy-friendly network without borders
Repo       : fedora
Matched from:
Filename   : /usr/libexec/cjdns/mkpasswd

mkpasswd-5.5.15-3.fc38.x86_64 : Encrypt a password with crypt(3) function
using a salt
Repo       : fedora
Matched from:
Filename   : /usr/bin/mkpasswd
Filename   : /usr/share/doc/mkpasswd
Filename   : /usr/share/licenses/mkpasswd
```

If you are using a Red Hat–based Linux distribution, such as Fedora, CentOS, AlmaLinux, or Rocky Linux, you can create a salted password using Python. Python provides a built-in module called "crypt" that can be used to generate a salted hash for a given password. This can improve the security of your system by making it harder for attackers to crack user passwords.

```
python3 -c 'import crypt; print(crypt.crypt("Ansible54321", crypt.
mksalt(crypt.METHOD_SHA512)))'
```

```
[jdoe@f38s1 ch07]$ python3 -V
Python 3.11.2
[jdoe@f38s1 ch07]$ python3 -c 'import crypt; print(crypt.
crypt("Ansible54321", crypt.mksalt(crypt.METHOD_SHA512)))'
<string>:1: DeprecationWarning: 'crypt' is deprecated and slated for
removal in Python 3.13
$6$V1dA.5p.ZdpKmq8I$f/qqX83U1BfEoqDvuOwhSh5kyN/kZjV4A.
EtQ7DbeMpqxWi2u55VOT3UGlAdZ4DYMP8/lXmNRNjJbi9N1uPlK1
```

After generating the salted password using Python, you can create a new user account on your Red Hat–based Linux distribution, such as Fedora, CentOS, AlmaLinux, or Rocky Linux, using Ansible's user module and argument name and password parameters; take special attention to the use of the single and double quotations.

```
ansible all -m user -a 'name=jane password="$6$V1dA.5p.ZdpKmq8I$f/
qqX83U1BfEoqDvuOwhSh5kyN/k
ZjV4A.EtQ7DbeMpqxWi2u55VOT3UGlAdZ4DYMP8/lXmNRNjJbi9N1uPlK1"' -b -K
```

```
[jdoe@f38s1 ch07]$ ansible all -m user -a 'name=jane
password="$6$V1dA.5p.ZdpKmq8I$f/qqX83U1BfEoqDvuOwhSh5kyN/kZjV4A.
EtQ7DbeMpqxWi2u55VOT3UGlAdZ4DYMP8/lXmNRNjJbi9N1uPlK1"' -b -K
BECOME password: ***************
192.168.127.162 | CHANGED => {
    "ansible_facts": {
        "discovered_interpreter_python": "/usr/bin/python3"
    },
    "changed": true,
    "comment": "",
```

```
    "create_home": true,
    "group": 1002,
    "home": "/home/jane",
    "name": "jane",
    "password": "NOT_LOGGING_PASSWORD",
    "shell": "/bin/sh",
    "state": "present",
    "system": false,
    "uid": 1002
}
[... omitted for brevity]
```

After creating a new user account with the salted password, you can verify that the password has been stored securely by checking the /etc/shadow file on your Red Hat–based Linux distribution, such as Fedora, CentOS, AlmaLinux, or Rocky Linux. The /etc/shadow file stores password hashes for user accounts and is only accessible by the root user.

ansible all -m shell -a "sudo tail /etc/shadow" -b -K

```
[jdoe@f38s1 ch07]$ ansible all -m shell -a "sudo tail /etc/shadow" -b -K
BECOME password: ***************
192.168.127.161 | CHANGED | rc=0 >>
syslog:!:19435::::::
uuidd:!:19435::::::
tcpdump:!:19435::::::
tss:!:19435::::::
landscape:!:19435::::::
fwupd-refresh:!:19435::::::
brendan:$6$KZXDxIh6lwewjP8v$sdwOODIVUbdOMsbcN4F/rdYvLFjsInWNy
8G5djQdTBTL4LBd9jYguEZiMGP1HjEHA8bXmAISku54tv5R67rpB/:19435:0:99999:7:::
lxd:!:19435::::::
jdoe:$y$j9T$jqB4oyOA8hkkVA7jzPUjq.$OwSVHk/
tQcbDHDBYtXRTsJSTDtjxO3jgWTsCWST6Ou4:19442:0:99999:7:::
jane:$6$V1dA.5p.ZdpKmq8I$f/qqX83U1BfEoqDvuOwhSh5kyN/kZjV4A.
EtQ7DbeMpqxWi2u55VOT3UGlAdZ4DYMP8/lXmNRNjJbi9N1uPlK1:19443:0:99999:7:::
```

```
192.168.127.162 | CHANGED | rc=0 >>
```
[... omitted for brevity]

To check if the salted password has been stored successfully, you can open the /etc/
shadow file using a text editor or a command-line utility, such as cat or less, and look for
the line corresponding to the user account you just created. The salted password will be
located in the second field of the line, between two consecutive colons (:), represented
by a long string of characters.

Now, to create a group called "dragonfly" using an Ansible ad hoc command, you
can run the following command:

ansible all -m group -a "name=dragonfly state=present" -b -K

```
[jdoe@f38s1 ch07]$ ansible all -m group -a "name=dragonfly
state=present" -b -K
BECOME password: ***************
192.168.127.162 | CHANGED => {
    "ansible_facts": {
        "discovered_interpreter_python": "/usr/bin/python3"
    },
    "changed": true,
    "gid": 1003,
    "name": "dragonfly",
    "state": "present",
    "system": false
}
```
[... omitted for brevity]
```
[jdoe@f38s1 ch07]$ ansible fedora -m shell -a "tail /etc/group -n 3" -b -K
BECOME password: ***************
192.168.127.151 | CHANGED | rc=0 >>
jdoe:x:1001:
jane:x:1002:
dragonfly:x:1003:
[jdoe@f38s1 ch07]$ ansible ubuntu -m shell -a "tail /etc/group -n 3" -b -K
BECOME password: ***************
192.168.127.162 | CHANGED | rc=0 >>
```

```
jdoe:x:1001:
jane:x:1002:
dragonfly:x:1003:
192.168.127.161 | CHANGED | rc=0 >>
jdoe:x:1001:
jane:x:1002:
dragonfly:x:1003:
```

To create a user named "hugh" on Fedora servers only, you can assign them to the "dragonfly" group and create a home directory for them. To do this, run the following command:

```
ansible fedora -m user -a "name=hugh group=dragonfly
ansible fedora -m shell -a "tail /etc/passwd -n 2"
ansible fedora -m shell -a "ls /home/"
[jdoe@f38s1 ch07]$ ansible fedora -m user -a "name=hugh group=dragonfly
createhome=yes" -b -K
BECOME password: ***************
192.168.127.151 | CHANGED => {
    "ansible_facts": {
        "discovered_interpreter_python": "/usr/bin/python3"
    },
    "changed": true,
    "comment": "",
    "create_home": true,
    "group": 1003,
    "home": "/home/hugh",
    "name": "hugh",
    "shell": "/bin/bash",
    "state": "present",
    "system": false,
    "uid": 1003
}
[jdoe@f38s1 ch07]$ ansible fedora -m shell -a "tail /etc/passwd -n 2"
192.168.127.151 | CHANGED | rc=0 >>
jane:x:1002:1002::/home/jane:/bin/bash
```

```
hugh:x:1003:1003::/home/hugh:/bin/bash
[jdoe@f38s1 ch07]$ ansible fedora -m shell -a "ls /home/"
192.168.127.151 | CHANGED | rc=0 >>
brendan
hugh
jane
janedoe
jdoe
[jdoe@f38s1 ch07]$
```

To create a directory called "tadpole" under the directory of the user "jdoe" on Ubuntu nodes, you can use a similar method as before. Run the following command on each Ubuntu node where you want to create the directory:

ansible ubuntu -m file -a "path=/home/jdoe/tadpole state=directory

mode=0755" -b -K

```
[jdoe@f38s1 ch07]$ ansible ubuntu -m file -a "path=/home/jdoe/tadpole
state=directory mode=0755" -b -K
BECOME password: ***************
192.168.127.162 | CHANGED => {
    "ansible_facts": {
        "discovered_interpreter_python": "/usr/bin/python3"
    },
    "changed": true,
    "gid": 0,
    "group": "root",
    "mode": "0755",
    "owner": "root",
    "path": "/home/jdoe/tadpole",
    "size": 4096,
    "state": "directory",
    "uid": 0
}
[... omitted for brevity]

[jdoe@f38s1 ch07]$ ansible ubuntu -m shell -a "ls -lh /home/jdoe/"
```

```
192.168.127.161 | CHANGED | rc=0 >>
total 4.0K
drwxr-xr-x 2 root root 4.0K Mar 27 14:15 tadpole
192.168.127.162 | CHANGED | rc=0 >>
total 4.0K
drwxr-xr-x 2 root root 4.0K Mar 27 14:15 tadpole
```

To create a file under the newly created directory on Ubuntu nodes, run the following command, specifying the name and contents of the file as needed:

ansible ubuntu -m file -a "path=/home/jdoe/tadpole/frogeggs.txt

state=touch

mode=0755" -b -K

```
[jdoe@f38s1 ch07]$ ansible ubuntu -m file -a "path=/home/jdoe/tadpole/
frogeggs.txt state=touch mode=0755" -b -K
BECOME password: ***************
192.168.127.161 | CHANGED => {
    "ansible_facts": {
        "discovered_interpreter_python": "/usr/bin/python3"
    },
    "changed": true,
    "dest": "/home/jdoe/tadpole/frogeggs.txt",
    "gid": 0,
    "group": "root",
    "mode": "0755",
    "owner": "root",
    "size": 0,
    "state": "file",
    "uid": 0
}
[... omitted for brevity]

[jdoe@f38s1 ch07]$ ansible ubuntu -m shell -a "ls -lh /home/jdoe/tadpole/"
192.168.127.161 | CHANGED | rc=0 >>
total 0
```

```
-rwxr-xr-x 1 root root 0 Mar 27 14:15 frogeggs.txt
192.168.127.162 | CHANGED | rc=0 >>
total 0
-rwxr-xr-x 1 root root 0 Mar 27 14:15 frogeggs.txt
```

At this stage, we want to check the free disk space of servers to make sure that we have enough space. To do this, you can use the following command:

ansible all -a "df -h"
ansible fedora -m shell -a 'free -m'

```
[jdoe@f38s1 ch07]$ ansible all -a "df -h"
192.168.127.162 | CHANGED | rc=0 >>
Filesystem                          Size  Used Avail Use% Mounted on
tmpfs                               391M  1.6M  390M   1% /run
/dev/mapper/ubuntu--vg-ubuntu--lv    29G  8.1G   19G  31% /
tmpfs                               2.0G     0  2.0G   0% /dev/shm
tmpfs                               5.0M     0  5.0M   0% /run/lock
/dev/sda2                           2.0G  296M  1.5G  17% /boot
tmpfs                               391M  4.0K  391M   1% /run/user/1001
192.168.127.161 | CHANGED | rc=0 >>
Filesystem                          Size  Used Avail Use% Mounted on
tmpfs                               391M  1.6M  390M   1% /run
/dev/mapper/ubuntu--vg-ubuntu--lv    29G  8.1G   19G  31% /
tmpfs                               2.0G     0  2.0G   0% /dev/shm
tmpfs                               5.0M     0  5.0M   0% /run/lock
/dev/sda2                           2.0G  296M  1.5G  17% /boot
tmpfs                               391M  4.0K  391M   1% /run/user/1001
192.168.127.151 | CHANGED | rc=0 >>
Filesystem                Size  Used Avail Use% Mounted on
devtmpfs                  4.0M     0  4.0M   0% /dev
tmpfs                     977M     0  977M   0% /dev/shm
tmpfs                     391M  1.3M  390M   1% /run
/dev/mapper/fedora-root    15G  2.4G   13G  17% /
tmpfs                     977M   96K  977M   1% /tmp
/dev/nvme0n1p2            960M  282M  679M  30% /boot
tmpfs                     196M     0  196M   0% /run/user/1001
```

```
[jdoe@f38s1 ch07]$ ansible fedora -m shell -a 'free -m'
192.168.127.151 | CHANGED | rc=0 >>
               total        used        free      shared  buff/cache   available
Mem:            1953         247        1279           1         426        1558
Swap:           1952           0        1952
[jdoe@f38s1 ch07]$ ansible ubuntu -m shell -a 'free -m'
192.168.127.161 | CHANGED | rc=0 >>
               total        used        free      shared  buff/cache   available
Mem:            3906         493        3319           1         324        3413
Swap:           3881           0        3881
192.168.127.162 | CHANGED | rc=0 >>
               total        used        free      shared  buff/cache   available
Mem:            3906         495        3317           1         323        3411
Swap:           3881           0        3881
[jdoe@f38s1 ch07]$
```

We want to install the "tree" package on our Linux servers, which will allow users to view directory structures in a more organized and user-friendly way. To install this package, you can use the "yum" module on Fedora servers and the "apt" module on Ubuntu nodes.

ansible fedora -m yum -a name=tree -b -K

```
[jdoe@f38s1 ch07]$ ansible fedora -m yum -a name=tree -b -K
BECOME password: ***************
192.168.127.151 | SUCCESS => {
    "ansible_facts": {
        "discovered_interpreter_python": "/usr/bin/python3"
    },
    "changed": false,
    "msg": "Nothing to do",
    "rc": 0,
    "results": []
}
[jdoe@f38s1 ch07]$ ansible fedora -m shell -a 'tree'
192.168.127.151 | CHANGED | rc=0 >>
.
```

```
0 directories, 0 files
[jdoe@f38s1 ch07]$ ansible ubuntu -m apt -a "name=tree state=present" -b -K
BECOME password: ****************
192.168.127.161 | CHANGED => {
    "ansible_facts": {
        "discovered_interpreter_python": "/usr/bin/python3"
    },
    "cache_update_time": 1679802650,
    "cache_updated": false,
    "changed": true,
    "stderr": "",
[... omitted for brevity]

[jdoe@f38s1 ch07]$ ansible ubuntu -m shell -a 'tree' # run the tree command
using ansible ad hoc
192.168.127.162 | CHANGED | rc=0 >>
.
└── tadpole
    └── frogeggs.txt

2 directories, 1 file
192.168.127.161 | CHANGED | rc=0 >>
.
└── tadpole
    └── frogeggs.txt

2 directories, 1 file
[jdoe@f38s1 ch07]$
```

Please ensure that you are following the book's guidelines while working on
your development environment on your PC. Let's remove the software using the
"state=absent" parameter to remove the package tree and check the service status.

ansible fedora -m yum -a "name=tree state=absent" -b -K

```
[jdoe@f38s1 ch07]$ ansible fedora -m yum -a "name=tree state=absent" -b -K
BECOME password: ****************
192.168.127.151 | CHANGED => {
```

```
    "ansible_facts": {
        "discovered_interpreter_python": "/usr/bin/python3"
    },
    "changed": true,
    "msg": "",
    "rc": 0,
    "results": [
        "Removed: tree-2.1.0-2.fc38.x86_64"
    ]
}
[jdoe@f38s1 ch07]$ ansible fedora -m shell -a 'tree'
192.168.127.151 | FAILED | rc=127 >>
/bin/sh: line 1: tree: command not foundnon-zero return code

[jdoe@f38s1 ch07]$ ansible ubuntu -m apt -a "name=tree state=absent" -b -K
BECOME password: ****************
192.168.127.162 | CHANGED => {
    "ansible_facts": {
        "discovered_interpreter_python": "/usr/bin/python3"
    },
    "changed": true,
    "stderr": "",
    "stderr_lines": [],
[... omitted for brevity]
[jdoe@f38s1 ch07]$ ansible ubuntu -m shell -a 'tree'
192.168.127.161 | FAILED | rc=127 >>
/bin/sh: 1: tree: not foundnon-zero return code
192.168.127.162 | FAILED | rc=127 >>
/bin/sh: 1: tree: not foundnon-zero return code
```

After issuing the command, open the VMware Workstation terminal console for all nodes and see them rebooting. The rebooting will take some time, so your script looks like it hung, but when the servers come back online, it will confirm the successful reboot and complete the ad hoc command execution. Give a minute or two and you will see the CHANGED message as shown here:

```
ansible all -m reboot -a reboot_timeout=600 -u jdoe -b -K
```

```
[jdoe@f38s1 ch07]$ ansible all -m reboot -a reboot_timeout=600 -u
jdoe -b -K
BECOME password: ***************
192.168.127.151 | CHANGED => {
    "changed": true,
    "elapsed": 51,
    "rebooted": true
}
192.168.127.161 | CHANGED => {
    "changed": true,
    "elapsed": 61,
    "rebooted": true
}
192.168.127.162 | CHANGED => {
    "changed": true,
    "elapsed": 62,
    "rebooted": true
}
```

Expand your knowledge:

A full breakdown of Ansible ad hoc command for better understanding

Let's break down the command used previously to understand all parts of the command; the command used previously was "ansible all -m reboot -a reboot_timeout=600 -u jdoe -b -K", and here is a full breakdown:

ansible: Ansible command that is used to manage infrastructure, automate tasks, and deploy software.

all: Refers to the target hosts or inventory groups that the command will be applied to. In this case, all refers to all hosts that are defined in our inventory file.

-m reboot: reboot is an Ansible module that will be used to perform the task of rebooting the target hosts.

-a reboot_timeout=600: This is an argument or option for an Ansible module that will be passed to the reboot module. In this case, it sets the "reboot_timeout" parameter to 600 seconds (10 minutes). This means that the target hosts will wait for up to ten minutes for a reboot before timing out and resuming normal operations. If you don't define this value, the timeout value will default to 600 seconds.

-u jdoe: jdoe is the remote user account that will be used to authenticate to the target hosts.

-b: Specifies that the sudo (or equivalent) command should be used to execute the task with elevated privileges.

-K: Prompts the user to enter the password for the remote user account specified with the -u option.

In a single sentence, this command instructs Ansible to reboot all the hosts defined in the inventory file, with a maximum wait time of ten minutes, and use the jdoe user account with sudo privileges. Please increase the time in the production if you believe that any server reboot will take more than ten minutes.

This command will **shut down your systems** immediately, so use it with care. If you are running a such command on live production servers, you may need out-of-band console access or admin access to the vCenter to manually start your servers. We are performing everything in a safe lab environment, so run the command and see the effects of the command.

ansible all -m shell -a "sudo shutdown now" -b -K

```
[jdoe@f38s1 ch07]$ ansible all -m shell -a "sudo shutdown now" -b -K
BECOME password: ***************
192.168.127.161 | UNREACHABLE! => {
    "changed": false,
    "msg": "Failed to connect to the host via ssh: Shared connection to
    192.168.127.161 closed.",
```

```
    "unreachable": true
}
192.168.127.151 | UNREACHABLE! => {
    "changed": false,
    "msg": "Failed to connect to the host via ssh: Shared connection to
    192.168.127.151 closed.",
    "unreachable": true
}
192.168.127.162 | UNREACHABLE! => {
    "changed": false,
    "msg": "Failed to connect to the host via ssh: Shared connection to
    192.168.127.162 closed.",
    "unreachable": true
}
```

Now, manually power on the nodes from the VMware Workstation console.

To check the system uptime using the shell module, you can use the "uptime" argument. Make sure to enclose the argument in double quotation marks to ensure proper execution. This command will display the current uptime of the system.

ansible all -m shell -a "uptime"

```
[jdoe@f38s1 ch07]$ ansible all -m shell -a "uptime"
192.168.127.162 | CHANGED | rc=0 >>
 13:24:57 up 2 min,  1 user,  load average: 0.25, 0.27, 0.11
192.168.127.161 | CHANGED | rc=0 >>
 13:24:57 up 2 min,  1 user,  load average: 0.28, 0.35, 0.16
192.168.127.151 | CHANGED | rc=0 >>
 00:24:57 up 3 min,  1 user,  load average: 0.49, 0.52, 0.24
```

First, create a new file named "ymmysnails.txt". Next, use the copy module to transfer the file from the Control Machine to all the managed nodes. You can then check if the file was successfully transferred by running a quick shell command on the managed nodes. The ad hoc command for this task may be lengthy, but you can simplify the process by using the cut-and-paste feature of your SSH.

```
ansible all -m copy -a "src=/home/jdoe/ch07/yummysnails.txt dest=/home/
jdoe/yummysnails.txt owner=jdoe group=jdoe mode=0644" -b -K
```

```
[jdoe@f38s1 ch07]$ cat > yummysnails.txt
French cuisine includes yummy buttered snails.
Yummy buttery snails.
I love yummy snails.
[jdoe@f38s1 ch07]$ ls
ansible.cfg  inventory  yummysnails.txt
[jdoe@f38s1 ch07]$ ansible all -m copy -a "src=/home/jdoe/ch07/yummysnails.
txt dest=/home/jdoe/yummysnails.txt owner=jdoe group=jdoe mode=0644" -b -K
BECOME password: ****************
192.168.127.161 | CHANGED => {
    "ansible_facts": {
        "discovered_interpreter_python": "/usr/bin/python3"
    },
    "changed": true,
    "checksum": "5d03a68ad64bf5397dd0efb6440d058b6349ff32",
    "dest": "/home/jdoe/yummysnails.txt",
    "gid": 1000,
    "group": "jdoe",
    "md5sum": "daa13fe86fdfc2154ee4b96cb4d84ac6",
    "mode": "0644",
    "owner": "jdoe",
    "size": 94,
    "src": "/home/jdoe/.ansible/tmp/ansible-
    tmp-1680096489.3677917-1731-222689413444096/source",
    "state": "file",
    "uid": 1000
}
192.168.127.162 | CHANGED => {
[... omitted for brevity]

[jdoe@f38s1 ch07]$ ansible all -m shell -a "cat /home/jdoe/yummysnails.txt"
192.168.127.161 | CHANGED | rc=0 >>
French cuisine includes yummy buttered snails.
```

```
Yummy buttery snails.
I love yummy snails.
192.168.127.162 | CHANGED | rc=0 >>
[... omitted for brevity]
```

Install chrony to transition to Ansible-playbook Demo, and install the time server using the yum or dnf package manager on Fedora, f38c1 only. chrony is a time synchronization tool for Linux that offers fast synchronization, hardware timestamping, and dual-server modes. It can synchronize time with remote servers or local hardware clocks and is useful in unstable network situations or when strict timing is required. NTP services usually use TCP port 123.

```
ansible fedora -m yum -a "name=chrony state=installed" -b -K
```

```
[jdoe@f38s1 ch07]$ ansible fedora -m yum -a "name=chrony
state=installed" -b -K
BECOME password: ***************
192.168.127.151 | SUCCESS => {
    "ansible_facts": {
        "discovered_interpreter_python": "/usr/bin/python3"
    },
    "changed": false,
    "msg": "Nothing to do",
    "rc": 0,
    "results": []
}
```

Tip

Converting the ad hoc "ansible fedora -m yum -a "name=chrony

state=installed" -b -K" command into a YAML playbook

To convert the preceding Ansible ad hoc command into a YAML playbook, we can create a file with a ".yml" or ".yaml" file extension and define the necessary parameters in YAML format. For example, the playbook could look like this:

```
---
- name: Install chrony package on Fedora hosts
  hosts: fedora
become: true
  become_method: sudo
  vars:
    ansible_become_pass: Super5ecretPa55word!

  tasks:
    - name: Install chrony package
      yum:
        name: chrony
        state: installed
```

This Ansible playbook is designed to install the "chrony" package on the hosts in the "fedora" group. It has a descriptive name of "Install chrony package on Fedora hosts" to indicate its purpose. The playbook includes one task to achieve its objective.

The task is named "Install chrony package". This task uses the "yum" module to install the "chrony" package on each target host. The desired state of the package is set to "installed" to ensure that the package is installed.

To execute this playbook, it targets the hosts in the "fedora" group. It also sets the become parameter to true, which allows the playbook to run with escalated privileges, and specifies the become_method as "sudo". This is done to ensure that the playbook has the necessary permissions to install the "chrony" package. The playbook also defines a variable named ansible_become_pass and sets its value to "Super5ecretPa55word!", which is used as the password for privilege escalation.

Use the Ansible command to start the "chronyd" service on hosts that are members of the "fedora" group, which only contains a single node, f38c1. In reverse, if you want to stop the chronyd's NTP service, then you simply need to change the "state=started" to "state=stopped".

Tip

Converting the ad hoc "ansible fedora -m service -a "name=chronyd

state=started" -b -K" command into a YAML playbook

This Ansible playbook is designed to check whether the "chronyd" service is running on the hosts in the "fedora" group. It has a descriptive name of "Check if chronyd is running" to indicate its purpose. The playbook includes two tasks to achieve its objective.

```
---
- name: Check if chronyd is running
  hosts: fedora
  become: true
  become_method: sudo
  vars:
    ansible_become_pass: Super5ecretPa55word!

  tasks:
    - name: Check chronyd status
      service:
        name: chronyd
        state: started
      register: chronyd_status

    - name: Print chronyd status
      debug:
        msg: "chronyd service is {{ chronyd_status.state }} on {{
        inventory_hostname }}"
```

The first task is named "Check chronyd status". This task uses the "service" module to check the status of the "chronyd" service on each target host. The desired state of the service is set to "started" to ensure that the service is running. The result of this task is registered in a variable named chronyd_status for future use.

The second task is named "Print chronyd status". This task uses the "debug" module to print a message that includes the status of the "chronyd" service and the hostname of the target host. The message is constructed using the value of chronyd_status.state and the inventory_hostname variable, which refers to the hostname of the current target host.

To execute this playbook, it targets the hosts in the "fedora" group. It also sets the become parameter to true, which allows the playbook to run with escalated privileges, and specifies the become_method as "sudo". This is done to ensure that the playbook has the necessary permissions to check the status of the "chronyd" service. The playbook also defines a variable named ansible_become_pass and sets its value to "Super5ecretPa55word!", which is used as the password for privilege escalation.

Use the Ansible command to stop the "chronyd" service on hosts that are members of the "fedora" group, which only contains a single node, f38c1. In reverse, if you want to start the chronyd's NTP service, then you simply need to change the "state=stopped" to "state=started".

ansible fedora -m service -a "name=chronyd state=stopped" -b -K

```
[jdoe@f38s1 ch07]$ ansible fedora -m service -a "name=chronyd
state=stopped" -b -K
BECOME password: ***************
192.168.127.151 | CHANGED => {
    "ansible_facts": {
        "discovered_interpreter_python": "/usr/bin/python3"
    },
    "changed": true,
    "name": "chronyd",
    "state": "stopped",
    "status": {
        "AccessSELinuxContext": "system_u:object_r:chronyd_unit_file_t:s0",
        "ActiveEnterTimestamp": "Thu 2023-03-30 23:12:31 AEDT",
        "ActiveEnterTimestampMonotonic": "20346690",
        "ActiveExitTimestampMonotonic": "0",
        "ActiveState": "active",
[... omitted for brevity]
```

In the previous example, we used an Ansible ad hoc command to check the status of the chronyd service. However, we can create a more structured and reusable solution by writing an Ansible playbook that achieves the same task. Here's an example of a YAML playbook that checks if the chronyd service is running.

Tip

Converting the ad hoc "ansible fedora -m service -a "name=chronyd

state=stopped" -b -K" command into a YAML playbook

The following Ansible playbook achieves the same objective as the previous example, which was to manage the state of the "chronyd" service on target hosts. However, this time the playbook sets the desired state to "stopped" using the same service module. The YAML script is largely self-explanatory and easy to follow.

```
---
- name: Check if chronyd is running
  hosts: fedora
  become: true
  become_method: sudo
  vars:
    ansible_become_pass: Super5ecretPa55word!

  tasks:
    - name: Check chronyd status
      service:
        name: chronyd
        state: stopped
      register: chronyd_status

    - name: Print chronyd status
      debug:
        msg: "chronyd service is {{ chronyd_status.state }}
        on {{ inventory_hostname }}"
```

This completes the Ansible ad hoc practice chapter.

Tip

Terminology confusion over Ansible Control Machine and Ansible Managed Nodes?

To reduce confusion regarding the terminology used in Ansible, it is important to understand that there are different terms used to refer to the same concept. In Ansible, the machine used to manage the automation of tasks on remote hosts is commonly referred to as the Ansible Control Machine or Ansible control node. However, the more commonly used term in official documentation and certification programs is "Ansible Control Machine."

Similarly, the remote hosts that are being managed by Ansible are referred to as Ansible Machines or Ansible Nodes. However, the more commonly used term is "Ansible Managed Node," which is used to refer to the machines or systems that are being managed by Ansible.

To provide clarity and consistency throughout this book, we will consistently use the terms "Ansible Control Machine" to refer to the server and "Ansible Managed Node" to refer to remote nodes. This will help readers to better understand the concepts being discussed and avoid any potential confusion that might arise from using different terms interchangeably.

7.1 Summary

This chapter focused on teaching readers how to work with Ansible ad hoc commands on multiple machines. Completing the last two chapters is fundamental to the success to the rest of the book, to say the least. The chapter began by guiding readers through setting up a working directory for Ansible ad hoc command practice and running the Ansible ping ad hoc command. The chapter also covered how to specify a user and prompt for their password when running an ad hoc command. Throughout the chapter, readers practiced a range of ad hoc commands, including testing the SSH connection to the managed nodes, checking the distribution of the operating system, gathering facts from all servers, and checking the system uptime of remote hosts. The chapter also covered how to create and delete users on Linux, create a user group and assign a user, install and remove software, and reboot and shut down Linux systems. Readers learned the correct terminology for the Ansible Control Machine and Ansible Managed Nodes. Additionally, the chapter helped readers understand the difference between ICMP ping and Ansible ping test. By the end of the chapter, readers were able to convert Ansible ad hoc commands into a simple working Ansible playbook. This chapter was a critical step toward mastering Ansible, and the knowledge gained will help readers automate their IT infrastructure.

## CHAPTER 8

Learning Ansible Basic Concepts II: Using when, Improving Playbook, and Targeting Nodes

In this chapter, we will delve deeper into the basics of Ansible by exploring topics such as improving your playbook, using when conditionals, and targeting specific nodes. We will first review the considerations you should make before writing your Ansible playbooks, such as understanding idempotency, familiarizing yourself with Ansible error messages, and using the verbose mode to gain more information about Ansible's operation. We will then discuss how to add more tasks to your existing playbook and keep packages always up to date using "state: latest". Additionally, we will cover how to use your existing playbook to create an uninstall playbook and how to write a working playbook for both Ubuntu and Fedora. Next, we will explore how to use "when" conditionals to add another OS type to your playbook and how to target a specific host or group of hosts. We will also discuss how to refactor an Ansible playbook to make it more efficient. Finally, we will examine how to target specific nodes and check services from the control node. We will also cover how to print output using Ansible's debug module and how to use "ignore_errors: yes" in your play to ignore errors and let your play complete. To apply these concepts in practice, we will show you how to install Samba and create a Samba user on a Fedora client using a playbook.

© Brendan Choi and Erwin Medina 2023
B. Choi and E. Medina, *Introduction to Ansible Network Automation*,
https://doi.org/10.1007/978-1-4842-9624-0_8

In the previous chapters, you've gained a solid understanding of Ansible ad hoc commands and learned how to convert them into simple playbooks. With these foundational skills in place, we can now dive into the next level of Ansible automation. In this chapter, we will focus on writing Ansible playbooks, which allow us to automate complex tasks and manage our infrastructure more efficiently. We'll explore the powerful "when" module, which enables us to add conditional statements to our playbooks, making them more flexible and adaptable to different scenarios. Throughout this chapter, we'll gradually enhance our playbooks and learn how to target specific nodes in our infrastructure. By the end of this chapter, you'll have a comprehensive understanding of writing working Ansible playbooks and be able to apply these skills to different scenarios. This chapter is one of the most important chapters in this book. So let's get started and take your Ansible automation skills to the next level!

8.1 Considerations Before Writing Your Ansible Playbook

An Ansible playbook is an essential tool for automating infrastructure tasks. By leveraging the YAML format, playbooks can effectively describe the desired state of a system rather than focusing on the steps necessary to achieve that state. Writing an Ansible playbook requires a combination of scripting and declarative statements. While YAML is not a full-fledged programming language, it provides a series of declarative statements to put your system in the desired state. Actual tasks are completed by package managers, systemd, or service applications running on the operating system. As we have discussed in previous chapters, mastering the skills required to create an Ansible playbook can significantly improve your infrastructure automation. Playbooks allow you to automate complex tasks and manage your infrastructure effortlessly. By understanding YAML syntax and its unique features, you can create efficient, effective, and robust playbooks that will streamline your processes and save valuable time and effort.

Let's take a closer look at the basic steps for writing an Ansible playbook using a simple example playbook.

First, define the hosts: The initial step in writing an Ansible playbook is to identify the hosts that the playbook will be executed against. You can specify a single host or a group of hosts in the playbook's header using the "hosts" keyword. You can also define a group of hosts in the inventory file.

Second, define the tasks: Once you've identified the hosts, the next step is to define the tasks that will be executed against them. Each task should have a name, a module, and a set of arguments. Ansible offers a wide range of modules that you can use to perform different tasks, such as installing a package, creating a file, or managing users.

In addition, you can use the "when" keyword to add conditional statements to your tasks. This allows you to execute certain tasks only when specific conditions are met, making your playbooks more flexible and adaptable.

Third, combine the hosts and tasks: Finally, you can combine the hosts and tasks to define your playbook. This can be achieved by using the "hosts" and "tasks" keywords in the playbook's YAML syntax. You can also use additional keywords like "vars" and "roles" to define variables and reusable sets of tasks, respectively.

In summary, writing an Ansible playbook involves identifying the hosts, defining the tasks that will be executed against them, and combining the two to create the playbook. By utilizing modules and conditional statements, you can create powerful and flexible playbooks that can be easily customized and adapted to different scenarios.

Here's an example of a simple Ansible playbook creation steps that installs the Apache web server on a group of hosts:

Throughout this chapter, it is essential to note that only SSH access to the Ansible Control Machine, f38s1, with an IP address of 192.168.127.150, is required. One of the main advantages of using Ansible is the ability to control, manage, and orchestrate multiple client nodes from a single control machine. By using the control machine as the central point of administration, we eliminate the need to log into each client node individually, saving time and effort.

By using Ansible, we can effectively manage a large number of hosts, automate complex tasks, and ensure that our infrastructure is maintained in the desired state. With the proper understanding of Ansible's core concepts and tools, we can effectively manage and orchestrate our infrastructure, streamline our processes, and improve our overall efficiency.

Tip

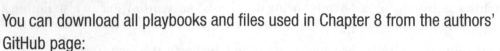

Download playbooks from the authors' GitHub page.

You can download all playbooks and files used in Chapter 8 from the authors'
GitHub page:

https://github.com/ansnetauto/appress_ansnetauto/blob/main/
ch08_files.zip

8.2 Creating and Running a New Playbook in Ansible

To apply the basic steps for writing an Ansible playbook, let's create a new playbook
in YAML and execute it. We will begin by creating a new working directory and then
creating a local inventory and ansible.cfg files for Ansible to read the information from.
In this example, we will demonstrate how to install the apache2 package on Ubuntu
client nodes, specifically u23c1 and u23c2. By following the YAML format and utilizing
the appropriate modules, we can easily execute this task and ensure that the desired
state is achieved on these nodes. By understanding the fundamentals of writing an
Ansible playbook, we can automate various tasks across multiple hosts, streamlining
our processes and saving valuable time and effort. Whether you are a seasoned
DevOps professional or a novice, mastering Ansible playbooks is an essential skill for
infrastructure automation.

```
$ mkdir ch08 && cd ch08
$ pwd
/home/jdoe/ch08

$ vi inventory
$ cat inventory
192.168.127.161
192.168.127.162
```

```
$ vi ansible.cfg
$ cat ansible.cfg
[defaults]
inventory = ./inventory # specify that you want to use the inventory file
in the present working location
private_key_file = /home/jdoe/.ssh/ansible    # for some OS, it is
important that you specify the full file path

$ ansible all -m ping # run a simple Ansible ping to test the connectivity
192.168.127.161 | SUCCESS => {
    "ansible_facts": {
        "discovered_interpreter_python": "/usr/bin/python3"
    },
    "changed": false,
    "ping": "pong"
}
192.168.127.162 | SUCCESS => {
    "ansible_facts": {
        "discovered_interpreter_python": "/usr/bin/python3"
    },
    "changed": false,
    "ping": "pong"
}
```

If the preceding Ansible ad hoc command worked, create the first playbook for this chapter named "8.1_install_apache.yml".

```
$ vi 8.2_install_apache.yml
$ cat 8.2_install_apache.yml
```

Once you have completed your playbook, it should resemble the following file and be saved with a .yml extension:

```
---

- hosts: all
  become: true
```

```
tasks:

- name: Install apache2 package on Ubuntu servers
  ansible.builtin.apt:
    name: apache2
```

This playbook defines a single task that utilizes the apt module to install the apache2 package. The "hosts" keyword specifies that the task should be executed on all hosts, and the "become" keyword instructs Ansible to elevate privileges before executing the task.

To execute this playbook, save the file and run the following command:

$ **ansible-playbook 8.2_install_apache.yml**

```
PLAY [all] ************************************************************

TASK [Gathering Facts] ***********************************************
fatal: [192.168.127.161]: FAILED! => {"msg": "Missing sudo password"}
fatal: [192.168.127.162]: FAILED! => {"msg": "Missing sudo password"}

PLAY RECAP ***********************************************************
192.168.127.161        : ok=0     changed=0    unreachable=0    failed=1
skipped=0     rescued=0    ignored=0
192.168.127.162        : ok=0     changed=0    unreachable=0    failed=1
skipped=0     rescued=0    ignored=0
```

What happened in the preceding example? We forgot to include the "--ask-become-pass" option. Let's re-run the playbook with this option now.

$ **ansible-playbook --ask-become-pass 8.2_install_apache.yml**
```
BECOME password: ***************

PLAY [all] ************************************************************

TASK [Gathering Facts] ***********************************************
ok: [192.168.127.162]
ok: [192.168.127.161]

TASK [Install apache2 package on Ubuntu servers] ********************
changed: [192.168.127.162]
changed: [192.168.127.161]
```

```
PLAY RECAP *********************************************************
192.168.127.161    : ok=2    changed=1    unreachable=0    failed=0
skipped=0    rescued=0    ignored=0
192.168.127.162    : ok=2    changed=1    unreachable=0    failed=0
skipped=0    rescued=0    ignored=0
```

You have now executed your playbook and successfully installed the Apache services
on your Ubuntu servers. To confirm that the packages have been installed correctly from
the control machine, f38s1, try the command in the following tip.

Tip

How can you verify whether the apache2 package has been installed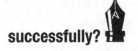

successfully?

To check the installation history from the controlled nodes, you can navigate to
/var/log/apt/history.log. To do so, execute the following command:

```
$ ansible all -a "tail /var/log/apt/history.log"
```

Now, you have full control over the controlled nodes (f38c1, u23c1, and u23c2)
from the control machine (f38s1). You can run commands, check files, update
packages, reboot, and shut down the client nodes as needed.

After confirming that the apache2 packages are installed by checking the history.
log, you can verify the functionality of the Apache server by opening your favorite web
browser and entering the IP addresses of the client nodes. To check the operational
status, use HTTP and the host IPs. If the web services are working correctly, you should
see the working Apache2 Ubuntu Default Page, similar to the one shown in Figure 8-1.

Note that the services start automatically after installation on Ubuntu, so we don't
need to start them. However, on Fedora or any Red Hat distributions, we need to start the
service manually after installation.

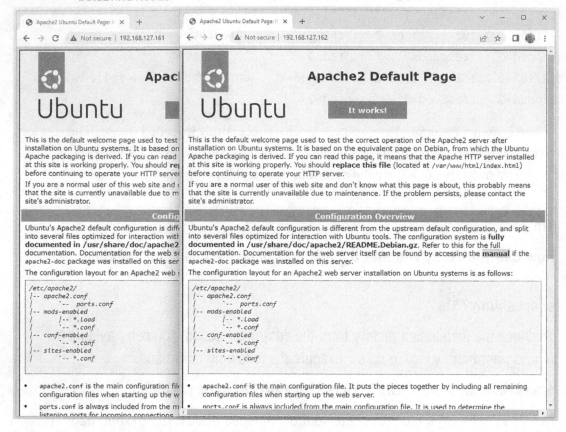

Figure 8-1. *Apache2 Web services on u23c1 and u23c2*

Let us now explore the concept of idempotency in Ansible and its crucial role in configuration management.

8.3 Idempotency Is a Key Feature of Ansible Tasks

Idempotency guarantees the consistency and stability of system configurations and administration tasks. Ansible's idempotency ensures that executing a playbook or task multiple times will not alter the system's state unless there is a change in the configuration. This means that running the same playbook or task repeatedly will result in the same desired outcome, ensuring a consistent and predictable system state. Ansible's idempotency reduces the risk of human error and misconfiguration, preventing unnecessary downtime or disruptions to the system. Maintaining the stability of the system and avoiding unexpected or unnecessary changes help ensure the same

result each time the playbook or task is run (source: https://docs.ansible.com/
ansible/latest/reference_appendices/glossary.html#term-Idempotency).

When re-executing the same playbook, Ansible's idempotency ensures that the
system remains unchanged unless there are changes in the configuration. Consequently,
the playbook's output will display "changed=0", indicating that no significant changes
have been made to the system. Let's quickly verify this visually.

```
$ ansible-playbook --ask-become-pass 8.2_install_apache.yml
BECOME password: ***************

PLAY [all] *******************************************************************

TASK [Gathering Facts] *******************************************************
ok: [192.168.127.162]
ok: [192.168.127.161]

TASK [Install apache2 package on Ubuntu servers] ****************************
ok: [192.168.127.161]
ok: [192.168.127.162]

PLAY RECAP *******************************************************************
192.168.127.161        : ok=2    changed=0    unreachable=0    failed=0
skipped=0    rescued=0    ignored=0
192.168.127.162        : ok=2    changed=0    unreachable=0    failed=0
skipped=0    rescued=0    ignored=0
```

The idempotency property is a critical feature of Ansible, as demonstrated by the
playbook run previously. It reduces the risk of unexpected or unnecessary changes
to the system, improving system stability and reducing the potential for downtime
or disruptions. By executing only the necessary tasks, Ansible helps maintain system
consistency and reliability. Ansible's idempotency ensures that the system remains in
a consistent and desired state, regardless of how many times the playbook or task is
executed, providing a reliable and efficient means of configuration management.

To quickly refresh and improve your ad hoc command skills, try the following
commands from your Ansible Control Machine. You'll be surprised at how quickly and
easily you can extract the desired system information from the client nodes. In Ansible,
the goal is to perform almost all tasks from the control machine, avoiding the need to log
into the client nodes, particularly when managing a large number of devices.

Expand your knowledge

More helpful Ansible ad hoc commands?

```
# Here are some more very helpful ansible ad hoc commands to get you
excited about Ansible. Give each one a try and find out what they can do
for you.
# to list all hosts content
$ ansible all --list-hosts
  hosts (2):
    192.168.127.161
    192.168.127.162

# to see all servers' facts using the gather_facts module
$ ansible all -m gather_facts
# to see specific server facts only
$ ansible all -m gather_facts --limit 192.168.127.161
# to see the Linux version using the 'gather_facts' module, 'filter',
and '-a' (arguments) option. '--ask-become-pass' will prompt you for the
server's sudo user password
$ ansible all -m gather_facts -a 'filter=ansible_distribution_version'
-b --ask-become-pass
# you can also use the 'setup' module in place of the 'gather_facts' module
$ ansible all -m setup -a 'filter=ansible_distribution_version' -b
--ask-become-pass
# use the wildcard character, *, to see more about your Linux system.
$ ansible all -m setup -a 'filter=ansible_distribution*' -b --ask-
become-pass
```

As we haven't yet mastered how to use the Ansible Password Vault feature, we will be using the --ask-become-pass option throughout the chapter. However, there is a way to remove the hassle of entering longer commands and to avoid entering the password, as shown in the following Warning. Keep in mind that saving a sudo user's password in a text file for an Ansible application is against best security practices. In a production environment, taking the easy way out can pose a security risk, so following standard best practices is always the recommended approach.

Warning!

Simplifying your playbook command

If you prefer not to use the --ask-become-pass option when running the playbook,
you can add a [all:vars] variable for all nodes in the inventory file. This way, the
password will be automatically read and referenced from the inventory file under
the [all:vars] variable. However, it's important to note that embedding a password
in a file like this is not considered the best security practice. We should always
exercise caution and follow security best practices. For now, we will continue using
the --ask-become-pass option until we discuss the Ansible Password Vault feature.

```
$ cat inventory
192.168.56.91
192.168.56.92

[all:vars]
ansible_become_password=SuperSecretPassword
```

8.4 Getting Familiar with Ansible Error Messages

Did you know that if your playbook contains typos, incorrect spacing, or references
to non-existent packages, Ansible will alert you to the errors? Ansible is an incredibly
helpful program that will always let you know what went wrong so that you can correct
the issues. In this section, we will intentionally trigger Ansible errors to become familiar
with them and learn how to use Ansible's verbose mode to diagnose errors.

Let's begin by coming up with a fake package name, "dragonball", and seeing what
error message Ansible returns when attempting to install it. Since the package name is
not recognized by the client system, we expect to receive a "No package matching" error.

To create this chapter's second YAML playbook to install the fake package, simply
copy the first playbook to save time and reduce typing errors.

```
$ cp 8.2_install_apache.yml 8.4_install_dragonball.yml
$ vi 8.4_install_dragonball.yml
$ cat 8.4_install_dragonball.yml
```

Your second playbook will look like this:

```
---

- hosts: all
  become: true

  tasks:
  - name: Install dragonball package on Ubuntu servers
    ansible.builtin.apt:
      name: dragonball
```

Now run the new playbook, 8.4_install_dragonball.yml.

```
$ ansible-playbook --ask-become-pass 8.4_install_dragonball.yml
BECOME password: ***************

PLAY [all] **************************************************************

TASK [Gathering Facts] **************************************************
ok: [192.168.127.162]
ok: [192.168.127.161]

TASK [Install dragonball package on Ubuntu servers] *********************
fatal: [192.168.127.161]: FAILED! => {"changed": false, "msg": "No package
matching 'dragonball' is available"}
fatal: [192.168.127.162]: FAILED! => {"changed": false, "msg": "No package
matching 'dragonball' is available"}

PLAY RECAP *************************************************************
192.168.127.161      : ok=1    changed=0    unreachable=0    failed=1
skipped=0    rescued=0    ignored=0
192.168.127.162      : ok=1    changed=0    unreachable=0    failed=1
skipped=0    rescued=0    ignored=0
```

8.5 Getting More Information About Ansible Operation Using the Verbose Mode

In Section 8.4, we deliberately caused an error to demonstrate an Ansible error. This is an excellent opportunity to introduce you to the verbose mode feature in Ansible. When running an Ansible playbook, you can use the -v option to activate the verbose mode, which provides additional information about the tasks executed by Ansible. To use this feature, you simply append -v at the end of the playbook command. By appending more v's to the -v option, you can increase the level of detail provided. Up to seven v's can be used to get the maximum level of information.

Refer to Table 8-1 for a summary of the different verbosity levels and their respective levels of detail.

Table 8-1. *Ansible verbose modes*

Level	# of v's	Explanation
0	None	Verbose mode not in use
1	-v	Displays the details of tasks being executed, including task results as "succeeded" or "failed"
2	-vv	Adds details about the variables being set within each task and values
3	-vvv	Adds details about the connection and task execution
4	-vvvv	Adds details about the playbook and its execution
5	-vvvvv	Adds details about the inventory being used
6	-vvvvvv	Adds details about the modules being executed and their parameters
7	-vvvvvvv	Adds details about the Python API being used by Ansible

It is worth noting that using higher levels of verbosity can result in a substantial amount of output. Therefore, it is advisable to redirect the output to a file or use a utility such as the less command to browse through the output comfortably.

To observe the changes brought about by Ansible's verbose mode, execute the playbook from Section 8.4 and add the -v option to it.

```
$ ansible-playbook --ask-become-pass 8.4_install_dragonball.yml -v
Using /home/jdoe/ch08/ansible.cfg as a config file
BECOME password: ***************
[Same output as before]
[... omitted for brevity]
```

To obtain even more detailed output, you can add an additional -v option to the
previous command and execute it again. This will provide a higher level of verbosity,
including information such as the exact commands being executed on the remote host
and any variables being set during the playbook run. This level of detail can be helpful
when troubleshooting complex issues or understanding the exact steps being taken
by Ansible during the playbook execution. However, it is important to note that with
increased verbosity comes increased output, so use this option judiciously and only
when necessary.

```
$ ansible-playbook --ask-become-pass 8.4_install_dragonball.yml -vv
ansible-playbook [core 2.14.4]
  config file = /home/jdoe/ch08/ansible.cfg
  configured module search path = ['/home/jdoe/.ansible/plugins/modules',
  '/usr/share/ansible/plugins/modules']
  ansible python module location = /usr/lib/python3.11/site-
  packages/ansible
  ansible collection location = /home/jdoe/.ansible/collections:/usr/share/
  ansible/collections
  executable location = /usr/bin/ansible-playbook
  python version = 3.11.3 (main, Apr  5 2023, 00:00:00) [GCC 13.0.1
  20230401 (Red Hat 13.0.1-0)] (/usr/bin/python3)
  jinja version = 3.0.3
libyaml = True
Using /home/jdoe/ch08/ansible.cfg as config file
BECOME password: ***************
Skipping callback 'default', as we already have a stdout callback.
Skipping callback 'minimal', as we already have a stdout callback.
Skipping callback 'oneline', as we already have a stdout callback.
PLAYBOOK: 8.3_install_dragonball.yml ***********************************
```

```
1 plays in 8.3_install_dragonball.yml

PLAY [all] **********************************************************

TASK [Gathering Facts] *********************************************
task path: /home/jdoe/ch08/8.3_install_dragonball.yml:3
ok: [192.168.127.161]
ok: [192.168.127.162]

TASK [Install dragonball package on Ubuntu servers] ***********************
task path: /home/jdoe/ch08/8.3_install_dragonball.yml:7
fatal: [192.168.127.162]: FAILED! => {"changed": false, "msg": "No package
matching 'dragonball' is available"}
fatal: [192.168.127.161]: FAILED! => {"changed": false, "msg": "No package
matching 'dragonball' is available"}
```

Adding an extra -v to the command will provide you with even more detailed
information in the verbose output. This can be useful when troubleshooting issues or
trying to understand the exact steps that Ansible is taking during playbook execution.

```
$ ansible-playbook --ask-become-pass 8.4_install_dragonball.yml -vvv
ansible-playbook [core 2.14.4]
  config file = /home/jdoe/ch08/ansible.cfg
  configured module search path = ['/home/jdoe/.ansible/plugins/modules',
  '/usr/share/ansible/plugins/modules']
  ansible python module location = /usr/lib/python3.11/site-
  packages/ansible
  ansible collection location = /home/jdoe/.ansible/collections:/usr/share/
  ansible/collections
  executable location = /usr/bin/ansible-playbook
  python version = 3.11.3 (main, Apr  5 2023, 00:00:00) [GCC 13.0.1
  20230401 (Red Hat 13.0.1-0)] (/usr/bin/python3)
  jinja version = 3.0.3
libyaml = True
Using /home/jdoe/ch08/ansible.cfg as config file
BECOME password: ***************
```

```
host_list declined parsing /home/jdoe/ch08/inventory as it did not pass its
verify_file() method
script declined parsing /home/jdoe/ch08/inventory as it did not pass its
verify_file() method
auto declined parsing /home/jdoe/ch08/inventory as it did not pass its
verify_file() method
Parsed /home/jdoe/ch08/inventory inventory source with ini plugin
Skipping callback 'default', as we already have a stdout callback.
Skipping callback 'minimal', as we already have a stdout callback.
Skipping callback 'oneline', as we already have a stdout callback.
PLAYBOOK: 8.3_install_dragonball.yml ************************************
1 plays in 8.3_install_dragonball.yml

PLAY [all] *************************************************************

TASK [Gathering Facts] ************************************************
task path: /home/jdoe/ch08/8.3_install_dragonball.yml:3
<192.168.127.161> ESTABLISH SSH CONNECTION FOR USER: None
<192.168.127.161> SSH: EXEC ssh -C -o ControlMaster=auto -o
ControlPersist=60s -o 'IdentityFile="/home/jdoe/.ssh/ansible"' -o
KbdInteractiveAuthentication=no -o PreferredAuthentications=gssapi-with-
mic,gssapi-keyex,hostbased,publickey -o PasswordAuthentication=no -o
ConnectTimeout=10 -o 'ControlPath="/home/jdoe/.ansible/cp/68f4fa8f2e"'
192.168.127.161 '/bin/sh -c '"'"'echo ~ && sleep 0'"'"''
...
```

[Output is too long ... omitted for brevity]

Experiment with all seven levels of verbosity at your leisure, but keep in mind that
the output size increases progressively with each additional -v option. If you want to
save the level 5 verbose output of a command to an external file named "output.log", you
can use shell redirection. However, be sure to remove the "--ask-become-pass" option
from the command, as it will prevent the output from being saved to the file. Here's the
command you should execute:

```
$ ansible-playbook 8.4_install_dragonball.yml -vvvvv > output.log 2>&1
```

```
$ ansible-playbook 8.4_install_dragonball.yml -vvvvv > output.log 2>&1
$ ls -lh output.log
-rw-r--r--. 1 jdoe jdoe 80K Apr 20 22:53 output.log
```

In Chapters 2 and 3, you learned about the redirection and append features of
the Linux command line. In the provided command, the ">" symbol is used for shell
redirection, which redirects the standard output of the command to a file named output.
log. The "2>&1" portion redirects any error messages to the same file, ensuring that both
standard output and errors will be captured in output.log.

It's important to note that when using shell redirection, if the specified file already
exists, it will be overwritten by the new output. If you want to append the output to an
existing file instead of overwriting it, you can use ">>" instead of ">" as the redirection
operator.

Additionally, it's worth keeping in mind that if the command being redirected
generates a lot of output; the resulting file could be quite large and potentially consume
a lot of disk space. It's a good practice to periodically check and clean up any such log
files to free up space on the system.

8.6 Disabling gather_facts to Speed Up the Playbook

Here, we will learn how to speed up playbooks by disabling gather_facts, but before that,
let's create a new playbook with two tasks and try to run it to observe how the changed=
status changes. We will be adding a new task to update the repository cache. To do
this, you can simply copy the first playbook, 8.2_install_apache.yml, and create a new
playbook called 8.6_update_repo_index.yml.

```
$ cp 8.2_install_apache.yml 8.6_update_repo_index.yml
$ vi 8.6_update_repo_index.yml
$ cat 8.6_update_repo_index.yml
```

Your new playbook, 8.6_update_repo_index.yml, should look like this:

```
---
- hosts: all # target all hosts
  become: true # run the playbook with an elevated privilege level

  tasks:
  - name: Update repository index # specify the name of the task
    ansible.builtin.apt: # Ansible module
      update_cache: yes # update the repository index

  - name: Install apache2 package
    ansible.builtin.apt:
      name:   apache2
```

In Ansible, when running a task, the output will indicate whether changes were made to the target system or not. The "changed=1" in the output indicates that the task modified the state of the system, such as updating the repository index, installing a package, modifying a configuration file, or restarting a service. When a task makes changes, Ansible records those changes in a file on the managed host called the "fact cache," which allows Ansible to determine whether a task needs to be run again in future playbooks.

On the other hand, "changed=0" means that the task did not make any changes to the system, as it was already in the desired state. This can happen if the task is idempotent, which means it will produce the same result regardless of how many times it is run. An example of an idempotent task is checking if a package is installed – if it is already installed, the task will report "changed=0" since no action was needed. Idempotent tasks are important because they allow playbooks to be run repeatedly without causing unintended changes to the system.

It's worth noting that the "changed" value only reflects the state of the system immediately after the task has run. Subsequent tasks in the playbook or future playbooks may modify the system in a way that overrides the changes made by the current task. Therefore, it's important to carefully design and test playbooks to ensure that the desired state of the system is achieved and maintained over time.

```
$ ansible-playbook -ask-become-pass 8.6_update_repo_index.yml
BECOME password: *****************

PLAY [all] ***************************************************************

TASK [Gathering Facts] **************************************************
ok: [192.168.127.161]
ok: [192.168.127.162]

TASK [Update repository index] ******************************************
changed: [192.168.127.162]
changed: [192.168.127.161]

TASK [Install apache2 package] ******************************************
ok: [192.168.127.162]
ok: [192.168.127.161]

PLAY RECAP **************************************************************
192.168.127.161         : ok=3    changed=1    unreachable=0    failed=0
skipped=0    rescued=0    ignored=0
192.168.127.162         : ok=3    changed=1    unreachable=0    failed=0
skipped=0    rescued=0    ignored=0
```

It's important to maintain the idempotence of playbooks in Ansible, ensuring that they can be run multiple times without causing unintended changes or side effects to the target system. Understanding whether a task has made changes or not is crucial to achieving this. In Ansible, when running a task, the output indicates whether changes were made to the target system or not. A "changed=1" in the output means that the task modified the state of the system, while "changed=0" means that the task did not make any changes to the system as it was already in the desired state.

By default, when running a playbook in Ansible, the gather_facts option is enabled, meaning that facts about the target system are collected before executing any tasks. This process can take some time, leading to longer playbook run times. To speed up playbook runs, you can disable the gather_facts option by setting it to false, using "gather_facts: false". Disabling gather_facts can significantly improve the playbook's speed, especially in large and complex environments where gathering facts can be time-consuming. Therefore, you can improve the performance of your last playbook by disabling gather_facts and running it again to observe the improvement.

```yaml
---
- hosts: all
  become: true
gather_facts: false # Disable gather_facts

  tasks:
  - name: Update repository index
    ansible.builtin.apt:
      update_cache: yes

  - name: Install apache2 package
    ansible.builtin.apt:
      name:  apache2
```

When you execute the playbook with "gather_facts: false", the output response on the
screen will be quicker compared to the previous playbook run, where gather_facts were
enabled. By disabling gather_facts, you skip the step where Ansible collects information
about the target system, which saves time and can make a significant difference in
playbook execution time, especially in large-scale environments. Therefore, it's a
good practice to disable gather_facts when you don't need them, as it can significantly
improve the playbook's performance.

```
ansible-playbook –ask-become-pass 8.6_update_repo_index.yml
BECOME password: *****************

PLAY [all] ********************************************************
# No facts gathered message here!
TASK [Update repository index] ***********************************
changed: [192.168.127.162]
changed: [192.168.127.161]
[...output omitted for brevity]
```

However, keep in mind that gather_facts provides important system information that
some tasks may depend on, so disabling it may affect certain tasks. It's recommended to
evaluate whether gather_facts are necessary for your playbook before disabling them.

8.7 Adding More Tasks to Your Existing Playbook

To make our playbook more useful, let's add more tasks, this time to install PHP
packages. To save time, you can copy the last YAML file and create a new one to add
another play specifically for installing the PHP service.

```
$ cp 8.6_update_repo_index.yml 8.7_update_install_apache_php.yml
$ vi 8.7_update_install_apache_php.yml
$ cat 8.7_update_install_apache_php.yml
```

After successfully adding another task to install the PHP package, your playbook will
resemble the following YAML playbook:

```
---
- hosts: all
become: true
gather_facts: false

  tasks:
  - name: update repository index
    ansible.builtin.apt:
      update_cache: yes

  - name: install apache2 package
    ansible.builtin.apt:
      name: apache2

  - name: add php support for apache2
    ansible.builtin.apt:
      name: libapache2-mod-php
```

To observe the execution of the playbook, run it and pay close attention to the
output. This will allow you to see each task as it is executed and identify any errors or
issues that may arise during the process.

```
$ ansible-playbook  --ask-become-pass 8.7_update_install_apache_php.yml
BECOME password: **************
```

```
PLAY [all] *********************************************************

TASK [Update repository index] *************************************
changed: [192.168.127.162]
changed: [192.168.127.161]

TASK [Install apache2 package] *************************************
ok: [192.168.127.161]
ok: [192.168.127.162]

TASK [add php support for apache2] *********************************
changed: [192.168.127.161]
changed: [192.168.127.162]

PLAY RECAP ********************************************************
192.168.127.161        : ok=3    changed=2    unreachable=0    failed=0
skipped=0    rescued=0    ignored=0
192.168.127.162        : ok=3    changed=2    unreachable=0    failed=0
skipped=0    rescued=0    ignored=0
```

If your playbook ran successfully, you would see an output similar to the one shown
previously. It's important to observe that both the updating repository index and PHP
tasks were installed successfully, and the "changed" value is 2 for both clients. This
indicates that changes were made to the target system as desired. Now, let's explore how
we can ensure that packages are updated to their latest version every time we run the
playbook.

8.8 Keeping Packages Always Up to Date Using "state: latest"

In Ansible, the "state" parameter is used to define the desired state of a resource. As
shown in Table 8-2, several different state values can be used in your playbook. The
specific state value to be used will depend on the task you want to perform and the
module you are using. To get you up to speed with Ansible's state values, let's quickly
cover some commonly used values. The table contains simple descriptions of each
value, along with examples for each one. By using these state values in your playbook,

you can ensure that the resources you manage are always in the desired state. This is a key aspect of idempotence, which ensures that running the same playbook multiple times has the same effect as running it once.

Table 8-2. *Ansible state commonly used values*

Value	Description	Example

present	The default value. Used with resources, the specified resource should be present on the target system; if the specified resource is not present, Ansible will create it	- name: Install nginx package
		  apt:
		    name: nginx
		    state: **present**

absent	The specified resource should not be present on the host. If the resource is present, Ansible will remove it	- name: Remove apache2 package
		  apt:
		    name: apache2
		    state: **absent**

started/ stopped/ reloaded	Used with **services**, starts (stops/reloads) the service, or it continues to run	- name: Start(Stop/Reload) nginx service
		  service:
		    name: nginx
		    state: **started(stopped/reloaded)**

enabled	Used with **services** and **systemd** units, the service is enabled at boot time. This is like auto-on at start-up	- name: Enable nginx service
		  systemd:
		    name: nginx
		    enabled: yes

disabled	Used with **services** and **system** units, the service is disabled at boot time. This is like auto-off at start-up	- name: Disable nginx service
		  systemd:
		    name: nginx
		    enabled: no

(continued)

347

Table 8-2. (*continued*)

Value	Description	Example

file	Used with **copy module**, the file should be a regular file	- name: Ensure nginx.conf is a regular file
		file:
		    path: /etc/nginx/nginx.conf
		    state: **file**

directory	Used with the **file module**, the file should be a directory	- name: Ensure html directory exists
		file:
		    path: /var/www/html
		    state: **directory**

hard	Used with the **file module**, the file should be a hard link, a mirror copy of the original file	- name: Create a hard link for mylink
		file:
		    src: /home/jdoe/mylink
		    dest: /usr/local/bin/mylink
		    state: **hard**

link	Used with the **file module**, the file should be a symbolic (soft) link, a special file that points to another file	- name: Create a soft link for mylink
		file:
		    src: /home/jdoe/mylink
		    dest: /usr/local/bin/mylink
		    state: **link**

mounted/ unmounted	Used with the **mount** module, the file system should be mounted	- name: (Un)Mount mydata file system
		mount:
		    path: /mnt/mydata
		    state: **mounted** (/**unmounted**)

latest	Used with the **yum** or **apt** module, the latest package version should be installed	- name: Install latest nginx package
		yum:
		    name: nginx
		    state: **latest**

(*continued*)

Table 8-2. (*continued*)

Value	Description	Example
present/ absent	Used with the **user** module, the user should be either present or absent on the system	- name: User account exists or doesn't exist user: name: jdoe state: **present** (/**absent**)

In a production environment, it is important to keep all software versions up to date
for various reasons. To accomplish this, you can add "state: latest" to your playbook,
which ensures that packages are always up to date every time the playbook is run.

To demonstrate the use of Ansible's "state" parameter, let's create another playbook
by copying the previous playbook and making a small modification. This will help us
see how we can use the "state" parameter to update packages to their latest version each
time we run the playbook.

```
$ cp 8.7_update_install_apache_php.yml

8.8_update_install_apache_php_latest.yml
$ vi 8.8_update_install_apache_php_latest.yml
$ cat 8.8_update_install_apache_php_latest.yml
```

To ensure that your software packages are up to date, you can simply add "state:
latest" to the relevant tasks in your playbook. This tells Ansible to update the packages
to their latest version each time the playbook is run. After modifying your playbook with
this parameter, it should look similar to the following:

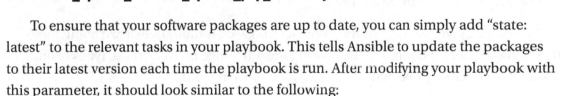

```
---
- hosts: all
become: true
gather_facts: false

  tasks:
  - name: update repository index
    ansible.builtin.apt:
      update_cache: yes
```

```
- name: install apache2 package
  ansible.builtin.apt:
    name: apache2
    state: latest

- name: add php support for apache2
  ansible.builtin.apt:
    name: libapache2-mod-php
    state: latest
```

After modifying your playbook to include "state: latest" for updating packages, save the changes and execute the playbook to apply the updates to the target systems. As before, you can use the "ansible-playbook" command followed by the path to your playbook file. Keep in mind that this task may take some time to complete, depending on the number of packages that need to be updated and the speed of the network connection between the Ansible control node and the target systems. Therefore, it's essential to be patient and wait for the playbook to finish executing before proceeding with any further actions on the target systems.

$ ansible-playbook --ask-become-pass

8.8_update_install_apache_php_latest.yml

[...output omitted for brevity]

Before we move on to the next section, let's take a few minutes to learn about hard links and soft links in Linux. Understanding the difference between these types of links is essential to effectively managing files and directories in Linux.

Expand your knowledge:

The difference between the hard and symbolic links in layman's terms

The decision to use either a hard link or a soft link depends on specific scenarios and your requirements. While both types of links serve a similar purpose of pointing to a file or directory, there are distinct differences between them that make them suitable for different use cases. Therefore, it's important for you to carefully evaluate the situation and choose the appropriate type of link that best fits the needs of the system.

If you're interested in expanding your concept on file linking in Linux, we
recommend checking out this informative article on the Red Hat website:

`www.redhat.com/sysadmin/linking-linux-explained`

8.9 Creating an Uninstall Playbook Using the Existing Playbook

To create an uninstall playbook, you can leverage the existing playbook that you have
created in Section 8.8. This playbook will help you uninstall the software packages
that were previously installed using Ansible. Creating an uninstall playbook is
straightforward and can be done by following a few simple steps.

First, copy the previous playbook and create a new file called "8.9_uninstall.yml".
Then, make a small modification to the playbook by replacing the "state: latest"
parameter with "state: absent". This will ensure that the specified software packages are
removed from the target systems. With these changes, your uninstall playbook is now
ready to be executed.

```
$ cp 8.8_update_install_apache_php_latest.yml  8.9_uninstall.yml
$ vi 8.9_ uninstall.yml
$ cat 8.9_ uninstall.yml
```

Your new playbook should look similar to the following:

```
---
- hosts: all
  become: true
  gather_facts: false

  tasks:
  - name: update repository index
    ansible.builtin.apt:
```

```
    update_cache: yes

  - name: Remove apache2 package
    ansible.builtin.apt:
      name: apache2
      state: absent

  - name: Remove php support for apache2
    ansible.builtin.apt:
      name: libapache2-mod-php
      state: absent
```

Let's execute the new playbook and observe how the software is uninstalled right in front of our eyes.

```
$ ansible-playbook -ask-become-pass 8.9_uninstall.yml
BECOME password: ****************

PLAY [all] *************************************************************

TASK [Update repository index] ****************************************
changed: [192.168.127.162]
changed: [192.168.127.161]

TASK [Remove apache2 package] *****************************************
changed: [192.168.127.162]
changed: [192.168.127.161]

TASK [Remove php support for apache2] *********************************
changed: [192.168.127.161]
changed: [192.168.127.162]

PLAY RECAP ************************************************************
192.168.127.161        : ok=3    changed=3    unreachable=0    failed=0
skipped=0    rescued=0    ignored=0
192.168.127.162        : ok=3    changed=3    unreachable=0    failed=0
skipped=0    rescued=0    ignored=0
```

To confirm that the software has been successfully uninstalled, try accessing the websites using your preferred web browser by entering the following URLs: http://192.168.127.161/ and http://192.168.127.162/. If you are using Google Chrome, you will receive a "This site can't be reached" message. Similarly, if you are using Firefox, you will see a similar connection error message, as shown in Figure 8-2.

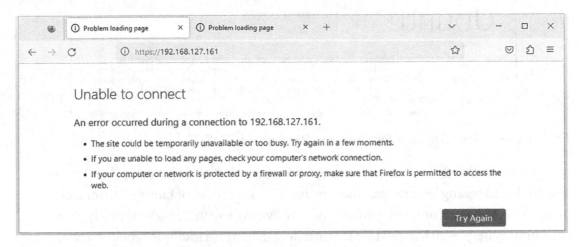

Figure 8-2. *Unable to connect error on u23c1 and u23c2*

To reinstall the Apache2 and PHP services on the Ubuntu client nodes, simply run the installation playbook again. It's a straightforward process that can be done at any time.

```
$ ansible-playbook --ask-become-pass
8.8_update_install_apache_php_latest.yml
BECOME password: ****************
```

[...output omitted for brevity]

As you can see in Figure 8-3, the Apache2 service has been reinstalled and is immediately available on the Firefox browser.

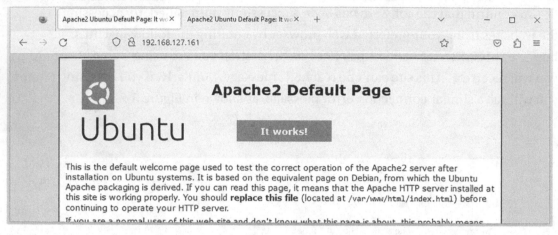

Figure 8-3. *Working web services on u23c1 and u23c2*

Let's make things more interesting by adding the Fedora client node (f38c1) to our
playbook and seeing how we can manage two different types of Linux distributions.
In a production environment, you may not always work with a single device type and
operating system, so it's important to learn how to manage multiple types of devices
simultaneously. This will increase productivity and allow us to use a single playbook to
manage multiple operating systems or device types.

8.10 Add Another OS Type and Use the "when" Conditional in Your Playbook

Up until now, we've only worked with two client hosts running a single type of Linux
distribution, Ubuntu 23.04. This has helped to keep our explanations and understanding
simple. However, in a real production environment, you'll need to manage a variety of
systems running different operating systems. To better prepare for this scenario and
make our playbooks more comprehensive, let's power on a second virtual machine
running Fedora and add it to our inventory with the name "f38c1", as shown here:

```
                                    >_ f38s1
ch08]$  nano inventory
ch08]$  ansible all --list-hosts
  hosts (3):
    192.168.127.161
    192.168.127.162
    192.168.127.151
```

Now, let's execute the first installation playbook (8.1_install_apache.yml) and observe
the response from Ansible. It's expected to see error messages due to the different package
managers used by different Linux distributions. For example, Ubuntu (Debian) derivatives
use apt (new)/apt-get (old), while Fedora (Red Hat/CentOS) uses dnf (new)/yum (old).

```
$ ansible-playbook --ask-become-pass 8.1_install_apache.yml
BECOME password: **************

PLAY [all] ***************************************************************

TASK [Gathering Facts] **************************************************
ok: [192.168.127.161]
ok: [192.168.127.151]
ok: [192.168.127.162]

TASK [Install apache2 package on Ubuntu servers] ************************
[WARNING]: Updating cache and auto-installing missing dependency: python3-apt
fatal: [192.168.127.151]: FAILED! => {"changed": false, "cmd": "apt-get
update", "msg": "[Errno 2] No such file or directory: b'apt-get'", "rc": 2,
"stderr": "", "stderr_lines": [], "stdout": "", "stdout_lines": []}
ok: [192.168.127.161]
ok: [192.168.127.162]

PLAY RECAP *************************************************************
192.168.127.151      : ok=1    changed=0    unreachable=0    failed=1
skipped=0    rescued=0    ignored=0
192.168.127.161      : ok=2    changed=0    unreachable=0    failed=0
skipped=0    rescued=0    ignored=0
192.168.127.162      : ok=2    changed=0    unreachable=0    failed=0
skipped=0    rescued=0    ignored=0
```

In an Ansible playbook, the "apt" module is designed to work only with Debian-
based distributions such as Ubuntu, Pop!_OS, and Linux Mint. However, package
managers used in Linux distributions can vary depending on the base distribution. For
instance, Red Hat–based distributions use yum or dnf, while Arch Linux uses pacman,
among others. Therefore, we cannot use Ansible's apt module to install packages on
Fedora, and the error message we received is due to package manager incompatibility.
So how can we solve this problem?

To begin with, let's first understand how Ansible reads the OS information by running a simple Ansible ad hoc command, which we have learned in the earlier chapters.

```
$ ansible all -m setup -a 'filter=ansible_distribution*' --ask-become-pass
```

```
BECOME password: ***************

192.168.127.161 | SUCCESS => {
    "ansible_facts": {
        "ansible_distribution": "Ubuntu",
        "ansible_distribution_file_parsed": true,
        "ansible_distribution_file_path": "/etc/os-release",
        "ansible_distribution_file_variety": "Debian",
        "ansible_distribution_major_version": "23",
        "ansible_distribution_release": "lunar",
        "ansible_distribution_version": "23.04",
        "discovered_interpreter_python": "/usr/bin/python3"
    },
    "changed": false
}
[... omitted for brevity]
192.168.127.151 | SUCCESS => {
    "ansible_facts": {
        "ansible_distribution": "Fedora",
        "ansible_distribution_file_parsed": true,
        "ansible_distribution_file_path": "/etc/redhat-release",
        "ansible_distribution_file_variety": "RedHat",
        "ansible_distribution_major_version": "38",
        "ansible_distribution_release": "",
        "ansible_distribution_version": "38",
        "discovered_interpreter_python": "/usr/bin/python3"
    },
    "changed": false
}
```

Now, let's use another useful ad hoc command to check the installed package managers on our client nodes. We can check the availability of the apt package manager on the systems with the following command:

```
$ ansible all -a 'which apt' --ask-become-pass
BECOME password: ***************

192.168.127.161 | CHANGED | rc=0 >>
/usr/bin/apt
192.168.127.162 | CHANGED | rc=0 >>
/usr/bin/apt
192.168.127.151 | FAILED | rc=1 >>
which: no apt in (/home/jdoe/.local/bin:/home/jdoe/bin:/usr/local/bin:/usr/
bin:/usr/local/sbin:/usr/sbin)non-zero return code
```

Next, let's check the availability of the yum package manager on our client nodes using another useful ad hoc command:

```
$ ansible all -a 'which yum' --ask-become-pass
BECOME password: ***************

192.168.127.161 | FAILED | rc=1 >>
non-zero return code
192.168.127.162 | FAILED | rc=1 >>
non-zero return code
192.168.127.151 | CHANGED | rc=0 >>
/usr/bin/yum
```

The "when" conditional in Ansible playbooks is a useful feature that allows you to control whether a task should be executed based on a condition. The condition can be a Jinja2 expression that evaluates to true or false. In our example, we will use the "when" statement based on the gathered facts to run the "apt" command only if the distribution is "Ubuntu". The syntax for the "when" statement, in this case, would be "when: ansible_distribution == 'Ubuntu'". You can modify this condition to match the names of other distributions as required. If the operating system is not Ubuntu, the playbook will skip the Fedora servers and execute only on the Ubuntu servers.

```
$ cp 8.1_install_apache.yml 8.10_when.yml
$ vi 8.10_when.yml
$ cat 8.10_when.yml
```

```yaml
---
- hosts: all
  become: true

  tasks:
  - name: Install apache2 package on Ubuntu servers
    ansible.builtin.apt:
      name: apache2
    when: ansible_distribution=='Ubuntu'
```

Once you have made the necessary modifications to your new playbook file, as
shown previously, you can run the playbook 8.9_when.yml and observe the output. You
will notice that the play will skip the task for installing the Apache2 server on the Fedora-
based client but will still run on the Ubuntu-based clients. This is because we have used
Ansible's "when" conditional to control the execution of the task based on the operating
system type. As a result, the playbook will only run the "apt" command on the Ubuntu-
based clients and skip the Fedora-based client.

```
$ ansible-playbook --ask-become-pass 8.10_when.yml
BECOME password: ***************

PLAY [all] ************************************************************

TASK [Gathering Facts] ***********************************************
ok: [192.168.127.161]
ok: [192.168.127.162]
ok: [192.168.127.151]

TASK [Install apache2 package on Ubuntu servers] ********************
skipping: [192.168.127.151]
ok: [192.168.127.161]
ok: [192.168.127.162]
```

```
PLAY RECAP  ************************************************************
192.168.127.151      : ok=1     changed=0    unreachable=0    failed=0
skipped=1    rescued=0    ignored=0
192.168.127.161      : ok=2     changed=0    unreachable=0    failed=0
skipped=0    rescued=0    ignored=0
192.168.127.162      : ok=2     changed=0    unreachable=0    failed=0
skipped=0    rescued=0    ignored=0
```

If you have multiple systems based on the same base distribution, such as Debian, Ubuntu, and Pop!_OS, which all use the same package manager, you can use a Python list to shorten the YAML file. The "when" statement can be written as follows:

`when: ansible_distribution in ['Debian', 'Ubuntu', 'Pop!_OS']`

This code simplifies the "when" statement by using a Python list to check whether the value of "ansible_distribution" is present in the list of distributions specified in the statement. If the value matches any of the distributions in the list, the task will be executed. Otherwise, the task will be skipped. Using this approach can make the code more maintainable, especially when dealing with multiple flavors of the same Linux distribution.

8.11 Targeting a Specific Host or Group of Hosts

When using Ansible to target a specific host or group of hosts, you can be very specific in your playbook. Building upon the example from Section 8.9, let's say you want to target a particular distribution and version. You can achieve this by adding "when" conditionals to your playbook. For instance, if you only want to update the package cache on servers running Fedora 38, you can create a playbook with the following "when" conditionals:

$ **`vi 8.11_update_cache_fedora_38.yml`**

```
---
- name: Update package cache on Fedora 38 servers
  hosts: all
  become: true
```

```
  tasks:
    - name: Update package cache
      ansible.builtin.dnf:
        update_cache: yes
      when: ansible_distribution == 'Fedora' and ansible_distribution_
      major_version == '38'
```

This playbook demonstrates how to target specific hosts based on their operating
system and version. It updates the package cache only on hosts in the "fedora38" group
running Fedora version 38, using the "dnf" module instead of "apt" for Debian-based
distributions. By checking if the operating system is Fedora and the major version is
38 before running the "dnf" module, the playbook ensures that the task is executed
only where it's intended to. This approach allows for very targeted playbook execution,
performing only the necessary tasks on specific hosts.

```
$ ansible-playbook --ask-become-pass 8.11_update_cache_fedora_38.yml
```

```
BECOME password: ***************

PLAY [Update package cache on Fedora 38 servers] *************************

TASK [Gathering Facts] **************************************************
ok: [192.168.127.161]
ok: [192.168.127.162]
ok: [192.168.127.151]

TASK [Update package cache] *********************************************
skipping: [192.168.127.161]
skipping: [192.168.127.162]
ok: [192.168.127.151]

PLAY RECAP **************************************************************
192.168.127.151     : ok=2    changed=0    unreachable=0    failed=0
skipped=0    rescued=0    ignored=0
192.168.127.161     : ok=1    changed=0    unreachable=0    failed=0
skipped=1    rescued=0    ignored=0
192.168.127.162     : ok=1    changed=0    unreachable=0    failed=0
skipped=1    rescued=0    ignored=0
```

To update the package cache for both Ubuntu and Fedora systems using a single playbook, copy the last YAML file and modify it as shown in the following. The updated playbook uses the "when" conditional to execute the "apt" module for Ubuntu-based systems and the "dnf" module for Fedora-based systems:

```yaml
---

- name: Update package cache on all Debian or Red Hat based OS
  hosts: all
  become: true

  tasks:
    - name: Update package cache on Red Hat distros
      ansible.builtin.dnf:
        update_cache: yes
      when: ansible_distribution in ['Fedora', 'Red Hat', 'CentOS']

    - name: Update package cache on Debian distros
      ansible.builtin.apt:
        update_cache: yes
      when: ansible_distribution in ['Ubuntu', 'Debian',  'Pop!_OS']
```

After modifying the YAML file as shown in the previous step, the playbook will update the package cache on both Ubuntu and Fedora systems based on their respective package managers. The "when" conditionals ensure that the playbook executes only on the intended hosts, making it more efficient and targeted. With this single playbook, you can target various distribution names with different package manager modules in a single play. After modifying the YAML file, run the playbook and observe the outputs.

Note that the output has been removed from this book to keep it brief.

```
$ ansible-playbook --ask-become-pass 8.11_update_cache_all.yml
BECOME password: ***************
PLAY [Update package cache on all Debian or Red Hat based OS]
********************

[output omitted for brevity]
```

The "when" conditional in Ansible provides the ability to control when tasks should be executed based on a specific condition. As mentioned earlier, this condition can be a Jinja2 expression that evaluates to True or False. If the condition is True, the task will be executed, and if the condition is False, the task will be skipped. It is worth noting that the when conditional supports other Jinja2 expressions such as comparisons (>, >=, <, <=, ==, !=) and Boolean operators (and, or, not). These expressions are written in Jinja2, but the operators themselves are Python comparison operators, and True and False are Boolean values in Python. Therefore, knowing Python can be beneficial when working with Ansible. In short, the when conditional provides flexibility to your playbooks, enabling you to avoid unnecessary tasks that could slow down automation. It is a powerful tool that can help you to write more efficient and targeted playbooks.

8.12 Writing a Working Playbook for Both Ubuntu and Fedora

Let's use the playbook from Section 8.11 as a basis to create a new playbook that updates the repository cache on all systems and installs web services on both Ubuntu and Fedora clients. However, it's essential to note that the Ansible modules and packages to be installed are different for each distribution. For example, we'll use the "apt" module to install the "apache2" package on Ubuntu clients, while we'll use the "dnf" module to install the "httpd" package on Fedora clients.

After writing your playbook, it should look similar to the following example:

```
$ cp 8.11_update_cache_fedora_38.yml 8.12_update_install_http.yml
$ vi 8.12_update_install_http.yml
$ cat 8.12_update_install_http.yml
---
- hosts: all
  become: true
  collections:
    - ansible.builtin
```

```
tasks:
    - name: Update package cache on Red Hat distros
      dnf:
        update_cache: yes
      when: ansible_distribution in ['Fedora', 'Red Hat', 'CentOS']

    - name: Update package cache on Debian distros
      apt:
        update_cache: yes
      when: ansible_distribution in ['Ubuntu', 'Debian',  'Pop!_OS']

    - name: Install apache2 package on Ubuntu
      apt:
        name: apache2
      when: ansible_distribution == "Ubuntu"

    - name: Install httpd package on Fedora
      dnf:
        name: httpd # The package name is different
      when: ansible_distribution == "Fedora"
```

To execute the latest playbook, run the following command in the terminal:

```
$ ansible-playbook –ask-become-pass 8.12_update_install_http.yml
BECOME password: **************

PLAY [all] *********************************************************
[...omitted for brevity]
TASK [Install httpd package on Fedora] *****************************
skipping: [192.168.127.161]
skipping: [192.168.127.162]
changed: [192.168.127.151]
```

```
PLAY RECAP  *************************************************************
192.168.127.151       : ok=3     changed=1     unreachable=0     failed=0
skipped=2     rescued=0     ignored=0
192.168.127.161       : ok=3     changed=1     unreachable=0     failed=0
skipped=2     rescued=0     ignored=0
192.168.127.162       : ok=3     changed=1     unreachable=0     failed=0
skipped=2     rescued=0     ignored=0
```

Upon reviewing the PLAY RECAP, we can see that all tasks have been completed successfully, as indicated by the "ok=3" status for all client nodes. We have already confirmed that the web services are working on the Ubuntu servers, so this time, let's check the web service on the Fedora server (f38c1) using the URL http://192.168.127.151/. However, as you can see in Figure 8-4, we encountered a connection timed-out error from the server. What could have caused this issue? For Red Hat–based distributions using the httpd package, we need to perform additional steps to enable the web services. Specifically, we need to open the correct port using systemctl.

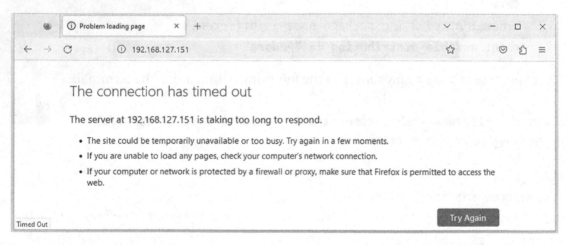

Figure 8-4. *Connection timed-out error on f38c1*

If you're manually performing this task on f38c1, you would need to run the following commands in sequence. However, if you had to perform this task on 30 servers, you would likely need to write a simple shell/Python/Perl script to automate the process. Now that you know about Ansible, you can achieve the same result without having to learn or touch a programming language.

```
# This is a reference only. Please DO NOT run these commands.
[jdoe@f38c1 ~]$ systemctl status httpd # check the HTTP service
[jdoe@f38c1 ~]$ sudo systemctl enable httpd # Start service at system
start-up
[jdoe@f38c1 ~]$ sudo systemctl start httpd # Start HTTP service
[jdoe@f38c1 ~]$ systemctl status httpd # check the HTTP service
[jdoe@f38c1 ~]$ su - # login as the root user
Password: ***************
[root@f38c1 ~]$ firewall-cmd –add-service=http # open http port using the
service name
OR
[root@f38c1 ~]$ firewall-cmd –add-port=80/tcp # open http port using the
port number &      protocol type
```

We will now update the previous playbook by adding a task to enable the HTTP
service at startup and open the firewall port for port 80.

```
$ cp 8.12_update_install_http.yml 8.12_update_install_enable_http.yml
$ vi 8.12_update_install_enable_http.yml
$ cat 8.12_update_install_enable_http.yml
```

```
[...omitted for brevity]
    - name: Install httpd package on Fedora
      dnf:
        name: httpd # the package name is different
      when: ansible_distribution == "Fedora"

  - name: Ensure httpd is running on Fedora
    service:
      name: httpd # the package name is different
      state: started # ensure the service is running
    when: ansible_distribution == "Fedora"
```

```yaml
- name: Open http port 80 on Fedora
  firewalld: # Ansible module
    service: http
    permanent: true # make this a permanent setting
    state: enabled # ensure the service starts at start-up
  when: ansible_distribution == "Fedora"

- name: Restart firewalld service for new service to kick-in
  service:
    name: firewalld # service name
    state: restarted # restart firewalld service
  when: ansible_distribution == "Fedora"
```

After running the aforementioned playbook, the output on f38c1 should resemble
this, indicating that all tasks have been completed:

```
$ ansible-playbook –ask-become-pass 8.12_update_install_enable_http.yml
```

```
BECOME password: ***************

[...omitted for brevity]
TASK [Ensure httpd is running on Fedora] *********************************
skipping: [192.168.127.161]
skipping: [192.168.127.162]
changed: [192.168.127.151]

TASK [Open http port 80 on Fedora] **************************************
skipping: [192.168.127.161]
skipping: [192.168.127.162]
changed: [192.168.127.151]

TASK [Restart firewalld service for new service to kick-in] ***************
skipping: [192.168.127.161]
skipping: [192.168.127.162]
changed: [192.168.127.151]
```

```
PLAY RECAP ***********************************************************
192.168.127.151      : ok=6      changed=3      unreachable=0      failed=0
skipped=2     rescued=0     ignored=0
192.168.127.161      : ok=3      changed=1      unreachable=0
failed=0     skipped=5     rescued=0     ignored=0
192.168.127.162      : ok=3      changed=1      unreachable=0      failed=0
skipped=5     rescued=0     ignored=0
```

If everything goes as planned, you should now be able to refresh the web page,
and it will display a working Fedora Webserver Test Page, similar to the one shown in
Figure 8-5.

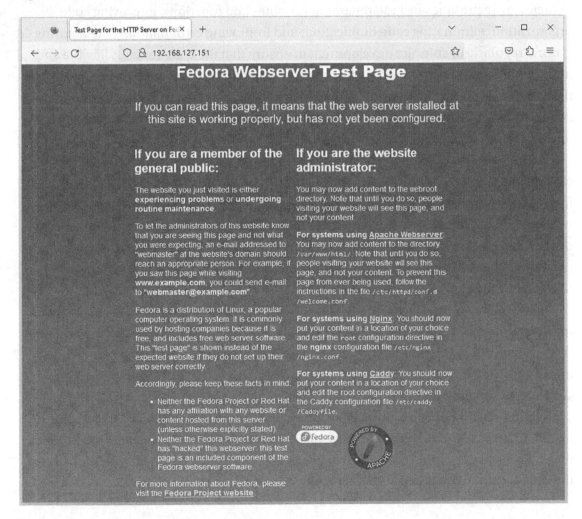

Figure 8-5. *Working web page on f38c1*

At this stage, all three client nodes are providing the web services and are working fine. However, upon reviewing the last playbook, it appears to be quite lengthy. Therefore, we should ask ourselves whether there is any way to simplify or shorten it. Our last playbook was quite lengthy. Let's simplify and shorten it by refactoring.

8.13 Refactoring a Playbook

Refactoring in programming refers to the process of restructuring and improving existing code without changing its original functionality. It involves simplifying the code, improving its readability and maintainability, and reducing its complexity. Refactoring techniques include renaming variables and functions, improving code organization, eliminating code duplication, and improving error handling. Refactoring is done regularly in software development to ensure that the code remains flexible and maintainable over time. It helps to improve the quality of the code and makes it easier to maintain and modify. Even though an Ansible playbook written in YAML is not exactly code, we can still apply the concept of refactoring from programming to improve our inefficient and unappealing playbook.

When writing Ansible playbooks, there are several ways to enhance readability, maintainability, and performance, such as utilizing variables, roles, and tags. By following these best practices, playbooks can become more flexible, modular, and maintainable, ultimately saving time and effort. Although we'll cover these concepts in depth later, for now, we'll use a gradual refactoring approach to simplify the previous playbook. This will demonstrate the significant changes and performance improvements that refactoring can bring to playbooks.

Before we start the refactoring process, a simple way to simplify the plays is to break the YAML playbook into multiple functional files. In our case, we can break the original 8.12_update_install_enable_http.yml into two files: one file to update the cache and install software and another file to enable, start, and open the HTTP port on Fedora servers as a separate playbook.

When breaking the 8.12_update_install_enable_http.yml file into two files, 8.13_install_main.yml and 8.13_enable_http_on_fedora.yml, we will also clean up the files to make them easy to understand. We will be using 8.13_install_main.yml to demonstrate the refactoring concept in the next section.

```
$ cat 8.13_install_main.yml

- hosts: all
become: true
collections:
    - ansible.builtin

  tasks:
    - name: Update package cache on Ubuntu
      apt:
        update_cache: yes
      when: ansible_distribution=='Ubuntu'

    - name: Install apache2 package on Ubuntu
      apt:
        name: apache2
      when: ansible_distribution == "Ubuntu"

    - name: Update package cache on Fedora
      dnf:
        update_cache: yes
      when: ansible_distribution=='Fedora'

    - name: Install httpd package on Fedora
      dnf:
        name: httpd
      when: ansible_distribution == "Fedora"
```

```
cat 8.13_enable_http_on_fedora.yml

---
- hosts: all
  become: true
  collections:
    - community.general
```

369

```yaml
tasks:
  - name: Ensure httpd is running on Fedora
    ansible.builtin.service:
      name: httpd
      state: started
    when: ansible_distribution == "Fedora"

  - name: Open http port 80 on Fedora
    community.general.firewalld: # Ansible module
      service: http
      permanent: true
      state: enabled
    when: ansible_distribution == "Fedora"

  - name: Restart firewalld service for new service to kick-in
    ansible.builtin.service:
      name: firewalld
      state: restarted
    when: ansible_distribution == "Fedora"
```

Let's begin the refactoring process by making a simple improvement that involves utilizing a list. Ansible provides a list in the form of a dash, which allows for installing multiple packages in a single statement by looping through the list of package names.

8.13_install_main.yml (original)	Refactoring 1: 8.13_install_main_rf1.yml

```
---
- hosts: all
  become: true
  collections:
  - ansible.builtin

  tasks:
  - name: Update package cache
    on Ubuntu
    apt:
      update_cache: yes
    when: ansible_
    distribution=='Ubuntu'

  - name: Install apache2
package on Ubuntu
    apt:
      name: apache2
    when: ansible_distribution
    == "Ubuntu"

  - name: Update package cache
    on Fedora
    dnf:
      update_cache: yes
    when: ansible_
    distribution=='Fedora'

  - name: Install httpd package
    on Fedora
    dnf:
      name: httpd
    when: ansible_distribution
    == "Fedora"
```

```
---
- hosts: all
  become: true
  collections:
  - ansible.builtin

  tasks:
  - name: Update package cache on Ubuntu
    apt:
      update_cache: yes
    when: ansible_distribution=='Ubuntu'

  - name: Install packages on Ubuntu
    apt:
      name:
        - apache2
        - libapache2-mod-php
        - tmux
        - tree
      state: latest
    when: ansible_distribution == "Ubuntu"

  - name: Update package cache on Fedora
    dnf:
      update_cache: yes
    when: ansible_distribution=='Fedora'

  - name: Install packages on Fedora
    dnf:
      name:
        - httpd
        - php
        - tmux
        - tree
      state: latest
    when: ansible_distribution == "Fedora"
```

371

The Ansible playbook "8.13_install_main_rf1.yml" has undergone refactoring in the "install packages" section using a list of package names. This enables the installation of multiple packages in a single play by looping through the list using either the "apt" or "dnf" package manager.

When you execute the refactored playbook, you can observe the changes in the output and learn the intricacies of refactoring. The process involves iterating over the previous script to make it more concise and easier to understand.

```
$ ansible-playbook --ask-become-pass 8.13_install_main_rf1.yml
BECOME password: ***************
```

[...omitted for brevity]

It's worth noting that Ansible supports two types of YAML list syntax. The first method uses a hyphen followed by the item name, while the second method uses a Python-like syntax that encloses the items in square brackets. Both methods are valid and can be used interchangeably, depending on personal preference or organizational conventions.

8.13_install_main_rf1.yml	Refactoring 1: 8.13_install_main_rf2.yml

```yaml
---
- hosts: all
  become: true
  collections:
  - ansible.builtin

tasks:
  - name: Update package cache on Ubuntu
   apt:
    update_cache: yes
   when: ansible_distribution=='Ubuntu'

  - name: Install packages on Ubuntu
   apt:
    name:
     - apache2
     - libapache2-mod-php
     - tmux
     - tree
    state: latest
   when: ansible_distribution == "Ubuntu"

  - name: Update package cache on Fedora
   dnf:
    update_cache: yes
   when: ansible_distribution=='Fedora'

  - name: Install packages on Fedora
   dnf:
    name:
     - httpd
     - php
     - tmux
     - tree
    state: latest
   when: ansible_distribution == "Fedora"
```

```yaml
---
- hosts: all
  become: true
  collections:
  - ansible.builtin

tasks:
  - name: Update package cache
   on Ubuntu
   apt:
    update_cache: yes
   when: ansible_
   distribution=='Ubuntu'

  - name: Install packages on Ubuntu
   apt:
    name: [apache2, libapache2-
    mod-php, tmux, tree]
    state: latest
   when: ansible_distribution ==
   "Ubuntu"

  - name: Update package cache
   on Fedora
   dnf:
    update_cache: yes
   when: ansible_
   distribution=='Fedora'

  - name: Install packages on Fedora
   dnf:
    name: [httpd, php, tmux,
    tree]
    state: latest
   when: ansible_distribution ==
   "Fedora"
```

By executing the refactored playbook, you can observe the changes and learn the intricacies of refactoring. This process involves iterating over the previous script to make it more concise and easier to understand. So run the playbook and analyze the output to see how the use of variables and other refactoring techniques has simplified the playbook.

```
$ ansible-playbook --ask-become-pass 8.13_install_main_rf2.yml
BECOME password: ***************
```

[...omitted for brevity]

The third refactoring involves simplifying the playbook even further by using the "update_cache: yes" option. This option is used to update the package cache before installing packages, which eliminates the need for a separate task to update the cache. This makes the playbook more concise and efficient, as it combines two tasks into one. By implementing this change, the playbook becomes more streamlined and easier to read, making it more manageable for future modifications.

8.13_install_main_rf2.yml	Refactoring 2: 8.13_install_main_rf3.yml

```
---
- hosts: all
  become: true
  collections:
  - ansible.builtin

  tasks:
  - name: Update package cache on Ubuntu
    apt:
      update_cache: yes
    when: ansible_distribution=='Ubuntu'

  - name: Install packages on Ubuntu
    apt:
      name: [apache2, libapache2-mod-php,
      tmux, tree]
      state: latest
    when: ansible_distribution == "Ubuntu"

  - name: Update package cache on Fedora
    dnf:
      update_cache: yes
    when: ansible_distribution=='Fedora'

  - name: Install packages on Fedora
    dnf:
      name: [httpd, php, tmux, tree]
      state: latest
    when: ansible_distribution == "Fedora"
```

```
---
- hosts: all
  become: true
  collections:
  - ansible.builtin

  tasks:
  - name: Install packages on
    Ubuntu
    apt:
      name: [apache2, libapache2-
      mod-php, tmux, tree]
      state: latest
      update_cache: yes
    when: ansible_distribution
    == "Ubuntu"

  - name: Install packages on
    Fedora
    dnf:
      name: [httpd, php, tmux,
      tree]
      state: latest
      update_cache: yes
    when: ansible_distribution
    == "Fedora"
```

In the previous example, we demonstrated how a play consisting of four lines of YAML code could be simplified to a single "update_cache: yes" option. If you understand the parameters available under specific circumstances, you can optimize your playbook. In the refactored example on the right, "update_cache: yes" is used with the apt/dnf module to indicate that Ansible should update the local package cache on the target

machine before installing the specified packages. When "update_cache" is set to "yes",
Ansible runs the "apt/dnf update" command on the target machine to ensure that the
local package cache is up to date with the latest package versions available from the
configured repositories. This ensures that the apt/dnf module can install the latest
versions of the specified packages.

To observe the changes and learn the intricacies of refactoring, execute the
refactored playbook, and examine the output. This process involves iterating over the
previous script to make it more concise and easier to understand.

```
$ ansible-playbook --ask-become-pass 8.13_install_main_rf3.yml
BECOME password: ***************
```

[...omitted for brevity]

Fourth and final refactoring: To reduce the play into a single play, use variables
and move them into the inventory file. Change the playbook as shown in the following,
replacing "apt" or "dnf" with "package". Ansible's package module enables the playbook
to use whichever package manager the underlying OS is using. First, declare the
variables inside the inventory. See the following:

```
[jdoe@f38s1 ch08]$ vi inventory
[jdoe@f38s1 ch08]$ cat inventory
192.168.127.161 apache_package=apache2 php_package=libapache2-mod-php tmux_
package=tmux tree_package=tree
192.168.127.162 apache_package=apache2 php_package=libapache2-mod-php tmux_
package=tmux tree_package=tree
192.168.127.151 apache_package=httpd php_package=php tmux_package=tmux
tree_package=tree
```

In the preceding inventory file, four variables have been defined: apache_package,
php_package, tmux_package, and tree_package. The correct package names must be
specified for each variable based on the package manager being used by the server. By
defining the variables in the inventory file, the playbook becomes less convoluted.

After refactoring the 8.13_install_main_rf3.yml file and restructuring it as shown in
8.13_install_main_rf4.yml, a single, amazingly efficient playbook will be left. Comparing
the final version to the original playbook created, it is evident that the concept of
refactoring pays off when working with Ansible YAML playbooks.

8.13_install_main_rf3.yml	Refactoring 3: 8.13_install_main_rf4.yml

``yaml
--- 	
- hosts: all
  become: true
  collections:
   - ansible.builtin
 	
  tasks:
   - name: Install packages on Ubuntu
     apt:
      name: [apache2, libapache2-mod-
      php, tmux, tree]
      state: latest
      update_cache: yes
     when: ansible_distribution ==
     "Ubuntu"
 	
   - name: Install packages on Fedora
     dnf:
      name: [httpd, php, tmux, tree]
      state: latest
      update_cache: yes
     when: ansible_distribution ==
     "Fedora"
``
	``yaml
	--- 	
	- hosts: all
	  become: true
	  collections:
	   - ansible.builtin
	
	  tasks:
	   - name: Install packages on Linux
	     package: # package is an
	     Ansible Module
	      name:
	        - "{{ apache_package }}" # a
	          variable
	        - "{{ php_package }}" # a
	          variable
	        - "{{ tmux_package }}" # a
	          variable
	        - "{{ tree_package }}" # a
	          variable
	      state: latest
	      update_cache: yes
	``

To make a script more concise and easier to understand, you can use the process of refactoring. By executing the refactored playbook and examining the output, you can observe the changes and learn about the intricacies of refactoring.

```
$ ansible-playbook --ask-become-pass 8.13_install_main_rf4.yml
BECOME password: ***************

[...omitted for brevity]
```

377

To prepare for the next exercise, it is necessary to uninstall the packages that
were previously installed. This can be achieved by running the appropriate uninstall
commands for each package. Once the packages have been successfully uninstalled, the
system will be ready for the next task.

```
$ cp 8.13_install_main_rf4.yml 8.13_uninstall_main_rf4.yml
$ vi 8.13_uninstall_main_rf4.yml
$ cat 8.13_uninstall_main_rf4.yml
---
- hosts: all
  become: true

  tasks:
    - name: Uninstall packages on Linux
      Ansible.builtin.package: # package is an Ansible Module
        name:
          - "{{ apache_package }}"  # a variable
          - "{{ php_package }}"  # a variable
          - "{{ tmux_package }}" # a variable
          - "{{ tree_package }}" # a variable
        state: absent
        update_cache: yes
```

The installation playbook can be easily transformed into an uninstallation playbook.
Simply modify the playbook to remove the packages instead of installing them. By
running the uninstall playbook, we can remove the installed packages and prepare for
the next exercise.

```
$ ansible-playbook --ask-become-pass 8.13_uninstall_main_rf4.yml
BECOME password: ***************

[...omitted for brevity]
```

Great work on mastering the concept of refactoring in Ansible playbooks! Refactoring
helps simplify code, improves its readability and maintainability, and reduces its
complexity. The goal is to make playbooks easily understandable and optimized for
performance. In addition to simplification, there are several techniques you can use to

refactor your Ansible playbooks, such as extracting common tasks into separate roles, reducing duplicate code, and using variables and loops effectively.

When refactoring Ansible playbooks, testing is also crucial. Regular testing ensures that your playbook runs smoothly and without errors. You can use tools like Molecule to test your playbooks in isolated environments. In summary, refactoring is a critical step in creating efficient and maintainable Ansible playbooks. By applying various refactoring techniques and testing regularly, you can create playbooks that are easy to understand and maintain over time.

Expand your knowledge:

Documentation on package module

Referring to Red Hat's official Ansible documentation is an excellent idea, as it provides a plethora of useful information. However, with so many topics to cover, it's easy to get lost in the vast amount of information, leading to days of reading, studying, and testing to grasp Ansible concepts based on the documentation. To simplify this process, here's a link to the package module that we used in the previous playbook to refactor and simplify our code:

https://docs.ansible.com/ansible/latest/collections/ansible/builtin/package_module.html

---

8.14 Ansible, Targeting Specific Nodes

Let's explore how to target specific nodes by modifying the inventory file to focus on different servers based on their roles. Building upon the previous exercise, we can create functional groups of client hosts in the inventory file as follows:

```
$ vi inventory
$ cat inventory

[web_server]
192.168.127.161
192.168.127.162
```

[file_server]

`192.168.127.151`

[db_server]

In this exercise, we'll create a new playbook that installs three useful Linux command tools: htop (a process viewer), nmon (a system monitor, tuner, and benchmark tool), and iftop (a network traffic and bandwidth usage tool). You can choose between two methods to create the playbook: the YAML folded block scalar method or the simpler YAML inline sequence method. In the "hosts" section, we'll specify the "file_server" group only, which will target the client node with the IP address 192.168.127.151. Although there are differences between the two file creation methods, you only need to create one playbook file named 8.14_install_tools.yml. In this book, we'll stick to the first method, which is the more commonly used list method.

$ **vi 8.14_install_tools.yml**

```
#YAML folded block scalar
- name: Install useful Linux tools
  hosts: file_server
  become: true

  tasks:
    - name: Install htop, nmon, and iftop packages
      ansible.builtin.package:
        name:
          - htop
          - nmon
          - iftop
        state: latest
        update_cache: yes
```

As mentioned earlier, optionally, the YAML folded block scalar method can be simplified by using the YAML inline sequence method, which makes the playbook more concise and reduces the line length.

$ **vi 8.14_install_tools.yml**

```
# YAML inline sequence
- name: Install useful Linux tools
  hosts: file_server
  become: true

  tasks:
    - name: Install htop, nmon, and iftop packages
      ansible.builtin.package:
        name: ['htop', 'nmon', 'iftop']
        state: latest
        update_cache: yes
```

When running the playbook, only the specified packages will be installed on the
"file_server" client group. This is because the playbook has been configured to target a
specific node within that group, which happens to be the Fedora client server. The other
Ubuntu nodes will not have these packages installed unless they are also members of the
"file_server" group.

$ **ansible-playbook --ask-become-pass 8.14_install_tools.yml**
BECOME password: **************

PLAY [Install useful Linux tools] ***************************************

TASK [Gathering Facts] **
ok: [192.168.127.151]

TASK [Install htop, nmon, and iftop packages] ***************************
changed: [192.168.127.151]

PLAY RECAP ***
192.168.127.151   : ok=2   changed=1   unreachable=0
failed=0   skipped=0   rescued=0   ignored=0

Expanding the scope of the installation to other nodes or groups is easy. Simply
modify the playbook to target the desired groups or nodes. If you want to install the
packages on all nodes, regardless of their group or operating system, you can change the
"hosts" section to "all". Alternatively, you can target multiple groups by appending them

after the comma separator, like this: "hosts: file_server, web_server". This will install the
packages on all nodes belonging to both groups.

By making these changes, the playbook becomes more versatile and can be used
to install packages on a wide range of nodes and groups. However, keep in mind that
installing packages on all nodes could potentially have unintended consequences, so it's
important to carefully consider the scope of the installation before making any changes
to the playbook.

$ **vi 8.14_install_tools.yml**

```
#YAML folded block scalar
- name: Install useful Linux tools
  hosts: file_server, web_server
  become: true

  tasks:
    - name: Install htop, nmon, and iftop packages
      ansible.builtin.package:
        name:
          - htop
          - nmon
          - iftop
        state: latest
        update_cache: yes
```

After updating the playbook to target the "file_server" and "web_server" groups,
execute the playbook to install the Linux tools on all nodes within those groups. You will
be able to observe the installation process on each node and verify that the tools have
been successfully installed by running their respective commands.

$ **ansible-playbook --ask-become-pass 8.14_install_tools.yml**
BECOME password: **************

[...omitted for brevity]

Creating a new playbook that includes the "pre_tasks" section is easy. Simply make a
copy of the existing playbook and modify it as needed. When you run the new playbook,
the tasks specified under "pre_tasks" will be executed before the main playbook tasks.

This feature is particularly useful for ensuring that your system repository is up to date before installing new packages.

By using "pre_tasks" in your playbook, you can ensure that any necessary updates are applied before proceeding with the rest of the tasks. This helps to avoid potential conflicts or errors that might occur if the system repository is not updated before package installation.

Overall, "pre_tasks" can be a valuable tool in your Ansible playbook arsenal, providing a way to perform important setup tasks before executing the main playbook tasks.

```
$ cp 8.14_install_tools.yml 8.14_install_tools_w_pre_tasks.yml
$ vi 8.14_install_tools_w_pre_tasks.yml
$ cat 8.14_install_tools_w_pre_tasks.yml
---
- hosts: all
  become: true
  pre_tasks: # mandates this play to run with priority.
  collections:
    - ansible.builtin

  - name: install updates (Ubuntu)
    apt:
      upgrade: dist
      update_cache: yes
    when: ansible_distribution == "Ubuntu"

  - name: install updates (Fedora)
    dnf:
      update_only: yes
      update_cache: yes
    when: ansible_distribution == "Fedora"

#YAML folded block scalar
- name: Install useful Linux tools
  hosts: file_server
  become: true
```

```
tasks:
  - name: Install htop, nmon, and iftop packages
    package:
      name:
        - htop
        - nmon
        - iftop
      state: latest
```

The playbook "8.14_install_tools_w_pre_tasks.yml" consists of two plays, each with a set of tasks to be executed on the target hosts. The first play targets all hosts and runs with elevated privileges using become: true. It also includes a pre_tasks section that ensures the target systems are up to date before proceeding with the rest of the playbook tasks. This section has two tasks: one for Ubuntu and one for Fedora, which updates the system's package cache and applies any available upgrades using their respective package managers.

The second play targets hosts belonging to the file_server group and also runs with become: true. It installs three useful Linux tools, htop, nmon, and iftop, using the package manager.

Make sure to run the playbook and verify that it's working as expected.

```
$ ansible-playbook --ask-become-pass 8.14_install_tools_w_pre_tasks.yml
```

```
BECOME password: **************
```

[...omitted for brevity]

Now, we want to make f38c1 (192.168.127.151) and u23c1 (192.168.127.161) database servers running MariaDB.

```
$ vi inventory
$ cat inventory
```

```
[web_server]
192.168.127.161
192.168.127.162
```

[file_server]
192.168.127.151

[db_server]
192.168.127.151
192.168.127.161

Instead of creating the playbook from scratch, let's use the last playbook as a base and create our playbook to install MariaDB. This will save us time and reduce the risk of typos.

```
$ cp  8.14_install_tools_w_pre_tasks.yml  8.14_install_mariadb.yml
$ vi 8.14_install_mariadb.yml
$ cat 8.14_install_mariadb.yml
---
- hosts: db_server # specify target group here
  become: true
  collections:
    - ansible.builtin

  pre_tasks: # mandates this play to run with priority.

  - name: install updates (Ubuntu)
    apt:
      upgrade: dist
      update_cache: yes
    when: ansible_distribution == "Ubuntu"

  - name: install updates (Fedora)
    dnf:
      update_only: yes
      update_cache: yes
    when: ansible_distribution == "Fedora"

#YAML folded block scalar
- name: Install useful Linux tools
  hosts: db_server # specify target group here
  become: true
```

```
tasks:
  - name: Install htop, nmon, and iftop packages
    package:
      name:
        - htop
        - nmon
        - iftop
      state: latest

  - name: install mariadb package (Ubuntu) # install maridDB on
Ubuntu nodes
    apt:
      name: mariadb-server # be careful with the package name
      state: latest
    when: ansible_distribution == "Ubuntu"

  - name: install mariadb package (Fedora)     # install maridDB on
Fedora nodes
    dnf:
      name:
        - mariadb # be careful with the package names
        - mariadb-server # be careful with the package names
      state: latest
    when: ansible_distribution == "Fedora"
```

After executing the playbook, if your output is similar to or the same as the following output, then your MariaDB installation on your DB servers has been completed successfully.

```
$ ansible-playbook --ask-become-pass 8.14_install_mariadb.yml
BECOME password: ***************

PLAY [db_server] ***************************************************

TASK [Gathering Facts] *********************************************
ok: [192.168.127.161]
ok: [192.168.127.151]
```

```
TASK [install updates (Ubuntu)] ****************************************
skipping: [192.168.127.151]
ok: [192.168.127.161]

TASK [install updates (Fedora)] ****************************************
skipping: [192.168.127.161]
ok: [192.168.127.151]

PLAY [Install useful Linux tools] **************************************

TASK [Gathering Facts] *************************************************
ok: [192.168.127.161]
ok: [192.168.127.151]

TASK [Install htop, nmon, and iftop packages] *************************
ok: [192.168.127.161]
ok: [192.168.127.151]

TASK [install mariadb package (Ubuntu)] *******************************
skipping: [192.168.127.151]
changed: [192.168.127.161]

TASK [install mariadb package (Fedora)] *******************************
skipping: [192.168.127.161]
changed: [192.168.127.151]

PLAY RECAP ************************************************************
192.168.127.151            : ok=5    changed=1    unreachable=0    failed=0
skipped=2    rescued=0    ignored=0
192.168.127.161            : ok=5    changed=1    unreachable=0    failed=0
skipped=2    rescued=0    ignored=0
```

8.15 Check Services from the Control Node

To check the newly installed DB service, you can go to the u20sn2 node and run the
"systemctl status" MariaDB command. However, if you want to check this from the
control machine (f38s1), you can create a simple Ansible playbook.

To create a new YAML playbook to start and check the status of the service, follow
these steps:

$ **8.15_check_db_service.yml**

```
---
- hosts: db_server
  become: true
  collections:
    - ansible.builtin

  tasks:
  - name: Start MariaDB service
    systemd: # Ansible module for Red Hat distros
      name: mariadb
      state: started
      enabled: true
    when: ansible_distribution == "Fedora"

  - name: Start MariaDB service
    service: # Ansible module for Debian distros
      name: mariadb
      state: started
      enabled: true
    when: ansible_distribution == "Ubuntu"

  - name: Check the status of the MariaDB service
    service_facts: # Ansible module
    register: service_state # Use register and debug to print out the
    result on the screen
  - debug:
      var: service_state.ansible_facts.services["mariadb.service"].state
```

It is essential to learn how to write YAML playbooks, but it is equally important to
write them in a way that is suitable for you and your team. When writing playbooks, it's
a good practice to add comments using the # symbol to explain tasks or provide context.
This can help you and your team better understand the playbook's purpose and make
modifications or updates more manageable in the future.

Execute the playbook and observe for any errors or alerts to ensure that the service is started successfully.

```
$ ansible-playbook --ask-become-pass 8.15_check_db_service.yml
BECOME password: ***************

PLAY [db_server] *******************************************************
[...omitted for brevity]
TASK [debug] ***********************************************************
ok: [192.168.127.151] => {
    "service_state.ansible_facts.services[\"mariadb.service\"].state":
    "running"
}
ok: [192.168.127.161] => {
    "service_state.ansible_facts.services[\"mariadb.service\"].state":
    "running"
}

PLAY RECAP *************************************************************
192.168.127.151          : ok=4    changed=1    unreachable=0    failed=0
skipped=1    rescued=0    ignored=0
192.168.127.161          : ok=4    changed=0    unreachable=0    failed=0
skipped=1    rescued=0    ignored=0
```

By now, you should be familiar with the various outputs provided by Ansible and what each item value in the PLAY RECAP section means. Understanding these outputs is always helpful in troubleshooting any issues that may arise while running your playbook.

8.16 Printing Output Using Ansible Debug Module

In Ansible, the ability to print output using the debug module is extremely useful for troubleshooting playbook runs and ensuring optimal performance without errors. The register and debug modules can also be used to check services from an Ansible playbook by storing the output in a variable and then printing it using the debug module. This allows for valuable information to be obtained during playbook runs, which can help in maintaining and improving the performance of your playbook.

Let's create a playbook to check the services running on the Fedora client node belonging to the "db_server" group.

$ **vi 8.16_check_fedora_services.yml**

```
---
- hosts: db_server
  become: true
  collections:
    - ansible.builtin

  tasks:
  - name: Checking service status
    command: systemctl status "{{ item }}"
    with_items:
    - sshd # service name is sshd for fedora
    - mariadb
    when: ansible_distribution == "Fedora"
    register: service_state
    ignore_errors: yes # allows the playbook to continue executing even if
    a task fails.

  - name: Display service state
    debug:
     var: service_state
```

Run the playbook and observe the output you receive. You may notice some errors for services that are not currently running on the servers.

$ **ansible-playbook --ask-become-pass 8.16_check_fedora_services.yml**
BECOME password: ***************

[...omitted for brevity]

Create a new playbook to check services running on the Ubuntu servers only by using the first playbook as a base. Simply copy the file "8.16_check_fedora_services.yml" and name it "8.16_check_ubuntu_services.yml" using the command "cp 8.16_check_fedora_services.yml 8.16_check_ubuntu_services.yml". Take special care with the service names for Ubuntu as the OpenSSH service name is "ssh" instead of "sshd".

```
$ cp 8.16_check_fedora_services.yml 8.16_check_ubuntu_services.yml
$ vi 8.16_check_ubuntu_services.yml
$ cat 8.16_check_ubuntu_services.yml
---
- hosts: db_server
  become: true
  collections:
    - ansible.builtin

  tasks:
  - name: Checking service status
    command: systemctl status "{{ item }}"
    with_items:
    - ssh # service name changed to ssh for Ubuntu
    - mariadb # service name is the same as fedora
    when: ansible_distribution == "Ubuntu"
    register: service_state
    ignore_errors: yes # allows the playbook to continue executing even if
    a task fails

  - name: Display service state
    debug:
      var: service_state
```

Execute the playbook and verify that there are no unexpected errors or alerts.

```
$ ansible-playbook --ask-become-pass 8.17_test_ignore_errors.yml
BECOME password: ***************
```

[...omitted for brevity]

We only have two more sections left in this chapter, and you deserve a well-deserved break from your computer. It's essential to take breaks in between your reading and lab sessions and get plenty of water, fresh air, and sometimes a new perspective in life to make the most of your pursuit of IT greatness.

8.17 Using "ignore_errors: yes" to Allow Playbook Completion Despite Errors

In Ansible, the "ignore_errors" parameter is a helpful feature that allows a playbook to continue executing even if some tasks encounter errors. This can be beneficial when you expect certain errors to occur or when there are transient issues that do not need to stop the playbook from running. Similar to Python's "continue" syntax, this feature enables the program to skip over errors and continue with execution.

For example, let's say you have a task that tries to delete a file that may not exist. Typically, this task would fail and interrupt the playbook execution. However, if you specify "ignore_errors: yes" for that task, the playbook will proceed and finish successfully. The "ignore_errors: yes" parameter in Ansible works similarly to the continue statement in Python, which allows you to skip over an iteration in a loop if a particular condition is met without stopping the loop itself.

It's important to exercise caution when using "ignore_errors" because ignoring errors can have unexpected consequences and create problems in the long run. It's recommended to use this feature only when necessary and to thoroughly test the playbook after implementing it. It's essential to assess the scenario and determine if using this feature is appropriate based on the usage.

$ **8.17_test_ignore_errors.yml**

```
---
- name: Test playbook for ignore_errors
  hosts: all
  gather_facts: false
  become: true

  tasks:
    - name: Failing task
      ansible.builtin.command: /bin/DodgyApp
```

```
#        ignore_errors: yes

   - name: Non-failing task
     debug:
        msg: "Work hard, play hard, and always keep at school!"
```

To proceed, you can first execute the playbook without the "ignore_errors" parameter by commenting it out with the "#" symbol. This will disable the line in the YAML playbook. Then, carefully observe the output. You should encounter an error, and your playbook will be interrupted without completely running the plays.

```
$ ansible-playbook --ask-become-pass 8.17_test_ignore_errors.yml
BECOME password: ***************

PLAY [Test playbook for ignore_errors] ***********************************

TASK [Failing task] ******************************************************
fatal: [192.168.127.161]: FAILED! => {"ansible_facts": {"discovered_
interpreter_python": "/usr/bin/python3"}, "changed": false, "cmd": "/bin/
DodgyApp", "msg": "[Errno 2] No such file or directory: b'/bin/DodgyApp'",
"rc": 2, "stderr": "", "stderr_lines": [], "stdout": "", "stdout_
lines": []}
fatal: [192.168.127.162]: FAILED! => {"ansible_facts": {"discovered_
interpreter_python": "/usr/bin/python3"}, "changed": false, "cmd": "/bin/
DodgyApp", "msg": "[Errno 2] No such file or directory: b'/bin/DodgyApp'",
"rc": 2, "stderr": "", "stderr_lines": [], "stdout": "", "stdout_
lines": []}
fatal: [192.168.127.151]: FAILED! => {"ansible_facts": {"discovered_
interpreter_python": "/usr/bin/python3"}, "changed": false, "cmd": "/bin/
DodgyApp", "msg": "[Errno 2] No such file or directory: b'/bin/DodgyApp'",
"rc": 2, "stderr": "", "stderr_lines": [], "stdout": "", "stdout_
lines": []}

PLAY RECAP ***************************************************************
```

```
192.168.127.151          : ok=0    changed=0    unreachable=0    failed=1
skipped=0    rescued=0    ignored=0
192.168.127.161          : ok=0    changed=0    unreachable=0    failed=1
skipped=0    rescued=0    ignored=0
192.168.127.162          : ok=0    changed=0    unreachable=0    failed=1
skipped=0    rescued=0    ignored=0
```

To activate the "ignore_errors" feature, simply remove the "#" symbol that was used to comment it out in the previous step. The updated code should look like the example shown here:

$ **8.17_test_ignore_errors.yml**

```
---
- name: Test playbook for ignore_errors
  hosts: all
  gather_facts: false
  become: true

  tasks:
    - name: Failing task
      ansible.builtin.command: /bin/DodgyApp
      ignore_errors: yes

    - name: Non-failing task
      debug:
        msg: "Work hard, play hard, and always keep at school!"
```

If you run the same playbook again with the "ignore_errors" parameter activated, any errors encountered will be ignored, and the playbook will continue to execute all the tasks in the play.

$ **ansible-playbook --ask-become-pass 8.17_test_ignore_errors.yml**
BECOME password: **************

```
PLAY [Test playbook for ignore_errors] ************************************

TASK [Failing task] ******************************************************
fatal: [192.168.127.162]: FAILED! => {"ansible_facts": {"discovered_
interpreter_python": "/usr/bin/python3"}, "changed": false, "cmd": "/bin/
DodgyApp", "msg": "[Errno 2] No such file or directory: b'/bin/DodgyApp'",
"rc": 2, "stderr": "", "stderr_lines": [], "stdout": "", "stdout_
lines": []}
...ignoring
fatal: [192.168.127.161]: FAILED! => {"ansible_facts": {"discovered_
interpreter_python": "/usr/bin/python3"}, "changed": false, "cmd": "/bin/
DodgyApp", "msg": "[Errno 2] No such file or directory: b'/bin/DodgyApp'",
"rc": 2, "stderr": "", "stderr_lines": [], "stdout": "", "stdout_
lines": []}
...ignoring
fatal: [192.168.127.151]: FAILED! => {"ansible_facts": {"discovered_
interpreter_python": "/usr/bin/python3"}, "changed": false, "cmd": "/bin/
DodgyApp", "msg": "[Errno 2] No such file or directory: b'/bin/DodgyApp'",
"rc": 2, "stderr": "", "stderr_lines": [], "stdout": "", "stdout_
lines": []}
...ignoring

TASK [Non-failing task] **************************************************
ok: [192.168.127.161] => {
    "msg": "Work hard, play hard and always keep at school!"
}
ok: [192.168.127.162] => {
    "msg": "Work hard, play hard and always keep at school!"
}
ok: [192.168.127.151] => {
    "msg": "Work hard, play hard and always keep at school!"
}
```

```
PLAY RECAP ***********************************************************************
192.168.127.151              : ok=2     changed=0    unreachable=0    failed=0
skipped=0     rescued=0    ignored=1
192.168.127.161              : ok=2     changed=0    unreachable=0    failed=0
skipped=0     rescued=0    ignored=1
192.168.127.162              : ok=2     changed=0    unreachable=0    failed=0
skipped=0     rescued=0    ignored=1
```

Congratulations, now you have learned how to use "ignore_errors" to your advantage in Ansible playbooks. However, it's essential to weigh the pros and cons before using this feature in your playbook. Ignoring errors can have unintended consequences and create problems in the long run, so it's recommended to use this feature only when necessary and to thoroughly test the playbook after implementing it.

8.18 Install Samba and Create a Samba User on the Fedora Client Using a Playbook

Samba is a fantastic software that facilitates sharing of files and printers between Linux and Windows systems on a network. On Fedora Linux, Samba can be installed as a file server, allowing Samba users to access shared files and directories. It should be noted that the Samba user accounts are separate from the Linux user accounts. It supports multiple protocols such as SMB, CIFS, and FTP and can integrate with authentication systems like Active Directory. Samba promotes easy file sharing and collaboration among network users, making it ideal for personal and some business applications. For full functioning, the typical ports used for Samba file sharing – 137, 138, 139, and 445 – must be open in any firewalls running on the server or client machines.

Here, let's complete our chapter by installing the Samba package on f38c1 (a member of the file_server group). The package name is Samba, and we also need to add the task of creating a SambaShare group, a Samba user, and a password. Please create the following playbook:

```
$ vi 8.18_install_samba.yml
$ cat 8.18_install_samba.yml

---
- name: Install and enable Samba on Fedora and create a Samba user account
```

```yaml
hosts: file_server
become: true
collections:
  - community.general

tasks:
  - name: Install Samba packages
    community.general.dnf:
      name: [samba, samba-client] # Note, we are using the list method
      state: present

  - name: Enable Samba service
    ansible.builtin.systemd: # We need systemd module for Fedora
      name: smb # service name is smb
      state: started # Ensure that the service is started
      enabled: yes # start at start-up

  - name: Ensure sambashare group exists
    ansible.builtin.group:
      name: sambashare
      state: present

  - name: Create Samba user account
    ansible.builtin.user: # 'user' is an Ansible module
      name: sambajdoe
      password: "{{ 'Super5cretPassw0rd' | password_hash('sha512_crypt',
      'SaltyFish') }}"
      shell: /sbin/nologin
      groups: sambashare
      append: yes

  - name: Add sambajdoe to smbpasswd file
    ansible.builtin.command: echo -ne "Super5cretPassw0rd\
    nSuper5cretPassw0rd\n" | smbpasswd -a -s sambajdoe
```

When you execute the preceding playbook, you may notice an annoying
[DEPRECATION WARNING] message. Ansible kindly informs us of what to do to
suppress this message.

```
$ ansible-playbook --ask-become-pass 8.18_install_samba.yml
BECOME password: ***************
```

[...omitted for brevity]
*TASK [Create Samba user account] **
[DEPRECATION WARNING]: Encryption using the Python crypt module is
deprecated. The Python crypt module is
deprecated and will be removed from Python 3.13. Install the passlib
library for continued encryption
functionality. This feature will be removed in version 2.17. **Deprecation
warnings can be disabled by setting
deprecation_warnings=False in ansible.cfg.**
changed: [192.168.127.151]*

*TASK [Add sambajdoe to smbpasswd file] **********************************
changed: [192.168.127.151]*

*PLAY RECAP ***
192.168.127.151   : ok=6   changed=2   unreachable=0   failed=0
skipped=0   rescued=0   ignored=0*

To open the "ansible.cfg" file and add the last line as shown here, use a text editor
such as vi or any other preferred editor:

```
$ vi ansible.cfg
$ cat ansible.cfg
```

```
[defaults]
inventory = ./inventory
private_key_file = /home/jdoe/.ssh/ansible
deprecation_warnings=False # Suppress any deprecation warnings in the play
```

To confirm that the deprecation message no longer appears, execute the "8.18_
install_samba.yml" playbook one last time in this chapter. If the "ignore_warnings"
parameter was correctly set in the "ansible.cfg" file, you should not see the deprecation
message anymore.

```
$ ansible-playbook --ask-become-pass 8.18_install_samba.yml
BECOME password: ***************
```

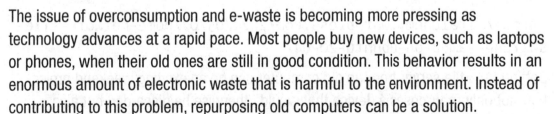

[...omitted for brevity]
TASK [Create Samba user account] ***
ok: [192.168.127.151]

TASK [Add sambajdoe to smbpasswd file] **
changed: [192.168.127.151]

PLAY RECAP **
192.168.127.151   : ok=6   changed=1   unreachable=0
failed=0   skipped=0   rescued=0   ignored=0

Configuring the Samba server is beyond the scope of this lesson, as this was a simple demonstration of how to install different packages using groups. You have now learned how to install services and check their status, all from the comfort of the control node. If you are interested in configuring the Samba server on Ubuntu, feel free to read the next TIP.

Tip

Bring your old or neglected PC/laptop/NUC back to life.

Give it a purpose as a Samba server for efficient file sharing and storage.

The issue of overconsumption and e-waste is becoming more pressing as technology advances at a rapid pace. Most people buy new devices, such as laptops or phones, when their old ones are still in good condition. This behavior results in an enormous amount of electronic waste that is harmful to the environment. Instead of contributing to this problem, repurposing old computers can be a solution.

In the IT industry, it is well known that technology has a life span, which means that certain devices become obsolete within a few years. However, there are still people who appreciate the value of old technology and collect vintage laptops or computers. Instead of letting these devices gather dust in a corner, why not put them to good use?

One way to repurpose old computers is to turn them into home file servers. A file server is a computer that stores files, such as photos or documents, and allows them to be accessed by other devices on a network. With the help of some simple steps, it is easy to set up a Samba server on an old PC, laptop, Next Unit of Computing (NUC, see Figure 8-6), or Raspberry Pi.

Both Fedora and Ubuntu are Linux-based operating systems that are commonly used in servers. The main author's blog provides an excellent guide on how to install Ubuntu and set up a Samba server. The Samba server allows you to transfer files from your phone or computer and store them safely on the old device. With the prices of SSDs at an all-time low, you can create a very quiet and energy-efficient file server system that runs in the background, waiting for you to upload and share files. Why pay for public cloud storage when you can build your own at home?

Figure 8-6. *Repurpose an old Intel NUC as a Samba server*

```
https://italchemy.wordpress.com/2021/05/02/home-network-file-
sharing-samba-on-ubuntu-20-04/
```

Setting up a file server from an old computer can be an exciting weekend project that not only repurposes a device that would otherwise be discarded but also provides a useful and practical solution for storing important files. Moreover, it can also be a fun learning experience that introduces you to the world of Linux and server administration.

8.19 Summary

In this chapter, you have expanded your knowledge of Ansible by learning how to
improve your playbook, add more tasks, and target specific nodes. You have discussed
the importance of idempotency, familiarized yourself with Ansible error messages,
and used the verbose mode. Additionally, you have covered conditional statements,
playbook refactoring, and error handling to ensure your plays are complete. This chapter
is one of the most significant chapters, and it is expected that you grasp and comprehend
as much as possible. If you are struggling with any part of the chapter, take your time to
understand it.

   To put these concepts into practice, we have demonstrated how to install Samba
and create a Samba user on a Fedora client using a playbook. By understanding these
concepts, you can create efficient and effective playbooks that can automate various
tasks on multiple hosts. With this knowledge, you can streamline your processes and
save valuable time and effort.

CHAPTER 9

Learning Ansible Basic Concepts III: Git, Tags, Managing Files, and Services

In this chapter, we delve into some more basic concepts in Ansible, including using GitHub to upload and share your playbooks or backing up your important work files. You will start with a step-by-step guide on how to get started with GitHub, create and upload playbooks, and utilize the cowsay feature. Next, we explore the Ansible tag concept, which allows you to selectively run specific tasks in a playbook, saving you time and improving performance. We then move on to managing files and services with Ansible, demonstrating how to create and update text files and configure services like Apache HTTP Server. Finally, we round off the chapter by illustrating how to copy and update text files with an Ansible playbook, which makes it easier to manage multiple servers. This chapter is dynamite as it also introduces you to some more Linux applications, such as neofetch, and exposes you to write a simple Python application to be integrated and used with an Ansible playbook at the end of this chapter. Whether you're new to Ansible or an experienced user, this chapter provides valuable insights and techniques to help you better manage your infrastructure.

© Brendan Choi and Erwin Medina 2023
B. Choi and E. Medina, *Introduction to Ansible Network Automation*,
https://doi.org/10.1007/978-1-4842-9624-0_9

When working with programming languages, it's essential to have a strategy for version controlling your files. This becomes even more critical when working in a team environment. Version control tools enable developers to track changes to source code over time, collaborate with other developers, and manage different versions of their code. In 2005, Linus Torvalds created Git, a distributed version control system designed to replace the proprietary BitKeeper system. Git has become the most widely used version control tool for source code management. Popular platforms such as GitHub, GitLab, Bitbucket, GitKraken, SourceForge, AWS CodeCommit, and Azure DevOps are all built on top of Git.

While this book is not primarily focused on software development, it's important to be familiar with at least one version control tool. GitHub is one of the most popular tools and offers free access after account registration. It allows developers to upload, store, and practice version control on a free account. With GitHub, you can create repositories, manage branches, commit changes, and collaborate with others through pull requests. By familiarizing yourself with Git and GitHub, you can easily manage your code, collaborate with others, and ensure the integrity of your code over time.

Getting Started with GitHub

GitHub is a powerful tool that can be used to upload, download, and version control your code using its web interface. However, you can also use Git commands from the command line to manage your repositories. Table 9-1 shows some Git commands that you can use to interact with your GitHub repository.

Table 9-1. Basic Git commands

Git command	Description
git clone	Clones a Git directory from the remote GitHub repository onto your local machine
git status	Displays the status of the files in your local repository, showing any uncommitted changes
git diff file_name	Displays the differences between the current version of the file in your local repository and the most recent commit to the repository

(continued)

Table 9-1. (*continued*)

Git command	Description
git add file_name	Adds a file to the staging area in your local repository, which prepares it for committing
git commit -m "message"	Commits the changes in the staging area to your local repository with a descriptive commit message
git push origin main	Sends the changes from your local repository to the remote GitHub repository on the main branch
git pull	Pulls the most recent changes from the remote GitHub repository down to your local repository

By using these Git commands in Table 9-1, you can perform the basic GitHub repository management from the command line. Whether you're working on a team project or just want to keep track of changes to your code, Git and GitHub provide powerful tools for version control and collaboration.

The first step to getting started with GitHub is to create an account using your email address. Here's a quick guide to help you create your account and start using GitHub:

Step 1: If you don't already have a GitHub account, go to `https://github.com/join` and create one by providing your email address, username, and password.

Step 2: Once you've successfully created your account, you can log in using your credentials and begin exploring the platform's many features. To create your first repository on GitHub, navigate to the top right corner of the page and click on the "+" icon, as shown in Figure 9-1. From the drop-down menu, select "New repository" to begin the setup process. This will allow you to define the repository's name, description, and other important details.

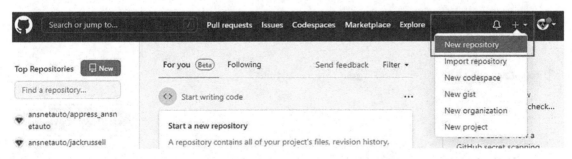

Figure 9-1. *Create a new GitHub repository 1*

405

Step 3: As shown in Figure 9-2, provide a name and brief description for your repository, and select whether you want it to be public or private. This choice will determine who can view and contribute to your repository.

Create a new repository

A repository contains all project files, including the revision history. Already have a project repository elsewhere? Import a repository.

Owner *   Repository name *

[ansnetauto ▾] / [repo1]

         ✔ repo1 is available.

Great repository names are short and memorable. Need inspiration? How about jubilant-garbanzo?

Description (optional)

[Ansible playbook repository 1]

○ 🔖 **Public**
    Anyone on the internet can see this repository. You choose who can commit.

○ 🔒 **Private**
    You choose who can see and commit to this repository.

Initialize this repository with:

☑ **Add a README file**
    This is where you can write a long description for your project. Learn more about READMEs.

Add .gitignore

[.gitignore template: None ▾]

Choose which files not to track from a list of templates. Learn more about ignoring files.

Choose a license

[License: None ▾]

A license tells others what they can and can't do with your code. Learn more about licenses.

This will set ⑂ main as the default branch. Change the default name in your settings.

ⓘ You are creating a public repository in your personal account.

[**Create repository**]

Figure 9-2. *Create a new GitHub repository 2*

We have selected "public" for full visibility, as we plan to share this project with our readers. However, it's important to take the time to consider the nature of your project and the level of access you want to grant to others before making your decision. By selecting the appropriate visibility setting, you can ensure that your code is accessible to the right audience and protected from unwanted access.

9.1 Creating and Uploading Playbooks to GitHub, Featuring cowsay

Now that we have a GitHub account and a brand-new repository to store our playbooks and other files, it's time to create two directories for this exercise. We'll create a "ch09" directory as our working directory and a "repo1" directory to be used as our GitHub base directory. In this exercise, we'll create a base directory with the same name as the GitHub repository to keep things simple. We'll also create a few files along the way, starting with the installation of cowsay on our control machine (f38s1) and the creation of a cowsay01.txt file. Next, we'll create a new ansible.cfg, inventory, and playbook files before executing the playbook to create three extra files that gather system information about our client nodes' OS using neofetch.

The grand plan for this section is to have some fun with cowsay, neofetch, and GitHub. You can pick up on different components of GitHub and make this exercise more visible and interesting.

Step 1: Create new directories named "ch09" and "repo1" on your Ansible Control Machine (f38s1) and enter the commands provided to follow along with the exercise.

```
[jdoe@f38s1 ~]$ mkdir ch09 repo1
[jdoe@f38s1 ~]$ cd ch09
[jdoe@f38s1 repo1]$ pwd
/home/jdoe/ch09
```

```
[jdoe@f38s1 ch09]$ sudo dnf install cowsay -y
[jdoe@f38s1 ch09]$ cowsay "Learning Ansible is fun!" > cowsay01.txt
[jdoe@f38s1 ch09]$ cowsay "Learning Ansible is fun!"
```

You will need to install cowsay on your control machine to see Figure 9-3 on your screen. The same package will be used to display the ASCII art when you execute your playbooks in Ansible.

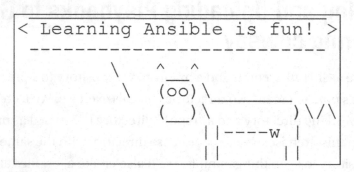

Figure 9-3. *cowsay learning Ansible is fun!*

Step 2: Create a new ansible.cfg file and a new inventory file, as shown here:

```
[jdoe@f38s1 repo1]$ vi ansible.cfg
```

```
[jdoe@f38s1 repo1]$ cat ansible.cfg
```

```
[defaults]
inventory = ./inventory
private_key_file = /home/jdoe/.ssh/ansible
deprecation_warnings=False
# nocows = 1 # The default is 0 or enabled. Remove '#' to disable cowsay,
cow_selection = random # the cowsay ASCII art characters will randomly change
forks=30 # The default parallel forked processes is 5. The maximum number
of parallel processes
```

Step 3: Create a new inventory file and simplify the servers based on their OS distribution type. Add them under the parent group "Linux".

```
[jdoe@f38s1 repo1]$ vi inventory
```

```
[jdoe@f38s1 repo1]$ cat inventory
```

```
[all:vars]
```

[fedora] # a client node group for Fedora
f38c1 ansible_host=192.168.127.151 # When the ansible_host parameter is used, we can specify the hostname, when the playbook runs, the hostname is displayed. If DNS is available, we can also use DNS or another option is to use Linux host files, but this is a lot easier.

[ubuntu] # a client node group for Ubuntu
u23c1 ansible_host=192.168.127.161
u23c2 ansible_host=192.168.127.162

[linux:children] # Assign children groups under this main group
fedora
ubuntu

Step 4: Create a simple playbook named "9.1_install_neofetch.yml" to install a system information tool, neofetch.

[jdoe@f38s1 ch09]$ **vi 9.1_install_neofetch.yml**
[jdoe@f38s1 ch09]$ **ls**
9.1_install_neofetch.yml ansible.cfg inventory
[jdoe@f38s1 ch09]$ **cat 9.1_install_neofetch.yml**

- name: Install and run neofetch command # Playbook name
  hosts: all # Target hosts
  gather_facts: false # Disable fact gathering
  become: true # Become root user to run tasks
  collections:
    - ansible.builtin

  tasks:
    - name: Install neofetch package # Task name
      package: # Ansible package module
        name: neofetch # Package name to install
        state: present # Ensure the package is installed

    - name: Run neofetch command and save output # Task name
      shell: neofetch # Run neofetch command
      register: neofetch_output # Capture the output of the command

409

```
    delegate_to: "{{ inventory_hostname }}" # Delegate the task to each
    host individually

- name: Save neofetch output to file on Control Machine # Task name
    local_action: # Run action on the control machine, not the
    target hosts
        module: copy # Ansible copy module
        content: "{{ neofetch_output.stdout }}" # Copy the output of the
        neofetch command
        dest: "./neofetch_output_{{ inventory_hostname }}.txt" # Save the
        output to a file, appending the hostname of each client node to the
        filename in the current working directory
```

In the preceding playbook, we are simplifying module names with the "collections" keyword, which lets us to define a list of collections that our playbook should search for unqualified module and action names. In our case, it is the "ansible.builtin" collection which is part of ansible-core, so you can use the collections keyword and then simply refer to short-form names of modules throughout our playbook (*source: https:// docs.ansible.com/ansible/latest/collections_guide/collections_using_ playbooks.html*).

If you need to save the output of the preceding playbook on each client node instead of the Ansible Control Machine, please refer to the following tip.

Tip

Do you want to save the output on the client nodes?

In the "9.1_install_neofetch.yml" playbook, we used "delegate_to:" and "local_ action:" to copy the output and save it in the control machine's local directory. However, if you want to save the files on each client machine as well, you can append the following playbook. After executing the playbook once again, it will also save the output from the neofetch command to the /tmp/ directory. The main difference between the two playbooks is the use of a different module.

```
- name: Save neofetch output to file on client nodes
  copy: # runs the copy on the client node, not on Control Machine
    content: "{{ neofetch_output.stdout | trim }}"
    dest: "/tmp/neofetch_output{{ inventory_hostname }}.txt"
```

Step 5: Execute the playbook to create three additional files with information about the client nodes' system using the neofetch tool.

```
$ ansible-playbook --ask-become-pass 9.1_install_neofetch.yml
BECOME password: ***************

[...output omitted for brevity]
```

Step 6: Check the number of files in the /home/jdoe/ch09/ directory. After running the last playbook successfully, you should now have seven files: ansible.cfg, inventory, the 9.1_install_neofetch.yml playbook, cowsay01.txt, and three files with system information for each client node created by the playbook.

```
[jdoe@f38s1 ch09]$ ll -lt
```

```
total 28
-rw-r--r--. 1 root root 2291 Apr 29 15:32 neofetch_output_f38c1.txt
-rw-r--r--. 1 root root 2451 Apr 29 15:32 neofetch_output_u23c1.txt
-rw-r--r--. 1 root root 2451 Apr 29 15:32 neofetch_output_u23c2.txt
-rw-r--r--. 1 jdoe jdoe  756 Apr 29 15:31 9.1_install_neofetch.yml
-rw-r--r--. 1 jdoe jdoe  168 Apr 29 15:30 inventory
-rw-r--r--. 1 jdoe jdoe  150 Apr 29 15:30 ansible.cfg
-rw-r--r--. 1 jdoe jdoe  210 Apr 29 15:30 cowsay01.txt
```

Step 7: On your Ansible Control Machine, f38s1, retrieve your public key for id_ed25519.pub and copy it to the clipboard.

```
[jdoe@f38s1 ch09]$ cd ..
```

```
[jdoe@f38s1 ~]$ ls
ch08   ch09
[jdoe@f38s1 ~]$ ls -a
```

```
.  ..  .ansible  .bash_history  .bash_logout  .bash_profile  .
bashrc  ch08  .config  repo1  .ssh  .viminfo
[jdoe@f38s1 ~]$ ls .ssh
ansible  ansible.pub  id_ed25519  id_ed25519.pub  known_hosts  known_
hosts.old
[jdoe@f38s1 ~]$ cat .ssh/id_ed25519.pub
ssh-ed25519 AAAAC3NzaC1lZDI1NTE5AAAAIKaBKRacKDPr5WCIpiG5ZHyyRIIuecM7AHZYG7A
u+yuU jdoe default
```

Step 8: Navigate to GitHub and click on your profile icon at the top right corner of the page. From the drop-down menu, select "Settings". Next, select "SSH and GPG keys" from the menu on the left. Click on the "New SSH Key" button and add your SSH key, making sure to include a descriptive title and the key itself, starting with "ssh-ed25519" or "ssh-rsa". See Figure 9-4 for an example.

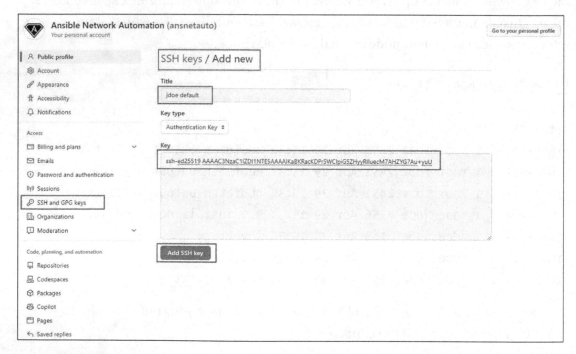

Figure 9-4. *Adding a new SSH key on GitHub*

Step 9: Clone the Git repository onto your Ansible Control Machine by going to the repository directory on GitHub and copying the SSH URL address, as shown in Figure 9-5.

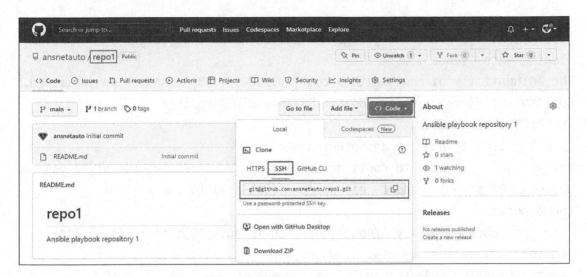

Figure 9-5. *Copy the SSH URL address on GitHub*

Step 10: Navigate to the home directory of jdoe and attempt to run the "git clone" command. You will be prompted with a "command not found" error as git is not installed by default on Fedora. Install the latest version of git using the command "sudo dnf install git -y".

```
[jdoe@f38s1 ~]$ pwd
/home/jdoe
[jdoe@f38s1 ~]$ ls
ch08   ch09
[jdoe@f38s1 ~]$ git clone git@github.com:ansnetauto/repo1.git
-bash: git: command not found
[jdoe@f38s1 ~]$ sudo dnf install git -y
[sudo] password for jdoe: ***************
[...installation output omitted for brevity]
[jdoe@f38s1 ~]$ git --version
git version 2.40.1
```

Step 11: Now, run the "git clone" command again using the SSH URL copied in step 9. Make sure the passphrase for your id_ed25519 key, created in an earlier chapter, is correct and functioning. If you have forgotten the passphrase you entered, then you will need to reset it by referring to Chapter 6.

413

```
[jdoe@f38s1 ~]$ git clone git@github.com:ansnetauto/repo1.git
Cloning into 'repo1'...
The authenticity of host 'github.com (20.248.137.48)' can't be established.
ED25519 key fingerprint is SHA256:+DiY3wvvV6TuJJhbpZisF/
zLDAOzPMSvHdkr4UvCOqU.
This key is not known by any other names
Are you sure you want to continue connecting (yes/no/[fingerprint])? yes
Warning: Permanently added 'github.com' (ED25519) to the list of
known hosts.
Enter passphrase for key '/home/jdoe/.ssh/id_ed25519': ***************
remote: Enumerating objects: 3, done.
remote: Counting objects: 100% (3/3), done.
remote: Total 3 (delta 0), reused 0 (delta 0), pack-reused 0
Receiving objects: 100% (3/3), done.
[jdoe@f38s1 ~]$ ll
total 8
drwxr-xr-x. 2 jdoe jdoe 4096 Apr 28 18:31 ch08
drwxr-xr-x. 2 jdoe jdoe 4096 Apr 29 15:32 ch09
drwxr-xr-x. 3 jdoe jdoe   35 Apr 29 16:09 repo1
[jdoe@f38s1 ~]$ ll repo1/
total 4
-rw-r--r--. 1 jdoe jdoe 38 Apr 29 16:09 README.md
```

Since we have a README.md file in our repository, it will be downloaded from the GitHub server in the cloud.

Step 12: Let's quickly modify the README.md file and update it from our Ansible Control Machine. Your README.md file should look like Figure 9-6.

```
[jdoe@f38s1 ~]$ cowsay "ANSIBLE IS AWESOME!" > repo1/README.md
[jdoe@f38s1 ~]$ cat repo1/README.md
```

```
  < ANSIBLE IS AWESOME! >
   --------------------
      \     ^__^
       \   (oo)_____
          (__)\        )\/\
              ||----w |
              ||      ||
```

Figure 9-6. *Update README.md*

Step 13: Use the "git diff" command to check the difference between the original README.md file and the updated file on the local machine. Your output should look similar to Figure 9-7 below.

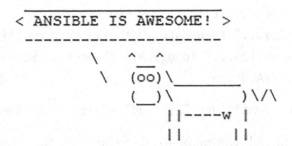

```
[jdoe@f38s1 ~]$ cd repo1/
[jdoe@f38s1 repo1]$ git diff README.md
```

```
diff --git a/README.md b/README.md
index 532b082..d096c40 100644
--- a/README.md
+++ b/README.md
@@ -1,2 +1,8 @@
-# repo1
-Ansible playbook repository 1
+ _____
+< ANSIBLE IS AWESOME! >
+ ------------------------
+      \     ^__^
+       \   (oo)_____
+          (__)\        )\/\
+              ||----w |
+              ||      ||
```

Figure 9-7. *Check the README.md file difference*

Step 14: Check the status using the "git status" command.

```
[jdoe@f38s1 repo1]$ git status
On branch main
Your branch is up to date with 'origin/main'.
```

```
Changes not staged for commit:
  (use "git add <file>..." to update what will be committed)
  (use "git restore <file>..." to discard changes in working directory)
        modified:   README.md

no changes added to commit (use "git add" and/or "git commit -a")
```

Step 15: Use the "git add" command to add a single file. Note that the change will not take place until we use the "git commit" command.

```
[jdoe@f38s1 repo1]$ git add README.md
[jdoe@f38s1 repo1]$ git status
On branch main
Your branch is up to date with 'origin/main'.

Changes to be committed:
  (use "git restore --staged <file>..." to unstage)
        modified:   README.md

[jdoe@f38s1 repo1]$ git commit -m "My First git commit"
Author identity unknown

*** Please tell me who you are.

Run

  git config --global user.email "you@example.com"
  git config --global user.name "Your Name"

to set your account's default identity.
Omit --global to set the identity only in this repository.

fatal: unable to auto-detect email address (got 'jdoe@f38s1.(none)')
```

Step 16: Git expects us to complete the missing configuration for the user email and name. Please add your details carefully by following the commands:

```
[jdoe@f38s1 repo1]$ git config --global user.email ansnetauto@gmail.com
[jdoe@f38s1 repo1]$ git config --global user.name "John Doe"
[jdoe@f38s1 repo1]$ git commit -m "My First git commit"
```

```
[main 38a0a18] My First git commit
 1 file changed, 8 insertions(+), 2 deletions(-)
[jdoe@f38s1 repo1]$ git push origin main
Enter passphrase for key '/home/jdoe/.ssh/id_ed25519': ***************
Enumerating objects: 5, done.
Counting objects: 100% (5/5), done.
Compressing objects: 100% (2/2), done.
Writing objects: 100% (3/3), 336 bytes | 336.00 KiB/s, done.
Total 3 (delta 0), reused 0 (delta 0), pack-reused 0
To github.com:ansnetauto/repo1.git
   9c7ee95..38a0a18  main -> main
```

Step 17: Go to your GitHub page, refresh the browser, and check the README.md file, as shown in Figure 9-8.

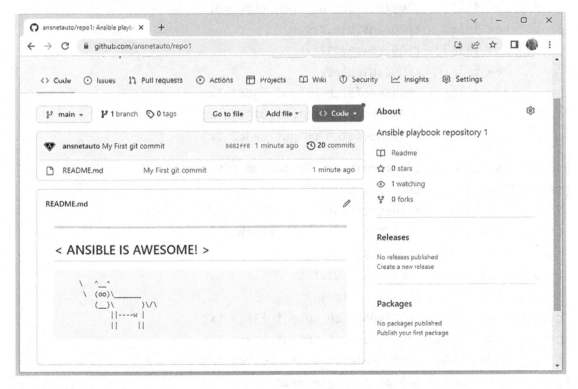

Figure 9-8. *Check the updated README.md file*

417

Step 18: Move the ch09 directory to the repo1 directory and use the "git add ." command to add all the files and directories. Don't forget the "." or the period after the git add command.

```
[jdoe@f38s1 repo1]$ mv ../ch09 .
[jdoe@f38s1 repo1]$ ls
ch09  README.md
[jdoe@f38s1 repo1]$ git add .
[jdoe@f38s1 repo1]$ git status
On branch main
Your branch is up to date with 'origin/main'.

Changes to be committed:
  (use "git restore --staged <file>..." to unstage)
        new file:   ch09/9.1_install_neofetch.yml
        new file:   ch09/ansible.cfg
        new file:   ch09/cowsay01.txt
        new file:   ch09/inventory
        new file:   ch09/neofetch_output_f38c1.txt
        new file:   ch09/neofetch_output_u23c1.txt
        new file:   ch09/neofetch_output_u23c2.txt

[jdoe@f38s1 repo1]$ git commit -m "My second git commit"
[main 591a800] My second git commit
 7 files changed, 178 insertions(+)
 create mode 100644 ch09/9.1_install_neofetch.yml
 create mode 100644 ch09/ansible.cfg
 create mode 100644 ch09/cowsay01.txt
 create mode 100644 ch09/inventory
 create mode 100644 ch09/neofetch_output_f38c1.txt
 create mode 100644 ch09/neofetch_output_u23c1.txt
 create mode 100644 ch09/neofetch_output_u23c2.txt
[jdoe@f38s1 repo1]$ git push origin main
Enter passphrase for key '/home/jdoe/.ssh/id_ed25519': ***************
Enumerating objects: 11, done.
Counting objects: 100% (11/11), done.
```

```
Compressing objects: 100% (10/10), done.
Writing objects: 100% (10/10), 2.49 KiB | 510.00 KiB/s, done.
Total 10 (delta 1), reused 0 (delta 0), pack-reused 0
remote: Resolving deltas: 100% (1/1), done.
To github.com:ansnetauto/repo1.git
   38a0a18..591a800  main -> main
```

Step 19: Go back to your GitHub page and verify that all the files in the ch09 directory have been successfully uploaded, as shown in Figure 9-9.

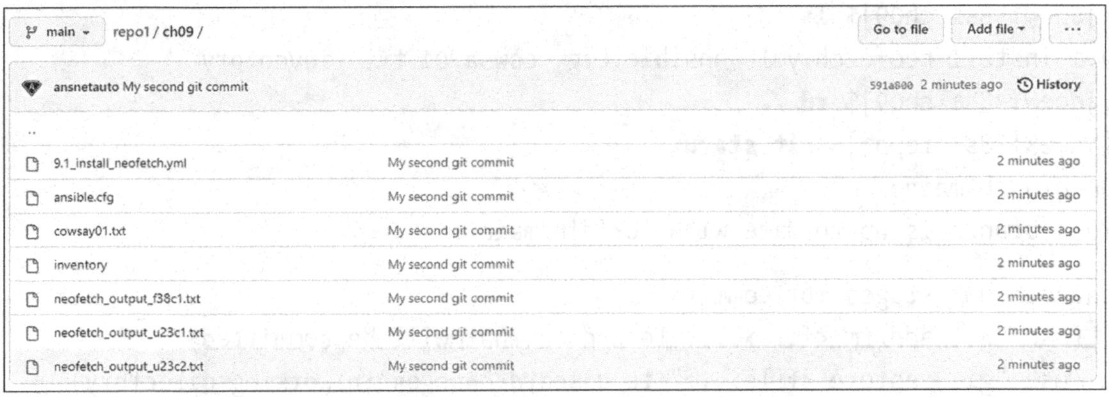

Figure 9-9. *The GitHub repo1/ch09 directory*

Step 20: Optionally, repeat the previous steps for the ch08 directory and upload it to GitHub. The ch08 directory has already been moved under the /home/jdoe/repo1/ directory, and the last processes have been repeated to upload the ch08 directory with all the playbooks and files from the previous chapter, as shown in Figure 9-10.

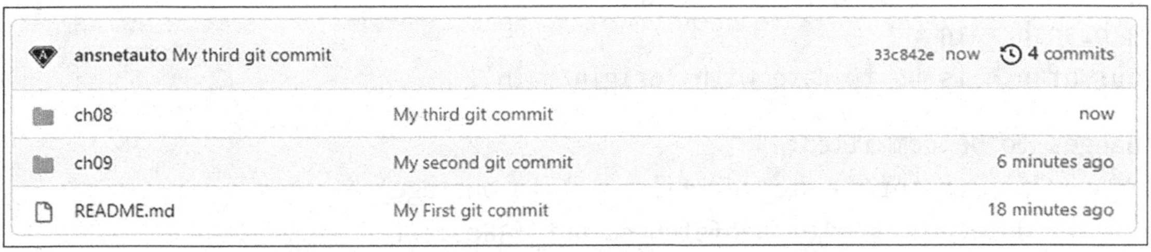

Figure 9-10. *GitHub after uploading the ch08 directory and files*

Step 21: Here, you will learn how to delete files on GitHub. First, you need to remove the three output files under the ch09 directory. Then, run the following Git commands:

```
[jdoe@f38s1 repo1]$ cd ch09
[jdoe@f38s1 ch09]$ ls
9.1_install_neofetch.yml  ansible.cfg  cowsay01.txt  inventory  neofetch_
output_f38c1.txt  neofetch_output_u23c1.txt  neofetch_output_u23c2.txt
[jdoe@f38s1 ch09]$ rm -rf neofetch_output_* # Remove 3 system
information files
[jdoe@f38s1 ch09]$ ls
9.1_install_neofetch.yml  ansible.cfg  cowsay01.txt  inventory
[jdoe@f38s1 ch09]$ cd ..
[jdoe@f38s1 repo1]$ git status
On branch main
Your branch is up to date with 'origin/main'.

Changes not staged for commit:
  (use "git add/rm <file>..." to update what will be committed)
  (use "git restore <file>..." to discard changes in working directory)
        deleted:    ch09/neofetch_output_f38c1.txt
        deleted:    ch09/neofetch_output_u23c1.txt
        deleted:    ch09/neofetch_output_u23c2.txt

no changes added to commit (use "git add" and/or "git commit -a")

[jdoe@f38s1 repo1]$ git add ch09
[jdoe@f38s1 repo1]$ git status
On branch main
Your branch is up to date with 'origin/main'.

Changes to be committed:
  (use "git restore --staged <file>..." to unstage)
        deleted:    ch09/neofetch_output_f38c1.txt
        deleted:    ch09/neofetch_output_u23c1.txt
        deleted:    ch09/neofetch_output_u23c2.txt
```

```
[jdoe@f38s1 repo1]$ git commit -m "Fourth git commit, delete 3 files"
[main 48d01b2] Fourth git commit, delete 3 files
 3 files changed, 124 deletions(-)
 delete mode 100644 ch09/neofetch_output_f38c1.txt
 delete mode 100644 ch09/neofetch_output_u23c1.txt
 delete mode 100644 ch09/neofetch_output_u23c2.txt

[jdoe@f38s1 repo1]$ git push origin main
Enter passphrase for key '/home/jdoe/.ssh/id_ed25519': **************
Enumerating objects: 5, done.
Counting objects: 100% (5/5), done.
Compressing objects: 100% (3/3), done.
Writing objects: 100% (3/3), 292 bytes | 292.00 KiB/s, done.
Total 3 (delta 2), reused 0 (delta 0), pack-reused 0
remote: Resolving deltas: 100% (2/2), completed with 2 local objects.
To github.com:ansnetauto/repo1.git
   33c842e..48d01b2  main -> main
```

Step 22: Check if the files have been deleted from your GitHub account, as shown in Figure 9-11.

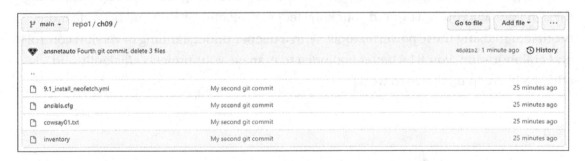

Figure 9-11. *GitHub – after removing three system information files*

Step 23: Create a file on GitHub and perform a pull action to confirm that the base directory is in sync with the GitHub directory.

```
[jdoe@f38s1 repo1]$ git pull
Enter passphrase for key '/home/jdoe/.ssh/id_ed25519': **************
Already up to date.
```

Step 24: To ensure that the cowsay feature doesn't interfere with your work, it's important to disable it. You can do this by removing the "#" from your inventory file. Disabling cowsay will allow you to focus solely on the task at hand and ensure that your progress is not impeded by unnecessary distractions. Your inventory file should look like the following example:

```
[defaults]
inventory = ./inventory
private_key_file = /home/jdoe/.ssh/ansible
deprecation_warnings=False
nocows = 1 # Disable cowsay
# cow_selection = random # Redundant configuration, disabled
forks=30
```

Congratulations on completing the mini GitHub basic training that featured cowsay! Remember to save your files frequently to ensure that you always have the latest valid copies on GitHub. This will help you avoid potential setbacks or loss of work. If you have more time, we highly recommend that you take advantage of the extensive Git and GitHub learning resources page available at the following URL: https://docs.github.com/en/get-started/quickstart/git-and-github-learning-resources. By exploring these resources, you can expand your knowledge of Git and GitHub and become more proficient in using these powerful tools. With a deeper understanding of version control and collaboration, you'll be better equipped to manage your projects efficiently and effectively. Keep up the good work!

Tip

What is neofetch?

Neofetch is a command-line utility that provides a wealth of information about a Linux system in a single command. It displays details such as the Linux distribution, kernel version, desktop environment, window manager, theme, and icon set, as well as CPU and GPU information. Neofetch is highly customizable, allowing users to modify its display options and add custom ASCII art or logos to their output. It supports a variety of operating systems, including Linux, macOS, and BSD, and is available in the repositories of many Linux distributions. With its ease of use and comprehensive system information, Neofetch is a popular tool among Linux users and system administrators. See Figure 9-12.

```
jdoe@u23c1:~$ neofetch
            .-/+oosssssoo+/-.              jdoe@u23c1
        `:+ssssssssssssssssss+:`           ----------
      -+ssssssssssssssssssyyssss+-         OS: Ubuntu 23.04 x86_64
    .ossssssssssssssssssdMMMNysssso.       Host: VMware Virtual Platform None
   /ssssssssshdmmNNmmyNMMMMhssssss/        Kernel: 6.2.0-20-generic
  +ssssssssshmydMMMMMMMNddddyssssssss+     Uptime: 10 hours, 18 mins
 /sssssssshNMMMyhhyyyyhmNMMMNhssssssss/    Packages: 794 (dpkg), 5 (snap)
.ssssssssdMMMNhsssssssssshNMMMdssssssss.   Shell: bash 5.2.15
+sssshhhyNMMNysssssssssssyNMMMysssssss+    Resolution: 1280x800
ossyNMMMNyMMhsssssssssssssshmmmhssssssso   Terminal: /dev/pts/0
ossyNMMMNyMMhsssssssssssssshmmmhssssssso   CPU: Intel i7-6700HQ (2) @ 2.591GHz
+sssshhhyNMMNysssssssssssyNMMMysssssss+    GPU: 00:0f.0 VMware SVGA II Adapter
.ssssssssdMMMNhsssssssssshNMMMdssssssss.   Memory: 299MiB / 3899MiB
 /sssssssshNMMMyhhyyyyhdNMMMNhssssssss/
  +sssssssssdmydMMMMMMMMdddddyssssssss+
   /ssssssssssshdmNNNNmyNMMMMhssssss/
    .ossssssssssssssssssdMMMNysssso.
      -+sssssssssssssssssyyyssss+-
        `:+ssssssssssssssssss+:`
            .-/+oossssoo+/-.
```

Figure 9-12. *Neofetch system information example*

9.2 Ansible Tags Explained

Every time you execute an Ansible playbook, you have to run it against all nodes. If you use tags, you can specifically run the playbook on tagged (targeted) nodes. Tags add some more flexibility to how the playbook is used in our plays, and this feature saves time as you only need to run the set of playbooks at specific targets. In Ansible, tags are used to selectively run specific tasks or plays within a playbook. Tags can be used to filter tasks or plays by a particular label or name, making it easier to run specific parts of a playbook or exclude certain tasks from being executed. Using tags in Ansible can help you selectively run specific tasks or plays within a playbook, making it easier to manage and maintain your automation workflows.

To add a tag to a task or play, you simply add the "tags" parameter to the task or play definition in your playbook. Here's an example:

```
$ vi 9.2_tags.yml
$ cat 9.2_tags.yml

---
- hosts: all # Set hosts to target and become the root user
  become: true
  collections:
    - ansible.builtin

  - name: install updates (Ubuntu)
    tags: always
    apt:
      upgrade: dist # Upgrade all packages to the latest version
      update_cache: yes # Update the local package cache
    when: ansible_distribution == "Ubuntu" # Only run on Ubuntu

  - name: install updates (Fedora)
    tags: always
    dnf:
      update_only: yes # Only update packages, don't install new ones
      update_cache: yes # Update the local package cache
    when: ansible_distribution == "Fedora" # Only run on Fedora

- hosts: linux # Set hosts to target and become the root user
become: true

  - name: install apache2 & PHP packages for Ubuntu
    tags: ubuntu,apache  # Add tags for easy identification
    apt:
      name:
        - apache2
        - libapache2-mod-php # Install Apache2 and PHP packages
      state: latest # Install the latest available version
    when: ansible_distribution == "Ubuntu" # Only run on Ubuntu
```

```
- name: install httpd & php packages for Fedora/CentOS
  tags: fedora,httpd  # Add tags for easy identification
  dnf:
    name:
      - httpd
      - php  # Install HTTPD and PHP packages
    state: latest  # Install the latest available version
  when: ansible_distribution == "Fedora"  # Only run on Fedora
```

This playbook is an example of using Ansible tags to selectively run specific tasks in a playbook based on the tags defined for those tasks. Tags allow for better organization, filtering, and selective execution of tasks in a playbook. The playbook has two plays: one for updating packages and another for installing Apache2 and PHP packages on different Linux distributions. The tasks in each play are tagged with specific tags, which enable the selection and execution of only the tasks that have those tags. For instance, the first play has tasks tagged with always, which means that these tasks will always be executed regardless of any tag filters applied. The second play has tasks tagged with apache, apache2, ubuntu, fedora, and httpd for easy identification and filtering.

During playbook execution, tags can be used to filter which tasks should be executed based on their assigned tags. For example, executing only tasks tagged with ubuntu will ensure that only tasks relevant to Ubuntu will be executed. This selective execution feature is useful in cases where only a subset of tasks needs to be run, such as when updating specific packages on certain hosts, without running other unrelated tasks. Ansible tags in Ansible allow for better organization, filtering, and selective execution of tasks in a playbook. The use of tags in this playbook enables the selection and execution of only the relevant tasks based on their assigned tags.

To see the tags defined in an Ansible playbook, you can run the command "ansible-playbook --list-tags <playbook.yml>". This will list all the tags used in the playbook, along with their description. You can also use tags to run a specific set of tasks in the playbook by specifying the tags with the "--tags" option. For example, if you only want to run tasks with the "apache" tag, you can use the command "ansible-playbook <playbook.yml> --tags apache". This can be useful when you want to run a subset of tasks in a large playbook or when you want to skip certain tasks. Additionally, using tags in your playbook can make it easier to organize and understand the tasks, especially when dealing with complex playbooks.

```
$ ansible-playbook --list-tags 9.2_tags.yml
```

```
playbook: 9.2_tags.yml

  play #1 (all): all            TAGS: []
      TASK TAGS: [always]

  play #2 (linux): linux           TAGS: []
      TASK TAGS: [apache, fedora, httpd, ubuntu]
```

To run specific tasks in an Ansible playbook, you can use tags. The "--tags" option is used to run only the tasks with specific tags when running the playbook. For example, if you want to run only the tasks with the "fedora" tag, you would use the following command:

```
$ ansible-playbook myplaybook.yml --tags fedora
```

This command would run only the tasks with the "fedora" tag and skip any other tasks in the playbook.

You can also use the "--skip-tags" option to skip tasks with a specific tag. For example, to skip tasks with the "apache" tag, you would use the following command:

```
$ ansible-playbook myplaybook.yml --skip-tags apache
```

Furthermore, you can add multiple tags to a task or play and use multiple tags when running the playbook to execute only the tasks that have any of the specified tags. This can help you to quickly and easily execute specific parts of your playbook based on their tags.

Use the tag name "--tags fedora" to only run the playbook on Fedora servers.

```
$ ansible-playbook -tags fedora --ask-become-pass 9.2_tags.yml
BECOME password: ***************
```

```
[...omitted for brevity]

< TASK [install httpd & php packages for Fedora/CentOS] >
 ---------------------------------------------------------
skipping: [u23c1] # skipped Ubuntu server
skipping: [u23c2] # skipped Ubuntu server
```

```
changed: [f38c1] # Executed on Fedora server only
[...omitted for brevity]
```

The preceding execution has two plays; the first play will execute on all servers with the always tag, and the second play will only execute on the servers with the tag, fedora only, and skip the Ubuntu servers which do not contain the specified tag.

Target more than single controlled nodes by using multiple tags separated by a comma and enclosed in quotation marks, for example, "--tags "apache, httpd"".

$ ansible-playbook --tags "apache, httpd" --ask-become-pass 9.2_tags.yml

```
BECOME password: ***************

[...omitted for brevity]
< TASK [install apache2 & PHP packages for Ubuntu] >
------------------------------------------------------

skipping: [f38c1]
changed: [u23c2]
changed: [u23c1]
_____

< TASK [install httpd & php packages for Fedora/CentOS] >
--------------------------------------------------------

skipping: [u23c1]
skipping: [u23c2]
ok: [f38c1]
```

[...omitted for brevity]

Automating repetitive tasks with Ansible can save a significant amount of time and effort in managing IT infrastructure. As you work with Ansible, take note of tasks that are performed repeatedly, as they are prime candidates for automation. In this playbook, we saw how tags could be used to run specific tasks on targeted nodes only, making it easier to manage a large infrastructure with many nodes.

By automating repetitive tasks and using tags effectively, you can streamline your IT operations, improve efficiency, and reduce the risk of errors. Ansible also provides other features like roles, templates, and modules that can help you automate more complex tasks and manage infrastructure more effectively.

Moving on to managing files, you will learn how to use Ansible to copy, move, and delete files and directories, as well as change their ownership and permissions. This will further enhance your ability to automate infrastructure management and increase the speed and efficiency of your IT operations.

9.3 Managing Files

When it comes to administering servers and network devices, file management is a crucial aspect of the job. Often, IT professionals need to transfer files between different nodes, whether it's to update software, transfer data, or make backups. Fortunately, Ansible playbooks can simplify this process by providing a streamlined method for copying, uploading, and downloading files. There are several file management tasks that Ansible can handle, including copying files to a server, uploading files to specific nodes, and downloading files from the Internet.

To copy a file to a server, an IT professional can use Ansible to transfer the file to a designated storage space on the target node. This allows for efficient and secure file management across different nodes. Uploading files to controlled nodes can also be done using Ansible. In this case, the IT professional can use the playbook to upload a file to specific nodes, such as f38c1, u23c1, and u23c2, from the control node f38s1.

Finally, Ansible can also be used to download a zip file from the Internet, unpack it, and install Terraform using a playbook. This can save time and streamline the installation process for IT professionals who need to install Terraform on multiple nodes. Overall, Ansible is a powerful tool for managing files between different nodes in a network, making file management more efficient and less time-consuming.

Step 1: Create a directory to store files and then create a simple HTML file in the "/home/jdoe/repo1/ch09/files" directory. The directory must be named "files" as Ansible will be searching for this directory name by default. In other words, if you do not specify the file storage path, Ansible will look for a directory named "files".

```
[jdoe@f38s1 ch09]$ mkdir files # Important! Name the directory as 'files'.
```

```
[jdoe@f38s1 ch09]$ cd files
[jdoe@f38s1 files]$ pwd
/home/jdoe/repo1/ch09/files # take a note of the present working directory
[jdoe@f38s1 files]$ vi default_site.html
```

```
[jdoe@f38s1 files]$ cat default_site.html
<!DOCTYPE html>
<html>
    <body>
        <h1>ANSIBLE LEARNING DEFAULT PAGE</h1>
        <p>You're on a roll!</p>
        <p>Stay the course!</p>
        <p>Keep your nose to the grindstone!</p>
    </body>
</html>
```

Step 2: Let's copy and reuse the previous playbook to create a new one for this section. You will append a new task to copy the HTML file and run the Ansible playbook.

```
[jdoe@f38s1 files]$ cd ..
[jdoe@f38s1 ch09]$ pwd
/home/jdoe/repo1/ch09
[jdoe@f38s1 ch09]$ cp 9.2_tags.yml 9.3_copy_file.yml
[jdoe@f38s1 ch09]$ vi 9.3_copy_file.yml
[jdoe@f38s1 ch09]$ cat 9.3_copy_file.yml
---
[...omitted for brevity]

  - name: copy default html file to web servers
    tags: apache,httpd
    copy:
      src: default_site.html # Ansible assumes source files are under the
      "files" directory
      dest: /var/www/html/index.html # The file name does not have to be
      the same
      owner: root # owner
      group: root # group
      mode: 0644 # permission

- hosts: fedora # target only fedora for this play
  become: true # run as the root user
  gather_facts: false # disable gather_facts to save time
```

```
  tasks:
  - name: Restart web services
    service: # use Ansible service module
      name: httpd # target service to restart
      state: restarted # restart the service
```

Step 3: Execute the Ansible playbook named 9.3_copy_file.yml to transfer the files to the designated client nodes. Ensure that you have properly configured the playbook to include the correct source and destination paths for the files you want to copy. Once the playbook has been executed, you can verify that the files have been successfully transferred by logging into the client nodes or web servers and checking the specified destination directories.

```
[jdoe@f38s1 ch09]$ ansible-playbook --ask-become-pass 9.3_copy_file.yml
```

```
BECOME password: ***************

[...omitted for brevity]

TASK [copy default html file to web servers]
*************************************************************************
changed: [u23c1]
changed: [u23c2]
changed: [f38c1]

PLAY RECAP
*************************************************************************
f38c1   : ok=5   changed=1   unreachable=0   failed=0   skipped=2
rescued=0   ignored=0
u23c1   : ok=5   changed=1   unreachable=0   failed=0   skipped=2
rescued=0   ignored=0
u23c2   : ok=5   changed=1   unreachable=0   failed=0   skipped=2
rescued=0   ignored=0
```

Step 4: Create a new playbook to check whether the files have been successfully uploaded to the client nodes or web servers.

```
[jdoe@f38s1 ch09]$ vi 9.3_check_files.yml
[jdoe@f38s1 ch09]$ cat 9.3_check_files.yml

---
- hosts: all
  become: true
  gather_facts: false
  collections:
    - ansible.builtin

  tasks:
  - name: get contents of a file
    command: cat /var/www/html/index.html # command to run
    register: file_output # register read content
    become: true

  - name: View the file contents
    debug: # debug captuere message
      msg: "{{file_output.stdout .split('\n') }}" # by adding .split('\n')
      reads the output line by line
```

Step 5: Now, run the playbook with the -l option to target a specific group. Here, we only want to run the playbook against the servers under the "fedora" device group. Since we only have one server, f38c1, the play will only target this single device.

```
[jdoe@f38s1 ch09]$ ansible-playbook -l fedora --ask-become-pass 9.3_check_
files.yml
BECOME password: ***************

PLAY [all]
**************************************************************************

TASK [get contents of file]
**************************************************************************
changed: [f38c1]
```

```
TASK [View the file contents]
************************************************************************
ok: [f38c1] => {
    "msg": [
        "<!DOCTYPE html>",
        "<html>",
        "    <body>",
        "        <h1>ANSIBLE LEARNING DEFAULT PAGE</h1>",
        "        <p>You're on a roll!</p>",
        "        <p>Stay the course!</p>",
        "        <p>Keep your nose to the grindstone!</p>",
        "    </body>",
        "</html>"
    ]
}

PLAY RECAP
************************************************************************
f38c1      : ok=2    changed=1    unreachable=0    failed=0    skipped=0
rescued=0    ignored=0
```

Now run the "ansible-playbook -l ubuntu --ask-become-pass 9.3_check_files.yml"
command to check the files on Ubuntu Web Servers too.

[jdoe@f38s1 ch09]$ **ansible-playbook -l ubuntu --ask-become-pass 9.3_check_**
files.yml
BECOME password: **************

[...omitted for brevity]

Step 6: Open your favorite web browser and check the new default web
page at the following URLs: http://192.168.127.151, http://192.168.127.161, and
http://192.168.127.162. If you have followed each step, you should see a similar default
page to Figure 9-13.

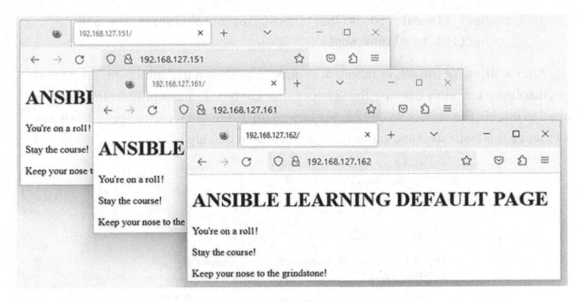

Figure 9-13. *Updated web page for testing*

Step 7: If you restart the Fedora web server (f38c1) for any reason, the service will stop because we have not yet enabled the service in our script. This is because we have not yet issued the "systemctl enable httpd" command on the affected web server. Let's quickly write a reboot playbook and test our theory.

```
[jdoe@f38s1 ch09]$ vi 9.3_reboot.yml
[jdoe@f38s1 ch09]$ cat 9.3_reboot.yml

- hosts: fedora  # target host group named fedora
become: yes  # run the playbook with superuser privileges
gather_facts: false
  collections:
    - ansible.builtin

tasks:
  - name: Reboot Fedora server
    reboot:  # The Ansible module
      reboot_timeout: 600  # The time in seconds to wait for the system
      to reboot
      test_command: uptime  # test whether the system has rebooted
      successfully
```

```
      connect_timeout: 60  # The timeout for establishing the SSH
      connection to client nodes
```

After waiting for the server reboot to complete, as shown in Figure 9-14, the page is not displayed correctly because the service is not enabled at startup. To fix this issue, we need to enable the service. We will cover how to do this in the services section. For now, let's leave this issue as is and move on to the next step quickly.

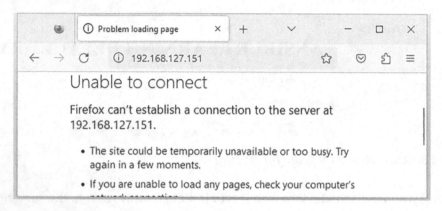

Figure 9-14. *The f38c1 web page after a system reboot*

Step 8: Terraform is an open source infrastructure as code (IaC) tool that enables users to define, provision, and manage cloud infrastructure using a high-level configuration language in a declarative manner. We want to explore Terraform's features, so we will install it on one of our client machines, f38c1, and assign it as the Terraform server.

We have chosen Terraform installation because we need to download the source files from HashiCorp's official download page and install them on our machine. This can be considered a type of file handling in Ansible. Let's quickly create a playbook to install the latest version of Terraform on our server. You don't have to use the same version used here (Terraform 15.5), but if a newer version is available, update the source address to pull the files from the correct location to ensure you install the latest Terraform version.

```
[jdoe@f38s1 ch09]$ vi 9.3_install_terraform.yml
[jdoe@f38s1 ch09]$ cat 9.3_install_terraform.yml

---
- hosts: f38c1
  become: true
```

```
gather_facts: false
collections:
  - ansible.builtin

tasks:
- name: Install unzip
  package:
    name: unzip # Install unzip on f38c1

- name: Install Terraform
  unarchive:
    src: https://releases.hashicorp.com/terraform/0.15.5/
    terraform_0.15.5_linux_amd64.zip
    dest: /usr/local/bin # File destination directory
    remote_src: yes # Tell Ansible that this is a remote source
    owner: root
    group: root
```

As this book is not solely focused on Terraform, we will not go beyond the package installation. However, if you have the time and resources to learn Terraform, it's a good idea to start from their official documentation site at www.terraform.io/docs/index.html.

Step 9: Now execute the installation playbook.

```
[jdoe@f38s1 ch09]$ ansible-playbook --ask-become-pass 9.3_install_
terraform.yml
BECOME password: *************

PLAY [f38c1]
***************************************************************************

TASK [Install unzip]
***************************************************************************
ok: [f38c1]

TASK [Install Terraform]
***************************************************************************
```

```
changed: [f38c1]
[...ommitted for brevity]

PLAY RECAP
***************************************************************************
f38c1   : ok=5    changed=1    unreachable=0    failed=0    skipped=0
rescued=0    ignored=0
```

By successfully downloading and installing Terraform on your client nodes, you have demonstrated the importance of Linux knowledge when working with Ansible. As we have seen in Chapter 3, downloading files from the Internet is a common task in automation, and this knowledge is critical when writing playbooks and testing Ansible. These concepts are also essential when automating network devices.

By utilizing Ansible to automate tasks, we can apply the same principles of copying files and installing software to our network infrastructure. In this way, we can manage our network devices and cloud infrastructure consistently and reliably. The ability to automate network infrastructure can improve network uptime, reduce errors, and improve overall efficiency.

As you continue to explore Ansible and automation, you will see that the same core principles apply to a variety of systems and technologies. By building your knowledge of Linux and, by extension, automation strategies, you can create powerful, reliable, and scalable automation solutions that can simplify complex tasks and help you to manage your IT infrastructure more effectively.

9.4 Managing Services

Instead of manually logging into each client node and running individual commands, our goal is to perform all administration tasks using Ansible playbooks. This approach allows us to execute versatile ad hoc commands or write a playbook to accomplish the desired task from the terminal console of the control server, f38s1. However, some tasks may still require manual login to check the system or service status, and this particular task is one such example. When SSHing into f38c1, we can see that the httpd service is in a "disabled" state, which prevents the successful execution of the "systemctl status httpd" command.

In step 7 of Section 9.3, we left the web service broken after the system reboots, and we will continue troubleshooting the issue here. Computer systems, whether running on hardware, virtual machines, or the cloud, all function in a similar manner. The differences between them lie in the services they provide to users. For our example, we turned all three client nodes into web service servers in the previous section. However, we noticed different behaviors between the two different OS types. Ubuntu runs and enables the Apache web service automatically, but Fedora requires manual intervention. Therefore, we had to add a section to start the services in our playbook, "9.3_copy_file.yml".

Step 1: We will write a simple playbook that uses the command module in Ansible to run a Linux command. By default, Ansible uses the client machine's default shell when executing commands.

```
[jdoe@f38s1 ch09]$ vi 9.4_check_status_httpd.yml
[jdoe@f38s1 ch09]$ cat 9.4_check_status_httpd.yml

---
- name: Check httpd status
  hosts: fedora
  become: true
  gather_facts: true # This is the default setting but only a
  declarative line
  collections:
    - ansible.builtin

  tasks:
  - name: Run systemctl status command and store output in a variable
    command: systemctl status httpd # The command we want to run
    register: apache_status_output # save the output of the command saved
    in a variable

  - name: Print httpd status
    debug: # prints the value of a variable
      var: apache_status_output.stdout_lines # specifies the variable to
      be printed
```

Step 2: Execute the playbook and review the output, paying attention to any errors that may occur. In this case, the error message indicates that the "systemctl status httpd" command returned a nonzero return code, specifically code 3, which indicates that the httpd service is not currently active on the target host. When working with Ansible and playbooks, it is common to encounter errors related to various issues. It is important to get used to seeing errors from Ansible and be prepared to troubleshoot them to successfully manage your infrastructure with Ansible.

```
[jdoe@f38s1 ch09]$ ansible-playbook --ask-become-pass 9.4_check_status_
httpd.yml
BECOME password: ***************

PLAY [Check httpd status]
************************************************************************

TASK [Gathering Facts]
************************************************************************
ok: [f38c1]

TASK [Run systemctl status command and store output in variable]
************************************************************************
fatal: [f38c1]: FAILED! => {"changed": true, "cmd": ["systemctl",
"status", "httpd"], "delta": "0:00:00.033170", "end": "2023-04-30
14:15:56.811688", "msg": "non-zero return code", "rc": 3, "start":
"2023-04-30 14:15:56.778518", "stderr": "", "stderr_lines": [], "stdout":
"○ httpd.service - The Apache HTTP Server\n    Loaded: loaded (/usr/
lib/systemd/system/httpd.service; disabled; preset: disabled)\n    Drop-
In: /usr/lib/systemd/system/service.d\n              └─10-timeout-
abort.conf\n            /usr/lib/systemd/system/httpd.
service.d\n              └─php-fpm.conf\n    Active: inactive (dead)\n
Docs: man:httpd.service(8)", "stdout_lines": ["○ httpd.service - The
Apache HTTP Server", "    Loaded: loaded (/usr/lib/systemd/system/httpd.
service; disabled; preset: disabled)", "    Drop-In: /usr/lib/systemd/
system/service.d", "              └─10-timeout-abort.conf", "            /
usr/lib/systemd/system/httpd.service.d", "              └─php-fpm.conf",
"    Active: inactive (dead)", "      Docs: man:httpd.service(8)"]}
```

```
PLAY RECAP
**************************************************************************
f38c1    : ok=1    changed=0   unreachable=0    failed=1    skipped=0
rescued=0    ignored=0
```

Step 3: Before running the playbook again to check its status, you can try starting
the httpd service using the "systemctl start httpd" command. To ensure that the service
starts before running the playbook, let's modify the code to include a task that starts the
service, followed by our original task to check its status.

[jdoe@f38s1 ch09]$ **cat 9.4_check_status_httpd.yml**

```
---
- name: Check httpd status
  hosts: fedora
  become: true
  gather_facts: true # This is the default setting but only a
  declarative line
  collections:
    - ansible.builtin

tasks:
  - name: Start httpd service
    systemd:
      name: httpd
      state: started # httpd service must be started so you can run the
      'systemctl status httpd' command

  - name: Run systemctl status command and store output in a variable
    command: systemctl status httpd # The command we want to run
    register: httpd_status_output # save the output of the command saved in
    a variable

  - name: Print httpd status
    debug: # prints the value of a variable
      var: httpd_status_output.stdout_lines # specifies the variable to
      be printed
```

Step 4: After executing the preceding playbook, the service status changes to
"Active: active (running)". However, the service "enabled" status remains "disabled".
Consequently, if there is a reboot of the server, the service will not start automatically.
Optionally, you can log in to the "f38c1" client node and run "systemctl stop httpd",
followed by "systemctl status httpd". This will change the "Active: active (running)" status
to "Active: inactive (dead)".

```
[jdoe@f38s1 ch09]$ ansible-playbook --ask-become-pass 9.4_check_status_
httpd.yml
BECOME password: ***************

PLAY [Check httpd status]
*************************************************************************

TASK [Gathering Facts]
*************************************************************************
ok: [f38c1]

TASK [Start httpd service]
*************************************************************************
changed: [f38c1]

TASK [Run systemctl status command and store output in variable]
*************************************************************************
changed: [f38c1]

TASK [Print httpd status]
*************************************************************************
ok: [f38c1] => {
    "httpd_status_output.stdout_lines": [
        "● httpd.service - The Apache HTTP Server",
        "     Loaded: loaded (/usr/lib/systemd/system/httpd.service;
          disabled; preset: disabled)",
        "    Drop-In: /usr/lib/systemd/system/service.d",
        "             └─10-timeout-abort.conf",
        "             /usr/lib/systemd/system/httpd.service.d",
        "             └─php-fpm.conf",
```

```
"        Active: active (running) since Sun 2023-04-30 14:26:46 AEST;
        1s ago",
"          Docs: man:httpd.service(8)",
"      Main PID: 5415 (httpd)",
"        Status: \"Started, listening on: port 80\"",
"         Tasks: 177 (limit: 2296)",
"        Memory: 13.5M",
"           CPU: 107ms",
"        CGroup: /system.slice/httpd.service",
"                ├─5415 /usr/sbin/httpd -DFOREGROUND",
"                ├─5416 /usr/sbin/httpd -DFOREGROUND",
"                ├─5417 /usr/sbin/httpd -DFOREGROUND",
"                ├─5418 /usr/sbin/httpd -DFOREGROUND",
"                └─5419 /usr/sbin/httpd -DFOREGROUND",
"",
"Apr 30 14:26:45 f38c1 systemd[1]: Starting httpd.service - The
Apache HTTP Server...",
"Apr 30 14:26:45 f38c1 httpd[5415]: AH00558: httpd: Could not
reliably determine the server's fully qualified domain name, using
fe80::20c:29ff:fe45:a9db%ens160. Set the 'ServerName' directive
globally to suppress this message",
"Apr 30 14:26:46 f38c1 systemd[1]: Started httpd.service - The
Apache HTTP Server.",
"Apr 30 14:26:46 f38c1 httpd[5415]: Server configured, listening
on: port 80"
    ]
}

PLAY RECAP
*********************************************************************************
f38c1    : ok=4    changed=2    unreachable=0    failed=0    skipped=0
rescued=0    ignored=0
```

Step 5: To ensure that the httpd service starts automatically at boot time, we can add the parameter "enabled: yes" to our playbook. This will enable the service to start automatically whenever the system reboots. The following is the updated version of the 9.4_check_status_httpd.yml playbook with the "enabled: yes" parameter:

```
$ vi 9.4_check_status_httpd.yml
$ cat 9.4_check_status_httpd.yml

---
- name: Check httpd status
  hosts: fedora
  become: true
  gather_facts: true
  collections:
    - ansible.builtin

  tasks:
  - name: Start httpd service
    systemd:
      name: httpd
      state: started  # Ensure the service is in started state
      enabled: yes # the service or daemon is enabled to start
      automatically at boot time

  - name: Run systemctl status command and store output in a variable
    command: systemctl status httpd
    register: httpd_status_output

  - name: Print httpd status
    debug:
      var: httpd_status_output.stdout_lines
```

By adding "enabled: yes", we are ensuring that the httpd service is not only started but also enabled at boot time. This will ensure that the service is automatically started whenever the system reboots without requiring any manual intervention.

Step 6: Execute the 9.4_enable_httpd.yml playbook, and you can verify that the service has been enabled. Even after the system reboots, the httpd service will always start at boot time. Carefully examine the output of the command. Note that the "disabled" status for the httpd service may not be updated in the printout.

```
[jdoe@f38s1 ch09]$ ansible-playbook --ask-become-pass 9.4_check_status_
httpd.yml
BECOME password: **************

PLAY [Check httpd status]
**************************************************************************

TASK [Gathering Facts]
**************************************************************************
ok: [f38c1]

TASK [Start httpd service]
**************************************************************************
changed: [f38c1]

TASK [Run systemctl status command and store output in variable]
**************************************************************************
changed: [f38c1]

TASK [Print httpd status]
**************************************************************************
ok: [f38c1] => {
    "httpd_status_output.stdout_lines": [
        "● httpd.service - The Apache HTTP Server",
        "     Loaded: loaded (/usr/lib/systemd/system/httpd.service;
          enabled; preset: disabled)",
        "     Drop-In: /usr/lib/systemd/system/service.d",
        "             └─10-timeout-abort.conf",
        "             /usr/lib/systemd/system/httpd.service.d",
        "             └─php-fpm.conf",
        "     Active: active (running) since Sun 2023-04-30 14:26:46 AEST;
          1h 36min ago",
        "       Docs: man:httpd.service(8)",
```

```
"     Main PID: 5415 (httpd)",
"       Status: \"Total requests: 0; Idle/Busy workers
        100/0;Requests/sec: 0; Bytes served/sec:    0 B/sec\"",
"        Tasks: 177 (limit: 2296)",
"       Memory: 13.5M",
"          CPU: 2.932s",
"       CGroup: /system.slice/httpd.service",
"               ├─5415 /usr/sbin/httpd -DFOREGROUND",
"               ├─5416 /usr/sbin/httpd -DFOREGROUND",
"               ├─5417 /usr/sbin/httpd -DFOREGROUND",
"               ├─5418 /usr/sbin/httpd -DFOREGROUND",
"               └─5419 /usr/sbin/httpd -DFOREGROUND",
"",
"Apr 30 14:26:45 f38c1 systemd[1]: Starting httpd.service - The
 Apache HTTP Server...",
"Apr 30 14:26:45 f38c1 httpd[5415]: AH00558: httpd: Could not
 reliably determine the server's fully qualified domain name, using
 fe80::20c:29ff:fe45:a9db%ens160. Set the 'ServerName' directive
 globally to suppress this message",
"Apr 30 14:26:46 f38c1 systemd[1]: Started httpd.service - The
 Apache HTTP Server.",
"Apr 30 14:26:46 f38c1 httpd[5415]: Server configured, listening
 on: port 80"
  ]
}

PLAY RECAP
**************************************************************************
f38c1   : ok=4    changed=2    unreachable=0    failed=0    skipped=0
rescued=0    ignored=0
```

Ansible's service modules, including systemd, service, upstart, launchctl, openrc, rcng, runit, system-analyze, system-journal, and initctl, are not only crucial for managing server infrastructure but also play a vital role in network device configuration management and administration. Many vendors, including Cisco, Palo Alto, Fortinet, and others, provide Ansible modules for their network devices, allowing for automated management and configuration. Ansible's service modules enable the automation of service management tasks that would otherwise require manual intervention, saving time and reducing human error. The modules allow for the management of services in different states, such as started, stopped, enabled, and disabled, ensuring consistency across multiple devices.

In addition to service management, Ansible's automation capabilities extend to network device configuration management and administration, making it a versatile tool for network infrastructure management. Ansible's network modules enable the automation of device configuration, enabling quick and efficient configuration changes across multiple devices. By using Ansible for network infrastructure management, network administrators can ensure consistency across their devices, reduce errors, and increase the efficiency of their operations. The importance of understanding the various states of services and device configuration management cannot be overstated, as it helps maintain the uptime of network infrastructure and prevents disruptions.

9.5 Copying and Updating Text Files with Ansible Playbook

In this section, we'll explore how Ansible can be used to automate the process of updating a text file on a single client node (f38c1). Manually updating configuration files on multiple systems can be a tedious and time-consuming task, which is why automation is a critical component in system administration. With Ansible, we can leverage the line module with regular expressions to search for and update specific text within a file.

In this example, we'll update the ServerAdmin email address in the httpd.conf file and restart the service to implement the change. While we'll be working with a single server for this demonstration, imagine having to update 50 web servers httpd. conf files with the same information – the time savings and reduction in workload for administrators can be significant.

To begin, we'll create a playbook to fetch the httpd.conf file from the client node (f38c1) and identify the line in the text file that we want to update. Our playbook will copy the httpd.conf file from the client machine's /etc/httpd/conf/httpd.conf directory and save it on our Ansible Control Machine.

Step 1: Create a new playbook to copy a file from the client node. To begin, we need to create an Ansible playbook that will copy the target file from the client node to our

Ansible Control Machine. This playbook will use the fetch module to copy the file and save it in the current working directory of the control machine. With this playbook, we can easily make a copy of the target file from any number of client nodes without having to manually copy the file from each server.

[jdoe@f38s1 ch09]$ **vi 9.5_copy_file.yml**

```
- name: Copy httpd.conf file from edora to a local directory
  hosts: fedora # fedora group devices
gather_facts: false
collections:
  - ansible.builtin

  tasks:
    - name: Copy httpd.conf file
      fetch: # Ansible module
        src: /etc/httpd/conf/httpd.conf # file to copy
        dest: ./ # copy the file to the current working directory
        flat: yes # copy the file to the destination directory on the
        control node without creating a directory structure
```

Step 2: Run the "9.5_copy_file.yml" playbook to copy the file from the client node to the control machine.

[jdoe@f38s1 ch09]$ **ansible-playbook --ask-become-pass 9.5_copy_file.yml**

```
BECOME password: ***************

PLAY [Copy httpd.conf file from fedora to local directory]
*************************************************************************

TASK [Copy httpd.conf file]
*************************************************************************
changed: [f38c1]

PLAY RECAP
*************************************************************************
f38c1     : ok=1    changed=1    unreachable=0    failed=0    skipped=0
rescued=0    ignored=0
```

Step 3: Now that we have the file in our Ansible Control Machine, f38s1, let's open it using the "set number" option in vi, which will provide us with line numbers. This will help us locate the ServerAdmin email address and observe what the line looks like. Our goal is to update this information on the client node, f38c1.

```
[jdoe@f38s1 ch09]$ ls -lh httpd.conf
-rw-r--r--. 1 jdoe jdoe 12K Apr 30 17:25 httpd.conf
[jdoe@f38s1 ch09]$ vi -c "set number" httpd.conf
[...omitted for brevity]
87 # ServerAdmin: Your address, where problems with the server should be
 88 # e-mailed.  This address appears on some server-generated pages, such
 89 # as error documents.  e.g. admin@your-domain.com
 90 #
 91 ServerAdmin root@localhost # Target text to update, want to update the
    email address
 92
 93 #
 94 # ServerName gives the name and port that the server uses to
    identify itself.
 95 # This can often be determined automatically, but we recommend
    you specify
 96 # it explicitly to prevent problems during startup.
 97 #
 98 # If your host doesn't have a registered DNS name, enter its IP
    address here.
 99 #
100 #ServerName www.example.com:80
[...omitted for brevity]
```

Step 4: Now that we have located our target text to replace, let's write another playbook to update the email address of ServerAdmin. After updating the text, we need to restart the service to make the changes take effect. We will add the necessary lines to restart the httpd service on the client node.

```
[jdoe@f38s1 ch09]$ vi 9.5_update_email.yml
[jdoe@f38s1 ch09]$ cat 9.5_update_email.yml
```

```
- hosts: fedora   # Run only on hosts in the fedora group
  become: true    # Run tasks with privilege escalation to become root
  collections:
    - ansible.builtin

  tasks:
  - name: change the e-mail address for httpd admin  # Task name
    tags: apache,fedora,httpd # Tags for task
    lineinfile:
      path: /etc/httpd/conf/httpd.conf  # Path of file to update
      regexp: '^ServerAdmin'  # Regular expression to locate line beginning
      with "ServerAdmin"
      line: ServerAdmin jdoe@ansnetauto.com  # Replacing line
    when: ansible_distribution == "Fedora"  # Only run this task if the OS
    is Fedora
    register: httpd  # Register this task's result as "httpd"

  - name: restart httpd for Fedora  # Task name
    tags: apache,fedora,httpd # Tags for task
    service:
      name: httpd # Name of the service to restart
      state: restarted  # Restart the service
    when: httpd.changed  # Only run this task if the "httpd" task changed
    the file
```

The regular expression used here is "^ServerAdmin". This pattern matches any line that begins with the string "ServerAdmin", where the ^ (caret) symbol is used to match the beginning of a line that starts with the string "ServerAdmin". Since this is running on Linux, the string search is case-sensitive. However, if you need to do a case-insensitive regular expression search in Ansible, you can use the "(?i)" option key. For example, "(?i)^ServerAdmin". But this is not necessary for our use case since after reviewing the contents of our file, we found that there is only a single line that begins with the string "ServerAdmin". The "line" module's parameter will replace the matched line with the new information.

It's important to note that if you're new to regular expressions, it may take some time to get used to the syntax and meanings behind their metacharacters. Learning regular expressions can be challenging, but it's a valuable skill to have. As the saying goes, "No pain, no gain." To become proficient in using regular expressions, you'll need to put in many hours of practice and study. Unfortunately, there's no shortcut or easy way to learn it. You are the only person who can put in the effort and dedication required to master this skill.

Step 5: Execute the playbook named 9.5_update_email.yml to update the email alias of the ServerAdmin.

```
[jdoe@f38s1 ch09]$ ansible-playbook --ask-become-pass 9.5_update_email.yml

BECOME password: ***************

PLAY [all]
************************************************************************

PLAY [fedora]
************************************************************************

TASK [Gathering Facts]
************************************************************************
ok: [f38c1]

TASK [change e-mail address for httpd admin]
************************************************************************
changed: [f38c1]

TASK [restart httpd for Fedora]
************************************************************************
changed: [f38c1]

PLAY RECAP
************************************************************************
f38c1      : ok=3    changed=2    unreachable=0    failed=0    skipped=0
rescued=0    ignored=0
```

Step 6: Use the "mv" command to rename the httpd.conf file to httpd.conf.back to mark it as a backup or redundant file. This is done in case we want to compare the original file with the updated file of the same name, so the original file does not get overwritten with the new file.

```
[jdoe@f38s1 ch09]$ mv httpd.conf httpd.conf.bak
[jdoe@f38s1 ch09]$ ls -lh httpd*
```

```
-rw-r--r--. 1 jdoe jdoe 12K Apr 30 17:25 httpd.conf.bak
```

Step 7: Run playbook 9.5_copy_file.yml one more time to copy the updated file.

```
[jdoe@f38s1 ch09]$ ansible-playbook --ask-become-pass 9.5_copy_file.yml
```

```
BECOME password: **************

PLAY [Copy httpd.conf file from f38c1 to local directory]
*************************************************************************

TASK [Copy httpd.conf file]
*************************************************************************
changed: [f38c1]

PLAY RECAP
*************************************************************************
f38c1      : ok=1    changed=1    unreachable=0    failed=0    skipped=0
rescued=0    ignored=0
```

Step 8: If you check the files starting with the word httpd, now we should have two files as shown here:

```
[jdoe@f38s1 ch09]$ ls -lh httpd*
```

```
-rw-r--r--. 1 jdoe jdoe 12K Apr 30 18:01 httpd.conf
-rw-r--r--. 1 jdoe jdoe 12K Apr 30 17:25 httpd.conf.bak
```

Step 9: To do a final check, run a simple diff command to compare the old file (httpd.conf.bak) and the new file (httpd.conf). If the result is the same as shown in the following, it indicates that the email update has been successful.

[jdoe@f38s1 ch09]$ **diff httpd.conf.bak httpd.conf**

91c91

< ServerAdmin root@localhost

> ServerAdmin jdoe@ansnetauto.com

Step 10: To verify the changes made to line 91, run the command "vi -c "set number" httpd.conf" once again and confirm that the line number is updated as expected. See Figure 9-15.

[jdoe@f38s1 ch09]$ **vi -c "set number" httpd.conf**

```
 80 #
 81 # All of these directives may appear inside <VirtualHost> containers,
 82 # in which case these default settings will be overridden for the
 83 # virtual host being defined.
 84 #
 85
 86 #
 87 # ServerAdmin: Your address, where problems with the server should be
 88 # e-mailed.  This address appears on some server-generated pages, such
 89 # as error documents.  e.g. admin@your-domain.com
 90 #
 91 ServerAdmin jdoe@ansnetauto.com
 92
 93 #
 94 # ServerName gives the name and port that the server uses to identify itself.
 95 # This can often be determined automatically, but we recommend you specify
 96 # it explicitly to prevent problems during startup.
 97 #
 98 # If your host doesn't have a registered DNS name, enter its IP address here.
 99 #
100 #ServerName www.example.com:80
101
102 #
103 # Deny access to the entirety of your server's filesystem. You must
104 # explicitly permit access to web content directories in other
105 # <Directory> blocks below.
```

Figure 9-15. *Email updated httpd.conf on f38c1*

The following exercise is an **optional** component, but it will teach you how to create an external script and integrate it with an Ansible playbook to increase the capabilities of Ansible. When we combine Ansible with other applications written in programming languages, it becomes an even more powerful tool. In step 9, we saw the Linux diff in action, and the result was rather boring. Here, we will create a Python application that compares the same two files and outputs the result to an HTML file, which compares the output side by side for easy comparison. This Python application will use Python's difflib to turn the comparison result into a single HTML file to be opened in your web browser. The compare.py Python script used here will be reused during our network automation playbooks in later chapters, so please follow along to learn how to run an external Python application from a playbook and double the power of Ansible.

Step 11: Let's create a Python application called "compare.py" that will compare two files and output the result to an HTML file. Even if you don't understand Python, please follow along, as you ought to learn it in the near future. The code explanation is embedded in the script, and you can either download "compare.py" from the author's GitHub page or write each line in a text editor such as vi. The choice is yours.

Tip

Use this command to download "compare.py" to save time:

```
curl -O https://raw.githubusercontent.com/ansnetauto/appress_ansnetauto/
main/compare.py
```

You can also create this Python application by typing them in vi and saving the file with a .py extension, like this:

```
[jdoe@f38s1 ch09]$ vi compare.py
[jdoe@f38s1 ch09]$ cat compare.py
```

```
import difflib

# File names variables
file01 = "httpd.conf.bak"
file02 = "httpd.conf"

# Read the contents of the first file
with open(f'./{file01}', 'r') as f1:
    file1_contents = f1.readlines()
```

```
# Read the contents of the second file
with open(f'./{file02}', 'r') as f2:
    file2_contents = f2.readlines()

# Compute the differences between the files with PEP8 column with of 79
differences = difflib.HtmlDiff(wrapcolumn=79).make_file(file1_contents,
file2_contents)

# Write the differences to an HTML file
with open(f'./{file01}_{file02}_compared.html', 'w') as html_file:
    html_file.write(differences)
```

Step 12: Python 3 is already installed on your Fedora 38 server (f38s1), and the Python 3 difflib library is included in the Python 3 standard library, so there's no need to install it separately with pip. Let's create an Ansible playbook to run the preceding Python application, compare.py, from the local machine. While you could simply run "python3 compare.py" in this case, our goal is to teach you how to execute an external application written in another programming language. This knowledge will allow you to integrate external tools to trigger tasks that cannot be achieved by Ansible alone. Although Ansible is a highly versatile tool, it is not always perfect or completely customizable for any scenario.

```
[jdoe@f38s1 ch09]$ vi 9.5_diff2html.yml
[jdoe@f38s1 ch09]$ cat 9.5_diff2html.yml
```

```
---
- name: Run compare.py
  hosts: localhost # run on the local machine (f38s1)
  become: true
  collections:
    - ansible.builtin

  tasks:
    - name: Run compare.py
      command: python3 ./compare.py # runs compare.py script to compare two
      files and output the result to an HTML file
```

Step 13: Execute the playbook. Ensure that all of the files are in the same directory as we are using the ./ directory; you can change the file paths as you wish if you want to be more specific with the location of the file paths.

```
[jdoe@f38s1 ch09]$ ansible-playbook --ask-become-pass 9.5_diff2html.yml
```

```
BECOME password: ***************

PLAY [Run compare.py]
*************************************************************************

TASK [Gathering Facts]
*************************************************************************
ok: [localhost]

TASK [Run compare.py]
*************************************************************************
changed: [localhost]

PLAY RECAP
*************************************************************************
localhost      : ok=2    changed=1    unreachable=0    failed=0    skipped=0
rescued=0    ignored=0
```

Step 14: After successfully executing the playbook, you should find an additional file that starts with "httpd" and is named "httpd.conf.bak_httpd.conf_compared.html". This file contains the comparison output of the two files in HTML format.

```
[jdoe@f38s1 ch09]$ ls -lh httpd*
```

```
-rw-r--r--. 1 jdoe jdoe  12K Apr 30 18:01 httpd.conf
-rw-r--r--. 1 jdoe jdoe  12K Apr 30 17:25 httpd.conf.bak
-rw-r--r--. 1 root root 122K May  1 22:24 httpd.conf.bak_httpd.conf_
compared.html
```

Step 15: To transfer the output file of the comparison, "httpd.conf.bak_httpd.conf_compared.html", from the Fedora server to your Windows 11 host machine, you can use the SFTP protocol via a file transfer client like WinSCP. If you don't have it installed yet, you can download the latest version of WinSCP from their website (`https://winscp.net/eng/downloads.php`) and install it on your PC. After that, you can use WinSCP to log into the server with the credentials of the "jdoe" user and navigate to the directory where the compared.html file is located. Finally, simply drag and drop the file to a local folder on your Windows machine, as shown in Figure 9-16.

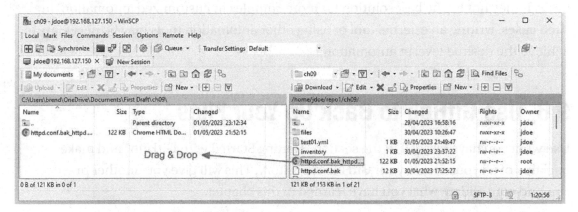

Figure 9-16.   *WinSCP drag and drop httpd.conf.bak_httpd.conf_compared.html*

Step 16: Open the httpd.conf.bak_httpd.conf_compared.html file in your web browser to view the differences. Python's difflib library is simple yet powerful, producing an easily identifiable cross-checking method, as shown in Figure 9-17.

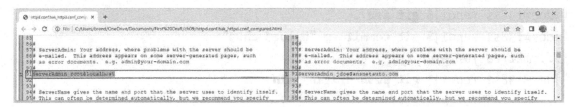

Figure 9-17.   *Open httpd.conf.bak_httpd.conf_compared.html on the web browser*

The purpose of the preceding exercise was to introduce the concept of writing an external application in another programming language to complement Ansible's features. Although Ansible is a powerful tool, it has some limitations when it comes to customization for certain scenarios. It is not intended to be used for the automation of every task, and there will be situations where Ansible's capabilities may fall short of the user's expectations, requiring the use of an external application.

Ansible's limitations in customization stem from the fact that it is a high-level tool designed to simplify the process of managing IT infrastructure. However, this comes at the cost of not being the most customizable and comprehensive solution. There may be scenarios where Ansible cannot cover 100% of the system and network automation requirements, leaving the need for an external tool.

Therefore, it is important to understand the strengths and weaknesses of Ansible when considering it for automation. While Ansible is great for repetitive, predictable tasks, it may not be the best solution for more complex or customized automation. In such cases, writing an external tool or using other automation tools may be necessary to achieve the desired level of automation.

9.6 Use GitHub to Back Up Your Files

Use what you have learned in the section "Getting Started with GitHub" and make backups of all your files to your GitHub repository. This will give you another practice run and consolidate what you have learned in this chapter.

```
[jdoe@f38s1 ch09]$ cd ..
[jdoe@f38s1 repo1]$ pwd
/home/jdoe/repo1
[jdoe@f38s1 repo1]$ git status
[...omitted for brevity]
[jdoe@f38s1 repo1]$ git add .
[jdoe@f38s1 repo1]$ git commit -m "Upload ch09"
[...omitted for brevity]
[jdoe@f38s1 repo1]$ git push origin main
[...omitted for brevity]
[jdoe@f38s1 repo1]$ git status
On branch main
Your branch is up to date with 'origin/main'.

nothing to commit, working tree clean
```

Congratulations on completing part 3 of Ansible basic concepts in this book! There is only one more chapter left on Ansible's basic concepts, and then we will dive right into the practicals of network automation. If you have made it this far and have completed all of the tasks, you are almost there! Now it's time to start working on simple network automation using Ansible. However, we would like to remind you that automation is easier said than done, especially when dealing with a mix of legacy and new products coexisting in the production network. To add to the complexity, there is an urgency to move everything into the cloud, and the tools required for automation in different cloud environments can vary. In these changing times, it is important to learn the concepts of automation and how to apply your ideas using different tools. As they say, the tools are only as good as the handyman. We have a plethora of different automation tools, but there is no single tool that fits all bills. Therefore, you need to be willing to learn and be equipped with several tools, including learning a couple of programming languages, so that you can write, decode, and use them in real production environments. You have gained essential knowledge and techniques that will enable you to manage your infrastructure more efficiently. By completing Ansible's basic concepts III and moving on to Chapter 10, you will be one step closer to becoming an Ansible expert who can automate complex tasks and manage infrastructure more effectively. So keep going and enhance your skills!

9.7 Summary

This chapter covered a variety of key concepts related to Ansible playbooks, equipping you with the essential knowledge to manage your infrastructure more effectively. We started with an exploration of GitHub, learning how to create a repository to store your Ansible playbooks. From there, we moved on to the use of the cowsay tool to create a simple playbook and upload it to GitHub. We then delved into the topic of Ansible tags and their usefulness in organizing and executing specific tasks within a playbook. We also discussed how to manage files and services with Ansible, exploring the copy and template modules for copying and updating file contents, as well as the service module for managing system services. Furthermore, we demonstrated how to integrate an external Python application into an Ansible playbook to compare two files containing similar information and output the results to an HTML file for easier viewing and comparison. Lastly, we provided a brief recap on using GitHub to back up your Ansible files, ensuring a secure and easily accessible repository for your playbooks. By mastering the concepts covered in this chapter, you will have a solid foundation for managing your infrastructure more efficiently with Ansible.

CHAPTER 10

Learning Ansible Basic Concepts IV: Users, Roles, Host Variables, Templates, and Password Vault

This chapter concludes the Ansible concepts series in this book, and we will soon move on to the Network Automation Practical Primer Labs. In this chapter, we will cover intermediate topics such as creating users, bootstrapping a Linux server, using roles, exploring variable options and handlers, working with templates, and managing passwords in Ansible using the password vault. Additionally, you will learn how to install, configure, and test FTP and SFTP servers on Linux. This chapter may be the most challenging one, but it's packed with valuable information, so grab a cup of coffee or an energy drink and dive right in.

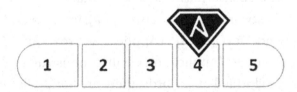

Welcome to the final chapter of Ansible concepts! Congratulations on reaching this point – you've already completed half point of the book! You've learned how to build an Ansible learning lab with four virtual machines, each running either Fedora (RHEL/CentOS) or Ubuntu (Debian) Linux distribution. We hope you've found the learning experience enjoyable and easy to master various Ansible basic concepts.

© Brendan Choi and Erwin Medina 2023
B. Choi and E. Medina, *Introduction to Ansible Network Automation*,
https://doi.org/10.1007/978-1-4842-9624-0_10

However, it's important to keep in mind that automation is not a silver bullet for all enterprise challenges and problems, despite what IT evangelists and gurus may claim. Implementing enterprise IT automation requires specific skills, and effective execution of the plan requires clear communication with stakeholders. As the person doing the work, you must possess the necessary skills to execute the plan.

In this chapter, we'll focus on the remaining fundamental concepts of Ansible that are crucial for efficiently automating IT infrastructure. You will explore users, roles, host variables, templates, and password management in Ansible, which provides a scalable and maintainable approach to infrastructure automation by organizing and structuring Ansible playbooks. Users and roles help define access control and implement role-based permissions across multiple systems. Host variables enable dynamic and flexible inventory management, while templates offer a powerful mechanism for generating configuration files and other resources. As always, this chapter includes hands-on exercises so that you can follow along and learn as you go. Get ready to dive into the final chapter of Ansible concepts and learn the remaining essential concepts to efficiently automate your IT infrastructure!

In the last three chapters, we've executed Ansible playbooks using the command "ansible-playbook --ask-become-pass <playbook_name>". While we demonstrated how to pre-configure the password in the inventory file to save time and typing, storing passwords and sensitive data in clear text files is not considered a best industry practice. Instead, we encourage readers to use the full command for each execution to become familiar with the Ansible command syntax. This approach will also give new readers a true sense of working with Ansible every day.

When we think about the current enterprise IT buzzwords related to network programmability, key terms such as network programmability, network automation and orchestration, SDN (software-defined networking), intent-based networking (IBN), NetDevOps (Network DevOps), API (Application Programming Interface), IaC (infrastructure as code), and ACI (Application Centric Infrastructure) come to mind. However, behind all these glorified buzzwords, there are hundreds and thousands of programmers and IT engineers working day and night behind their keyboards to keep everything afloat and operational. The actual jobs are not as glamorous as these buzzwords may suggest, and we will explore this topic further in the upcoming chapters.

Now that you have experienced the drills, let's focus on simplifying our daily tasks and save time. One easy way to achieve this is by creating aliases for long ansible commands. You can create simple aliases under the "~/.bashrc" file as outlined in the following tip. **This will help you save time and reduce the number of keystrokes needed to execute your commands.** We encourage you to set up your aliases as soon as possible to streamline your workflow.

Tip

Creating an alias for "ansible-playbook --ask-become-pass" to

save time

```
[jdoe@f38s1 ~]$ pwd
/home/jdoe
[jdoe@f38s1 ~]$ ls -a
.    .ansible    .bash_logout    .bashrc  .gitconfig  .
python_history  .ssh      .wget-hsts
..  .bash_history  .bash_profile  .config  .
lesshst    repo1              .viminfo
[jdoe@f38s1 ~]$ vi ~/.bashrc
[jdoe@f38s1 ~]$ cat .bashrc
# .bashrc
[...omitted for brevity]
unset rc
alias anp='ansible-playbook' # shortened to anp
alias anpap='ansible-playbook --ask-become-pass' # shortend
to anpap
[jdoe@f38s1 ~]$ source .bashrc # apply the change to take effect on .bashrc
```

If you can spare ten minutes, we highly recommend reading the following thread on Stack Overflow. It contains valuable information that can help you extend your knowledge and improve your understanding of the topic. We encourage you to take the time to read it before moving on, as it may help you in your current or future projects.

Expand your knowledge:

Difference between OS and network/security device bootstrapping

Bootstrapping is the process of setting up a basic working environment that
enables further configuration and management. In the context of OS system
deployment, it involves initializing and configuring the system with a set of basic
settings and packages required for the system to function properly. Network/
security device deployments involve configuring the device with basic network
settings, access control settings, and management settings to allow remote access
and management. The process of bootstrapping helps to establish a common
starting point that can be used to build and customize the environment to meet
specific requirements.

Read this Stack Overflow discussion: `https://stackoverflow.com/`
`questions/1254542/what-is-bootstrapping`.

10.1 Users

Ansible's user modules enable you to manage users on remote systems by creating,
modifying, and deleting users, as well as managing user attributes such as passwords,
home directories, and SSH keys. Automating these tasks with Ansible ensures that your
systems are consistently configured and secure, saving time and effort by avoiding
manual configuration on each system individually.

To add users to your Ansible-managed systems and prepare a playbook for
bootstrapping, you can use Ansible's user modules to manage users on multiple systems
simultaneously, ensuring consistency across your entire infrastructure. This knowledge
is essential for efficiently managing a large number of systems and streamlining your
workflow, as it enables you to ensure consistent management across your entire
infrastructure.

By the end of this lesson, you will have a solid understanding of how to create and
manage users on multiple systems using Ansible. You will also learn how to automate
the process of preparing these systems for future management by Ansible. It's important

to note that the Ansible concepts used in a Linux environment can be extended to network and security automation. Therefore, novice Ansible users must start their journey from Linux OS system automation.

Knowledge is power, and as a network engineer, if you're trying to automate your network infrastructure without understanding how Linux works or how Ansible works with various Linux OS, your efforts will only go so far. In this book, we cover all the necessary grounds to guide you on the right path to network automation in the mid-to-long term. If you start taking shortcuts, you'll miss out on asking and answering important questions, which will hinder your journey.

Let's get started and learn how to add users and prepare for bootstrapping with Ansible!

Step 1: Before creating an Ansible playbook to add a new user, it is important to verify the current user configurations on each client node. To do so, we can use Ansible's register and debug modules to check the last three lines of the /etc/passwd file on each client node. In Linux, user configurations are stored in the /etc/passwd file, and passwords are stored in the /etc/shadow file. To avoid duplicating effort, we can copy and reuse the ansible.cfg and inventory files from the previous chapter.

```
[jdoe@f38s1 ~]$ cd repo1/
[jdoe@f38s1 repo1]$ mkdir ch10
[jdoe@f38s1 repo1]$ cp ch09/inventory ch10/ && cp ch09/ansible.cfg ch10/
[jdoe@f38s1 repo1]$ cd ch10/
[jdoe@f38s1 ch10]$ ls
ansible.cfg   inventory
[jdoe@f38s1 ch10]$ vi 10.1_read_passwd.yml
[jdoe@f38s1 ch10]$ cat 10.1_read_passwd.yml
---
- hosts: all # run against all client nodes
  become: true
  gather_facts: false # do not gather facts to speed up playbook run

  tasks:
  - name: Read file content
    ansible.builtin.command: cat /etc/passwd # shell command to run
    register: file_output # output container/holder
```

```
- name: View the last three lines of the file
  ansible.builtin.debug: # print the contents of the file_output variable
    msg: "{{ file_output.stdout_lines[-3:] }}" # -3 is negative indexing,
    means the last three lines
```

Step 2: After creating the Ansible playbook, execute the playbook and observe the last line of the output. Then proceed to the next step, where we will add a new user using another Ansible playbook and observe how it affects the output. Remember to note the last lines in each output.

```
[jdoe@f38s1 ch10]$ anpap 10.1_read_passwd.yml
BECOME password: **************

[...omitted for brevity]
ok: [f38c1] => {
    "msg": [
        "nginx:x:988:988:Nginx web server:/var/lib/nginx:/sbin/nologin",
        "mysql:x:27:27:MySQL Server:/var/lib/mysql:/sbin/nologin",
        "sambajdoe:x:1004:1005::/home/sambajdoe:/sbin/nologin"
    ]
}
[...omitted for brevity]
```

Step 3: Here, we will create a new playbook to add a new sudo user named "jsmith" on each client node. We have briefly covered this topic in a previous chapter, so you should already be familiar with the code.

```
[jdoe@f38s1 ch10]$ vi 10.1_add_user.yml
[jdoe@f38s1 ch10]$ cat 10.1_add_user.yml

---
- hosts: all
  become: true
  gather_facts: false

  tasks:
  - name: create a new user
    ansible.builtin.user: # Ansible user module
```

464

```
    name: jsmith # new user name
    group: root # make this user a sudoer
```

Step 4: To add the new user, we need to execute the 10.1_add_user.yml
playbook now.

```
[jdoe@f38s1 ch10]$ anpap 10.1_add_user.yml
BECOME password: ***************
```

[...omitted for brevity]

Step 5: If your playbook is completed without errors, use the 10.1_read_passwd.yml
playbook to verify the changes in the /etc/passwd file. If you encountered any errors in
step 4, you will need to check for typos in the inventory or ansible.cfg file or review your
playbook.

```
[jdoe@f38s1 ch10]$ anpap 10.1_read_passwd.yml
BECOME password: ***************
```

[...omitted for brevity]
```
TASK [View the last three lines of the file] *****************************
ok: [f38c1] => {
    "msg": [
        "mysql:x:27:27:MySQL Server:/var/lib/mysql:/sbin/nologin",
        "sambajdoe:x:1004:1005::/home/sambajdoe:/sbin/nologin",
        "jsmith:x:1005:0::/home/jsmith:/bin/bash" # new user jsmith added
        to f38c1
    ]
}
ok: [u23c1] => {
    "msg": [
        "jane:x:1002:1002::/home/jane:/bin/sh",
        "mysql:x:109:116:MySQL Server,,,:/nonexistent:/bin/false",
        "jsmith:x:1003:0::/home/jsmith:/bin/sh" # new user jsmith added
        to u23c1
    ]
}
```

```
ok: [u23c2] => {
    "msg": [
        "jdoe:x:1001:1001:John Doe,,,:/home/jdoe:/bin/bash",
        "jane:x:1002:1002::/home/jane:/bin/sh",
        "jsmith:x:1003:0::/home/jsmith:/bin/sh" # new user jsmith added
        to u23c2
    ]
}
```
[...omitted for brevity]

Step 6: In previous chapters, you learned how to create a new user named jdoe and grant him the sudoer privileges by adding him to the wheel group on Fedora and the sudo group for Ubuntu. Another approach to grant a user sudoer privileges on Linux is by using a sudoer file tailored to that user's profile. The first step in doing this is to create a sudoer_jsmith file that can be uploaded to the client nodes. Follow the following steps to create the sudoer_jsmith file for uploading, making sure to first create the files directory and then create the sudoer_jsmith file under the files directory.

```
[jdoe@f38s1 ch10]$ mkdir files # the new directory name has to be named,
"files"
[jdoe@f38s1 ch10]$ vi files/sudoer_jsmith # create a new sudoer file for
user jsmith
[jdoe@f38s1 ch10]$ cat files/sudoer_jsmith
jsmith ALL=(ALL) NOPASSWD: ALL
```

Step 7: On Linux systems, when you add a sudoer file for a user, you can control their sudo access permissions by adding or removing files from their specific sudoers directory. Each user's sudoer files are stored in the /etc/sudoers.d/ directory. If you run the "sudo ls -l /etc/sudoers.d" command, you will see an empty directory on a Fedora server or only a README file on an Ubuntu server. To verify this, quickly create a playbook to check the directory and execute it against the three client nodes.

```
[jdoe@f38s1 ch10]$ vi 10.1_ls_sudoers.yml
[jdoe@f38s1 ch10]$ cat 10.1_ls_sudoers.yml

---
- name: Run ls -l /etc/sudoers.d command and output to screen
```

```
hosts: all
become: true

tasks:
  - name: Run ls -l /etc/sudoers.d command
    ansible.builtin.shell: ls -l /etc/sudoers.d # shell command to run
    register: sudoers_output # capture output

  - name: Output result to screen
    ansible.builtin.debug:
      var: sudoers_output.stdout_lines # print output
```

If you execute the preceding playbook successfully, you should see the same or similar output to what is shown here:

```
[jdoe@f38s1 ch10]$ anpap 10.1_ls_sudoers.yml
BECOME password: ***************

PLAY [Run ls -l /etc/sudoers.d command and output to screen] **************

TASK [Gathering Facts] ***************************************************
ok: [u23c1]
ok: [u23c2]
ok: [f38c1]

TASK [Run ls -l /etc/sudoers.d command] **********************************
changed: [u23c1]
changed: [u23c2]
changed: [f38c1]

TASK [Output result to screen] *******************************************
ok: [f38c1] => {
    "sudoers_output.stdout_lines": [
        "total 0"
    ]
}
ok: [u23c1] => {
    "sudoers_output.stdout_lines": [
        "total 4",
```

```
        "-r--r----- 1 root root 1096 Feb 18 12:03 README"
    ]
}
ok: [u23c2] => {
    "sudoers_output.stdout_lines": [
        "total 4",
        "-r--r----- 1 root root 1096 Feb 18 12:03 README"
    ]
}

PLAY RECAP ***********************************************************
f38c1 : ok=3 changed=1 unreachable=0  failed=0  skipped=0  rescued=0  ignored=0
u23c1 : ok=3 changed=1 unreachable=0  failed=0  skipped=0  rescued=0  ignored=0
u23c2 : ok=3 changed=1 unreachable=0  failed=0  skipped=0  rescued=0  ignored=0
```

Step 8: Now, let's add the public SSH key for the new user jsmith and assign ownership of the directory to him. First, let's copy the Ansible public SSH key and add it to the playbook. We will be using the public key that we created for the Ansible user, which is located in the file "~/.ssh/ansible.pub".

```
[jdoe@f38s1 ch10]$ cat ~/.ssh/ansible.pub

ssh-ed25519 AAAAC3NzaC1lZDI1NTE5AAAAIFvayxHfA8pjZTldlXQdVPEK+fdjFekSPx
9E4bnbPlOb ansible
```

The preceding key is unique to this demonstration only, and your key will be different. Therefore, make sure to use your key and include it in step 9 of your next playbook.

Step 9: Copy the base Ansible playbook, the 10.1_add_user.yml file, and create a new playbook called 10.1_enable_user.yml. This playbook will create the user, add the SSH public key for jsmith, and copy the sudoer_jsmith file that we created in the ./files/ directory. The new YAML text should be highlighted in bold, and you need to append it to the existing playbook.

```
[jdoe@f38s1 ch10]$ cp 10.1_add_user.yml 10.1_enable_user.yml
[jdoe@f38s1 ch10]$ vi 10.1_enable_user.yml
[jdoe@f38s1 ch10]$ cat 10.1_enable_user.yml
---
```

```
- hosts: all
  become: true
  gather_facts: false

  tasks:
  - name: create a new user
    ansible.builtin.user:
      name: jsmith
      group: root

  - name: add ssh key for jsmith
    tags: always
    ansible.posix.authorized_key: # Ansible authorized_key module
      user: jsmith
      key: "ssh-ed25519 AAAAC3NzaC1lZDI1NTE5AAAAIFvayxHfA8pjZTldlXQdVPEK+
      fdjFekSPx9E4bnbPl0b ansible"

  - name: add sudoers file for jsmith
    tags: always
    ansible.builtin.copy: # uses Ansible copy module
      src: sudoer_jsmith # source file under /files/
      dest: /etc/sudoers.d/jsmith # file destination on the client node
      owner: root # owner
      group: root # user permission
      mode: 0440 # file permission, the file owner has read permission and
      the file group has read permission, but neither has write or execute
      permission. This means that only the owner and members of the file
      group can read the file, but they cannot modify or execute it.
```

Step 10: Now, it's time to execute the playbook to upload the file and grant sudoer privileges to the new user, jsmith. Please ensure that you are running the playbook from the correct directory.

```
[jdoe@f38s1 ch10]$ anpap 10.1_enable_user.yml
BECOME password: ***************

PLAY [all] ************************************************************
```

```
TASK [create a new user] ********************************************
ok: [u23c1]
ok: [u23c2]
ok: [f38c1]

TASK [add ssh key for jsmith] ***************************************
changed: [u23c1]
changed: [u23c2]
changed: [f38c1]

TASK [add sudoers file for jsmith] **********************************
changed: [u23c1]
changed: [u23c2]
changed: [f38c1]

PLAY RECAP *********************************************************
f38c1 : ok=3 changed=2 unreachable=0 failed=0  skipped=0  rescued=0  ignored=0
u23c1 : ok=3 changed=2 unreachable=0 failed=0  skipped=0  rescued=0  ignored=0
u23c2 : ok=3 changed=2 unreachable=0 failed=0  skipped=0  rescued=0  ignored=0
```

Step 11: Time to check if the sudoer file for jsmith has been uploaded correctly. You can use the same playbook used in step 7, 10.1_ls_sudoers.yml.

```
[jdoe@f38s1 ch10]$ anpap 10.1_ls_sudoers.yml
BECOME password: ****************

PLAY [Run ls -l /etc/sudoers.d command and output to screen] **************

TASK [Gathering Facts] *********************************************
ok: [u23c1]
ok: [u23c2]
ok: [f38c1]

TASK [Run ls -l /etc/sudoers.d command] ****************************
changed: [u23c1]
changed: [u23c2]
changed: [f38c1]
```

```
TASK [Output result to screen] *****************************************
ok: [f38c1] => {
    "sudoers_output.stdout_lines": [
        "total 4",
        "-r--r-----. 1 root root 31 May  3 22:31 jsmith"
    ]
}
ok: [u23c1] => {
    "sudoers_output.stdout_lines": [
        "total 8",
        "-r--r----- 1 root root   31 May  3 12:31 jsmith",
        "-r--r----- 1 root root 1096 Feb 18 12:03 README"
    ]
}
ok: [u23c2] => {
    "sudoers_output.stdout_lines": [
        "total 8",
        "-r--r----- 1 root root   31 May  3 12:31 jsmith",
        "-r--r----- 1 root root 1096 Feb 18 12:03 README"
    ]
}

PLAY RECAP *************************************************************
f38c1 : ok=3  changed=1  unreachable=0  failed=0  skipped=0  rescued=0  ignored=0
u23c1 : ok=3  changed=1  unreachable=0  failed=0  skipped=0  rescued=0  ignored=0
u23c2 : ok=3  changed=1  unreachable=0  failed=0  skipped=0  rescued=0  ignored=0
```

Step 12: As a shortcut, let's use an Ansible ad hoc command as the user jsmith and use the private key located at /home/jdoe/.ssh/ansible to ping all client nodes. If we receive a successful response of "ping": "pong", then the user can log into each server successfully. It is important to remember how to run ad hoc Ansible commands. If you discover exemplary ad hoc commands, make sure to save them to your notepad, OneNote, or blog for future reference to save time.

```
[jdoe@f38s1 ch10]$ ansible all -u jsmith --private-key=/home/jdoe/.ssh/
ansible -m ping
```

```
u23c2 | SUCCESS => {
    "ansible_facts": {
        "discovered_interpreter_python": "/usr/bin/python3"
    },
    "changed": false,
    "ping": "pong" # SSH is working fine
}
u23c1 | SUCCESS => {
    "ansible_facts": {
        "discovered_interpreter_python": "/usr/bin/python3"
    },
    "changed": false,
    "ping": "pong" # SSH is working fine
}
f38c1 | SUCCESS => {
    "ansible_facts": {
        "discovered_interpreter_python": "/usr/bin/python3"
    },
    "changed": false,
    "ping": "pong" # SSH is working fine
}
```

Step 13: Simplify the ansible-playbook executions by modifying the ansible.cfg file, and add the "remote_user=jsmith" configuration. This will specify the Ansible management user account and make the process more streamlined.

```
[jdoe@f38s1 ch10]$ cp ansible.cfg ansible.cfg.bak # always make a back up

[jdoe@f38s1 ch10]$ vi ansible.cfg
[jdoe@f38s1 ch10]$ cat ansible.cfg
[defaults]
inventory = ./inventory
private_key_file = /home/jdoe/.ssh/ansible
```

```
deprecation_warnings=False
nocows = 1
# cow_selection = random
forks=30
```
remote_user = jsmith # we define the remote_user here in ansible.cfg file

Step 14: If you re-run the last playbook without the "--ask-become-pass" option, it
will run automatically using the private and public SSH key pairs. Remember that the
shorthand "anp" command stands for "ansible-playbook".

[jdoe@f38s1 ch10]$ **anp 10.1_enable_user.yml**

```
PLAY [all] *********************************************************

TASK [create a new user] ******************************************
ok: [u23c1]
ok: [u23c2]
ok: [f38c1]

TASK [add ssh key for jsmith] *************************************
ok: [u23c1]
ok: [u23c2]
ok: [f38c1]

TASK [add sudoers file for jsmith] ********************************
ok: [u23c2]
ok: [u23c1]
ok: [f38c1]

PLAY RECAP ********************************************************
f38c1  : ok=3   changed=0   unreachable=0   failed=0   skipped=0   rescued=0   ignored=0
u23c1  : ok=3   changed=0   unreachable=0   failed=0   skipped=0   rescued=0   ignored=0
u23c2  : ok=3   changed=0   unreachable=0   failed=0   skipped=0   rescued=0   ignored=0
```

A successful playbook run without errors or password prompts indicates that you
have correctly followed along, and your playbook ran as written declaratively.

Step 15: Let's apply everything we've learned so far by creating a new playbook
called 10.1_bootstrap.yml that incorporates the playbooks we have worked with
previously. By modifying the copied file, we can ensure that each server is updated and

provisioned with a new user, SSH key, and sudoer file that is copied across to each node
before managing the controlled nodes from your Ansible control node. As you're already
familiar with these playbooks, there isn't a need for many embedded explanation lines.

```
[jdoe@f38s1 ch10]$ vi 10.1_bootstrap.yml
[jdoe@f38s1 ch10]$ cat 10.1_bootstrap.yml

---

- hosts: all
  become: true

  pre_tasks: # a list of tasks to be executed before the main tasks
  - name: install updates (Ubuntu)
    tags: always
    ansible.builtin.apt:
      upgrade: dist
      update_cache: yes
    when: ansible_distribution == "Ubuntu"

  - name: install updates (Fedora)
    tags: always
    ansible.builtin.dnf:
      update_only: yes
      update_cache: yes
    when: ansible_distribution == "Fedora"

- hosts: all
  become: true
  tasks:

  - name: create a new user - jsmith
    tags: always
    ansible.builtin.user:
      name: jsmith
      groups: root
```

```
- name: add ssh key for jsmith
  tags: always
  ansible.posix.authorized_key:
    user: jsmith
    key: "ssh-ed25519 AAAAC3NzaC1lZDI1NTE5AAAAIFvayxHfA8pjZTldlXQdVPEK+
    fdjFekSPx9E4bnbPlOb ansible"

- name: add sudoers file for jsmith
  tags: always
  ansible.builtin.copy:
    src: sudoer_jsmith
    dest: /etc/sudoers.d/jsmith
    owner: root
    group: root
    mode: 0440
```

Once you have completed the user bootstrap playbook mentioned previously, run the playbook using the shortened command "anpap" (ansible-playbook --ask-become-pass). If the playbook runs successfully, you can proceed to the next step.

```
[jdoe@f38s1 ch10]$ anpap 10.1_bootstrap.yml
BECOME password: ****************

[...omitted for brevity]
TASK [create new user - jsmith] *****************************************
changed: [u23c1]
changed: [u23c2]
changed: [f38c1]

TASK [add ssh key for jsmith] *******************************************
ok: [u23c2]
ok: [u23c1]
ok: [f38c1]

TASK [add sudoers file for jsmith] **************************************
ok: [u23c1]
ok: [u23c2]
ok: [f38c1]
```

```
PLAY RECAP  **********************************************************
f38c1  : ok=6  changed=1  unreachable=0  failed=0  skipped=1  rescued=0  ignored=0
u23c1  : ok=6  changed=2  unreachable=0  failed=0  skipped=1  rescued=0  ignored=0
u23c2  : ok=6  changed=2  unreachable=0  failed=0  skipped=1  rescued=0  ignored=0
```

Step 16: After you have completed the process of bootstrapping the servers, which involves updating packages and creating a new sudo user (in this case, jsmith), you can proceed to run a provisioning playbook to install the software of your choice. In this example, we will create a simple playbook named "10.1_bootstrap_post_install.yml". This playbook will install nmap for network scanning and troubleshooting, as well as vsftp to turn all three client nodes into FTP servers. Please note that we will not be configuring the FTP user or user settings in this section. We leave this task for you to complete at your own pace and to your satisfaction. Additionally, if necessary, the playbooks 10.1_bootstrap.yml and 10.1_bootstrap_post_install.yml can be combined into a single playbook.

```
[jdoe@f38s1 ch10]$ vi 10.1_bootstrap_post_install.yml
[jdoe@f38s1 ch10]$ cat 10.1_bootstrap_post_install.yml

---
- hosts: all
  become: true

  tasks:
    - name: install packages
      ansible.builtin.package: # Notice the simplification here
        state: latest
        name:
          - nmap
          - vsftpd
      when: ansible_distribution in ["Fedora", "Ubuntu"] # Notice the
      simplification
```

In the preceding playbook, we simplified it by using the package module, which eliminates the need for two different modules. The package module automatically uses the OS native package manager, such as dnf or apt, to install packages based on the OS type. Also, notice the use of a list for OS types. What could have been a long, winding code becomes simpler, as you learned in the refactoring exercise earlier.

Now, you can run the preceding playbook without a sudoer password, as the sudo user and SSH key exchange have already been completed with the run of the 10.1_bootstrap.yml playbook. This time, run the simplified playbook with the "anp" (ansible-playbook) command. Don't forget that we have already configured "remote_user=jsmith" under our inventory file, so this user is used in this play.

```
[jdoe@f38s1 ch10]$ anp 10.1_bootstrap_post_install.yml
BECOME password: *****************

PLAY [all] *********************************************************

TASK [Gathering Facts] *********************************************
ok: [u23c2]
ok: [u23c1]
ok: [f38c1]

TASK [install packages] *******************************************
changed: [f38c1]
changed: [u23c2]
changed: [u23c1]

PLAY RECAP ********************************************************
f38c1 : ok=2  changed=1  unreachable=0  failed=0  skipped=0  rescued=0  ignored=0
u23c1 : ok=2  changed=1  unreachable=0  failed=0  skipped=0  rescued=0  ignored=0
u23c2 : ok=2  changed=1  unreachable=0  failed=0  skipped=0  rescued=0  ignored=0
```

If your playbook has been executed successfully, your output should resemble the example shown previously. Now, it's time to move on and learn about the concept of roles in Ansible.

10.2 Roles

Roles in Ansible are used to organize and modularize playbooks and related files in a way that simplifies the management of complex configurations across multiple systems. A role is a collection of tasks, handlers, variables, files, templates, and defaults, all of which are stored in structured directories. Using roles enables teams to collaborate more effectively, improve code reuse, and make playbooks more flexible, scalable, and maintainable.

Roles are extensively used in Ansible playbooks to group related tasks, handlers, files, templates, and variables into reusable and self-contained units. They can be included or imported as needed to build up a larger set of tasks and configurations. In addition to playbooks, roles are a core concept in the Ansible Automation Platform, where they can be easily managed, versioned, and shared through the platform's web UI and API. Since this book's main focus is on Ansible Engine, after completing this book, we hope your interest will extend to the Ansible Automation Platform and you will be able to provision a GUI-based general tool for your teams in your organizations.

Creating a role for configuring a specific software stack, such as a web server or a database server, is a good use case for roles. This role could include all the necessary tasks, files, and variables to install, configure, and manage the software stack. The role could then be reused across different projects and environments, reducing duplication and manual effort. Roles also allow for the efficient organization of tasks by breaking them down and assigning them to each functional role. Instead of having all plays in a single YAML file, roles disperse the functions and assign different tasks based on their roles. Typically, roles are structured in a tree-like directory path.

To practice and learn how roles work in Ansible, you can follow these steps.

Step 1: We have previously installed the "tree" package on our Ansible Control Machine. If you haven't installed it yet, you can use the "sudo dnf install tree" command to install it. Though this tool is not mandatory, it can help explain roles and templates better. Therefore, if you haven't installed it on your server already, please proceed to do so.

```
[jdoe@f38s1 ch10]$ tree -version
tree v2.1.0 © 1996 - 2022 by Steve Baker, Thomas Moore, Francesc Rocher,
Florian Sesser, Kyosuke Tokoro
```

Step 2: Create a subdirectory for each role you want to define within the "roles" directory. Name each subdirectory after the role it represents. Take special care so you don't make typos.

```
[jdoe@f38s1 ch10]$ mkdir roles
[jdoe@f38s1 ch10]$ cd roles/ # Ensure that you move to the roles
directory here!
[jdoe@f38s1 roles]$ mkdir base db_servers file_servers web_servers
```

```
[jdoe@f38s1 roles]$ mkdir base/tasks db_servers/tasks file_servers/tasks
web_servers/tasks
[jdoe@f38s1 roles]$ cd .. # Move up to parent directory
[jdoe@f38s1 ch10]$ tree roles # Check directory structure under the 'roles'
directory
roles
├── base
│   └── tasks
├── db_servers
│   └── tasks
├── file_servers
│   └── tasks
└── web_servers
    └── tasks

9 directories, 0 files
```

As you can see, we have created five roles, including the base role, and for each role, we have created a subdirectory called "tasks" within its respective directory.

Step 3: Next, navigate to the ../roles/base/tasks directory and create a task file named main.yml. Unlike playbooks, YAML files used in roles are configured as task files, so it is unnecessary to specify the target nodes in roles; also putting the three hypens, "---", at the beginning of the YAML file is optional.

For base role:

```
[jdoe@f38s1 ch10]$ vi roles/base/tasks/main.yml
[jdoe@f38s1 ch10]$ cat roles/base/tasks/main.yml
```

```
- name: add ssh key for jsmith
  tags: always
  ansible.posix.authorized_key:
    user: jsmith
    key: "ssh-ed25519 AAAAC3NzaC1lZDI1NTE5AAAAIFvayxHfA8pjZTldlXQdVPEK+
    fdjFekSPx9E4bnbPlOb ansible"
```

For **db_server role:**

```
[jdoe@f38s1 ch10]$ vi roles/db_servers/tasks/main.yml
[jdoe@f38s1 ch10]$ cat roles/db_servers/tasks/main.yml

- name: install mariadb package
  ansible.builtin.package:
    name: "{{ 'mariadb-server' if ansible_distribution == 'Ubuntu' else
    'mariadb' }}"
    state: latest
  tags: mariadb
```

For **file_server role:**

```
[jdoe@f38s1 ch10]$ vi roles/file_servers/tasks/main.yml
[jdoe@f38s1 ch10]$ cat roles/file_servers/tasks/main.yml

- name: install samba package
  tags: samba
  ansible.builtin.package:
    name: samba
    state: latest
```

For **web_server role:** If you do not want to type all the directives, use the
downloaded copy from the author's GitHub site.

```
[jdoe@f38s1 ch10]$ vi roles/web_servers/tasks/main.yml
[jdoe@f38s1 ch10]$ cat roles/web_servers/tasks/main.yml

- name: install httpd and PHP packages
  ansible.builtin.package:
    name:
      - "{{ 'apache2' if ansible_distribution == 'Ubuntu' else 'httpd' }}"
      - "{{ 'libapache2-mod-php' if ansible_distribution == 'Ubuntu' else
      'php' }}"
    state: latest
  tags: [apache, httpd, ubuntu, fedora]
```

```yaml
- name: start httpd for Fedora/CentOS/Red Hat
  tags: [apache, httpd, fedora]
  ansible.builtin.service:
    name: "{{ 'httpd' if ansible_distribution == 'Fedora' else omit }}"
    state: started
    enabled: yes
  when: ansible_distribution == "Fedora"

- name: change e-mail address for httpd admin
  tags: [apache, httpd, fedora]
  ansible.builtin.lineinfile:
    path: /etc/httpd/conf/httpd.conf
    regexp: '^ServerAdmin'
    line: ServerAdmin admin@ansnetauto.com
  when: ansible_distribution == "Fedora"
  register: httpd

- name: restart httpd for Fedora
  tags: [apache, httpd, fedora]
  ansible.builtin.service:
    name: httpd
    state: restarted
  when: httpd.changed

- name: copy default html file from site
  tags: [apache, httpd, apache2]
  ansible.builtin.copy:
    src: default_site.html
    dest: /var/www/html/index.html
    owner: root
    group: root
    mode: '0644'
```

Step 4: To use the default_site.html file in the web-servers role, it needs to be copied from the Chapter 9 exercise. First, check if the default_site.html file still exists under the ch09/files directory. Then, in the ch10 directory, execute the command cp ../ch09/files/default_site.html files/ to copy the file to the /home/jdoe/repo1/ch10/files/ directory.

481

```
[jdoe@f38s1 ch10]$ tree ../ch09/files
```

```
../ch09/files
└── default_site.html
```

```
1 directory, 1 file
```

Create a new directory called "files" under the "roles/web_servers/" directory, and then copy the "default_site.html" file from the Chapter 9 exercise to this newly created "files" directory.

```
[jdoe@f38s1 ch10]$ mkdir roles/web_servers/files
[jdoe@f38s1 ch10]$ cp ../ch09/files/default_site.html roles/web_
servers/files/
[jdoe@f38s1 ch10]$ tree roles/web_servers/
roles/web_servers/
├── files
│   └── default_site.html
└── tasks
    └── main.yml
```

```
3 directories, 2 files
```

At the end of the Roles assignment, the file structure under the "roles" directory should look similar to the following tree output. Each role should have a "tasks" directory with a "main.yml" file, and the "web_servers" role should have a "files" directory containing the "default_site.html" file. Your directory structure should resemble this:

```
[jdoe@f38s1 ch10]$ tree roles
```

```
roles
├── base
│   └── tasks
│       └── main.yml
├── db_servers
│   └── tasks
│       └── main.yml
│
```

```
├── file_servers
│    └── tasks
│         └── main.yml
└── web_servers
     ├── files
     │    └── default_site.html
     └── tasks
          └── main.yml
```

`10 directories, 5 files`

Step 5: To begin, let's create a backup of the current inventory file used in the Chapter 10 exercises. After that, we can create a new inventory file based on the roles of our servers for this exercise. Please follow the example provided here:

```
[jdoe@f38s1 ch10]$ cp inventory inventory.bak
[jdoe@f38s1 ch10]$ vi inventory
[jdoe@f38s1 ch10]$ cat inventory
[db_servers]
u23c1 ansible_host=192.168.127.161

[file_servers]
f38c1 ansible_host=192.168.127.151

[web_servers]
u23c1 ansible_host=192.168.127.161
u23c2 ansible_host=192.168.127.162
```

Step 6: Now that we have properly structured our roles, we can create the main playbook file and run the "ansible-playbook" command. If you have organized your roles correctly, the playbook should run smoothly without errors. The name of the playbook file here is "10.2a_provision_roles.yml", which is the longer version of the provisioning playbook before refactoring. In step 8, we will refactor this playbook and compare its effects with the original version.

```
[jdoe@f38s1 ch10]$ vi 10.2a_provision_roles.yml
[jdoe@f38s1 ch10]$ cat 10.2a_provision_roles.yml

---
```

```yaml
- hosts: all
  become: true

  pre_tasks:
  - name: install updates (Ubuntu)
    tags: always
    ansible.builtin.apt:
      update_cache: yes
    changed_when: false
    when: ansible_distribution == "Ubuntu"

  - name: install updates (Fedora)
    tags: always
    ansible.builtin.dnf:
      update_cache: yes
    changed_when: false
    when: ansible_distribution == "Fedora"

- hosts: all
  become: true
  roles: # Define all servers and assign a "base" role
    - base  # role to perform base configuration on all servers

- hosts: db_servers
  become: true
  roles: # Assign "db_servers" role to database servers
    - db_servers  # role to configure database servers

- hosts: file_servers
  become: true
  roles: # Assign "file_servers" role to file servers
    - file_servers  # role to configure file servers

- hosts: web_servers
  become: true
  roles: # Assign "web_servers" role to web servers
    - web_servers  # role to configure web servers
```

Step 7: After creating the playbook, ensure to run it to verify that it runs without errors.

[jdoe@f38s1 ch10]$ **anp 10.2a_provision_roles.yml**

[...omitted for brevity]

Step 8: Now it's time to refactor the 10.2a_provision_roles.yml playbook and create a shorter version named 10.2b_provision_roles.yml. The refactored playbook should achieve the same outcome as the longer version did.

[jdoe@f38s1 ch10]$ **cp 10.2a_provision_roles.yml 10.2b_provision_roles.yml**

[jdoe@f38s1 ch10]$ **vi 10.2b_provision_roles.yml**
[jdoe@f38s1 ch10]$ **cat 10.2b_provision_roles.yml**

```
---
- hosts: all # Target all hosts in the inventory
  become: true # Run tasks with elevated privileges
  tasks:
    - name: update package cache # Task name
      ansible.builtin.package: # Use the package module
        update_cache: yes # Update the package cache
      changed_when: false # Consider the task successful even if no changes
      were made
      tags: [always, update] # Assign tags to the task

- hosts: all
  become: true
  roles: # notice the use of the list to shorten the roles
    - base
    - db_servers
    - file_servers
    - web_servers
```

Step 9: Execute the refactored version of the provisioning playbook, 10.2b_
provision_roles.yml.

```
[jdoe@f38s1 ch10]$ anp 10.2b_provision_roles.yml

[...omitted for brevity]
```

If your refactored roles playbook has been executed successfully without any
errors, you can move on to the next concepts: variables, host_vars, and handlers. These
concepts will allow you to define reusable values with variables, host-specific variables
with host_vars, and execute tasks with handlers that are triggered by notifications. Using
these concepts can make your playbooks more modular and save time. Let's see how
they work at the base level.

10.3 Variable Options in Ansible

Ansible, although not a fully fledged programming language like Python, JavaScript,
Perl, or even Shell Scripting, utilizes YAML to make declarative statements that take
advantage of OS-specific and built-in tools. While learning Ansible and its playbook
features, you will quickly notice that programming concepts remain relevant and extend
to Ansible. It cannot be stressed enough that Ansible alone cannot be the ultimate
automation and orchestration tool; one must use it wisely with other programming
languages to achieve the best results. Therefore, our recommendation is to use Python as
Ansible's supporting tool since Ansible is built on top of Python. Python is an excellent
complement to Ansible because it offers a wide range of modules and libraries that one
can use to extend Ansible's capabilities. With Python, one can create custom modules,
perform complex tasks, and manipulate data more efficiently. Additionally, it has a vast
and active community that shares solutions to various automation challenges, making it
easier to find answers to problems one may encounter.

In this section, we will explore the concept of variables in Ansible and delve into
four different use cases to help extend your understanding of how variables can be used
in playbooks. Imagine that you are a network engineer who recently joined a company
and has been tasked by your manager to deploy some FTP servers on three Linux
machines. One machine is based on the Red Hat distribution, and the other two are
based on the Debian distribution. However, before installing them on the production
servers, you want to test them in your POC (proof-of-concept) environment using the

Red Hat distribution. In our case, it is the Fedora 38 server (f38c1). In this scenario, we can leverage Ansible's variable features to build the necessary scripts. Using variables in Ansible provides a way to store and reuse values across different parts of your playbook, making your automation more flexible and maintainable. For example, you can define variables to specify the package names, versions, directories, and other configuration settings for your FTP servers. By using variables, you can make your playbook more dynamic and adaptable to different environments or scenarios. This flexibility allows you to reuse your playbook for other use cases or even scale it up to manage hundreds or thousands of servers. Here, we will look at different ways of using variables in Ansible and how they can be applied to various tasks and scenarios. By the end of this section, you will have a solid understanding of how to use variables effectively in your Ansible playbooks.

Expand your knowledge:

Exploring Variable Precedence: Understanding Ansible's Vars Hierarchy

Understanding variable precedence is essential in Ansible as it plays a crucial role in determining which variable takes precedence over others. When the same variable is defined at multiple levels with the same name, a defined order of precedence is followed. Here is a tabulated overview of variable precedence as shown in Table 10-1, listed from highest to lowest.

Table 10-1. *Ansible vars precedence*

Precedence	Source	Example
1	Extra Variables (-e)	ansible-playbook hi_ken.yml -e "my_variable=Barbie"
2	Role Variables	In a role: roles/my_role/vars/main.yml defining my_variable: Barbie
3	Play Variables	In a playbook: vars: section defining my_variable: Barbie
4	Block Variables	Within a block: block: section defining my_variable: Barbie
5	Task Variables	Within a task: vars: parameter defining my_variable: Barbie
6	Host Variables	In the inventory or host_vars directory: my_host.yml file defining my_variable: Barbie
7	Facts Variables	Automatically gathered facts about the remote system, such as ansible_facts["ansible_distribution"]
8	Role Default Variables	In a role: roles/my_role/defaults/main.yml defining my_variable: Barbie

Take an active approach to learning by physically typing out and practicing each of the given examples.

Precedence 1: Extra Variables (-e)

Execute the Ansible command with the "-e" flag to override other variables with the same variable name; the -e option takes the highest precedence.

```
[jdoe@f38s1 ch10]$ mkdir vars_precedence && cd vars_precedence
[jdoe@f38s1 vars_precedence]$ mkdir ken1 && cd ken1
[jdoe@f38s1 ken1]$ vi 10.3_hi_ken1.yml
[jdoe@f38s1 ken1]$ cat 10.3_hi_ken1.yml
---
- hosts: localhost
  gather_facts: false
  tasks:
    - name: Print Hi, Ken!
```

```
    debug:
        msg: "Hello, {{ my_variable | default('Ken') }}!"
```

```
[jdoe@f38s1 ken1]$ anp 10.3_hi_ken1.yml -e "my_variable=Jane"
[...omitted for brevity]
TASK [Print Hello, World!] *******************************************
ok: [localhost] => {
    "msg": "Hi, Jane!"
[...omitted for brevity]
```

```
[jdoe@f38s1 ken1]$ anp 10.3_hi_ken1.yml # If you execute playbook
without -e flag, it will print "Hi, Ken!" by default.
[...omitted for brevity]
TASK [Print Hello, World!] *******************************************
ok: [localhost] => {
    "msg": "Hi, Ken!"
[...omitted for brevity]
```

Precedence 2: Role Variables

Create the roles/my_role/var directory and create a main.yml file with "my_
variable: 'Barbie'"; then create the 10.3_hi_ken2.yml file and include roles in the
playbook; this will take precedence over the default variable value, Ken, and will
output "Hi, Barbie!".

```
[jdoe@f38s1 ken1]$ cd ..
[jdoe@f38s1 vars_precedence]$ mkdir ken2 && cd ken2
[jdoe@f38s1 ken2]$ mkdir -p roles/my_role/vars
[jdoe@f38s1 ken2]$ vi roles/my_role/vars/main.yml
[jdoe@f38s1 ken2]$ cat roles/my_role/vars/main.yml
my_variable: 'Barbie'
[jdoe@f38s1 ken2]$ vi 10.3_hi_ken2.yml
[jdoe@f38s1 ken2]$ cat 10.3_hi_ken2.yml
---
- hosts: localhost
  gather_facts: false
  roles:
```

```
      - my_role
    tasks:
      - name: Print Hi, Ken!
        ansible.builtin.debug:
          msg: "Hi, {{ my_variable | default('Ken') }}!"
```

```
[jdoe@f38s1 ken2]$ anp 10.3_hi_ken2.yml
[...omitted for brevity]
TASK [Print Hi, Ken!] *************************************************
ok: [localhost] => {
    "msg": "Hi, Barbie!"
}
[...omitted for brevity]
```

Precedence 3: Play Variables

The variable defined under the vars module will take third precedence, and in this
example, my_variable will override the default value "Ken".

```
[jdoe@f38s1 ken2]$ cd ..
[jdoe@f38s1 vars_precedence]$ mkdir ken3 && cd ken3
[jdoe@f38s1 ken3]$ vi 10.3_hi_ken3.yml
[jdoe@f38s1 ken3]$ cat 10.3_hi_ken3.yml
---
- hosts: localhost
  gather_facts: false
  vars:
    my_variable: 'Barbie'
  tasks:
    - name: Print Hi, Ken!
      ansible.builtin.debug:
        msg: "Hi, {{ my_variable | default('Ken') }}!"
```

```
[jdoe@f38s1 ken3]$ anp 10.3_hi_ken3.yml
[...omitted for brevity]
TASK [Print Hi, Ken!] *************************************************
ok: [localhost] => {
```

```
    "msg": "Hi, Barbie!"
}
```
[...omitted for brevity]

Precedence 4: Block Variables

You can also use the block module to set the precedence and override the default variable "Ken". In this example, the variable was set using the set_fact module.

```
[jdoe@f38s1 ken3]$ cd ..
[jdoe@f38s1 vars_precedence]$ mkdir ken4 && cd ken4
[jdoe@f38s1 ken4]$ vi 10.3_hi_ken4.yml
[jdoe@f38s1 ken4]$ cat 10.3_hi_ken4.yml
---
- hosts: localhost
  gather_facts: false
  tasks:
    - block:
        - name: Set my_variable within the block
          ansible.builtin.set_fact:
            my_variable: 'Barbie'
      always:
        - name: Print Hi, Ken!
          ansible.builtin.debug:
            msg: "Hi, {{ my_variable | default('Ken') }}!"

[jdoe@f38s1 ken4]$ anp 10.3_hi_ken4.yml
```
[...omitted for brevity]
```
TASK [Print Hi, Ken!] ************************************************
ok: [localhost] => {
    "msg": "Hi, Barbie!"
}
```
[...omitted for brevity]

Precedence 5: Task Variables

You can also configure the variable under a task variable, and it will overwrite the default variable.

```
[jdoe@f38s1 ken4]$ cd ..
[jdoe@f38s1 vars_precedence]$ mkdir ken5 && cd ken5
[jdoe@f38s1 ken5]$ vi 10.3_hi_ken5.yml
[jdoe@f38s1 ken5]$ cat 10.3_hi_ken5.yml
---
- hosts: localhost
  gather_facts: false
  tasks:
    - name: Print Hi, Ken!
      ansible.builtin.debug:
        msg: "Hi, {{ my_variable | default('Ken') }}!"
      vars:
        my_variable: 'Barbie'
```

```
[jdoe@f38s1 ken5]$ anp 10.3_hi_ken5.yml
[...omitted for brevity]
TASK [Print Hi, Ken!] ************************************************
ok: [localhost] => {
    "msg": "Hi, Barbie!"
}
[...omitted for brevity]
```

In above playbook execution, you will get [WARNING] messages, you can ignore the messages.

Precedence 6: Host Variables

Create an inventory.ini file and also a localhost.yml file under the host_vars directory; then use the "-I inventory" when executing the new playbook.

```
[jdoe@f38s1 ken5]$ cd ..
[jdoe@f38s1 vars_precedence]$ mkdir ken6 && cd ken6
[jdoe@f38s1 ken6]$ vi inventory.ini
```

```
[jdoe@f38s1 ken6]$ cat inventory.ini
[my_hosts]
localhost
[jdoe@f38s1 ken6]$ mkdir -p host_vars
[jdoe@f38s1 ken6]$ vi host_vars/localhost.yml
[jdoe@f38s1 ken6]$ cat host_vars/localhost.yml
my_variable: 'Barbie'
[jdoe@f38s1 ken6]$ vi 10.3_hi_ken6.yml
[jdoe@f38s1 ken6]$ cat 10.3_hi_ken6.yml
---
- hosts: my_hosts
  gather_facts: false
  tasks:
    - name: Print Hi, Ken!
      ansible.builtin.debug:
        msg: "Hi, {{ my_variable | default('Ken') }}!"

[jdoe@f38s1 ken6]$ anp -i inventory.ini 10.3_hi_ken6.yml
[...omitted for brevity]
TASK [Print Hi, Ken!] *************************************************
ok: [localhost] => {
    "msg": "Hi, Barbie!"
}
[...omitted for brevity]
```

Precedence 7: Facts Variables

You can also use the set_fact to override the default value.

```
[jdoe@f38s1 ken6]$ cd ..
[jdoe@f38s1 vars_precedence]$ mkdir ken7 && cd ken7
[jdoe@f38s1 ken7]$ mkdir ken7 && cd ken7
[jdoe@f38s1 ken7]$ cat 10.3_hi_ken7.yml
---
- hosts: localhost
  gather_facts: false
  tasks:
```

493

```
  - name: Set my_variable fact
    ansible.builtin.set_fact:
      my_variable: 'Barbie'
  - name: Print Hi, Ken!
    ansible.builtin.debug:
      msg: "Hi, {{ my_variable | default('Ken') }}!"
```

[jdoe@f38s1 ken7]$ **anp 10.3_hi_ken7.yml**
[...omitted for brevity]
TASK [Print Hi, Ken!] **
ok: [localhost] => {
    "msg": "Hi, Barbie!"
}
[...omitted for brevity]

In above playbook execution, you will get [WARNING] messages, you can ignore the messages.

Precedence 8: Role Default Variables

Lastly, you can use the role default variable. Immerse yourself in the learning process by actively typing and practicing each of the given examples to enhance your understanding.

[jdoe@f38s1 ken7]$ **cd ..**
[jdoe@f38s1 vars_precedence]$ **mkdir ken8 && cd ken8**
[jdoe@f38s1 ken8]$ **mkdir -p roles/my_role/defaults**
[jdoe@f38s1 ken8]$ **vi roles/my_role/defaults/main.yml**
[jdoe@f38s1 ken8]$ **cat roles/my_role/defaults/main.yml**
my_variable: 'Barbie'
[jdoe@f38s1 ken8]$ **vi 10.3_hi_ken8.yml**
[jdoe@f38s1 ken8]$ **cat 10.3_hi_ken8.yml**

- hosts: localhost
  gather_facts: false
  roles:
    - my_role

```
tasks:
  - name: Print Hi, Ken!
    ansible.builtin.debug:
      msg: "Hi, {{ my_variable | default('Ken') }}!"
```

[jdoe@f38s1 ken8]$ **anp 10.3_hi_ken8.yml**
[...omitted for brevity]

```
TASK [Print Hi, Ken!] *********************************************
ok: [localhost] => {
    "msg": "Hi, Barbie!"
}
```
[...omitted for brevity]

In the preceding playbook execution, you will get [WARNING] messages; you can ignore the messages.

Now that we have explored each of the examples, it's time to put the precedence to the test. You can now experiment with two or three of the methods mentioned previously to witness the precedence in action firsthand and confirm its behavior. I encourage you to try out different scenarios at your own pace and observe how the variables are prioritized. Take your time to conduct these tests and gain a deeper understanding of how precedence works in practice. Enjoy exploring and experimenting!

Let us use the vsftpd (Very Secure FTP Daemon) server installation on a Fedora server as an example. The examples shown here are for explanatory purposes only, and you do not have to execute these playbooks. Read along to understand the different ways you can use variables in Ansible playbooks. At the end of this section, we have included a quick exercise. Additionally, the next section contains another exercise related to host_vars and handlers.

Using Variables in Ansible 1 – Declaration in Playbooks: The first way to use variables in an Ansible playbook is by defining them within the main playbook itself, using the "vars" keyword followed by the variable declarations. You can study variable declaration in playbooks using the following playbook as an example. In this playbook, the variables "ftp_users", "ftp_root_dir", and "ftp_port" are declared and initialized to their respective values. These variables are then used in the subsequent tasks to install and configure the vsftpd server. You will be able to see the full playbook in action at the end of this section.

```
[...omitted for brevity]
  vars:
    ftp_users:
      - name: jsparrow
        password: LizSwann2003
      - name: ppan
        password: TinkerBell1902
    ftp_root_dir: /var/ftp
    ftp_port: 21
[...omitted for brevity]
```

If we examine the variables shown previously, we can see that they take the form of a nested dictionary in Python, where the outermost key is "vars", and its value is another dictionary containing the variables declared in the YAML code. The "ftp_users" key has a value of a list of two dictionaries, each representing an FTP user with a "name" and "password" key-value pair. The "ftp_root_dir" and "ftp_port" keys have string values. You can compare these variables to the following Python nested dictionary with the variable name "vars".

```
vars = { "ftp_users": [{"name": "jsparrow", "password": "LizSwann2003"},
        {"name": "ppan", "password": "TinkerBell1902"}],
    "ftp_root_dir": "/var/ftp",
    "ftp_port": 21}
```

Using Variables in Ansible 2 – Variable Declaration in Inventory: As you have seen in previous exercises, variables can also be declared in the inventory file. Using the same FTP server installation example, we can move these variables to the inventory file, as shown in the following example. In this example, the variables ftp_port and ftp_root_dir are declared and initialized for each host in the ftp_servers group. These variables are then used in subsequent tasks to install and configure the vsftpd server.

```
[ftp_servers]
ftp1 ansible_host=192.168.1.100 ftp_port=2121 ftp_root_dir=/var/ftp
ftp2 ansible_host=192.168.1.101 ftp_port=21 ftp_root_dir=/var/ftp
```

Using Variables in Ansible 3 – Variable Declaration in External Files: The third way to use variables is to declare them in an external YAML file under a separate directory, such as group_vars, and reference that information in your playbooks. As you may have guessed, the information is typically stored in the form of dictionaries with their respective keys and values. In the following example, we have nested dictionaries. The ftp_users, ftp_root_dir, and ftp_port variables are declared and initialized in a file called ftp_servers.yml under the group_vars directory. These variables are then automatically applied to all hosts in the ftp_servers group.

```
# group_vars/ftp_servers.yml
---
ftp_users:
  - name: barbie
    password: barbie12345
  - name: ken
    password: ken67890
ftp_root_dir: /var/ftp
ftp_port: 21
```

If we convert the preceding information into Python variables and data types, we will end up with three variables with corresponding values. The first variable would be a list of dictionaries, while the other two variables would be simple one-to-one variables. "/var/ftp" is a string data type, and 21 is a digit data type.

```
ftp_users = [{"name": "jsparrow", "password": "LizSwann2003"}, {"name": "ppan", "password": "TinkerBell1902"}]
ftp_root_dir = "/var/ftp"
ftp_port = 21
```

Using Variables in Ansible 4 – Variable Declaration on the Command Line: You may have encountered this form of a variable while practicing ad hoc commands. It involves declaring variables through a command line using arguments. In the following example, the ftp_port variable is overridden with a value of 2121 for the current execution of the install_ftp.yml playbook.

```
ansible-playbook -i inventory.yml install_ftp.yml -e "ftp_port=2121"
```

Having seen four examples of variables in Ansible, it is time to put them into practice by writing a playbook that installs an FTP server on our file servers. Let's include only the f38c1 (192.168.127.151) client node in the group and turn it into a functional FTP server for now.

```
[jdoe@f38s1 ch10]$ vi 10.3_install_config_ftp_server.yml
[jdoe@f38s1 ch10]$ cat 10.3_install_config_ftp_server.yml
---
- name: Install and configure vsftpd server
  hosts: file_servers
  become: true

  vars: # Define variables at the beginning
    ftp_users:
      - name: jsparrow
        password: LizSwann2003
      - name: ppan
        password: TinkerBell1902
    ftp_root_dir: /var/ftp
    ftp_port: 21

  tasks:
    - name: Install vsftpd server
      ansible.builtin.yum: # Use yum package manager to install vsftpd on
      the Fedora machine
        name: vsftpd
        state: present

    - name: Create vsftpd.conf file
      ansible.builtin.file: # create file module to create vsftpd.conf
      configuration file
        path: /etc/vsftpd.conf
        state: touch

    - name: Configure vsftpd server
      ansible.builtin.lineinfile: # Use lineinfile to write information to
      vsftpd.conf file
```

```
  path: /etc/vsftpd.conf
  line: "{{ item.key }}={{ item.value }}"
with_dict: # loop through and use the key:value pairs to write lines
  - anonymous_enable: 'NO'
    local_enable: 'YES'
    write_enable: 'YES'
    local_umask: '022'
    secure_chroot_dir: '/var/run/vsftpd/empty'
    pam_service_name: 'vsftpd'
    rsa_cert_file: "'/etc/pkillow_writeable_chroot' 'YES'"

- name: Create FTP Users
  ansible.builtin.user: # Use user module to create FTP users, since we
  have two users, we have to use the variable substitution or variable
  interpolation, that is using "{{ }}"
    name: "{{ item.name }}" # name of new FTP user
    password: "{{ item.password | password_hash('sha512') }}" #
    password of new FTP user
    createhome: yes # create user's folder to upload/download files
    home: "{{ ftp_root_dir }}/{{ item.name }}" # creates /var/ftp/
    jsparrow and /var/ftp/ppan
    shell: /bin/bash # specify bash shell as the default shell
  loop: "{{ ftp_users }}" # ftp_users point to the vars on the top of
  this playbook

- name: Configure FTP Directory Permissions
  ansible.builtin.file:
    path: "{{ ftp_root_dir }}/{{ item.name }}" # variables are recalled
    and used multiple times
    state: directory
    mode: '2775' # The 2 in 2775 indicates that the setgid bit is set,
    which causes new files and directories created within the directory
    to inherit the group ownership of the parent directory (ftp in this
    case). This ensures that all files and directories created by the
    FTP users have the correct group ownership, allowing both the FTP
    user and the FTP group to read, write, and execute them.
```

```
    owner: "{{ item.name }}" # variables are recalled and used
    multiple times
    group: "{{ item.name }}" # variables are recalled and used
    multiple times
  loop: "{{ ftp_users }}" # variables are recalled and used
  multiple times

- name: Allow FTP through Firewall
  ansible.posix.firewalld: # need port 21 to be opened and in
  listening state
    service: ftp
    permanent: yes
    state: enabled # service is enabled so automatically starts at OS
    start-up
    immediate: yes

- name: Restart vsftpd service
  ansible.builtin.service:
    name: vsftpd
    state: restarted # restart vsftpd service, equivalent to 'systemctl
    restart vsftpd'
```

With your newfound knowledge of variables in playbooks, you can now confidently run the playbook and quickly test it to ensure everything is working as expected.

[jdoe@f38s1 ch10]$ **anp 10.3_install_config_ftp_server.yml**

[...omitted for brevity]

After running the playbook successfully, you may wonder how to verify if the FTP server is functioning correctly. Fortunately, there are two simple ways to test the FTP server's functionality. **The first and easiest method** involves using a Windows host PC, as shown in Figures 10-1 and 10-2. You can use WinSCP with the FTP protocol and log in using one of the FTP users you created in your playbook.

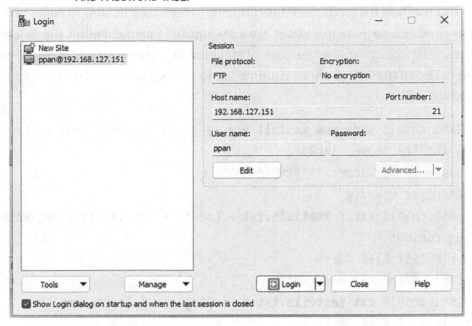

Figure 10-1. *WinSCP FTP login*

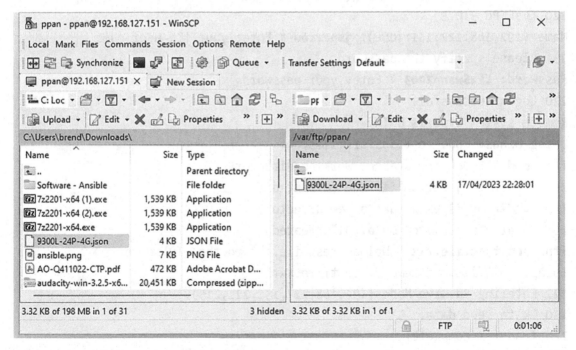

Figure 10-2. *WinSCP FTP file transfers*

Another method to test the FTP functionality, which may be new to some people, is also easy and can be done from your Ansible Control Machine. Follow the following steps to test FTP from your Ansible Control Machine. If you choose this method, you will need to install the FTP client by running "sudo yum install ftp -y" on your Ansible Control Machine.

```
[jdoe@f38s1 ch10]$ sudo yum install ftp -y # ftp is ftp client package,
vsftp is the ftp server package
[sudo] password for jdoe: ***************
[...omitted for brevity]
[jdoe@f38s1 ch10]$ cat > testfile.txt # Create a new testfile.txt with the
following content
THIS IS FTP TEST FILE ONLY!
[Press Ctrl +D to save and exit]
[jdoe@f38s1 ch10]$ cat testfile.txt # Display the file content
THIS IS FTP TEST FILE ONLY!
[jdoe@f38s1 ch10]$ ftp 192.168.127.151
Connected to 192.168.127.151 (192.168.127.151).
220 (vsFTPd 3.0.5)
Name (192.168.127.151:jdoe): jsparrow # Enter your ftp user name
331 Please specify the password.
Password: LizSwann2003 # Enter your password
230 Login successful.
Remote system type is UNIX.
Using binary mode to transfer files.
ftp> pwd # Check the present working directory
257 "/var/ftp/jsparrow" is the current directory
ftp> mkdir my_dir01 # Make a new directory
257 "/var/ftp/jsparrow/my_dir01" created
ftp> put testfile.txt # Upload testfile.txt to the FTP server
local: testfile.txt remote: testfile.txt
227 Entering Passive Mode (192,168,127,151,221,215).
150 Ok to send data.
226 Transfer complete.
28 bytes sent in 0.000127 secs (220.47 Kbytes/sec)
ftp> ls
```

```
227 Entering Passive Mode (192,168,127,151,196,91).
150 Here comes the directory listing.
drwxr-sr-x    2 1006      1006            6 May 07 11:12 my_dir01
-rw-r--r--    1 1006      1006           28 May 07 11:12 testfile.txt
226 Directory send OK.
ftp> rename testfile.txt ftpfile.bak # change the name of the test.txt file
to ftpfile.bak
350 Ready for RNTO.
250 Rename successful.
ftp> ls # list items in /var/ftp/jsparrow directory
227 Entering Passive Mode (192,168,127,151,44,146).
150 Here comes the directory listing.
-rw-r--r--    1 1006      1006           28 May 07 11:18 ftpfile.bak
drwxr-sr-x    2 1006      1006            6 May 07 11:18 my_dir01
226 Directory send OK.
ftp> get ftpfile.bak # download the renamed ftpfile.bak onto Ansible
Control machine
local: ftpfile.bak remote: ftpfile.bak
227 Entering Passive Mode (192,168,127,151,56,213).
150 Opening BINARY mode data connection for ftpfile.bak (28 bytes).
226 Transfer complete.
28 bytes received in 5.8e-05 secs (482.76 Kbytes/sec)
ftp> rmdir my_dir01 # delete my_dir01
250 Remove directory operation successful.
ftp> delete ftpfile.bak.txt # delete ftpfile.bak
250 Delete operation successful.
ftp> ls # list empty directory /var/ftp/jsparrow
227 Entering Passive Mode (192,168,127,151,59,101).
150 Here comes the directory listing.
226 Directory send OK.
ftp> bye # exit FTP session
221 Goodbye.
[jdoe@f38s1 ch10]$ ls -lh ftpfile.bak
-rw-r--r--. 1 jdoe jdoe 28 May  7 21:20 ftpfile.bak
```

If you're encountering issues with your FTP server, there exist a few troubleshooting tips you can try before seeking further assistance. These tips may help you resolve the issue without requiring external help. However, if you continue to experience issues, you can always search the Internet for additional troubleshooting resources.

Extend your knowledge:

Still having trouble uploading/downloading files from your FTP server?

Step 1. To manually allow FTP traffic through port 21 on a Fedora/Red Hat/CentOS Linux system, you can execute a sequence of commands that involves opening the port and reloading the firewall-cmd service. Port 21 is commonly used for File Transfer Protocol (FTP) traffic. First, use the command to add a rule to the firewall configuration that permits incoming TCP traffic on port 21. The "--permanent" option ensures that the change is permanent across reboots. Next, reload the firewall configuration with the command to apply the changes made with the previous command. Finally, use the command to list the open ports on the system, confirming that port 21 is now open for TCP traffic.

```
[jdoe@f38c1 ~]$ sudo firewall-cmd --permanent --add-port=21/tcp
[sudo] password for jdoe:***************
success
[jdoe@f38c1 ~]$ sudo firewall-cmd -reload
success
[jdoe@f38c1 ~]$ sudo firewall-cmd --list-ports
21/tcp
```

Step 2. If step 1 does not resolve the issue, you can try the following step to grant the FTP user access to create, delete, and modify files and directories in /var/ftp/. Linux is known for its secure operating system, where ports are closed by default, and access to specific services and directories is regulated by SELinux (Security-Enhanced Linux). SELinux is a mandatory access control system that uses the setsebool command to set SELinux Boolean values. It offers an additional layer of security beyond conventional file permissions by implementing a system-wide security policy that governs which actions are authorized or denied. It labels files and system resources with security contexts that determine their sensitivity and integrity. Policies control the processes that can access resources based on their labels and specify the actions they can perform. Developed by the NSA, SELinux is now a standard feature of many Linux distributions, adding an extra layer of protection to the operating system that can be tailored to meet specific security requirements.

```
[jdoe@f38c1 ~]$ sudo yum install -y policycoreutils-python selinux-
policy-targeted
[jdoe@f38c1 ~]$ sudo setsebool -P ftpd_full_access on
[jdoe@f38c1 ~]$ sudo systemctl restart vsftpd
```

Visit the following URLs to extend your SELinux information:

```
https://en.wikipedia.org/wiki/Security-Enhanced_Linux
```

and

```
www.redhat.com/en/topics/linux/what-is-
selinux#:~:text=Security%2DEnhanced%20Linux%20
(SELinux),Linux%20Security%20Modules%20(LSM).
```

10.4 host_vars and handler

In the previous exercise, we explored four different ways to use variables in Ansible, and we practiced using variables in a playbook. Additionally, we learned how to set up an FTP server and validate FTP services on a Fedora server, which is a Red Hat–based Linux distribution. Moving forward, let's delve into two crucial Ansible concepts: host_vars and handlers. Host_vars are variables that apply to a specific host or group of hosts, while handlers are tasks that execute only if one or more notified tasks report a changed state. You can define host_vars in YAML files named after the target hosts or target groups, and Ansible applies them to the relevant hosts or groups when running a playbook.

Using host_vars and handlers can significantly improve the efficiency and flexibility of your Ansible workflows. Host_vars enable you to define variables on a per-host or per-group basis, allowing you to apply specific configurations and settings to different hosts or groups. Meanwhile, handlers ensure that only necessary actions are executed,

improving the speed and reliability of your playbook runs. Implementing host_vars
and handlers can also make your automation workflows more organized and easier
to maintain, especially when dealing with complex infrastructure. As responsible
engineers, our job is to provide reliable and honest solutions to our clients. While
honesty is always the best policy, in the world of sales and marketing, it may not always
be possible to reveal the whole truth to customers. This creates a dilemma for engineers
who want to provide the best solutions possible while also being transparent with their
clients. However, by continuing to learn, grow, and improve our skills, we can provide
the best possible solutions while still being honest and transparent.

In this example, we will only scratch the surface of the host_vars and handler
concepts, and we encourage readers to extend their knowledge of these concepts as
they work on more complex automation projects. On-the-job training and applying the
concepts learned from resources like this book to real-world production playbooks or
scripts are essential for mastering Ansible and maximizing its potential in managing
infrastructure.

Let's dive into an exercise to better understand the Ansible concept of host_vars and
handlers.

Step 1: To utilize host variables in Ansible, it is necessary to create a dedicated file for
the variables to be used by each host or group of hosts. This file should be named after
the target host or group and stored in the host_vars directory within your Ansible project.
By structuring your variables in this manner, you can easily apply specific configurations
and settings to different hosts or groups, which can enhance the efficiency and
effectiveness of your infrastructure management.

```
[jdoe@f38s1 ch10]$ mkdir host_vars
[jdoe@f38s1 ch10]$ cd host_vars/
[jdoe@f38s1 host_vars]$ pwd
/home/jdoe/repo1/ch10/host_vars
[jdoe@f38s1 host_vars]$ vi f38c1.yml
[jdoe@f38s1 host_vars]$ vi u23c1.yml
[jdoe@f38s1 host_vars]$ cp u23c1.yml u23c2.yml
```

As you are aware, package names for installing Apache web servers may differ
between various Linux distributions, such as Fedora and Ubuntu. To account for this
difference, we will create three separate YAML files under the host_vars directory, each

containing the package names for a specific Linux distribution. By doing so, we can
ensure that the correct package names are used for each server based on its operating
system. The three YAML files we will create are

```
[jdoe@f38s1 host_vars]$ cat f38c1.yml
http_package_name: httpd
http_service: httpd
php_package_name: php

[jdoe@f38s1 host_vars]$ cat u23c1.yml
http_package_name: apache2
http_service: apache2
php_package_name: libapache2-mod-php

[jdoe@f38s1 host_vars]$ cat u23c2.yml
http_package_name: apache2
http_service: apache2
php_package_name: libapache2-mod-php
```

Step 2: To streamline the web_servers playbook, it is recommended to refactor
the primary script (found at roles/web_servers/tasks/main.yml) using the package
module. Additionally, it is suggested to use variable names that match the package
names specified in the host_vars directory. This approach simplifies the playbook and
facilitates maintenance, allowing for quick package installation and configuration on the
designated servers.

```
[jdoe@f38s1 host_vars]$ cd ..
[jdoe@f38s1 ch10]$ vi roles/web_servers/tasks/main.yml
[jdoe@f38s1 ch10]$ cat roles/web_servers/tasks/main.yml
```

```
- name: install httpd and PHP packages
  ansible.builtin.package:
    name:
      - "{{ http_package_name }}" # Only change the highlighted
      - "{{ php_package_name }}" # Only change the highlighted
    state: latest
  tags: [apache, httpd, ubuntu, fedora]
```

[...omitted for brevity] # Leave the entire playbook as is, only change the
highlighted.

Step 3: Let's now use the playbook from exercise 10.3 (10.3b_provision_roles.
yml) and run it with the host_vars files we just created. Although the output may not
appear different, the playbook is now retrieving the host variables from the host_vars/
directory and utilizing them in the play. This enables finer control over variables and
configurations while also making the playbook more concise and manageable.

`[jdoe@f38s1 ch10]$ anp 10.3b_provision_roles.yml`

`[...omitted for brevity]`

Now that you have practiced and seen the concept of host_vars in action, let's move
on to understanding the handler concept in Ansible.

10.4.1 Concept of the Handler in Ansible

Ansible handlers ensure idempotency by executing only when triggered by the notify
directive and when there is a change in the state of the task. Handlers run in the order
defined in the handlers section and execute only if there is a state change. It's crucial
to name them uniquely to avoid duplicate names. Handlers are useful for restarting,
reloading, starting, or stopping services on target nodes and help ensure the playbook
runs efficiently by avoiding unnecessary restarts. To define a handler, use the notify and
handlers directives. Handlers are typically grouped using the listen keyword and called
using a single notify statement. By default, handlers run at the end of the play once all
regular tasks have been executed. If you want handlers to run before the end of the play
or between tasks, add a meta task to flush them using the meta module.

Overall, handlers are tasks that execute only if one or more notified tasks report a
changed state. This concept is particularly useful for actions that should execute only
once at the end of a playbook or when a change has occurred, such as restarting a service
or reloading a configuration file. By using handlers, you can ensure that these actions are
only executed when needed, improving the efficiency and reliability of your playbook
executions. Despite the significance of this concept, most available materials on Ansible
handlers are carbon copies of the official documentation's examples, which mostly rely
on high-level explanations and standard HTTPD, Apache, or Nginx examples. Hence, we
spent a week creating better explanations for the Ansible handler concept with practical
examples that allow you to learn and practice the concept. This simplified approach will
help you grasp the fundamental concept of the handler more easily using only two Linux
servers: the Ansible Control Machine (f38s1) and Fedora client node (f38c1).

Step 1: Create a new directory called "10.4_handler" for Section 10.4. Change your working directory to the newly created directory and create a new inventory file that only includes "f38c1". Additionally, create an "ansible.cfg" file with the exact information shown in this exercise. If you're feeling tired, you can copy both files from "/home/jdoe/repo1/ch10".

```
[jdoe@f38s1 ch10]$ mkdir 10.4_handler # create a new working
directory
[jdoe@f38s1 ch10]$ cd 10.4_handler # change the working directory
[jdoe@f38s1 10.4_handler]$ vi inventory # create inventory file and add a
single target host
[jdoe@f38s1 10.4_handler]$ cat inventory
f38c1 ansible_host=192.168.127.151 # only contains a single client node
```

Ensure that your ansible.cfg file is configured properly.

```
[jdoe@f38s1 ch10]$ cp ../ansible.cfg . # copy the ansible.cfg file from the
parent directory
[jdoe@f38s1 10.4_handler]$ vi ansible.cfg # modify the file as shown below
[jdoe@f38s1 10.4_handler]$ cat ansible.cfg # display the content of
the file
[defaults]
inventory = ./inventory # use the inventory in the working directory
private_key_file = /home/jdoe/.ssh/ansible # use the private key in this
directory
deprecation_warnings=False
nocows = 1 # disable cowsay
```

Step 2: To proceed, create a new Ansible playbook as shown here:

```
[jdoe@f38s1 10.4_handler]$ vi 10.4_top5_handler.yml
[jdoe@f38s1 10.4_handler]$ cat 10.4_top5_handler.yml

---
- hosts: f38c1 # target host
  become: true # run as root user
  gather_facts: false
```

```
vars:
  file_path: "./top5.txt" # specify the file name and path, will use /
  home/jdoe/
  file_contents: | # file contents variable to be entered into top5.
  txt file
    London
    Paris
    New York
    Sydney
    Tokyo

tasks:
  - name: check if the file exists
    ansible.builtin.stat: # stat module is used to check the file exists
      path: "{{ file_path }}"
    register: file_info

  - name: create the file if it does not exist
    ansible.builtin.file: # file module to create a new file if it does
    not exist (using when)
      path: "{{ file_path }}"
      state: touch
      mode: "0666" # the file is readable and writable by all, including
      the owner, group, & others.
    when: not file_info.stat.exists # only create file, top5.txt if file
    does not exist

  - name: ensure the file has specific contents
    ansible.builtin.copy:
      dest: "{{ file_path }}" # destination of the file
      content: "{{ file_contents }}" # make sure the top 5 cities are
      all intact
    notify: file_changed # if the content is different, notify will
    trigger the handler to run
```

```
handlers:
  - name: file_changed # this name must be exactly the same as the
  parameter used in notify
    ansible.builtin.command: echo "Your file has been changed!"
```

The preceding playbook creates a text file named "top5.txt" that contains my top five secret cities around the world. It checks whether the file exists, and if it doesn't, it creates a new file. Additionally, it uses the copy and content modules to verify if the file's content has changed. If the content hasn't changed, the handler won't run. However, if it detects a change in the file's content, the handler will overwrite the modified information. This mechanism is particularly useful when you need to keep some configuration files with specific information that other users cannot modify for a good reason. By running this playbook, you ensure that the file always contains your favorite five cities, and not someone else's.

Step 3: Create a second playbook that removes the first line of the "top5.txt" file. This will allow us to modify the content and test the concept of handlers. When you run this playbook, it will remove the first line (which contains London as the city in the first line) from the file. This, in turn, triggers the handler action, which notifies the "ensure file has specific contents" task. Simply create the second playbook, and then we'll execute both playbooks in different orders to go through the sequence.

```
[jdoe@f38s1 10.4_handler]$ vi 10.4_top5_remove_one.yml
[jdoe@f38s1 10.4_handler]$ cat 10.4_top5_remove_one.yml

---
- hosts: f38c1
  become: true
  vars:
    file_path: "./top5.txt"

  tasks:
    - name: remove first line from file
      ansible.builtin.shell: "tail -n +2 {{ file_path }} > {{ file_path }}
      .tmp && mv {{ file_path }}.tmp {{ file_path }}" # shell tail command
      is run to remove the first line of the top5.txt

    - name: read file
```

```
    become: true
    register: file_contents # hold the content from the command run
    ansible.builtin.shell: cat {{ file_path }} # run the concatenate
    command to display the content
    check_mode: no

  - name: display file contents
    ansible.builtin.debug: # display the content of the command run
      var: file_contents.stdout_lines
```

Step 4: Execute the "10.4_top5_handler.yml" playbook for the first time and observe the output. You will notice that the handler is triggered and the message "RUNNING HANDLER [file_changed]" is executed, as highlighted in the following output:

```
[jdoe@f38s1 10.4_handler]$ anpap 10.4_top5_handler.yml
BECOME password: ****************

PLAY [f38c1] *********************************************************

TASK [check if file exists] *****************************************
ok: [f38c1]

TASK [create file if it does not exist] *****************************
changed: [f38c1]

TASK [ensure the file has specific contents] ************************
changed: [f38c1]

RUNNING HANDLER [file_changed] **************************************
changed: [f38c1]

PLAY RECAP **********************************************************
f38c1 : ok=4  changed=3  unreachable=0  failed=0  skipped=0  rescued=0  ignored=0
```

Step 5: Run the same playbook again, and you will notice that the handler is not executed because the file created during the first run remains unchanged. This proves our theory that as long as the file "top5.txt" remains unchanged, the handler will not execute.

```
[jdoe@f38s1 10.4_handler]$ anpap 10.4_top5_handler.yml
BECOME password: ****************

PLAY [f38c1] ***************************************************************

TASK [check if file exists] ***********************************************
ok: [f38c1]

TASK [create file if it does not exist] ***********************************
skipping: [f38c1]

TASK [ensure the file has specific contents] ******************************
ok: [f38c1]

PLAY RECAP ****************************************************************
f38c1 : ok=2  changed=0  unreachable=0  failed=0  skipped=1  rescued=0  ignored=0
```

Step 6: Go to the client node f38c1, and check the file top5.txt located under /home/jdoe. You will see that the file contains the expected five cities.

```
[jdoe@f38c1 ~]$ cat top5.txt

London
Paris
New York
Sydney
Tokyo
```

Step 7: Now back at the Ansible control node, f38s1, run the playbook (10.4_top5_remove_one.yml), which removes the first line or the first city from the file. This playbook will print the remaining cities after removing the first city, as you can see from the output:

```
[jdoe@f38s1 10.4_handler]$ anpap 10.4_top5_remove_one.yml
BECOME password: ****************

PLAY [f38c1] ***************************************************************

TASK [Gathering Facts] ****************************************************
ok: [f38c1]
```

```
TASK [remove first line from file] ************************************
changed: [f38c1]

TASK [read file] *******************************************************
changed: [f38c1]

TASK [display file contents] ******************************************
ok: [f38c1] => {
    "file_contents.stdout_lines": [
        "Paris",
        "New York",
        "Sydney",
        "Tokyo"
    ]
}

PLAY RECAP ************************************************************
f38c1 : ok=4  changed=2  unreachable=0  failed=0  skipped=0  rescued=0  ignored=0
```

Step 8: If you insist on checking the same information from the client node, f38c1, run the concatenate or more command to view the contents of the file, top5.txt.

```
[jdoe@f38c1 ~]$ cat top5.txt
```

```
Paris
New York
Sydney
Tokyo
```

Step 9: Go back to the control node and run the handler playbook, 10.4_top5_handler.yml, again. You will see the handler execute in front of your eyes. If it works correctly, then it will rewrite the top five cities as before, with London reinstated, as seen in step 6.

```
[jdoe@f38s1 10.4_handler]$ anpap 10.4_top5_handler.yml
BECOME password: ***************

PLAY [f38c1] *********************************************************
```

```
TASK [check if file exists] ********************************************
ok: [f38c1]

TASK [create file if it does not exist] **********************************
skipping: [f38c1]

TASK [ensure the file has specific contents] ****************************
changed: [f38c1]

RUNNING HANDLER [file_changed] ****************************************
changed: [f38c1]

PLAY RECAP ***********************************************************
f38c1  : ok=3  changed=2  unreachable=0  failed=0  skipped=1  rescued=0  ignored=0
```

Step 10: Now, back at the client node, f38c1, check the top5.txt file again. Voila! London is back at the top of the list of the other four favorite cities. Thus, we have successfully demonstrated that the handler worked by using the notify directive in our playbook.

[jdoe@f38c1 ~]$ **cat top5.txt**

```
London
Paris
New York
Sydney
Tokyo
```

The preceding example provided a simple demonstration of using Ansible host_vars and handlers. However, to effectively apply these concepts to real-world production environments, it's crucial to continue learning and extending your knowledge. Remember that skills that are not practiced are only as good as skills learned solely from books. Staying engaged with the IT field and practicing what you have learned will help you level up your skills and become a better engineer.

To extend the concept of handlers, there are several other aspects to consider. For instance, multiple tasks in a playbook might require multiple handlers, and it's important to name them uniquely to avoid duplicate names. In such cases, you can group handlers using the "listen" keyword and call them using a single notify statement.

You should also understand when handlers run. By default, handlers run at the end of the play after all regular tasks have been executed. However, if you want handlers to run before the end of the play or between tasks, you can add a meta task to flush them using the meta module.

Additionally, it's crucial to handle task errors that may arise during playbook execution with notify directives. You can use the failed_when parameter to specify the conditions under which a task should fail, and the ignore_errors parameter to ignore errors and continue playbook execution. Finally, it's important to note that handlers are like other tasks in a playbook, but they are only run when triggered by the notify directive and when there is a change of state. They help ensure idempotency and efficient playbook execution by avoiding unnecessary restarts or other actions.

To learn more about handlers and these additional aspects, explore Ansible's official documentation and practice with practical examples.

10.5 Templates

In Ansible, templates are used to generate dynamic configuration files based on variables and data from the playbook or inventory. Templates are written in the Jinja2 template language, which allows for the use of variables, loops, conditionals, and other dynamic constructs. Templates are important as they provide a way to generate dynamic configuration files or scripts based on variables or other dynamic data. Using templates can simplify the process of managing and configuring large numbers of hosts. They allow for the use of variables, loops, conditionals, and other dynamic constructs, making it easy to standardize the configuration of the same or similar systems. Without templates, you would need to manually create and maintain multiple versions of your configuration files for different servers or environments, which can be time-consuming and error-prone.

By using templates, you can define a single source file with placeholders for variables and then use Ansible to render the file for each target server or environment with the appropriate values. This helps to ensure consistency and accuracy in your configuration management process.

Here, we will use a simple example to practice using templates while configuring f38c1 as a new SFTP server. As the target server already has OpenSSH-server installed, there is no need to install it again. The SFTP server uses the same services and port number as the OpenSSH server, making it unnecessary to install any additional software.

Step 1: Create a new working directory named 10.5_template. This will help us isolate our new files for this exercise and enhance your understanding with less clutter.

```
[jdoe@f38s1 ch10]$ mkdir 10.5_template
[jdoe@f38s1 ch10]$ cd 10.5_template
[jdoe@f38s1 10.5_template]$ pwd
/home/jdoe/repo1/ch10/10.5_template
```

Step 2: After changing your directory, create a simple list of controlled nodes like this to control the nodes in your environment:

```
[jdoe@f38s1 10.5_template]$ vi inventory
[jdoe@f38s1 10.5_template]$ cat inventory

f38c1 ansible_host=192.168.127.151
```

Step 3: You can create the ansible.cfg file from scratch or copy it from the previous exercise. For this exercise, we will create it from scratch.

```
[jdoe@f38s1 10.5_template]$ vi ansible.cfg
[jdoe@f38s1 10.5_template]$ cat ansible.cfg

[defaults]
inventory = ./inventory
private_key_file = /home/jdoe/.ssh/ansible
deprecation_warnings=False
nocows = 1
```

Step 4: Now, this is the most critical part of this section, and it requires your full attention while creating this template. However, if you want to save time, you can use the downloaded copy of the Jinja2 template file named "sshd_config.j2".

```
[jdoe@f38s1 10.5_template]$ vi sshd_config.j2
[jdoe@f38s1 10.5_template]$ cat sshd_config.j2

# Original settings # These were the original configurations or enabled
features
Include /etc/ssh/sshd_config.d/*.conf # Include additional configuration
files from this directory
```

```
AuthorizedKeysFile .ssh/authorized_keys # Specify the file containing
authorized public keys for user authentication
Subsystem sftp /usr/libexec/openssh/sftp-server # Define the SFTP subsystem
and specify the path to the SFTP server binary

### ADDED BY Network Automation ADMIN ### # New configurations to
enable SFTP
Match User {{sftp_user}} # Apply the following settings only to the
specified user
ForceCommand internal-sftp # Force the use of SFTP and prevent shell access
PasswordAuthentication yes # Allow password authentication for the
specified user
ChrootDirectory {{sftp_dir}} # Set the root directory for the specified
user to the specified directory
PermitTunnel no # Disable tunneling
AllowAgentForwarding no # Disable agent forwarding
AllowTcpForwarding no # Disable TCP forwarding
X11Forwarding no # Disable X11 forwarding
```

Step 5: One of the author's blogs (www.italchemy.wordpress.com) shares how to install, configure, and test an SFTP server manually on Linux. You can read about the manual SFTP server configuration from the following URL: https://wordpress.com/post/italchemy.wordpress.com/4525. Additionally, there are many interesting topics on the same blog page.

The following Ansible playbook is an attempt to replicate the SFTP server installation, configuration, and verification steps shared on the author's WordPress site. With the help of Ansible, setting up a new SFTP server on a single server or ten servers becomes easy. If you are a serious network or systems engineer, you must understand how files can be transferred between different systems on your network and also have a full grasp of how to set up and fine-tune each file-sharing server. This will add flexibility to your work and help others in your organization too. With a good working knowledge of file sharing in an enterprise network environment, you will always have an edge over your peers and shine like a northern star.

Since this playbook is quite lengthy, it's important to focus your attention when writing and understanding the following YAML codes to ensure accuracy and completeness. If you want to save time typing, you can find the same code on the authors' GitHub page at https://github.com/ansnetauto/repo1.

```
[jdoe@f38s1 10.5_template]$ vi 10.5_install_sftp_server.yml
[jdoe@f38s1 10.5_template]$ cat 10.5_install_sftp_server.yml

---
- name: Install SFTP server on Fedora/CentOS/Red Hat/EC2 Linux
  hosts: all
  become: true
  vars: # add your variables here
    sftp_user: sftpuser # username is sftpuser
    sftp_dir: /var/sftp # this is where all sftp directories will reside
    sftp_data_dir: /var/sftp/sftpdata # this is where all the data will be
    shared for sftpuser

  tasks:
    - name: Add a new user and set the password
      ansible.builtin.user:
        name: "{{ sftp_user }}"
        password: "{{ 'B3llaVita!@#' | password_hash('sha512') }}" #
        Remember your password
        update_password: always

    - name: Create the SFTP directory
      ansible.builtin.file:
        path: "{{ sftp_dir }}"
        state: directory

    - name: Create the SFTP data directory
      ansible.builtin.file:
        path: "{{ sftp_data_dir }}"
        state: directory

    - name: Set ownership of SFTP directories
      ansible.builtin.file:
        path: "{{ item.path }}"
        owner: "{{ item.owner }}"
        group: "{{ item.group }}"
        mode: "{{ item.mode }}"
```

```yaml
      loop: # use the loop to read the dictionaries below to set correct
      directory ownership
        - { path: "{{ sftp_dir }}", owner: "root", group: "root",
        mode: "0755" } # for root user
        - { path: "{{ sftp_data_dir }}", owner: "{{ sftp_user }}", group:
        "{{ sftp_user }}", mode: "0700" } # for sftp_user

    - name: Copy sshd_config.j2 file from current working directory to /
    etc/ssh/
      ansible.builtin.copy:
        src: sshd_config.j2
        dest: /etc/ssh/
        mode: '0600'
        owner: root
        group: root

    - name: Modify sshd_config file # use jinja2 template file to update
    the sshd_config file
      ansible.builtin.template:
        src: sshd_config.j2
        dest: /etc/ssh/sshd_config
        owner: root
        group: root
        mode: '0600'
      notify: restart sshd # did you notice that we are suing a
      handler here

    - name: Check sshd_config file syntax
      ansible.builtin.command: sshd -t
      register: sshd_config_syntax
      ignore_errors: yes

  handlers: # we are using handler to restart the sshd service
    - name: restart sshd
      ansible.builtin.systemd:
        name: sshd
        state: restarted
```

```
when: sshd_config_syntax.rc == 0 # execute if the previous task
returned an rc value of 0, which indicates that the syntax of the
sshd_config file is correct
```

Step 6: After creating and verifying all the necessary files, you are now ready to execute your playbook and transform your Linux server into a fully functioning SFTP server. **Since we are working with an existing SSH server to add the SFTP service and user, it's recommended to take a snapshot of your virtual machines using VMware Workstation's snapshot feature, if you have been following the book step-by-step.** This will allow you to easily restore to the working state in case of any issues during the execution of the playbook.

Once you are ready, run the playbook and check the output. If your output matches the example provided in the book, then everything is working correctly. However, if you encounter any errors, you can troubleshoot the issue and re-run the playbook until it executes successfully.

```
[jdoe@f38s1 10.5_template]$ anpap 10.5_install_sftp_server.yml
BECOME password: ***************

PLAY [Install SFTP server on Fedora/CentOS/Red Hat/EC2 Linux] *************

TASK [Gathering Facts] ****************************************************
ok: [f38c1]

TASK [Add a new user and set the password] *******************************
changed: [f38c1]

TASK [Create the SFTP directory] *****************************************
changed: [f38c1]

TASK [Create the SFTP data directory] ************************************
changed: [f38c1]

TASK [Set ownership of SFTP directories] *********************************
ok: [f38c1] => (item={'path': '/var/sftp', 'owner': 'root', 'group':
'root', 'mode': '0755'})
changed: [f38c1] => (item={'path': '/var/sftp/sftpdata', 'owner':
'sftpuser', 'group': 'sftpuser', 'mode': '0700'})
```

521

```
TASK [Copy sshd_config.j2 file from current working directory to /etc/ssh/]
*********************************
changed: [f38c1]

TASK [Modify sshd_config file] ********************************************
changed: [f38c1]

TASK [Check sshd_config file syntax] *************************************
changed: [f38c1]

RUNNING HANDLER [restart sshd] ********************************************
changed: [f38c1]

PLAY RECAP ***************************************************************
f38c1    : ok=9  changed=8  unreachable=0  failed=0  skipped=0  rescued=0  ignored=0
```

Step 7: After successfully running your playbook, it is important to conduct a
verification test to ensure that your new SFTP user is unable to log in to the server
using the SSH protocol. It is a best security practice to keep the administration account
separate from the application user account, such as the one created here. If you attempt
to log in to the server using sftpuser's credentials, it should fail. A failed login attempt is
expected by design and indicates that the configuration is working as intended.

```
[jdoe@f38s1 10.5_template]$ ssh sftpuser@192.168.127.151
sftpuser@192.168.127.151's password: B3llaVita!@#

This service allows sftp connections only.
Connection to 192.168.127.151 closed.
```

Step 8: On the other hand, if you use the SFTP protocol or command, you will be
able to log in and perform general administrative tasks, including file and directory
housekeeping. You will be logging into your SFTP root directory, as shown in the
following, and will be allowed to move to the data sharing directory "sftpdata". Voila! We
confirmed that our SFTP server is working properly; we should be able to use this SFTP
server in our future Ansible networking labs.

```
[jdoe@f38s1 10.5_template]$ sftp sftpuser@192.168.127.151
sftpuser@192.168.127.151's password: B3llaVita!@#

Connected to 192.168.127.151.
sftp> pwd
Remote working directory: /
sftp> ls
sftpdata
sftp> cd sftpdata/
sftp> # Use Ctrl+Z to stop the SFTP session.
```

Step 9: Like the FTP server that we configured and tested earlier, the newly configured SFTP server can also be accessed, and files can be transferred between the Windows host PC and Linux server using the WinSCP SFTP client. This is particularly useful when transferring image files and log files between two different systems. When logging into WinSCP, refer to Figures 10-3 and 10-4 for guidance.

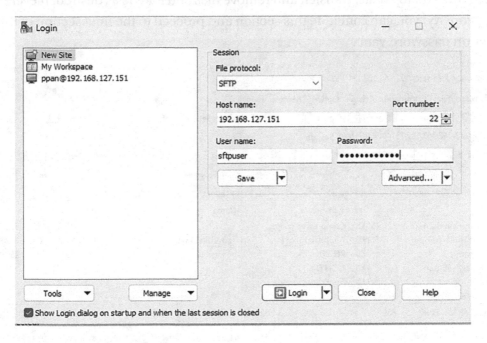

Figure 10-3. *SFTP server login*

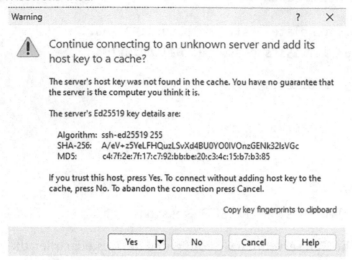

Figure 10-4. *SFTP server – accept to add the host key*

Step 10: As shown in Figure 10-5, test the functionality of the SFTP server to ensure that it allows you to create, transfer, and remove files and folders as desired. If everything works properly, you can conclude this section and proceed to the final section of this chapter on password vault.

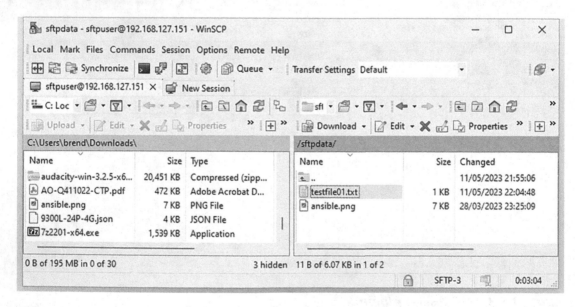

Figure 10-5. *SFTP server – test file creation and file transfers*

Congratulations! By completing this tutorial, you have gained a solid understanding of how to use Ansible and Ansible templates to install and configure an SFTP server on Linux. You have also become proficient in testing the functionality of your newly configured SFTP server. An SFTP server is an essential component of any Network, Systems, and Security domain for day-to-day operations, as well as a critical tool for engineers dealing with system administration at a large scale. With the knowledge you have gained, you can now confidently deploy and manage SFTP servers to support your organization's needs.

While the previous example was a simple demonstration of using templates in Ansible, **the real challenge lies in applying Ansible concepts to complex production scenarios that meet business requirements and achieve business objectives to a high standard.** To become an expert in network automation, it's crucial to connect the dots between different Ansible concepts and apply them effectively to your work needs. Continuously practicing and exploring the vast capabilities of Ansible is the key to improving your automation skills and becoming proficient in network automation.

Tip

Are the best things in life really free? Binge watching free IT training videos

on YouTube

As a tech lead and technical book author, I understand the importance of having high-quality study resources to advance your IT career. There are many paid and free IT training resources out there, but one of the most popular forms of training for many IT professionals is the free IT training videos on YouTube. Some video contents are as good or even better than the paid content offered by CBT Nuggets and IPTV training videos. For instance, Jeremey's IT Lab on CCNA (`www.youtube.com/channel/UC0Q7Hlz75NYhYAuq6OOfqHw`) is an excellent example of a YouTube channel that provides great content for novice network engineers.

Although using video training can help you complete a whole CCNA certification without attending Cisco's official Training courses, it is important to note that you will still need to read the good old Cisco CCNA textbooks to cover the finer details.

Therefore, it is crucial to consider if you are utilizing YouTube videos to their full potential as an IT student or professional. You need to evaluate if the videos you are watching, whether lounging on your couch or bed, in your car, or even on the toilet, are adding any value to your career.

While YouTube is technically "free," the company collects your data for marketing purposes, and you may often encounter advertisements prompting you to purchase products. However, YouTube still provides a vast selection of valuable IT training videos that can benefit anyone seeking to enhance their skills.

If you're determined to make a career in IT and elevate your skills to the next level, it is necessary to take a proactive approach to learning. Don't just watch IT training videos casually in your spare time; treat them like formal training sessions. Sit at your desk, take notes, and practice the skills you learn to absorb the information better. Investing your time and resources in education can lead to new heights in your IT career. It's up to you to convert those experiences into meaningful opportunities for growth and success.

Remember, "imitation is the source of creativity," and it's crucial to apply what you learn to practical work situations. So go beyond merely scrolling and make the most of the valuable IT training resources available to you. Industry insiders say that experience is everything when it comes to learning, so don't shy away from opportunities to apply your knowledge to real-world situations. With the right mindset and approach, you can achieve success and advance your IT career to new heights (B.C. May 2023).

10.6 Managing Password on Ansible

As you become more familiar with Ansible, you'll notice that there are multiple ways to handle and use passwords within the Ansible Control Machine. So far, we've used the "--ask-become-pass" option, which has worked well for us during our journey through learning Ansible. However, in a production environment, your organization will likely follow one of several information security standards, such as ISO/IEC 27001,

NIST SP800-53, CIS Controls, PCI DSS, HIPAA, or GDPR. While there's no need to delve into the details of each standard, the IT industry recognizes that information security, including password management in the enterprise IT infrastructure ecosystem, is a critical and long-standing issue.

Up until now, we've tediously used the "--ask-become-pass" option on the command line to familiarize readers with other Ansible concepts instead of focusing solely on password management. This option prompts the Ansible playbook to request a password for privilege escalation when executing commands requiring "sudo" or "su" commands on client (target) nodes. By default, Ansible executes commands with the current user's password, but in some cases, the user may lack sufficient privileges to run specific commands, and thus, the "--ask-become-pass" option is used. It's important to take special care when manually entering passwords on the command line as they may be recorded in shell history or logs. To mitigate this risk, it's recommended that you store your passwords securely using Ansible Vault or an external password store. Remember, when it comes to password management, more security is always better than less.

Now, let's explore other ways of using passwords in Ansible, deepen our understanding, and gain the knowledge and experience required to use them effectively in our playbooks. We have tabulated multiple ways how passwords are used in Table 10-2 for your reference.

Table 10-2. *Multiple ways to use passwords in Ansible*

No.	Passwd method	Option used	Explanation
1	**Remote user password**	ansible_ssh_pass	To establish an SSH connection, the user needs to provide the password for the remote user. This password can be set by using the "ansible_ssh_pass" variable in either the inventory or playbook
2	**Become password**	ansible_become_pass	When you provide a become password, you can escalate privileges on a remote host to the "sudo" or "su" level. You can set the "ansible_become_pass" variable in either the inventory or playbook to specify this password. This has the same effect as using the "--ask-become-pass" option
3	**Vault password**	--ask-vault-pass	Ansible Vault is a feature that enables the encryption of sensitive data, such as passwords, API keys, and certificates. To use Ansible Vault, you can encrypt the data using the "ansible-vault" command-line tool or the "vault" keyword in the playbook and provide the vault password when running the playbook using the "--ask-vault-pass" option
4	**Privilege escalation password**	ansible_password	You can set a privilege escalation password for specific tasks using the "ansible_password" variable. This variable can be used in addition to the "ansible_become_pass" option for privilege escalation
5	**Password lookup plug-in**	password lookup plug-ins	Passwords can be retrieved from external sources such as password managers, credential stores, or external services using password lookup plug-ins. To use these plug-ins, you can specify them in your playbook or inventory as required

This is the last topic that we will cover on basic Ansible concepts. As you are already somewhat familiar with the first two methods, we will focus on the encrypt and decrypt password methods, using two Ansible Vault examples. An API-key example will be demonstrated in one of the upcoming Palo Alto Security labs.

10.6.1 Password Vault

Ansible Vault is a feature that enables file encryption using AES256 and password file encryption. This eliminates the need to use plain text–based passwords, enhancing security. With Ansible Vault, you can create a new vault file with the "ansible-vault create" command, check encryption using the "cat" command, view the content of the file with "ansible-vault view", update the password using "ansible-vault rekey", and change the content of the file using "ansible-vault edit". Using Ansible Vault to store passwords can significantly reduce security risks associated with storing passwords in plain text, making it a vital component of any organization's password management strategy.

Here is a quick list of the ansible-vault commands you will be using in the next exercise for encryption and decryption of your password. Please read the commands and explanations in Table 10-3 before moving to the next task.

Table 10-3. *Working with ansible-vault*

Ansible-vault command	Explanation
ansible-vault create vault_pass.yml	Create a new vault file called "vault_pass.yml"
cat vault_pass.yml	Check encryption used
ansible-vault view vault_pass.yml	Display/view the content of the file
ansible-vault rekey vault_pass.yml	Update the password to open the vault_pass.yml file
ansible-vault edit vault_pass.yml	Change the content of the file

Extend your knowledge:

Ensure security of sensitive data using the vault-id feature.

Ansible Vault-id is a popular feature that allows you to specify the source of encryption keys or passwords for decrypting sensitive data. By separating this information from playbooks and storing it in external files or plug-ins, it ensures the security of sensitive data. The vault-id option enables you to precisely define the location or method of retrieving the decryption keys or passwords. This approach provides a robust and secure mechanism for handling confidential information within Ansible playbooks and configurations, safeguarding against unauthorized access and ensuring the privacy of sensitive data.

Let's say you have an encrypted Ansible Vault file named my_secrets.yml that contains sensitive data. You can create a vault password file named my_vault_pass.txt with the decryption password stored in it.

To run a playbook using the vault password file, you can use the --vault-id option:

```
ansible-playbook --vault-id @my_vault_pass.txt my_
playbook.yml
```

In this example, @my_vault_pass.txt specifies the vault password file location. Ansible will read the decryption password from the my_vault_pass.txt file and use it to decrypt the vaulted data in my_secrets.yml during playbook execution.

10.6.1.1 Encrypting ansible_become_pass Only Using ansible-vault

Let's practice using ansible-vault by following this exercise. It's a simple example that focuses on encrypting the ansible_become_pass only. So go ahead and give your fingers some practice!

Step 1: Begin by creating a new working directory specifically for practicing password vault, and then change your current working directory to this newly created directory.

```
[jdoe@f38s1 ch10]$ pwd
/home/jdoe/repo1/ch10
[jdoe@f38s1 ch10]$ mkdir 10.6_password_vault
[jdoe@f38s1 ch10]$ cd 10.6_password_vault/
[jdoe@f38s1 10.6_password_vault]$
```

Step 2: Create a vault_pass.yaml file by executing the command "ansible-vault create vault_pass.yml".

```
[jdoe@f38s1 10.6_password_vault]$ ansible-vault create vault_pass.yml
```

```
New Vault password: ***************
Confirm New Vault password: ***************  # Don't forget this password!
ansible_become_pass: SuperSecretPassword
```

After executing the "ansible-vault create vault_pass.yml" command in the previous step, a new file named "vault_pass.yml" will be created in your working directory. This file will be encrypted using the Ansible Vault and will require a password to be decrypted and accessed.

```
[jdoe@f38s1 10.6_password_vault]$ ls
```

```
vault_pass.yml
```

Step 3: To verify the encryption, check that ansible-vault is using AES256 to encrypt data. The password you provided when creating the vault is used to generate the private key for password encryption. If you see a bunch of numbers, that's exactly what we expect to see from the cat command output.

```
[jdoe@f38s1 10.6_password_vault]$ cat vault_pass.yml
```

```
$ANSIBLE_VAULT;1.1;AES256
65623537656266383032303239383965666639306339613832393438316234353834366365
643631
[...omitted for brevity]
31313562633032396162326533663763353264366643661363734
```

Step 4: To view the content of the vault_pass.yml file, use the ansible-vault view command. This will display the actual content of the file in the terminal.

```
[jdoe@ansible-server ~]$ ansible-vault view vault_pass.yml
```

```
Vault password: **********

ansible_become_pass: SuperSecretPassword

# Optionally, if you want to assign passwords individually, you can do so
like this.
# f38c1_become_password: SuperSecret123 # optional, so hashed out
```

```
# u23c1_become_password: SuperSecret234 # optional, so hashed out
# u23c2_become_password: SuperSecret456 # optional, so hashed out
```

Step 5: Practice updating the key by using the ansible-vault rekey command. This will allow you to change the password used to unlock the vault_pass.yml file.

```
jdoe@f38s1 10.6_password_vault]$ ansible-vault rekey vault_pass.yml

Vault password: ***************
New Vault password: ********
Confirm New Vault password: ********
Rekey successful
```

Step 6: If you wish to update the actual password stored in the vault_pass.yml file, you can use the ansible-vault edit command. Let's update our password using this command."

```
[jdoe@f38s1 10.6_password_vault]$ ansible-vault edit vault_pass.yml
Vault password: ********

ansible_become_pass: 5uper5ecret8assword!@# # updated password
```

Step 7: Now, let's create a basic ansible.cfg file. You can carefully create the file by following the explanations provided in gray.

```
[jdoe@f38s1 10.6_password_vault]$ vi ansible.cfg
[jdoe@f38s1 10.6_password_vault]$ cat ansible.cfg

[default]
inventory = ./inventory # Don't forget the ./
private_key_file = /home/jdoe/.ssh/ansible # get private key from this path
deprecation_warnings=False
nocows = 1 # 1 disables cowsay
forks=30 # default folks are 5
```

Step 8: Let's create a new inventory file. It should look like the example shown in the following. We will include the ansible_become_pass inside the inventory file. Modify the inventory file to retrieve the password from the vault_pass.yml file. The variable name in the inventory file should match the one in the vault_pass.yml file word for word.

```
[jdoe@f38s1 10.6_password_vault]$ vi inventory
```

```
[jdoe@f38s1 10.6_password_vault]$ cat inventory
```

[all:vars]
ansible_become_pass='{{ ansible_become_pass }}' # take special care, type in word-by-word
ansible_user='{{ user_name }}' # optional, so hashed out
ansible_become=yes   # optional, so hashed out
ansible_become_method=sudo # optional, so hashed out

[all]
f38c1 ansible_host=192.168.127.151
u23c1 ansible_host=192.168.127.161
u23c2 ansible_host=192.168.127.162

Step 9: To perform a system reboot on all client nodes using Ansible, you can create a basic playbook. However, **note that this playbook will initiate the reboot process without user confirmation.** Therefore, if this playbook is going to be used in a production environment, it's crucial to inform the business well in advance and disable any monitoring systems to prevent unnecessary alerts and notifications. **It is highly recommended that any system reboots in a production environment should be carried out under an approved change window, following the ITIL 4.0 framework.** ITIL processes are a set of best practices for IT service management (ITSM), which help organizations achieve their IT service objectives efficiently. To ensure minimal disruption, the engineer should exercise caution when executing service-interrupting playbooks and follow the relevant ITIL processes.

```
[jdoe@f38s1 10.6_password_vault]$ vi 10.6_reboot.yml
```

```
[jdoe@f38s1 10.6_password_vault]$ cat 10.6_reboot.yml
```

```
---
- hosts: all
  become: true

  tasks:
    - name: reboot all nodes
      ansible.builtin.reboot:
```

Step 10: Execute the ansible-playbook with the –ask-vault-pass option as shown here:

```
[jdoe@f38s1 10.6_password_vault]$ ansible-playbook 10.6_reboot.yml --ask-
vault-pass -e@./vault_pass.yml
Vault password: ********

PLAY [all] *********************************************************

TASK [Gathering Facts] *********************************************
ok: [u23c1]
ok: [u23c2]
ok: [f38c1]

TASK [reboot all nodes] ********************************************
changed: [f38c1]
changed: [u23c1]
changed: [u23c2]

PLAY RECAP *********************************************************
f38c1 : ok=2  changed=1  unreachable=0  failed=0  skipped=0  rescued=0  ignored=0
u23c1 : ok=2  changed=1  unreachable=0  failed=0  skipped=0  rescued=0  ignored=0
u23c2 : ok=2  changed=1  unreachable=0  failed=0  skipped=0  rescued=0  ignored=0
```

It's important to note that the "Gathering Facts" module, also known as "gather_facts," is enabled by default in our playbook. While this module may slow down the playbook's speed, it is recommended to keep it enabled, especially in cases where there may be errors or typos in the playbook, ansible.cfg, or inventory file. Enabling this module can help check the sanity of your files and stop the play before running the main tasks, which can save time and prevent potential errors.

Step 11: During the reboot process, you will notice that all client nodes are rebooting on the VMware Workstation consoles as shown in Figure 10-6. The servers should reboot in sequence, but it is so quick that it may appear as if they are all rebooting in parallel. Please wait until the server reboots are completed before proceeding. Once the reboot is finished, you should see the same output as in step 10.

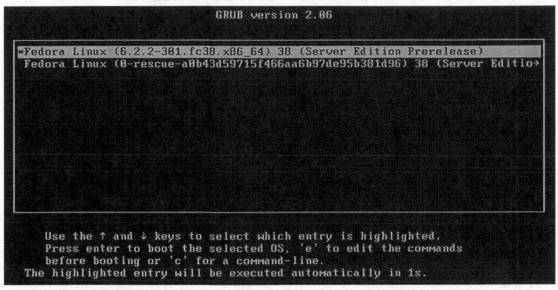

Figure 10-6. *f38c1 rebooting screen example*

Tip

All playbooks and files are available from the following GitHub site:

https://github.com/ansnetauto/repo1

10.6.1.2 Encrypting vars.yml with Ansible Vault

Ansible Vault is a powerful tool that enables the encryption of sensitive information in
your playbooks, adding an extra layer of security to your infrastructure. When dealing
with confidential data, we can create a separate vars.yml file and encrypt it with Ansible
Vault. Subsequently, we can refer to this file in our playbook using the vars_files option,
which loads the encrypted parameters. This approach not only protects the sensitive
data but also enables the creation of clean and concise playbooks, with specific
information, which can aid in the event of a playbook failure. It is a recommended
practice to use Ansible Vault to encrypt sensitive information in playbooks, especially
when dealing with production systems.

Step 1: Use the same ansible.cfg file as before.

```
[jdoe@f38s1 10.6_password_vault]$ vi ansible.cfg
[jdoe@f38s1 10.6_password_vault]$ cat ansible.cfg

[defaults]
inventory = ./inventory
private_key_file = /home/jdoe/.ssh/ansible
deprecation_warnings=False
nocows = 1
forks=30
```

Step 2: You need to update the inventory file to ensure that it only contains the hosts listed under the [all] group.

```
[jdoe@f38s1 10.6_password_vault]$ cat inventory
[jdoe@f38s1 10.6_password_vault]$ vi inventory

[all]
f38c1 ansible_host=192.168.127.151
u23c1 ansible_host=192.168.127.161
u23c2 ansible_host=192.168.127.162
```

Step 3: Create a vars.yml file and specify the variables that you want to use in your playbook in dictionary format.

```
[jdoe@f38s1 10.6_password_vault]$ vi vars.yml
[jdoe@f38s1 10.6_password_vault]$ cat vars.yml

---
ansible_user: jdoe
ansible_become: yes
ansible_become_method: sudo
ansible_become_pass: 5uper5ecret8assword!@#
```

Step 4: To encrypt the vars.yml file using Ansible Vault, run the following command:

```
[jdoe@f38s1 10.6_password_vault]$ ansible-vault encrypt vars.
yml
```

```
New Vault password: ********
Confirm New Vault password: ********
Encryption successful
```

If you try to view the encrypted file, it will output as a long string of numbers.

```
[jdoe@f38s1 10.6_password_vault]$ cat vars.yml
```

```
$ANSIBLE_VAULT;1.1;AES256
3434303630343830343362616262565654663132333165623266643763646138613530356533
336261
```
```
[...omitted for brevity]
```
```
62373934656665646335
```

Optionally, you may choose to decrypt the vars.yml file, but it's not necessary for the next steps of creating and executing the playbook. If you did decrypt the file, remember to encrypt it again before moving to the next step.

```
[jdoe@f38s1 10.6_password_vault]$ ansible-vault decrypt vars.yml
```

```
Vault password: ********

Decryption successful
```

Check the content of the file using the concatenate command.

```
[jdoe@f38s1 10.6_password_vault]$ cat vars.yml
```

```
---
ansible_user: jdoe
ansible_become: yes
ansible_become_method: sudo
ansible_become_pass: 5uper5ecret8assword!@#
```

Step 5: To create the new reboot playbook, use the "vars_files" option, which loads information from "vars.yml". If you have more than one variable file to load, you can add them to the list. However, in our case, we only have one variable file, so you only need to specify that particular file.

```
[jdoe@f38s1 10.6_password_vault]$ vi 10.6_reboot_vars.yml
[jdoe@f38s1 10.6_password_vault]$ cat 10.6_reboot_vars.yml

- name: Reboot servers
  hosts: all
  become: yes
  become_method: sudo

  vars_files:
    - vars.yml
  tasks:
    - name: Reboot servers
      ansible.builtin.reboot:
```

Step 6: It's time to execute your playbook with the --ask-vault-pass option. Since we're using specific parameters read from the encrypted vars.yml, we'll run the command "ansible-playbook" (or "anp") followed by the playbook name and the --ask-vault-pass option. This command will prompt you to enter the Ansible Vault password that was used to encrypt the vars.yml file.

```
[jdoe@f38s1 10.6 password_vault]$ anp 10.6_reboot_vars.yml --ask-vault-
pass
Vault password: ********

PLAY [Reboot servers] ***********************************************

TASK [Gathering Facts] **********************************************
ok: [u23c1]
ok: [u23c2]
ok: [f38c1]
```

```
TASK [Reboot servers] ***********************************************
changed: [f38c1]
changed: [u23c1]
changed: [u23c2]

PLAY RECAP **********************************************************
f38c1  : ok=2  changed=1  unreachable=0  failed=0  skipped=0  rescued=0  ignored=0
u23c1  : ok=2  changed=1  unreachable=0  failed=0  skipped=0  rescued=0  ignored=0
u23c2  : ok=2  changed=1  unreachable=0  failed=0  skipped=0  rescued=0  ignored=0
```

Ansible Vault is an effective way to securely store sensitive data alongside your regular playbooks in source control. Encrypting your data offers minimal risk, as long as you use a strong password. It is also recommended to rotate the encryption password frequently to enhance security, as with any shared secret. Additionally, Ansible provides advanced features for Vaults, such as the ability to use different passwords for different Vaults. Exploring Ansible's documentation can help you leverage its native capabilities and secure your secrets effectively.

Furthermore, you can use an API key for authentication to make the process more user-friendly. During the playbook execution in interactive mode, you can prompt the user to enter the API key. If your organization already uses an enterprise password manager with custom modules for interaction, you can integrate it with Ansible to secure sensitive data. Some popular enterprise password managers include HashiCorp Vault, CyberArk Vault, Thycotic Secret Server, LastPass Enterprise, and Keeper Security. However, integrating with a custom password manager is beyond the scope of this book, as every organization has its security tools and policies.

Extend your knowledge:

Dive deeper to extend your knowledge and use Ansible's official documentation.

To extend your knowledge and deepen your understanding of Ansible Vault, it"s recommended to use Ansible"s official documentation. While it can be confusing for beginners, it"s still a valuable learning resource that"s available for free. Here are some links you can visit to learn more about Ansible Vault and password management:

Official Ansible Vault documentation: `https://docs.ansible.com/ansible/2.8/user_guide/vault.html#id6`

Handling secrets in your Ansible playbooks:

`www.redhat.com/sysadmin/ansible-playbooks-secrets`

By leveraging these resources, you can further enhance your Ansible skills and develop a better understanding of how to manage sensitive information in your playbooks.

In preparation for Chapter 11 and your Network Automation lab, it is highly recommended to back up your data using your GitHub account. It is crucial to regularly and frequently back up both your source code and data to avoid the risk of data loss. As a reminder, let's take a quick look at an example of the GitHub data backup process. Later in the book, we will demonstrate the use of API keys in action, but for now, let's conclude this chapter.

```
[jdoe@f38s1 10.6_password_vault]$ cd ../..
[jdoe@f38s1 repo1]$ git status
[jdoe@f38s1 repo1]$ git add .
[jdoe@f38s1 repo1]$ git commit -m "Upload Ch10"
[jdoe@f38s1 repo1]$ git push origin main
```

The Ansible concepts covered in the previous four chapters are essential building blocks for automating tasks and managing infrastructure with Ansible. While these concepts are not all-inclusive, they provide a solid foundation for readers to build upon. With Chapter 10 now complete, you have gained valuable knowledge on intermediate topics such as creating users, bootstrapping servers, using roles, exploring variables and handlers, templates, and password management. If you are new to Ansible, it is recommended to practice these concepts on a Linux OS first before expanding to network and security automation. In the next chapters, you will dive into practical examples of Ansible Network Automation using enterprise networking devices and apply the concepts you have learned in this book to real-world scenarios. So get ready to have some fun and put your newfound skills into action.

10.7 Summary

This chapter marks the end of the Ansible concepts series in this book, covering intermediate topics such as user creation, Linux server bootstrapping, role usage, variable options and handlers, template, and password management with Ansible Vault. The chapter also provided instructions on installing, configuring, and testing FTP and SFTP servers on Linux using Ansible playbooks. While these concepts are essential for automating complex tasks and managing large-scale infrastructure, it's important to remember that they build on the foundational knowledge from previous chapters. If you're new to Ansible, it's recommended to practice different Ansible concepts on a Linux OS first before expanding out to network and security automation. With this chapter completed, the Ansible basics series has concluded. The next chapters will focus on practical Network Automation labs using enterprise networking devices and applying the concepts learned in this book to Ansible Network Automation.

CHAPTER 11

Building an Ansible Learning Environment for Network Automation

In this chapter, we will guide you through the process of constructing a powerful Ansible learning environment for network automation. Our focus will be on key components such as Cisco Modeling Labs (CML) with routing and switch focus, Palo Alto and Fortinet firewalls installed on GNS3 with a security focus, and the configuration and connection testing of Palo Alto PA-VM and Fortinet FortiGate firewalls. Additionally, we will create Cisco c8000v edge router virtual machines on VMware Workstation with a patch management focus and a Cisco Wireless LAN Controller (WLC) VM on ESXi 7 with wireless and patch management purposes. By the end of this chapter, you'll have a robust learning environment consisting of routers, switches, firewalls, edge routers, and a WLC. This comprehensive setup will empower you to embark on your network automation journey with Ansible. Get ready to unlock the full potential of Ansible and transform your network automation capabilities. Prepare to unlock the immense potential of Ansible in network automation!

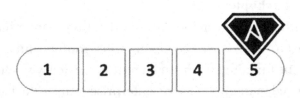

Welcome to the Network Automation Lab Preparation chapter, where we will embark on a journey of hands-on experience and practical exploration. In this chapter, we will shift our focus from Linux OS-related networking topics to the next level of learning: setting up major network devices in our virtual lab for Ansible Network Automation.

© Brendan Choi and Erwin Medina 2023
B. Choi and E. Medina, *Introduction to Ansible Network Automation*,
https://doi.org/10.1007/978-1-4842-9624-0_11

Brace yourself, as this chapter is a true powerhouse when it comes to building labs and gaining valuable experience. Our primary objective is to guide you through the process of constructing a functional virtualized lab environment that specifically caters to Ansible Network Automation. While we continue to create small testing playbooks to ensure smooth login and connectivity, the main goal here is to provide you with a valuable resource for learning Ansible and network automation. Additionally, this lab environment will also serve as a fertile ground for exploring the initialization of routers, switches, firewalls, Wireless LAN Controllers, and other crucial IT concepts. Throughout this chapter, you can expect to encounter a wide range of technologies, including wired and wireless LAN, as well as security. You will also dive into numerous files and integration tasks, leveraging both open source and proprietary software. Get ready to embark on an exciting journey of lab building and practical exploration as we equip you with the necessary skills for network automation and beyond!

Building a lab environment like this is highly involved and requires special attention to detail to ensure both open source and proprietary software work seamlessly on a single PC/laptop. It's important to note that most of the components will be installed on a single laptop, but the Cisco virtual Wireless LAN Controller (vWLC) will be installed on an external ESXi 7 server due to software compatibility issues. Although we aimed to keep everything within a single PC setup, due to software compatibility, unsolved software bugs, and licensing protection issues, labs for Cisco WLC and Palo Alto PAN-OS upgrading chapters will be demonstrated on external platforms. For the most part, you will be installing routers, switches, and firewalls on GNS3, as well as edge router VMs running on VMware Workstation 17 Pro. We could have chosen to exclude these topics, but we believe that exposing our readers to a real production-like environment is important and still better than no exposure. **Given the breadth of the topics covered in this chapter and the effort required to complete a full lab environment, we have assigned a difficulty rating of five out of five for this chapter.**

To provide you with more information about what this chapter has to offer, we will begin by installing Cisco's CML (Cisco Modeling Labs) routers and switches. The CML IOSv image provides the functionality of an L3 routing device with all the Cisco IOS-XE features, commonly used in many of Cisco's enterprise routing devices. On the other hand, the CML IOSvl2 image will provide the functionality of managed L2 (and L3) switching device features that are found on Cisco IOS-XE enterprise switches. These CML routers and switches will be used for simple routing and switching Ansible labs. After that, we will guide you through installing Palo Alto's PA-VM and Fortinet's FortiGate on GNS3 for our security Ansible labs. Next, we will install Cisco Catalyst 8000V routers as a regular virtual machine on VMware Workstation. The first router will be cloned to make the second virtual router, and these two routers will be used in IOS-XE upgrading Ansible lab in Chapter 15. Finally, we will install the Cisco vWLC in VMware ESXi 7.0 for WLC upgrading Ansible lab in Chapter 16. These installations will give you access to a diverse range of networking platforms to effectively test and learn network automation using Ansible.

By the end of this chapter, you will have several networking devices ready for testing Ansible playbooks in the upcoming chapters. Additionally, you will be able to add various major vendor virtual machines to both GNS3 and VMware Workstation for your future learning. Let's dive into the lab preparation processes for our Ansible Network Automation endeavors. If you have already read the prequel, *Introduction to Python Network Automation: The First Journey* by Brendan Choi (2021), you will already be familiar with the process of installing virtual Cisco networking devices on the VMware Workstation environment. Even without prior experience in building virtual routers or switches, you will be able to follow the instructions provided in the accompanying installation guidelines and the book. Be sure to refer to the guidelines provided in this book to successfully set up our network testing lab.

Tip

Your key to unlocking the next ten chapters

We cannot emphasize enough the importance of readers completing this chapter for their success. This particular chapter holds significant importance within the book as it serves as the glue that connects the first half and second half of the book. The success of the upcoming practical labs heavily depends on your comprehension and completion of this chapter in its entirety.

To optimize your time, we recommend downloading all four installation guides from the authors' GitHub page and reviewing them in advance. Building a working IT lab yourself requires some project management skills. Careful planning is essential to effectively complete this chapter, making it essentially another book within the book. Some software is open source, while others are highly proprietary with limited access to the public. Completing all the required tasks within one to two days would be exceptional, but for most readers, it may take more time as they locate and download various software and files throughout this chapter.

For your convenience, the installation guides are divided into four parts. You may choose to approach this chapter in four separate parts, following each guide for a step-by-step progression. Alternatively, if you are eager to tackle the entire chapter at once, that option is also available to you.

As a helpful tip, we recommend first downloading and reviewing all installation guides for Chapter 11. This will allow you to better understand what software and files are required and how to tackle each part. By doing so, you can plan and ensure successful installation and integration. Completion of Chapter 11 acts as a key (Figure 11-1) to unlocking the next ten chapters, which build upon the knowledge gained in this pivotal chapter. Consider this chapter as your key to unlocking the upcoming chapters and expanding your understanding of the subject matter.

Figure 11-1. *Your key to the next ten chapters*

Visit the authors' GitHub site and download the installation guides and a config file:

[GitHub Link: `https://github.com/ansnetauto/appress_ansnetauto`]

Ch11_Pre-task1_Cisco_CML_Router_Switch_Installation_on_GNS3.pdf

Ch11_Pre-task2_PaloAlto_and_Fortinet_Firewall_Installation_on_GNS3.pdf

Ch11_Pre-task3_Cisco_c8kv_Router_VM_Creation_on_VMware_WS.pdf

Ch11_Pre-task4_Cisco_Wireless_LAN_Controller(WLC)_VM_Creation_on_VMware_ESXi.pdf

Ch11_Pre-task5_Host_PC_Loopback_GNS3_Installation_Optional.pdf

Ch11_r1_r2_sw1_sw2_Initialization_configs.txt

To condense the chapter length, we have provided all the installation guides as downloadable supplementary PDF files. It is crucial that you thoroughly read and diligently follow the instructions outlined in these guides to complete all tasks successfully. This ensures that your environment is properly prepared and ready for the ten subsequent practical chapters. Please note that completing this chapter is mandatory if you wish to engage in the practical labs. However, if you prefer a more casual approach without participating in hands-on labs, you have the option to skip this chapter. Nevertheless, it is important to be aware that this decision may limit your learning experience and the knowledge you acquire. It is widely acknowledged that the most effective way to learn is through practical application – learning by doing. Engaging in hands-on activities allows you to truly grasp the concepts and understand their practical implications. If you aspire to become a Subject Matter Expert (SME), there is no substitute for actively engaging in practical tasks. This approach offers the most comprehensive understanding of the subject matter.

Now, let's proceed with the installation of Cisco routers and switches on GNS3.

11.1 Cisco CML (Cisco Modeling Labs) Router and Switch Installation on GNS3

Familiarizing yourself with building network labs using network emulators is a crucial aspect of IT learning, whether you are a student or a professional aiming to obtain certifications from major network vendors such as Cisco, Juniper, HPE, Palo Alto, Fortinet, and others. Throughout your career as an IT engineer, this skill will remain essential, particularly if your work involves closely managing enterprise IT infrastructure. The traditional reliance on physical hardware or paying significant fees for renting pre-built lab racks from leasing providers is no longer the preferred choice for many students. Thanks to advancements in personal computing and emulator technology, anyone can now build a personalized and customized IT lab environment using various software to thoroughly test vendor products. The only thing that may be missing is a true passion for exploring and learning different technologies, which can significantly expand one's horizons and open new opportunities. If you are truly passionate about your work, especially in the field of IT, success tends to favor dedicated learners. So it is important to consistently invest your time and effort into learning and improving your skills if you aspire to excel as an IT engineer.

For example, Cisco offers subscriptions for Cisco Modeling Labs (CML) and provides access to Cisco dCloud (`https://dcloud.cisco.com/`), which offers pre-built lab scenarios. However, before diving into these options, it's important to consider a few factors. One drawback of relying solely on Cisco's pre-built labs is the lack of knowledge about their construction and the individuals who built them. By relying exclusively on these pre-built labs, you may miss out on gaining a deep understanding of the intricate details involved in setting up and configuring lab environments. It's like being a mechanic who can only perform basic maintenance tasks without truly comprehending how all the components of a car work together. Furthermore, it's essential to note that CML is a yearly subscription service that comes at a cost. While it offers excellent materials at an affordable price for those focusing on Cisco technology, it may not provide the same value for young job-seeking future network engineers.

On the other hand, using pre-built labs does save time and effort in setting up the lab infrastructure. You can focus more on the content and exercises provided by Cisco, delving into the specific topics and technologies covered by certification exams. However, without knowledge of how the lab is built, you may lack a comprehensive understanding of how the various network components interact and operate. To truly grasp the intricacies of network operations, it is highly recommended to learn how to build and configure your lab environments. Just like a skilled mechanic who can disassemble and rebuild an entire engine, being able to create your network lab from the ground up grants you a deeper understanding of networking concepts. It provides an opportunity to experiment, troubleshoot, and explore different scenarios, ultimately enhancing your overall knowledge and skills. Consider investing your time into building a proper networking or IT lab, as it's akin to learning how to fish rather than solely relying on pre-prepared meals.

By utilizing network emulators like GNS3 and EVE-NG, you can create your own virtualized lab environments. These emulators offer a wide range of flexibility, allowing you to design complex topologies and experiment with various technologies. This approach eliminates the need for expensive subscriptions or leasing rack hours, and it empowers you to fully control and customize your lab experience. By the way, the topologies used throughout this book use one of the simplest topologies as the focus is teaching the readers how to master managing various devices using Ansible plays; once you have mastered the Ansible basics, you can re-apply the concepts and skills learned to more complex topologies and production environment to your heart's content.

Our current objective is to integrate Cisco's CML switch and router images with GNS3. To begin, please visit the authors' GitHub page at https://github.com/ansnetauto/appress_ansnetauto and locate the integration guide titled "Ch11_Pre-task1_Cisco_CML_Router_Switch_Installation_on_GNS3.pdf". This guide is part of the prequel book, *Introduction to Python Network Automation: The First Journey* by Brendan Choi (2021). It is important to carefully follow the instructions provided in the guide, as it will guide you through the process of installing GNS3 and integrating the CML router and switch images on the GNS3 VM running on VMware Workstation. The steps involved in setting up CML with the newer version of GNS3 have slightly changed and require careful attention.

For a successful installation of CML routers and switches on GNS3, you will need the essential files listed in Table 11-1.

Table 11-1. *Required files for CML router and switch installation on GNS3*

Description	File name	File size
Cisco CML L2 Switch	vios_l2-adventerprisek9-m.vmdk.SSA.152-4.0.55.E	92.3 MB
Cisco CML L3 Router	vlos-adventerprisek9-m.vmdk.SPA.157-3.M3.qcow2	127 MB
	IOSv_startup_config	1 MB
JunOS L2 Switch (optional)	JunOS Olive-disk1.vmdk	272 MB

Assuming you have completed the GNS3 CML and VMware integration using the first installation guide for Chapter 11, you are now ready to begin a new GNS3 project. The focus of this task is to create a simple network topology that connects our Ansible Control Machine to the routers and switches running on GNS3 VM. Although this task is relatively straightforward, it requires attention to detail. To establish the connection, we will use the NAT1 cloud to connect to the VMnet8 interface of VMware Workstation, which is configured on the 192.168.127.0/24 subnet. Our goal is to power on f38s1 (192.168.127.150) and establish communication with the topology we will be creating on GNS3's topology canvas.

Now let's dive right in and get started!

Step 1: To begin a new project in GNS3, navigate to File ➤ New Blank Project (or use the shortcut Ctrl + N). Alternatively, you can close and restart GNS3, and you will be prompted to start at the new Project screen. Give your new project a meaningful name, considering that it will serve as the foundation for our lab and encompass most of the exercises. Let's keep it simple and name this project "ansnetauto_lab01". Once you have selected a suitable name for your project, click the [OK] button. Refer to Figure 11-2 for a visual representation.

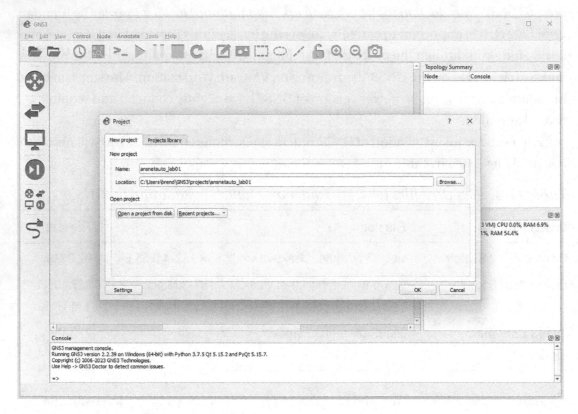

Figure 11-2. *Starting a new GNS3 project*

Step 2: Next, go to the left icon menus and click "All devices" to display the available devices. Locate the **NAT icon** and drag it onto the workspace. When you drop the NAT icon, a prompt will appear asking you to select the server to run on. Make sure to choose your local host PC name as the server. This ensures proper communication between the topology and the virtual machines running on VMware Workstation 17 Pro. Keep in mind that your server's name will be different and should match the name of your host PC. As shown in Figure 11-3, our hostname is LP50BC, but your server name will be different.

Figure 11-3. *Selecting your hostname as the server for NAT1*

Step 3: Drag and drop GNS3's built-in **Ethernetswitch** (Switch1) to the center of the canvas. In the device settings, choose GNS3 VM as the server to host this device, as illustrated in Figure 11-4.

Figure 11-4. *Selecting GNS3 VM as the server for the Ethernet switch (Switch1)*

Step 4: Drag and drop two Cisco IOSv routers from the "All devices" section to the left of Switch1 and two Cisco IOSvL2 switches to the right. To rename the devices, simply place your mouse over a device, right-click, and select "Rename hostname" from the menu, as shown in Figure 11-5.

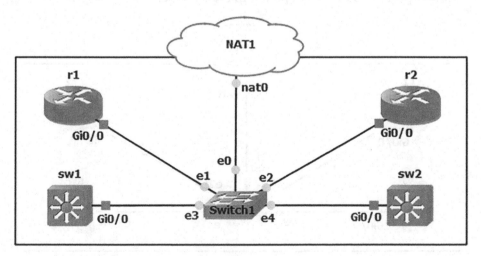

Figure 11-5. *Connecting two routers and two switches to the GNS3 topology*

Step 5: To power on the devices, begin by placing your mouse over "r1" and right-clicking. From the menu, select the "Start" option as shown in Figure 11-6. Allow a few seconds for the device to power on. Repeat this process for "r2," "sw1," and "sw2" to ensure that all four devices are powered on. Please be patient as it may take a few minutes for all devices to complete the startup process. Once all devices are powered on, we can proceed to configure their IP addresses and create a brief Ansible playbook for connectivity testing.

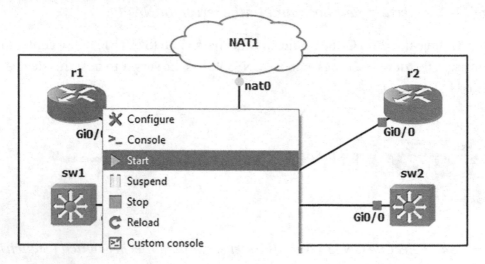

Figure 11-6. *Powering on one device at a time*

Step 6: Once all four devices have successfully powered on, as indicated in Figure 11-7, double-click on the Cisco router and switch icons to open the console. The console should open in PuTTY, as depicted in Figure 11-8.

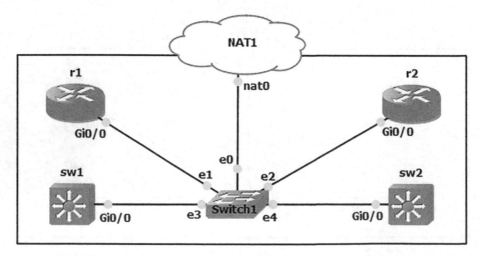

Figure 11-7. *All devices powered on*

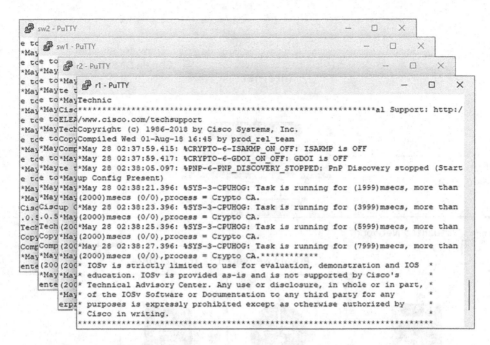

Figure 11-8. *Opening terminal console on PuTTY*

Step 7: Proceed to the main window of the VMware Workstation and power on the Ansible Control Machine, f38s1 (192.168.127.150). This step is necessary to test the internal connectivity between this node and the powered-on Cisco devices, as depicted in Figure 11-9.

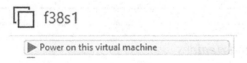

Figure 11-9. *Powering on Ansible Control Machine, f38s1*

Step 8: Refer to Figure 11-10 for initial router and switch configurations. Let's change the hostnames, assign IP addresses and unshut the connected interfaces, and test connectivity between each device to the Ansible control node. Also, we will create a local user account, jdoe, with a secret and then save the running configuration to the startup configuration.

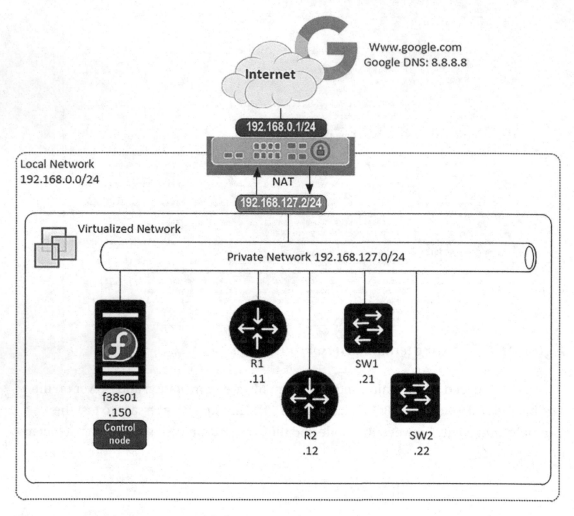

Figure 11-10. *Connected devices*

As our readers are Cisco students or experienced professionals in the field, we assume that you have a basic understanding of Cisco router and switch operations. However, if you are new to these commands, don't worry! You can still follow along and learn how to establish communication between our Ansible control node and network devices.

To begin, please double-click on the router and switch icons to open the Console sessions in PuTTY. We will guide you through the process of initializing the configuration for each network device using the provided settings, ensuring they are ready for our labs. Take care to enter the configuration accurately and avoid any typos.

Once the configuration is complete, we will proceed to write a simple Ansible playbook on the Ansible Control Machine and test our connectivity. Let's get started!

Note   We encourage you to manually configure your Cisco devices, as it provides valuable hands-on experience. However, if you're a seasoned network engineer well versed in the commands, we understand that time is valuable. In that case, to expedite the process, we have shared the initialization configuration file on the authors' GitHub page. Visit the GitHub site at `https://github.com/ansnetauto/appress_ansnetauto` and locate a text file named "Ch11_r1_r2_sw1_sw2_Initialization_configs.txt".

CONFIGURE R1 TO COMMUNICATE ON THE GNS3 NETWORK.

```
!Configure hostname, interface Gi0/0, assign IP, unshut Gi0/0 interface
Router#configure terminal
Router(config)#hostname r1
r1(config)#interface GigabitEthernet 0/0
r1(config-if)#ip address 192.168.127.11 255.255.255.0
r1(config-if)#no shut
r1(config-if)#end
!Test connectivity to the Ansible Control node, f38s1 at 192.168.127.150
r1#ping 192.168.127.150
Type escape sequence to abort.
Sending 5, 100-byte ICMP Echos to 192.168.127.150, timeout is 2 seconds:
.!!!!
Success rate is 80 percent (4/5), round-trip min/avg/max = 1/3/6 ms
!Configure user jdoe with secret
r1#config t
r1(config)#username jdoe pri 15 secret 5uper5cret9asswOrd
! Configure SSH lines and enable SSH 2.0 server
r1(config)#line vty 0 15
r1(config-line)#login local
r1(config-line)#transport input ssh
r1(config-line)#exit
r1(config)#ip domain-name ansnetauto.net
```

r1(config)#**crypto key generate rsa**
The name for the keys will be: r1.ansnetauto.net
Choose the size of the key modulus in the range of 360 to 4096 for your
  General Purpose Keys. Choosing a key modulus greater than 512 may take
  a few minutes.

How many bits in the modulus [512]: **1024**
% Generating 1024 bit RSA keys, keys will be non-exportable...
[OK] (elapsed time was 1 seconds)

*May 28 05:25:58.934: %SSH-5-ENABLED: SSH 1.99 has been enabled
r1(config)#**ip ssh time-out 60**
r1(config)#**ip ssh authentication-retries 2**
! Configure default gateway
r1(config)#**ip route 0.0.0.0 0.0.0.0 192.168.127.2**
! To allow domain lookup, enable DNS lookup and configure DNS server
r1(config)#**ip domain-lookup**
r1(config)#**ip name-server 192.168.127.2** ! Default Gateway IP of VMnet 8
r1(config)#**do ping www.google.com** ! Test connection to Google.com
Translating "www.google.com"...domain server (192.168.127.2) [OK]

Type escape sequence to abort.
Sending 5, 100-byte ICMP Echos to 142.250.204.4, timeout is 2 seconds:
!!!!!
Success rate is 100 percent (5/5), round-trip min/avg/max = 13/15/21 ms
r1(config)#**do ping 8.8.8.8**
Type escape sequence to abort.
Sending 5, 100-byte ICMP Echos to 8.8.8.8, timeout is 2 seconds:
!!!!!
Success rate is 100 percent (5/5), round-trip min/avg/max = 13/18/25 ms
r1(config)#**exit**
! Save the configuration to the startup-config
r1#**copy running-config startup-config**
Destination filename [startup-config]?
Building configuration...
   [OK]

REFER TO THE R1 CONFIGURATION AND CONFIGURE R2.

```
Router#conf t
Router(config)#hostname r2
r2(config)#int GigabitEthernet 0/0
r2(config-if)#ip add 192.168.127.12 255.255.255.0
r2(config-if)#no shut
[... Refer to the r1 configuration above and repeat the same
configuration for r2]
```

CONFIGURE SW1 TO ALLOW COMMUNICATION.

```
!Configure hostname, interface vlan 1, assign IP, unshut vlan 1 interface
Switch>en
Switch#config t
Switch(config)#hostname sw1
sw1(config)#int vlan 1
sw1(config-if)#ip add 192.168.127.21 255.255.255.0
sw1(config-if)#no shut
sw1(config-if)#end
!Test connection to f38s1 at 192.168.127.150
sw1#ping 192.168.127.150
Type escape sequence to abort.
Sending 5, 100-byte ICMP Echos to 192.168.127.150, timeout is 2 seconds:
.!!!!
Success rate is 80 percent (4/5), round-trip min/avg/max = 4/7/15 ms
!Configure user jdoe with secret
sw1#config t
sw1(config)#username jdoe pri 15 secret 5uper5cret9assw0rd
! Configure SSH lines and enable SSH 2.0 server
sw1(config)#line vty 0 15
sw1(config-line)#login local
sw1(config-line)#transport input ssh
sw1(config-line)#exit
sw1(config)#ip domain-name ansnetauto.net
sw1(config)#crypto key generate rsa
```

The name for the keys will be: sw1.ansnetauto.net

Choose the size of the key modulus in the range of 360 to 4096 for your
    General Purpose Keys. Choosing a key modulus greater than 512 may take
    a few minutes.

How many bits in the modulus [512]: **1024**

% Generating 1024 bit RSA keys, keys will be non-exportable...

[OK] (elapsed time was 0 seconds)

*May 28 06:22:11.395: %SSH-5-ENABLED: SSH 1.99 has been enabled

sw1(config)#**ip ssh time-out 60**

sw1(config)#**ip ssh authentication-retries 2**

! Disable IP Routing on the switch to make this device strictly L2 switch and
configure the default gateway using the ip default-gateway command

sw1(config)#**no ip routing**

sw1(config)#**ip default-gateway 192.168.127.2**

! To allow domain lookup, enable DNS lookup and configure DNS server

r1(config)#**ip domain-lookup**

r1(config)#**ip name-server 192.168.127.2** ! Default Gateway IP of VMnet 8

sw1(config)#**do ping www.google.com**

Translating "www.google.com"...domain server (192.168.127.2) [OK]

i

Type escape sequence to abort.

Sending 5, 100-byte ICMP Echos to 142.250.204.4, timeout is 2 seconds:

!!!!!

Success rate is 100 percent (5/5), round-trip min/avg/max = 7/14/28 ms

! Save the configuration to the startup-config

sw1(config)#**exit**

sw1#**copy run start**

Destination filename [startup-config]?

Building configuration...

  Compressed configuration from 3794 bytes to 1780 bytes[OK]

USE SW1'S CONFIGURATION AS YOUR REFERENCE AND CONFIGURE SW2.

```
Switch>en
Switch#conf t
Switch(config)#hostname sw2
sw2(config)#int vlan 1
sw2(config-if)#ip add 192.168.127.22 255.255.255.0
sw2(config-if)#no shut
[... Refer to the sw1 configuration above and repeat the same configuration
for sw2]
```

You have completed the initial configuration for routers r1 and r2 and switches sw1 and sw2. Now, let's SSH into our Ansible Control Machine (f38s1) and create a few simple Ansible playbooks to test the end-to-end functionality.

Tip

SSH login from one Cisco device to another

```
sw2>en
sw2#ssh -l jdoe -p 22 192.168.127.11
[...omitted for brevity]
Password: 5uper5cret9assw0rd
[...omitted for brevity]
R1#exit
[Connection to 192.168.127.11 closed by foreign host]
sw2#ssh -l jdoe -p 22 192.168.127.12
[...omitted for brevity]
sw2#ssh -l jdoe -p 22 192.168.127.21
[...omitted for brevity]
```

Step 9: Move to the repo1 directory and create a new subdirectory named ana_lab, which stands for Ansible Network Automation Lab. Then create a new ansible.cfg file shown in this example. Notice that we are not using host key checking and also disabled cowsay.

```
[jdoe@f38s1 ~]$ cd repo1/
[jdoe@f38s1 repo1]$ mkdir ana_lab && cd ana_lab
[jdoe@f38s1 ana_lab]$ vi ansible.cfg
[jdoe@f38s1 ana_lab]$ cat ansible.cfg
[defaults]
inventory=inventory
host_key_checking=False
nocows = 1
```

Step 10: Create a new inventory file as shown in the following. We will hard-code or specify OS type, user, password, and connection type under the inventory's variable section so we can write a cleaner main playbook later.

```
[jdoe@f38s1 ana_lab]$ vi inventory
[jdoe@f38s1 ana_lab]$ cat inventory

[ios_devices:vars]
ansible_network_os=ios
ansible_user=jdoe
ansible_password=5uper5cret9assw0rd
ansible_connection=network_cli

[routers]
r1 ansible_host=192.168.127.11
r2 ansible_host=192.168.127.12

[switches]
sw1 ansible_host=192.168.127.21
sw2 ansible_host=192.168.127.22

[ios_devices:children]
routers
switches
```

Step 11: Let's create a simple show clock playbook to test the connectivity to our network devices.

```
[jdoe@f38s1 ana_lab]$ vi 11.1_show_clock.yml
[jdoe@f38s1 ana_lab]$ cat 11.1_show_clock.yml

---

- name: Cisco show clock example
  hosts: ios_devices
  gather_facts: false

  tasks:
    - name: run show clock on the routers
      cisco.ios.ios_command:
        commands: show clock
      register: output

    - name: print output
      ansible.builtin.debug:
        var: output.stdout_lines
```

Step 12: Execute the show clock playbook and observe the output.

```
[jdoe@f38s1 ana_lab]$ anp 11.1_show_clock.yml

PLAY [Cisco show clock example]
********************************************************************************

TASK [run show clock on the routers]
********************************************************************************
fatal: [r2]: FAILED! => {"changed": false, "msg": "ssh connection failed:
ssh connect failed: kex error : no match for method kex algos: server
[diffie-hellman-group-exchange-sha1,diffie-hellman-group14-sha1], client
[curve25519-sha256,curve25519-sha256@libssh.org,ecdh-sha2-nistp256,
ecdh-sha2-nistp384,ecdh-sha2-nistp521,diffie-hellman-group-exchange-sha256,
diffie-hellman-group14-sha256,diffie-hellman-group16-sha512,diffie-hellman-
group18-sha512]"}
```

```
fatal: [r1]: FAILED! => {"changed": false, "msg": "ssh connection failed:
ssh connect failed: kex error : no match for
```
[...*omitted for brevity*]

Oops! An error message indicates a failure to establish an SSH connection to all network devices. The specific issue identified is a key exchange (kex) algorithm mismatch between the server (r1, r2, sw1, and sw2) and the client (f38s1), where the Ansible control node is acting as the client. Before proceeding with the playbook execution, it's crucial to troubleshoot and resolve this problem.

Step 13: We can troubleshoot this issue by adding a single KexAlgorithms configuration line to the ssh_config file located in the /etc/ssh/ directory. The server or Cisco network devices specifically request the diffie-hellman-group-exchange-sha1 and diffie-hellman-group14-sha1 key exchange algorithms. Therefore, we need to add a line at the top of the /etc/ssh/ssh_config file using sudo privileges to modify it. Go ahead and add the first line highlighted in gray.

```
[jdoe@f38s1 ana_lab]$ sudo vi /etc/ssh/ssh_config
[sudo] password for jdoe: ***************
[jdoe@f38s1 ana_lab]$ cat ansible.cfg
KexAlgorithms diffie-hellman-group-exchange-sha1,diffie-hellman-
group14-sha1
#        $OpenBSD: ssh_config,v 1.35 2020/07/17 03:43:42 dtucker Exp $

# This is the ssh client system-wide configuration file.  See
# ssh_config(5) for more information.  This file provides defaults for
```

Step 14: Execute the "show clock" playbook again and closely observe the output.

```
[jdoe@f38s1 ana_lab]$ anp 11.1_show_clock.yml

PLAY [Cisco show clock example]
************************************************************************

TASK [run show clock on the routers]
************************************************************************
[WARNING]: ansible-pylibssh not installed, falling back to paramiko
[WARNING]: ansible-pylibssh not installed, falling back to paramiko
[WARNING]: ansible-pylibssh not installed, falling back to paramiko
```

```
[WARNING]: ansible-pylibssh not installed, falling back to paramiko
ok: [r2]
ok: [r1]
ok: [sw2]
ok: [sw1]
TASK [print output]
*************************************************************************
ok: [r2] => {
    "output.stdout_lines": [
        [
            "*10:26:04.759 UTC Sun May 28 2023"
        ]
    ]
}
[...omitted for brevity]
PLAY RECAP
*************************************************************************
r1    : ok=2    changed=0   unreachable=0   failed=0   skipped=0   rescued=0   ignored=0
r2    : ok=2    changed=0   unreachable=0   failed=0   skipped=0   rescued=0   ignored=0
sw1   : ok=2    changed=0   unreachable=0   failed=0   skipped=0   rescued=0   ignored=0
sw2   : ok=2    changed=0   unreachable=0   failed=0   skipped=0   rescued=0   ignored=0
```

You can observe that initially, Ansible attempts to use the ansible-pylibssh library. However, since it fails to locate the package, Ansible automatically switches to using Python's paramiko SSH library. Now, let's explore the implications of installing the ansible-pylibssh library.

Step 15: If you prefer to utilize ansible-pylibssh as the SSH transport library, you can install it by executing the following command. Pip serves as the package installation manager for Python. Run the provided pip command here to complete the installation process.

```
[jdoe@f38s1 ana_lab]$ pip install ansible-pylibssh

efaulting to user installation because normal site-packages is not
writeable
Collecting ansible-pylibssh
```

```
Downloading ansible_pylibssh-1.1.0-cp311-cp311-manylinux_2_24_x86_64.whl
(2.3 MB)
---------------------------------------- 2.3/2.3 MB 5.1 MB/s eta 0:00:00
Installing collected packages: ansible-pylibssh
Successfully installed ansible-pylibssh-1.1.0
```

After the installation, you can utilize the **pip freeze** command to check the installed packages. If you wish to remove the ansible-pylibssh package, you can run pip uninstall ansible-pylibssh as an optional step.

[jdoe@f38s1 ana_lab]$ **pip freeze**

```
ansible==7.4.0
ansible-core==2.14.4
ansible-pylibssh==1.1.0
argcomplete==2.0.0
```
[...omitted for brevity]

Step 16: Now, on the third attempt, luck is on our side. Let's run the "show clock" playbook once more and carefully observe the output.

[jdoe@f38s1 ana_lab]$ **anp 11.1_show_clock.yml**

```
PLAY [Cisco show clock example]
***************************************************************************

TASK [run show clock on the routers]
***************************************************************************
ok: [r1]
ok: [r2]
ok: [sw2]
ok: [sw1]
TASK [print output]
***************************************************************************
```

```
ok: [r1] => {
    "output.stdout_lines": [
        [
            "*10:59:50.842 UTC Sun May 28 2023"
        ]
    ]
}
[...omitted for brevity]
PLAY RECAP
*************************************************************************
r1    : ok=2   changed=0   unreachable=0   failed=0   skipped=0   rescued=0   ignored=0
r2    : ok=2   changed=0   unreachable=0   failed=0   skipped=0   rescued=0   ignored=0
sw1   : ok=2   changed=0   unreachable=0   failed=0   skipped=0   rescued=0   ignored=0
sw2   : ok=2   changed=0   unreachable=0   failed=0   skipped=0   rescued=0   ignored=0
```

Step 17: This exercise is optional, but if you want to be prompted for the username and password when executing the playbook, you can try the following.

First, create a backup of your existing inventory file. Then, remove the ansible_user and ansible_password lines in the inventory file, resulting in a new inventory file that looks like this:

```
[jdoe@f38s1 ana_lab]$ cp inventory inventory_bak
[jdoe@f38s1 ana_lab]$ vi inventory
[jdoe@f38s1 ana_lab]$ cat inventory
[ios_devices:vars]
ansible_network_os=ios
ansible_connection=network_cli

[routers]
r1 ansible_host=192.168.127.11
r2 ansible_host=192.168.127.12

[switches]
sw1 ansible_host=192.168.127.21
sw2 ansible_host=192.168.127.22
```

```
[ios_devices:children]
routers
switches
```

Step 18: To prompt the user for input when executing this playbook, utilize the vars_ prompt module. Start by copying the 11.1_show_clock.yml file and creating a new file called 11.1_show_clock2.yml. Modify the new file as follows. Additionally, take note that we have changed the host from "ios_devices" to "routers,switches" to demonstrate that this format is also supported.

```
[jdoe@f38s1 ana_lab]$ cp 11.1_show_clock.yml 11.1_show_clock2.yml
[jdoe@f38s1 ana_lab]$ cat 11.1_show_clock2.yml

---
- name: Cisco show version example
  hosts: routers,switches
  gather_facts: false

  vars_prompt:
    - name: ansible_user
      prompt: "Enter the ansible_user name:"
      private: no

    - name: ansible_password
      prompt: "Enter the ansible_password:"
      private: yes

  tasks:
    - name: run show clock on the routers
      cisco.ios.ios_command:
        commands: show clock
      register: output

    - name: print output
      ansible.builtin.debug:
        var: output.stdout_lines
```

Step 19: Now, execute the new playbook, and it will prompt you for the username and password before proceeding with the playbook execution. Enter both pieces of information and press the [Enter] key.

```
[jdoe@f38s1 ana_lab]$ anp 11.1_show_clock2.yml
Enter the ansible_user name:: jdoe
Enter the ansible_password::***************
PLAY [Cisco show version example] ****************************************

TASK [run show clock on the routers] ************************************
ok: [r1]
ok: [r2]
ok: [sw2]
ok: [sw1]
[...omitted for brevity]
```

Congratulations! You've accomplished a significant milestone by completing all the exercises and reaching this point. You have successfully installed Cisco CML routers and switches, configuring them to establish communication with the Ansible control node and the Internet. SSH services have been enabled on all four network devices, and you have verified connectivity and SSH logins between each device. Furthermore, you have developed a simple "show clock" playbook, along with ansible.cfg and a structured inventory file, to test login functionality and manage all four network devices.

While this lab is conducted on a single laptop, utilizing two routers and two switches for demonstration purposes, it's crucial to recognize that the same playbooks can be executed on a larger scale of 20, 200, or even 2000 devices of the same type in a production environment. When creating your playbook, always bear scalability in mind. The two routers and two switches utilized in this lab serve as a valuable learning experience, providing a training ground to enhance your skills as a confident Ansible network engineer.

11.2 Palo Alto and Fortinet Firewall Installation on GNS3

When it comes to enterprise security, several prominent vendor names come to mind, including Palo Alto, Check Point, Fortinet, and Cisco. These companies have established themselves as market leaders in traditional hard-based firewalls and, more recently, cloud security virtual devices that protect enterprise networks from malicious actors. Security has become a critical aspect of the entire enterprise IT ecosystem, and if you work in an IT-related field and are involved in enterprise networking, security technologies are talked about every day and all day long. As they say, it only takes one security breach to compromise the hardware that your company's security team has worked hard to implement over the years. As an IT engineer, it is essential to have an interest in security technologies, gain the right exposure and experience, and implement the best enterprise security solutions offered by these vendors. If you haven't taken enterprise security seriously, then perhaps it's time to dip your toes into it by exploring Palo Alto and Fortinet firewalls.

Although this book is not solely focused on enterprise security, we will cover some basics of working with firewalls from the most popular vendors in the market as of 2023: Palo Alto and Fortinet. Additionally, we will run some Ansible labs against their operating systems to get a feel for handling different OS from different security vendors. While we won't delve into the full range of security concepts and applications in this book, readers will be exposed to some Ansible applications in enterprise firewall scenarios. If you are an enterprise security engineer, learn the basics by reading Chapters 17 to 21 and apply your experience to a real production environment.

In the later part of this book, we have chosen to focus on Palo Alto and Fortinet firewalls for several reasons using Ansible playbooks. Firstly, Palo Alto has emerged as one of the largest players in the enterprise firewall market in recent times, renowned for providing top-notch performance and security. On the other hand, Fortinet, although a market follower until recent years, has gained significant market share in the enterprise security market. To stay ahead in their careers, many network engineers are now recommended to study either Palo Alto or Fortinet security certification tracks, or even both, to gain a comprehensive understanding of these industry-leading solutions.

What's more, both Palo Alto Networks and Fortinet have recognized the true power of Red Hat's Ansible, and their development teams have been creating and contributing to the development of various vendor-specific Ansible modules. These modules make it easier to manage and automate tasks supported by Palo Alto and Fortinet devices using the Ansible Automation Platform and Ansible Engine. To delve deeper into the latest modules supported for Ansible regarding Palo Alto and Fortinet products, you can visit the following links for further reading:

Ansible and Palo Alto Networks: `www.ansible.com/integrations/networks/palo-alto`

Ansible and Fortinet: `www.ansible.com/integrations/security/fortinet`

While Check Point and Cisco Firepower are also excellent security products, Palo Alto and Fortinet have gained more popularity among most enterprise CTOs and IT managers. So if you are new to the IT industry, you will hear more about Palo Alto and Fortinet in the years to come. Studying market-leading vendor products and understanding their capabilities will provide valuable insights and enhance the skill set of network engineers in the dynamic field of enterprise security. In the last decade, IT professionals like us have been told to study network security, and in the next ten years, we have been warned about the importance security plays in corporate networks. It is crucial to keep up to date on the subject of security, which includes cyber security.

The files required to complete your Palo Alto (PA-VM) and Fortinet (FortiGate) firewall installations are listed in Table 11-2."

Table 11-2. *Required files for Palo Alto and Fortinet firewall installation on GNS3*

Description	File name	File size
Palo Alto PA-VM	Pan-vm-fw.gns3a	8 KB
	PA-VM-KVM-10.1.0.qcow2	3.4 GB
Fortinet	Fortigate.gns3a	22 KB
FortiGate	empty30G.qcow2	192.5 KB
	FGT_VM64_KVM-v7.2.4.F-build1396-FORTINET.out.kvm.qcow2	90.8 MB

Let's begin by installing the latest Palo Alto and Fortinet virtual firewalls on our GNS3 network emulator to learn and test with Ansible.

11.2.1 Palo Alto PA-VM Initial Configuration and Connection Test

Step 1: To proceed with the installation of Palo Alto and Fortinet firewalls on GNS3, you should visit the authors' GitHub site and download the installation guide. The guide you need to download and follow is titled "Ch11_Pre-task2_PaloAlto_and_Fortinet_Firewall_Installation_on_GNS3.pdf". This file provides detailed instructions for the installation process.

After downloading the guide from the following URL (GitHub link): `https://github.com/ansnetauto/appress_ansnetauto`, carefully follow each step outlined in the guide. This will help you install the required image and create your virtual firewalls.

Step 2: At this point, we will assume that you have successfully followed the instructions and completed the installation for Palo Alto PA-VM 10.1.0 and FortiGate 7.2.4 on your GNS3. Now that you have both virtual devices available in your GNS3's All devices, let's drag and drop each firewall onto the Topology canvas to continue building our lab, ansnetauto_lab01 project. After connecting and powering on both firewalls, your GNS3 topology should resemble Figure 11-11.

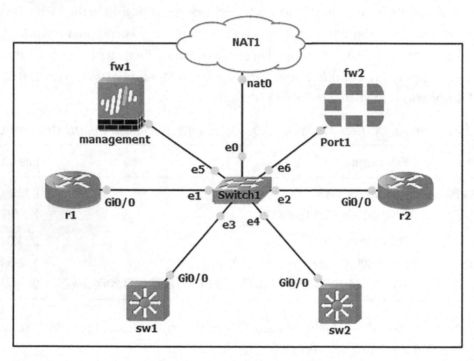

Figure 11-11.   *Powering on all GNS3 devices example*

Tip

Ensuring the smooth operation of the GNS3 labs

If your laptop is struggling to run all the VMs and GNS3 devices simultaneously, it is advisable to keep only the relevant devices powered on. This approach will ensure smooth lab operation and conserve processing power. **It is not necessary to run all VMs on VMware Workstation and all networking devices on GNS3 at the same time.** Depending on your laptop's specifications, available memory, and CPU capability, you should exercise discretion in running the lab based on your available resources. If your laptop has lower specifications, limited memory, or a lower-grade CPU, it becomes even more important to manage your resources wisely to optimize performance and prevent any system issues. By selectively running the necessary devices, you can still achieve effective hands-on practice without overburdening your laptop's capabilities.

Step 3: Please refer to Figure 11-12 to focus on the relevant devices. In this section, we will be using the host PC, f38s1, u23c2, r1, Switch1, fw1, and fw2, as depicted in Figure 11-12. This means you can keep the rest of the unused devices such as sw1, sw2, and r2. It's worth noting that this setup allows you to run your lab effectively using a single laptop and leverage multiple cutting-edge technologies simultaneously.

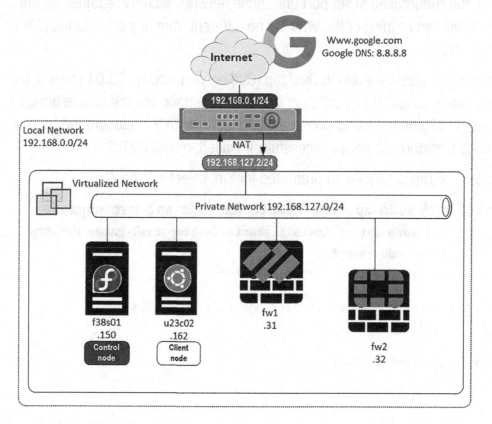

Figure 11-12. *Building Ansible learning lab*

Expand your knowledge:

Installing GUI on the Ubuntu 23.04 server (Gnome Desktop)

In preparation for testing HTTPS login to PA-VM (fw1) and FortiGate (fw2), let's install the Gnome Desktop on our Ubuntu client node, u23c1 (192.168.127.162). We will use this virtual machine to verify the web page functionalities of each firewall and ensure they are working correctly (see Figure 11-13). If you have a support contract associated with your vendor's web account, you can download the .ova file and install it as a virtual machine. Ultimately, these firewalls are Linux based and repurposed to support enterprise network security features, so the installation and running of the VMs are no different from any other Linux VMs on hypervisors.

All it takes to install a working Desktop (GUI) on your Ubuntu 23.04 Linux is three lines of commands. The installation of the GUI interface will take some time, so you need to issue the install command and let it run in the background for a while. After the Desktop has been successfully installed, reboot u23c2.

Update your repository. When prompted for Y/n, select Y to continue.

```
jdoe@u23c2:$ sudo apt-get update && sudo apt-get upgrade
jdoe@u23c2:$ sudo apt -y install ubuntu-desktop task-gnome-desktop
jdoe@u23c2:~$ sudo reboot
[sudo] password for jdoe: ***************

Broadcast message from root@u23c2 on pts/1 (Mon 2023-05-29
06:30:34 UTC):
```

The system will reboot now!

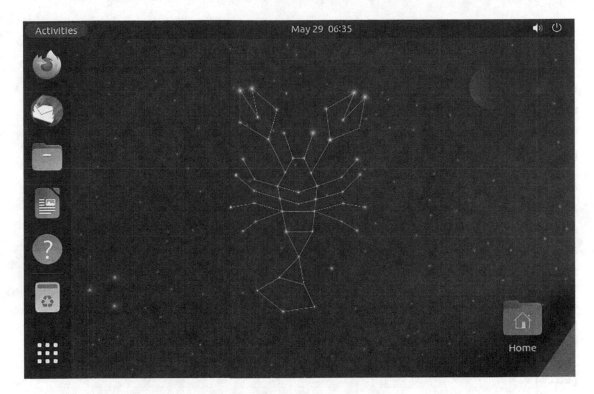

Figure 11-13. *Ubuntu Gnome Desktop on u23c2*

An alternative way to test HTTPS connection is to use the host PC's Windows 11. However, this requires the use of the Microsoft Loopback interface to connect to one of the routers and establish a connection via GNS3's Cloud connection. A complete installation and configuration guide will be provided on the authors' GitHub page as a complementary guide. You can find the file named "Ch11_Pre-task5_Host_PC_Loopback_GNS3_Installation_Optional.pdf". This guide will enable you to SSH or HTTP into the virtual devices running on GNS3 VM. **Adding flexibility is key to successful lab building and IT study.** The knowledge gained through practice and proof of concept extends to the quality of your actual work. So please take the time to build proper proof-of-concept labs and practice, practice, and practice.

Step 4: To initialize our Palo Alto PA-VM, we need to configure the device from the command line. You can refer to the official documentation provided here for detailed instructions:

Official documentation: https://docs.paloaltonetworks.com/pan-os/10-1/pan-os-cli-quick-start/cli-cheat-sheets/cli-cheat-sheet-networking

Here is the initial configuration for our PA-VM to establish communication on our network within the current topology. After following the installation guide, you have **reset the factory default admin password (admin/admin)**. However, if you wish to update your password, you can do so by executing the "set mgt-config users admin password" command to reset your password.

```
admin@PA-VM> configure
admin@PA-VM# set deviceconfig system type static
admin@PA-VM# set deviceconfig system ip-address 192.168.127.31 netmask
255.255.255.0 default-gateway 192.168.127.2 dns-setting servers primary
192.168.127.2

admin@PA-VM# set mgt-config users admin password
Enter password   : **************
Confirm password : **************

[edit]
admin@PA-VM# commit
Commit job 2 is in progress. Use Ctrl+C to return to command prompt
...............................................55%......................60%.
75%........98%.............[ 3871.852828] netlink: 12 bytes leftover after
parsing attributes in process `ip'.
.......................................100%
Configuration committed successfully
```

Step 5: To ensure a successful lab experience in the later part of this book, it is important to validate the reachability of various nodes and addresses. First, validate the reachability to the Ansible control node, f38s1 (192.168.127.150), and the client node with GUI, u23c1 (192.168.127.162). Additionally, confirm the reachability of the Google DNS IP, 8.8.8.8, and the Google URL, www.google.com. All these addresses must be reachable from your Palo Alto PA-VM. Verifying the reachability of these nodes and addresses ensures that your lab setup is functional and ready for the subsequent sections of this book.

```
admin@PA-VM# exit
admin@PA-VM> ping host 192.168.127.150
PING 192.168.127.150 (192.168.127.150) 56(84) bytes of data.
64 bytes from 192.168.127.150: icmp_seq=1 ttl=64 time=3.59 ms
[...omitted for brevity]
admin@PA-VM> ping host 192.168.127.162
PING 192.168.127.162 (192.168.127.162) 56(84) bytes of data.
64 bytes from 192.168.127.162: icmp_seq=1 ttl=64 time=2.12 ms
[...omitted for brevity]
admin@PA-VM> ping host 8.8.8.8
PING 8.8.8.8 (8.8.8.8) 56(84) bytes of data.
64 bytes from 8.8.8.8: icmp_seq=1 ttl=128 time=17.5 ms
[...omitted for brevity]
admin@PA-VM> ping host www.google.com
PING www.google.com (142.250.204.4) 56(84) bytes of data.
64 bytes from syd09s25-in-f4.1e100.net (142.250.204.4): icmp_seq=1 ttl=128
time=13.0 ms
[...omitted for brevity]
```

Step 6: Go to the u23c2 client node on VMware Workstation's main window, log in with your credentials, and open the Firefox web browser. Navigate to the Palo Alto PA-VM web page at https://192.168.127.31. If the page loads without errors, you are now ready to tackle the Palo Alto Ansible labs later in this book (see Figure 11-14).

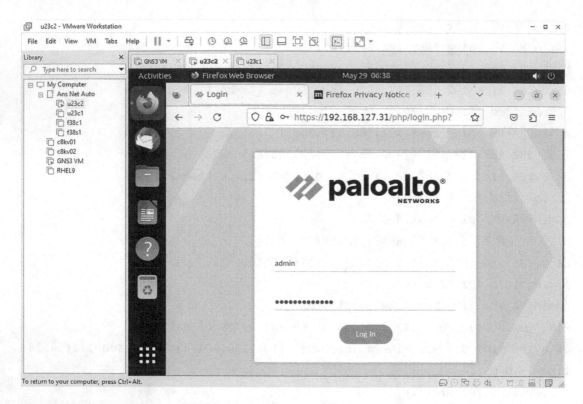

Figure 11-14. *Opening a PAN-OS login page on the Firefox browser running on u23c2*

We will reserve the first PAN-OS playbook for Chapter 17. Now that you have confirmed the reachability of your PA-VM and successfully accessed the Web Admin page, you can proceed with the initial configuration of Fortinet's FortiGate. This configuration is similar to the process followed for Palo Alto PA-VM. Let's proceed and complete this step to ensure we can utilize FortiGate for our Ansible learning labs.

11.2.2 Fortinet FortiGate Initial Configuration and Connection Test

This section provides a step-by-step guide to configuring your FortiGate's network settings for the first time using the CLI. For more detailed information about each command, please refer to Fortinet's official FortiOS CLI reference. **The factory default password for FortiGate is "admin" with a blank password.** Let's swiftly configure the device by setting the static IP address, DNS, and default gateway and perform simple ICMP ping tests for connection validation.

FortiOS CLI reference: https://docs.fortinet.com/document/fortigate/7.4.0/
cli-reference/84566/fortios-cli-reference

Step 1: To start the task, log in and set your password for the first time.

```
FortiGate-VM64-KVM login: admin
Password: blank
You are forced to change your password. Please input a new password.
New Password:***************
Confirm Password: :***************
Welcome!
```

Step 2: Now enter the configuration mode and configure your new FortiGate firewall.

```
FortiGate-VM64-KVM # config system interface
FortiGate-VM64-KVM (interface) # edit port1
FortiGate-VM64-KVM (port1) # set mode static
FortiGate-VM64-KVM (port1) # set ip 192.168.127.32 255.255.255.0
FortiGate-VM64-KVM (port1) # set allowaccess https ping ssh
FortiGate-VM64-KVM (port1) # end
FortiGate-VM64-KVM # config system dns
FortiGate-VM64-KVM (dns) # set primary 192.168.127.2
FortiGate-VM64-KVM (dns) # set secondary 8.8.8.8
FortiGate-VM64-KVM (dns) # end
FortiGate-VM64-KVM # execute ping 192.168.127.150
PING 192.168.127.150 (192.168.127.150): 56 data bytes
64 bytes from 192.168.127.150: icmp_seq=0 ttl=64 time=7.3 ms
[...omitted for brevity]
```

Step 3: Configure the default gateway for port1.

```
FortiGate-VM64-KVM # config router static
FortiGate-VM64-KVM (static) # edit 1
new entry '1' added
FortiGate-VM64-KVM (1) # set device port1
FortiGate-VM64-KVM (1) # set gateway 192.168.127.2
FortiGate-VM64-KVM (1) # next
The destination is set to 0.0.0.0/0 which means all IP addresses.
FortiGate-VM64-KVM (static) # end
```

```
FortiGate-VM64-KVM # execute ping 8.8.8.8
PING 8.8.8.8 (8.8.8.8): 56 data bytes
64 bytes from 8.8.8.8: icmp_seq=0 ttl=128 time=12.0 ms
[...omitted for brevity]
```

Step 4: Save the configuration to prevent any loss of settings and ensure that the device boots up with the correct configurations.

```
FortiGate-VM64-KVM # config system global
FortiGate-VM64-KVM (global) # set cfg-save automatic
FortiGate-VM64-KVM (global) # end
FortiGate-VM64-KVM # exit
```

Step 5: Run the "show system interface" command to check the current configurations. Additionally, refer to the vendor-provided Administration Guide to explore FortiOS and learn about the various features of FortiGate's command lines. You can access the guide at https://docs.fortinet.com/document/fortigate/7.4.0/ administration-guide/954635/getting-started.

```
FortiGate-VM64-KVM # show system interface
config system interface
    edit "port1"
        set vdom "root"
        set ip 192.168.127.31 255.255.255.0
        set allowaccess ping https ssh http telnet
        set type physical
        set snmp-index 1
[...omitted for brevity]
```

Step 6: If all configurations and ping tests have been successful, proceed to u23c2 in VMware Workstation. Open the URL https://192.168.127.32 and verify if the page loads correctly. Additionally, you can try logging in using your credentials (refer to Figure 11-15) to ensure proper access.

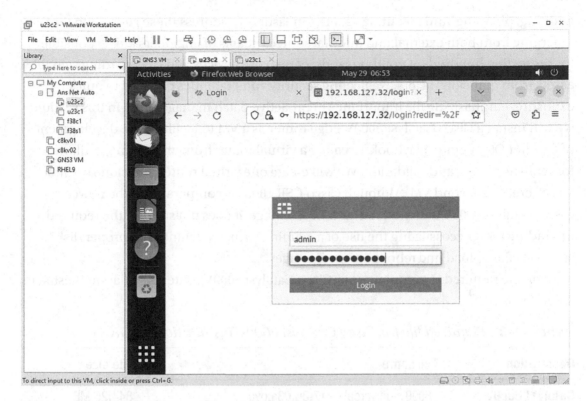

Figure 11-15. *FortiGate Web Login page from Firefox running on u23c2*

Now that you have completed the initial configuration and connectivity tests for Fortinet's FortiGate VM, you are ready to dive into writing some playbooks to interact with a Fortinet firewall. We will leave the first FortiGate playbook for a later chapter.

Next, we will proceed with the installation of the Cisco Catalyst 8000V Edge router virtual machine, which will be used for an IOS-XE upgrade lab in the future. While the GNS3 images are excellent, certain features may not be fully supported in this setup. Therefore, we need to create a new virtual machine specifically for our lab testing, including OS upgrades. Let's get started!

11.3 Cisco c8000v Edge Router VM Creation on VMware Workstation

In today's rapidly evolving cyber-security landscape, securing enterprise networks has become paramount due to the constant stream of security vulnerabilities in vendor products. IT engineers are facing increased workloads, encompassing tasks such as auditing, planning, and executing security measures to address these gaps. With threats emerging from both external and internal sources, teams of engineers are responsible for protecting hundreds, if not thousands, of network devices and safeguarding valuable assets from malicious actors. Neglecting security vulnerabilities can lead to quick exposure, emphasizing the importance of proactive patch management. In this section, we will install a Cisco Catalyst 8000V Edge router as a VM to facilitate the development of a router OS upgrade playbook. Creating a virtual router from an ISO image allows for realistic testing and validation. We will create one virtual router and clone the first VM to create a second VM. Although Cisco CSR 1000v is comparable to the newer Cisco Catalyst 8000V and available as a GNS3 image, it does not support the required upgrading task, necessitating the use of a genuine virtual machine with proper disk space for file upload and reboot into new images.

The file required to complete your Cisco Catalyst 8000V router installation is listed in Table 11-3.

Table 11-3. *Required file for Cisco Catalyst 8000V installation on GNS3*

Description	File name	File size
Catalyst 8000V (for creating VM)	c8000v-universalk9.17.06.03a.ova (MD5: 09b8f40158f79b793690bad8a534ad0e)	844.25 MB

Please note that the Cisco Catalyst 8000V images are proprietary software and you will need to source the software through the genuine channel or find a suitable alternative to proceed with the virtual router creations. If you encounter difficulties in obtaining the proprietary software used, you can still use the GNS3 to test parts of the upgrade playbooks. However, for now, let's focus on installing the Cisco Catalyst 8000V image and creating two routers directly on VMware Workstation 17 Pro.

Step 1: Before you begin, visit the authors' GitHub site and download the "Ch11_Pre-task3_Cisco_c8kv_Router_VM_Creation_on_VMware_WS.pdf", which is the installation guide for the Cisco Catalyst 8000V Edge router.

GitHub link: `https://github.com/ansnetauto/appress_ansnetauto`

Step 2: Please review the downloaded document carefully and complete the installation. The guide provides detailed instructions for the installation process. Once the download is complete, follow each step outlined in the guide meticulously to install the required image and create your virtual routers.

Step 3: Once you have completed the router installation and cloning processes, you will have two fully functional Cisco Catalyst 8000V routers: c8kv01 with an IP address of 192.168.127.171 and c8kv02 with an IP address of 192.168.127.172. Please refer to Figure 11-16.

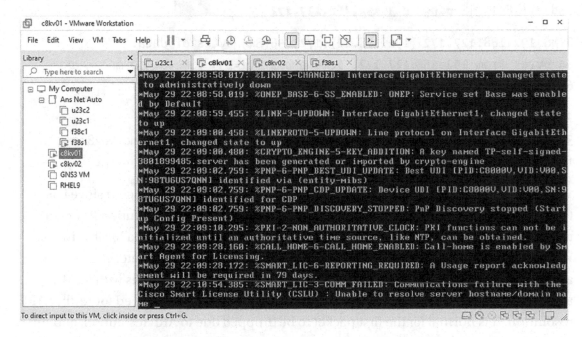

Figure 11-16. *Two Cisco Catalyst 8000V routers installed*

Step 4: Power on the virtual machines f38s1, c8kv01, and c8kv02.

Step 5: We have already configured the management IP addresses on c8kv01 and c8kv02, so technically, we should be able to ping these routers from f38s1 if all of the interface configurations have been strictly followed according to the installation guide. Since these are all running on a flat network of 192.168.127.0/24, as long as the routers' interfaces are correctly configured, the Ansible Control Machine (f38s1) should be able to communicate with these two routers.

```
[jdoe@f38s1 ~]$ ping -c 3 192.168.127.171

PING 192.168.127.171 (192.168.127.171) 56(84) bytes of data.
64 bytes from 192.168.127.171: icmp_seq=2 ttl=255 time=0.689 ms
64 bytes from 192.168.127.171: icmp_seq=3 ttl=255 time=7.22 ms
```

```
--- 192.168.127.171 ping statistics ---
3 packets transmitted, 2 received, 33.3333% packet loss, time 2015ms
rtt min/avg/max/mdev = 0.689/3.953/7.218/3.264 ms
```

[jdoe@f38s1 ~]$ **ping -c 3 192.168.127.172**

```
PING 192.168.127.172 (192.168.127.172) 56(84) bytes of data.
64 bytes from 192.168.127.172: icmp_seq=2 ttl=255 time=0.450 ms
64 bytes from 192.168.127.172: icmp_seq=3 ttl=255 time=0.587 ms

--- 192.168.127.172 ping statistics ---
3 packets transmitted, 2 received, 33.3333% packet loss, time 2028ms
rtt min/avg/max/mdev = 0.450/0.518/0.587/0.068 ms
```

The first packet loss in a ping command should not be a major concern since it is typically a result of ARP resolution. In networking, ARP (Address Resolution Protocol) is utilized to discover the MAC address associated with an IP address on a local network. When you initiate a ping, the source device sends an ARP request to determine the MAC address of the destination device. The destination device then responds with its MAC address, enabling subsequent packets to be transmitted without the need for further ARP resolution. It is normal for the first packet to be dropped due to ARP resolution, and this occurrence does not indicate any issues with the network. However, if you re-execute the same command, the first packet will not be dropped because the MAC address has already been learned from the previous ICMP communication.

Step 6: With the connectivity between the Ansible control node and the two routers verified, proceed to SSH into f38s1. Once logged in, create a new directory named "ch11", and within it, create three essential files: ansible.cfg, inventory, and 11.1_icmp.yml.

[jdoe@f38s1 ~]$ **cd repo1/**
[jdoe@f38s1 repo1]$ **cd ana_lab**
[jdoe@f38s1 ana_lab]$ **vi ansible.cfg**
[jdoe@f38s1 ana_lab]$ **cat ansible.cfg**
[defaults]
inventory=inventory
host_key_checking=False
nocows = 1

Step 7: Using the previous inventory file from the "show clock" playbook for GNS3 routers and switches, we will modify the inventory slightly to group different types of routers into different groups and then add both router types as ios_device's children. Use the provided example here as your reference. Separating the routers into different models or types can help you to target only the devices which are of the same model.

```
[jdoe@f38s1 ana_lab]$ vi inventory
[jdoe@f38s1 ana_lab]$ cat inventory

[ios_devices:vars]
ansible_network_os=ios
ansible_user=jdoe
ansible_password=5uper5cret9assw0rd
ansible_connection=network_cli

[router_type1]
r1 ansible_host=192.168.127.11
r2 ansible_host=192.168.127.12

[router_type2]
c8kv01 ansible_host=192.168.127.171
c8kv02 ansible_host=192.168.127.172

[switches]
sw1 ansible_host=192.168.127.21
sw2 ansible_host=192.168.127.22

[ios_devices:children]
router_type1
router_type2
switches
```

Step 8: Let's create an ICMP (ping) test playbook for the routers using the ping module.

```
[jdoe@f38s1 ana_lab]$ vi 11.3_icmp1.yml
[jdoe@f38s1 ana_lab]$ cat 11.3_icmp1.yml

---
```

```
- hosts: router_type2
  gather_facts: true # we want gather_fact to execute, so specified true

  tasks:
  - name: Test reachability to Cisco IOS XE Routers
    ansible.builtin.ping:
```

Step 9: Execute the ICMP playbook and observe the output. Since we already installed the ansible-pylibssh or Python SSH Library on the Ansible control node, it will use the same SSH library. In other words, it will not give us the "[WARNING]: ansible-pylibssh not installed, falling back to paramiko" message and we are expecting a clean playbook run.

```
[jdoe@f38s1 ana_lab]$ anp 11.3_icmp1.yml

PLAY [router_type2]
***************************************************************************

TASK [Gathering Facts]
***************************************************************************
ok: [c8kv01]
ok: [c8kv02]

TASK [Test reachability to Cisco IOS XE Routers]
***************************************************************************
ok: [c8kv01]
ok: [c8kv02]

PLAY RECAP
***************************************************************************
c8kv01     : ok=2    changed=0    unreachable=0    failed=0    skipped=0
rescued=0    ignored=0
c8kv02     : ok=2    changed=0    unreachable=0    failed=0    skipped=0
rescued=0    ignored=0
```

Step 10: Let's proceed to create the second connectivity test playbook, which will utilize the net_ping module. Name the file as "11.3_icmp2.yml". In this playbook, we will be using the Ansible net_ping module and specify the destination parameter.

```
[jdoe@f38s1 ana_lab]$ vi 11.3_icmp2.yml
[jdoe@f38s1 ana_lab]$ cat 11.3_icmp2.yml
```

```
---
- hosts: router_type2
  gather_facts: true # by default gather_facts is on, but want to be
specific, so added a statement

  tasks:
  - name: Test reachability to Cisco IOS XE Routers
    ansible.netcommon.net_ping:
      dest: "{{ ansible_host }}"
```

Step 11: Execute the playbook "11.3_icmp2.yml" to perform a test on the login and connectivity from the Ansible Control Machine.

```
[jdoe@f38s1 ana_lab]$ anp 11.3_icmp2.yml
```

[The result should be the same as in Step 8.] [...omitted for brevity]

Step 12: Now, let's utilize the playbook "11.1_show_clock.yml" as the foundation for creating another playbook that will be used to check the IOS-XE versions. We will name this new playbook "11.3_show_version.yml".

```
[jdoe@f38s1 ana_lab]$ cp  11.1_show_clock.yml  11.3_show_version.yml
[jdoe@f38s1 ana_lab]$ vi 11.3_show_version.yml
[jdoe@f38s1 ana_lab]$ cat 11.3_show_version.yml
---
```

```
- name: Display Cisco IOS versions
  hosts: router_type2
  gather_facts: true # specifying true to run gather_facts

  tasks:
    - name: run show version on target devices
      cisco.ios.ios_command:
        commands: show version | incl IOS XE Software
      register: output
```

```
    - name: print output
      ansible.builtin.debug:
        var: output.stdout_lines
```

Step 13: Execute the aforementioned playbook and carefully observe the resulting output.

```
[jdoe@f38s1 ana_lab]$ anp 11.3_show_version.yml

[...omitted for brevity]
TASK [print output]
*****************************************************************************
ok: [c8kv01] => {
    "output.stdout_lines": [
        [
            "Cisco IOS XE Software, Version 17.06.03a"
        ]
    ]
}
ok: [c8kv02] => {
    "output.stdout_lines": [
        [
            "Cisco IOS XE Software, Version 17.06.03a"
        ]
    ]
}
[...omitted for brevity]
```

If you have completed the tasks successfully, now you are ready to perform the configuration management and task automation on Cisco routers from our Ansible control node.

Congratulations on successfully learning how to write connection-testing playbooks and utilize Ansible to check the IOS-XE version. Through this process, you have gained valuable knowledge on using different Ansible modules to ensure connectivity between target nodes (c8kv01 and c8kv02) and the Ansible control node (f38s1).

The steps involved in setting up ansible.cfg, creating an inventory with flexibility, and composing functional Ansible playbooks are similar to those covered in previous chapters for Linux playbooks. We encourage readers to start their journey by comprehensively understanding Ansible Linux automation, as the concepts you have mastered can now be effectively applied to a wide range of network and security devices.

By leveraging the knowledge acquired in Ansible Linux automation, you have established a strong foundation for automating tasks across various systems. Whether it entails managing Linux servers, routers, switches, firewalls, or other devices, the principles you have learned can be readily applied. Proficiency in Ansible empowers you to streamline and standardize configuration management, provisioning, and deployment processes, resulting in enhanced efficiency, consistency, and scalability in managing diverse systems within your infrastructure.

Next, we will explore the process of creating a Cisco Wireless LAN Controller (WLAN) on a VMware Workstation, following a similar approach as the one demonstrated for the Cisco Catalyst 8000V Edge router VM creation mentioned earlier.

11.4 Cisco Wireless LAN Controller (WLC) VM Creation on VMware ESXi 7

In our opinion, Cisco stands out as one of the industry leaders in providing robust and high-performance enterprise-level wireless solutions and hardware. Their products seamlessly connect wireless and mobile devices to enterprise networks. While there are competitors in the enterprise wireless market, such as Aruba Networks (a subsidiary of HP), Ruckus Wireless, Juniper Networks, Extreme Networks, Huawei Technologies, and Meraki (a subsidiary of Cisco), Cisco has maintained its market leadership in WAN, LAN, and WLAN technologies.

Cisco's expertise in LAN technology translates well to their wireless solutions, giving them a competitive edge over their rivals. Cisco's wireless products are renowned for their reliability and performance, making them a preferred choice for enterprises, governments, the military, and organizations that require robust and secure wireless networks. Cisco's Technical Assistance Center (TAC) support for their wireless devices is highly regarded and known for its exceptional quality.

Cisco vWLC (virtual Wireless LAN Controller) is a software-based version of popular Cisco hardware-based Wireless LAN Controllers. It is designed to provide centralized management and control for wireless networks. The vWLC is typically deployed as a virtual machine and can be run on various hypervisors such as VMware ESXi, Microsoft Hyper-V, or KVM. At the core of Cisco's wireless technology is its WLCs, which serve as a central management system for wireless networks. Whenever there is a field notice or security vulnerability alert related to Cisco WLCs, wireless engineers must prioritize patching the WLC to safeguard their organization's wireless network from potential security threats and malicious actors. In recent times, Cisco has introduced Cisco Catalyst 9800 WLAN Controller running on IOS-XE, which is marketed for small-medium businesses; this software is geared toward smaller offices and buildings. The software that will be installed in this section is the enterprise-level virtual WLC, which has been replacing the aging Cisco 5500's and 2500's WLCs in the production network.

We have been trying to integrate all software to run on VMware Workstation, but this installation is one of the two exceptions in this book, that you have to install Type I hypervisors (or bare metal) for our testing. We are forced to install the virtual WLC on VMware's ESXi environment due to VMware Workstation (a Type 2 or hosted hypervisor) and WLC software compatibility. The authors have been testing the vWLC software installation on VMware Workstation 17 Pro with partial success, meaning the software can be installed and pingable; however, the management web GUI and SSH access were inaccessible while spending a whole day discovering and troubleshooting the issue; this is an old known issue on the VMware workstations, and the students have to fall back onto the Type 1 hypervisor for the testing. If you have access to any of the Type 1 hypervisors such as ESXi, Hyper-V, or KVM, use those platforms to import the virtual machine files. If you have one of the AWS, Azure, or GCP accounts, you can install Cisco's vWLC there and execute your Ansible playbooks. As an alternative, we could have used the 9800 WLC, but the OS is based on the IOS-XE catalyst OS, which works in the same way as the Catalyst switches. If you want to give it a try, you should be looking for Catalyst 9800-CL Wireless Controller for Cloud on Cisco's download page and look for a file with a file name similar to C9800-CL-universalk9.17.06.05.ova.

In this context, we will be creating a working Cisco WLC on my vCenter and ESXi 7.0.3 environment using the VMware .ova file, which has been downloaded from Cisco's website. Later on, in subsequent chapters, we will update the software using the .aes file. You only need a single .aes file to upgrade a running Cisco WLC. We understand that this snag of software compatibility issue is a little drawback for some of our readers; however, this also gives the readers the opportunity to expand and study more on the Type I hypervisors as well as the offerings of the Public Cloud service providers capabilities to support Cisco's appliance-based wireless devices.

The file required to complete your Cisco Wireless LAN Controller installation is listed in Table 11-4.

Table 11-4. *Required files for Cisco WLC installation on vSphere 6.7 or above*

Description	File name	File size
Cisco WLC **(for creating VM)**	AIR_CTVM-K9_8_8_130_0.ova (MD5: 2e3754fb18230b897fe4074c60028944)	357.71 MB

Let's proceed with creating the vWLC in preparation for Chapter 16. This is the final task that you need to accomplish. Let's get started!

Step 1: As always, start by visiting the authors' GitHub site and downloading the installation guide for Pre-task 4 from the provided link.

GitHub link: https://github.com/ansnetauto/appress_ansnetauto

Ch11_Pre-task4_Cisco_Wireless_LAN_Controller(vWLC)_VM_Creation_on_VMware_ESXi.pdf

This file provides comprehensive instructions for the installation process. After downloading it, carefully follow each step outlined in the guide to install the required image and create your virtual Wireless LAN Controller.

Please keep in mind that the installation needs to be performed on an ESXi environment or a Public/Private cloud platform.

Step 2: For our installation, we have used the following information to create a vWLC on ESXi 7.0.3. Keep your wireless server-related information handy for later tasks in Chapter 16.

```
WLC name: wlc01
Username: admin
Password: Super5cret9assw0rd <<< Meet minimum requirements
Management interface: Management interface
Mgt interface IP: 192.168.0.201/24 <<< Same subnet as others
Default Gateway: 192.168.0.1
DHCP IP: 192.168.0.1
Service interface IP: 192.168.127.201/24 <<< This is only a placeholder
configuration
```

Step 3: To ensure future access if needed, make use of PuTTY to establish SSH sessions and verify their functionality (refer to Figure 11-17). This step allows you to log in securely and guarantees smooth remote connections. By utilizing PuTTY, you can maintain a reliable SSH setup for future use, providing convenience and accessibility whenever required.

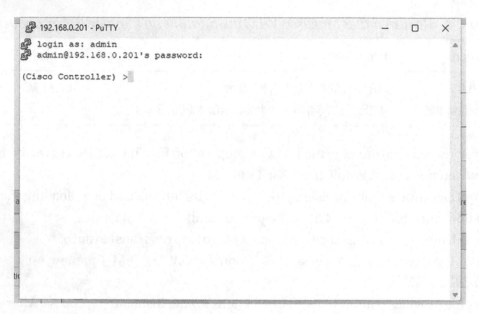

Figure 11-17. SSH login to Cisco vWLC

Step 4: Take a moment to sign in to the Web Administration page and explore the various menu options. For wireless engineers, this will be a familiar territory – a playground for you to navigate with ease. However, if you are new to Cisco Wireless and haven't studied it before, this will be an exhilarating and novel experience for you (refer to Figure 11-18). Embrace the opportunity to dive into this new domain and discover the exciting possibilities it holds.

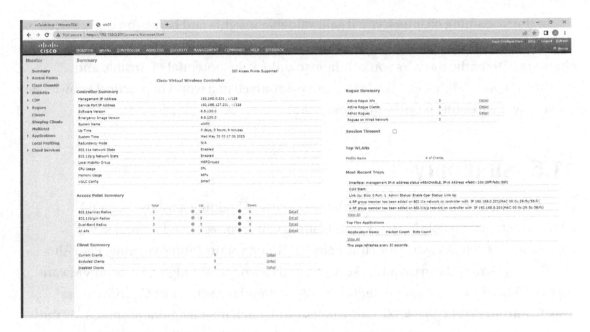

Figure 11-18. *Cisco vWLC Web login – Summary page*

If you are new to Cisco Wireless Technology and have never had a serious interest in wireless technology, now is the perfect time to explore and delve into this exciting field. Just by looking at the vWLC Web interface, you can already appreciate why Cisco has been the market leader in this space. The interface is incredibly intuitive and user-friendly. However, it's important to note that GUI interfaces are gradually being replaced by APIs. As IT professionals often say, APIs are the new GUI for administrators. While GUIs are fantastic, they have a major limitation when it comes to running batch or custom jobs at a large scale.

Congratulations on reaching this point in the chapter! You've truly earned your key to unlocking the next ten chapters. Although this chapter may not be the longest, it involved a multitude of moving parts, including installation guides and various software for integration and setup. If this is your first experience building such a lab, welcome to the world of IT engineers! We warmly welcome you and wish you a fantastic journey in your IT career in this field. It has been an incredible ride to reach this milestone, and now you have an exciting opportunity to delve into the next ten chapters. Brace yourself for practical fun with Ansible as you dive deeper into its world.

In the upcoming chapters, you'll gain valuable insights and hands-on experiences that will further enhance your network automation skills. Embrace the remaining chapters with enthusiasm as you continue to unlock the potential of Ansible and transform your abilities. Get ready to immerse yourself in a world of practical knowledge and enjoy the exciting journey that lies ahead!

11.5 Summary

In this chapter, we guided you through the process of building a robust learning environment for Ansible Network Automation. Our focus revolved around key components such as Cisco Modeling Labs (CML) for routing and switching, Palo Alto and Fortinet firewalls on GNS3 for security, and Cisco c8000v edge routers on VMware Workstation for patch management. We also explored the setup of a Cisco Wireless LAN Controller (WLC) on ESXi 7 for wireless and patch management purposes. By the end of this chapter, you acquired a comprehensive learning environment consisting of enterprise-level routers, switches, firewalls, edge routers, and a WLC. This setup empowers you to embark on your network automation journey with Ansible and IT in general. Prepare to unlock the immense potential of Ansible in network automation and elevate your capabilities in managing and automating your network infrastructure.

PART III

The Practical

## CHAPTER 12

Cisco Router and Switch Configuration with Ansible

In this chapter, we will explore Cisco router and switch configuration using Ansible, an efficient configuration management and automation tool. Through hands-on labs, you will gain practical experience in deploying Ansible playbooks to configure Cisco IOS-XE routers and switches. You will build all GNS3-based labs from the ground up, starting with initial device configurations and then using Ansible to perform tasks that are typically done manually. These labs offer both manual and Ansible automated configuration tasks while also teaching the configuration validation processes along the way. Lab 1 focuses on creating an EIGRP lab topology from scratch and configuring routers with EIGRP routing enabled using Ansible playbooks. Lab 2 builds an OSPF lab from the ground up, configuring routers with OSPF dynamic routing using Ansible playbooks. By leveraging Ansible's "when" module, we can target specific hosts for configuration. In Lab 3, we dive into Cisco L2 switch configuration, exploring VLAN, VTP, and trunking configurations using a single Ansible playbook. Ansible-vault is utilized to protect user credentials. Lab 4 is an optional challenge lab for those eager to configure five Cisco routers and have a go at configuring Access Control Lists (ACL) with Ansible. Throughout the chapter, we will apply Ansible concepts to streamline network management, enhance efficiency and scalability, and free up your time to focus on more value-adding work.

Welcome to the first of our ten chapters on Ansible Network Automation Practical Primer Labs! We're thrilled to have you here and can't wait for you to dive into the practical side of the book. Each chapter will cover basic to intermediate networking topics, with a strong emphasis on the interaction between the Ansible Control Machine and the enterprise-level networking devices in our labs.

© Brendan Choi and Erwin Medina 2023
B. Choi and E. Medina, *Introduction to Ansible Network Automation*,
https://doi.org/10.1007/978-1-4842-9624-0_12

In this particular chapter, we'll begin each section by presenting you with a lab topology for your review. You'll then set up the topology in GNS3 to initialize the lab environment. As our primary focus is on Ansible and its communication to other devices, we won't delve into an in-depth discussion of networking concepts. Rest assured, there are numerous networking books, training videos, YouTube channels, and blogs available to study those concepts. Our goal here is to equip you with the skills to effectively use Ansible to interact with networking devices in action, in particular Cisco IOS-XE-based routers and switches.

To enrich your learning experience, we have methodically chosen two labs dedicated to basic router configuration: one lab focused on basic switch configuration and one hands-on lab for you to try yourself, specifically designed for router ACL configuration. While these labs only scratch the surface of the vast field of networking, they serve as a solid starting point. **After all, taking the first step is essential in any learning process. It's better to begin with a solid foundation than to postpone indefinitely.** Remember, action speaks louder than words, and we're here to help you take the first step. Now, without further ado, let's dive right in and get started on this exciting journey!

Warning!

Be advised, all labs in this book are using a /24 subnet.

Please take note that all labs are using a /24 subnet configuration, following the principle of simplicity and effectiveness. If the IP addressing scheme used in this book clashes with your existing network, you should consider changing the third portion of the subnet. For example, for the VM network, you can update the address from 192.168.127.11/24 to 192.168.27.11/24. Similarly, for the home network, if you are not using the 192.168.0.0/24 subnet, you should update it to match your current LAN IP addressing scheme. It's worth acknowledging that sometimes, embracing a straightforward and uncomplicated approach yields the best results!

12.1 Configuring EIGRP Using Ansible

EIGRP (Enhanced Interior Gateway Routing Protocol) is a powerful routing protocol developed by Cisco, commonly taught to students during CCNA certification studies. It is often categorized as an advanced distance vector or hybrid routing protocol, incorporating the strengths of both distance vector and link-state protocols. Notably, EIGRP utilizes the Diffusing Update Algorithm (DUAL), enhancing routing efficiency and stability. Compared to RIP (Routing Information Protocol), EIGRP surpasses it by offering advanced features and capabilities. One significant advantage is its support for unequal cost load balancing, setting it apart from protocols like RIP or OSPF (Open Shortest Path First). This means that EIGRP can optimize network links by simultaneously utilizing multiple paths with varying metric values, effectively utilizing backup router bandwidth when needed. Unlike OSPF, EIGRP does not employ a specific protocol number in the IP header, such as OSPF's protocol number 89. Instead, EIGRP uses its proprietary encapsulation method and does not rely on a predefined protocol number assignment. It's important to recognize that EIGRP is a proprietary routing protocol exclusive to Cisco devices and is not an industry standard. Consequently, compatibility with non-Cisco routers and networking equipment may be limited. However, due to its robustness and advanced capabilities, EIGRP remains a popular choice in Cisco-centric network environments, serving as a valuable tool for network administrators. While a network designer selects a routing protocol, this selection is entirely dependent on the specific requirements of the company. While there is much more to learn about EIGRP, our focus in this context is on Ansible Network Automation, so we won't delve into further details about EIGRP.

Let's go through the steps to set up, configure, write, and execute Ansible playbooks together. Specifically for this EIGRP lab, we will provide detailed, step-by-step instructions to help you get started. In OSPF and switch configuration labs, we will first present the network topology and then provide the corresponding instructions. Let's dive in and explore EIGRP configuration with Ansible playbooks.

Step 1: To kick-start the process, open GNS3 and wait for the GNS3 VM to power on in VMware Workstation. Allow a few minutes for the process to complete. Create a new project with a name that holds personal significance, or if you prefer to follow the book, name your project "ch12.1_lab1_eigrp", as exemplified in Figure 12-1. A meaningful name is needed for easier identification of your lab for future reference.

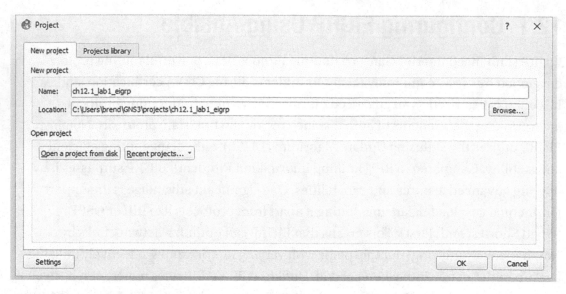

Figure 12-1. *Creating a GNS3 project for an EIGRP lab*

Step 2: Before you start, take a moment to thoroughly examine the provided lab topology, Figure 12-2. Pay close attention to the IP addressing scheme depicted in the diagram, recalling the concepts and steps outlined in the previous chapter that guided you in setting up the lab environment. It is crucial to accurately configure this topology on the GNS3 topology canvas and initialize the devices before proceeding to write your Ansible playbook.

In this EIGRP configuration lab, you will work with three interconnected routers. These routers are linked via their GigabitEthernet interfaces. It's important to note that the GigabitEthernet 0/0 (Gi0/0) interfaces on each router will connect to the 192.168.127.0/24 network, serving as the out-of-band management subnet. This subnet facilitates communication between the Ansible control node and the networking devices for control and management purposes. Throughout this book, we will utilize this same management network configuration to manage our target devices whenever possible. The remaining GigabitEthernet ports on the routers are interconnected following a precise IP addressing scheme, as illustrated in Figure 12-2.

Take approximately ten minutes to thoroughly examine the following topology, refreshing your memory about the setup process outlined in Chapter 11. By recalling the configuration steps performed to establish the lab environment, you will ensure a seamless transition from the topology to GNS3, or vice versa if you prefer to set up this lab in reverse.

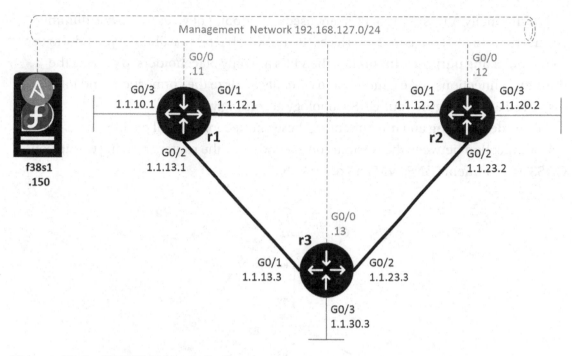

Figure 12-2. EIGRP lab topology

Lab 1: EIGRP Lab Topology

Step 3: Now, head over to GNS3 and drag and drop, and then arrange the devices on the blank canvas, replicating the lab topology. It's crucial to refer to the previous chapter for guidance and instructions on how to configure the devices accurately. As mentioned before, Chapter 11 holds the key to all the labs in this book. By reviewing and implementing the knowledge gained from Chapter 11, you'll be ready to proceed with confidence and successfully prepare the foundation for writing your Ansible playbook.

To enable communication between the Ansible control node (f38s1, 192.168.127.150) and the three routers, we need to establish a connection through the NAT1 cloud. This cloud resides on the host PC/laptop and is connected to the unmanaged Switch1 within the GNS3 VM. This setup enables seamless communication between the Linux virtual machines and any routers and switches present in the GNS3 topology. The highlighted rectangle in Figure 12-3 represents the replicated network topology depicted in Figure 12-2.

Additionally, VPCs (Virtual PCs) are used as endpoint devices to provide dummy connectivity to the configured interfaces. In the switch lab, we will show you how to use VPCs for testing purposes. In this lab, the VPCs are only placeholders to provide the dummy connections. Take a moment to carefully analyze the connections and interfaces displayed and configure your GNS3 topology accordingly.

By understanding and implementing these connections, you'll enable communication between the Ansible control node and the routers running within your GNS3 environment (GNS3 VM and other VMs).

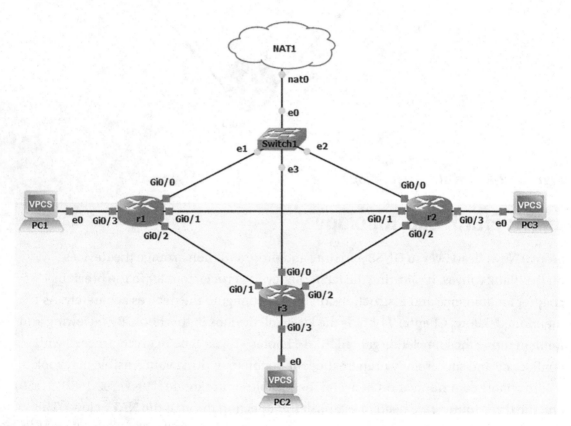

Figure 12-3.   *EIGRP GNS3 topology*

Lab 1: GNS3 Device Connections

Step 4: In GNS3, power on all devices, allowing them enough time to undergo the Power-On Self-Test (POST) processes. It's important to ensure that your routers have successfully loaded the IOS-XE image and become stable before proceeding. Once the devices have completed the boot process and are ready, proceed by opening the terminal consoles. Simply double-click on the icons representing routers r1, r2, and r3 to access their command-line interface (CLI). Opening these consoles will grant you the necessary access to execute commands and interact with the routers effectively.

Step 5: To configure the routers, start with r1 and reference the provided configuration. You can utilize the same information when configuring r2 and r3, except for hostnames and IP addresses for the GigabitEthernet 0/0 interface on each router. This configuration aligns with the setup used during the testing of our GNS3 lab environment build. By implementing this configuration, you will establish the crucial connectivity required between the Ansible Machine and the routers, facilitating control and management functionalities.

```
                                    R1

Router#conf t
Router(config)#hostname r1
r1(config)#ip domain name ansnetauto.net
r1(config)#ip name-server 192.168.127.2
r1(config)#username jdoe privilege 15 secret 5uper5cret9assw0rd
r1(config)#no ip http server
r1(config)#no ip http secure-server
r1(config)#ip route 0.0.0.0 0.0.0.0 192.168.127.2
r1(config)#line vty 0 15
r1(config-line)#login local
r1(config-line)#transport input ssh
r1(config-line)#logging synchronous
r1(config-line)#exit
r1(config)#interface GigabitEthernet0/0
r1(config-if)#ip address 192.168.127.11 255.255.255.0
r1(config-if)#no shut
r1(config-if)#exit
r1(config)#crypto key generate rsa
The name for the keys will be: r1.ansnetauto.net
Choose the size of the key modulus in the range of 360 to 4096 for your
    General Purpose Keys. Choosing a key modulus greater than 512 may take
    a few minutes.
```

```
How many bits in the modulus [512]: 1024
% Generating 1024 bit RSA keys, keys will be non-exportable...
[OK] (elapsed time was 2 seconds)

r1(config)#ip ssh time-out 60
r1(config)#ip ssh authentication-retries 2
r1(config)#exit
r1#copy running-config startup-config
```

Referring to the aforementioned instructions, proceed with the configuration of r2. The only differences between the configurations of r1 and r2 are the hostname and the last digit of the IP address. Ensure that the hostname and IP address are correctly configured, maintaining consistency with the naming and IP addressing scheme. **A well-defined host naming convention and a consistent IP addressing scheme are always beneficial as they ensure everyone is on the same page. This becomes even more crucial in a production environment where clear communication and uniformity are paramount.**

```
Router#conf t
Router(config)#hostname r2
[...omitted for brevity]
r2(config)#interface GigabitEthernet0/0
r2(config-if)#ip address 192.168.127.12 255.255.255.0
[...omitted for brevity]
```

Similarly, configure r3 following the same guidelines as before. Make sure to adjust the hostname to reflect r3 and modify the IP address accordingly, considering the established addressing scheme.

```
Router#conf t
Router(config)#hostname r3
[...omitted for brevity]
r3(config)#interface GigabitEthernet0/0
r3(config-if)#ip address 192.168.127.13 255.255.255.0
[...omitted for brevity]
```

If you want to save time, you can use the initialization file.

Tip

Make your router initialization easy.

To save time, you have the option to download the ch12.1_r1_r2_r3_Initialization. txt file from the authors' GitHub site. By doing so, you can simply perform a cut-and-paste operation to complete the configuration in one go:

https://github.com/ansnetauto/appress_ansnetauto

Step 6: Proceed to the Ansible control node, f38s1 (192.168.127.150). Here, you need to create new ansible.cfg and inventory files. While you can work from any directory, for the sake of simplicity, we will create a new directory called ch12 under /home/jdoe/ repo1. Within this directory, you will further create subdirectories for each lab. For instance, for this lab, you will create the directory /home/jdoe/repo1/ch12/1_eigrp. This directory structure will aid in organizing your Ansible-related files and ensure a systematic approach throughout the book.

ANSIBLE.CFG

```
[defaults]
inventory=inventory
host_key_checking=False
nocows = 1
```

INVENTORY

```
ansible_network_os=ios
ansible_user=jdoe
ansible_password=5uper5cret9assw0rd
ansible_connection=network_cli

[router_type1]
r1 ansible_host=192.168.127.11
r2 ansible_host=192.168.127.12
r3 ansible_host=192.168.127.13
```

Step 7: In this router configuration lab, we will use one file per each router's configuration. In your working directory, create individual configuration files for each router (r1.yml, r2.yml, r3.yml) with the following structure. If you are configuring additional routers of the same type, you can replicate this process by creating more router configuration variable files and saving them accordingly. Consider the scenario where you are involved in a new router deployment or refresh project, tasked with configuring 50 routers of the same model and type. In such cases, Ansible configuration management becomes even more beneficial, providing efficient and streamlined management for you and your company. You no longer have to SSH into each device to configure all 50 routers; instead Ansible serves as the centralized configuration manager.

```
                              R1.YML

---
interface1:
  description: "To r2"
  ip_address: "1.1.12.1"
  subnet_mask: "255.255.255.0"

interface2:
  description: "To r3 "
  ip_address: "1.1.13.1"
  subnet_mask: "255.255.255.0"

interface3:
  description: "To r1 local"
  ip_address: "1.1.10.1"
  subnet_mask: "255.255.255.0"
```

```
                              R2.YML

---
interface1:
  description: "To r1"
  ip_address: "1.1.12.2"
  subnet_mask: "255.255.255.0"
```

```
interface2:
  description: "To r3 "
  ip_address: "1.1.23.2"
  subnet_mask: "255.255.255.0"

interface3:
  description: "To r2 local"
  ip_address: "1.1.20.2"
  subnet_mask: "255.255.255.0"
```

R3.YML

```
---
interface1:
  description: "To r1"
  ip_address: "1.1.13.3"
  subnet_mask: "255.255.255.0"

interface2:
  description: "To r2 "
  ip_address: "1.1.23.3"
  subnet_mask: "255.255.255.0"

interface3:
  description: "To r3 local"
  ip_address: "1.1.30.3"
  subnet_mask: "255.255.255.0"
```

Step 8: Now, let the drum rolls commence as we present our primary Cisco IOS-XE router interface configuration Ansible playbook. This playbook is designed to configure the interfaces (GigabitEthernet0/1, GigabitEthernet0/2, GigabitEthernet0/3) of three Cisco IOS-XE routers (r1, r2, r3) by reading router-specific configuration files. If you are configuring different interfaces, feel free to modify the playbook accordingly to meet your specific requirements.

```
12.1_CONFIG_INT.YML
```

```yaml
---
- name: Configure Cisco IOS-XE routers' interfaces
  hosts: router_type1 # group of hosts
  gather_facts: false

  tasks:
    - name: Load config files # Load config variables from each router config
      YAML files
      include_vars: # Assign .yml file to the variable r_config
        file: "{{ inventory_hostname }}.yml" # the inventory_hostname must
        match the router name
        name: r_config

    - name: Configure GigabitEthernet interfaces 0/1-0/3
      cisco.ios.ios_command: # Execute a series of IOS commands to
      target nodes
        commands: # A series of IOS commands to run on target nodes
          - "configure terminal"
          - "interface GigabitEthernet0/1"
          - "description {{ r_config.interface1.description }}" # Insert
            description on Gi0/1
          - "ip address {{ r_config.interface1.ip_address }} {{ r_config.
            interface1.subnet_mask }}" # Insert ip and subnet mask on Gi0/1
          - "no shutdown" # Enable interface Gi0/1
          - "interface GigabitEthernet0/2"
          - "description {{ r_config.interface2.description }}"
          - "ip address {{ r_config.interface2.ip_address }} {{ r_config.
            interface2.subnet_mask }}"
          - "no shutdown"
          - "interface GigabitEthernet0/3"
          - "description {{ r_config.interface3.description }}"
          - "ip address {{ r_config.interface3.ip_address }} {{ r_config.
            interface3.subnet_mask }}"
          - "no shutdown"
          - "end"
```

In the preceding playbook, the "hosts" parameter is defined in our inventory file, which contains the hostnames or IP addresses of the three routers. Also, note that "ansible_connection=network_cli" has been configured under inventory to apply it to all targeted nodes. We completed this task in step 6. Additionally, the "username" and "password" are also defined in the same inventory file, although this approach raises some security concerns. However, rest assured, we will address this concern in the switch lab by implementing the password vault feature we have learned from Chapter 10.

Step 9: Now, let's copy the 11.1_show_clock.yml playbook from Chapter 11, located in the ana_lab directory, and update the "hosts" parameter to "router_type1". We will rename the file to 12.1_show_clock.yml using the command "cp /home/jdoe/repo1/ ana_lab/11.1_show_clock.yml ./12.1_show_clock.yml". As you have become more familiar with Linux commands and many of the Ansible playbook modules by now, we will gradually reduce the need to provide step-by-step instructions or explanations for every line, assuming you are getting accustomed to working with Ansible on Linux OS.

12.1_SHOW_CLOCK.YML

```
---
- name: Cisco show clock example
  hosts: router_type1
  gather_facts: false

  tasks:
    - name: run show clock on the routers
      cisco.ios.ios_command:
        commands: show clock
      register: output

    - name: print output
      ansible.builtin.debug:
        var: output.stdout_lines
```

Step 10: Execute the 12.1_show_clock.yml playbook and verify its successful execution. If the playbook runs without any errors, you can proceed to the next step and run the 12.1_config_int.yml playbook. However, if you encounter an error message during the execution of the show clock playbook, it is essential to troubleshoot the error before moving forward. Ensure that all necessary configurations and dependencies are in place and address any issues or inconsistencies that may have caused the error. If all went well as planned, go to the next step to execute the 12.1_config_int.yml playbook. Executing non-configuration-related and non-impacting playbook such as this to probe for any communication issues or system errors is a good DevOps and production work habit to adopt.

```
[jdoe@f38s1 1_eigrp]$ anp 12.1_show_clock.yml
[...omitted for brevity]
```

Step 11: This is the first of the main playbooks in this lab; execute the 12.1_config_int.yml playbook and carefully observe the output. This playbook was designed to configure the specified interfaces on the routers based on the predefined parameters. As the playbook runs, pay close attention to the displayed output, which will provide valuable information about the execution process and any potential errors or warnings encountered. If you want more feedback from the plays, enable the verbose mode by adding the "-v", up to seven v's. By closely monitoring the output, you can ensure that the interface configurations are applied correctly and troubleshoot any issues that may arise during the execution of the playbook.

```
[jdoe@f38s1 1_eigrp]$ anp 12.1_config_int.yml
[...omitted for brevity]
```

Step 12: If the execution of your interface configuration playbook was successful, proceed to create a playbook that displays the configured interfaces. This playbook will allow you to verify all the interfaces to check the status from a single playbook. We have named this playbook 12.1_show_ip_int_bri.yml. By executing this playbook, you will be able to review the outputs and confirm the status of the interfaces on all three routers, ensuring that they are functioning as expected.

12.1_SHOW_IP_INT_BRI.YML

```
---
- name: Run show ip interface brief
  hosts: router_type1
  gather_facts: false
```

```
tasks:
  - name: Execute show ip interface brief
    cisco.ios.ios_command:
      commands:
        - show ip interface brief
    register: show_output

  - name: Print show ip interface brief output
    ansible.builtin.debug:
      var: show_output.stdout_lines
```

Once again, imagine if you had 100 routers to configure, imagine running the show ip interface brief command manually 100 times. You can add any show commands to this playbook to run and check the different aspects of your routers, and this is all via SSH connection and no agent software needs to be installed on your platform.

If your playbook is executed successfully, you should observe interface information similar to the output provided here:

```
[jdoe@f38s1 1_eigrp]$ anp 12.1_show_ip_int_bri.yml
[...omitted for brevity]
TASK [Print show ip interface brief output] ******************************
ok: [r1] => {
    "show_output.stdout_lines": [
        [
            "Interface          IP-Address      OK? Method Status  Protocol",
            "GigabitEthernet0/0  192.168.127.11  YES NVRAM  up      up       ",
            "GigabitEthernet0/1  1.1.12.1        YES manual up      up       ",
            "GigabitEthernet0/2  1.1.13.1        YES manual up      up       ",
            "GigabitEthernet0/3  1.1.10.1        YES manual up      up       "
[...omitted for brevity]
```

This simple playbook was designed to check the interface status of all three routers. However, if you still have doubts or would like to further validate the results, you can open the GNS3 terminal consoles for each router and manually run the "show ip interface brief" command. This manual verification method has been the preferred method of confirming the status of the interfaces for traditional command-line warriors and ensure that the configuration changes have taken effect as expected. Trust your eyes, but feel free to validate the results through direct examination if desired.

Step 13: Before enabling EIGRP routing, it is crucial to validate the routing tables on the routers. To achieve this, modify the previous playbook and execute the following playbook to check the routing table on the routers. By running the playbook, you will be able to inspect the routing tables and ensure that the expected routes are present or absent. This validation step provides an opportunity to verify the correctness of the routing configurations before enabling the EIGRP routing on our routers.

12.1_SHOW_IP_ROUTE.YML

```
---
- name: Run show ip route
  hosts: router_type1
  gather_facts: false

  tasks:
    - name: Execute show ip route
      cisco.ios.ios_command:
        commands:
          - show ip route
      register: show_output

    - name: Print show ip route output
      ansible.builtin.debug:
        var: show_output.stdout_lines
```

Step 14: Execute the preceding playbook to validate the routing tables on the routers.

```
[jdoe@f38s1 1_eigrp]$ anp 12.1_show_ip_route.yml
[...omitted for brevity]
TASK [Print show ip route output] ****************************************
ok: [r1] => {
    "show_output.stdout_lines": [
```

[...omitted for brevity]
```
          "Gateway of last resort is 192.168.127.2 to network 0.0.0.0",
          "",
          "S*     0.0.0.0/0 [1/0] via 192.168.127.2",
          "       1.0.0.0/8 is variably subnetted, 6 subnets, 2 masks",
          "C        1.1.10.0/24 is directly connected, GigabitEthernet0/3",
          "L        1.1.10.1/32 is directly connected, GigabitEthernet0/3",
          "C        1.1.12.0/24 is directly connected, GigabitEthernet0/1",
          "L        1.1.12.1/32 is directly connected, GigabitEthernet0/1",
          "C        1.1.13.0/24 is directly connected, GigabitEthernet0/2",
          "L        1.1.13.1/32 is directly connected, GigabitEthernet0/2",
```
[...omitted for brevity]

Step 15: At this stage, we have successfully configured all relevant interfaces, and they are in an up/up state. However, if you test connectivity between routers, you will only be able to reach the directly connected interfaces. From the perspective of router r1, this means that it can only communicate with the interfaces 1.1.12.2, 1.1.13.3, and 1.1.10.1. All other interfaces are currently unreachable since we have not yet enabled dynamic routing, such as EIGRP, in our lab environment.

To test the communication between the interfaces of routers r1, r2, and r3 from the perspective of r1, you can use the ICMP (ping) commands provided in the following. Please note that if you perform similar ICMP tests from routers r2 and r3, you can expect to see an identical output pattern. This will allow you to verify the connectivity between the interfaces of the routers and ensure that the necessary communication paths are established.

```
r1#ping 1.1.12.2
r1#ping 1.1.13.3
r1#ping 1.1.30.3
r1#ping 1.1.30.2
r1#ping 1.1.30.3
r1#ping 1.1.23.2
r1#ping 1.1.23.3
```

Let's proceed with enabling EIGRP to establish communication between all routers and other parts of the network.

Step 16: This is the second of the main playbooks in this lab. To simplify the process, we will create a single eigrp_config file that contains the configuration for all three routers. This will make the configuration management more efficient. For demonstration purposes, we will create this configuration playbook using no variables and will not refactor it, so this gives the users the rawness of a draft playbook. Write and execute the main playbook, named 12.1_enable_eigrp.yml (feel free to rename it to something meaningful to you), to enable EIGRP on routers r1, r2, and r3. This playbook will ensure that EIGRP is properly configured and activated on each router, allowing for seamless communication within the network. By executing this playbook, you will enable EIGRP and pave the way for effective routing across your network infrastructure.

12.1_CONFIG_EIGRP.YML

```
---
- name: Enable EIGRP on routers
  hosts: router_type1
gather_facts: false

  tasks:
    - name: Configure EIGRP on r1
      when: inventory_hostname == 'r1'
      cisco.ios.ios_command:
        commands:
          - "conf t"
          - "router eigrp 1"
          - "network 1.1.10.1 0.0.0.0"
          - "network 1.1.12.1 0.0.0.0"
          - "network 1.1.13.1 0.0.0.0"
          - "end"

    - name: Configure EIGRP on r2
      when: inventory_hostname == 'r2'
      cisco.ios.ios_command:
        commands:
          - "conf t"
          - "router eigrp 1"
          - "network 1.1.12.2 0.0.0.0"
```

```
        - "network 1.1.20.2 0.0.0.0"
        - "network 1.1.23.2 0.0.0.0"
        - "end"

    - name: Configure EIGRP on r3
      when: inventory_hostname == 'r3'
      cisco.ios.ios_command:
        commands:
          - "conf t"
          - "router eigrp 1"
          - "network 1.1.13.3 0.0.0.0"
          - "network 1.1.23.3 0.0.0.0"
          - "network 1.1.30.3 0.0.0.0"
          - "end"
```

Notice the use of the "when" module in the playbook to specifically target individual devices. Execute the preceding command, and if your playbook runs as expected without any errors or issues, proceed to the verification step.

```
[jdoe@f38s1 1_eigrp]$ anp 12.1_config_eigrp.yml
[...omitted for brevity]
```

Verification is an essential part of the configuration process to ensure that the desired configuration changes have taken place in the desired service state. By proceeding to the next step, you will be able to confirm whether EIGRP has been enabled correctly on the specified routers and validate the functionality of the network.

Step 17: To verify the changes made to the IP routing table after enabling EIGRP, you can use the previously used playbook, 12.1_show_ip_route.yml. Execute this playbook again and compare the output with the previous routing table information obtained before running the playbook.

By comparing the outputs, you will be able to observe any changes in the routing table entries. Specifically, you should see new routes added or modified routes reflecting the EIGRP routing protocol. This step allows you to confirm that the routing changes have been successfully applied and that the routers are now utilizing EIGRP for dynamic routing within the network.

```
[jdoe@f38s1 1_eigrp]$ anp 12.1_show_ip_route.yml
[...omitted for brevity]
TASK [Print show ip route output] ****************************************
ok: [r1] => {
[...omitted for brevity]
        "L      1.1.13.1/32 is directly connected,
                GigabitEthernet0/2",
        "D      1.1.20.0/24 [90/3072] via 1.1.12.2, 00:02:58,
                GigabitEthernet0/1",
        "D      1.1.23.0/24 [90/3072] via 1.1.13.3, 00:02:58,
                GigabitEthernet0/2",
        "               [90/3072] via 1.1.12.2, 00:02:58,
                    GigabitEthernet0/1",
        "D      1.1.30.0/24 [90/3072] via 1.1.13.3, 00:02:58,
                GigabitEthernet0/2",
        "    192.168.127.0/24 is variably subnetted, 2 subnets,
                2 masks",
[...omitted for brevity]
```

At this point, we haven't saved the configuration changes made to the routers. If you wish to practice this lab one more time, do not save the running-config, you can simply reload the routers. However, if you would like to save the current configuration and proceed to the next lab, you can manually run the "write memory" or "copy running-config startup-config" command. Alternatively, you can execute the following playbook, which will automatically save the configuration for you before powering down your routers.

Please note that we are not using the "copy running-config startup-config" command in the following playbook to avoid any user confirmation prompts. Instead, we are using the "write memory" command to go around the prompt problem. If you know the exact prompt and responses you want to give, you could use the "copy running-config startup-config" command.

12.1_SAVE_CONFIG.YML

```
---
- name: Copy running-config to startup-config
  hosts: router_type1
  gather_facts: false
  tasks:
    - name: Copy running-config to startup-config
      cisco.ios.ios_command:
        commands:
          - "write memory"
```

Congratulations on successfully completing the EIGRP configuration Ansible lab! By working through this lab, you have acquired valuable hands-on experience in configuring Cisco routers using Ansible and implementing EIGRP routing within a network. Your meticulous step-by-step approach has ensured that you started off on the right foot and gained a solid understanding of the concepts involved.

Now, let's transition to the OSPF lab. This lab will be relatively quick and straightforward since the overall process is similar to what you have just learned. However, please note that the lab will feature a different topology, providing you with a fresh challenge and an opportunity to expand your knowledge. By continuing with the OSPF lab, you will further enhance your skills in network configuration and Ansible playbook development. So let's dive right in and explore the power of OSPF dynamic routing using Ansible.

Tip

Looking for ansible-core cisco collections?

If you have followed along the book, your Ansible control node already has most of the required collections as cisco.iso collection gets installed as part of the ansible package in ansible-core. To check the installed collection list, you can run the "ansible-galaxy collection list" command as shown here:

```
[jdoe@f38s1 ~]$ ansible -version
ansible [core 2.14.4]
[...omitted for brevity]
[jdoe@f38s1 ~]$ ansible-galaxy collection list
# /usr/lib/python3.11/site-packages/ansible_collections
Collection                   Version
---------------------------- -------
[...omitted for brevity - only cisco collections shown]
cisco.aci                    2.4.0
cascaras                     4.0.0
cisco.dnac                   6.6.4
cisco.intersight             1.0.24
cisco.ios                    4.4.0
cisco.iosxr                  4.1.0
cisco.ise                    2.5.12
cisco.meraki                 2.15.1
cisco.mso                    2.2.1
cisco.nso                    1.0.3
cisco.nxos                   4.1.0
cisco.ucs                    1.8.0
[...omitted for brevity - only cisco collections shown]
```

Collection Index/Collections in the Cisco Namespace/Cisco.Ios

Source: https://docs.ansible.com/ansible/latest/collections/
cisco/ios/index.html#plugins-in-cisco-ios

12.2 Configuring OSPF Using Ansible

OSPF (Open Shortest Path First) is a link-state routing protocol. It advertises necessary information to determine the overall network configuration of other routers. Unlike distance vector routing protocols, OSPF does not support split horizon or automatic summarization. The most commonly used OSPF version is OSPFv2, specified in RFC 2328. OSPF uses protocol number 89 in IP packets to transmit routing information. It is a standard protocol widely supported by most vendors, making it the most used Interior

Gateway Protocol (IGP). It is supported by leading vendors including Cisco, Juniper, Arista Networks, Extreme Networks, and Huawei. This widespread support ensures interoperability and seamless integration in multi-vendor network environments. It's important to note that OSPF is a standard protocol, while specific implementations and features may vary among vendors. OSPF operates using areas, allowing for stable operation even in large-scale networks. By dividing the network into multiple areas, such as a backbone area and several branch areas, OSPF prevents network changes occurring in a specific area from being propagated to other areas through appropriate settings. This ensures the stability and scalability of the network. For example, OSPF routers exchange Link State Advertisements (LSAs) to share information about their directly connected networks, such as network topology, link costs, and available bandwidth. This enables routers to build a complete map of the network and calculate the shortest paths to reach different destinations. Compared to distance vector routing protocols like RIP and IGRP, OSPF offers advantages such as fast convergence, reduced routing loops, scalability, support for Variable Length Subnet Masks (VLSM), and hierarchical design.

Although OSPF offers a wealth of additional interesting topics to explore and is usually discussed over a couple of chapters in traditional networking books, our current focus within the context of Ansible Network Automation does not involve delving into further details about OSPF. So let's begin our lab by reviewing the lab topology and GNS3 device connections first.

Lab 2: OSPF Lab Topology

The OSPF lab topology presented in Figure 12-4 and the Ansible Control Machine, f38s1, have access to all four routers through the management network. We have used a GNS3's built-in unmanaged layer 2 switch in the middle to connect r1, r2, and r3, so you have to configure the devices according to the diagrams shown in GNS3 topology canvas. The OSPF areas have been specified in two separate ovals to give you reference. All IP addresses are as shown in the diagram. The subnets 1.1.10.0/24 and 1.1.40.0/24 represent the local networks for routers r1 and r4, respectively.

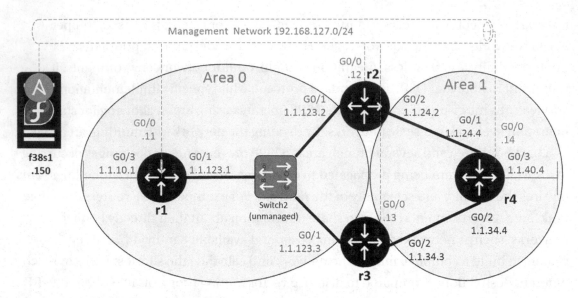

Figure 12-4. *OSPF lab topology*

In GNS3, you would configure the preceding OSPF topology as shown in Figure 12-5. Drag and drop the devices, make the connections according to the figure, and power on all devices to begin the configuration processes. The only caveat to be mindful of is that while all devices are running on the GNS3 VM, the NAT1 cloud must be configured to run on your host PC. The highlighted rectangle represents our OSPF testing topology, and the connection to NAT1 connects the network to 192.168.127.0/24; hence, f38s1 can control the routers while running on VMware Workstation. Note that the initial management IP configuration will have to be completed manually in step 2.

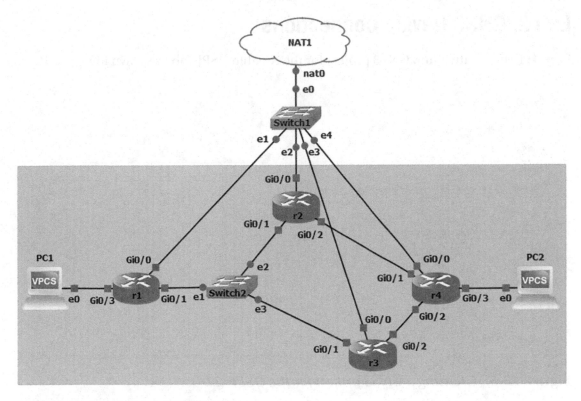

Figure 12-5. *GNS3 OSPF topology*

Lab 2: GNS3 Device Connections

Step 1: Let's create a new GNS3 project for the Ansible OSPF lab as shown in Figure 12-6.

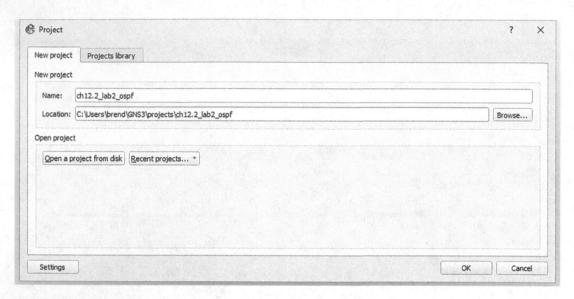

Figure 12-6. *Creating a GNS3 project for the OSPF lab*

Step 2: To ensure centralized control and management, we need to configure the management interfaces of each device on their GigabitEthernet0/0 (Gi0/0) interfaces. This will allow us to control all four routers (r1, r2, r3, and r4) from the Ansible control node, which has the IP address 192.168.127.150 (f38s1). If you haven't done so already, please download the **Ch12.2_r1_r2_r3_r4_Initialization_configs.txt** file from the authors' GitHub repository. Once downloaded, open the console of each router by double-clicking on their respective icons in GNS3. Then, initialize r1, r2, r3, and r4 using the cut-and-paste method, pasting the configuration from the downloaded file.

You can access the authors' GitHub repository via the following link (GitHub link): https://github.com/ansnetauto/appress_ansnetauto.

Step 3: Before creating the main playbook, let's create a new ICMP playbook that will help you to test the connectivity to each router's management IP addresses from the Ansible Control Machine (local). We will write the playbook to ping routers and save the output to a file. This will allow you to effectively assess the connectivity between the Ansible Control Machine and the management IP addresses of the routers, confirming the readiness of the OSPF lab.

```
[jdoe@f38s1 1_eigrp]$ cd ..
[jdoe@f38s1 ch12]$ mkdir 2_ospf && cd 2_ospf
[jdoe@f38s1 2_ospf]$ vi 12.2_icmp_mgt_int.yml
[jdoe@f38s1 2_ospf]$ cat 12.2_icmp_mgt_int.yml
---
- name: Ping hosts and save output  # playbook name
  hosts: localhost  # this machine
  gather_facts: false  # no gathering facts

  tasks:
    - name: Ping hosts  # task name
      ansible.builtin.raw: ping -c 4 192.168.127.{{ item }}  # ping 4 times
      to each IP address
      register: ping_output  # Stores the command output in the 'ping_
      output' variable
      with_sequence: start=11 end=14  # Iterates from 11 to 14, using each
      value as an 'item'
      changed_when: false  # task is not considered 'changed' if executed
      failed_when: false  # task is not considered 'failed' even if runs
      into errors

    - name: Save output to file  # task name
      ansible.builtin.copy:
        content: "{{ ping_output.results | map(attribute='stdout') |
        join('\n') }}"  # Extracts the 'stdout' attribute from each item in
        'ping_output.results' and joins them with newlines
        dest: 12.2_icmp_output.txt  # save the output to current directory
```

Step 4: To test and validate the connectivity between the control node and routers, execute the 12.2_icmp_mgt_int.yml playbook. Alternatively, you can utilize the show clock or ICMP playbooks that were developed in earlier chapters. As an added twist, we are testing communication from the local Linux server to multiple network devices; by modifying your playbooks slightly, you can create a simple yet extremely effective playbook capable of testing connectivity to hundreds or even thousands of devices in a single execution. This is the advantage of transitioning from manual tasks to infrastructure as code (IaC) and adopting DevOps practices. By automating repetitive tasks through scripted automation, we achieve enhanced efficiency and scalability.

This approach facilitates seamless testing and validation of connectivity throughout our network. However, it is important to consider that in certain environments such as DMZ or highly secure corporate networks, ICMP (Internet Control Message Protocol) may be disabled by network administrators for valid reasons.

Execute the playbook to check the management network connectivity.

```
[jdoe@f38s1 2_ospf]$ anp 12.2_icmp_mgt_int.yml
[...omitted for brevity]
```

If your playbook ran successfully, you will find an output file named 12.2_icmp_output.txt in your current working directory. This file will contain the results of the ICMP test conducted on your routers' management interfaces. It provides valuable information regarding the connectivity status leading up to device configuration.

```
[jdoe@f38s1 2_ospf]$ ls
12.2_icmp_mgt_int.yml   12.2_icmp_output.txt
[jdoe@f38s1 2_ospf]$ cat 12.2_icmp_output.txt
PING 192.168.127.11 (192.168.127.11) 56(84) bytes of data.
64 bytes from 192.168.127.11: icmp_seq=1 ttl=255 time=4.07 ms
64 bytes from 192.168.127.11: icmp_seq=2 ttl=255 time=4.41 ms
64 bytes from 192.168.127.11: icmp_seq=3 ttl=255 time=6.78 ms
64 bytes from 192.168.127.11: icmp_seq=4 ttl=255 time=4.70 ms
[..omitted for brevity]
```

Step 5: Having verified the reachability of the management interfaces from the Ansible Control Machine (f38s1), proceed to copy the ansible.cfg and inventory files from the previous lab. Simply add the relevant information for r4 in the inventory file, and you can use both files immediately. This allows you to save time and effort in setting up the Ansible environment for your OSPF lab.

```
[jdoe@f38s1 2_ospf]$ cp ../1_eigrp/ansible.cfg . && cp ../1_eigrp/
inventory .
[jdoe@f38s1 2_ospf]$ vi inventory
jdoe@f38s1 2_ospf]$ cat inventory
[router_type1:vars]
ansible_network_os=ios
ansible_user=jdoe
ansible_password=5uper5cret9assw0rd
```

```
ansible_connection=network_cli

[router_type1]
r1 ansible_host=192.168.127.11
r2 ansible_host=192.168.127.12
r3 ansible_host=192.168.127.13
r4 ansible_host=192.168.127.14
```

Step 6: Now, let's revisit Figure 12-4 to examine the configurations that need to be applied to each router. Take some time to analyze the pattern and devise your strategy. Thoroughly review the following configurations, as they must be implemented on the routers before proceeding to the next step. It is important to approach this task with care and attention to detail. **Analyzing the configuration of a single critical network device is important, but when it comes to automation, analyzing the configuration for multiple critical devices becomes even more crucial. In other words, the power of automation, when entrusted to underprepared and inexperienced individuals, can potentially cause significantly more damage than one can envision.**

Outlined here is the necessary configuration for r1.

R1

```
interface GigabitEthernet0/1
ip address 1.1.123.1 255.255.255.0
no shutdown
!
interface GigabitEthernet0/3
ip address 1.1.10.1 255.255.255.0
no shutdown
```

The subsequent configuration is essential for r2.

R2

```
interface GigabitEthernet0/1
ip address 1.1.123.2 255.255.255.0
no shutdown
!
```

623

```
interface GigabitEthernet0/2
ip address 1.1.24.2 255.255.255.0
no shutdown
```

In the following, you will find the required configuration for r3.

R3

```
interface GigabitEthernet0/1
ip address 1.1.123.3 255.255.255.0
no shutdown
!
interface GigabitEthernet0/2
ip address 1.1.34.3 255.255.255.0
no shutdown
```

Please refer to the following mandatory configuration for r4.

R4

```
interface GigabitEthernet0/1
ip address 1.1.24.4 255.255.255.0
no shutdown
!
interface GigabitEthernet0/2
ip address 1.1.34.4 255.255.255.0
no shutdown
!
interface GigabitEthernet0/3
ip address 1.1.40.4 255.255.255.0
no shutdown
```

Step 7: Starting from step 6, we have reviewed the configuration patterns mentioned earlier and identified the necessary steps to configure the interfaces with the specific information provided. Given that the routers' names correspond to the last digit of the IP addressing scheme, we can leverage this information to our advantage and incorporate it into our playbook. By utilizing the last digit information, we can accurately configure the interfaces as required.

Task 1: Configure the Gi0/1 interfaces of r1, r2, and r3 on the 1.1.123.0/24 subnet.

Task 2: Configure the Gi0/2 interface of r2 on the 1.1.24.0/24 subnet.

Task 3: Configure the Gi0/1 interface of r4 on the 1.1.24.0/24 subnet.

Task 4: Configure the Gi0/2 interfaces of r3 and r4 on the 1.1.34.0/24 subnet.

Task 5: Configure the G0/3 interface of r1 on the 1.1.10.0/24 subnet and the G0/3 interface of r4 on the 1.1.40.0/24 subnet.

Step 8: If we convert the plays from step 7 into a working Ansible playbook, it may look similar to the example provided. However, there are different ways to structure YAML playbooks, and it is ultimately up to the administrator to decide the length and complexity of their playbook. There is no right or wrong answer in terms of playbook length; some playbooks may be more efficient or concise than others, depending on the specific requirements and preferences of the administrator.

12.2_CONFIGURE_INT.YML

```yaml
---
- name: Configure Cisco IOS-XE routers in group router_type1
  hosts: router_type1
  gather_facts: false

  tasks:
    - name: Configure r1, r2, and r3's Gi0/1 interfaces on 1.1.123.0/24
    # Task 1
      cisco.ios.ios_command:
        commands:
          - "configure terminal"
          - "interface GigabitEthernet0/1"
          - "ip address 1.1.123.{{ inventory_hostname[-1] }} 255.255.255.0"
          - "no shutdown"
          - "end"
      when: inventory_hostname in ['r1', 'r2', 'r3']

    - name: Configure r2's Gi0/2 interface on 1.1.24.0/24 # Task 2
      cisco.ios.ios_command:
```

```
        commands:
            - "configure terminal"
            - "interface GigabitEthernet0/2"
            - "ip address 1.1.24.{{ inventory_hostname[-1] }} 255.255.255.0"
            - "no shutdown"
            - "end"
        when: inventory_hostname == 'r2'

    - name: Configure r4's Gi0/1 interface on 1.1.24.0/24 # Task 3
      cisco.ios.ios_command:
        commands:
            - "configure terminal"
            - "interface GigabitEthernet0/1"
            - "ip address 1.1.24.{{ inventory_hostname[-1] }} 255.255.255.0"
            - "no shutdown"
            - "end"
        when: inventory_hostname == 'r4'

    - name: Configure r3 and r4's Gi0/2 interfaces on 1.1.34.0/24 # Task 4
      cisco.ios.ios_command:
        commands:
            - "configure terminal"
            - "interface GigabitEthernet0/2"
            - "ip address 1.1.34.{{ inventory_hostname[-1] }} 255.255.255.0"
            - "no shutdown"
            - "end"
        when: inventory_hostname in ['r3', 'r4']

    - name: Configure r1's G0/3 on 1.1.10.0/24 and r4's G0/3 interfaces on
      1.1.40.0/24 # Task 5
      cisco.ios.ios_command:
        commands:
            - "configure terminal"
            - "interface GigabitEthernet0/3"
            - "ip address 1.1.{{ inventory_hostname[-1] }}0.{{ inventory_
              hostname[-1] }} 255.255.255.0"
            - "no shutdown"
```

```
        - "end"
    when: inventory_hostname in ['r1', 'r4']
```

Did you notice something interesting? As mentioned before, we are using the last digit of the hostname in our playbook by using the expression {{ inventory_hostname[-1] }}. This allows us to dynamically incorporate the last digit as a parameter in the playbook. Additionally, you may have noticed that we are judiciously using the when parameter to control the execution of commands. This ensures that specific commands are only run on the intended target nodes.

Step 9: Once your playbook has been executed successfully, you can proceed to copy the "show ip interface brief" playbook from the previous EIGRP lab and execute it. This will allow you to verify the status of the interfaces and ensure that all the expected interfaces are in the desired "up/up" state.

```
[jdoe@f38s1 2_ospf]$ cp ../1_eigrp/12.1_show_ip_int_bri.yml ./12.2_show_ip_
int_bri.yml
[jdoe@f38s1 2_ospf]$ anp 12.2_show_ip_int_bri.yml
[...omitted for brevity]
ok: [r4] => {
    "show_output.stdout_lines": [
        [
            "Interface         IP-Address      OK? Method   Status Protocol",
            "GigabitEthernet0/0 192.168.127.14  YES NVRAM    up     up         ",
            "GigabitEthernet0/1 1.1.24.4        YES manual   up     up         ",
            "GigabitEthernet0/2 1.1.34.4        YES manual   up     up         ",
            "GigabitEthernet0/3 1.1.40.4        YES manual   up     up         "
        ]
    ]
}
[...omitted for brevity]
```

Step 10: Instead of appending all the OSPF configuration in a single lengthy playbook in the previous playbook, we have chosen to separate this playbook from the interface configuration playbook. The objective is to configure OSPF 1 on all routers, facilitating end-to-end communication between devices. This configuration ensures that r1, for example, can successfully ping r4's local network with IP address 1.1.40.4, and likewise, r4 can ping r1's local network with IP address 1.1.10.1. By setting up OSPF, we establish a dynamic routing protocol that enables efficient and reliable routing within our network using industry standard routers.

Here is our OSPF configuration for r1.

R1 (# TASK 1)

```
router ospf 1
router-id 1.1.1.1
network 1.1.10.1 0.0.0.0 area 0
network 1.1.123.1 0.0.0.0 area 0
```

In the following, you will find the OSPF configuration we have set up for r2.

R2 (# TASK 2)

```
router ospf 1
router-id 2.2.2.2
network 1.1.123.2 0.0.0.0 area 0
network 1.1.24.1 0.0.0.0 area 1
```

Provided here is the OSPF configuration we've established for r3.

R3 (# TASK 3)

```
router ospf 1
router-id 3.3.3.3
network 1.1.123.3 0.0.0.0 area 0
network 1.1.34.3 0.0.0.0 area 1
```

Presented here is the OSPF configuration we have for r4.

```
R4 (# TASK 4)
```

```
router ospf 1
router-id 4.4.4.4
network 1.1.24.4 0.0.0.0 area 1
network 1.1.34.4 0.0.0.0 area 1
network 1.1.40.4 0.0.0.0 area 1
```

Each router has its own unique networks to configure, and we will utilize the router's last digit as a differentiator to ensure uniqueness. To achieve this, we will treat each router as a separate play in our playbook. Consequently, there will be a total of four plays in our playbook, which are outlined in the following.

Step 11: Now, we will proceed to write the main playbook and leverage the fact that the hostnames contain the last digit of the corresponding IP address. By using the expression "{{ inventory_hostname[-1] }}" within our playbook, we can dynamically access and utilize this information. This approach allows us to streamline our configuration process and make it more efficient. The following playbook strategy builds upon the interface configuration playbook and incorporates the use of "when" parameters as well as the hostname's last digit as a variable in our plays.

```
12.2_CONFIGURE_OSPF.YML
```

```
---
- name: Configure OSPF 1 on Cisco IOS-XE routers
  hosts: router_type1
  gather_facts: false

  tasks:
    - name: Configure OSPF on routers # Task 1
      cisco.ios.ios_command:
        commands:
          - "router ospf 1"
          - "router-id {{ inventory_hostname[-1] }}.{{ inventory_hostname[-1]
            }}.{{ inventory_hostname[-1] }}.{{ inventory_hostname[-1] }}"
          - "network 1.1.{{ inventory_hostname[-1] }}0.{{ inventory_
            hostname[-1] }} 0.0.0.0 area 0"
```

```
        - "network 1.1.123.{{ inventory_hostname[-1] }} 0.0.0.0 area 0"
      when: inventory_hostname in ['r1']

  - name: Configure OSPF on routers # Task 2
    cisco.ios.ios_command:
      commands:
        - "router ospf 1"
        - "router-id {{ inventory_hostname[-1] }}.{{ inventory_hostname[-1]
        }}.{{ inventory_hostname[-1] }}.{{ inventory_hostname[-1] }}"
        - "network 1.1.123.{{ inventory_hostname[-1] }} 0.0.0.0 area 0"
        - "network 1.1.24.{{ inventory_hostname[-1] }} 0.0.0.0 area 1"
      when: inventory_hostname in ['r2']

  - name: Configure OSPF on routers # Task 3
    cisco.ios.ios_command:
      commands:
        - "router ospf 1"
        - "router-id {{ inventory_hostname[-1] }}.{{ inventory_hostname[-1]
        }}.{{ inventory_hostname[-1] }}.{{ inventory_hostname[-1] }}"
        - "network 1.1.123.{{ inventory_hostname[-1] }} 0.0.0.0 area 0"
        - "network 1.1.34.{{ inventory_hostname[-1] }} 0.0.0.0 area 1"
      when: inventory_hostname in ['r3']

  - name: Configure OSPF on routers # Task 4
    cisco.ios.ios_command:
      commands:
        - "router ospf 1"
        - "router-id {{ inventory_hostname[-1] }}.{{ inventory_hostname[-1] }}.
        {{ inventory_hostname[-1] }}.{{ inventory_hostname[-1] }}"
        - "network 1.1.24.{{ inventory_hostname[-1] }} 0.0.0.0 area 1"
        - "network 1.1.34.{{ inventory_hostname[-1] }} 0.0.0.0 area 1"
        - "network 1.1.{{ inventory_hostname[-1] }}0.{{ inventory_
        hostname[-1] }} 0.0.0.0 area 1"
      when: inventory_hostname in ['r4']
```

Step 12: Give a couple of minutes for the OSPF neighborship to be formed between the four routers. Then, execute the 12.2_show_ip_route.yml playbook to verify the OSPF routes formed in the routing tables of each router. This playbook will provide valuable information regarding the directly connected connections and dynamically learned routes through OSPF.

```
[jdoe@f38s1 2_ospf]$ cp ../1_eigrp/12.1_show_ip_route.yml ./12.2_show_ip_
route.yml
[jdoe@f38s1 2_ospf]$ anp ./12.2_show_ip_route.yml
[...omitted for brevity]
ok: [r3] => {
[...omitted for brevity]
            "Gateway of last resort is 192.168.127.2 to network 0.0.0.0",
            "",
            "S*    0.0.0.0/0 [1/0] via 192.168.127.2",
            "      1.0.0.0/8 is variably subnetted, 7 subnets, 2 masks",
            "O        1.1.10.0/24 [110/2] via 1.1.123.1, 00:00:27,
            GigabitEthernet0/1",
            "O        1.1.24.0/24 [110/2] via 1.1.34.4, 00:42:00,
            GigabitEthernet0/2",
            "C        1.1.34.0/24 is directly connected,
            GigabitEthernet0/2",
            "L        1.1.34.3/32 is directly connected,
            GigabitEthernet0/2",
            "O        1.1.40.0/24 [110/2] via 1.1.34.4, 00:42:00,
            GigabitEthernet0/2",
            "C        1.1.123.0/24 is directly connected,
            GigabitEthernet0/1",
            "L        1.1.123.3/32 is directly connected,
            GigabitEthernet0/1",
            "      192.168.127.0/24 is variably subnetted, 2 subnets,
            2 masks",
            "C        192.168.127.0/24 is directly connected,
            GigabitEthernet0/0",
            "L        192.168.127.13/32 is directly connected,
            GigabitEthernet0/0"
        ]
    ]
} [...omitted for brevity]
```

Step 13: Finally, perform the ping test between all four routers. While we are only showing the ping test results between r1 and r4, feel free to test the communication between different devices at your convenience.

R1#PING 1.1.40.4

```
Type escape sequence to abort.
Sending 5, 100-byte ICMP Echos to 1.1.40.4, timeout is 2 seconds:
!!!!!
Success rate is 100 percent (5/5), round-trip min/avg/max = 10/15/28 ms
```

R4#PING 1.1.10.1

```
Type escape sequence to abort.
Sending 5, 100-byte ICMP Echos to 1.1.10.1, timeout is 2 seconds:
!!!!!
Success rate is 100 percent (5/5), round-trip min/avg/max = 7/13/24 ms
```

Now that you have completed the Ansible OSPF configuration lab, let's quickly move onto the last lab of this chapter, which involves a simple Switch VLAN and VTP configuration. This lab will provide you with hands-on experience in configuring VLANs on switches using Ansible playbook.

12.3 Switch VLAN Configuration Lab

VLANs (Virtual Local Area Networks) in Cisco IOS and IOS-XE switches are used to logically segment a network into separate virtual LANs. VLANs provide numerous benefits in enterprise networks. They enable traffic isolation by grouping devices based on logical requirements, enhancing security by preventing unauthorized access to sensitive data or systems. VLANs create distinct broadcast domains, reducing the volume of broadcast traffic and improving network performance. Moreover, VLANs improve network efficiency by grouping devices with similar traffic patterns, optimizing communication, and minimizing unnecessary network traffic. VLAN trunking allows VLANs to extend across multiple switches, ensuring VLAN continuity by enabling the transmission of VLAN-tagged packets between switches. Inter-VLAN routing, performed by layer 3 devices like routers or layer 3 switches (a.k.a. srouter), is necessary for devices in different VLANs to communicate with each other by routing traffic between VLANs. Overall, VLANs in enterprise networks provide traffic isolation, control over broadcast domains, improved network performance, VLAN continuity across switches via trunking, and inter-VLAN communication facilitated by routing. In the case of the CML IOS-XE switch images used here, the IP routing feature is enabled by default, and we need to disable it to make them function solely as layer 2 switches. You can verify the IP routing status by executing the "show ip protocols" command.

In this switching lab, we will configure end-to-end VLANs in the network using Ansible playbooks. The goal is to enable communication between PC1 with IP address 1.1.10.3 in VLAN 10 and PC2 with IP address 1.1.20.3 in VLAN 20, with the default gateway being r1. In this topology, r1 acts as the only routing device used to route between two disparate logical local area networks, while all four switches operate at layer 2 and have IP routing disabled. This means that even though PC1 and PC2 are physically connected on the adjacent ports on the same switch, they belong to different logical local area networks due to their respective VLAN assignments.

To get started, let's manually configure the lab settings on the Ansible Control Machine, allowing it to communicate with all devices through the management network 192.168.127.0/24. Then, we can proceed with the switch configurations using Ansible. You will need to use the provided information in VLAN lab topology and GNS3 device connections to complete your configuration tasks. IP addresses and VLAN details have been provided to ensure the successful configuration of end-to-end VLAN in the network, enabling PC1 and PC2 to communicate via r1's G0/3 trunking interface.

First, take a moment to study the VLAN lab topology depicted in Figure 12-7.

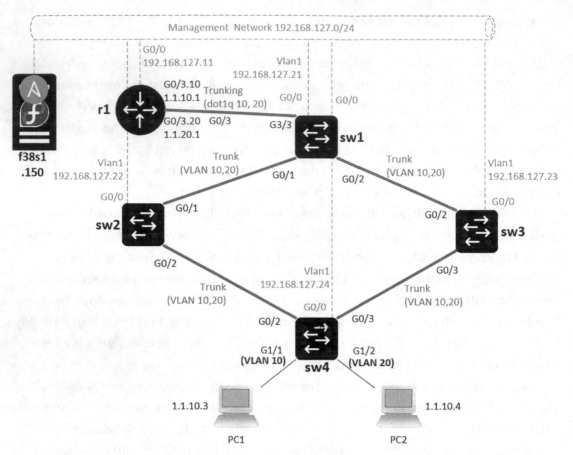

Figure 12-7. VLAN lab topology

Lab 3: VLAN Lab Topology

After visualizing the tasks in your mind, let's review Figure 12-8, GNS3 device connections, and begin constructing the VLAN lab from the ground up. Rest assured, each step will be provided as a guideline, so you just need to focus and follow along attentively.

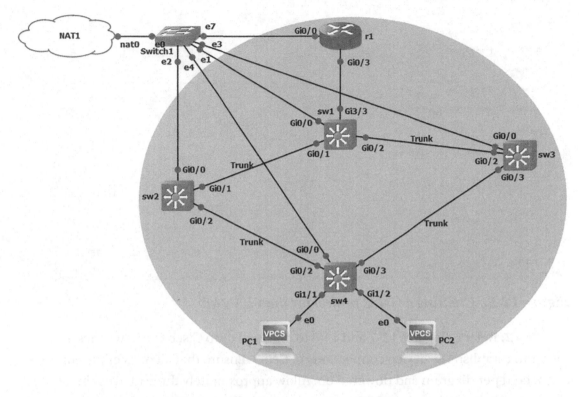

Figure 12-8. *GNS3 VLAN device connections*

Lab 3: GNS3 Device Connections

Refer to the figures as you go through the steps to build the VLAN lab from scratch. Each step will guide you on what needs to be done. Just stay focused and follow along.

Follow these steps to complete the end-to-end VLAN configuration lab:

Step 1: Open GNS3 and wait for the GNS3 VM to power on in VMware Workstation. Allow a moment for the process to complete. Once the VM is up and running, create a new GNS3 project for your switch lab. As shown in Figure 12-9, we have given this project an intuitive name, "ch12.3_lab3_vlan". Give the project a meaningful name that is relevant to you.

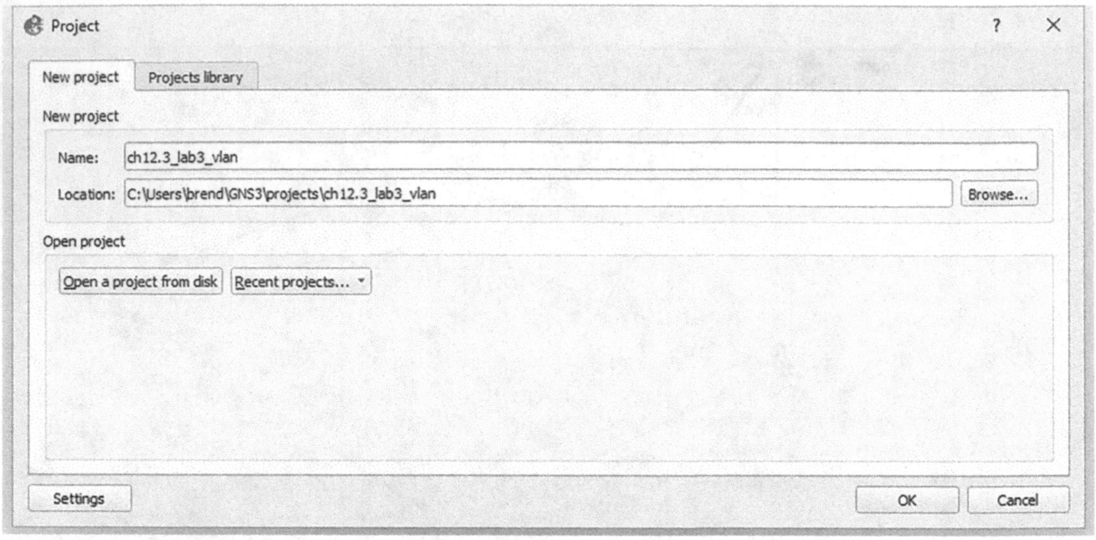

Figure 12-9. *Creating a GNS3 project for the VLAN lab*

Step 2: Refer to Figures 12-7 and 12-8 to drag and drop Cisco CML switches and a router to establish the device connections in GNS3. Ensure that all devices are correctly connected per diagram and powered on. Allow approximately three to five minutes for the devices to complete the POST process and settle down.

Step 3: Next, configure the management interfaces on r1, sw1, sw2, sw3, and sw4 as depicted in Figure 12-7. Assign the IP address 192.168.127.11/24 to r1's G0/0 interface. For the switches, use VLAN 1 as the management interface and assign the following IP addresses: 192.168.127.21 for sw1, 192.168.127.22 for sw2, 192.168.127.23 for sw3, and 192.168.127.24 for sw4. Please note that this task needs to be done manually as it cannot be automated using the Ansible Control Machine.

If you want to speed up this process, locate the file named "**Ch12.3_r1_sw_1-4_ initialization_configs.txt**" and use the cut-and-paste function to complete the device initializations.

R1

```
configure terminal
hostname r1
username jdoe privilege 15 secret 5uper5cret9assw0rd
ip domain-name ansnetauto.net
crypto key generate rsa
```

```
1024
line vty 0 15
login local
transport input ssh
logging synchronous
interface Gi0/0
ip address 192.168.127.11 255.255.255.0
no shutdown
```

SW1

```
enable
configure terminal
hostname sw1
username jdoe privilege 15 secret 5uper5cret9assw0rd
no ip routing #disable ip routing
ip domain-name ansnetauto.net
crypto key generate rsa
1024
line vty 0 15
login local
transport input ssh
logging synchronous
interface vlan 1
ip address 192.168.127.21 255.255.255.0
no shutdown
```

SW2

```
enable
configure terminal
hostname sw2
[...omitted for brevity, refer to sw1]
interface vlan 1
ip address 192.168.127.22 255.255.255.0
no shutdown
```

SW3

```
enable
configure terminal
hostname sw3
[...omitted for brevity, refer to sw1]
interface vlan 1
ip address 192.168.127.23 255.255.255.0
no shutdown
```

SW4

```
enable
configure terminal
hostname sw4
[...omitted for brevity, refer to sw1]
interface vlan 1
ip address 192.168.127.24 255.255.255.0
no shutdown
```

Step 4: Proceed to your Ansible Control Machine, f38s1, to verify the connection to each device simultaneously using the 12.2_icmp_mgt_int.yml playbook. Execute the playbook from your local machine. Make a copy of the playbook and rename it as 12.3_icmp_mgt_int.yml. Then, make slight modifications to the playbook by incorporating a loop since the IP address of the router does not follow the same pattern as the rest of the switches' IPs.

```
[jdoe@f38s1 ch12]$ mkdir 3_vlan && cd 3_vlan
[jdoe@f38s1 3_vlan]$ cp ../2_ospf/12.2_icmp_mgt_int.yml ./12.3_icmp_
mgt_int.yml
[jdoe@f38s1 3_vlan]$ vi 12.3_icmp_mgt_int.yml
[jdoe@f38s1 3_vlan]$ cat 12.3_icmp_mgt_int.yml
---
- name: Ping r1, sw1-sw4 and save output to a file
  hosts: localhost
  gather_facts: false
```

```
tasks:
  - name: Ping hosts
    ansible.builtin.raw: ping -c 4 {{ item }}
    register: ping_output
    loop:
      - 192.168.127.11
      - 192.168.127.21
      - 192.168.127.22
      - 192.168.127.23
      - 192.168.127.24
    failed_when: false
  - name: Save output to file
    ansible.builtin.copy:
      content: "{{ ping_output.results | map(attribute='stdout') |
      join('\n') }}"
      dest: 12.3_icmp_output.txt
```

You should not need any additional files to run this playbook as the playbook is ran by the f38s1. Execute the modified ping test playbook. Please note that if you don't have the ansible.cfg file in the directory, and if you have cowsay installed, you might see the cows appearing during the playbook execution. The default ansible.cfg file will be used, which is located under /etc/ansible/.

[jdoe@f38s1 3_vlan]$ **anp 12.3_icmp_mgt_int.yml**
[*...omitted for brevity*]

If your playbook is executed successfully, you will find a new output file in your working directory. Open this file to validate the communication between your Ansible control node and all network devices.

[jdoe@f38s1 3_vlan]$ **cat 12.3_icmp_output.txt**
PING 192.168.127.11 (192.168.127.11) 56(84) bytes of data.
64 bytes from 192.168.127.11: icmp_seq=1 ttl=255 time=2.82 ms
64 bytes from 192.168.127.11: icmp_seq=2 ttl=255 time=2.76 ms
64 bytes from 192.168.127.11: icmp_seq=3 ttl=255 time=3.77 ms
64 bytes from 192.168.127.11: icmp_seq=4 ttl=255 time=3.39 ms

```
--- 192.168.127.11 ping statistics ---
4 packets transmitted, 4 received, 0% packet loss, time 3004ms
rtt min/avg/max/mdev = 2.759/3.183/3.767/0.416 ms
```
[...omitted for brevity]

Step 5: Copy the ansible.cfg and inventory files from the previous lab and make slight modifications to the inventory file.

```
[jdoe@f38s1 3_vlan]$ cp ../2_ospf/ansible.cfg ./ && cp ../2_ospf/
inventory ./
[jdoe@f38s1 3_vlan]$ ls
12.3_icmp_mgt_int.yml  12.3_icmp_output.txt  ansible.cfg  inventory
```

In the following inventory file, both devices are using the same IOS-XE software, and the username and password used are the same as the router_type1 devices. The switches have been placed in their group named switch_type1, and then the router and switch groups are grouped under the ios_xe_devices group as child groups. This grouping is done to simplify the playbooks and is an important concept to master.

```
[jdoe@f38s1 3_vlan]$ vi inventory
[jdoe@f38s1 3_vlan]$ cat inventory
[ios_xe_devices:vars]
ansible_network_os=ios
ansible_user=jdoe # to be password vaulted in step 6
ansible_password=5uper5cret9assw0rd # to be password vaulted in step 6
ansible_connection=network_cli

[router_type1]
r1 ansible_host=192.168.127.11

[switch_type1]
sw1 ansible_host=192.168.127.21
sw2 ansible_host=192.168.127.22
sw3 ansible_host=192.168.127.23
sw4 ansible_host=192.168.127.24

[ios_xe_devices:children]
router_type1
switch_type1
```

In the next step, we will enhance the security of our inventory file by removing the username and password information and using a password vault instead.

To accomplish this, we'll utilize the good old show clock playbook that we used in Lab 12.1 to validate the SSH connections to all five devices before proceeding further.

```
[jdoe@f38s1 3_vlan]$ cp ../1_eigrp/12.1_show_clock.yml ./12.3_show_clock.yml
[jdoe@f38s1 3_vlan]$ cat 12.3_show_clock.yml
---

- name: Cisco show clock example
  hosts: router_type1,switch_type1 # note, you can replace this with ios_
xe_devices
  gather_facts: false

  tasks:
    - name: run show clock on the routers
      cisco.ios.ios_command:
        commands: show clock
      register: output

    - name: print output
      ansible.builtin.debug:
        var: output.stdout_lines
```

Run the show clock playbook to validate the login credentials and ensure that the SSH connections are established successfully. The playbook must run without any SSH connection errors, such as "ssh connection failed: Failed to authenticate public key". If the operation is successful, it means that your Ansible playbook now has full control over these devices through SSH connections.

```
[jdoe@f38s1 3_vlan]$ anp 12.3_show_clock.yml
[...omitted for brevity]
```

Step 6: To enhance security and adhere to industry best practices, it is important to remove the embedded username and password from the inventory file. This eliminates the risk of exposing sensitive information. In Chapter 10, we learned about the password vault and its importance. If you need a refresher, please revisit the section on the password vault.

In this step, we will use the encrypted vars_files method, which is the easiest approach to secure our credentials.

```
[jdoe@f38s1 3_vlan]$ vi inventory
[jdoe@f38s1 3_vlan]$ cat inventory
[ios_xe_devices:vars]
ansible_network_os=ios
ansible_connection=network_cli #removed the ansible_user and ansible_
password from here

[router_type1]
r1 ansible_host=192.168.127.11

[switch_type1]
sw1 ansible_host=192.168.127.21
sw2 ansible_host=192.168.127.22
sw3 ansible_host=192.168.127.23
sw4 ansible_host=192.168.127.24

[ios_xe_devices:children]
router_type1
switch_type1
```

Next, we will create an encrypted vars.yml file using the ansible-vault create command. This will ensure that the information we enter in this file is encrypted and protected. In this file, we want to safeguard our username and password. It is important to note that the data format for the user should be a list. Pay close attention to this detail, as it is crucial for the successful execution of the playbook.

```
[jdoe@f38s1 3_vlan]$ ansible-vault create vars.yml
New Vault password: ***************
Confirm New Vault password: ***************
---
ansible_user: jdoe # Note, a colon is used to make this into a dictionary
ansible_password: 5uper5cret9assw0rd # Note, a colon is used to make this
into a dictionary
```

Now, for testing purposes, let's add the vars_files module to our playbook and specify the encrypted vars.yml file. This will allow us to access the encrypted variables during playbook execution.

```
[jdoe@f38s1 3_vlan]$ vi 12.3_show_clock.yml
[jdoe@f38s1 3_vlan]$ cat 12.3_show_clock.yml
---

- name: Cisco show clock example
  hosts: router_type1,switch_type1
  gather_facts: false

  vars_files: # Don't forget to add these two lines to your testing
  playbook
    - vars.yml

  tasks:
    - name: run show clock on the routers
      cisco.ios.ios_command:
        commands: show clock
      register: output

    - name: print output
      ansible.builtin.debug:
        var: output.stdout_lines
```

To execute the test playbook with the encrypted vars.yml file, use the --ask-vault-pass option to unlock the file during playbook execution. If your playbook runs successfully without any errors, it's time to write and test the playbooks for automating the configuration of VLAN-related tasks on multiple switches.

```
[jdoe@f38s1 3_vlan]$ anp 12.3_show_clock.yml --ask-vault-pass
Vault password: ***************
[...omitted for brevity]
```

If the preceding playbook executed successfully and you have confirmed all the system times on all devices, you are ready to move to the next step.

Step 7: Now, let's enable the router, r1's Gi0/3 interface, and configure it as a trunking interface, as used in the router-on-a-stick configuration. To achieve this, we need to create sub-interfaces on Gi0/3 and assign IP addresses to each sub-interface. If you prefer to configure a single device using the same router configuration playbook used in previous labs, you can do so. However, to save time, we will configure it manually in this lab.

R1

```
r1#conf t
r1(config)#int Gi0/3
r1(config-if)#no shutdown
r1(config-subif)#encapsulation dot1Q 10
r1(config-subif)#ip address 1.1.10.1 255.255.255.0
r1(config-subif)#interface g0/3.20
r1(config-subif)#encapsulation dot1Q 20
r1(config-subif)#ip address 1.1.20.1 255.255.255.0
```

Step 8: Now, let's configure the two VPCs in GNS3, which will be used as our endpoint testing devices. While using two routers to replace two VPCs is an option, it requires a significant amount of processing power, so you can use VPCs. It is recommended that you familiarize yourself with using VPCs on GNS3 to optimize your lab experience with this tool.

For this lab, we will configure PC1 and PC2 as follows:

- Assign the IP address 1.1.10.5/24 to PC1's Ethernet 0 interface, with the default gateway set to 1.1.10.1 (r1's dot1Q 10 IP address).

- Assign the IP address 1.1.20.8/24 to PC2's Ethernet 0 interface, with the default gateway set to 1.1.20.1 (r1's dot1Q 20 IP address).

PC1

```
PC1> ip 1.1.10.5 255.255.255.0 1.1.10.1
Checking for duplicate address...
PC1 : 1.1.10.5 255.255.255.0 gateway 1.1.10.1

PC1> show ip
```

```
NAME        : PC1[1]
IP/MASK     : 1.1.10.5/24
GATEWAY     : 1.1.10.1
DNS         :
MAC         : 00:50:79:66:68:00
LPORT       : 20129
RHOST:PORT  : 127.0.0.1:20130
MTU         : 1500
```

Now, out of curiosity, let's configure PC2 with the IP address 1.1.10.8 and perform a quick connectivity test to 1.1.10.5. If the connectivity is successful, we can proceed to assign PC2 the actual IP address of 1.1.20.8. However, it's important to note that once PC2 is assigned to the 1.1.20.0/24 subnet, PC1 and PC2 will no longer be able to communicate with each other. This is because they will be on different subnets; even though they are connected to adjacent ports on the same switch, they are connected to the different logical connections, which requires L3 routing devices such as a router or L3 switch.

PC2

```
PC2> ip 1.1.10.8 255.255.255.0 1.1.10.1
Checking for duplicate address...
PC2 : 1.1.10.8 255.255.255.0 gateway 1.1.10.1

PC2> ping 1.1.10.5

84 bytes from 1.1.10.5 icmp_seq=1 ttl=64 time=11.422 ms
84 bytes from 1.1.10.5 icmp_seq=2 ttl=64 time=16.059 ms
84 bytes from 1.1.10.5 icmp_seq=3 ttl=64 time=12.582 ms
84 bytes from 1.1.10.5 icmp_seq=4 ttl=64 time=15.869 ms
84 bytes from 1.1.10.5 icmp_seq=5 ttl=64 time=49.163 ms

PC2> ip 1.1.20.8 255.255.255.0 1.1.20.1
Checking for duplicate address...
PC2 : 1.1.20.8 255.255.255.0 gateway 1.1.20.1

PC2> ping 1.1.10.5

host (1.1.20.1) not reachable
```

```
PC2> show ip

NAME        : PC2[1]
IP/MASK     : 1.1.20.8/24
GATEWAY     : 1.1.20.1
DNS         :
MAC         : 00:50:79:66:68:01
LPORT       : 20163
RHOST:PORT  : 127.0.0.1:20164
MTU         : 1500
```

Now that the setup is complete, we can use the Ansible playbook to configure the four switches according to the provided network topology.

To enable communication between PC1 and PC2 via end-to-end VLAN implementation and the router-on-a-stick using r1's Gi0/3 interface, we need to perform the following tasks:

- Configure trunk ports on sw1, sw2, sw3, and sw4.

- Configure the VTP domain as a best practice.

- Create VLAN 10 and VLAN 20 on sw1 and assign VLAN 10 to r4's interface Gi1/1 and VLAN 20 to r4's interface Gi1/2.

Step 9: For trunk port configuration on all four switches, you will need to configure the following interfaces to allow traffic to travel through VLAN 10 and VLAN 20. Pay close attention to the port numbers and try to determine how many plays are needed to configure these trunk ports. Finding the common denominator is key to writing a precise Ansible playbook. Also, make sure to include interface Gi3/3 in the configuration for sw1.

SW1

```
interface range g0/1, g0/2, g3/3
switchport trunk encapsulation dot1q
switchport mode trunk
switchport trunk allowed vlan 10,20
```

```
                                 SW2

interface range g0/1, g0/2
switchport trunk encapsulation dot1q
switchport mode trunk
switchport trunk allowed vlan 10,20
```

```
                                 SW3

interface range g0/2, g0/3
switchport trunk encapsulation dot1q
switchport mode trunk
switchport trunk allowed vlan 10,20
```

```
                                 SW4

interface range g0/2, g0/3
switchport trunk encapsulation dot1q
switchport mode trunk
switchport trunk allowed vlan 10,20
```

Since the trunks between sw1 and sw2 are connected through Gi0/1 and Gi0/2, they can be configured in a single play. Similarly, for sw3 and sw4, their trunks are connected using Gi0/2 and Gi0/3, so they can also be configured in a single play. However, we need to configure sw1's Gi3/3, which connects to r1's trunking ports, separately as the port naming is unique to this port only. To target specific switches based on their device names, we can make use of the "when" module.

SW1, SW2, SW3 AND SW4 (TASKS 1, 2 AND 3)

```
    - name: Configure trunk ports on sw1's Gi3/3 # Task 1
      cisco.ios.ios_command:
        commands:
          - "configure terminal"
          - "interface g3/3"
          - "switchport trunk encapsulation dot1q"
          - "switchport mode trunk"
          - "switchport trunk allowed vlan 10,20"
      when: inventory_hostname=='sw1'

    - name: Configure trunk ports on sw1 and sw2 # Task 2
      cisco.ios.ios_command:
        commands:
          - "configure terminal"
          - "interface range g0/1, g0/2"
          - "switchport trunk encapsulation dot1q"
          - "switchport mode trunk"
          - "switchport trunk allowed vlan 10,20"
      when: inventory_hostname in ['sw1', 'sw2']

    - name: Configure trunk ports on sw3 and sw4 # Task 3
      cisco.ios.ios_command:
        commands:
          - "configure terminal"
          - "interface range g0/2, g0/3"
          - "switchport trunk encapsulation dot1q"
          - "switchport mode trunk"
          - "switchport trunk allowed vlan 10,20"
      when: inventory_hostname in [sw3', 'sw4']
```

Step 10: Configuring the VTP domain and password is relatively straightforward in this playbook, as all four switches will be configured with the same information. This simplifies the configuration process and ensures consistency across the switches.

SW1, SW2, SW3 AND SW4

```
vtp domain ansible-vtp01
vtp password ansible
```

Adding the VTP domain and password to all four switches can be accomplished with just one play. This play will ensure that the VTP settings are applied uniformly across the switches, making the configuration process efficient and consistent.

SW1, SW2, SW3 AND SW4 (TASK 4)

```
- name: Configure VTP on all switches # Task 4
  cisco.ios.ios_command:
    commands:
      - "configure terminal"
      - "vtp domain ansible-vtp01"
      - "vtp password ansible"
```

Step 11: To configure VLAN 10 and VLAN 20 on sw1, we need to address the trunk port G0/3 on r1, which is connected to sw1's G3/3. This specific configuration task will be handled in a separate play within our playbook.

SW1

```
vlan 10
name VLAN-10
vlan 20
name VLAN-20
end
```

PC1 and PC2 are currently connected to sw4's Gi1/1 and Gi1/2 ports, respectively, and these ports need to be configured as access switchports. We will assign VLAN 10 to Gi1/1 and VLAN 20 to Gi1/2. This configuration task will be included as another play in our Ansible playbook.

```
                              SW4
```

```
interface Gi1/1
switchport mode access
switchport access vlan 10
interface Gi1/2
switchport mode access
switchport access vlan 20
```

If we write the preceding two plays into our YAML file, they will look similar to the following plays:

```
                    SW1 AND SW4 (TASKS 5 AND 6)
```

```yaml
    - name: Configure VLANs on sw1 # Task 5
      cisco.ios.ios_command:
        commands:
          - "configure terminal"
          - "vlan 10"
          - "name VLAN-10"
          - "vlan 20"
          - "name VLAN-20"
      when: inventory_hostname == 'sw1'

    - name: Configure access ports on sw4 # Task 6
      cisco.ios.ios_command:
        commands:
          - "configure terminal"
          - "interface Gi1/1"
          - "switchport mode access"
          - "switchport access vlan 10"
          - "interface Gi1/2"
          - "switchport mode access"
          - "switchport access vlan 20"
      when: inventory_hostname == 'sw4'
```

These plays will configure VLAN 10 and 20 on sw1 and set the access ports on sw4 to use the appropriate VLANs for PC1 and PC2.

Step 12: Let's combine all the plays into a single YAML file and execute our playbook. Make sure to include the vars_files parameter to reference the encrypted vars.yml file.

Here's an example of how the playbook file may look like:

10.3_CONFIG_SWITCHES.YML

```
---
- name: Configure IOS-XE switches
  hosts: switch_type1
  gather_facts: no

  vars_files:
    - vars.yml

tasks:
    - name: Configure trunk port on sw1's Gi3/3
      cisco.ios.ios_command:
        commands:
          - "configure terminal"
          - "interface g3/3"
          - "switchport trunk encapsulation dot1q"
          - "switchport mode trunk"
          - "switchport trunk allowed vlan 10,20"
      when: inventory_hostname=='sw1'

    - name: Configure trunk ports on sw1, sw2
      cisco.ios.ios_command:
        commands:
          - "configure terminal"
          - "interface range g0/1,g0/2"
          - "switchport trunk encapsulation dot1q"
          - "switchport mode trunk"
          - "switchport trunk allowed vlan 10,20"
      when: inventory_hostname in ['sw1', 'sw2']

    - name: Configure trunk ports on sw3, sw4
      cisco.ios.ios_command:
        commands:
          - "configure terminal"
```

```
        - "interface range g0/2,g0/3"
        - "switchport trunk encapsulation dot1q"
        - "switchport mode trunk"
        - "switchport trunk allowed vlan 10,20"
      when: inventory_hostname in ['sw3', 'sw4']

  - name: Configure VTP on all switches
    cisco.ios.ios_command:
      commands:
        - "configure terminal"
        - "vtp domain ansible-vtp01"
        - "vtp password ansible"
    register: output3

  - name: Configure VLANs on sw1
    cisco.ios.ios_command:
      commands:
        - "configure terminal"
        - "vlan 10"
        - "name VLAN-10"
        - "vlan 20"
        - "name VLAN-20"
      when: inventory_hostname == 'sw1'

  - name: Configure access ports on sw4
    cisco.ios.ios_command:
      commands:
        - "configure terminal"
        - "interface Gi1/1"
        - "switchport mode access"
        - "switchport access vlan 10"
        - "interface Gi1/2"
        - "switchport mode access"
        - "switchport access vlan 20"
      when: inventory_hostname == 'sw4'
```

You may have noticed that we have consistently used the "ios_command" Ansible module in all three of our labs. However, if you prefer, there is another useful module called "ios_config". The advantage of using this module is that it automatically escalates the privilege level to the configuration mode, eliminating the need for users to run the "configure terminal" command explicitly. Nonetheless, the choice of which module to use and how you structure your playbook is entirely up to you, as long as your work is executed efficiently.

Additionally, it's worth noting that while automation has flourished in the world of systems engineering, it has traditionally faced resistance in the realm of network engineering. However, the tide is slowly turning, and now is the time to wholeheartedly embrace automation. Automating the manual tasks that traditional network engineers have been performing for over 50 years will bring tremendous benefits and significantly improves overall efficiency.

Step 13: Once you have assembled the playbook, execute it using the following command, providing the vault password when prompted:

```
[jdoe@f38s1 3_vlan]$ anp 10.3_config_switches.yml--ask-vault-pass
Vault password: ***************
PLAY [Configure IOS-XE switches] ****************************************

TASK [Configure trunk port on sw1's Gi3/3] ****************************
skipping: [sw2]
skipping: [sw3]
skipping: [sw4]
ok: [sw1]

TASK [Configure trunk ports on sw1, sw2] ****************************
skipping: [sw3]
skipping: [sw4]
ok: [sw2]
ok: [sw1]

TASK [Configure trunk ports on sw3, sw4] ****************************
skipping: [sw1]
skipping: [sw2]
ok: [sw3]
ok: [sw4]

TASK [Configure VTP on all switches] ****************************
ok: [sw2]
```

```
ok: [sw1]
ok: [sw4]
ok: [sw3]

TASK [Configure VLANs on sw1] *****************************************
skipping: [sw2]
skipping: [sw3]
skipping: [sw4]
ok: [sw1]

TASK [Configure access ports on sw4] *************************************
skipping: [sw1]
skipping: [sw2]
skipping: [sw3]
ok: [sw4]

PLAY RECAP ***********************************************************************
sw1                        :
ok=4    changed=0    unreachable=0    failed=0    skipped=2    rescued=0    ignored=0
sw2                        :
ok=2    changed=0    unreachable=0    failed=0    skipped=4    rescued=0    ignored=0
sw3                        :
ok=2    changed=0    unreachable=0    failed=0    skipped=4    rescued=0    ignored=0
sw4                        :
ok=3    changed=0    unreachable=0    failed=0    skipped=3    rescued=0    ignored=0
```

Step 14: To close out this lab, perform a manual ping test and traceroute from PC1 (1.1.10.5) and PC2 (1.1.20.8). This will help verify if there is successful communication between PC1 and PC2 after the VLAN configuration.

On PC1, open a command prompt and execute the following commands:

PC1

```
PC1> ping 1.1.20.8
 84 bytes from 1.1.20.8 icmp_seq=1 ttl=63 time=152.194 ms
 84 bytes from 1.1.20.8 icmp_seq=2 ttl=63 time=96.122 ms
```

```
84 bytes from 1.1.20.8 icmp_seq=3 ttl=63 time=111.680 ms
84 bytes from 1.1.20.8 icmp_seq=4 ttl=63 time=101.526 ms
84 bytes from 1.1.20.8 icmp_seq=5 ttl=63 time=104.935 ms

PC1> trace 1.1.20.8
trace to 1.1.20.8, 8 hops max, press Ctrl+C to stop
  1    1.1.10.1   90.944 ms   54.665 ms   34.507 ms
  2   *1.1.20.8    73.080 ms (ICMP type:3, code:3, Destination port unreachable)
```

On PC2, open a command prompt and execute the following commands:

PC2

```
PC2> ping 1.1.10.5
84 bytes from 1.1.10.5 icmp_seq=1 ttl=63 time=97.333 ms
84 bytes from 1.1.10.5 icmp_seq=2 ttl=63 time=90.749 ms
84 bytes from 1.1.10.5 icmp_seq=3 ttl=63 time=116.250 ms
84 bytes from 1.1.10.5 icmp_seq=4 ttl=63 time=99.555 ms
84 bytes from 1.1.10.5 icmp_seq=5 ttl=63 time=81.174 ms

PC2> trace 1.1.10.5
trace to 1.1.10.5, 8 hops max, press Ctrl+C to stop
  1    1.1.20.1   45.123 ms   38.847 ms   58.702 ms
  2   *1.1.10.5    90.906 ms (ICMP type:3, code:3, Destination port
unreachable)
```

Step 15: Optionally, you can run the following commands to validate the changes:
On the switches:

- Run **show interface trunk** to verify the trunk ports and their associated VLANs.

- Run **show vtp status** to check the VTP domain configuration and verify that it matches the desired settings.

- Run **show cdp neighbors** to see the neighboring devices and confirm the connectivity between switches and other devices.

These commands provide additional information about the trunking, VTP configuration, and neighboring devices. They can help you ensure that the VLAN configuration and connectivity are correctly applied.

Congratulations on successfully completing all three recommended labs in Chapter 12! You've gained valuable hands-on experience in configuring various aspects of router and switch configuration using Ansible. As an additional challenge, we have prepared an extra lab for you to explore at your leisure and put your skills to the test. Take your time and enjoy the opportunity to further enhance your knowledge and expertise. If you think you have learned enough and are ready to give it a go, that is fantastic! However, if you feel like you need a little bit more preparation, you can always come back to this challenge later. Well done to everyone who has reached this page after completing all of the tasks.

12.4 Lab 4 Challenge: Configure New Routers and Access Control List (ACL)

Challenge Scenario: You work as a senior network engineer in the IT department of a rapidly growing international pharmaceutical company. Initially, the company chose Huawei routers for cost-cutting purposes when it was new to the market. However, with an increase in customers signing significant contracts and the need for superior Technical Assistance Center (TAC) support, the company has decided to upgrade its aging fleet of edge routers to top-of-the-line routers. This decision is also influenced by security announcements and changes in Federal laws. Moreover, the Huawei routers are nearing their End-of-Life (EoL) in six months, and there are security concerns regarding certain models potentially containing chipsets capable of sniffing traffic and sending it back to China, which cannot be undetectable by end users.

To determine the replacement routers, your IT department has planned to test products from various vendors. Additionally, in line with recent developments, a dedicated SRE/DevOps team has been formed in your department to restructure IT operations. This team, composed of highly skilled engineers, aims to adopt an automation framework and automate tasks to initiate the company's automation journey.

Both the CTO and VP of your company are enthusiastic about systems and networking automation. They have been informed, through their connections in the business community, that adopting an automation framework along with tools like the Ansible Automation Platform offers numerous benefits for IT departments. As a result, your bosses want to explore Ansible as a tool and its ability to manage configurations and automate tasks across the company's network, which includes hundreds of network routers and switches. Your task is to develop a proof-of-concept lab that demonstrates the power of Ansible. This lab will serve as a preliminary step before the company fully commits to implementing automation and orchestration tools within the IT department. Furthermore, you have been instructed to demonstrate the lab environment using Cisco IOS-XE virtual routers, which will replace the old Huawei routers.

The Challenge: Originally, your network architect was assigned the task of creating the demo. However, since they come from a traditional networking background and are unfamiliar with Ansible, you have been asked to assist in creating a proof-of-concept (POC) lab for routing. The lab should consist of five routers. The specific requirements for the demo are outlined here, and it is crucial to meet all these requirements before the demonstration:

Demo Lab Requirements:

- The IP addressing must strictly adhere to the Lab network topology as depicted in Figure 12-10.

- Configure the management interfaces on GigabitEthernet 0/0 interfaces to allow the Ansible Control Machine (f38s1, IP: 192.168.127.150) to control all five routers.

- Use an Ansible playbook to configure all interfaces.

- Use an Ansible playbook to enable dynamic routing using OSPF 99.

- Use an Ansible playbook to assign OSPF router IDs, where the ID consists of the last digit of the hostname (e.g., for r3, the ID is 3.3.3.3, and for r5, the ID is 5.5.5.5).

- Use an Ansible playbook to configure an Access Control List (ACL) on the G0/2 interface of r2, allowing inbound traffic from r3 with source IP addresses of 1.1.3.3, 1.1.23.3, and 1.1.30.3.

Lab 4: ACL Network Topology

Please refer to Figure 12-10, which depicts the network topology provided by your architect. The information presented in this figure should be consulted.

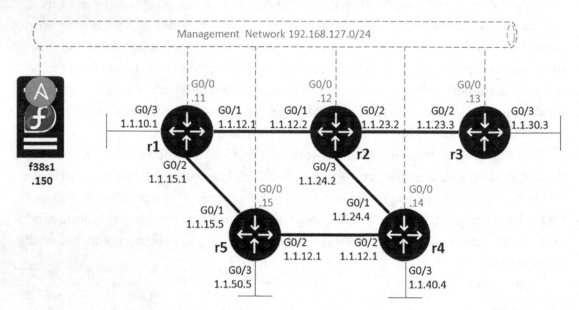

Figure 12-10.   ACL topology

Lab 4: GNS3 Device Connections

To assist you in configuring the ACL POC on your GNS3 environment, the GNS3 network topology is also depicted in Figure 12-11.

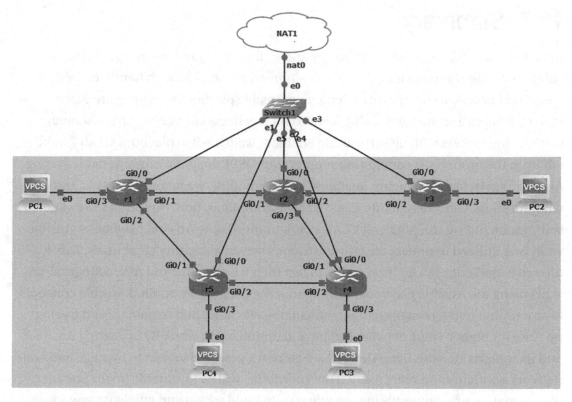

Figure 12-11. *GNS3 ACL topology*

Please note that there is no right or wrong playbook for this challenge; the goal is to create more efficient playbooks. Once you have written your initial set of playbooks, attempt to refactor them to reduce the number of lines to a minimum. Enjoy the challenges as you carry them out.

In the upcoming chapter, Chapter 13, we will dive deep into the process of creating network device configuration backups for Cisco routers and switches. You'll have the opportunity to learn how to handcraft an Ansible application that will efficiently back up the configurations for you and your team. This promises to be an exciting chapter, as you gain valuable insights and practical skills to enhance your configuration management practices. Get ready to embark on this thrilling journey that will empower you to safeguard critical network settings with confidence!

12.5 Summary

In this chapter, we explored Cisco router and switch configuration using Ansible, an efficient configuration management and automation tool. Through hands-on labs, we gained practical experience in deploying Ansible playbooks to configure Cisco IOS-XE routers and switches. Lab 1 focused on creating a lab topology from scratch, configuring routers with EIGRP routing enabled using Ansible playbooks. Lab 2 built a lab from the ground up, configuring routers with OSPF dynamic routing enabled using Ansible playbooks. Leveraging Ansible's "when" module, we targeted specific hosts for configuration. Lab 3 delved into Cisco L2 switch configuration, exploring VLAN and VTP settings, including trunking and VLAN configuration using Ansible playbooks. Ansible-vault was utilized to protect the administrator's sensitive security credentials. Lab 4 offered a challenge lab for those eager to test their Cisco router and ACL configuration skills using the Ansible playbook. Throughout the chapter, we applied Ansible concepts to streamline network management, enhancing efficiency and scalability and freeing up time for higher-value network design and optimization work. By mastering Ansible and its integration with Cisco devices, we gained a powerful toolset to manage and scale network configurations effectively. This knowledge will be invaluable in our pursuit of automation and orchestration, enabling us to build robust and efficient network infrastructures.

Network Device Backup Ansible Playbook

Chapter 13 of our book, titled "Network Device Backup Ansible Playbook," highlights the importance of critical network device configuration backups, such as routers, switches, WLCs, and firewalls, for all organizations. We emphasize the significance of disaster recovery and troubleshooting by having a reference of these backups. The chapter begins with instructions on setting up the lab environment in GNS3 and configuring the initial routers and switches. We then delve into the process of securely backing up the Cisco router and switch configurations to an SCP file server. While showcasing the capabilities of Ansible as a network device configuration backup tool, we also discuss its limitations. Additionally, we explore the application of ansible-vault encryption for enhanced security and address challenges related to key exchange and cipher compatibility when working with new servers and legacy network devices. Lastly, we demonstrate the backup synchronization to a single SCP server initially and then expand it to three SCP servers, ensuring the protection of critical running-config information for efficient disaster recovery and easy referencing. Join us in Chapter 13 to gain valuable insights and practical implementation guidance for network device backups using Ansible playbooks.

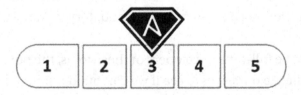

In the ever-evolving world of Information and Communication Technology (ICT), IT engineers and their teams rely on a wide range of tools to perform specific tasks. These tools come in various forms, including proprietary, free, and open source solutions.

© Brendan Choi and Erwin Medina 2023
B. Choi and E. Medina, *Introduction to Ansible Network Automation*,
https://doi.org/10.1007/978-1-4842-9624-0_13

One of the most important tools for network engineers at work is network device configuration management, which includes device backup tools as a subset of the device configuration management tool. When it comes to backing up critical network devices, network engineers and their IT teams have several options to choose from based on their IT budget and disaster recovery strategies.

One common interest for all network engineers is how the network devices' configurations are backed up and managed. Many network device configuration management tools, such as SolarWinds, Cacti, RANCID, Kiwi CatTools, and Oxidized, have emerged to address this need. Most of these tools offer configuration change tracking and version control of the device backups. Although the terminology used by each of these tools may vary, they essentially perform the backup by running an automated script using a scheduler such as a cron job or Windows scheduler. The scheduled automatic backups run at specific intervals, with the option to save the running, startup, or both configurations to FTP (File Transfer Protocol), SFTP (Secure File Transfer Protocol), or SCP (Secure Copy Protocol) servers. Some of these tools also provide configuration comparison tools using a type of diff tool usually written in any one of the programming languages of the vendor's choice. These tools are used for comparing and finding differences between text in two different files. Most often, these tools provide a user-friendly GUI for user interaction and are an essential tool in the network engineers' arsenal.

At the true business end of all these tools, they are used to store network device configurations as files in a safe place. When the hardware fails, the system's OS is attacked or runs into a bug and becomes unrecoverable, or an engineer performs a change that brings down a device, and hence the whole network, these backed-up files serve as the last known good configuration to recover the system in the shortest time possible. Device backup is one of the least interesting topics of current networking technologies, and not everyone wants to know about it, but they must know how to make backups of critical networking devices as it is a mandatory task, not an option for any network engineer.

While we may not be full-time developers of these tools, the purpose of this lab is to explore and challenge ourselves to see if we can build a simple tool using an Ansible playbook. It presents an interesting challenge as Ansible is not a fully fledged configuration management tool and will not be as good as some of the product sets mentioned previously. However, by understanding the concept of file backup and seeing some of the tools in action, we can enhance our ability to safeguard critical network device configurations. Moreover, once we have written something in YAML, it becomes an application that we can reuse over and over, and since this is written by you, you understand the fine details of your tool.

Hence, in this lab, we will focus on exploring the Cisco router and switch configuration backup using the simple "show running-config" command and then save the file to the Ansible control node as the primary place to store the running configurations of all our network devices. Once the files are saved to our backup directory, we will then send the file to the SCP file server, which will act as the primary network device configuration server. If you want to build more redundancies to prevent data loss due to a system failure, we can use another SCP file server to share the backed-up configurations, making this solution amazingly scalable. The good thing about Ansible is that the provided module keeps the files synchronized, so there is little danger of duplicating the same files. We will also delve into the automation of backup jobs using cron jobs in Chapter 14, a scheduling utility commonly found in Unix-like operating systems. By automating the backup jobs using cron jobs, we can streamline the process, ensuring regular and reliable backups without manual intervention. Throughout this lab, we will uncover valuable insights and best practices for securing network device configurations. We will learn how to leverage the power of technology to minimize the risk of configuration loss, improve disaster recovery capabilities, and maintain network stability by always keeping the up-to-date known good running configuration.

In production network and data center operations, the gathering of running configuration backups plays a vital role as it provides snapshots of critical network devices. These backups are crucial for network troubleshooting purposes, serving as a valuable point of reference. They allow for easy comparison and analysis of configurations, aiding in the identification and resolution of issues within the network infrastructure. By maintaining an up-to-date collection of running configuration backups, network administrators and engineers can ensure a more efficient and effective troubleshooting process, leading to improved network performance and reliability.

Let's embark on this chapter to learn how to effectively protect network configurations, automate backup processes, and ensure stability by regularly making backups of all our devices.

13.1 Setting Up Network Device Configuration Backup Lab

The proposed study flows for this lab include the following tasks in which you will engage:

1. Set up a new GNS3 project specifically for the router and switch configuration backup lab.

2. Verify the connectivity between devices.

3. Write Ansible playbook part 1 to run the "show running-config" command and save the file to the backup directory. If no backup directory exists, detect it and create one.

4. Write Ansible playbook part 2 to test file upload to the SCP file server at 192.168.127.151 and test the synchronization.

5. Add two more SCP file servers and synchronize the backup directory and backup files on three different servers.

6. Validate the backed-up configuration files to ensure their accuracy and completeness.

To provide a clear overview of the lab setup, here is a simple topology for your reference. Additionally, we will provide suggestions on how to connect devices within GNS3 to prepare for this lab. Let's commence our journey.

13.1.1 Network Device Configuration Backup Lab Topology and Connections

In this chapter, we have a single lab, and our emphasis will be on the backup of the running configuration. As our main focus is on the backup process, the devices will only require minimal configurations. This will enable the Ansible control node to execute the backup playbook, utilizing the backup module on each network device and saving the configurations with a timestamp to the local directory named "backup." Therefore, there is no need to establish connections between networking devices; we only require the management plane to be operational for our testing and development lab.

Follow these instructions to set up the GNS3 lab according to Figures 13-1 and 13-2:

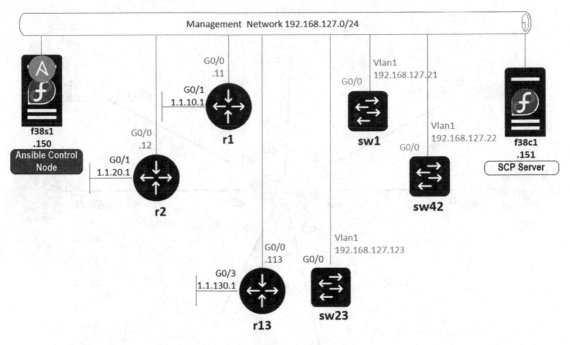

Figure 13-1. *Device backup lab topology*

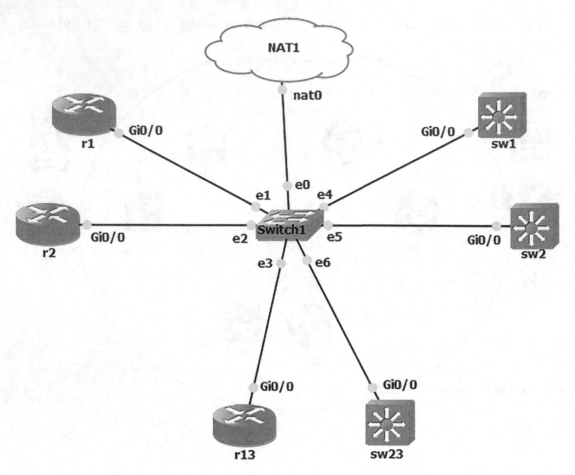

Figure 13-2. *GNS3 topology*

Step 1: Start VMware Workstation and power on the Ansible Control Machine (f38s1) with the IP address 192.168.127.150, as well as the SCP file server (f38c1) with the IP address 192.168.127.151.

Step 2: Refer to Figure 13-1 for a comprehensive overview of the hostnames and IP addresses.

Step 3: Launch GNS3 and create a new lab topology by referencing Figure 13-2.

Step 4: Download and open the Chapter 13 device initialization file (Ch13_routers_switches_initialization_configs.txt). This file contains the necessary configurations for the management interfaces of all devices, as well as the SSH configuration to enable communication between the Ansible Control Machine and the three routers and three switches. Please note that it may take some time for the network devices to boot up and stabilize, so allow approximately five to ten minutes for this process. If you are practicing these labs on a PC/laptop with lower specifications, you can reduce the number of powered-on devices to two routers and two switches.

You can download the files used in this chapter from the following URL: `https://github.com/ansnetauto/appress_ansnetauto`.

At this stage, both Linux servers and the four to six network devices should be powered on and connected to the same network. You are now ready to proceed with the router and switch backup lab.

13.2 Cisco Router and Switch Configuration Backup to File Server (SCP)

SCP (Secure Copy) is a protocol based on SSH (Secure Shell) that provides secure file transfers between a client and a server. It offers authentication and encryption, making it a reliable alternative to FTP (File Transfer Protocol) for secure file management and transfer. SCP operates on port 22, the same port used by SSH, eliminating the need for additional configuration. FTP, although widely used, has security vulnerabilities as it transmits data in plain text, making it susceptible to interception. To enhance security, alternative protocols like SFTP (SSH File Transfer Protocol) and FTPS (FTP Secure) have been introduced. SFTP incorporates SSL/TLS encryption for secure control and data connections, while FTPS also provides encryption for secure file transfers.

In the context of backing up Cisco networking device configurations, using FTP or SFTP can pose challenges due to the limitations of out-of-the-box Ansible modules and the handling of various prompts. It is important to note that backing up Cisco networking devices using FTP or SFTP can sometimes be challenging or even impossible with the current out-of-the-box Ansible modules. Additional configuration is required to ensure that Cisco IOS and IOS-XE devices use the same SSH Kex Algorithms and handle all possible prompts correctly. The Ansible official documentation suggests using the ansible.netcommon.cli_command module to handle the command output and prompts, but this module is still a work in progress. Users may encounter issues when dealing with the details of key exchange algorithms and newer Linux servers that do not support smaller RSA key sizes. These are areas where further support from Red Hat Ansible is needed.

Read about ansible-netcommon-cli-command-module here:

https://docs.ansible.com/ansible/latest/collections/ansible/netcommon/
cli_command_module.html#ansible-collections-ansible-netcommon-cli-
command-module

Cisco IOS and IOS-XE devices require additional configuration and handling of specific prompts to enable FTP or SFTP backups. As a workaround, many network engineers who work with Ansible have discovered a workaround solution to back up router and switch configurations by running the "show run" command and saving the output to the Ansible control node's directory. We adopt the same approach and demonstrate how to make backups of running configurations, but we will go one step beyond just making the backup.

In this lab, we will recreate the playbook to save the running configurations of each device to our directory. Additionally, we will create a separate playbook to send these files to our file server, f38c1, using the Secure Copy (SCP) protocol. Since SCP operates over SSH and utilizes port 22, there is no need for further configuration. Once we have written and confirmed that both playbooks are functioning properly, we can combine them into a single playbook for a more streamlined backup process.

Step 1: To proceed with Chapter 13, create a new working directory. Start by copying the ping playbook from the previous lab, Lab 12.2. Once you have copied the playbook, make the necessary modifications to test the reachability of all management IP addresses from the Ansible Control Machine.

```
[jdoe@f38s1 repo1]$ mkdir ch13 && cd ch13
[jdoe@f38s1 ch13]$ cp /home/jdoe/repo1/ch12/2_ospf/12.2_icmp_mgt_int.yml
./13_icmp_mgt_int.yml
[jdoe@f38s1 ch13]$ vi 13_icmp_mgt_int.yml
---
- name: Ping hosts and display output
  hosts: localhost
  gather_facts: false

  tasks:
    - name: Ping hosts
      ansible.builtin.raw: ping -c 4 {{ item }}
      register: ping_output
      loop:
```

```
    - 192.168.127.151 # SCP server
    - 192.168.127.11 # r1
    - 192.168.127.12 # r2
    - 192.168.127.113 # r13
    - 192.168.127.21 # sw1
    - 192.168.127.22 # sw2
    - 192.168.127.123 # sw23
  changed_when: false # Important setting to let the failed message
  display on the screen

- name: Display output
  ansible.builtin.debug:
    var: ping_output.results | map(attribute='stdout_lines') | list #
    Modify the last line
```

Step 2: Execute the 13_icmp_mgt_int.yml playbook by its name. This playbook will display the ping results on your screen, instead of saving the output as before. Check if all devices are reachable from the control node. If all devices are reachable, you can proceed to the next step.

```
[jdoe@f38s1 ch13]$ anp 13_icmp_mgt_int.yml
[...omitted for brevity]
TASK [Display output] **************************************************
ok: [localhost] => {
    "ping_output.results | map(attribute='stdout_lines') | list": [
        [
            "PING 192.168.127.150 (192.168.127.150) 56(84) bytes of data.",
            "64 bytes from 192.168.127.150: icmp_seq=1 ttl=64 time=0.038 ms",
            "64 bytes from 192.168.127.150: icmp_seq=2 ttl=64 time=0.042 ms",
            "64 bytes from 192.168.127.150: icmp_seq=3 ttl=64 time=0.111 ms",
            "64 bytes from 192.168.127.150: icmp_seq=4 ttl=64 time=0.056 ms",
            "",
            "--- 192.168.127.150 ping statistics ---",
            "4 packets transmitted, 4 received, 0% packet loss, time 3104ms",
            "rtt min/avg/max/mdev = 0.038/0.061/0.111/0.029 ms"
        ],
[...omitted for brevity]
```

Step 3: While attempting to SSH into other servers from your Ansible server, you might encounter key exchange errors. To save time during the initial stages of this lab, let's include the KexAlgorithms options for all three SCP servers. If you come across additional key exchange messages requiring you to add different cipher types, you can add them at the end after a comma without a space.

```
[jdoe@f38s1 ch13]$ cat ~/.ssh/config

Host 192.168.127.151
    KexAlgorithms +diffie-hellman-group1-sha1

Host 192.168.127.161
    KexAlgorithms +diffie-hellman-group1-sha1

Host 192.168.127.162
    KexAlgorithms +diffie-hellman-group1-sha1
```

Before proceeding to step 4, I hope you can spare a few minutes to read this helpful tip.

Tip

Do you want to SSH into Cisco Legacy routers or switches from Ansible Control Machine? ✒️

When it comes to cipher and encryption for SSH, Cisco devices are not always up to the latest and greatest. However, the newer Linux and Windows systems are usually one or two steps ahead of Cisco in this area. Therefore, if you are using newer operating systems like RHEL 9.1–based systems or any of the newer Debian distributions, you may encounter difficulties when logging into Cisco routers and switches via SSH on port 22. This can be attributed to the key exchange algorithm settings and RSA key size supported by these newer systems.

To enable SSH login from your Ansible server, please add the following configuration to the "~/.ssh/config" file:

Host 192.168.127.11
    KexAlgorithms +diffie-hellman-group-exchange-sha1

```
    PubkeyAcceptedAlgorithms +ssh-rsa
    HostkeyAlgorithms +ssh-rsa
    RequiredRSASize 1024
```

This configuration addition ensures that the correct key exchange algorithm and RSA key size are used when establishing SSH connections between your Ansible server and Cisco devices.

When you attempt to SSH without the aforementioned settings, you will encounter an "ssh-rsa" message or a similar error message.

```
[jdoe@f38s1 ch13]$ ssh jdoe@192.168.127.11
```

Unable to negotiate with 192.168.127.11 port 22: no matching host key type found. Their offer: ssh-rsa

By adding the key exchange algorithm settings to the configuration file of your devices, you will be able to establish an SSH connection between your Cisco devices and the Ansible Control Machine, as depicted in Figure 13-3.

```
[jdoe@f38s1 ch13]$ ssh jdoe@192.168.127.11

**************************************************************************
* IOSv is strictly limited to use for evaluation, demonstration and IOS  *
* education. IOSv is provided as-is and is not supported by Cisco's       *
* Technical Advisory Center. Any use or disclosure, in whole or in part,  *
* of the IOSv Software or Documentation to any third party for any        *
* purposes is expressly prohibited except as otherwise authorized by      *
* Cisco in writing.                                                       *
(jdoe@192.168.127.11) Password:  *****************************************

**************************************************************************
* IOSv is strictly limited to use for evaluation, demonstration and IOS  *
* education. IOSv is provided as-is and is not supported by Cisco's       *
* Technical Advisory Center. Any use or disclosure, in whole or in part,  *
* of the IOSv Software or Documentation to any third party for any        *
* purposes is expressly prohibited except as otherwise authorized by      *
* Cisco in writing.                                                       *
**************************************************************************
r1#
r1#
```

Figure 13-3. *SSH login to router r1*

Step 4: Now, let's prepare the vars.yml, ansible.cfg, and inventory files to be used for this lab. Start by creating an encrypted vars.yml file in the current working directory. This file will contain the same information as the vars.yml file used in lab 12.3, but let's make slight modifications to enable the Ansible control node to send files to our SCP server using a passphrase_response. Make sure you use the colon when entering the passphrase_response. Don't forget the Vault password as this will be used to run the playbook later.

```
[jdoe@f38s1 ch13]$ ansible-vault create vars.yml
New Vault password: ***************
Confirm New Vault password: ***************
---
ansible_user: jdoe # Using the same user name for both network devices and
SCP servers
ansible_password: 5uper5cret9assw0rd # Network device password/secret
passphrase_response: Secur3P@ssw0rd # SCP server password
```

Next, let's copy and reuse the ansible.cfg file from the last lab of Chapter 12. You can either copy the ansible.cfg file used in Chapter 12 or create a brand-new one for practice.

```
[jdoe@f38s1 ch13]$ cp ../ch12/3_vlan/ansible.cfg ./ansible.cfg
[jdoe@f38s1 ch13]$ vi ansible.cfg
[defaults]
inventory=inventory
host_key_checking=False
nocows = 1
```

Similarly, you have the option to either duplicate and modify the inventory file from the previous lab in Chapter 12 or create a new inventory file from scratch. However, please keep in mind that with the increased number of devices, some adjustments will be necessary for the inventory file. Additionally, since we will be utilizing the actual IP addresses of the SCP servers for file copying, there is no requirement to include the SCP servers in the inventory file. **One important consideration is to increase the default timeout value for ansible_command_timeout to ensure that sufficient time is provided for the network devices to respond to the command.** The default timeout value is 30 seconds, but in our lab environment, we may require more than 30 seconds for all six devices to respond promptly.

```
[jdoe@f38s1 ch13]$ cp ../ch12/3_vlan/inventory ./inventory
[jdoe@f38s1 ch13]$ vi inventory
[ios_xe_devices:vars]
ansible_network_os=ios
ansible_connection=network_cli
ansible_command_timeout=300 # Default timeout value is only 30 secs,
increase to 5 mins

[router_type1]
r1 ansible_host=192.168.127.11
r2 ansible_host=192.168.127.12
r13 ansible_host=192.168.127.113 # r13 is the correct hostname

[switch_type1]
sw1 ansible_host=192.168.127.21
sw2 ansible_host=192.168.127.22
sw23 ansible_host=192.168.127.123  # sw23 is the correct hostname

[ios_xe_devices:children]  # The OS is the same IOS-XE, so group similar
devices together
router_type1
switch_type1
```

Step 5: Now let's write the main Ansible playbook to create backups of the currently running configuration on the Ansible Control Machine's local storage. First, we will check if a directory named "backup" exists in the current working directory. If the directory does not exist, we will create it. Next, we will use the ios_config module with backup_options to create a backup of the running configuration. During this process, we will save the running-config files in timestamped directories using the format "yyyymmdd-hh-mm". This approach ensures that the files within each directory are easily identifiable based on the time they were initially created, even if the directories are copied and moved across different systems. Later on, you have the flexibility to modify this format according to your preference.

13.2_BACKUP_RUNNING_CONFIG_TO_ACM.YML

```
---
- name: Check and create a backup directory on the Ansible Control Machine
  hosts: localhost # Run on Ansible Control Machine, f38s1
  gather_facts: false

  tasks:
    - name: Check if the backup directory exists
      ansible.builtin.stat:
        path: ./backup
      register: backup_dir

    - name: Create backup directory
      ansible.builtin.file:
        path: ./backup
        state: directory
      when: not backup_dir.stat.exists

- name: Backup Cisco IOS-XE Router and Switch configurations
  hosts: ios_xe_devices  # Targeted devices
  gather_facts: false

  vars_files:
    - vars.yml

  vars:
    timestamp: "{{ lookup('pipe', 'date +%Y%m%d-%H%M') }}"
  tasks:
    - name: Run show run and save to a file
      cisco.ios.ios_config:
        backup: yes
        backup_options:
          filename: "{{ inventory_hostname }}-running-config.cfg"
          dir_path: ./backup/{{ timestamp }}_backup

    - name: Print message when completed
      ansible.builtin.debug: msg="{{ inventory_hostname }} - Backup to local
      storage completed"
```

Step 6: Now execute the preceding playbook, "13.2_save_sh_run_to_f38s1.yml", and ensure that the playbook functions correctly. If your playbook does not work, you must troubleshoot the issue before proceeding to the next step.

```
[jdoe@f38s1 ch13]$ anp 13.2_backup_running_config_to_acm.yml --ask-
vault-pass
Vault password: ***************
[...omitted for brevity]
```

After successfully backing up the files, check them. Since the playbook ran with the default forks parameter of 5 and also ran for over one minute, the configuration backups have been saved in two separate directories. One backup directory was created at 5:09 PM, which contains five backup configurations. The last device backup was performed at 5:10 PM, and the corresponding directory only contains a single file. The Ansible forks parameter determines the number of parallel tasks that Ansible can perform simultaneously. In other words, when running a playbook, Ansible can execute up to five tasks concurrently by default. Note that increasing the number of forks also requires more system resources, such as CPU and memory power.

```
[jdoe@f38s1 ch13]$ ls -lh backup/
total 0
drwxr-xr-x. 2 jdoe jdoe 154 Jun  7 17:10 20230607-1709_backup
drwxr-xr-x. 2 jdoe jdoe  37 Jun  7 17:10 20230607-1710_backup

[jdoe@f38s1 ch13]$ ls -lh backup/20230607-1709_backup
total 20K
-rw-r--r--. 1 jdoe jdoe 3.4K Jun  7 17:10 r13-running-config.cfg
-rw-r--r--. 1 jdoe jdoe 3.4K Jun  7 17:10 r1-running-config.cfg
-rw-r--r--. 1 jdoe jdoe 3.3K Jun  7 17:10 r2-running-config.cfg
-rw-r--r--. 1 jdoe jdoe 3.8K Jun  7 17:10 sw1-running-config.cfg
-rw-r--r--. 1 jdoe jdoe 3.8K Jun  7 17:10 sw2-running-config.cfg
[jdoe@f38s1 ch13]$ ls -lh backup/20230607-1710_backup
total 4.0K
-rw-r--r--. 1 jdoe jdoe 3.8K Jun  7 17:10 sw23-running-config.cfg
```

This could pose a problem for us because we want to save all files in the same directory. The number of forks supported by Ansible depends on the CPU and memory size of the Ansible control node, as well as the specific use case. For your information, in an Ansible Automation Platform environment, as a general guideline, the recommendation is to have approximately 100 forks per 4 GB of memory usage and a baseline value of 4 forks per CPU core. The same recommendation might not apply to our ansible-playbook using command line. However, it's important to refer to Ansible's official documentation for the most up-to-date and accurate information regarding fork values and their implications in your specific environment. If you need to increase the level of parallelism, you can adjust the "forks" value to a higher number. It's crucial to consider the capacity of your system and the available resources when adjusting the "forks" value. Setting it too high can strain system resources and lead to performance issues, while setting it too low may result in slower task execution.

To correct this problem, since we are operating in our lab environment, we will be generous and increase the fork number to 50 in our ansible.cfg file.

```
[jdoe@f38s1 ch13]$ vi ansible.cfg
[defaults]
inventory=inventory
host_key_checking=False
nocows = 1
forks = 50 # Add this line to change the default fork value from 5 to 50
```

Step 7: Now that the files are stored in the backup directory on the Ansible Control Machine, we want to synchronize them with our SCP server. This will allow us to store the files semi-permanently and retrieve the information whenever necessary.

In most IT organizations, the general rule for retaining backup files or information is around seven years or thereabouts. However, this duration can vary depending on the organization's IT budget and recovery strategy. In some cases, router and switch configuration files may be kept for as little as 14 days before the information is purged.

Let's quickly write a simple playbook to copy and move the files across our SCP server.

```
┌─────────────────────────────────────────────────────────────────────┐
│               13.2_MOVE_FILES_TO_SCP_SERVER.YML                       │
└─────────────────────────────────────────────────────────────────────┘
```

```
---
- name: Run SCP command with automated passphrase
  hosts: localhost
  gather_facts: false
```

```
vars_files:
- vars.yml

tasks:
  - name: Run SCP command
    ansible.builtin.expect:
      command: scp -r ./backup jdoe@192.168.127.151:/home/jdoe/.
      responses:
        "Enter passphrase for key '/home/jdoe/.ssh/id_ed25519':": "{{
        passphrase_response }}"
    register: scp_output

  - name: Display SCP command output
    ansible.builtin.debug:
      var: scp_output.stdout_lines
```

The preceding playbook is using the ansible.builtin.expect module with the usual suspect, scp command with -r option. The -r flag is used to enable recursive copying, ensuring that all files and directories within the "backup" directory are included in the transfer. The playbook is executing an SCP command to copy the backup files from the local directory "./backup" to a remote server. The command is being run using the ansible.builtin.expect module, which allows for interactive commands that require user input. Additionally, the task includes a responses section that responds to a specific prompt during the SCP command execution. In this case, if the prompt "Enter passphrase for key '/home/jdoe/.ssh/id_ed25519':" appears, the value of the variable passphrase_response will be provided as the response. The output of this task is registered in the variable scp_output, which can be used for further processing or debugging if needed.

Execute the playbook "13.2_move_files_to_scp_server.yml" with the "--ask-vault-pass" option to decrypt the "vars.yaml" file.

```
[jdoe@f38s1 ch13]$ anp 13.2_move_files_to_scp_server.yml --ask-vault-pass
Vault password: ***************
[...omitted for brevity]
```

Go to the SCP file server, f38c1, and check the backed-up running-config files. These files are synchronized with the backup directory on f38s1. Even if you delete a file or the backup directory on f38s1, the files on f38c1 will remain unaffected and will not be removed. This makes it a simple and effective solution for companies in need of free network device backup solutions. It protects critical network devices such as firewalls, routers, switches, and Wireless LAN Controllers while also offering Linux and Windows file backup capabilities. **It's important to remember that Ansible was initially created with Linux OS in mind, and the support for network devices was an extension of Ansible's preexisting features. Hence, we embarked on our journey by studying the basics of Linux and Ansible concepts in a Linux environment.** We should consider ourselves fortunate to have such a powerful tool available for network engineering work.

```
[jdoe@f38c1 ~]$ ls
backup
[jdoe@f38c1 ~]$ ll backup/
total 0
drwxr-xr-x. 2 jdoe jdoe 154 Jun  7 17:29 20230607-1709_backup
drwxr-xr-x. 2 jdoe jdoe  37 Jun  7 17:29 20230607-1710_backup
[jdoe@f38c1 ~]$ ll backup/20230607-1709_backup
total 20
-rw-r--r--. 1 jdoe jdoe 3435 Jun  7 17:29 r13-running-config.cfg
-rw-r--r--. 1 jdoe jdoe 3432 Jun  7 17:29 r1-running-config.cfg
-rw-r--r--. 1 jdoe jdoe 3371 Jun  7 17:29 r2-running-config.cfg
-rw-r--r--. 1 jdoe jdoe 3853 Jun  7 17:29 sw1-running-config.cfg
-rw-r--r--. 1 jdoe jdoe 3853 Jun  7 17:29 sw2-running-config.cfg
[jdoe@f38c1 ~]$ ll backup/20230607-1710_backup
total 4
-rw-r--r--. 1 jdoe jdoe 3855 Jun  7 17:29 sw23-running-config.cfg
```

Step 8: If everything worked as planned, you can now combine the two playbooks into one. This consolidated playbook consists of multiple plays and various tasks. Please review the playbook carefully and pay attention to the details. Try to analyze each play and task to understand their respective objectives and actions. Since we have already discussed the previous two playbooks, this consolidation is simply merging them into one, so there isn't a lot of explanation to provide. You can refer to the name section of each play to understand what each play is aiming to accomplish.

13.2_BACKUP_RUNNING_CONFIG.YML

```
---
- name: Check and create a backup directory on the Ansible Control Machine
  hosts: localhost # Run on Ansible Control Machine, f38s1
  gather_facts: false

  tasks:
    - name: Check if the backup directory exists
      stat:
        path: ./backup
      register: backup_dir

    - name: Create backup directory
      ansible.builtin.file:
        path: ./backup
        state: directory
      when: not backup_dir.stat.exists

- name: Backup Cisco IOS-XE Router and Switch configurations
  hosts: ios_xe_devices  # Targeted devices
  gather_facts: false
  vars_files:
    - vars.yml

  vars:
    timestamp: "{{ lookup('pipe', 'date +%Y%m%d-%H%M') }}"

  tasks:
    - name: Run show run and save to a file
      cisco.ios.ios_config:
        backup: yes
        backup_options:
          filename: "{{ inventory_hostname }}-running-config.cfg"
          dir_path: ./backup/{{ timestamp }}_backup

    - name: Print message when completed
      ansible.builtin.debug: msg="{{ inventory_hostname }} - Backup to local
      storage completed"
```

```
- name: Copy backup files to the SCP server
  hosts: localhost  # Run locally
  gather_facts: false

  vars_files:
    - vars.yml

  tasks:
    - name: Run SCP command
      ansible.builtin.expect:
        command: scp -r ./backup jdoe@192.168.127.151:/home/jdoe/.
        responses:
          "Enter passphrase for key '/home/jdoe/.ssh/id_ed25519':": "{{
          passphrase_response }}"
      register: scp_output

    - name: Print message when completed
      ansible.builtin.debug: msg="Device backup file transfer to SCP
completed" # Simplified a little here
```

Step 9: It is time to execute the playbook mentioned previously and observe the result.

```
[jdoe@f38s1 ch13]$ anp 13.2_backup_running_config.yml --ask-vault-pass
Vault password:
[...omitted for brevity]
```

After successfully executing the playbook, if you check the primary backup folder on the Ansible Control Machine, you will notice a single directory that contains all six backup files. This outcome aligns with the expected result achieved by changing the forks parameter from 5 to 50.

```
[jdoe@f38s1 ch13]$ ll backup/
total 0
drwxr-xr-x. 2 jdoe jdoe 154 Jun  7 17:10 20230607-1709_backup
drwxr-xr-x. 2 jdoe jdoe  37 Jun  7 17:10 20230607-1710_backup
drwxr-xr-x. 2 jdoe jdoe 185 Jun  7 17:59 20230607-1758_backup
```

Now, swiftly navigate to the SCP file server and verify whether the backup directory has been synchronized and the latest running-config files are stored and accessible from the SCP server.

```
[jdoe@f38c1 ~]$ ll backup/
total 0
drwxr-xr-x. 2 jdoe jdoe 154 Jun  7 17:29 20230607-1709_backup
drwxr-xr-x. 2 jdoe jdoe  37 Jun  7 17:29 20230607-1710_backup
drwxr-xr-x. 2 jdoe jdoe 185 Jun  7 17:59 20230607-1758_backup
[jdoe@f38c1 ~]$ ll backup/20230607-1758_backup
total 24
-rw-r--r--. 1 jdoe jdoe 3435 Jun  7 17:59 r13-running-config.cfg
-rw-r--r--. 1 jdoe jdoe 3432 Jun  7 17:59 r1-running-config.cfg
-rw-r--r--. 1 jdoe jdoe 3371 Jun  7 17:59 r2-running-config.cfg
-rw-r--r--. 1 jdoe jdoe 3853 Jun  7 17:59 sw1-running-config.cfg
-rw-r--r--. 1 jdoe jdoe 3855 Jun  7 17:59 sw23-running-config.cfg
-rw-r--r--. 1 jdoe jdoe 3853 Jun  7 17:59 sw2-running-config.cfg
```

Apparently, with the execution of the preceding playbook, we encounter two underlying issues. Firstly, the Ansible control node shouldn't function as a file storage server, particularly in a production environment where multiple administrators will be sharing the same system to manage network devices and servers. Keeping sensitive running-config files on a busy server like this is not recommended. Therefore, it is crucial to promptly remove the files from the Ansible control node once the playbook has been successfully executed.

This brings us to the second problem. Currently, we only have a single SCP server to store the important running-config files for network device system failures or system recovery. However, if this server goes offline, it becomes a single point of failure. To address this, we can easily add more SCP servers by including additional IP addresses in our playbook, as long as the Ansible Control Machine has control over those machines.

To tackle these two issues, let's modify our previous playbook so that it copies the running configuration backup files of all our network devices to three different servers. Once the task **SSH into Cisco Legacy routers or switches** is completed, the backup folder and its contents on the Ansible Control Machine will be automatically deleted.

Step 10: Power on u23c1 (192.168.127.161) and u23c2 (192.168.127.162) Ubuntu servers. As these servers were utilized in earlier chapters, we are aware that Ansible can establish SSH access to these machines. In case you encounter any difficulties with this exercise, you may need to revert to your last known good running configuration using VMware Workstation snapshots.

Step 11: While the two Ubuntu servers are powering up in the background, let's promptly modify our playbook to address the two problems mentioned in step 10. You'll observe that there are only a few changes toward the end of this playbook. Additionally, we will retain the "backup" directory check play to create a new directory if it doesn't already exist. However, at the end of the playbook, the "backup" directory and its contents will always be deleted automatically.

13.2_BACKUP_RUNNING_CONFIG_MULTIPLE_SCP_CLEAN.YML

```
---
- name: Check and create a backup directory on the Ansible Control Machine
  hosts: localhost # Run on Ansible Control Machine, f38s1
  gather_facts: false

  tasks:
    - name: Check if the backup directory exists
      ansible.builtin.stat:
        path: ./backup
      register: backup_dir

    - name: Create backup directory
      ansible.builtin.file:
        path: ./backup
        state: directory
      when: not backup_dir.stat.exists

- name: Backup Cisco IOS-XE Router and Switch configurations
  hosts: ios_xe_devices  # Targeted devices
  gather_facts: false

  vars_files:
    - vars.yml
  vars:
    timestamp: "{{ lookup('pipe', 'date +%Y%m%d-%H%M') }}"
```

```yaml
  tasks:
    - name: Run show run and save to a file
      cisco.ios.ios_config:
       backup: yes
       backup_options:
          filename: "{{ inventory_hostname }}-running-config.cfg"
          dir_path: ./backup/{{ timestamp }}_backup

      - name: Print message when completed
        ansible.builtin.debug: msg="{{ inventory_hostname }} - Backup to local
        storage completed"

- name: Copy backup files to the SCP server
  hosts: localhost  # Run locally
  gather_facts: false

  vars_files:
    - vars.yml

  vars:
    scp_servers:
      - ip: "192.168.127.151"
        path: "/home/jdoe/"
      - ip: "192.168.127.161"
        path: "/home/jdoe/"
      - ip: "192.168.127.162"
        path: "/home/jdoe/"

  tasks:
    - name: Run SCP command
      ansible.builtin.expect:
        command: "scp -r ./backup jdoe@{{ item.ip }}:{{ item.path }}"
        responses:
          "Enter passphrase for key '/home/jdoe/.ssh/id_ed25519':": "{{
          passphrase_response }}"
      register: scp_output
      loop: "{{ scp_servers }}"
```

```
    - name: Print message when completed
      ansible.builtin.debug: msg="Device backup file transfer to SCP
      completed"

    - name: Remove "backup" directory on Ansible Control Machine
      ansible.builtin.file:
        path: "./backup/"
        state: absent
```

Step 12: Let's delete the backup directory from f38s1 and f38c1 before executing the preceding playbook.

Delete the backup directory from f38s1.

```
[jdoe@f38s1 ch13]$ rm -rf backup
[jdoe@f38s1 ch13]$ ls -lh backup
ls: cannot access 'backup': No such file or directory
```

Also, delete the backup directory from f38c1.

```
[jdoe@f38c1 ~]$ rm -rf backup
[jdoe@f38c1 ~]$ ls -lh backup
ls: cannot access 'backup': No such file or directory
```

Step 13: Execute the latest playbook with the --ask-vault-pass option.

```
[jdoe@f38s1 ch13]$ anp 13.2_backup_running_config_multiple_SCP_clean.yml
--ask-vault-pass
Vault password:
[...omitted for brevity]
```

Step 14: If you check the Ansible control node for the backup directory, it has been deleted after the playbook run. But if you check the other servers, you will be able to confirm that all three servers now have the same set of files.

On Ansible control node, f38s1:

```
[jdoe@f38s1 ch13]$ ls -lh backup
ls: cannot access 'backup': No such file or directory
```

SCP file server 1, f38c1:

```
[jdoe@f38c1 ~]$ ls -lh /home/jdoe/backup/20230608-0041_backup
total 24K
-rw-r--r--. 1 jdoe jdoe 3.4K Jun  8 00:42 r13-running-config.cfg
-rw-r--r--. 1 jdoe jdoe 3.4K Jun  8 00:42 r1-running-config.cfg
-rw-r--r--. 1 jdoe jdoe 3.3K Jun  8 00:42 r2-running-config.cfg
-rw-r--r--. 1 jdoe jdoe 3.8K Jun  8 00:42 sw1-running-config.cfg
-rw-r--r--. 1 jdoe jdoe 3.8K Jun  8 00:42 sw23-running-config.cfg
-rw-r--r--. 1 jdoe jdoe 3.8K Jun  8 00:42 sw2-running-config.cfg
```

SCP file server 2, u23c1:

```
jdoe@u23c1:~$ ls -lh /home/jdoe/backup/20230608-0041_backup
[...omitted for brevity]
```

SCP file server 3, u23c2:

```
jdoe@u23c2:~$ ls -lh /home/jdoe/backup/20230608-0041_backup
[...omitted for brevity]
```

While all servers may be in the same time zone, it's crucial to acknowledge that the date and time settings on Ubuntu and Fedora servers can vary. This distinction underscores the importance of incorporating date and time information into directories or file names to prevent any confusion. To address potential issues related to system time drift and time zones, deploying an NTP (Network Time Protocol) server and synchronizing the server times to a reliable time source with the correct stratum becomes essential. In a previous chapter, we covered the installation of the chrony server, which functions as a Linux NTP server. However, due to the focus on other significant topics, NTP will not be further discussed in this book.

To ensure the correct time zone is set on Linux servers, you can employ the "timedatectl" commands. These commands offer a convenient means to manage and configure the system's date and time settings. By utilizing "timedatectl", you can accurately set the time zone and avoid any discrepancies across your servers.

Tip

Changing the time zone on Linux

The following is an example of how to change the time zone on an Ubuntu server, but it's worth noting that the same command can be used for Fedora servers as well:

```
jdoe@u23c2:~$ date
Wed Jun  7 03:55:28 PM UTC 2023
jdoe@u23c2:~$ sudo timedatectl set-timezone Australia/Sydney
[sudo] password for jdoe: ***************
jdoe@u23c2:~$ date
Thu Jun  8 01:55:51 AM AEST 2023
```

Now that you have completed all the tasks in this chapter, you have gained valuable knowledge and skills. Throughout the process, you have learned how to construct a configuration backup lab using GNS3, develop an Ansible playbook for critical network devices running configuration backups on the Ansible Control Machine, and securely store the backup files on multiple file servers for disaster recovery and troubleshooting purposes.

Moving forward into Chapter 14, we will continue working with the same topology. In the upcoming chapter, you will delve into the concept of cron, which serves as a task scheduler. By combining the playbooks developed in this chapter with cron, you will be able to automate the execution of the playbook without any user interaction. This means that the backup of running configurations in your production environment will be autonomously backed up in the background of your network operations, eliminating the need for manual intervention.

The combination of Ansible playbooks and cron scheduling will empower you to streamline and automate critical backup processes, enhancing the efficiency and reliability of your network operations. Get ready to explore the power of cron in Chapter 14!

13.3 Summary

In conclusion, this chapter has provided valuable insights into network device backup using Ansible playbooks. We have stressed the importance of critical configuration backups for routers, switches, and firewalls, emphasizing their role in disaster recovery and operational fault troubleshooting. By setting up a lab environment in GNS3 and configuring the initial devices, readers have gained hands-on experience in preparing for the backup process. We explored the secure transfer of Cisco router and switch configurations to an SCP file server, addressing limitations and highlighting the power of Ansible as a network backup tool. The application of ansible-vault encryption has further enhanced security measures, while overcoming key exchange and cipher compatibility challenges has showcased adaptability. Finally, our demonstration of backup synchronization to multiple SCP servers ensures the safeguarding of vital running-config information. This chapter has equipped readers with the knowledge and practical skills to effectively implement network device backups, promoting efficient disaster recovery and serving as a valuable reference in network operations.

CHAPTER 14

Ansible Playbook Scheduling with Cron

In this chapter, we explore Ansible playbook scheduling with cron, providing a quick introduction to cron and its application to the Ansible playbook application. We delve into a practical lab environment, learning how to schedule playbooks using cron and gaining hands-on experience in operating and troubleshooting cron jobs. We also emphasize the importance of best security practices according to ISO 27001 and the SIEM model. The chapter highlights scheduling a cron job to test-drive the device backup playbook developed in Chapter 13 and setting up the system environment for seamless playbook execution. Additionally, we delve into two methods of Ansible playbook scheduling with a vaulted password: using a Shell script and a Python script. By understanding these techniques, you can safeguard playbooks and protect sensitive information. By the end of this chapter, you will have the knowledge and skills to efficiently schedule Ansible playbooks with cron, automate routine operations, and enhance infrastructure security. Join us as we explore the practical applications of cron and Ansible playbooks, empowering you to optimize your IT operations.

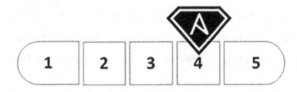

In this chapter, our focus is on automating the execution of Ansible playbooks from your Ansible Control Machine using the Linux job scheduler: cron. While hiring system administrators around the clock is an option if feasible, it can be dehumanizing and costly. Ansible relies on the underlying task scheduling mechanisms of the operating system, such as crontab and cron jobs, for managing and configuring scheduled tasks

© Brendan Choi and Erwin Medina 2023
B. Choi and E. Medina, *Introduction to Ansible Network Automation*,
https://doi.org/10.1007/978-1-4842-9624-0_14

on target systems. This approach ensures consistency and facilitates easy modification of tasks across multiple systems, combining the familiar cron syntax with Ansible's configuration management and automation capabilities.

To enable autonomous operation and maximize efficiency, we rely on built-in mechanisms like cron for task scheduling. In our case, we will schedule the backup application developed in Chapter 13. Linux cron, introduced in Version 7 Unix and developed by Brian Kernighan, has been a prominent job scheduler for Unix-like systems, including Linux. It has been widely adopted due to its ability to automate routine operations through the scheduling of recurring tasks. Notably, when Linus Torvalds developed Linux in the early 1990s, he incorporated many Unix principles, including the inclusion of the cron utility for task scheduling.

Cron utilizes the crontab configuration file to store schedule information and associated commands. Although cron operates through the command-line interface, it offers valuable capabilities once mastered. This chapter is a practical guide for scheduling Ansible playbooks and aims to demonstrate the effective utilization of cron for scheduling Ansible playbooks, empowering efficient task automation. Specifically, we will focus on scheduling the router and switch backup playbook at regular intervals, providing a reliable tool for your work and organization. While high-level scripted programming languages like JavaScript, Shell, Perl, or Python can also be used to develop similar network device configuration backup tools, we will emphasize the use of the Ansible playbook for this purpose. We will address the security challenges posed by embedding user credentials by employing an ansible-vault encrypted vars. yml file. Although not 100% secure, this approach offers improved security compared to embedding passwords directly into scripts. Further details on this topic will be discussed later in this chapter.

To facilitate your initial steps, we will begin with a simple Ansible playbook and cron, allowing you to familiarize yourself with the intricacies and features of task scheduling with cron. Let's embark on this journey together and unlock the full potential of automation!

14.1 Ansible Playbook Cron Lab Network Topology

We will continue using the same topology as in Chapter 13. However, for the final part of our lab, as depicted in Figure 14-1, you will need to power on two additional SCP servers: u23c1 (192.168.127.161) and u23c2 (192.168.127.162).

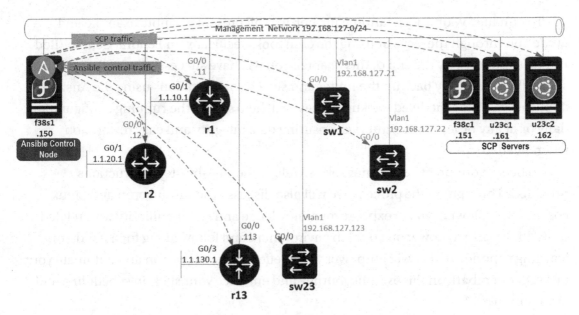

Figure 14-1. *Ansible cron lab network topology*

If you are using an older laptop with a previous-generation CPU and less than 16 GB of memory, it may struggle to run this lab. In such cases, you can run only four virtual devices: f38s1 (Ansible Control Machine), f38c1 (primary SCP file server), r1, and sw1. However, if your laptop meets the requirements, we encourage you to run the full lab to fully experience the power of the backup tool developed in Chapter 13, combined with the cron task scheduler.

Please note that the GNS3 topology remains unchanged from Chapter 13. Please take time to review the topology before moving on to the lab tasks.

14.2 Learning About Cron with a Simple Ansible Playbook

In the opening paragraphs, we briefly mentioned cron, recognizing that not everyone may be interested in delving into intricate details. Our main objective is to help you effectively utilize cron and provide practical training on scheduling tasks in real-world scenarios. To achieve this, we believe it's important to focus on hands-on experience with the tool, taking a more practical approach rather than purely theoretical. However, some theoretical aspects are inevitable and will be discussed as necessary.

To enhance your understanding further, we will present a simple example and guide you through the steps of using the cron tool specifically on Fedora/CentOS/Red Hat distributions. By the end of this chapter, you will have successfully implemented a schedule to regularly back up the router and switch configurations using the Ansible application. This scheduled backup process will help secure the running configuration daily or at any other desired interval, ensuring data integrity and easy restoration when needed.

To begin your practical journey, please follow the step-by-step instructions provided. Throughout the process, we will also discuss other useful cron and Linux commands, allowing you to expand your knowledge and gain familiarity with related tools. Make sure to power on your lab environment and follow along for a hands-on learning experience that will empower you to effectively utilize cron and automate your tasks. Let's embark on this exciting journey and enhance your skills in scheduling and automation!

Step 1: Let's create a simple playbook called hello_ansible.yml to perform a basic test and learn the practical side of cron. To simplify the paths, we will create the ch14 directory under /home/jdoe and work within that directory. Create another directory called learn_cron, and that's where you will have to practice and learn cron features.

```
[jdoe@f38s1 ~]$ mkdir ch14 && mkdir ch14/learn_cron && cd ch14/learn_cron
[jdoe@f38s1 learn_cron]$ vi hello_ansible.yml
[jdoe@f38s1 learn_cron]$ cat hello_ansible.yml
---
- name: Ansible Playbook for printing "Hello, Ansible!"
  hosts: localhost
  gather_facts: false

  tasks:
    - name: Print "Hello, Ansible!"
      ansible.builtin.debug:
        msg: "Hello, Ansible!"
```

Step 2: Since we want to use the default or global ansible.cfg file, let's locate the default ansible.cfg under /etc/ansible/ansible.cfg and disable cowsay (nocows).

```
[jdoe@f38s1 learn_cron]$ find /etc/ansible/ -name ansible.cfg
/etc/ansible/ansible.cfg
```

```
[jdoe@f38s1 learn_cron]$ sudo nano /etc/ansible/ansible.cfg
[sudo] password for jdoe: *****************
[jdoe@f38s1 learn_cron]$ sudo cat /etc/ansible/ansible.cfg
[...omitted for brevity]
[defaults]
nocows=1
```

Optionally, you can uninstall the cowsay from your system altogether using the
"sudo dnf remove cowsay" command. But we will leave it for the rest of the book as it
can sometimes help you to troubleshoot playbooks and where the playbooks reference
information from which ansible.cfg.

Step 3: Run the playbook to confirm that "Hello, Ansible!" prints on the screen.

```
[jdoe@f38s1 learn_cron]$ anp hello_ansible.yml
[WARNING]: provided hosts list is empty, only localhost is available. Note
that the implicit localhost does not match 'all'
[...omitted for brevity]
    "msg": "Hello, Ansible!"
[...omitted for brevity]
```

Step 4: Now, let's expand on the idea and create another playbook named "save_
hello_ansible.yml".

SAVE_HELLO_ANSIBLE.YML

```
---
- name: Hello Ansible Playbook for printing and appending to a file
  hosts: localhost
  gather_facts: false

  tasks:
    - name: Check if file exists
      ansible.builtin.stat:
        path: "hello_ansible.txt"
      register: file_stat

    - name: Create the file if it doesn't exist
      ansible.builtin.file:
```

```
      path: "hello_ansible.txt"
      state: touch
    when: file_stat.stat.exists == false

  - name: Get the current date and time
    ansible.builtin.command: date +"%Y-%m-%d %H:%M:%S"
    register: current_datetime
    changed_when: false

  - name: Append to file
    ansible.builtin.lineinfile:
      path: "hello_ansible.txt"
      line: "Hello Ansible! {{ current_datetime.stdout }}"
      insertafter: EOF
    delegate_to: localhost
```

The preceding playbook will perform the following actions: first, it will check if the file "hello_ansible.txt" exists in the current working directory. If the file doesn't exist, it will create a new file named "hello_ansible.txt" and append the line "Hello, Ansible! [date_time_stamp]" as the first entry. If the file already exists, the playbook will append "Hello, Ansible! [date_time_stamp]" as a new line at the end of the file (EOF).

The primary function of this playbook is monitoring cron service status, and it is also used for testing. By doing so, it ensures that our scheduled cron jobs are running smoothly. This approach provides an intuitive and straightforward way to determine if the cron service is in a good operational state with specific file types, thus saving us time in troubleshooting cron-related issues when scheduling script-based applications like our playbooks; the same idea can be applied to Python, Shell, JavaScript, and Perl file types. By constantly executing this playbook in the background through cron, we can verify that our scheduled tasks are functioning correctly. It serves as an effective method to monitor and validate the operational status of the cron service. By implementing this playbook in conjunction with cron, we can have confidence in the reliable execution of our scheduled tasks, thereby enhancing our automation processes and saving valuable troubleshooting time for any cron-related issues that may arise.

Step 5: On Fedora and most Linux distributions, cron is a pre-installed application. Let's utilize cron to schedule the execution of **save_hello_ansible.yml** every minute. To do this, you need to use the **crontab -e** command. We will soon delve into the meaning of the five stars/asterisks (* * * * *), but for now, think of it as representing every minute.

We will explore the details and significance of each star to gain a deeper understanding of the cron schedule.

```
[jdoe@f38s1 learn_cron]$ crontab -e
* * * * * ansible-playbook /home/jdoe/ch14/learn_cron/save_hello_
ansible.yml
```

Congratulations! You have successfully scheduled save_hello_ansible.yml to run every minute on your Ansible Control Machine. It's that simple! Enjoy the convenience of automated execution at regular intervals.

By default, the crontab file will open in the editor specified by the EDITOR environment variable, which is usually set to vi or vim. If you prefer to use a different text editor permanently, you can follow the following tip to change your text editor preference.

Tip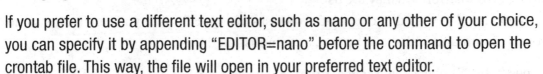

Changing the default text editor on your Linux server

If you prefer to use a different text editor, such as nano or any other of your choice, you can specify it by appending "EDITOR=nano" before the command to open the crontab file. This way, the file will open in your preferred text editor.

Here's an example:

```
[jdoe@f38s1 learn_cron]$ sudo dnf install nano -y
[jdoe@f38s1 learn_cron]$ EDITOR=nano crontab -e
* * * * * ansible-playbook /home/jdoe/ch14/learn_cron/save_hello_
ansible.yml
```

In the preceding example, the crontab -e command is used with the EDITOR=nano prefix to open the crontab file in the nano editor.

If you want to make nano your default editor permanently, you can add the line "export EDITOR=/usr/bin/nano" to either ~/.bashrc or ~/.bash_profile. After adding the line, you will need to log out and log back in for the changes to take effect.

Throughout this book, you have mastered the usage of the vi text editor. However, if you are interested in learning nano as your secondary editor, it can prove to be helpful rather than causing any harm. Switching to a different text editor, like nano, can bring benefits if you find it more user-friendly or if you are more comfortable with its features and commands. Each editor has its unique interface and functionality, and selecting the one that aligns with your preferences can enhance your overall editing experience and boost productivity.

Step 6: To view the scheduled tasks, you can use the **crontab -l** command, which will list all the scheduled tasks.

```
[jdoe@f38s1 learn_cron]$ crontab -l
* * * * * ansible-playbook /home/jdoe/ch14/learn_cron/save_hello_
ansible.yml
```

It's important to note that both Fedora (RHEL-based) and Ubuntu (Debian-based) systems provide consistent functionality for managing cron jobs using the crontab command. The -e option is used to edit cron jobs, while the -l option is used to list cron jobs. This consistency allows users to manage their scheduled tasks similarly regardless of the Linux distribution they are using.

If you need to view the scheduled cron tasks of a specific user, you can use the same crontab command with the -u option, as demonstrated here:

```
[jdoe@f38s1 learn_cron]$ sudo crontab -u jdoe -l
[sudo] password for jdoe: ***************
* * * * * ansible-playbook /home/jdoe/ch14/learn_cron/save_hello_
ansible.yml
```

By replacing "jdoe" with your username, you can view the cron tasks specific to that user. This feature comes in handy when you want to inspect and manage the cron jobs of individual users on your system.

Step 7: To effectively manage the crond services in Fedora, CentOS, and RHEL, you can utilize the following service management commands (systemctl). Most of these commands are self-explanatory, but for those that may require additional clarification, comments have been appended to the command lines. If you are using Debian or Ubuntu, simply drop the last letter "d" and use "cron" instead of "crond". Familiarizing yourself with these service management commands is crucial for troubleshooting any cron-related issues.

```
sudo systemctl disable crond # disable crond on system boot
sudo systemctl enable crond # enable crond on system boot
```

```
sudo systemctl reload crond # reload crond without interrupting
running jobs
sudo systemctl restart crond
sudo systemctl stop crond
sudo systemctl start crond
sudo systemctl status crond # check the status of crond
● crond.service - Command Scheduler
    Loaded: loaded (/usr/lib/systemd/system/crond.service; enabled;
preset: enabled)
   Drop-In: /usr/lib/systemd/system/service.d
            └─10-timeout-abort.conf
    Active: active (running) since Fri 2023-06-09 10:54:53 AEST; 1h
29min ago
  Main PID: 953 (crond)
     Tasks: 1 (limit: 4591)
    Memory: 2.2M
       CPU: 351ms
    CGroup: /system.slice/crond.service
            └─953 /usr/sbin/crond -n
```

The output of the "sudo systemctl status crond" command shown previously indicates that cron is enabled and running correctly. These commands offer essential control over the crond services, enabling effective configuration and management according to your specific requirements.

Tip

You can check the cron logs under /var/log/cron!

If you want to access all the cron job logs, they can be found at /var/log/cron. You can use the grep command to filter and print specific cron jobs. This powerful command allows you to search for particular keywords or patterns within the log files, helping you extract the relevant information you're interested in.

```
[jdoe@f38c1 ~]$ sudo tail /var/log/cron
sudo] password for jdoe: ***************
```

```
[...omitted for brevity]
Jun  9 18:01:01 f38c1 run-parts[1615]: (/etc/cron.hourly) finished 0anacron
Jun  9 18:01:01 f38c1 CROND[1614]: (root) CMDEND (run-parts /etc/
cron.hourly)
Jun  9 18:19:01 f38c1 crond[817]: (CRON) INFO (running with inotify support)

[jdoe@f38s1 learn_cron]$ sudo grep "save_hello_ansible.yml" /var/log/cron
[sudo] password for jdoe: ***************
Jun  9 19:00:03 f38s1 CROND[30550]: (jdoe) CMDEND (ansible-playbook /
home/jdoe/ch14/learn_cron/save_hello_ansible.yml)
[...omitted for brevity]
```

Step 8: If your cron is running correctly, it will automatically generate the hello_ansible.txt file in the current working directory and append "Hello, Ansible! [date_time_stamp]" to the end of each line.

After one-minute mark:

```
[jdoe@f38s1 learn_cron]$ cat hello_ansible.txt
Hello, Ansible! 2023-06-09 13:30:03
```

After three-minute mark:

```
[jdoe@f38s1 learn_cron]$ cat hello_ansible.txt
Hello, Ansible! 2023-06-09 13:30:03
Hello, Ansible! 2023-06-09 13:31:02
Hello, Ansible! 2023-06-09 13:32:03
```

Unless you cancel the cron job by using crontab -e again and removing the corresponding entry, the playbook will continue to run every minute indefinitely.

```
[jdoe@f38s1 learn_cron]$ cat hello_ansible.txt
Hello, Ansible! 2023-06-09 13:30:03
Hello, Ansible! 2023-06-09 13:31:02
Hello, Ansible! 2023-06-09 13:32:03
...
```

To cancel the task, you can simply use the # symbol to comment out the line in the cron table or delete the line completely. Here, we are demonstrating the method of commenting out the line to deactivate the task.

```
[jdoe@f38s1 learn_cron]$ crontab -l
# * * * * * ansible-playbook /home/jdoe/ch14/learn_cron/save_hello_
ansible.yml
```

To remove the crontab for the current user, jdoe, use the -r option.

```
[jdoe@f38s1 learn_cron]$ crontab -r
no crontab for jdoe
```

Step 9: You can also redirect or append the output to a file to track the specific cron job.

Redirecting output:

By default, the output of a cron job is sent via email to the owner of the crontab. However, you can redirect the output to a file by using the > symbol. For instance, to redirect the output to a file named hello_output.txt, you can use the following command:

```
[jdoe@f38s1 learn_cron]$ crontab -e
* * * * * ansible-playbook /home/jdoe/ch14/learn_cron/save_hello_ansible.
yml > /home/jdoe/ch14/learn_cron/hello_output.txt
```

When using the > symbol, the output of a command will overwrite the existing content in the file. This means that only the most recent output will be visible and previous outputs will be lost. If you wish to preserve the history of outputs, you can use the >> symbol instead, which appends the output to the file without overwriting it. This way, each output will be added to the file, allowing you to maintain a record of all the outputs over time.

```
[jdoe@f38s1 learn_cron]$ cat hello_output.txt
PLAY [Ansible Playbook for printing and appending to a file]
************************
[...omitted for brevity]
PLAY RECAP ************************************************************
localhost                  : ok=3  changed=1  unreachable=0  failed=0
skipped=1  rescued=0  ignored=0
```

This is useful if you are only interested in the output of the last cron job execution. The output size will remain constant and minimal.

Appending output:

To append the output of a cron job to a file without overwriting the existing content, you can use the >> symbol. This allows you to add the output to the end of the file without deleting any previous content. For example, to redirect the output to a file named hello_output.txt, you can use the following syntax:

```
[jdoe@f38s1 learn_cron]$ crontab -e
* * * * * ansible-playbook /home/jdoe/ch14/learn_cron/save_hello_ansible.
yml >> /home/jdoe/ch14/learn_cron/hello_output.txt
```

By using the >> symbol, the output will be appended to the file, ensuring that the previous content remains intact while adding the new output at the end of the file. This is particularly useful during the troubleshooting of cron services as it allows you to keep a history of the outputs. Unlike redirecting the output, which overwrites the existing content, appending the output immediately follows the last output, providing a convenient way to track the progress and results of your cron jobs over time. The output size will grow over time and requires administrators to delete old data from the output file.

Step 10: We have not set up email for the owner in our lab, but by default, cron sends email notifications for the output of each cron job to the owner. To disable email notifications, redirect the output to /dev/null.

```
[jdoe@f38s1 learn_cron]$ crontab -e
* * * * * ansible-playbook /home/jdoe/ch14/learn_cron/save_hello_ansible.
yml > /dev/null 2>&1
```

Step 11: Now is a good time to delve into the meaning behind the five asterisks (* * * * *) in the cron syntax. By understanding each position's significance, you can effectively schedule your cron jobs. Refer to Table 14-1 for a detailed breakdown of each position and study the examples provided. While it's not necessary to memorize each example, familiarizing yourself with the format will help you comprehend the purpose of each asterisk in the cron schedule.

In Table 14-1, you can find the meanings of each asterisk.

Table 14-1. *Meanings behind the five asterisks*

*	*	*	*	*
Minute: any	Hour: any	Day of the month: any	Month: any	Day of the week: any
0–59	0–23	1–31	1–12	0–7
				(both 0 and 7 represent Sunday)

Review the examples of crontab time configuration in Table 14-2 and try to familiarize yourself with the five values used in crontab time. The more you use it, the easier it becomes, but there are also many online tools available to assist with crontab time configuration.

Table 14-2. *Examples of crontab time configurations*

Crontab time	Explanation
* * * * *	Every minute
0 * * * *	At the top of every hour
0 0 * * *	Once a day at midnight
0 0 * * 0	Once a week on Sunday at midnight
0 0 1 * *	Once a month on the first day at midnight
0 0 1 1 *	Runs once a year on January 1 at midnight
*/5 * * * *	Every 5 minutes
*/30 * * * *	Every 30 minutes
0 */3 * * *	At minute 0 past every 3rd hour
0 */12 * * *	At minute 0 past every 12th hour
0 1 * * *	At 01:00 every day
30 5 * * 0	At 05:30 on Sunday
59 6 * 3 1	At 06:59 on Monday in March
0 2 * * 0/2	At 02:00 on every 2nd day of the week from Sunday through Sunday
0 0 28-31 * *	At 00:00 on every day of the month from 28 through 31
0 0 1 */3 *	At 00:00 on day-of-month 1 in every 3rd month
0 0 1 */6 *	At 00:00 on day-of-month 1 in every 6th month
0 0 1 1 *	At 00:00 on day-of-month 1 in January

We have covered the basics of cron using a real example playbook. To delve deeper and practice creating different cron schedules, I recommend visiting the Crontab Guru website (https://crontab.guru/). This site offers a user-friendly interface where you can experiment with specific values or utilize the * wildcard to create customized cron schedules. It provides a valuable resource for understanding cron syntax and generating the desired timing configurations for your cron jobs. By leveraging this tool and configuring the cron positions accordingly, you can create schedules that align perfectly with your specific timing requirements.

14.3 Ansible Playbook Scheduling Using Cron

In this section, we will provide a step-by-step guide to help you schedule your backup playbook using cron. By doing so, you can test your playbook with cron and transform it into a powerful configuration backup application. With this setup, your critical device configurations can be automatically backed up every night, eliminating the need for manual intervention from administrators. As mentioned in the previous chapter, while there are numerous proprietary configuration management tools available in the market, creating your tool has its advantages. Not only does it allow for customization, but it also enhances your development skills and deepens your understanding of the underlying technologies involved in device configuration management. So let's begin by creating a simple cron job without the use of encrypted vars password files.

Step 1: We will begin by copying the last working script from exercise 13.2, the "13.2_backup_running_config_multiple_SCP_clean.yml" playbook. However, we will simplify and modify it for our purposes. Let's give the new playbook a simpler name, "14_run_backup.yml".

In this modified playbook, we will make some adjustments and embed the credentials as variables to facilitate cron testing. After copying the file and modifying the necessary information, here is the reworked version of the YAML playbook:

```
[jdoe@f38s1 ch14]$ cd ..
[jdoe@f38s1 ch14]$
cp ../repo1/ch13/13.2_backup_running_config_multiple_SCP_clean.yml ./14_
run_backup.yml
[jdoe@f38s1 ch14]$ vi 14_run_backup.yml
[jdoe@f38s1 ch14]$ cat 14_run_backup.yml
---
- name: Check and create a backup directory on Ansible Control machine
# Play 1
  hosts: localhost
  gather_facts: false
```

```
    tasks:
      - name: Check if backup directory exists # Play 1, task 1
        ansible.builtin.stat:
          path: ./backup
        register: backup_dir

      - name: Create backup directory # Play 1, task 2
        ansible.builtin.file:
          path: ./backup
          state: directory
        when: not backup_dir.stat.exists

- name: Backup Cisco IOS-XE Router and Switch configurations # Play 2
  hosts: ios_xe_devices
  gather_facts: false

  vars:
    ansible_user: jdoe # login name for routers and switches
    ansible_password: 5uper5cret9assw0rd # password for routers and
    switches
    timestamp: "{{ lookup('pipe', 'date +%Y%m%d-%H%M') }}"
  tasks:
    - name: Run show run and save to a file # Play 2, task 1
      cisco.ios.ios_config:
        backup: yes
        backup_options:
          filename: "{{ inventory_hostname }}-running-config.cfg"
          dir_path: /home/jdoe/ch14/backup/{{ timestamp }}_backup # be very
          specific with dir_path

- name: Copy backup files to SCP server # Play 3
  hosts: localhost
  gather_facts: false

  vars:
    remote_user: jdoe # login name for SCP server login
    passphrase_response: Secur3P@ssw0rd # password for SCP server login
    scp_servers:
```

```
    - ip: "192.168.127.151"
      path: "/home/jdoe/"
    - ip: "192.168.127.161"
      path: "/home/jdoe/"
    - ip: "192.168.127.162"
      path: "/home/jdoe/"

  tasks:
    - name: Run SCP command # Play 3, task 1
      ansible.builtin.expect:
        command: "scp -r ./backup jdoe@{{ item.ip }}:{{ item.path }}"
        responses:
          "Enter passphrase for key '/home/jdoe/.ssh/id_ed25519':": "{{
          passphrase_response }}"
      register: scp_output
      loop: "{{ scp_servers }}"

- name: Remove the backup directory on Ansible Control Machine for security
# Play 4
  hosts: localhost
  gather_facts: false

  tasks:
    - name: Remove backup directory # Play 4, task 1
      ansible.builtin.file:
        path: "./backup/"
        state: absent
```

Pay special attention to the bold letters and highlighted sections mentioned previously. Additionally, ensure that you maintain proper spacing and follow the correct order when working with YAML files. Working with longer YAML files can be prone to typos and mistakes, so it's important to be diligent in reviewing your work for accuracy. Take your time to carefully check for any errors or inconsistencies to ensure the smooth functioning of your YAML files.

Step 2: Simplify the inventory file as shown here:

```
[jdoe@f38s1 ch14]$ cat inventory
[ios_xe_devices:vars]
```

```
ansible_network_os=ios
ansible_connection=network_cli
ansible_command_timeout=300

[ios_xe_devices]
r1 ansible_host=192.168.127.11
r2 ansible_host=192.168.127.12
r13 ansible_host=192.168.127.113
sw1 ansible_host=192.168.127.21
sw2 ansible_host=192.168.127.22
sw23 ansible_host=192.168.127.123
```

Step 3: We are going to use the global settings for the default Ansible configuration under /etc/ansible/. Change the global default settings in /etc/ansible/ansible.cfg.

```
[jdoe@f38s1 ch14]$ sudo vi /etc/ansible/ansible.cfg
[sudo] password for jdoe: **************
[jdoe@f38s1 ch14]$ sudo cat /etc/ansible/ansible.cfg
inventory = /home/jdoe/cronjob1/inventory # Be specific with the
inventory file
host_key_checking = False # Disable host key checking, this is important
nocows = 1
forks=30
```

Step 4: This is one of the most important steps to allow communication between the Ansible Control Machine and the rest of the devices on the network. Ensure that you have corrected the SSII config file for the local user jdoe, as this will be used for the key exchanges and cipher negotiations during our playbook.

```
[jdoe@f38s1 ch14]$ cat ~/.ssh/config
Host 192.168.127.11
    HostkeyAlgorithms +ssh-rsa
    StrictHostKeyChecking no

Host 192.168.127.12
    HostkeyAlgorithms +ssh-rsa
    StrictHostKeyChecking no

Host 192.168.127.113
```

```
    HostkeyAlgorithms +ssh-rsa
    StrictHostKeyChecking no

Host 192.168.127.21
    HostkeyAlgorithms +ssh-rsa
    StrictHostKeyChecking no

Host 192.168.127.22
    HostkeyAlgorithms +ssh-rsa
    StrictHostKeyChecking no

Host 192.168.127.123
    HostkeyAlgorithms +ssh-rsa
    StrictHostKeyChecking no

Host 192.168.127.151
    KexAlgorithms +diffie-hellman-group1-sha1
Host 192.168.127.161
    KexAlgorithms +diffie-hellman-group1-sha1

Host 192.168.127.162
    KexAlgorithms +diffie-hellman-group1-sha1
```

Step 5: Now, you are ready to schedule the configuration backup task using cron, using the "crontab -e" command. If you have any directory named "backup" under the /home/jdoe/ directory, remove them for this testing.

```
[jdoe@f38s1 ch14]$ crontab -e
[jdoe@f38s1 ch14]$ crontab -l
*/5 * * * * ansible-playbook -i /home/jdoe/ch14/inventory /home/jdoe/
ch14/14_run_backup.yml >> /home/jdoe/ch14/cron_log.txt 2>&1
```

The cron job expression "*/5 * * * *" indicates that the job will run every five minutes. Within this cron job, the command "ansible-playbook" is used to execute a specific playbook. The playbook being executed is "14_run_backup.yml" located at "/home/jdoe/ch14/". Additionally, the "-i /home/jdoe/ch14/inventory" option specifies the inventory file for Ansible to determine the target hosts. To capture the output and any errors generated by the command, the expression ">> /home/jdoe/ch14/cron_log.txt

2>&1" is used. The ">>" redirects the standard output to the file "/home/jdoe/ch14/ cron_log.txt" without overwriting the existing content. The "2>&1" redirects the standard error to the same location as the standard output. In short, this cron job executes the "14_run_backup.yml" playbook every five minutes using the specified inventory file. The output and any errors generated during execution are appended to the "cron_log. txt" file.

Step 6: Wait for five minutes to allow the cron job to run. After that, you can use the following commands to check the status of the crond and access the cron logs:

```
[jdoe@f38s1 ch14]$ systemctl status crond
[jdoe@f38s1 ch14]$ ls
[jdoe@f38s1 ch14]$ cat cron_log.txt
[jdoe@f38s1 ch14]$ sudo grep "14_run_backup.yml" /var/log/cron
[...omitted for brevity]
Jun  9 23:50:01 f38s1 CROND[220064]: (jdoe) CMD (ansible-playbook -i /home/
jdoe/ch14/inventory /home/jdoe/ch14/14_run_backup.yml >> /home/jdoe/ch14/
cron_log.txt 2>&1)
Jun  9 23:51:07 f38s1 CROND[220062]: (jdoe) CMDEND (ansible-playbook -i /
home/jdoe/ch14/inventory /home/jdoe/ch14/14_run_backup.yml >> /home/jdoe/
ch14/cron_log.txt 2>&1)
Jun  9 23:55:01 f38s1 CROND[221219]: (jdoe) CMD (ansible-playbook -i /home/
jdoe/ch14/inventory /home/jdoe/ch14/14_run_backup.yml >> /home/jdoe/ch14/
cron_log.txt 2>&1)
Jun  9 23:56:05 f38s1 CROND[221217]: (jdoe) CMDEND (ansible-playbook -i /
home/jdoe/ch14/inventory /home/jdoe/ch14/14_run_backup.yml >> /home/jdoe/
ch14/cron_log.txt 2>&1)
Jun 10 00:00:01 f38s1 CROND[222354]: (jdoe) CMD (ansible-playbook -i /home/
jdoe/ch14/inventory /home/jdoe/ch14/14_run_backup.yml >> /home/jdoe/ch14/
cron_log.txt 2>&1)
Jun 10 00:01:09 f38s1 CROND[222351]: (jdoe) CMDEND (ansible-playbook -i /
home/jdoe/ch14/inventory /home/jdoe/ch14/14_run_backup.yml >> /home/jdoe/
ch14/cron_log.txt 2>&1)
```

The provided log displays the execution of the cron job at 23:50, 23:55, and 00:01. This indicates that the playbook ran every five minutes as scheduled, resulting in a total of three routers and three switches running configuration backups being stored in the SCP file servers.

Furthermore, when the cron job runs, it creates a directory named "backup" in the current working directory. The contents of this directory are then copied to the SCP file servers and synchronized across all three SCP servers. Once the Ansible backup playbook completes its task, the "backup" directory is automatically deleted.

In case you encounter any interruptions or errors during the execution of the playbook, you can refer to the "cron_log.txt" file for troubleshooting purposes. This log file provides valuable information that can assist in diagnosing and resolving any issues that may arise.

```
[jdoe@f38s1 ch14]$ ls
14_run_backup.yml  backup        inventory   cron_log.txt  ...
```

Step 7: To stop the cron job, you can comment out the task line by adding a hash (#) symbol in front of it. This deactivates the task and prevents it from running. Once you have commented out the task line, save the changes and exit the editor.

After stopping the cron job, take a moment to review what has happened. By commenting out the task line, you have effectively deactivated the cron job, preventing it from executing as scheduled.

```
[jdoe@f38s1 ch14]$ crontab -e
[jdoe@f38s1 ch14]$ crontab -l
#*/5 * * * * ansible-playbook -i /home/jdoe/ch14/inventory /home/jdoe/
ch14/14_run_backup.yml >> /home/jdoe/ch14/cron_log.txt 2>&1
```

Step 8: Let's quickly check if the cron playbook executions have been successful by checking all three SCP files. The following are the ls command outputs on the second SCP server, u23c1. As you can see, we have three sets of configuration backups from the three routers and three switches.

```
┌─────────────────────────────────────────────────────────────────────┐
│                     U23C1 (SCP FILE SERVER 2)                         │
└─────────────────────────────────────────────────────────────────────┘
```

```
jdoe@u23c1:~$ ls -lh backup/
total 12K
drwxr-xr-x 2 jdoe jdoe 4.0K Jun  9 23:51 20230609-2350_backup
drwxr-xr-x 2 jdoe jdoe 4.0K Jun  9 23:56 20230609-2355_backup
drwxr-xr-x 2 jdoe jdoe 4.0K Jun 10 00:01 20230610-0000_backup

jdoe@u23c1:~$ ls -lh backup/20230610-0000_backup
total 24K
```

```
-rw-r--r-- 1 jdoe jdoe 3.3K Jun 10 00:01 r13-running-config.cfg
-rw-r--r-- 1 jdoe jdoe 3.3K Jun 10 00:01 r1-running-config.cfg
-rw-r--r-- 1 jdoe jdoe 3.4K Jun 10 00:01 r2-running-config.cfg
-rw-r--r-- 1 jdoe jdoe 3.8K Jun 10 00:01 sw1-running-config.cfg
-rw-r--r-- 1 jdoe jdoe 3.8K Jun 10 00:01 sw23-running-config.cfg
-rw-r--r-- 1 jdoe jdoe 3.8K Jun 10 00:01 sw2-running-config.cfg
```

The output on the third SCP file server, u23c2, is the same but has been omitted for brevity.

U23C2 (SCP FILE SERVER 3)

```
jdoe@u23c2:~$ ls -lh backup/

total 12K
drwxr-xr-x 2 jdoe jdoe 4.0K Jun  9 23:51 20230609-2350_backup
drwxr-xr-x 2 jdoe jdoe 4.0K Jun  9 23:56 20230609-2355_backup
drwxr-xr-x 2 jdoe jdoe 4.0K Jun 10 00:01 20230610-0000_backup
[...omitted for brevity]
```

The output on the first SCP file server also is the same as the second server. Now you have three copies of the critical network devices' running configurations in three different locations.

F38C1 (SCP FILE SERVER 1)

```
[jdoe@f38c1 ~]$ ls -lh backup/
total 0
drwxr-xr-x. 2 jdoe jdoe 185 Jun  9 23:51 20230609-2350_backup
drwxr-xr-x. 2 jdoe jdoe 185 Jun  9 23:56 20230609-2355_backup
drwxr-xr-x. 2 jdoe jdoe 185 Jun 10 00:01 20230610-0000_backup
[...omitted for brevity]
```

Imagine if your company had infrastructure or cloud services spread across three different locations. In such a scenario, it becomes paramount to ensure location redundancy by storing critical files in multiple locations, aligning with the principles of ISO 27001 for information security management. This approach aims to proactively prepare for potential disasters, such as network device failures or natural calamities, ensuring continuous data availability and business continuity. By leveraging the playbook, you can conveniently schedule regular backups of your device running configurations at your preferred time and securely store them across multiple platforms and more than two locations, thereby adhering to ISO 27001's emphasis on data protection, redundancy, and risk mitigation.

However, it's imperative to address a significant security concern. As mentioned earlier, the current practice of embedding usernames and passwords as variables in the playbook poses a notable security threat, particularly considering that the Ansible control node may be accessed by multiple users for various administrative tasks in a production environment. This approach does not comply with ISO 27001 security audit requirements, which necessitate a more robust and secure approach.

To bolster our security posture and ensure adherence to ISO 27001 guidelines, we must explore alternative methods that protect sensitive credentials and maintain the integrity of our information systems.

14.4 Ansible Playbook Scheduling Using Cron with a Vaulted Password

Maintaining the integrity of username and password protection is vital in enterprise infrastructure management, particularly when adhering to ISO 27001 compliance. Organizations must prioritize the safeguarding of administrative credentials to ensure the security of systems and data, protecting both company assets and customer information. In this context, Security Information and Event Management (SIEM) plays a crucial role. SIEM is a comprehensive approach to security management that involves collecting, monitoring, and analyzing security events and logs from various sources within an IT infrastructure. By implementing a SIEM solution, organizations can effectively detect and respond to security incidents, identify vulnerabilities, and ensure compliance with ISO 27001 requirements. Especially if you work for an organization

CHAPTER 14   ANSIBLE PLAYBOOK SCHEDULING WITH CRON

that adheres to ISO 27001 security standards, safeguarding administrative usernames and passwords becomes of utmost importance. These credentials must be handled and protected from unauthorized access to ensure the security of your systems and data. By doing so, you can effectively shield your company's and your customers' assets from malicious attacks.

In Section 14.3, we utilized embedded passwords in the playbook to test our cron job and tried to understand how to handle a working playbook in the job scheduler, cron. However, from the standpoint of security best practices, this approach falls well short of the required standards in any enterprise IT operations and production environment. To address this concern, we will create an encrypted vars.yml file to store the user credentials using ansible-vault; then this file will be utilized for scheduling the backup playbook. We will explore two methods: using a Shell script and a Python script to run the backup playbook with an encrypted vars.yml file. Although these methods may not provide the highest level of security for running the cron job, they introduce an additional layer of protection by encrypting and safeguarding the Ansible usernames and passwords using ansible-vault.

By implementing a combination of secure practices, including proper username and password protection, along with adopting SIEM best practices, organizations can significantly enhance their security posture, mitigate risks, and ensure compliance with ISO 27001 requirements.

Let's encrypt the usernames and passwords using ansible-vault and explore how we can schedule the playbook to run in our testing environment.

14.4.1 Shell Script Method

To run an Ansible playbook as a cron job using Shell and access the vars.yml file with a password, you can follow these steps:

Step 1: To create the vars.yml file and encrypt it using ansible-vault, use the following command. If you already have an unencrypted vars.yml file in the working folder, use the "ansible-vault encrypt vars.yml" command. If you already have an encrypted vars. yml file, use the "ansible-vault edit vars.yml" command. Since we don't have one, we will create a new encrypted vars.yml file.

```
[jdoe@f38s1 ch14]$ ansible-vault create vars.yml
New Vault password: ***************
```

```
Confirm New Vault password: ***************
ansible_user: jdoe # login name for routers and switches
ansible_password: 5uper5cret9assw0rd # password for routers and switches
remote_user: jdoe # login name for SCP server login
passphrase_response: Secur3P@ssw0rd # password for SCP server login
```

This will prompt you to set a password for encrypting the file. It is important to remember this password for future use.

Step 2: Now open the 14_run_backup.yml and update the playbook to remove the usernames and passwords.

```
[jdoe@f38s1 ch14]$ vi 14_run_backup.yml
[jdoe@f38s1 ch14]$ cat 14_run_backup.yml
[...omitted for brevity]
- name: Backup Cisco IOS-XE Router and Switch configurations # Play 2
  hosts: ios_xe_devices
  gather_facts: false

  vars_files: vars.yml # Update here

  vars: # Update (remove) here
    timestamp: "{{ lookup('pipe', 'date +%Y%m%d-%H%M') }}"

  tasks:
    - name: Run show run and save to a file # Play 2, task 1
      cisco.ios.ios_config:
        backup: yes
        backup_options:
          filename: "{{ inventory_hostname }}-running-config.cfg"
          dir_path: /home/jdoe/ch14/backup/{{ timestamp }}_backup # be very
          specific with dir_path
- name: Copy backup files to SCP server # Play 3
  hosts: localhost
  gather_facts: false

  vars_files: vars.yml # Update here

  vars: # Update (remove) here
```

```
scp_servers:
  - ip: "192.168.127.151"
    path: "/home/jdoe/"
  - ip: "192.168.127.161"
    path: "/home/jdoe/"
  - ip: "192.168.127.162"
    path: "/home/jdoe/"
```
[...omitted for brevity]

Step 3: Create a file named "sh_password.txt" in the "/home/jdoe/ch14/" directory. For demonstration purposes, we are creating this file in the same directory, but you can choose to place it in another directory in the system or hide it within the hidden directory "/home/jdoe/ch14/". In the Python example, we will utilize the hidden directory.

```
[jdoe@f38s1 ch14]$ vi sh_password.txt
[jdoe@f38s1 ch14]$ cat sh_password.txt
My5cret9assw0rd
```

Step 4: Next, you will need to create a Shell script that runs the backup playbook and provides the password to decrypt the vars.yml file. Create a new file, such as run_backup.sh, and include the following content:

```
[jdoe@f38s1 ch14]$ vi run_backup.sh
[jdoe@f38s1 ch14]$ cat run_backup.sh
#!/bin/bash

ansible-playbook -i /home/jdoe/ch14/inventory --vault-password-file /home/
jdoe/ch14/sh_password.txt /home/jdoe/ch14/14_run_backup.yml >> /home/jdoe/
ch14/run_backup_log.txt 2>&1
```

It is crucial to avoid any typos in the preceding Shell script. Please exercise caution and double-check your script for accuracy before executing it.

The following is a quick breakdown of the previous "run_backup.sh" file:

- #!/bin/bash: The line at the beginning of the file is called the shebang; it specifies the interpreter to be used to execute the script, which is, in this case, the bash shell.

- ansible-playbook: Ansible command to execute a playbook.

- -i /home/jdoe/ch14/inventory: Specifies the inventory file to be used for the playbook. It tells Ansible where to find the list of hosts to operate on.

- --vault-password-file /home/jdoe/ch14/sh_password.txt: The path to the file containing the password required to decrypt the encrypted variables (vault) in the playbook. It ensures that the playbook can access the encrypted variables securely.

- /home/jdoe/ch14/14_run_backup.yml: The path to the playbook file, which will be executed by Ansible.

- >> /home/jdoe/ch14/run_backup_log.txt 2>&1: Redirects the standard output (stdout) of the playbook execution to the file "/home/jdoe/ch14/run_backup_log.txt". The "2>&1" part redirects any error output (stderr) to the same file as well, so both standard output and error output are captured in the log file.

In short, the "run_backup.sh" script executes the Ansible playbook "14_run_backup.yml" using the specified inventory file, vault password file, and captures the output (both stdout and stderr) to a log file.

Step 5: To make the Shell script executable, use the command "chmod +x run_backup.sh". This grants permission to execute the script as a program, allowing you to run it by typing its name without specifying the interpreter explicitly. The script should include the program pointer, typically "#!/bin/bash", to indicate it should be interpreted using the bash shell.

Before running the "chmod +x" command, check the file permissions of your file.

```
[jdoe@f38s1 ch14]$ ls -lh run_backup.sh
-rw-r--r--. 1 jdoe jdoe    5 Jun 10 13:24 run_backup.sh
```

After running the "chmod +x" command, the file permission changes to an executable, and the file color changes to green.

```
[jdoe@f38s1 ch14]$ chmod +x run_backup.sh
[jdoe@f38s1 ch14]$ ls -lh run_backup.sh
-rwxr-xr-x. 1 jdoe jdoe 111 Jun 10 13:20 run_backup.sh
```

Warning!

Check if /etc/ansible/ansible.cfg has been updated per recommendation.

```
[defaults]
inventory = /home/jdoe/ch14/inventory
host_key_checking = False
nocows = 1
forks=50
```

Step 6: Add the following line to schedule the Shell script to run as a cron job:

```
[jdoe@f38s1 ch14]$ crontab -e
[jdoe@f38s1 ch14]$ crontab -l
*/5 * * * * /home/jdoe/ch14/run_backup.sh
```

Step 7: To temporarily disable the playbook, comment out the cron table entry, and then verify that the configuration backups have been successfully created on all SCP servers.

```
[jdoe@f38s1 ch14]$ crontab -e
[jdoe@f38s1 ch14]$ crontab -l
# */5 * * * * /home/jdoe/ch14/run_backup.sh
```

Step 8: To verify the success of your cron job for automated device configuration backups, log into the SCP server and check for the presence of directories containing the configuration files. If you find these directories with the config files inside, it indicates that your cron job was successful.

F38C1 (SCP FILE SERVER 1)

```
jdoe@u23c1:~$ ls -lh backup/
total 0
drwxr-xr-x 2 jdoe jdoe 4.0K Jun 10 14:11 20230610-1410_backup
drwxr-xr-x 2 jdoe jdoe 4.0K Jun 10 14:16 20230610-1415_backup
drwxr-xr-x 2 jdoe jdoe 4.0K Jun 10 14:21 20230610-1420_backup
[jdoe@f38c1 ~]$ ls -lh backup/20230610-1420_backup
```

```
total 24K
-rw-r--r--. 1 jdoe jdoe 3.3K Jun 10 14:21 r13-running-config.cfg
-rw-r--r--. 1 jdoe jdoe 3.3K Jun 10 14:21 r1-running-config.cfg
-rw-r--r--. 1 jdoe jdoe 3.4K Jun 10 14:21 r2-running-config.cfg
-rw-r--r--. 1 jdoe jdoe 3.8K Jun 10 14:21 sw1-running-config.cfg
-rw-r--r--. 1 jdoe jdoe 3.8K Jun 10 14:21 sw23-running-config.cfg
-rw-r--r--. 1 jdoe jdoe 3.8K Jun 10 14:21 sw2-running-config.cfg
```

U23C1 (SCP FILE SERVER 2)

```
jdoe@u23c1:~$ ls -lh backup/
total 12K
drwxr-xr-x 2 jdoe jdoe 4.0K Jun 10 14:11 20230610-1410_backup
drwxr-xr-x 2 jdoe jdoe 4.0K Jun 10 14:15 20230610-1415_backup
drwxr-xr-x 2 jdoe jdoe 4.0K Jun 10 14:21 20230610-1420_backup
[...omitted for brevity]
```

U23C2 (SCP FILE SERVER 3)

```
jdoe@u23c2:~$ ls -lh backup/
[...omitted for brevity]
```

Step 9: In our lab environment, we have configured the task to run every five minutes to thoroughly test its functionality. Once we have successfully validated its performance, we can proceed to replicate these settings in the production environment. In a busy production environment, it is recommended to schedule the cron job twice a day to ensure frequent backups of critical data. However, in a less active or nonbusy environment, scheduling the cron job once a day would be sufficient to meet the backup requirements. It is important to adapt the frequency of the cron job based on the specific needs and workload of your environment, ensuring that crucial data is backed up regularly without causing unnecessary strain on the system resources.

Run once at 00:00 (midnight):

```
[jdoe@f38s1 ch14]$ crontab -l
0 0 * * * /home/jdoe/ch14/run_backup.sh
```

Run twice a day, once at 05:00 AM and once at 10:00 PM:

```
[jdoe@f38s1 ch14]$ crontab -l
0 5 * * * /home/jdoe/ch14/run_backup.sh
0 22 * * * /home/jdoe/ch14/run_backup.sh
```

Congratulations! You have completed the scheduling of Ansible playbooks using an encrypted vars.yml file with the help of a Shell script. To ensure transparency and avoid creating a single point of failure, it is important to document the setup of cron jobs on your server and share this information with your team. Sharing knowledge and information with others is not only caring but also a virtue in the ICT world. By documenting and sharing your findings, you not only solidify your knowledge but also make the information official, allowing others to benefit from your expertise. Additionally, documenting your IT learnings and insights on a blog can be a great way to consolidate your knowledge and serve as a reference for future endeavors. If you find that your memory isn't the best, maintaining a blog can help you retain the information, and you can revisit your learnings at any time.

Extend your knowledge:

Unleash your IT passion and foster growth through sharing with others!

If you're interested, you can visit the author Brendan's blog by clicking here:

 https://italchemy.wordpress.com

ITalchemy – Pick my brain, share the love for IT.

Brendan has been blogging since 2014 after reading one of the articles on the Web about why you should blog, documenting his learnings and sharing them with the wider audience. Over the years, he has accumulated valuable knowledge, leading to the publication of his first, second, and third books. Remember, writing and sharing your passion is akin to maintaining a weekly diary. It allows you to reflect on your experiences, share insights, and contribute to the collective knowledge of the IT community. So don't hesitate to document and share your journey – it's a rewarding and fulfilling endeavor. Writing technical books may not make you instantly rich, but it offers numerous valuable rewards. It can establish you as an authority in your IT domain, inspiring upcoming IT engineers and opening up better job opportunities in the market. Most importantly, it provides a sense of self-fulfillment and satisfaction that cannot be measured solely in monetary terms.

Next, we will explore how to schedule the cron job for the same playbook using a Python script. The overall process will be almost identical, with the only difference being the use of a Python script instead of a Shell script. This is the final section of this chapter and will be a quick one.

14.4.2 Python Method

This will be the final topic of this chapter, and it will be a complementary section to further our understanding. If you prefer using Python instead of a Shell script, you can follow these steps to execute the Ansible playbook as a cron job and access the vars.yml file with a password using run_playbook.py. Since we will be using the same playbook and vars.yml file, we will focus on the main differences, as the overall process of preparing for playbook scheduling using cron and a Python script is similar to the Shell script case discussed earlier.

Step 1: To create or edit the vars.yml file using ansible-vault, use the following command:

```
[jdoe@f38s1 ch14]$ ansible-vault edit vars.yml
Vault password: *************
[...omitted for brevity]
```

Step 2: In contrast to the previous example, let's create a hidden file named .py_password.txt to enhance security and make it less obvious to others. Although you can create a new directory to store this file, for the sake of simplicity in this demonstration, we will create it in the same directory (./) or, in our case, /home/jdoe/ch14/.

```
[jdoe@f38s1 ch14]$ touch ./.py_password.txt
[jdoe@f38s1 ch14]$ vi ./.py_password.txt
[jdoe@f38s1 ch14]$ cat ./.py_password.txt
My5cret9assw0rd
```

Step 3: Create a Python script named "run_playbook.py" and include the following content. In this script, Python utilizes the shell command, similar to running a Shell script. However, the language used here is Python while still relying on the underlying bash shell for execution.

```
[jdoe@f38s1 ch14]$ vi run_backup.py
[jdoe@f38s1 ch14]$ cat run_backup.py
#!/usr/bin/env python3

import subprocess

with open("/home/jdoe/ch14/.py_password.txt", "r") as file:
    password = file.read().strip()

command = f"ansible-playbook -i /home/jdoe/ch14/inventory --vault-password-
file <(echo {password}) /home/jdoe/ch14/14_run_backup.yml >> /home/jdoe/
ch14/cron_log.txt 2>&1"

subprocess.run(command, shell=True)
```

You can find the breakdown of the Python code here:

- #!/usr/bin/env python3 – A shebang line that specifies the interpreter to be used for running the script (in this case, Python). Python code is easily recognizable as it always ends with the file extension .py.

- import subprocess – Imports the subprocess module, which allows you to run external commands from within Python. The subprocess module borrows the power of the underlying OS's processes.

- with open("/home/jdoe/ch14/.py_password.txt", "r") as file: – Opens the ".py_password.txt" file located at "/home/jdoe/ch14/" in read mode. The with statement ensures that the file is automatically closed after reading its contents.

- password = file.read().strip() – Reads the contents of the file and assigns it to the password variable. The strip() method is used to remove any leading or trailing whitespace.

- command = f" ansible-playbook -i /home/jdoe/ch14/inventory --
  vault-password-file /home/jdoe/ch14/password.txt /home/jdoe/
  ch14/14_run_backup.yml >> /home/jdoe/ch14/cron_log.txt
  2>&1" – Defines the command to be executed. It uses the ansible-
  playbook command to run a playbook, passing the inventory file,
  vault password file, and playbook file and redirecting the output to a
  log file.

- subprocess.run(command, shell=True) – Runs the command
  specified in the command variable using the subprocess.run()
  function. The shell=True argument allows the command to be
  executed in a shell environment.

Ultimately, this code reads the password from the ".password.txt" file, constructs the command to run the Ansible playbook, and then executes the command using the subprocess.run() function.

Step 4: Make the Python script executable using the chmod +x command.

```
[jdoe@f38s1 ch14]$ chmod +x run_backup.py
[jdoe@f38s1 ch14]$ ls -lh run_backup.py
-rwxr-xr-x. 1 jdoe jdoe 361 Jun 10 19:31 run_playbook.py
```

Now, the cron job will execute the Python script, which in turn runs the Ansible playbook by providing the password inline via the --vault-password-file option. This allows the playbook to access and decrypt the vars.yml file securely. Make sure that the Python script has the necessary permissions to access the required files and directories and that the password is handled securely.

Step 5: Set up the cron job by editing the crontab file with the following command. This time, we will schedule the cron job to run every three minutes.

```
[jdoe@f38s1 ch14]$ crontab -e
[jdoe@f38s1 ch14]$ crontab -l
*/3 * * * * /home/jdoe/ch14/run_backup.py # Just activated Python script
cron job
#*/5 * * * * /home/jdoe/ch14/run_backup.sh # Deactivated Shell script
cron job
```

Step 6: Run the Python cron job for approximately ten minutes, and you will have three copies of the same configuration files backed up to all three SCP file servers.

F38C1 (SCP FILE SERVER 1)

```
[jdoe@f38c1 ~]$ ls -lh backup/
total 0
drwxr-xr-x. 2 jdoe jdoe 185 Jun 10 14:11 20230610-1410_backup
drwxr-xr-x. 2 jdoe jdoe 185 Jun 10 14:15 20230610-1415_backup
drwxr-xr-x. 2 jdoe jdoe 185 Jun 10 14:21 20230610-1420_backup
drwxr-xr-x. 2 jdoe jdoe 185 Jun 10 20:00 20230610-2000_backup
drwxr-xr-x. 2 jdoe jdoe 185 Jun 10 20:03 20230610-2003_backup
drwxr-xr-x. 2 jdoe jdoe 185 Jun 10 20:06 20230610-2006_backup
```

U23C1 (SCP FILE SERVER 2)

```
jdoe@u23c1:~$ ls -lh backup/
total 24K
drwxr-xr-x 2 jdoe jdoe 4.0K Jun 10 14:11 20230610-1410_backup
drwxr-xr-x 2 jdoe jdoe 4.0K Jun 10 14:15 20230610-1415_backup
drwxr-xr-x 2 jdoe jdoe 4.0K Jun 10 14:21 20230610-1420_backup
drwxr-xr-x 2 jdoe jdoe 4.0K Jun 10 20:00 20230610-2000_backup
drwxr-xr-x 2 jdoe jdoe 4.0K Jun 10 20:03 20230610-2003_backup
drwxr-xr-x 2 jdoe jdoe 4.0K Jun 10 20:06 20230610-2006_backup
jdoe@u23c1:~$ ls -lh backup/20230610-2006_backup
total 24K
-rw-r--r-- 1 jdoe jdoe 3.3K Jun 10 20:06 r13-running-config.cfg
-rw-r--r-- 1 jdoe jdoe 3.3K Jun 10 20:06 r1-running-config.cfg
-rw-r--r-- 1 jdoe jdoe 3.4K Jun 10 20:06 r2-running-config.cfg
-rw-r--r-- 1 jdoe jdoe 3.8K Jun 10 20:06 sw1-running-config.cfg
-rw-r--r-- 1 jdoe jdoe 3.8K Jun 10 20:06 sw23-running-config.cfg
-rw-r--r-- 1 jdoe jdoe 3.8K Jun 10 20:06 sw2-running-config.cfg
```

```
┌─────────────────────────────────────────────────────────────────────┐
│                     U23C2 (SCP FILE SERVER 3)                          │
└─────────────────────────────────────────────────────────────────────┘
```

```
jdoe@u23c2:~$ ls -lh backup/
total 24K
drwxr-xr-x 2 jdoe jdoe 4.0K Jun 10 14:11 20230610-1410_backup
drwxr-xr-x 2 jdoe jdoe 4.0K Jun 10 14:16 20230610-1415_backup
drwxr-xr-x 2 jdoe jdoe 4.0K Jun 10 14:21 20230610-1420_backup
drwxr-xr-x 2 jdoe jdoe 4.0K Jun 10 20:00 20230610-2000_backup
drwxr-xr-x 2 jdoe jdoe 4.0K Jun 10 20:03 20230610-2003_backup
drwxr-xr-x 2 jdoe jdoe 4.0K Jun 10 20:06 20230610-2006_backup
```

Step 7: To complete this task, stop the Python cron job.

```
[jdoe@f38s1 ch14]$ crontab -e
[jdoe@f38s1 ch14]$ crontab -l
# */3 * * * * /home/jdoe/ch14/run_backup.py
#*/5 * * * * /home/jdoe/ch14/run_backup.sh
```

Congratulations on completing all the tasks and reaching this point! By completing the steps outlined in this chapter, you have successfully scheduled a cron job for your network device configuration backup playbook using the Python method. Once you have finalized your development in the lab environment and documented the necessary information to share with your team, you can proceed to implement this solution within your organization.

While it is true that many enterprises already utilize commercial tools for similar purposes, the beauty of Chapters 13 and 14 is that you have learned how to build a network running configuration backup tool for Cisco routers and switches from scratch using Ansible, cron, Shell, and Python code. This knowledge gives you the flexibility to tailor the solution to your specific needs and requirements.

Now is the time to start thinking about other areas where you can leverage cron jobs to automate mundane tasks. By conceptualizing a storyline and jotting down your ideas in a text file or on paper, you can identify additional opportunities to streamline and optimize your work processes, benefiting both you and your organization. Remember that Ansible, while not a programming language itself, can become even more powerful when combined with one or two interpreted scripting languages such as Python, Shell, JavaScript, or Perl.

As you continue your learning journey, consider exploring and expanding your knowledge in these scripting languages. Acquiring proficiency in scripting languages will greatly enhance your ability to leverage the full potential of Ansible, enabling you to accomplish even more in your automation endeavors.

14.5 Summary

In this chapter, we explore Ansible playbook scheduling with cron, providing a practical introduction to cron and its use cases with Ansible. We delve into a practical lab environment, learning how to schedule playbooks using cron and gaining hands-on experience in operating and troubleshooting cron jobs. Emphasizing the significance of best security practices according to ISO 27001 and the SIEM model, we highlight the scheduling of a cron job to test-drive the device backup playbook developed in Chapter 13 and the setup of the system environment for seamless playbook execution with cron and Ansible playbook. Additionally, we delve into two methods of Ansible playbook scheduling with a vaulted password: using a Shell script and a Python script. By understanding these techniques, engineers can safeguard playbooks and protect sensitive information. By the end of this chapter, you have gained the knowledge and skills to efficiently schedule Ansible playbooks with cron, automate routine operations, and enhance infrastructure security best practices.

As a reader, you have explored the practical applications of cron and Ansible, empowering you to develop skills in cron and optimize your IT operations. With this newfound expertise, you can streamline workflows, strengthen security measures, and unlock new levels of efficiency in your infrastructure management. The chapter concludes with a reflection on the transformative power of cron and Ansible playbooks, enabling you to propel your team's IT capabilities to new heights.

CHAPTER 15

Cisco Router Upgrading Playbook

This chapter focuses on the Cisco IOS-XE router Upgrading Ansible Playbook. With security being a top priority, the chapter highlights the importance of patch management and OS upgrades. The lab network topology includes Cisco routers, an SFTP server, and an Ansible control node. The workflow of upgrading Cisco IOS-XE router in bundle mode is explained, along with the benefits of using Ansible in network operations. The step-by-step Cisco IOS-XE Router Upgrade Lab guides readers through building the application using code snippets. The chapter concludes with the complete lab playbook in a single file, enabling readers to understand and modify it as needed. By following the guidelines, readers can enhance their Cisco network administration skills and can adopt automation in their critical network infrastructure upgrades, strengthening network security and performance.

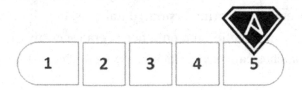

In today's interconnected digital landscape, the stability of network infrastructure plays a pivotal role in ensuring the smooth operation of businesses. Network service stability is crucial for a company, directly impacting its day-to-day operations and overall business longevity. However, network operational outages often stem from changes performed by internal engineers or, externally, the Internet service provider (ISP) due to poor planning or unforeseen issues during network changes for maintenance work. While the stance of "if it is not broken, then don't fix it" may seem appealing for network stability, this approach cannot be adopted when it comes to network security.

© Brendan Choi and Erwin Medina 2023
B. Choi and E. Medina, *Introduction to Ansible Network Automation*,
https://doi.org/10.1007/978-1-4842-9624-0_15

Network and systems engineers in the Information and Communication Technology (ICT) industry face significant pressure to keep their systems up to date with the latest technologies, reducing security vulnerabilities and minimizing the attack surface to protect both company and customer assets from malicious actors. Upgrading and patching enterprise network devices has become essential due to the heightened focus on enterprise network security. Even a single incident of a security breach can have irreversible consequences, damaging an organization's reputation and exposing both the company's and customers' confidential information. Therefore, reputable companies invest significant time and effort into performing system upgrades and patch management.

A substantial portion of a network engineer's time is dedicated to applying patches and upgrading aging infrastructures, ensuring increased security in critical devices such as firewalls, routers, switches, wireless controllers, access points, and any appliance servers. Patch management and system upgrades have now become the industry norm due to the constantly evolving landscape of cloud, data center, and enterprise network security threats. Recent high-profile security breaches and data compromises have significantly increased organizations' awareness of the importance of network security. The sharing of information through Common Vulnerabilities and Exposures (CVEs) has become crucial in proactively protecting against security vulnerabilities. Leading enterprise network vendors, including Cisco, Palo Alto, Check Point, Fortinet, and others, along with reputable endpoint protection software vendors like CrowdStrike, SentinelOne, Cylance, Carbon Black, and more, rely on and reference the same CVE and CVSS (Common Vulnerability Scoring System) databases. Regular releases of patches and updates address vulnerabilities and enhance overall security measures. Neglecting these upgrades and patches can leave critical network devices vulnerable to exploits and potential breaches.

The recent Log4j virus outbreak in December 2021 serves as an example that highlights the risks associated with outdated software and vulnerabilities. In Log4j 1.x's JMSSink component, attackers with write access to the configuration or accessible LDAP service can exploit a vulnerability to execute remote code using a configuration. It's important to note that this issue specifically affects Log4j 1.x when using JMSSink, not the default setting. Upgrading to Log4j 2 is crucial as it addresses this vulnerability and other issues from previous versions. Hackers also target servers and services, demanding ransom payments from organizations. Numerous cases involving major financial institutions demonstrate the significant loss of customer data and trust caused by network security compromises. Even a minor security breach can severely impact an organization's operations, underscoring the criticality of maintaining up-to-date patches and robust security measures to safeguard network infrastructure from malicious actors.

To maintain network stability and security, upgrading and patching critical devices is crucial. Network engineers prioritize system upgrades and effective patch management to protect organizations from breaches. Timely upgrades and proactive patching enhance network security, safeguard assets, and preserve sensitive information. This chapter focuses on upgrading Cisco IOS-XE router, traditionally a manual task performed by network engineers after hours. While Cisco aims to become more software-friendly, its proprietary tools for upgrades and patch management don't scale well for larger environments. In many cases, Ansible outperforms Cisco's tools in configuration and patch management. Despite this, network engineers remain responsible for patching and upgrading Cisco network devices due to the company's industry leadership. Cisco's network devices are extensively deployed in public, private, and hybrid networks, including the Internet itself. Although this chapter cannot cover all insights into upgrading and patching critical networks, it demonstrates how to upgrade Cisco IOS-XE routers using Ansible. Exploring Ansible's features here provides opportunities to apply them in other work areas.

15.1 Router Upgrade Lab Network Topology

The lab topology is illustrated in Figure 15-1. In this lab, we will control the devices from the Ansible Control Machine, **f38s1** (IP: 192.168.127.0.**150**), and attempt to upgrade two Cisco virtual c8000v routers directly on VMware Workstation. The routers are named **c8kv01** (IP: 192.168.127.0.**171**) and **c8kv02** (IP: 192.168.127.0.**172**). They currently run on IOS-XE 17.06.03a and will be upgraded to version 17.06.05 using the new IOS-XE router image named c8000v-universalk9.17.06.05.SPA.bin. This image is stored in the SFTP server, **f38c1** (IP: 192.168.127.0.**151**).

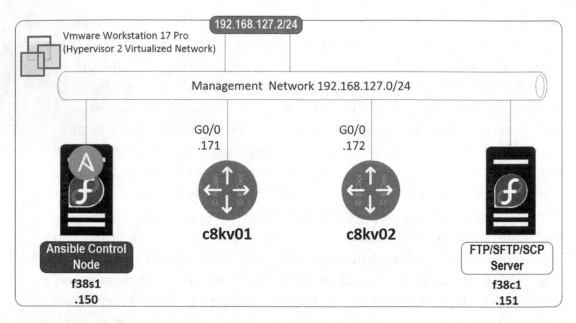

Figure 15-1. *Cisco IOS-XE router upgrade playbook lab topology*

The SFTP server, f38c1, functions as an all-in-one network file sharing server, combining FTP, SFTP, and SFTP services all in a single server. Therefore, you can select the File Transfer Protocol that suits your testing requirements. The workflow for this process will be discussed in the following section.

Expand your knowledge:

Cisco IOS-XE bundle vs. install mode

Cisco IOS-XE supports two modes: Install mode and Bundle mode. In Bundle mode, the router or switch boots directly from the .bin file, which contains the complete software image. This results in faster boot-up times as there is no need to unpack the firmware. Install mode involves booting the package files compressed within the .bin file, which takes longer to unpack and can contribute to longer boot-up times. Bundle mode offers faster boot times and simpler software management with a single .bin file. Install mode provides more flexibility and control over individual package files, allowing for independent software upgrades and feature management. The choice between the modes depends on specific requirements and preferences. The "show version" command can be used to determine the current mode of operation by displaying the output, including the mode (Install or Bundle) in which the IOS-XE software is running.

Refer to the following document for more information:

`www.cisco.com/c/en/us/td/docs/routers/C8000V/Configuration/ c8000v-installation-configuration-guide/m_upgrading_ c8000v.html`

15.2 Cisco IOS-XE Router Upgrade Workflow in Bundle Mode

We mentioned in the previous chapter that if we can document our tasks and processes on paper or in a text file, we can automate them. As a network engineer, if you can write down your tasks and specify the steps involved, automation becomes possible for many of those tasks, though not necessarily all of them. In our case, we use YAML to write Ansible playbooks. In this chapter, we will break down the actual tasks and discuss whether they can be automated using Ansible.

When upgrading an IOS-XE on a Cisco router, the procedures described in Table 15-1 outline a simplified version of the steps to upgrade from an earlier version to a new version (minor upgrade) using an SFTP file server. It is important to note that while the pre-check and post-check steps are simplified here, in actual upgrading scenarios, engineers dedicate their time to thoroughly perform these checks. Although we can demonstrate the pre-check and post-check process, for the sake of simplicity in this book, we will focus more on the actual upgrading of the target devices.

Table 15-1. *General IOS-XE router upgrading task breakdown*

#	Task description	Automation?
1	SSH into the router and check the current IOS-XE by running "show version". For this lab, we are using IOS-XE version 17.06.03a.	Yes
2	Log into the Cisco website and check the latest Gold image (the one with the star) and choose which version you will upgrade your system to.	No
3	Download the latest IOS-XE software image from the Cisco website with your CCO associated with an active support contract. For the upgrade, you need to download the file ending with .bin, that is, c8000v-universalk9.17.06.05.SPA.bin.	No
4	SSH verifies that the router's flash has enough space for a new IOS-XE image.	Yes
5	Set up an SFTP server on a server that is accessible from the router.	Yes
6	Copy the downloaded IOS-XE software image file to the SFTP server directory.	Yes
7	Create a backup of the router's current configuration using the copy running-config startup-config command. This step ensures that you can restore the configuration in case any issues arise during the upgrade process.	Yes
8	Enter the copy SFTP: command to initiate the file transfer from the SFTP server. Provide the SFTP server's IP address, the file name of the IOS-XE software image, and the destination file name on the router.	Yes
9	Enter the password when prompted to authenticate and start the file transfer process.	Yes
10	Wait for the file transfer to complete. This may take some time depending on the size of the software image.	Yes
11	Once the file transfer is successful, enter the configure terminal command to enter global configuration mode.	Yes
12	Update the boot system configuration to point to the newly transferred IOS-XE software image. Use the following command: `boot system flash:cisco-ios-xe-17.06.05.bin`	Yes
13	Save the configuration changes by entering the copy running-config startup-config command.	Yes

(continued)

Table 15-1. (*continued*)

#	Task description	Automation?
14	Verify that the new boot system configuration is set correctly by issuing the show bootvar command.	Yes
15	Restart the router to begin the upgrade process. Use the reload command and confirm the reload when prompted.	Yes
16	Wait for the router to reboot and complete the upgrade process. During this time, do not interrupt the router or perform any configuration changes.	Yes
17	After the reboot, log in to the router and enter the show version command to verify that the upgrade was successful. The output should display the newly installed version of the IOS-XE software.	Yes

Note that these steps provide a general overview, and it is crucial for each engineer to perform all the due diligence while preparing for their IOS-XE upgrade; it is recommended that if there is any clarification required, you reference Cisco's official documentation or open a Cisco TAC case for assistance. While the provided steps are comprehensive, it is important to highlight that the capturing of the pre-upgrade and post-upgrade running-config, interfaces, and IP routing information is among the most critical tasks. These verifications ensure that the network remains stable and continues to provide the same or enhanced services to the users after the upgrade.

In other words, performing an IOS-XE upgrade requires careful and thorough planning, as well as the know-how to best utilize Cisco's official documentation and Cisco TAC support. A well-thought-out, careful change planning and preparation provide engineers with piece of mind, avoiding potential pitfalls and traps that could result in catastrophic network outages. Even for an experienced engineer, it is essential to approach IOS-XE patching with caution and pay attention to every detail.

Tip

Humans pretend to be a computer.

In our honest opinion, a significant majority of network engineers in today's industry secure their positions based on their exceptional troubleshooting and patch management skills rather than relying on their physical appearance, charisma, or personal connections with managers. The nature of IT work often leads engineers to exhibit introverted traits. This stereotype has been prevalent for years, often ridiculed in movies and dramas, and is expected to persist as long as the IT industry thrives. To a large extent, this stereotype holds. While some IT technicians may possess extroverted characteristics, we wonder if you have encountered many individuals with similar traits in the field. It's important to note that this statement reflects our personal opinion and is part of a general discussion.

When working with computers and their languages (such as protocols), you will realize that they are human creations, with computing concepts and operations rooted in the human mind. Interestingly, IT technicians must assume the role of a computer and mimic its behavior during training and study. For example, understanding how enterprise routers make routing decisions based on their configuration and responses to different scenarios requires embodying the essence of a router. Therefore, when preparing for Cisco routers and switches, more experienced engineers strive to understand things from the device's perspective rather than relying solely on their viewpoint.

The term "cosplay" originates from combining the words "costume" and "play." In this sense, we can apply the cosplay analogy to network engineers. Just as cosplayers dress up as fictional characters, skilled network engineers "cosplay" as routers, switches, firewalls, or any other devices they manage in their environment. They immerse themselves in the role of the device, understanding its behavior, configurations, and decision-making processes.

Reference: `www.theliftedbrow.com/liftedbrow/humans-pretending-to-be-computers-pretending-to`

In the upcoming sections, we will guide you through the development of an Ansible YAML playbook that incorporates the aforementioned steps. By leveraging Ansible's powerful automation capabilities, you can streamline the IOS-XE upgrade process and unlock several key benefits for your network infrastructure administration. These are some key benefits of using Ansible in your network operation:

- Streamlined and efficient upgrades

- Consistency and standardization across devices and environments

- Increased scalability for handling upgrades on a larger scale

- Empowerment of less experienced engineers to confidently perform upgrades

- Cost-effective solution leveraging Ansible's open source capabilities

By automating the Cisco IOS-XE upgrade process using Ansible, you can achieve consistent, efficient, and scalable upgrades while empowering engineers at various skill levels. It's a valuable investment that can streamline operations, reduce downtime, and ensure the reliability of your network infrastructure.

Let's dive in and begin designing and writing small, functional playbooks. Afterward, we can integrate them into a cohesive application.

Warning!

Before you begin the lab, take snapshots of your routers, c8kv01 and c8kv02.

To do this, navigate to your VMware Workstation 17 Pro and take snapshots of your routers. This will enable you to practice your scripts in different scenarios. It is recommended to take snapshots regularly at important milestones to prevent any potential issues (see Figure 15-2).

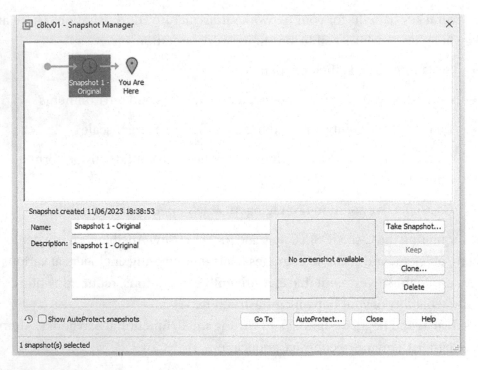

Figure 15-2. *Taking a snapshot before starting the IOS upgrading lab*

15.3 Cisco IOS-XE Router Upgrade Lab

To ensure simplicity and ease of understanding throughout the lab, we will develop an
IOS upgrading playbook using two files: vars.yml and 15_ios_upgrade.yml. By saving
most of the variables in the vars.yml file, the playbook will become cleaner and more
comprehensible from the student's perspective. Understanding the usage of variables at
different points in the playbook is crucial, and once you grasp this concept, you can choose
to embed the information as desired. However, for our demonstration, let's keep it simple.
This approach will help us focus on the core concepts without unnecessary complexity.

Tip

All files used in this book and chapters are available from the authors'

GitHub site.

Download link: `https://github.com/ansnetauto/repo1/tree/main`

15.3.1 Lab Setup

Step 1: Power on the following machines on VMware Workstation: f38s1 (192.168.127.150), f38c1 (192.168.127.151), c8kv01 (192.168.127.171), and c8kv02 (192.168.127.172). For this chapter, we will exclusively utilize VMware Workstation and won't require GNS3. Please ensure that all four VMs are up and running.

Step 2: Referencing Figure 15-3, utilize WinSCP on your host PC to copy the new IOS file to the SFTP file server, f38c1, with the IP address 192.168.127.151. Create a directory named "ios_files" under the /home/jdoe/ directory. In this example, we will be copying the "c8000v-universalk9.17.06.05.SPA.bin" file to /home/jdoe/ios_files. Once copied, the file will be accessible from the /ios_files directory within the SFTP perspective, as you will observe shortly.

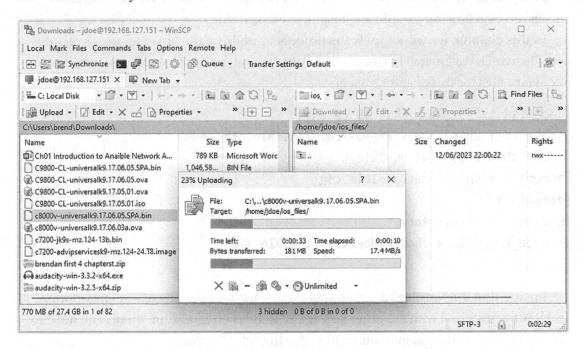

Figure 15-3. *Copying the new IOS image to the SFTP server, f38c1*

Step 3: Now, let's include c8kv01 (192.168.127.171) and c8kv02 (192.168.127.172) to ~/.ssh/config for smooth key exchange between our Ansible Control Machine and two new routers.

```
[jdoe@f38s1 ~]$ vi ~/.ssh/config
[jdoe@f38s1 ~]$ cat ~/.ssh/config
```

[...omitted for brevity]
Host 192.168.127.171
    HostkeyAlgorithms +ssh-rsa
    StrictHostKeyChecking no

Host 192.168.127.172
    HostkeyAlgorithms +ssh-rsa
    StrictHostKeyChecking no
[...omitted for brevity]

Step 4: In Chapters 13 and 14, we utilized the "jdoe" account for SSH authentication between the Ansible Control Machine and the SFTP servers. This required providing the passphrase "Enter passphrase for key '/home/jdoe/.ssh/id_ed25519':", which we addressed by using the passphrase_response workaround.

In this chapter, we will simplify the process by utilizing the "ansible" user's private_key_file, which we created in Chapter 10. Follow the steps here to copy and modify the necessary files for this chapter's usage:

```
[jdoe@f38s1 ~]$ mkdir ch15 && cd ch15
[jdoe@f38s1 ch15]$ cp ../repo1/ch10/ansible.cfg ./
[jdoe@f38s1 ch15]$ vi ansible.cfg
[jdoe@f38s1 ch15]$ cat ansible.cfg
[defaults]
inventory = ./inventory
private_key_file = /home/jdoe/.ssh/ansible
nocows = 1
```

Ensure that the "ansible" account was created without the id_ed25519 passphrase and has been shared with the other servers. With this configuration, there is no need to manually provide the passphrase, unlike with the "jdoe" account.

Step 5: Now, let's add the host information for our two IOS-XE routers. Open the "inventory" file using a text editor and add the following lines to specify the host information:

```
[jdoe@f38s1 ch15]$ cp ../repo1/ch10/inventory ./
[jdoe@f38s1 ch15]$ vi inventory
[jdoe@f38s1 ch15]$ cat inventory
[file_servers]
```

```
f38c1 ansible_host=192.168.127.151 # SFTP Server
```

```
[ios_xe_routers]
c8kv01 ansible_host=192.168.127.171 # Router 1
c8kv02 ansible_host=192.168.127.172 # Router 2
```

Save the file after adding the host information. This step ensures that Ansible knows the IP addresses of our two routers and can establish communication with them during the playbook execution.

Step 6: Before we proceed with writing a simple IOS upgrade playbook, let's save all our variables to the vars.yml file. This will allow our playbook to access the necessary data efficiently.

Open the "vars.yml" file using a text editor and add the relevant variables and their values.

For example:

VARS.YML

```
ansible_user: jdoe # Router user ID
ansible_password: 5uper5cret9assw0rd # Router password
sudoer_name: jdoe # f38c1, server sudo user
ansible_become_pass: Secure5cret9assw0rd # f38c1, sudo user password
sftp_server_ip: 192.168.127.151 # SFTP server IP
sftp_username: jdoe # SFTP user name
sftp_password: Secure5cret9assw0rd # SFTP password
ios_file_md5: f3dc5681ac6b66d807a36b3830569344 # New IOS file MD5 value
ios_file_name: c8000v-universalk9.17.06.05.SPA.bin # New IOS file name
new_ios_version: 17.06.05 # New IOS version number
```

Step 7: Either on your VMware Workstation console or SSH session to your routers, check the current IOS by running the command "show version" for your reference, as shown in Figure 15-4.

```
c8kv02#show version
Cisco IOS XE Software, Version 17.06.03a
Cisco IOS Software [Bengaluru], Virtual XE Software (X86_64_LINUX_IOSD-UNIVERSAL
K9-M), Version 17.6.3a, RELEASE SOFTWARE (fc1)
Technic8kv01#show ver
CopyriCisco IOS XE Software, Version 17.06.03a
CompilCisco IOS Software [Bengaluru], Virtual XE Software (X86_64_LINUX_IOSD-UNIVERSAL
      K9-M), Version 17.6.3a, RELEASE SOFTWARE (fc1)
      Technical Support: http://www.cisco.com/techsupport
Cisco Copyright (c) 1986-2022 by Cisco Systems, Inc.
All riCompiled Fri 08-Apr-22 04:51 by mcpre
licens
softwa
with ACisco IOS-XE software, Copyright (c) 2005-2022 by cisco Systems, Inc.
GPL coAll rights reserved.  Certain components of Cisco IOS-XE software are
documelicensed under the GNU General Public License ("GPL") Version 2.0.  The
or thesoftware code licensed under GPL Version 2.0 is free software that comes
softwawith ABSOLUTELY NO WARRANTY.  You can redistribute and/or modify such
      GPL code under the terms of GPL Version 2.0.  For more details, see the
      documentation or "License Notice" file accompanying the IOS-XE software,
ROM: Ior the applicable URL provided on the flyer accompanying the IOS-XE
      software.
c8kv02
Uptime
 --MorROM: IOS-XE ROMMON

    c8kv01 uptime is 14 minutes
    Uptime for this control processor is 16 minutes
    --More--
```

Figure 15-4. *Cisco IOS-XE version before the upgrade*

Now that you have completed the preparation work for this lab, let's write the main IOS upgrade playbook. This task requires your full attention, as the playbook is lengthy and involves numerous moving parts.

15.3.2 Writing the Main Playbook for Router Upgrade

The playbooks have been divided into 11 parts for a better explanation, with each part being explained first. Additionally, a complete version of the playbook will be provided at the end of this chapter, including brief explanations. To save time, please download the playbook from the authors' GitHub page.

Step 1: Let's begin with the IOS check and validation to determine if our current IOS version is older and requires an upgrade to a newer version. In this example, we will be upgrading from version 17.06.03a to 17.06.05, which is a minor version upgrade operating in Bundle mode. If you are planning an upgrade using Install mode, please refer to Cisco's documentation and plan accordingly using Ansible. Check the current IOS version and compare it with the new IOS version to ensure that the current IOS is up to date.

```
---
- name: Upgrade Cisco IOS-XE Routers
  hosts: ios_xe_routers
  gather_facts: true # By default true but specifying this to show our
  intention!

  vars_files: vars.yml # read vars.yml for variables.

  max_fail_percentage: 0 # If any host fails, the application will exit, in
  percentage.

  tasks:
    - name: Check current IOS-XE version from gathered IOS facts # Task 1
      ios_facts:

    - name: Debug current and new IOS versions # Task 2
      ansible.builtin.debug:
        msg:
          - "Current version: {{ ansible_net_version }}" # Informational
          - "New version    : {{ new_ios_version }}" # Informational

    - name: Quit playbook if ansible_net_version equals new_ios_version
    # Task 3
      block:
        - name: Fail if versions are equal or current IOS is newer
          ansible.builtin.fail:
            msg: "Current IOS version is already up to date."
          when: ansible_net_version >= new_ios_version

        - name: Debug Message
          ansible.builtin.debug:
            msg: "Continuing with the playbook, upgrading IOS version..."
          ignore_errors: true
```

The Ansible playbook provided previously is designed for upgrading Cisco IOS-XE routers. It begins by specifying the playbook name and the target hosts. Facts are gathered from the hosts to obtain information, and variables are loaded from a file named vars.yml. The playbook sets the maximum failure percentage to 0, meaning any host failure will cause the playbook to stop.

The tasks section consists of several steps: checking the current IOS-XE version using the ios_facts module, displaying the current and new versions with the debug module, and then a block that fails the playbook if the versions are equal or if the current IOS version is newer. If the conditions are not met, a debug message is displayed, and errors in this task are ignored.

Step 2: Create a backup directory for configurations on the SFTP server.

```
# Confinuing from previous step
- name: Create directories on the SFTP server
  hosts: f38c1

  tasks:
    - name: Get ansible date/time facts # Task 1
      ansible.builtin.setup:
        filter: "ansible_date_time"
        gather_subset: "!all"

    - name: Store DTG as a fact # Task 2
      ansible.builtin.set_fact:
        DTG: "{{ ansible_date_time.date }}"

    - name: Create Directory for backup # Task 3
      ansible.builtin.file:
        path: "~/ch15/{{ DTG }}" # e.g.) /home/jdoe/ch15/2023-06-14
        state: directory
        mode: "0775"
      run_once: true
```

The Ansible playbook provided previously is responsible for creating directories on our SFTP server, specifically under the name "f38c1". The playbook consists of three tasks. The first task, "Get Ansible date/time facts," utilizes the setup module to gather date and time facts from the Ansible controller. It filters the facts to retrieve only the "ansible_date_time" subset. The second task, "Store DTG as a fact," employs the set_fact module to store the current date in the "DTG" variable. This information is extracted from the previously gathered Ansible date/time facts. The third task, "Create Directory for backup," utilizes the file module to generate a directory path on the SFTP server. The path is constructed using the format "~/ch15/{{ DTG }}", where the "DTG" variable represents the stored date. Additionally, the task sets the directory's permissions to

"0775" to allow read, write, and execute access. The task is executed only once using the run_once parameter. These tasks collectively enable the creation of directories with dynamic names based on the current date on the SFTP server.

Step 3: Next, we will proceed to create backups of the running-config for each router using the "copy run-config sftp" command. Please ensure accuracy in your typing and spacing when executing this step.

```
# Confinuing from previous step
- name: Copy the running configuration
  hosts: ios_xe_routers
  gather_facts: false

  vars_files: vars.yml

  vars:
    file_name: "ch15/{{ hostvars['f38c1'].DTG }}/{{ inventory_hostname
    }}-confg-0"
    command_timeout: 600

  tasks:
    - name: Copy running configuration # Task 1
      ansible.netcommon.cli_command:
        command: "copy running-config sftp://{{ sftp_username }}:{{ sftp_
        password }}@{{ sftp_server_ip }}/{{ file_name }}"
        check_all: True
        prompt:
          - 'Address or name of remote host'
          - 'Destination username'
          - 'Destination filename'
        answer:
          - '{{ sftp_server_ip }}'
          - '{{ sftp_username }}'
          - '{{ file_name }}'
      register: copy_result

    - name: Display copy result # Task 2
      ansible.builtin.debug:
        var: copy_result
```

The preceding Ansible playbook is designed to copy the running configuration from Cisco IOS-XE routers to an SFTP server. It starts with the playbook name and specifies the target hosts as "ios_xe_routers". The playbook disables gathering facts by setting the "gather_facts" parameter to false. Variables are loaded from the "vars.yml" file, which includes the "file_name" variable representing the destination path on the SFTP server. This path is constructed based on the current date and the inventory hostname. Another variable, "command_timeout", is set to limit the maximum execution time for commands to 600 seconds. The playbook consists of two tasks. The first task utilizes the "ansible. netcommon.cli_command" module to execute a CLI command on the routers. This command copies the running configuration to the SFTP server, using the provided SFTP credentials and dynamically generated file paths. It handles prompts interactively and stores the result in the "copy_result" variable. The second task, "Display copy result," uses the "debug" module to print the value of the "copy_result" variable, providing information about the success or failure of the previous task.

Step 4: Before making any changes to the routers, save the running configuration.

```
# Confinuing from previous step
    - name: Save running-config to startup-config # Task 1
      cisco.ios.ios_config:
        save_when: always
```

The task "Save running-config to startup-config" utilizes the "ios_config" module. It is responsible for saving the running configuration to the startup configuration on Cisco IOS devices, ensuring persistence even after a reboot. The "save_when" parameter is set to "always," ensuring unconditional saving.

Step 5: In this step, we will extend the SSH session timer and copy the new IOS file to the routers' flash drive. As the files are being uploaded to the Cisco routers, you can monitor the progress of the file upload by using the **"show flash: | in 17.06.05"** command.

```
# Confinuing from previous step
    - name: Extend SSH timer to 99 mins # Task 1
      cisco.ios.ios_config:
        commands:
          - line vty 0 15
          - exec-timeout 99 0
```

```
- name: Copy new IOS from SFTP server 192.168.127.151 # Task 2
  ansible.netcommon.cli_command:
    command: 'copy sftp://{{ sftp_username }}:{{ sftp_password }}@{{
    sftp_server_ip }}/{{ ios_file_name }} flash:/{{ ios_file_name }}'
    check_all: True
    prompt:
      - 'Destination filename'
    answer:
      - '{{ ios_file_name }}'
```

The preceding Ansible playbook consists of two tasks. The first task, named
"Extend SSH timer to 99 minutes," utilizes the "ios_config" module. It executes a set
of commands on the IOS device to extend the SSH session timer to 99 minutes. The
commands executed are "line vty 0 15" and "exec-timeout 99 0". This task ensures
that SSH connections remain active for an extended duration, providing convenience
and uninterrupted access. The second task, named "Copy new IOS from SFTP server
192.168.127.151," uses the "cli_command" module. It executes a CLI command on the
IOS device to copy a new IOS image from an SFTP server. The command incorporates
the provided SFTP credentials, server IP address, and the specified "ios_file_name". The
task handles prompts encountered during the execution, particularly the "Destination
filename" prompt, and provides the answer as "{{ ios_file_name }}". This task facilitates
the seamless update of IOS images on the device from the designated SFTP server.
These tasks collectively ensure an extended SSH session timer and enable the effortless
retrieval of the latest IOS image from an SFTP server, enhancing the performance and
functionality of the IOS device.

Tip

Comparing FTP, SFTP, and SCP router file upload methods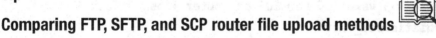

If you are interested in learning more about file uploading and downloading
methods, the primary author has shared information on all three methods on his
blog. You can visit the following links for further details:

1. Ansible IOS-XE File Upload – FTP Method

    Link: https://wordpress.com/post/italchemy.
    wordpress.com/5472

2. Ansible IOS-XE File Upload – SFTP Method

    Link: https://wordpress.com/post/italchemy.wordpress.
    com/5475

3. Ansible IOS-XE File Upload – SCP Method

    Link: https://wordpress.com/post/italchemy.wordpress.
    com/5478

These resources will provide you with in-depth insights into the different file-uploading methods and help you understand the nuances and benefits of each approach. Feel free to explore the links and expand your knowledge of file management in Ansible for IOS-XE routers.

___

Step 6: After the file upload finishes, verify the integrity of the new IOS file.

```
# Confinuing from previous step
  - name: Verify MD5 value on the flash # Task 1
    cisco.ios.ios_command:
      commands: verify /md5 flash:{{ ios_file_name }} {{ios_file_md5 }}
    register: ios_file_md5_flash_result

  - ansible.builtin.debug: # Task 2
      var: ios_file_md5_flash_result.stdout

  - name: Locate MD5 value of new IOS on router flash # Task 3
    ansible.builtin.set_fact:
      ios_file_md5_flash: "{{ ios_file_md5_flash_result.stdout[0] |
      regex_search('[a-f0-9]{32}') }}"

  - ansible.builtin.debug: # Task 4
      msg:
        - "ios_file_md5 [flash:/]          : {{ ios_file_md5_flash }}"
        - "ios_file_md5 [Correct Value]    : {{ ios_file_md5 }}"
```

```
    - name: Fail if MD5 Values are different # Task 5
      ansible.builtin.fail: msg="Failed, flash IOS MD5 value DOES NOT MATCH
      the correct IOS file MD5 value. "
      when: ios_file_md5_flash != ios_file_md5 or 'Verified' not in ios_
      file_md5_flash_result.stdout[0]

    - name: Pass if MD5 values are the same # Task 6
      ansible.builtin.debug:
        msg: Passed, flash IOS MD5 MATCH provided IOS file MD5.
      when: ios_file_md5_flash == ios_file_md5 and 'Verified' in ios_file_
      md5_flash_result.stdout[0]
```

The provided Ansible playbook focuses on verifying MD5 values on a router's flash memory as a means to halt the upgrade process in case of file corruption during the file transfer. The first task utilizes the "ios_command" module to verify the MD5 value of a specified file on the flash memory, storing the result. The second task displays the MD5 verification result obtained from the previous task. In the third task, the MD5 value is extracted from the result and assigned to a variable. Subsequently, the fourth task compares and displays the MD5 values from the router's flash memory and the correct MD5 value for comparison. To signal a failure, the fifth task uses the "fail" module, generating an error message if the MD5 values do not match or if the verification result does not contain the string "Verified". Conversely, the sixth task utilizes the "debug" module to present a success message if the MD5 values match and the verification result contains the string "Verified". This playbook ensures the detection of file corruption during the upgrade process by verifying MD5 values.

Step 7: Change the routers' boot variables so that they boot into the new IOS image.

```
# Confinuing from previous step
    - name: Clear the old boot variable # Task 1
      cisco.ios.ios_config:
        commands:
          - "no boot system"
        save_when: always

    - name: Change the boot variable to a new IOS image (.bin) # Task 2
      cisco.ios.ios_config:
        commands:
          - "boot system flash:{{ ios_file_name }}"
```

```
      save_when: always

  - name: Run show boot command # Task 3
    cisco.ios.ios_command:
      commands: show boot
      wait_for:
        - result[0] contains "{{ new_ios_version }}"
    register: show_boot1

  - ansible.builtin.debug: # Task 4
      var: show_boot1.stdout_lines
```

The given Ansible playbook consists of four tasks that focus on managing the boot variables and verifying the boot configuration on a Cisco IOS device. The first task, "Clear the old boot variable," utilizes the "ios_config" module to execute the command "no boot system" and remove any existing boot system configurations. The second task, "Change the boot variable to the new IOS image," uses the "ios_config" module to set the boot system configuration to the new IOS image file. It executes the command "boot system flash:{{ ios_file_name }}" to accomplish this. The third task, "Run the show boot command," employs the "ios_command" module to execute the command "show boot" and waits for the result to contain the string "{{ new_ios_version }}". The output of this command is stored in the variable "show_boot1" using the "register" keyword. The fourth task, "debug," displays the contents of the "show_boot1" variable, specifically the "stdout_lines" attribute. This provides visibility into the output of the "show boot" command.

Step 8: Save the configuration once more and issue the reload command.

```
# Confinuing from previous step
  - name: Save running-config to startup-config # Task 1
    cisco.ios.ios_config:
      save_when: always

  - name: Reload the device # Task 2
    cisco.ios.ios_command:
      commands:
        - command: "reload\r"
          prompt: 'Proceed with reload? [confirm]'
          answer: "\r"
```

The preceding Ansible playbook consists of two tasks related to saving the running configuration to the startup configuration and reloading a Cisco IOS device. The first task, "Save running-config to startup-config", utilizes the "ios_config" module with the "save_when" parameter set to "always". This ensures that the running configuration is saved to the startup configuration, persisting any changes made. The second task, "Reload the device," uses the "ios_command" module to execute the command "reload" on the device. It provides a prompt pattern to match the confirmation message of reloading and specifies the answer as "\r" (carriage return) to proceed with the reload. These tasks collectively enable the saving of the running configuration and perform a device reload, ensuring that any configuration changes take effect and the device is reloaded safely.

Step 9a: Although the recommended method to wait for the router to reload and detect open port 22 was attempted, it encountered some issues.

```
- name: Wait for the device to come back online. # Task 1
  ansible.builtin.wait_for:
    host: "{{ inventory_hostname }}"
    port: 22
    delay: 120
    timeout: 600
    state: started
  delegate_to: localhost
```

The preceding playbook presents the recommended approach for waiting until a device is back online. The task specifically waits for port 22 to become available after a 120-second delay. In our lab environment, where routers typically take around 3 minutes and 30 seconds to reboot, the probing begins at the 2-minute mark. This task utilizes the "wait_for" module to define the waiting conditions. Parameters such as the "host" parameter are set to "{{ inventory_hostname }}" to identify the specific host, while the "port" parameter is configured as 22 for establishing an SSH connection. The task incorporates a 120-second initial delay and a 600-second timeout for the maximum waiting duration. The "state" parameter is set to "started" to ensure the device is fully operational before proceeding. By delegating the task to the "localhost" machine, the device's status can be monitored. It's important to note that while this method may not work universally due to platform and Ansible version variations, alternative solutions can be employed to address specific issues. It's crucial to thoroughly test the "wait_for" module in your lab environment to determine its effectiveness. Since step 9a did not work in our lab, we are resorting to step 9b as a workaround.

Step 9b: If you are familiar with the booting-up time of your devices, you can estimate it and introduce a delay in your playbook accordingly.

```
# Confinuing from previous step
- name: Sleep for 5 minutes # Task 1
  hosts: localhost
  gather_facts: false
  tasks:
    - name: Pause for 5 minutes
      ansible.builtin.pause:
        seconds: 300
      run_once: true
```

The playbook serves the purpose of pausing the playbook execution for 5 minutes (300 seconds). It targets the "localhost" host and does not gather facts. The single task in the playbook is named "Pause for 5 minutes" and utilizes the "pause" module. The module is configured with the "seconds" parameter set to 300, representing the duration of the pause in seconds. Since my routers typically take between 3 minutes 30 seconds and 3 minutes 40 seconds before they come online, this deliberate pause allows for the necessary waiting time. The "run_once" parameter ensures that the task is executed only once, regardless of the number of hosts. By using this playbook, you can introduce a deliberate delay in the playbook execution, accommodating specific timing requirements or synchronization with external processes.

Step 10: After the five-minute wait, restore the SSH session times to the default ten minutes.

```
# Confinuing from previous step
- name: Copy the running configuration
  hosts: ios_xe_routers
  gather_facts: false

  vars_files: vars.yml

  vars:
    file_name: "ch15/{{ hostvars['f38c1'].DTG }}/{{ inventory_hostname
    }}-confg-1"
    command_timeout: 600
```

```
tasks:
  - name: Restore SSH timer to default value, 10 mins  # Task 1
    cisco.ios.ios_config:
      commands:
        - line vty 0 15
        - exec-timeout 10 0
      save_when: modified

  - name: Copy running configuration  # Task 2
    ansible.netcommon.cli_command:
      command: "copy running-config sftp://{{ sftp_username }}:{{ sftp_
      password }}@{{ sftp_server_ip }}/{{ file_name }}"
      check_all: True
      prompt:
        - 'Address or name of remote host'
        - 'Destination username'
        - 'Destination filename'
      answer:
        - '{{ sftp_server_ip }}'
        - '{{ sftp_username }}'
        - '{{ file_name }}'
    register: copy_result

  - name: Display copy result  # Task 3
    ansible.builtin.debug:
      var: copy_result
```

The preceding Ansible playbook is designed to copy the running configuration from IOS-XE routers to an SFTP server. Let's break down each component of the playbook. The playbook starts with the task named "Copy running configuration," which specifies the hosts as "ios_xe_routers" and sets "gather_facts" to false, indicating that no fact-gathering is required. The playbook includes the "vars_files" directive, which imports variables from the "vars.yml" file containing additional configuration data. In the "vars" section, two variables are defined: "file_name" and "command_timeout". "file_name" is constructed using the values of "hostvars['f38c1'].DTG" and "inventory_hostname" to form the file path for the copied configuration. "command_timeout" is set to 600 seconds. Task 1, named "Restore SSH timer to default value, 10 mins," uses the "ios_ config" module to execute commands that restore the SSH timer to its default value of ten minutes. The "save_when" parameter is set to "modified" to save the configuration when it is modified. Task 2, named "Copy running configuration," uses the "ansible. netcommon.cli_command" module to run the command that copies the running configuration to the specified SFTP server. The command includes variables for the SFTP username, password, server IP, and the constructed "file_name" variable. The "check_all" parameter is set to true to ensure all prompts are checked. Task 3, named "Display copy result," uses the "debug" module to print the value of the "copy_result" variable, which contains the output of the previous task. By executing this playbook, the running configuration of the IOS-XE routers will be copied to the designated SFTP server, and the playbook will provide information about the result of the copy operation.

Step 11: Verify that the new IOS version is correct.

```
# Confinuing from previous step
    - name: Check the new IOS version. # Task 1
      cisco.ios.ios_facts:

    - ansible.builtin.debug: # Task 2
        msg:
          - "Current version is {{ ansible_net_version }}"

    - name: Assert that the new ios version is correct. # Task 3
      vars:
        NEW_IOS_VERSION: "{{ new_ios_version }}"
      ansible.builtin.assert:
        that:
          - NEW_IOS_VERSION == ansible_net_version

    - ansible.builtin.debug: # Task 4
        msg:
          - "Cisco IOS-XE upgrade has been completed successfully."
```

The provided Ansible playbook includes multiple tasks that focus on checking and verifying the new IOS version. Task 1, titled "Check the new IOS version," employs the "ios_facts" module to gather information about the network devices, specifically their IOS versions. Task 2, labeled as "Debug," utilizes the "debug" module to display a message containing the current IOS version. It accesses the "ansible_net_version" variable to retrieve the version information. Task 3, named "Assert that the new IOS version is correct," defines a variable called "NEW_IOS_VERSION" with the desired new IOS version as its value, utilizing the "assert" module, and validates whether the "NEW_IOS_VERSION" matches the "ansible_net_version" variable. If the assertion fails, an error will be raised, indicating an incorrect new IOS version. Task 4, also utilizing the "debug" module, prints a success message confirming the successful completion of the Cisco IOS-XE upgrade. By executing this playbook, you can verify the current IOS version, compare it to the desired version, and ensure a successful upgrade. This playbook is designed to maintain consistency and accuracy in managing IOS versions across network devices.

Step 12: Now execute the "15_upgrade_router.yml" file. This process will take approximately 20 minutes from start to finish to upgrade the two routers in our lab environment. It is crucial to ensure that you have followed the chapter's instructions carefully and that your playbook reaches the final message, indicating a successful upgrade. If you need to refer to the complete playbook, it is included at the end of this chapter before the summary. Additionally, a copy of the playbook is available on GitHub to expedite the testing process (`https://github.com/ansnetauto/repo1/tree/main/ch15`). However, it is essential to focus on understanding the end-to-end playbook for a comprehensive understanding of the process.

```
[jdoe@f38s1 ch15]$ anp 15_upgrade_router.yml
[...omitted for brevity]
TASK [Assert that the new ios version is correct.] ************************
ok: [c8kv01] => {
    "changed": false,
    "msg": "All assertions passed"
}
ok: [c8kv02] => {
    "changed": false,
    "msg": "All assertions passed"
}

TASK [debug] *************************************************************
ok: [c8kv01] => {
    "msg": [
        "Cisco IOS-XE upgrade has been completed successfully."
    ]
}
```

```
ok: [c8kv02] => {
    "msg": [
        "Cisco IOS-XE upgrade has been completed successfully."
    ]
}

PLAY RECAP ************************************************************
c8kv01                          :
ok=27    changed=6  unreachable=0  failed=0  skipped=2  rescued=0  ignored=0
c8kv02                          :
ok=27    changed=6  unreachable=0  failed=0  skipped=2  rescued=0  ignored=0
f38c1                           :
ok=4     changed=0  unreachable=0  failed=0  skipped=0  rescued=0  ignored=0
localhost               :
ok=1     changed=0  unreachable=0  failed=0  skipped=0  rescued=0  ignored=0
```

Step 13: Either on your VMware Workstation console or SSH session to your routers, confirm the current IOS by running the command "show version" for your reference, as shown in Figure 15-5.

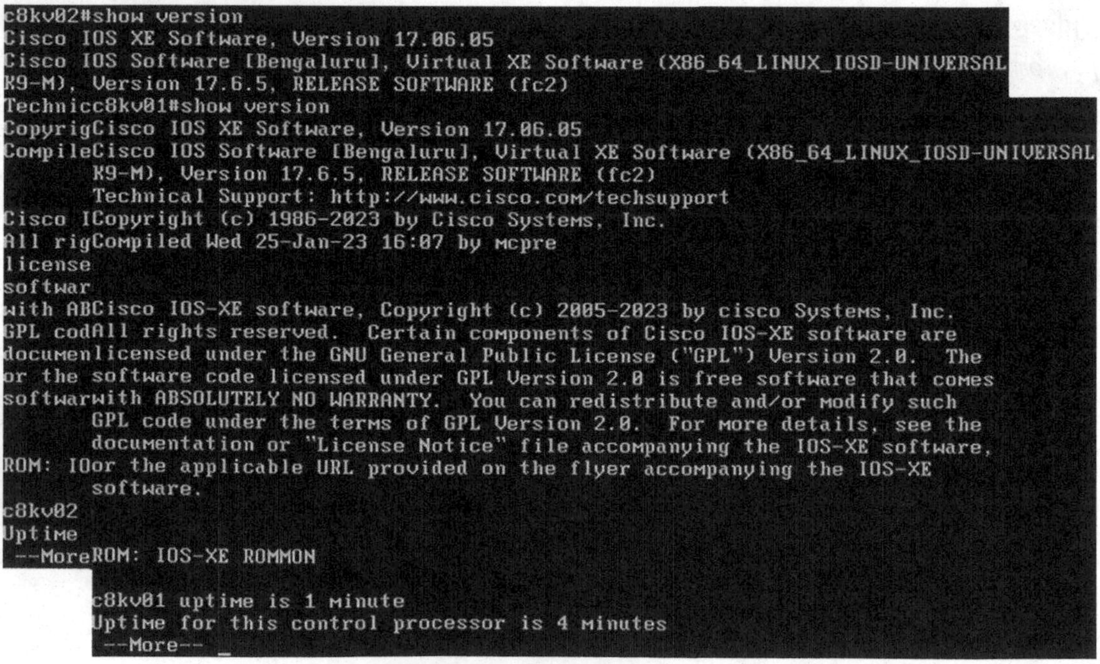

Figure 15-5. *Cisco IOS-XE version after the upgrade*

752

Step 14 [Optional]: You can make your playbook interactive using "vars_prompt".

Create a new working directory called "Chapter 15" or "ch15". In this directory, we will create a playbook that interacts with the user to collect important data. These collected values can then be used as variables in our Cisco IOS-XE upgrading playbook. By making the playbook interactive, we can add a level of engagement to the process, making it more interesting for the user.

15_COLLECT_DATA.YML

```
---
- hosts: localhost
  connection: local
  gather_facts: false

  # Collect credentials & new IOS file info to run on the local server
  vars_prompt: # Collect sudoer name, ansible become password, IOS-XE file
MD5 and name
      - name: "sudoer_name"
        prompt: "Sudoer name"
        private: no
      - name: "ansible_become_pass"
        prompt: "Sudo Password"
        private: yes # input will be hidden
        confirm: yes # Confirm by retyping the password
      - name: "ios_file_md5"
        prompt: "New IOS MD5 value"
        private: no # input will be visible
      - name: "ios_file_name"
        prompt: "New IOS File name (.bin)"
        private: no

  tasks:
    - name: Print User Entered Information # confirm your input after
    the typing
      ansible.builtin.debug:
        msg: |
          Sudoer name: {{ sudoer_name }}
```

```
        Sudo Password: {{ ansible_become_pass }}
        New IOS MD5 value: {{ ios_file_md5 }}
        New IOS File name (.bin): {{ ios_file_name }}
```

Execute the playbook created and enter the information and confirm that your user interactive playbook is working as designed.

```
[jdoe@f38s1 ch15]$ anp 15a_collect_data.yml
Sudoer name: jdoe
Sudo Password: ********
confirm Sudo Password: ********
New IOS MD5 value: f3dc5681ac6b66d807a36b3830569344
New IOS File name (.bin): c8000v-universalk9.17.06.05.SPA.bin

PLAY [localhost] ****************************************************

TASK [Print User Entered Information] ******************************
ok: [localhost] => {
    "msg": "Sudoer name: jdoe\nSudo Password: cisco123\nNew IOS MD5 value:
    f3dc5681ac6b66d807a36b3830569344\nNew IOS File name (.bin): c8000v-
    universalk9.17.06.05.SPA.bin\n"
}

PLAY RECAP *********************************************************
localhost                  :
ok=1    changed=0  unreachable=0  failed=0  skipped=0  rescued=0  ignored=0
```

Now that you have completed the development of a user interactive data collection tool using Ansible's vars_prompt module, you can use it to collect the administrator's credentials, as well as the IOS-XE file name and its MD5 information. This collected data will be utilized in our playbook. By incorporating this tool, the playbook becomes a versatile upgrade tool that can be used for different models with the same IOS-XE software, benefiting the entire team.

Step 15 [Optional]: You can also extract specific parts of a string using regular expression extraction. Here's an example demonstrating the extraction of the IOS version, such as "17.06.05" or "17.06.03a".

Create an Ansible playbook to extract the IOS version from the new IOS file (ios_
file_name).

15_EXTRACT_VERSION.YML

```
- name: Extract version from the file name
  hosts: localhost
  gather_facts: false

  vars:
    ios_file_name: "c8000v-universalk9.17.06.05.SPA.bin"  # Provide the file
    name here

  tasks:
    - name: Extract version from the file name
      ansible.builtin.set_fact:
        new_ios_version: "{{ ios_file_name | regex_search('\\d{2}\\.\\
        d{2}\\.\\d{2}[a-z]?') }}"

    - name: Print extracted version
      ansible.builtin.debug:
        var: new_ios_version
```

Execute the playbook and you will get the extracted IOS version from the ios_file_
name string.

```
[jdoe@f38s1 rp]$ anp 2_extract_version.yml
[...omitted for brevity]
TASK [Print extracted version] *******************************************
ok: [localhost] => {
    "new_ios_version": "17.06.05"
[...omitted for brevity]
```

Finally, presented here is the complete playbook for upgrading IOS-XE routers.
It is highly recommended to dedicate time to thoroughly understand each play and
its associated tasks. This playbook serves as a valuable resource for further study,
providing a comprehensive understanding of the upgrade process. It is essential to
grasp both the individual components and the overall flow of the script to gain a deep
understanding of its functionality. By comprehending the various code segments and

studying the playbook as a whole, you will develop profound insights into the upgrade process and enhance your ability to modify or adapt the playbook to meet your specific requirements. If desired, you can also refer to Chapter 10, specifically the "Roles" section, to break down this playbook into different roles and apply the concepts learned in the Ansible concept chapters.

15_UPGRADE_ROUTER.YML

```yaml
---
# 1
- name: Upgrade Cisco IOS-XE Routers # Playbook to upgrade IOS-XE routers
  hosts: ios_xe_routers
  gather_facts: true # Gather facts about hosts

  vars_files: vars.yml # Include variables from vars.yml

  max_fail_percentage: 0 # Maximum failure percentage

  tasks:
    - name: Check current IOS-XE version from gathered ios facts # Task to
    check current IOS-XE version
      cisco.ios.ios_facts:

    - name: Debug current and new IOS versions # Task to debug current and
    new IOS versions
      ansible.builtin.debug:
        msg:
          - "Current version: {{ ansible_net_version }}" # Print
          current version
          - "New version    : {{ new_ios_version }}" # Print new version

    - name: Quit playbook if ansible_net_version equals new_ios_version
    # Task to quit if versions are equal
      block:
        - name: Fail if versions are equal # Fail task if versions are equal
          ansible.builtin.fail:
            msg: "Current IOS version is already up to date." # Error message
          when: ansible_net_version >= new_ios_version # Condition to check
          versions
```

```
      - name: Debug Message # Task to debug message
        ansible.builtin.debug:
          msg: "Continuing with the playbook, upgrading IOS version..."
          # Print debug message
        ignore_errors: true # Ignore errors
# 2
- name: Create directories on SFTP server # Playbook to create directories on
SFTP server
  hosts: f38c1
  tasks:
    - name: Get ansible date/time facts # Task to get ansible date/time facts
      ansible.builtin.setup:
        filter: "ansible_date_time" # Filter facts
        gather_subset: "!all" # Gather only necessary facts

    - name: Store DTG as a fact # Task to store DTG as a fact
      ansible.builtin.set_fact:
        DTG: "{{ ansible_date_time.date }}" # Store DTG from ansible facts

    - name: Create Directory for backup # Task to create a directory
      for backup
      ansible.builtin.file:
        path: "~/ch15/{{ DTG }}" # Path for the directory
        state: directory # Create a directory
        mode: "0775" # Set directory permissions
      run_once: true # Run the task once
# 3
- name: Copy running configuration # Playbook to copy the running
configuration
  hosts: ios_xe_routers
  gather_facts: false # Disable facts gathering

  vars_files: vars.yml # Include variables from vars.yml

  vars:
    file_name: "ch15/{{ hostvars['f38c1'].DTG }}/{{ inventory_hostname
    }}-confg-0" # Define the file name for the copied configuration
    command_timeout: 600 # Set the command timeout
  tasks:
```

```
  - name: Copy running configuration # Task to copy the running
    configuration
    ansible.netcommon.cli_command:
      command: "copy running-config sftp://{{ sftp_username }}:{{ sftp_
      password }}@{{ sftp_server_ip }}/{{ file_name }}" # Command to copy
      running configuration using SFTP
      check_all: True # Check all prompts
      prompt:
        - 'Address or name of remote host' # Prompt for remote host
          address or name
        - 'Destination username' # Prompt for destination username
        - 'Destination filename' # Prompt for destination filename
      answer:
        - '{{ sftp_server_ip }}' # Answer for remote host address or name
        - '{{ sftp_username }}' # Answer for destination username
        - '{{ file_name }}' # Answer for destination filename
    register: copy_result # Register the result of the copy operation

  - name: Display copy result # Task to display the copy result
    ansible.builtin.debug:
      var: copy_result # Print the copy result
# 4
  - name: Save running-config to startup-config # Task to save running
    configuration to startup configuration
    cisco.ios.ios_config:
      save_when: always # Save the configuration always
# 5
  - name: Extend SSH timer to 99 mins # Task to extend SSH timer
    cisco.ios.ios_config:
      commands:
        - line vty 0 15 # Configure line VTY
        - exec-timeout 99 0 # Set exec-timeout to 99 minutes

  - name: Copy new IOS to SFTP server (192.168.127.151) # Task to copy new
    IOS to SFTP server
    ansible.netcommon.cli_command:
      command: 'copy sftp://{{ sftp_username }}:{{ sftp_password }}@{{
      sftp_server_ip }}/{{ ios_file_name }} flash:/{{ ios_file_name }}'
      # Command to copy IOS using SFTP
```

```
          check_all: True # Check all prompts
          prompt:
            - 'Destination filename' # Prompt for destination filename
          answer:
            - '{{ ios_file_name }}' # Answer for destination filename
# 6
  - name: Verify MD5 value on the flash # Task to verify MD5 value on flash
    cisco.ios.ios_command:
        commands: verify /md5 flash:{{ ios_file_name }} {{ios_file_md5 }}
        # Command to verify MD5 value on flash
      register: ios_file_md5_flash_result # Register the result of
      the command

  - ansible.builtin.debug:
        var: ios_file_md5_flash_result.stdout # Print the stdout of
        the command

  - name: Locate MD5 value of new IOS on router flash # Task to locate MD5
    value of new IOS on flash
    ansible.builtin.set_fact:
        ios_file_md5_flash: "{{ ios_file_md5_flash_result.stdout[0] | regex_
        search('[a-f0-9]{32}') }}" # Extract MD5 value using regex

  - ansible.builtin.debug:
      msg:
        - "ios_file_md5 [flash:/]          : {{ ios_file_md5_flash }}"
                                           # Print the MD5 value on flash
        - "ios_file_md5 [Correct Value]    : {{ ios_file_md5 }}" # Print
                                             the correct MD5 value

  - name: Fail if MD5 Values are different # Task to fail if MD5 values are
    different
    ansible.builtin.fail: msg="Failed, flash IOS MD5 value DOES NOT MATCH
    the correct IOS file MD5 value." # Fail with an error message
    when: ios_file_md5_flash != ios_file_md5 or 'Verified' not in ios_file_
    md5_flash_result.stdout[0] # Condition to trigger the failure

  - name: Pass if MD5 values are the same # Task to pass if MD5 values are
    the same
    ansible.builtin.debug:
```

```
    msg: Passed, flash IOS MD5 MATCH provided IOS file MD5. # Print a
    success message
  when: ios_file_md5_flash == ios_file_md5 and 'Verified' in ios_file_
  md5_flash_result.stdout[0] # Condition to trigger the success
```

 # 7

```
- name: Clear the old boot variable # Task to clear the old boot variable
  cisco.ios.ios_config:
    commands:
      - "no boot system" # Command to clear boot system
    save_when: always # Save the configuration always

- name: Change the boot variable to new IOS image (.bin) # Task to change
  the boot variable to new IOS
  cisco.ios.ios_config:
    commands:
      - "boot system flash:{{ ios_file_name }}" # Command to set boot
      system to new IOS image
    save_when: always # Save the configuration always

- name: Run show boot command # Task to run the show boot command
  cisco.ios.ios_command:
    commands: show boot # Command to show boot information
    wait_for:
      - result[0] contains "{{ new_ios_version }}" # Wait for the output
        to contain the new IOS version
  register: show_boot1 # Register the output

- ansible.builtin.debug:
    var: show_boot1.stdout_lines # Print the stdout_lines of the command
```

 # 8

```
- name: Save running-config to startup-config # Task to save running
  configuration to startup configuration
  cisco.ios.ios_config:
    save_when: always # Save the configuration always

- name: Reload the device # Task to reload the device
  cisco.ios.ios_command:
    commands:
      - command: "reload\r" # Command to reload the device
```

```
            prompt: 'Proceed with reload? [confirm]' # Prompt for reload
            confirmation
            answer: "\r" # Answer to confirm the reload
# 9
- name: Sleep for 5 minutes # Task to pause execution for 5 minutes
  hosts: localhost
  gather_facts: false
  tasks:
    - name: Pause for 5 minutes # Pause task for a specified duration
      ansible.builtin.pause:
        seconds: 300
      run_once: true
# 10
- name: Copy running configuration # Task to copy the running configuration
  hosts: ios_xe_routers
  gather_facts: false

  vars_files: vars.yml

  vars:
    file_name: "ch15/{{ hostvars['f38c1'].DTG }}/{{ inventory_hostname
    }}-confg-1" # Define file name using variables
    command_timeout: 600

  tasks:
    - name: Restore SSH timer to default value, 10 mins # Task to restore
      SSH timer
      cisco.ios.ios_config:
        commands:
          - line vty 0 15
          - exec-timeout 10 0
        save_when: modified

    - name: Copy running configuration # Task to copy the running
      configuration
      ansible.netcommon.cli_command:
        command: "copy running-config sftp://{{ sftp_username }}:{{ sftp_
        password }}@{{ sftp_server_ip }}/{{ file_name }}" # Command to copy
        running configuration
        check_all: True
```

761

```
      prompt:
        - 'Address or name of remote host'
        - 'Destination username'
        - 'Destination filename'
      answer:
        - '{{ sftp_server_ip }}'
        - '{{ sftp_username }}'
        - '{{ file_name }}'
    register: copy_result # Register the result of the copy operation
  - name: Display copy result # Task to display copy result
    ansible.builtin.debug:
      var: copy_result
# 11
    - name: Check the new IOS version. # Task to check new IOS version
    cisco.ios.ios_facts:

  - debug:
      ansible.builtin.msg:
        - "Current version is {{ ansible_net_version }}" # Print current
          IOS version

  - name: Assert that the new IOS version is correct. # Task to assert new
    IOS version
    vars:
      new_IOS_version: "{{ new_ios_version }}"

    ansible.builtin.assert:
      that:
        - new_IOS_version == ansible_net_version # Assert the equality of
          new and current IOS versions

  - ansible.builtin.debug:
      msg:
        - "Software upgrade has been completed successfully." # Print
          success message for software upgrade
```

Congratulations on reaching this page! You're making excellent progress, and your dedication is commendable. Keep up the good work as you continue through the rest of the book. In the upcoming chapter, we will delve into Cisco Wireless LAN Controller (WLC) upgrade procedures using the Ansible playbook. This chapter is especially valuable for those with a keen interest in enterprise wireless technologies. By exploring WLC upgrade procedures with Ansible, you will gain valuable insights into managing and upgrading wireless networks more efficiently. The Ansible playbook will provide a structured approach, enabling you to streamline the upgrade process and ensure smooth transitions for your wireless infrastructure. Stay motivated and eager to learn as we delve into the exciting world of Cisco Wireless LAN Controller upgrades. Your commitment to expanding your knowledge and skills will undoubtedly pay off in the realm of enterprise wireless technologies.

Get ready to fasten your seatbelt! In Chapter 16, we'll dive into the exciting world of Cisco Wireless LAN Controller's OS upgrade.

15.4 Summary

This chapter emphasized the significance of security in today's organizations. With the rise of computer viruses and security vulnerabilities added to the list of CVEs, vendors are collaborating with each other to safeguard enterprise infrastructure by sharing information. The chapter highlighted the importance of patch management and OS upgrades as essential measures for maintaining a secure network environment. The lab network topology, consisting of two Cisco c8000v routers, an SFTP server, and an Ansible control node, served as the foundation for exploring the Cisco IOS-XE router upgrade workflow in bundle mode. A breakdown of the general tasks involved in IOS-XE upgrading is provided, ensuring a comprehensive understanding of the process. Moreover, the chapter highlighted the key benefits of incorporating Ansible into network operations. By automating repetitive tasks, Ansible streamlines network management, improves efficiency, and reduces the likelihood of human error. The Cisco IOS-XE router Upgrade Lab offered a step-by-step guide for constructing the application. With detailed explanations and code snippets, readers can grasp the implementation process and gain the knowledge necessary to modify the playbook according to their specific requirements. To enhance comprehension, the chapter concluded with the provision of the Cisco IOS-XE Upgrade Lab playbook in a single file, enabling readers to study the playbook as a whole and facilitating easier customization. We demonstrated IOS-XE upgrades on two devices only, but in the real production environment, the number of devices could be exponential and the same script can be modified and tuned to upgrade tens and hundreds of IOS/IOS-XE routers to make your enterprise network devices more secure.

## CHAPTER 16

Cisco Wireless LAN Controller Upgrading Playbook

This chapter looks at Ansible playbook development for Cisco Wireless LAN Controller (WLC) upgrade in enterprise networks and the important role a WLC plays in enterprise networks. The WLC plays a pivotal role in managing wireless networks, ensuring seamless connectivity, and enabling secure and efficient data transmission. Regular upgrades are essential to keep the WLC protected against emerging security vulnerabilities and to leverage the latest features and enhancements offered by Cisco. We will explore the development of a simple WLC upgrading playbook, which automates the upgrade tasks, such as gathering inventory information, uploading new image files, and verifying the success of the upgrade. Executing and testing the playbook ensures the quality of our work while working on multiple devices and can reduce human error and downtime. Additionally, we will look at an example of a well-thought-out inventory file for managing multiple sites across a country, simplifying administration tasks, and enabling easier configuration management and upgrades. At the end of this chapter, you will have a solid understanding of the importance of the WLC upgrade in the enterprise network, the process of upgrading it using a playbook, and efficient inventory file management techniques for multi-site and multi-device environments.

© Brendan Choi and Erwin Medina 2023
B. Choi and E. Medina, *Introduction to Ansible Network Automation*,
https://doi.org/10.1007/978-1-4842-9624-0_16

Wireless networks play a vital role in modern enterprises, providing seamless communication and access to end users and endpoints. These networks have advanced through technologies such as Wi-Fi 6, Wi-Fi 6E, Bluetooth 5.x, and Zigbee 3.x. Wi-Fi 6 offers improved performance, capacity, and efficiency in high-density environments, while Wi-Fi 6E takes these capabilities to the next level by operating in the 6 GHz frequency band, providing higher connection speeds and lower latency. Bluetooth 5 extends the range, enhances data transfer speeds, and supports emerging IoT applications. Zigbee 3.0 provides reliable connectivity for low-powered and local applications, offering enhanced security and scalability for home automation and sensor networks.

Cisco provides comprehensive wireless solutions, including controllers and lightweight APs, enabling enhanced connectivity, mobility, and flexibility for users. Cisco WLCs play a key role in servicing access points for mobile devices within the LAN. They are widely deployed in medium-to-large enterprises to manage hundreds and thousands of wireless network access points (APs). Wireless networks are typically an extension of the Local Area Network (LAN), necessitating the same security practices as wired networks. The Cisco Catalyst 9800-CL Wireless Controller also supports cloud integration. However, wireless networks are susceptible to security threats, such as unauthorized access, data interception, and denial-of-service attacks. Regularly upgrading and patching Cisco WLCs and APs is crucial to address vulnerabilities and maintain network integrity. Securing mobile devices that connect to enterprise wireless networks presents unique challenges, requiring robust security measures to prevent unauthorized access, defend against malware, and enforce strong authentication. Keeping Cisco WLCs up to date is essential to protect against vulnerabilities and external threats. To emphasize the importance of securing enterprise wireless networks, consider the risk of unauthorized access and data manipulation through compromised access points. Such incidents can lead to data breaches, financial losses, and reputational damage. Protecting wireless networks requires implementing comprehensive security measures. This includes regular firmware upgrades, strong encryption, network segmentation, intrusion detection and prevention, and robust authentication mechanisms.

This chapter focuses on upgrading a Cisco WLC running on VMware ESXi 7 lab, but you can also run the same lab on a public or private cloud environment for testing purposes. You will learn how to write an Ansible playbook to upgrade an enterprise-level Cisco virtual Wireless LAN Controller (vWLC) run by AireOS. Traditionally, much of the Cisco WLC upgrades are performed through GUI or CLI by wireless engineers using the keyboard and mouse. This chapter serves as a playground for writing a Cisco WLC upgrading playbook in YAML format, which facilitates infrastructure as code (IaC). The chapter emphasizes the importance of transitioning from the manual keyboard and mouse approach to scripting and declarative statements in YAML format within a playbook. Developing an efficient and consistent upgrading process for critical wireless networks is extremely important for any organization. By implementing necessary security measures, organizations can ensure the confidentiality, integrity, and availability of wireless network resources while mitigating risks associated with wireless connectivity.

Warning!

This WLC upgrade lab was installed on ESXi 7 due to software compatibility.

Due to a software compatibility issue between the latest Cisco virtual Wireless LAN Controller and VMware Workstation 17 Pro, the development environment was set up in the VMware ESXi 7 environment. If you choose to install the latest Cisco WLC software using VMware Workstation, please note that the installation will be completed, but the administrator GUI may not function as expected. As a result, the steps and results described in this chapter may differ from those in the book.

If you are unable to set up a development environment as shown in this chapter, you can read this chapter as a future reference until you can build a proper testing environment for your playbook development.

Before we proceed, go to the following Cisco link, and study the general process to upgrade WLC manually and then let's first examine the lab topology.

Upgrade Process for AireOS Wireless LAN Controllers (WLCs):

`www.cisco.com/c/en/us/support/docs/wireless-mobility/wireless-lan-wlan/68835-wlc-upgrade.html`

16.1 WLC Lab Network Topology

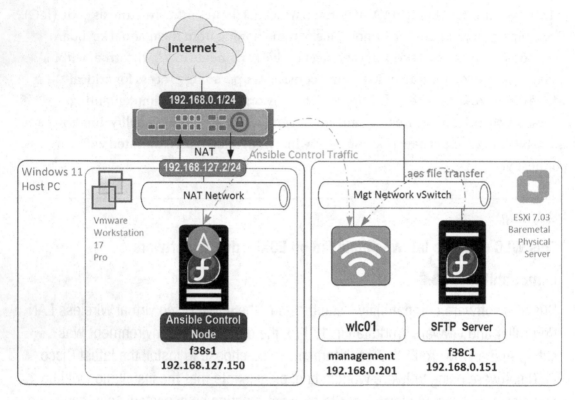

Figure 16-1. *Cisco WLC upgrading lab topology*

As you can see in Figure 16-1, we have the opportunity to work with virtual machines running on both Type 1 and Type 2 hypervisors in this lab. There are two types of hypervisors: Type 1 includes VMware ESXi 7, Microsoft Hyper-V, Citrix XenServer, and Proxmox VE. These hypervisors are designed to run directly on the hardware of a physical server, providing high-performance virtualization capabilities. On the other hand, Type 2 hypervisors include VMware Workstation, VMware Fusion, Oracle VirtualBox, and Parallels Desktop. These software applications are installed on an existing operating system and enable virtualization on a desktop or laptop computer.

We have configured a single Cisco vWLC (wlc01, 192.168.0.201) on an ESXi 7.03 bare-metal server and connected the server to a typical home network with a 192.168.0.0/24 subnet. Depending on your ISP and the home router/modem being used, your default home network IP could also be on the 192.168.1.0/24 subnet. The SFTP server f38c1 has been migrated to the ESXi 7 environment using the VMware

Converter, and the IP address has been updated to 192.168.0.151/24 with the default gateway of 192.168.0.1. Optionally, you can also install a brand-new server and follow the integration steps discussed in the earlier chapters. My laptop, which runs VMware Workstation 17 Pro, is connected to a natted subnet of 192.168.127.0/24. The Ansible Control Machine (f38s1) on my laptop can communicate with wlc01, which has an IP address of 192.168.0.201.

This setup is similar to other labs, but we have introduced a bare-metal ESXi 7 server on the local network to run the Cisco vWLC. If you wish to have the f38s1 server on the ESXi server, you can utilize VMware Converter to migrate these servers to the ESXi environment. After the migration is complete, make sure to adjust the IP address to align with the 192.168.0.0/24 subnet.

To install the latest Cisco WLC on an ESXi environment, please access the supplementary software installation guide provided on the authors' GitHub page.

URL: https://github.com/ansnetauto/appress_ansnetauto

Ch11_Pre-task4_Cisco_Wireless_LAN_Controller(vWLC)_VM_Creation_on_VMware_ESXi.pdf

---

Now let's look at the required files for this lab. Table 16-1 provides a list of files and software used for the preparation of this lab. The first virtual machine file, AIR_CTVM-K9_8_8_130_0.ova, was utilized to perform the initial installation of the software on VMware ESXi 7. However, for upgrading the Cisco WLC, the .ova (Open Virtual Appliance) file is not required. Instead, **we only need the actual Cisco WLC software, which is packaged in an encrypted format with the .aes (Advanced Encryption Standard) file extension**. The .aes file serves as an encrypted container for the Cisco WLC software, ensuring secure distribution and installation.

Table 16-1. *Cisco WLC software*

File name	MD5 values	File size
AIR_CTVM-K9_8_8_130_0.ova	2e3754fb18230b897fe4074c60028944	357.71 MB
AIR-CTVM-K9-8-10-185-0.aes	671ee89cdde98d9b86f124623468bdc0	494.02 MB

To obtain both files, you can download them from the official Cisco website after logging in with a valid software support contract. If you are affiliated with a Cisco Partner, you also have the option to participate in Cisco's NFR (Not for Resale) program. By paying the necessary subscription fees for your team, you can gain access to the NFR program, which provides the required files.

As emphasized in Chapter 1, it's important to note that these software files are proprietary to Cisco. Regrettably, the authors are unable to share any of the proprietary files with the readers due to licensing and intellectual property restrictions.

16.2 Preparing the Lab by Creating ansible.cfg and Inventory Files

It is always beneficial to write and prepare the necessary supplementary files in advance to run our main Ansible playbooks. Therefore, let's complete this task first so that we can concentrate solely on the WLC upgrading playbook afterward.

Step 1: As a standard procedure, let's create a new ansible.cfg file after setting up a new working directory named ch16.

```
[jdoe@f38s1 ~]$ mkdir ch16 && cd ch16
[jdoe@f38s1 ch16]$ vi ansible.cfg
[jdoe@f38s1 ch16]$ cat ansible.cfg
[defaults]
inventory = inventory    # Specifies the inventory file
host_key_checking=False    # Disables SSH host key checking for easier
automation
nocows = 1    # Disables cow ASCII art
deprecation_warnings = False    # Disables deprecation warnings
log_path = ./ansible.log    # Specifies the log file path for Ansible output
forks = 30    # Sets the maximum number of parallel processes to execute
interpreter_python=auto_silent    # Automatically detects & uses the
appropriate Python interpreter
```

Note that the log_path option has been enabled for troubleshooting purposes; you can review the output from the ansible-playbook executions by reviewing ansible.log.

Step 2: After creating the new working directory named ch16, the next step is to create a new inventory file.

```
[jdoe@f38s1 ch16]$ vi inventory
[jdoe@f38s1 ch16]$ cat inventory
[wlc:vars]
ansible_connection=network_cli    # Specifies the connection type as
                                   network_cli
ansible_network_os=aireos    # Specifies the network OS as aireos for Cisco
                             AireOS devices
ansible_command_timeout=180    # Increases the default command timeout from
                               30 to 180 s

[wlc]
wlc01 ansible_host=192.168.0.201    # Defines the wlc01 host with its
                                    IP address
```

Let's discuss the preceding file briefly. The ansible_network_os type is no longer "ios" for AireOS-based devices. Instead, it should be updated to "aireos" to accurately reflect the specific network operating system used by Cisco AireOS devices. AireOS has its roots in Aironet Communication, which Cisco acquired in February 1999. This acquisition played a vital role in enhancing Cisco's portfolio in wireless networking technology and expanding its offerings in the enterprise networking market. Following the acquisition, Aironet's products seamlessly integrated into Cisco's wireless solutions.

Over the years, the brand name "Aironet" has remained associated with Cisco's WLAN product line, showcasing the strong reputation and established market presence of Aironet Communication. Therefore, when working with AireOS devices in Ansible, it is important to set the ansible_network_os variable to "aireos" to align with the network operating system's specific requirements and functionalities. Additionally, make sure to specify the ansible_connection type as network_cli.

Step 3: Now, create a vars.yml file using the "ansible-vault create" command.

```
[jdoe@f38s1 ch16]$ ansible-vault create vars.yml
New Vault password: **************
Confirm New Vault password: **************
ansible_user: admin # Used to log into target WLC
ansible_ssh_pass: S3cr3tP4ssw0rd # WLC admin password
```

```
sftp_server: 192.168.0.151 # SFTP server
sftp_user: jdoe # SFTP user name
sftp_password: Secure9assw0rd # SFTP user password
aes_file_name: AIR-CTVM-K9-8-10-185-0.aes # upgrading file name
```

These are the three essential files required to execute our main playbook. Now, let's focus on developing the actual playbook(s).

16.3 Writing an Ansible Playbook for Cisco WLC Upgrading Ansible Playbook

In this example, we will keep our playbooks relatively simple to focus on discussing the inventory file later in this chapter. Therefore, let's create small playbooks for verification, uploading, and rebooting in three separate files.

Warning!

Take snapshots of your WLC now!

If you haven't already taken any snapshots of your WLC, now is an opportune moment to create a snapshot of your currently functioning virtual WLC. It is advisable to have snapshots for practice purposes, allowing you to iterate and refine your playbooks. Take a moment to capture a snapshot in your ESXi Web Console to ensure you have a stable starting point for further experimentation and playbook testing.

Step 1: Let's write a playbook to check the boot information and hence the software version.

```
[jdoe@f38s1 ch16]$ vi 16_aireos_show_boot.yml
[jdoe@f38s1 ch16]$ cat 16_aireos_show_boot.yml
---
- hosts: wlc
  gather_facts: no

  vars_files: vars.yml
```

```
vars:
  wlc_version: 8.10.185.0 # New AireOS version

  tasks:
    - name: Execute show boot command
      community.network.aireos_command:
        username: "{{ ansible_user }}"
        password: "{{ ansible_ssh_pass }}"
        commands: show boot
        wait_for:
          - result[0] not contains '{{ wlc_version }}' # not contains fails
            the playbook if the same version is found in the output.
      register: output1

    - ansible.builtin.debug:
        var: output1.stdout_lines
```

The preceding playbook runs and checks the wlc_version in the show boot output; if the same version is found, it will fail. If different version, then the playbook execution will be completed.

Let's quickly verify if the preceding playbook executes properly. When we execute this playbook, we can check the WLC version.

```
[jdoe@f38s1 ch16]$ anp 16_aireos_show_boot.yml --ask-vault-pass
Vault password: ***************
PLAY [wlc] *********************************************************

TASK [Execute show boot command] **********************************
ok: [wlc01]

TASK [debug] ******************************************************
ok: [wlc01] => {
    "output1.stdout_lines": [
        [
            "Primary Boot Image............. 8.8.130.0 (default) (active)",
            "Backup Boot Image............. 8.8.130.0"
        ]
    ]
}
```

```
PLAY RECAP ************************************************************
wlc01 : ok=2  changed=0  unreachable=0  failed=0  skipped=0  rescued=0  ignored=0
```

If you receive an output similar to the one shown previously, it indicates that your playbook has been executed successfully. This confirms that your Ansible control node is capable of managing the lab vWLC using playbooks through an SSH connection.

As you can see in Figure 16-2, upon accessing your Wireless LAN Controller's (WLC) web GUI and navigating to the "Config Boot" section under COMMANDS, you will encounter a screen displaying the Primary Image and Backup Image. In our case, both images initially have the same version number, which is 8.8.130.0. It is crucial to remember these values as we will compare them with the updated versions later on.

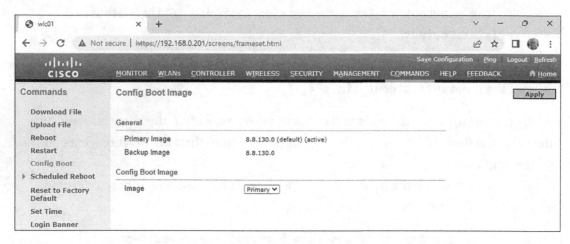

Figure 16-2. *WLC images before the upgrade*

Step 2: To gain further insights about our Wireless LAN Controller (WLC), let's refer to the Ansible documentation and incorporate some playbook snippets. This will allow us to gather more information before proceeding with the file upload and WLC reboot.

URL: https://docs.ansible.com/ansible/latest/collections/community/network/aireos_command_module.html

```
[jdoe@f38s1 ch16]$ vi 16_aireos_show_sysinfo_int.yml
[jdoe@f38s1 ch16]$ cat 16_aireos_show_sysinfo_int.yml
- hosts: wlc
  gather_facts: no

  vars_files: vars.yml
```

```
tasks:
- name: Run show sysinfo and check to see if the output contains Cisco
  Controller
  community.network.aireos_command:
    commands: show sysinfo
    wait_for: result[0] contains 'Cisco Controller'
  register: check_sysinfo_output

- name: Display check sysinfo output
  ansible.builtin.debug:
    var: check_sysinfo_output.stdout_lines

- name: Run multiple commands on remote nodes
  community.network.aireos_command:
    commands:
      - show interface summary
  register: multiple_commands_output

- name: Display multiple commands output
  ansible.builtin.debug:
    var: multiple_commands_output.stdout_lines
```

In the module mentioned previously, the community.network.aireos_command module is being used instead of aireos_command. These two modules, aireos_command and community.network.aireos_command, have distinct differences. While aireos_command is a module provided by Ansible, community.network.aireos_command is a community-driven version that offers more frequent updates and enhancements. By opting for community.network.aireos_command, you can leverage the benefits of an actively maintained and community-supported module that provides improved functionality and more timely updates compared to the standard Ansible module, aireos_command.

Execute the preceding playbook and you will be able to view all of the system information; this will help us to design our playbooks properly as we can turn the output information into variables.

```
[jdoe@f38s1 ch16]$ anp 16_aireos_show_sysinfo_int.yml --ask-vault-pass
Vault password: ***************
[...omitted for brevity]
```

```
ok: [wlc01] => {
    "check_sysinfo_output.stdout_lines": [
        [
            "Manufacturer's Name...................... Cisco Systems Inc.",
            "Product Name............................. Cisco Controller",
            "Product Version.......................... 8.8.130.0",
            "RTOS Version............................. 8.8.130.0",
            "Bootloader Version....................... 8.5.1.85",
            "Emergency Image Version.................. 8.8.130.0",
[...omitted for brevity]
            "Number of Interfaces.................... 3",
            "",
            "Interface Name    Port Vlan Id  IP Address       Type    Ap Mgr Guest",
            "----------------  ---- --------  ---------------  ------- ------ -----",
            "management        1    untagged  192.168.0.201    Static  Yes    N/A",
            "service-port      N/A  N/A       192.168.127.201  Static  No     N/A",
            "virtual           N/A  N/A       1.1.1.1          Static  No     N/A"
[...omitted for brevity]
```

Step 3: To initiate the upgrade process, follow the steps depicted in Figure 16-3. Use WinSCP from your Windows host PC to upload the "AIR-CTVM-K9-8-10-185-0.aes" file to the SFTP server, f38c1, at the IP address 192.168.0.151. In this scenario, we will employ WinSCP and log in with the SFTP user "jdoe" that was created in one of the earlier chapters.

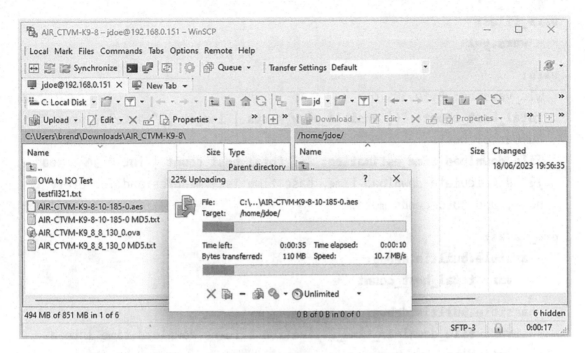

Figure 16-3. *Upload the new WLC .aes file onto the SFTP server's user directory*

Once the file has been successfully uploaded, you can verify the MD5 value using the following steps. This value must match the one provided by Cisco when you initially downloaded the file.

```
[jdoe@f38c1 ~]$ md5sum /home/jdoe/AIR-CTVM-K9-8-10-185-0.aes
671ee89cdde98d9b86f124623468bdc0  /home/jdoe/AIR-CTVM-K9-8-10-185-0.aes
```

Step 4: Let's create the File Upload Playbook, which will facilitate the uploading of the new WLC image file with the .aes extension. This playbook will execute the "show boot" command and analyze the results to compare the "wlc_version." If the version string matches, the playbook will report failure. However, if the software version does not match, the playbook will proceed with uploading the new WLC file.

```
[jdoe@f38s1 ch16]$ vi 16_aireos_file_download.yml
[jdoe@f38s1 ch16]$ cat 16_aireos_file_download.yml
---
- name: Cisco vWLC File upload playbook
  hosts: wlc
  gather_facts: no
```

```
vars_files:
  - vars.yml

vars:
  wlc_version: 8.10.185.0
  total_host_count: "{{ ansible_play_hosts | length }}" # Calculates
  number of hosts
  file_download_time_estimation: "{{ total_host_count | int * 30 + 300
  }}" # Calculate download time, base time is 5 minutes and for every
  host, add 30 seconds more.

pre_tasks:
  - ansible.builtin.debug:
      var: total_host_count

  - ansible.builtin.debug:
      var: file_download_time_estimation # Turns download time into a
      variable

tasks:
  - name: Execute show boot command
    community.network.aireos_command:
      username: "{{ ansible_user }}"
      password: "{{ ansible_ssh_pass }}"
      commands: show boot
      wait_for:
        - result[0] not contains '{{ wlc_version }}'
    register: output1

  - ansible.builtin.debug:
      var: output1.stdout_lines

  - name: Change WLC transfer settings # Changes setting for file
    download
    community.network.aireos_command:
      username: "{{ ansible_user }}"
      password: "{{ ansible_ssh_user }}"
      timeout: 30
```

```
    commands:
      - transfer download mode ftp
      - transfer download username "{{ sftp_user }}"
      - transfer download password "{{ sftp_password }}"
      - transfer download serverip "{{ sftp_server }}"
      - transfer download path /home/jdoe/
      - transfer download filename "{{ aes_file_name }}"

- name: Start new aireos file transfer # Transfers .aes file
  community.network.aireos_command:
    username: "{{ ansible_user }}"
    password: "{{ ansible_ssh_pass }}"
    timeout: "{{ file_download_time_estimation | int }}"
    commands:
      - command: 'transfer download start'
        prompt: '(y/N)'
        answer: 'y'
    wait_for: result[0] contains "File transfer is successful"

- name: Execute show boot command after file upload
  community.network.aireos_command:
    username: "{{ ansible_user }}"
    password: "{{ ansible_ssh_pass }}"
    commands:
      - show boot
  register: output2

- name: Image versions after the reload
  ansible.builtin.debug:
    var: output2.stdout_lines
```

Now, let's execute the aforementioned playbook to observe the changes in settings and upgrade our WLC with the new file.

```
[jdoe@f38s1 ch16]$ anp 16_aireos_file_download.yml --ask-vault-pass
Vault password: ***************
PLAY [Cisco vWLC File upload playbook] ***********************************
[...omitted for brevity]
PLAY RECAP **************************************************************
wlc01 : ok=8  changed=0  unreachable=0  failed=0  skipped=0  rescued=0  ignored=0
```

When the playbook executes the "Change WLC transfer settings" task, what you need to do is update the Download file set with the appropriate configuration for the new WLC software upload. This can be achieved by following the example illustrated in Figure 16-4, ensuring that the settings are correctly configured.

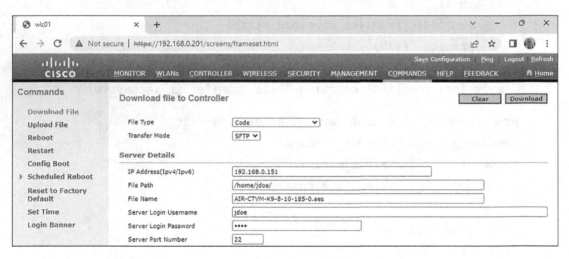

Figure 16-4. *WLC file transfer settings change the task*

Once the file downloading process from the SFTP server is complete, navigate to the COMMANDS menu and select "Config Boot" from the left-hand side. In doing so, you will observe that the Primary Image now reflects the newly downloaded version, which is 8.10.185.0 (default). However, the Backup Image remains the currently running version, which is 8.8.130.0 (active). This signifies that after the system reboots, it will boot into the default version, transforming 8.10.185.0 (default) into 8.10.185.0 (default) (active). We will verify this in the next step (see Figure 16-5).

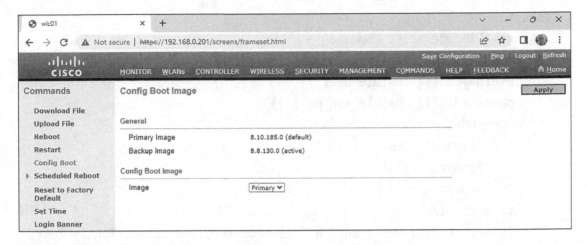

Figure 16-5. *Config Boot Image after file download*

Note that if you have prior experience with upgrading the WLC using the GUI, you are likely aware that Cisco WLC has its built-in file verification mechanism. Therefore, the MD5 verification and downloaded file integrity check are performed automatically. The WLC will only proceed with the upgrade if the file transfer was completed, and the file remains uncorrupted. Consequently, there is no need for us to manually verify the MD5 checksum during our upgrade process.

Optionally, if you wish to conduct additional testing, you can revert to the last snapshot to restore your image to the desired settings. This will enable you to execute the aforementioned playbook once again. However, if you are satisfied with your progress thus far, please proceed to step 5.

Step 5: Now, let's create the WLC Reset playbook. This playbook executes the "reset system" command on the WLCs. It is specifically designed to be used for resetting the system after the transfer of the new WLC file, regardless of whether it is for an upgrade or a downgrade.

```
[jdoe@f38s1 ch16]$ vi 16_aireos_reset.yml
[jdoe@f38s1 ch16]$ cat 16_aireos_reset.yml
---
- name: Hard reload (reboot) WLCs
  hosts: wlc
  gather_facts: no

  vars_files: vars.yml
```

```
tasks:
  - name: Execute reset command
    community.network.aireos_command:
      username: "{{ ansible_user }}"
      password: "{{ ansible_ssh_pass }}"
      commands:
        - command: 'reset system'
          prompt: '(y/N)'
          answer: 'y'
      timeout: 120
      ignore_errors: yes # When WLC is rebooted, the connection is lost,
      so we will simply ignore errors to complete our playbook.
```

If you access the terminal console of your WLC during the reboot, you will be able to see the WLC booting into the new image as seen in Figure 16-6.

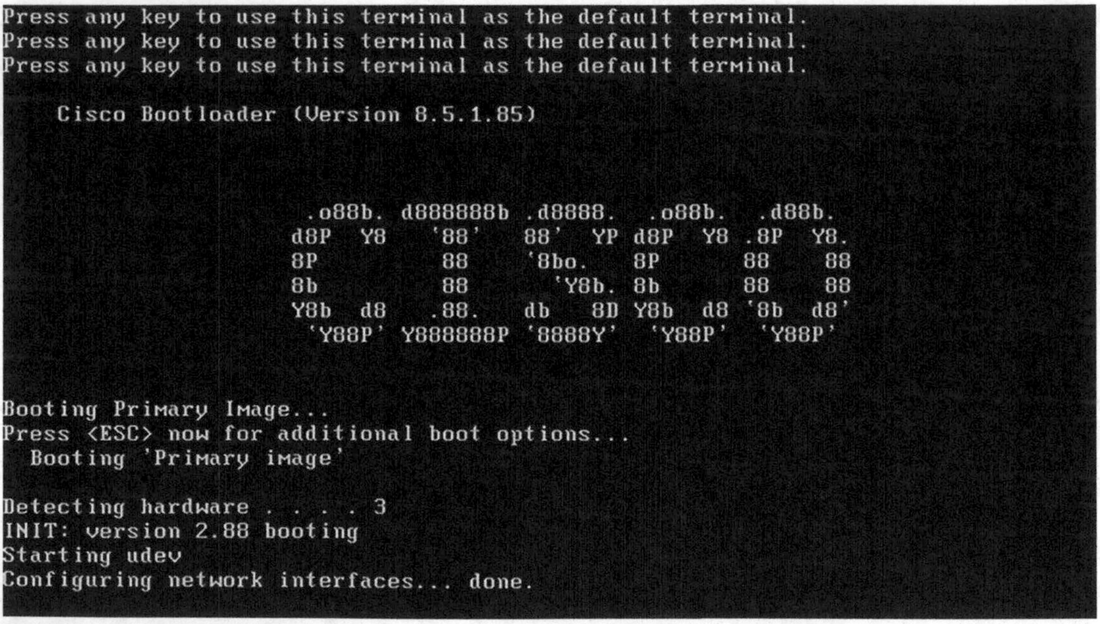

Figure 16-6. *The WLC booting process to complete the upgrade*

Figure 16-7 illustrates the Config Boot Image page within the COMMANDS menu on the rebooted WLC. It now displays the upgraded image, which is 8.10.185.0 (default) (active). It is worth noting that Cisco WLC always maintains two copies of the images in its flash. The previous version serves as the Backup Image, acting as a safeguard in case the Primary Image becomes corrupted or encounters issues.

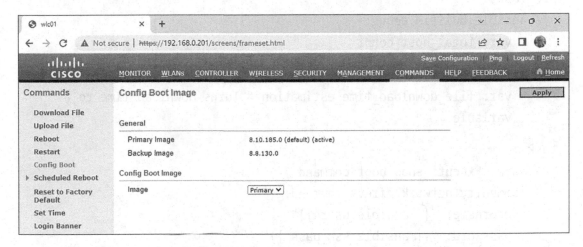

Figure 16-7. *WLC Config Boot Image information after the upgrade*

Step 6: At this stage, it is recommended to **revert to your previous snapshot for further testing**. In the next step, you will apply the final upgrade playbook and execute it once more to validate that all the playbook tasks are functioning as intended.

Step 7: Now combine 16_aireos_file_download.yml and 16_aireos_reset.yml files to create **16_aireos_upgrade.yml**.

```
[jdoe@f38s1 ch16]$ vi 16_aireos_upgrade.yml
[jdoe@f38s1 ch16]$ cat 16_aireos_upgrade.yml
---
- name: Cisco vWLC File upload playbook
  hosts: wlc
  gather_facts: no

  vars_files:
    - vars.yml
```

```yaml
vars:
  wlc_version: 8.10.185.0
  total_host_count: "{{ ansible_play_hosts | length }}"
  file_download_time_estimation: "{{ total_host_count | int * 30 + 300 }}"

pre_tasks:
  - ansible.builtin.debug:
      var: total_host_count

  - ansible.builtin.debug:
      var: file_download_time_estimation # Turns download time to a
      variable

tasks:
  - name: Execute show boot command
    community.network.aireos_command:
      username: "{{ ansible_user }}"
      password: "{{ ansible_ssh_pass }}"
      commands: show boot
      wait_for:
        - result[0] not contains '{{ wlc_version }}'
    register: output1

  - ansible.builtin.debug:
      var: output1.stdout_lines

  - name: Change WLC transfer settings
    community.network.aireos_command:
      username: "{{ ansible_user }}"
      password: "{{ ansible_ssh_user }}"
      timeout: 30
      commands:
        - transfer download mode ftp
        - transfer download username "{{ sftp_user }}"
        - transfer download password "{{ sftp_password }}"
        - transfer download serverip "{{ sftp_server }}"
        - transfer download path /home/jdoe/
        - transfer download filename "{{ aes_file_name }}"
```

```
- name: Start new aireos file transfer # Transfers .aes file
  community.network.aireos_command:
    username: "{{ ansible_user }}"
    password: "{{ ansible_ssh_pass }}"
    timeout: "{{ file_download_time_estimation | int }}"
    commands:
      - command: 'transfer download start'
        prompt: '(y/N)'
        answer: 'y'
    wait_for: result[0] contains "File transfer is successful"

- name: Execute show boot command after file upload
  community.network.aireos_command:
    username: "{{ ansible_user }}"
    password: "{{ ansible_ssh_pass }}"
    commands:
      - show boot
  register: output2

- name: Image versions after the reload
  ansible.builtin.debug:
    var: output2.stdout_lines

- name: Execute reset command
  community.network.aireos_command:
    username: "{{ ansible_user }}"
    password: "{{ ansible_ssh_pass }}"
    commands:
      - command: 'reset system'
        prompt: '(y/N)'
        answer: 'y'
    timeout: 120
  ignore_errors: yes
```

Step 8: If your playbook executed as intended, you should have encountered no errors and successfully reached the end of the playbook. However, it is possible to receive an "action failed" error message, as shown in the following. This is an expected behavior, and to ensure the completion of the playbook despite the error, we have enabled the ignore_errors directive, set to "yes". This allows the playbook to continue executing even if there are failures along the way.

```
[jdoe@f38s1 ch16]$ anp 16_aireos_upgrade.yml --ask-vault-pass
Vault password: *************
PLAY [Cisco vWLC File upload playbook] **********************************

TASK [debug] **********************************************************
ok: [wlc01] => {
    "total_host_count": "1"
}
[...omitted for brevity]
TASK [Image versions after the reload] **********************************
ok: [wlc01] => {
    "output2.stdout_lines": [
        [
            "Primary Boot Image.................... 8.10.185.0 (default)",
            "Backup Boot Image.................... 8.8.130.0 (active)"
        ]
    ]
}

TASK [Execute reset command] *******************************************
fatal: [wlc01]: FAILED! => {"changed": false, "msg": "The aireos_command
action failed to execute in the expected time frame (120) and was
terminated"}
...ignoring

PLAY RECAP ************************************************************
wlc01 : ok=9  changed=0  unreachable=0  failed=0  skipped=0  rescued=0  ignored=1
```

Step 9: In Ansible, idempotency is a crucial feature. However, in this particular scenario, we cannot rely solely on Ansible's idempotency, so we have implemented our circuit breaker mechanism to prevent unnecessary upgrades. To achieve this, we have utilized the wait_for directive along with the condition – result[0] not contains

'{{ wlc_version }}'. This combination ensures that the playbook is halted if the new IOS version is already present in the output of the show boot command. This circuit breaker acts as a safeguard, preventing unnecessary upgrades on WLCs that already have the same WLC versions. Execute the upgrade playbook again and confirm that no unnecessary files are uploaded to the WLC.

```
[jdoe@f38s1 ch16]$ anp 16_aireos_upgrade.yml --ask-vault-pass
Vault password: **************
PLAY [Cisco vWLC File upload playbook] **********************************

TASK [debug] **********************************************************
ok: [wlc01] => {
    "total_host_count": "1"
}

TASK [debug] **********************************************************
ok: [wlc01] => {
    "file_download_time_estimation": "330"
}

TASK [Execute show boot command] **************************************
fatal: [wlc01]: FAILED! => {"changed": false, "failed_conditions":
["result[0] not contains '8.10.185.0'"], "msg": "One or more conditional
statements have not been satisfied"}

PLAY RECAP ************************************************************
wlc01 : ok=2  changed=0  unreachable=0  failed=1  skipped=0  rescued=0  ignored=0
```

Congratulations on completing the Cisco Wireless LAN Controller upgrade playbook! Well done to all of you for reaching this point in the chapter. As a reward for your progress, let's delve into an interesting discussion on designing your inventory file to facilitate easier site or region management of dispersed locations. It is recommended that you read the remainder of the chapter before proceeding to the security labs starting from Chapter 17.

16.4 Ansible Inventory Configuration for Cisco WLC Enterprise Network

The Ansible inventory file holds significant importance in our playbooks. In Figure 16-8, we are presented with an enterprise wireless network consisting of five vWLCs spread across five cities in the United States. Each location has a WLC that serves both the local wireless network and acts as a secondary controller for the closest city. To streamline the configuration and patch management of these devices, you have been tasked with devising an inventory file design that allows for managing all devices collectively or organizing them based on regions or states. Now, let's dissect the inventory and examine the details of your new inventory file.

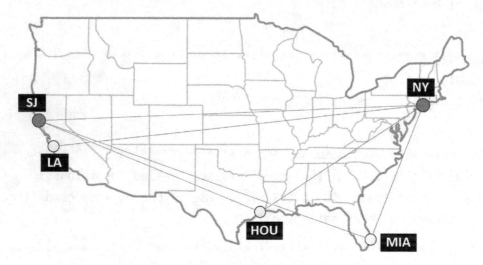

Figure 16-8. *US map with five major cities*

Let's take a quick look at our example inventory design. Following the inventory file, you will find a detailed explanation of its structure and organization.

```
                              INVENTORY

[all:vars]
ansible_user="{{ wlc_admin_user }}"
ansible_ssh_pass="{{ wlc_admin_password }}"

[wlc_tx:vars]
ansible_user="{{ wlc_admin_user77 }}"
ansible_ssh_pass="{{ wlc_admin_password77 }}"

[wlc_ny]
ny-slc10 ansible_host=10.10.10.254

[wlc_fl]
mia-wlc33 ansible_host=10.10.33.254

[wlc_tx]
hou-wlc77 ansible_host=10.10.77.254

[wlc_ca]
sj-wlc94 ansible_host=10.10.94.254
la-wlc90 ansible_host=10.10.90.254

[wlc_ec:children]
ny-slc10 ansible_host=10.10.10.254
mia-wlc33 ansible_host=10.10.33.254
hou-wlc77 ansible_host=10.10.77.254

[wlc_wc:children]
sj-wlc94 ansible_host=10.10.94.254
la-wlc90 ansible_host=10.10.90.254

[wlc_us:children]
wlc_ec
wlc_wc
```

1. [all:vars]: This section defines variables that apply to all hosts
    in the inventory. It sets the ansible_user and ansible_ssh_pass
    variables to the values of wlc_admin_user and wlc_admin_
    password, respectively.

2. [wlc_tx:vars]: This section defines variables specific to the hosts in the wlc_tx group. It sets the ansible_user and ansible_ssh_pass variables to the values of wlc_admin_user77 and wlc_admin_password77, respectively.

3. [wlc_ny]: This section defines a group named wlc_ny with a single host. The host is labeled as ny-slc10 and has the IP address 10.10.10.254.

4. [wlc_fl]: This section defines a group named wlc_fl with a single host. The host is labeled as mia-wlc33 and has the IP address 10.10.33.254.

5. [wlc_tx]: This section defines a group named wlc_tx with a single host. The host is labeled as hou-wlc77 and has the IP address 10.10.77.254.

6. [wlc_ca]: This section defines a group named wlc_ca with two hosts. The first host is labeled as sj-wlc94 and has the IP address 10.10.94.254. The second host is labeled as la-wlc90 and has the IP address 10.10.90.254.

7. [wlc_ec:children]: This section defines a group named wlc_ec that includes hosts from the wlc_ny, wlc_fl, and wlc_tx groups.

8. [wlc_wc:children]: This section defines a group named wlc_wc that includes hosts from the wlc_ca group.

9. [wlc_us:children]: This section defines a group named wlc_us that includes hosts from the wlc_ec and wlc_wc groups.

The inventory is organized based on geographical locations and functional groupings of the hosts. The [all:vars] section sets variables applicable to all hosts, while specific variables for individual groups are defined under [wlc_tx:vars]. The hosts are grouped by their respective state capital cities, such as New York (wlc_ny), Florida (wlc_fl), Texas (wlc_tx), and California (wlc_ca). Additionally, there are parent-child relationships defined between groups (wlc_ec, wlc_wc) and a higher-level group (wlc_us) that includes both child groups.

In the upcoming chapters (Chapters 17–21), we will focus on enterprise firewalls, specifically Palo Alto and Fortinet, two leading vendors in 2023. Through practical examples, we will explore how Ansible playbooks interact with these firewall platforms. With Ansible's capabilities, we'll discover the practical applications of network security automation. From simplifying firewall management to automating configurations and enhancing security policies, Ansible enables streamlined administration, improved efficiency, and robust firewall operations. Get ready for an engaging and hands-on experience as we dive into the world of network security automation with Palo Alto and Fortinet firewalls. Prepare to harness the power of Ansible and transform your firewall management and operations.

16.5 Summary

This chapter emphasized the importance of regular upgrades for the Cisco Wireless LAN Controller (WLC) in enterprise networks. Upgrading the WLC ensures wireless network security, unlocks advanced features, and maintains seamless connectivity for efficient data transmission. By utilizing an Ansible playbook, organizations benefit in multiple ways when upgrading the Cisco WLC. The playbook streamlines the upgrade process, automates tasks, and reduces errors. It enhances scalability and simplifies management across multiple devices, enabling coordinated upgrades. Ansible provides better control and visibility with validation steps and detailed logs for troubleshooting. Throughout the chapter, we explored the development of a WLC upgrading playbook and discussed efficient inventory file management techniques for multi-site and multi-device environments. Following these practices results in standardized upgrades, improved network security, optimized performance, and the ability to leverage the latest features from Cisco. By the end of this chapter, readers will have a solid understanding of the WLC's importance, the upgrade process using an Ansible playbook, and efficient inventory file management techniques.

## CHAPTER 17

Creating User Accounts on Palo Alto and Fortinet Firewalls

In this chapter, we will take a look at creating an administrator account using an Ansible playbook. We will also practice using ansible-vault. In today's digital landscape, securing sensitive data is of utmost importance, and ansible-vault provides a quick and easy way to encrypt and decrypt sensitive user information. Throughout the chapter, we will provide a guide that covers the entire thought process, starting from manual user creation and extending to writing an Ansible playbook for user creations. Detailed explanations of each section of Ansible snippets and outputs will be provided to help you understand the automation thought processes. Our goal is to equip you with the knowledge to confidently apply these concepts to secure your firewalls.

In Chapter 10, we explored the Ansible Vault, and in Chapters 12, 13, 14, and 16, we utilized the vault feature while managing Cisco devices. Now, in this chapter, we will leverage this feature to create user accounts on Palo Alto and FortiGate firewalls. Here, we delve into the automation of Palo Alto and Fortinet Firewall Administrator account creation using the Ansible playbook with ansible-vault. We begin by introducing ansible-vault as a tool for encrypting sensitive information and ensuring its security. Step-by-step, we guide you through the process of transitioning from manual account

© Brendan Choi and Erwin Medina 2023
B. Choi and E. Medina, *Introduction to Ansible Network Automation,*
https://doi.org/10.1007/978-1-4842-9624-0_17

setup to automated provisioning. You will learn how to develop a customized YAML playbook for creating administrator accounts on both firewall platforms. With practical examples and clear instructions, you will gain hands-on experience in crafting YAML code and incorporating ansible-vault for secure variable storage. The chapter culminates with the execution of the YAML playbook, showcasing the efficiency of automation in streamlining account creation. By the end of the chapter, you will have enough practice with ansible-vault, YAML playbook development, and the practical implementation of automation for managing administrator accounts.

For this chapter, our lab topology is simple, as depicted in Figure 17-1. We only require three virtual machines: the Ansible Control Machine, f38s1 (192.168.127.150), Palo Alto PAN-OS Firewall (192.168.127.31), and Fortinet FortiGate Firewall (192.168.127.32). For the remainder of this book, you will only work with two to three devices.

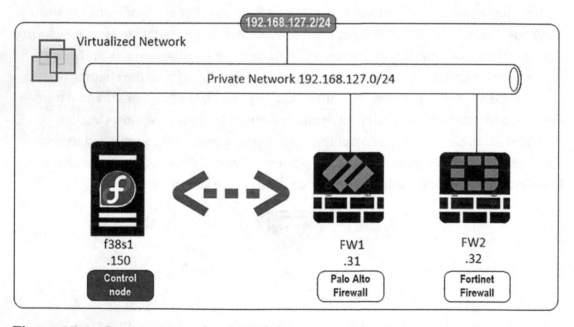

Figure 17-1. *Devices in use for this lab*

To replicate the topology on GNS3, follow these steps:

1.   Open the GNS3 topology canvas.

2.   Drag and drop the NAT cloud onto the canvas.

3. Place two Palo Alto firewalls and one Fortinet firewall onto the canvas.

4. Connect the firewalls using the GNS3 connection tool, as shown in Figure 17-2.

5. Take note of the following IP addresses for each firewall:

   - FW1: Palo Alto firewall with IP address 192.168.127.31/24

   - FW2: Fortinet firewall with IP address 192.168.127.32/24

   - FW3: Another Palo Alto firewall with IP address 192.168.127.33/24

We will be utilizing this GNS3 topology from Chapters 17 through 20. However, in each chapter, you will only need to power on one to two firewalls and will not need all three.

For this specific chapter, please ensure you have Palo Alto FW1 (192.168.127.31) and Fortinet FW2 (192.168.127.32) set up in your lab, as depicted in Figure 17-2 before you proceed.

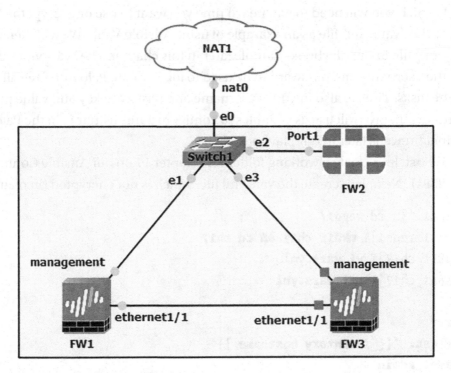

Figure 17-2. *GNS3 firewall lab topology*

17.1 Use Ansible Vault to Encrypt Sensitive Information

Ansible Vault is a feature in Ansible that allows you to encrypt sensitive data and store it securely. With Ansible Vault, you can encrypt variables, files, or even an entire playbook, ensuring that sensitive information is kept confidential. By using Ansible Vault, you can take your configuration management to the next level and safely store your sensitive information without worrying about unauthorized access. This is one of the most powerful features of Ansible, as it provides native content encryption capabilities. It also allows you to encrypt and decrypt arbitrary variables and files, making it a powerful tool for protecting sensitive information in your Ansible playbooks. With Ansible Vault, you can encrypt variable files that contain secrets or even an entire sensitive configuration file. This will provide an additional layer of security for your infrastructure. Ansible Vault offers many advanced features, but this section will focus on the basics.

To encrypt a standard YAML file containing plain text secrets, you can use the "ansible-vault encrypt" command. This will encrypt the file and prompt you for a password, which you will need to enter each time you want to use or decrypt the file. We will use the "vars.yml" file as an example of using Ansible Vault. We will then use the "vars.yml" file in our playbook example later in this chapter. The "vars.yml" file contains the username and password to be used to log in to the Palo Alto firewall and execute the tasks. The file also includes username and password key and value pairs of administrators that we will use as variables to configure administrators in the Palo Alto and Fortinet firewalls later in our playbook.

Step 1: First, let's create a working folder for Chapter 17 on our Ansible Control Machine, f38s1. Next, let's create the vars.yml file, which is not encrypted (in plain text).

```
[jdoe@f38s1 ~]$ cd repo1/
[jdoe@f38s1 repo1]$ mkdir ch17 && cd ch17
[jdoe@f38s1 ch17]$ vi vars.yml
[jdoe@f38s1 ch17]$ cat vars.yml
---
provider:
  ip_address: '{{ inventory_hostname }}'
  username: admin
  password: Palo123!
```

```
admins:
  deon:
    pan_username: deon
    pan_password: qwer@sed
  jenny:
    pan_username: jenny
    pan_password: dflgj#wl
  owen:
    pan_username: owen
    pan_password: Asdf@sew
  jachie:
    pan_username: jachie
    pan_password: Wq@esdf
  reeva:
    pan_username: reeva
    pan_password: Jkhu!kdfd
```

Step 2: Now, to encrypt the vars.yml file containing plain text passwords, we will use the "ansible-vault encrypt" command. This command will encrypt the file and prompt us for a password, which we will need to enter and use each time we access or decrypt the file. After encrypting the file, Ansible Vault will create a new version of the file with a .vault extension, which is encrypted.

```
[jdoe@f38s1 ch17]$ ansible-vault encrypt vars.yml
New Vault password: ***************
Confirm New Vault password: **************
Encryption successful
```

Step 3: Let's verify and use the "cat" command to view the file and check if it is encrypted.

```
[jdoe@f38s1 ch17]$ cat vars.yml
$ANSIBLE_VAULT;1.1;AES256
30306339633633626639633265563613736396632376466336330326235346130313031356332
[...omitted for brevity]
386463306330333132336566643564396331646264303662333934363335643839313834303038
489
```

Step 4: We will then use the "ansible-vault view" command to see the content of the encrypted file, and we will be prompted to enter our Vault password.

```
[jdoe@f38s1 ch17]$ ansible-vault view vars.yml
Vault password: **************
[...omitted for brevity]
```

Step 5: To edit the encrypted file, we can use the "ansible-vault edit" command.

```
[jdoe@f38s1 ch17]$ ansible-vault edit vars.yml
Vault password: **************
---
provider:
  ip_address: '{{ inventory_hostname }}'
  username: admin
  password: Palo123!

admins:
  deon:
    pan_username: deon
    pan_password: qwer@sed
[...omitted for brevity]
~
"~/.ansible/tmp/ansible-local-281187e8g5eq/tmpf9_u3be1.yml" 27L, 474C
```

Step 6: Lastly, to decrypt the encrypted file, we can use the "ansible-vault decrypt" command.

```
[jdoe@f38s1 ch17]$ ansible-vault decrypt vars.yml
Vault password: **************
Decryption successful
```

Step 7: Let's encrypt it again since we'll be using it in our examples.

```
[jdoe@f38s1 ch17]$ ansible-vault encrypt vars.yml
New Vault password: **************
Confirm New Vault password: **************
Encryption successful
```

Having defined and provided examples of using ansible-vault, let's now explore how we can use it to create Palo Alto and Fortinet Firewall Administrators, transitioning from manual to automation. By employing ansible-vault, we can securely store confidential information alongside our regular playbooks in source control. The beauty of this approach lies in the fact that the encrypted data mitigates risks as long as a strong password is chosen. To further bolster security, it is recommended to periodically rotate the encryption password, treating it as any other shared secret. Exploring Ansible's documentation can unveil additional ways to leverage its native capabilities and effectively safeguard your secrets.

17.2 Administrator Account Creation on Palo Alto Firewalls: From Manual to Automation

Before writing our playbook, let's quickly review the required fields for creating an account on the Palo Alto firewall. This step is crucial as it allows us to plan and gather the necessary information for our variables. By gaining a comprehensive understanding of how to manually administer the firewall interfaces, we can develop a relevant and effective Ansible playbook. If you don't possess complete knowledge in this area, it is always recommended to read the vendor's documentation and consult with your colleagues to obtain the assistance you require. Taking these steps ensures that you are well equipped to create a successful playbook and achieve your desired outcomes.

Step 1: To create an administrator account, go to **Device ➤ Administrators ➤ Add**. In the resulting window, fill out the required fields, such as the administrator's name, choose either an authentication profile or a password, and specify the administrator type as shown in Figure 17-3.

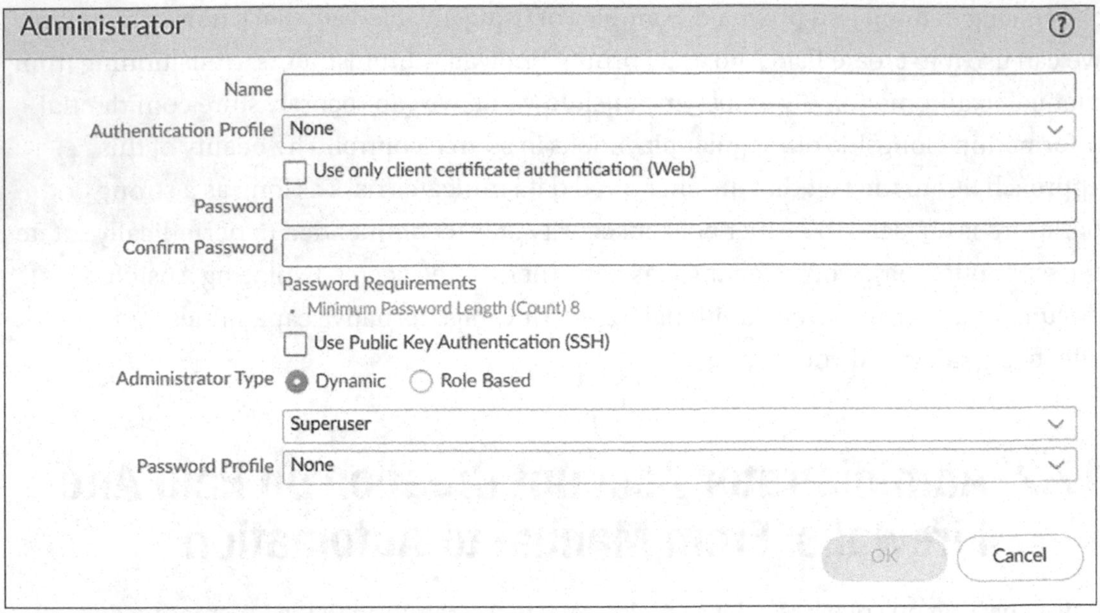

Figure 17-3. *Administrator account creation*

Additionally, you have the option to add a password profile to configure specific password settings, as demonstrated in Figure 17-4.

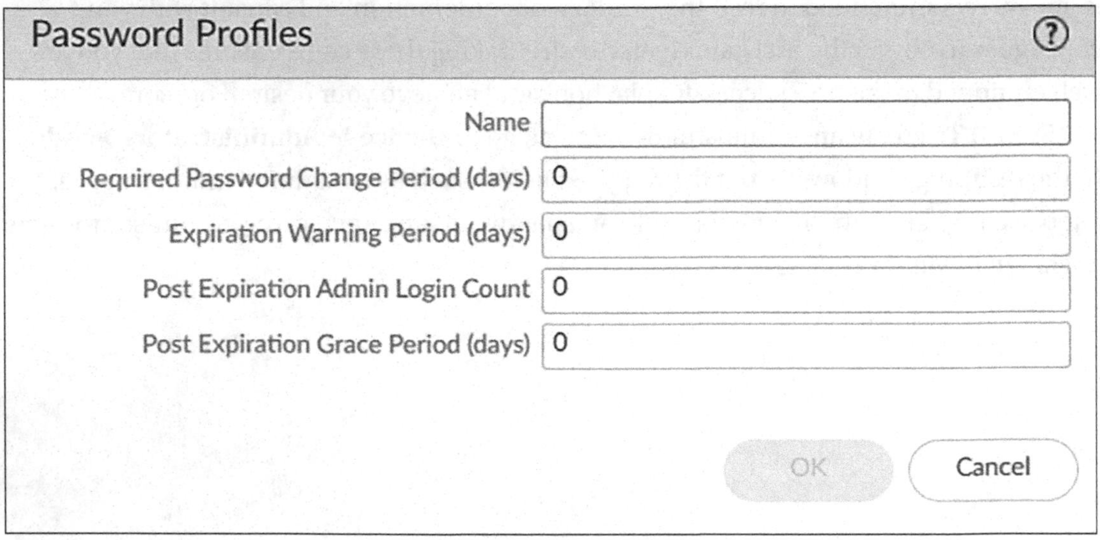

Figure 17-4. *Administrator account password profile*

Tip

Uninstall cowsay to keep things clean.

To keep things simple, we recommend you remove the cowsay so you do not have to disable it by specifying "nocows=1" in your ansible.cfg. For the rest of the book, cowsay will not be used.

```
[jdoe@f38s1 ch17]$ sudo dnf remove cowsay -y
```

17.3 Writing a YAML Playbook to Create an Administrator Account on a Palo Alto Firewall

Before diving into writing the YAML playbook, let's take a moment to perform a few preliminary steps. We will create the local ansible.cfg file, the inventory file, install paloaltonetworks.panos from ansible-galaxy, and install pan-os-python using the Python pip command. To ensure a smooth process, please follow the step-by-step instructions provided here:

Step 1: The **ansible.cfg** file is a configuration file to customize the behavior and settings in Ansible. The file is normally located in "**/etc/ansible/ansible.cfg**", and you would be able to see the default values when you read the file. However, to keep it simple, we will store all components in the same directory where our playbooks are stored. When Ansible runs, it will look for the ansible.cfg file to load any configuration settings specified within it. If there are no configuration settings defined, it will use its defaults. In this case, we have specified that our inventory, or what we call hosts, is named inventory.

```
[jdoe@f38s1 ch17]$ vi ansible.cfg
[jdoe@f38s1 ch17]$ cat ansible.cfg
[defaults]
inventory=inventory
```

Step 2: The **inventory** file is a file that contains the list of target hosts and groups. The file is normally located in "**/etc/ansible/hosts**", and you would be able to see examples of how you can build your inventory list when you read the file. In this case, we will define and name our host file as inventory as we have configured in the ansible. cfg file.

```
[jdoe@f38s1 ch17]$ vi inventory
[jdoe@f38s1 ch17]$ cat inventory
[palo]
192.168.127.31
```

Step 3: The **Roles** is a collection of modules that automates the configuration and operational tasks. For the Palo Alto firewall, we will need to install the role with the command "ansible-galaxy collection install paloaltonetworks.panos". It uses API calls using the Ansible framework.

```
[jdoe@f38s1 ch17]$ ansible-galaxy collection install paloaltonetworks.panos
[...omitted for brevity]
```

Step 4: The **SDK – software development kit** which is the Palo Alto Networks PAN-OS SDK for Python, is a package to help interact with Palo Alto Networks devices.

```
[jdoe@f38s1 ch17]$ pip3 install pan-os-python
[...omitted for brevity]
```

Also, install the xmltodict using the pip3 command to properly print out the output on your screen.

```
[jdoe@f38s1 ch17]$ pip3 install xmltodict
[...omitted for brevity]
```

Step 5: The **playbook**, named "17_create_pan_admins.yml", serves as our playbook written in YAML format. It defines and executes tasks targeted at specific hosts, as defined in our inventory file.

Before delving into the main playbook, let's create and test a simple playbook to ensure successful connectivity with the Palo Alto firewall. This preliminary playbook includes a script that runs the "show system info" operational command on the Palo Alto firewall and prints the resulting output.

By running this test playbook, we can verify the connectivity and ensure that the necessary prerequisites are in place before proceeding further.

```
[jdoe@f38s1 ch17]$ vi 17_show_system_info.yml
[jdoe@f38s1 ch17]$ cat 17_show_system_info.yml
---
- name: run the show command
  hosts: palo
  gather_facts: false
  connection: local
  vars_files: vars.yml

  tasks:
   - name: show system info
     paloaltonetworks.panos.panos_op:
       provider: '{{ provider }}'
       cmd: 'show system info'
     register: show_info

   - name: Print info
     debug:
       var: show_info.stdout
```

In the context of the playbook, the paloaltonetworks.panos.panos_op task requires a provider parameter to establish a connection with the device and execute the specified command (in this case, show system info). The provider variable is defined using the Ansible variable syntax {{ provider }}. Typically, the provider variable is defined elsewhere in the playbook, such as in the vars.yml file referenced in the vars_files section. It contains essential connection information, such as the device's IP address or hostname, username, password, and other authentication details. By passing the provider variable to the paloaltonetworks.panos.panos_op task, the task utilizes the provided connection details to establish a connection to the Palo Alto device and execute the specified command. The output of the command is then stored in the show_info variable, which can be accessed and printed using the debug task. Remember to appropriately define the provider variable in your playbook to establish a successful connection to your Palo Alto device.

Step 6: Now, let's execute the playbook and observe the successful execution of the command.

```
[jdoe@f38s1 ch17]$ anp --ask-vault-pass 17_show_system_info.yml
Vault password: ***************
PLAY [run show command] **************************************************

TASK [show system info] **************************************************
ok: [192.168.127.31]

TASK [Print info] ********************************************************
ok: [192.168.127.31] => {
    "show_info.stdout": {
        "response": {
            "@status": "success",
            "result": {
                "system": {
                    "app-version": "8402-6681",
                    "av-version": "0",
                    "cloud-mode": "non-cloud",
                    "default-gateway": "192.168.127.2",
                    "device-certificate-status": "None",
                    "device-dictionary-release-date": "2022/01/07
                    17:25:38 AEDT",
                    "device-dictionary-version": "40-305",
                    "devicename": "PA-VM",
                    "family": "vm",
                    "global-protect-client-package-version": "0.0.0",
                    "global-protect-clientless-vpn-version": "0",
                    "global-protect-datafile-release-date": "unknown",
                    "global-protect-datafile-version": "unknown",
                    "hostname": "PA-VM",
                    "ip-address": "192.168.127.31",
                    "ipv6-address": "unknown",
                    "ipv6-link-local-address": "fe80::20c:29ff:fe2c:
                    41f4/64",
                    "is-dhcp": "no",
```

```
              "logdb-version": "10.1.2",
              "mac-address": "00:0c:29:2c:41:f4",
              "model": "PA-VM",
              "multi-vsys": "off",
              "netmask": "255.255.255.0",
              "operational-mode": "normal",
[...omitted for brevity]

PLAY RECAP ************************************************************
192.168.127.31               : ok=2    changed=0    unreachable=0
failed=0    skipped=0    rescued=0    ignored=0
```

Moving on to our practical examples, in this scenario, you will come across an Ansible YAML script named "17_create_pan_admins.yml". It is essential to understand the contents of the YAML file to comprehend the objectives and execution of this playbook. The "17_create_pan_admins.yml" serves as an Ansible playbook specifically designed to create multiple administrator accounts. To ensure enhanced security, the administrator's username and password will be securely stored in an encrypted file called "vars.yml" using ansible-vault. This is an opportunity for you to thoroughly understand the significance of each line within the playbook, enabling you to readily grasp its meaning whenever you encounter similar lines in other playbooks.

As in all YAML files, **the three dashes indicate the start of a new document**.

```
---
```

With the use of **- name**, we can **describe what this YAML file does** or intends to do.

- name: Create Palo Alto Administrators

This specifies the target host(s) on which this playbook will run. In this case, it will run on a host named "palo". For this playbook, we will run it on a Palo Alto VM with IP 192.168.127.31. This IP is defined in our inventory as a member of the group-name named "palo".

hosts: palo

By default, the gather_facts module in Ansible is always enabled. However, if you don't require information from facts, you have the option to disable this module. Disabling gather_facts can help conserve processor resources and accelerate the execution of your playbook. When gather_facts is disabled, Ansible won't collect information about the target host(s) such as their IP address, operating system, installed packages, and other details. It's worth noting that the information gathered from the gather_facts module can be valuable as variables, allowing you to modify the behavior of your Ansible playbook. However, if you don't need this information for your specific use case, it's recommended to disable the gather_facts module to optimize the overall performance of your playbook.

```
gather_facts: false
```

The connection: local parameter in an Ansible playbook indicates that the playbook should be executed locally on the machine where Ansible is running, as opposed to being executed remotely on the target host(s). As a result, any tasks defined within the playbook will be executed on the Ansible control node itself instead of the target hosts. This feature proves advantageous for tasks that don't require remote execution or for conducting tests and validations.

```
connection: local
```

The vars_files: vars.yml parameter is utilized in the playbook 17_create_pan_admins. yml to specify the location of a YAML dictionary file that contains the required variables. These variables are crucial for acquiring the login credentials and administrator information, such as the username and password. By using a separate YAML dictionary file, the contents can be securely stored and encrypted, ensuring the protection of sensitive information.

```
vars_files: vars.yml
```

The Ansible task utilizes the "paloaltonetworks.panos.panos_administrator" module to create administrators on the Palo Alto firewall by providing their usernames and passwords. The values for the "pan_username" and "pan_password" parameters are obtained from the dictionary of admins defined in the vars.yml file. Additionally, the "superuser" parameter is set to "yes", granting the admin full access rights to the firewall. The "commit" flag is set to False, ensuring that the changes made by this task remain as a candidate configuration and are not immediately committed.

```
tasks:
- name: Create admins
  paloaltonetworks.panos.panos_administrator:
```

```
    provider: '{{ provider }}'
    admin_username: '{{ item.value.pan_username }}'
    admin_password: '{{ item.value.pan_password }}'
    superuser: 'yes'
    commit: 'False'
  loop: "{{ lookup('dict', admins) }}"
  no_log: 'True'
```

To iterate over the dictionary of admins, the task employs a loop. To conceal the username and password values from the output when executing the playbook, the "no_log" parameter is set to "True". This provides an extra layer of security by preventing the visibility of the username and password in plain text.

Once you have gained a comprehensive understanding of the YAML playbook, you can execute the "17_create_pan_admins.yml" playbook to verify the successful execution of the Ansible YAML script. Assuming there are no syntax errors or typos, you should observe output similar to the example provided in the following text. The playbook comprises a single task dedicated to creating administrators using the dictionary stored in the vars.yml file. The output provides a detailed explanation of each step involved in the playbook's execution.

17.4 Running the YAML Playbook to Create an Administrator Account on a Palo Alto Network Firewall

Before executing the playbook, it is evident that the administrators have not yet been configured on our designated Palo Alto Network firewall, which has an IP address of 192.168.127.31 (refer to Figure 17-5).

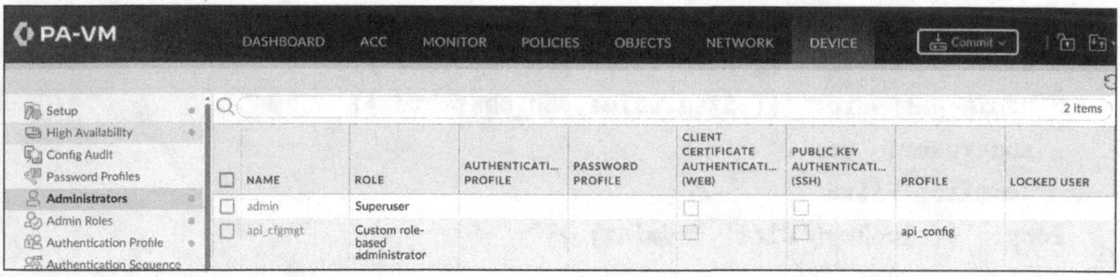

Figure 17-5. *PA-VM administrators before the configuration*

Step 1: For illustration and to gain a better understanding of the playbook, let's revisit the encrypted vars.yml file to examine the variables and the dictionary administrators created. We will utilize the ansible-vault view command, which will prompt us for the previously set Ansible Vault password. To log in to the Palo Alto firewall, the playbook will utilize the defined provider variables. The admins dictionary is populated with key-value pairs for each administrator.

```
[jdoe@f38s1 ch17]$ ansible-vault view vars.yml
Vault password: ***************
---
provider:
  ip_address: '{{ inventory_hostname }}'
  username: admin
  password: Palo123!

admins:
  deon:
    pan_username: deon
    pan_password: qwer@sed
  jenny:
    pan_username: jenny
    pan_password: dflgj#wl
  owen:
    pan_username: owen
    pan_password: Asdf@sew
  jachie:
    pan_username: jachie
    pan_password: Wq@esdf
```

```
reeva:
  pan_username: reeva
  pan_password: Jkhu!kdfd
```

Step 2: We will proceed to execute an Ansible playbook named "17_create_pan_admins.yml". To obtain the variables from the vars.yml file and utilize them within the playbook, we will use the "--ask-vault-pass" command. This command will decrypt the encrypted vars.yml file and retrieve the necessary variables for playbook execution. Ansible will prompt for the Vault password, ensuring that the entered password remains concealed for security purposes.

The "PLAY RECAP" section in the Ansible output summarizes the status of the tasks executed on each target host. In this example, the target host's IP address is 192.168.127.31. The output shows that there is one task executed on this host, and it was successful (ok=1). With this task, one change made a change to the system (changed=1), while 0 tasks were unreachable, failed, or skipped (unreachable=0, failed=0, skipped=0). Finally, no tasks required being rescued or ignored (rescued=0, ignored=0).

```
[jdoe@f38s1 ch17]$ ansible-playbook 17_create_pan_admins.yml --ask-
vault-pass
Vault password: ***************
PLAY [Create Palo Alto Administrators] ************************************

TASK [Create admins] *****************************************************
changed: [192.168.127.31] => (item=None)
changed: [192.168.127.31] => (item=None)
changed: [192.168.127.31] => (item=None)
changed: [192.168.127.31] => (item=None)
changed: [192.168.127.31] => (item=None)
changed: [192.168.127.31]

PLAY RECAP ***************************************************************
192.168.127.31             : ok=1    changed=1    unreachable=0
failed=0    skipped=0    rescued=0    ignored=0
```

Step 3: In Figure 17-6, it is evident that the administrators have been successfully configured according to the specifications defined in the admins dictionary. This configuration is now reflected in the candidate configuration of the Palo Alto Network firewall. As mentioned earlier, we have set each task with the "commit" parameter set to "False". This setting enables us to review the configuration before committing the changes. However, if desired, the parameter can be changed to "True" to automatically commit the configuration.

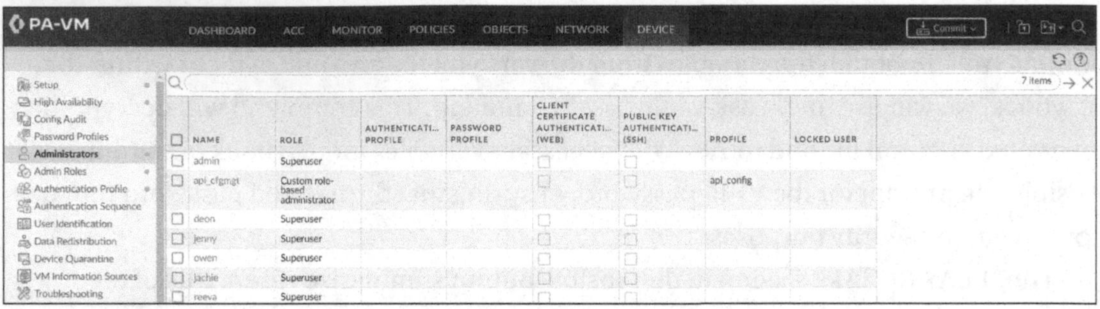

Figure 17-6. *PA-VM administrators after the configuration*

Here is the complete playbook of the "17_create_pan_admins.yml" file for your reference:

```
[jdoe@f38s1 ch17]$ vi 17_create_pan_admins.yml
[jdoe@f38s1 ch17]$ cat 17_create_pan_admins.yml
---
- name: Create Palo Alto Administrators
  hosts: palo
  gather_facts: false
  connection: local
  vars_files: vars.yml

  tasks:
  - name: Create admins
    paloaltonetworks.panos .panos_administrator:
      provider: '{{ provider }}'
      admin_username: '{{ item.value.pan_username }}'
      admin_password: '{{ item.value.pan_password }}'
      superuser: 'yes'
      commit: 'False'
    loop: "{{ lookup('dict', admins) }}"
    no_log: 'True'
```

We have practiced encrypting data using ansible-vault and have also examined a simple playbook for creating users on the Palo Alto firewall. Throughout this process, we analyzed each line of the playbook to comprehend the significance of every line in our code.

17.5 Administrator Account Creation on Fortinet Firewalls: From Manual to Automation

Let's quickly check how to create an administrator account manually through GUI, and you would follow these steps:

Step 1: Navigate to **System ➤ Administrators ➤ Create New ➤ Administrator**.

Step 2: In the resulting window, fill in the required fields, including the Username, Password, and Administration profile, as shown in Figure 17-7.

Step 3: Optionally, you can enable **Two-factor Authentication**, **Restrict login to trusted hosts**, and **Restrict admin to guest account provisioning only**.

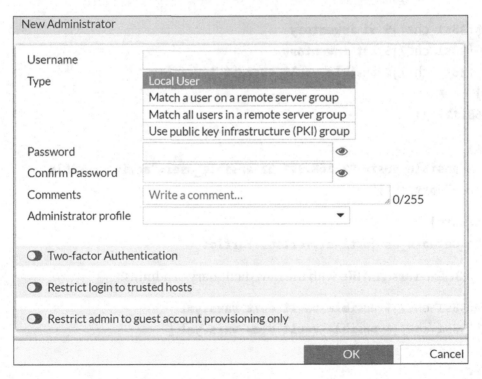

Figure 17-7. *Administrator account creation*

Now let's see how this is replicated and created using the Ansible playbook.

17.6 Writing a YAML Playbook to Create an Administrator Account on a Fortinet Firewall

We already have the ansible.cfg file in the same directory from the previous exercise. We will update our inventory and add the Fortinet device information. We will update the vars.yml file, the dictionary of admins and, lastly, the necessary installation needed to run our playbook on a Fortinet firewall.

Step 1: The **ansible.cfg** file is where we specify the name of our inventory, which we refer to as "hosts" in this case.

```
[jdoe@f38s1 ch17]$ cat ansible.cfg
[defaults]
inventory=inventory
```

Step 2: The **inventory** file is where we update and add the necessary information for the Fortinet firewall in this case. Additionally, we will encrypt it to ensure the security of sensitive information.

```
[jdoe@f38s1 ch17]$ vi inventory
[jdoe@f38s1 ch17]$ cat inventory
[jdoe@f38s1 ch17]$ ansible-vault encrypt inventory
[palo]
192.168.127.31

[forti]
Forti01 ansible_host=192.168.127.32 ansible_user="admin" ansible_
password="Forti123!"

[forti:vars]
ansible_network_os=fortinet.fortios.fortios
```

Step 3: The **vars.yml file** with the new dictionary of admins:

```
[jdoe@f38s1 ch17]$ ansible-vault edit vars.yml
[jdoe@f38s1 ch17]$ ansible-vault view vars.yml
---
admins:
 lifeng:
   forti_username: lifeng
```

```
  forti_password: qwer@sed
shannon:
  forti_username: shannon
  forti_password: dflgj#wl
osman:
  forti_username: osman
  forti_password: Asdf@sew
colin:
  forti_username: colin
  forti_password: Wq@esdf
```

Step 4: For the **Role** for the Fortinet firewall, we will need to install the role with the command "ansible-galaxy collection install fortinet.fortios".

```
[jdoe@f38s1 ch17]$ ansible-galaxy collection install fortinet.fortios
[...omitted for brevity]
```

Step 5: The **python library** for FortiGates/FortiOS devices, which, in this case, is the fortiosapi:

```
[jdoe@f38s1 ch17]$ pip3 install fortiosapi
[...omitted for brevity]
```

Step 6: The **playbook**, which is our application that is written in YAML format that defines and executes our tasks to our targeted hosts defined in our inventory file. In this case, our playbook is named "17_create_forti_admins.yml".

Again, before we go straight in, let's create and test a simple playbook to see if we can connect to the Fortinet firewall. We have a script to check the system status of the Fortinet firewall and print the output.

```
[jdoe@f38s1 ch17]$ vi 17_get_system_status.yml
[jdoe@f38s1 ch17]$ cat 17_ get_system_status.yml
---
- name: run get commands
  hosts: forti
  gather_facts: false
  connection: httpapi

  vars_files: vars.yml
```

```
  vars:
    ansible_httpapi_use_ssl: no
    ansible_httpapi_validate_certs: no
    ansible_httpapi_port: 80

  tasks:
  - name: get system status
    fortinet.fortios.fortios_monitor_fact:
      vdom:  "root"
      selectors:
        - selector: system_status
    register: system_info

  - name: print
    debug:
      msg: '{{ system_info }}'
```

Step 7: Now, let's run the playbook and observe the successful execution of the command.

```
[jdoe@f38s1 ch17]$ anp --ask-vault-pass 17_get_system_status.yml
Vault password: ***************
PLAY [run get commands] ************************************************

TASK [get system status] **********************************************
ok: [Forti01]

TASK [print] **********************************************************
ok: [Forti01] => {
    "msg": {
        "changed": false,
        "failed": false,
        "meta": [
            {
                "action": "",
                "build": 157,
                "http_method": "GET",
                "name": "status",
                "path": "system",
```

```
        "results": {
            "hostname": "FortiGate-VM64",
            "log_disk_status": "available",
            "model": "FGVM64",
            "model_name": "FortiGate",
            "model_number": "VM64"
        },
        "serial": "FGVMEVN35J1GBZ53",
        "status": "success",
        "vdom": "root",
        "version": "v7.0.1"
    }
  ]
}
}
```

```
PLAY RECAP ***********************************************************
Forti01 : ok=2     changed=0    unreachable=0    failed=0    skipped=0
rescued=0    ignored=0
```

Moving on to our practicals, in this example, you will find a comprehensive Ansible YAML script named "17_create_forti_admins.yml". The "17_create_forti_admins.yml" serves as an Ansible playbook designed to create multiple administrator accounts. The usernames and passwords of the administrators will be stored in an encrypted file called vars.yml using ansible-vault. Here is a brief explanation of each line in the playbook.

As with all YAML files, the three dashes "---" indicate the beginning of a new document.

```
---
```

With the use of - name, we can describe what this YAML file does or intends to do.

```
- name: Create Fortinet Administrators
```

This specifies the target host(s) on which this playbook will run. In this case, it will run on a host named "forti". For this playbook, we will run it on a Fortinet VM with IP 192.168.127.32. This IP is defined in our inventory as a member of the group-name named "forti".

```
hosts: forti
```

By default, Ansible's gather_facts module is enabled, but it can be disabled to conserve processor resources and speed up playbook execution. Disabling this module means that Ansible won't collect information about the target host(s), such as IP address, operating system, and installed packages. Although the gathered facts can be useful as variables to modify the Ansible playbook's flow, it's advisable to disable gather_facts if this information is not needed, thus optimizing playbook performance.

```
gather_facts: false
```

The connection: httpapi parameter in an Ansible playbook is a plug-in that offers methods for establishing a connection to a Fortinet FortiOS appliance or VM using the REST API.

```
connection: httpapi
```

The vars_files: vars.yml parameter defines variables stored in a YAML dictionary that are accessed by the playbook "17_create_forti_admins.yml" to retrieve administrator information, including the username and password. In this scenario, the YAML dictionary is created separately to ensure the security and encryption of its contents.

```
vars_files: vars.yml
```

The variables are configured here to establish a connection with the Fortinet firewall. Since we are using a VM evaluation license, we have set ansible_httpapi_use_ssl to "no", ansible_httpapi_validate_certs to "no", and ansible_httpapi_port to "80", which is not secure. If we have a valid license, we will set the SSL and certificate checks to "yes" and the port to "443".

```
vars:
  ansible_httpapi_use_ssl: no
  ansible_httpapi_validate_certs: no
  ansible_httpapi_port: 80
```

The Ansible task employs the "fortinet.fortios.fortios_system_admin" module to create administrators on the Fortinet firewall, providing the administrator's username and password. The vdom parameter is set to "root", and the state parameter is set to "present" to create the admin. The system_admin is a dictionary that retrieves the admin variables. The accprofile represents the administrator profile, which is set to "super_admin". The values of the forti_username and forti_password parameters are fetched from the dictionary of admins defined in the vars.yml file. The task loops through the module against the defined dictionary of admins. The no_log parameter is set to "True" to conceal the username and password values from the output when the playbook is executed. This ensures the security of the username and password by preventing them from being displayed in plain text.

```
  tasks:
  - name: Create admins
    fortinet.fortios.fortios_system_admin:
      vdom:   "root"
      state: "present"
      system_admin:
        accprofile: "super_admin"
        name: "{{ item.value.forti_username }}"
        password: "{{ item.value.forti_password }}"
    loop: "{{ lookup('dict',admins) }}"
    no_log: "True"
```

After gaining a thorough understanding of the YAML playbook, you can proceed to execute the "17_create_forti_admins.yml" playbook and verify the successful execution of the Ansible YAML script. If there are no syntax errors or typos, you should observe a similar output as shown in the following example. The playbook consists of a single task that creates administrators based on the dictionary stored in the vars.yml file. The output provides a detailed explanation of each step executed in the playbook.

17.7 Running the YAML Playbook to Create an Administrator Account on a Fortinet Firewall

Before executing the playbook, it is apparent that the administrators have not been set up on the target Fortinet firewall. The firewall, identified by the IP address 192.168.127.32 (see Figure 17-8), does not currently have the necessary configurations in place for the administrators.

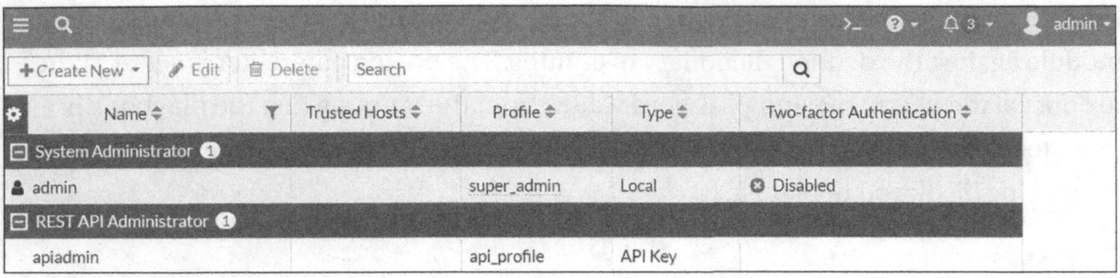

Figure 17-8. *Forti-VM administrators before the configuration*

Step 1: Firstly, let's take a look at the encrypted inventory file that contains the host information, including the username and password required for logging into the Fortinet firewall. Additionally, we have configured the network_os parameter as fortinet.fortios. fortios to enable the usage of modules and plug-ins specific to the Fortinet firewall.

```
[jdoe@f38s1 ch17]$ ansible-vault view inventory
Vault password: **************
[forti]
Forti01 ansible_host=192.168.127.32 ansible_user="admin" ansible_
password="Forti123!"

[forti:vars]
ansible_network_os=fortinet.fortios.fortios
```

Step 2: Next, let's examine the encrypted vars.yml file to review the variables and the dictionary of admins that were created. We can use the ansible-vault view command, which will prompt us to enter the previously set Ansible Vault password. The playbook will utilize the provider variables to establish a login connection with the Fortinet firewall. The admins dictionary contains the respective keys and values for each admin.

```
[jdoe@f38s1 ch17]$ ansible-vault view vars.yml
Vault password: **************
---
admins:
 lifeng:
   forti_username: lifeng
   forti_password: qwer@sed
```

```
shannon:
  forti_username: shannon
  forti_password: dflgj#wl
osman:
  forti_username: osman
  forti_password: Asdf@sew
colin:
  forti_username: colin
  forti_password: Wq@esdf
```

Step 3: Now, let's proceed to run the Ansible playbook named "17_create_forti_admins.yml". To execute the playbook successfully, we need to retrieve the variables from the vars.yml file. We can achieve this by using the "--ask-vault-pass" command, which will prompt us to provide the vault password for decrypting the encrypted vars. yml file and accessing the required variables. For security purposes, when entering the password, it will not be displayed on the screen.

The "PLAY RECAP" section in the Ansible output provides a summary of the task statuses on each target host. In this particular example, the target host is Forti01. The output reveals that a single task was executed successfully on this host (ok=1). Among the tasks, one change was made to the system (changed=1), while no tasks were unreachable, failed, or skipped (unreachable=0, failed=0, skipped=0). Furthermore, no tasks required being rescued or ignored (rescued=0, ignored=0).

```
[jdoe@f38s1 ch17]$ anp --ask-vault-pass 17_create_forti_admins.yml
Vault password: ***************
PLAY [Create Fortinet Administrators] ************************************

TASK [Create admins] ****************************************************
changed: [Forti01] => (item=None)
changed: [Forti01] => (item=None)
changed: [Forti01] => (item=None)
changed: [Forti01] => (item=None)
changed: [Forti01]

PLAY RECAP *************************************************************
Forti01  : ok=1    changed=1    unreachable=0    failed=0    skipped=0
rescued=0    ignored=0
```

Step 4: In Figure 17-9, a login test was conducted using one of the admin accounts named "lifeng". The test results indicate a successful login, confirming that the administrators have been configured according to the specifications outlined in the admins dictionary.

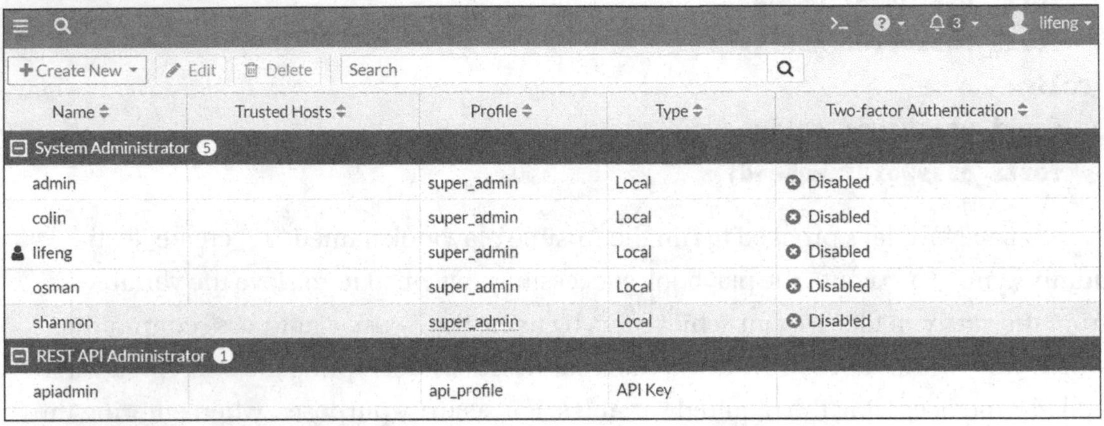

Name ⇕	Trusted Hosts ⇕	Profile ⇕	Type ⇕	Two-factor Authentication ⇕
System Administrator ⑤				
admin		super_admin	Local	⊗ Disabled
colin		super_admin	Local	⊗ Disabled
▲ lifeng		super_admin	Local	⊗ Disabled
osman		super_admin	Local	⊗ Disabled
shannon		super_admin	Local	⊗ Disabled
REST API Administrator ①				
apiadmin		api_profile	API Key	

Figure 17-9. *Forti-VM administrators after the configuration*

Here is the completed 17_create_forti_admins.yml file for your reference:

17_CREATE_FORTI_ADMINS.YML

```
---
- name: Create Fortinet Administrators
  hosts: forti
  gather_facts: false
  connection: httpapi
  vars_files: vars.yml

  vars:
    ansible_httpapi_use_ssl: no
    ansible_httpapi_validate_certs: no
    ansible_httpapi_port: 80

  tasks:
  - name: Create admins
    fortinet.fortios.fortios_system_admin:
      vdom:   "root"
```

```
    state: "present"
    system_admin:
      accprofile: "super_admin"
      name: "{{ item.value.forti_username }}"
      password: "{{ item.value.forti_password }}"
  loop: "{{ lookup('dict',admins) }}"
  no_log: "True"
```

We have explored the process of manually creating an administrator account on a FortiGate firewall, as well as how to accomplish the same task using an Ansible playbook. When comparing the user creation procedures for Palo Alto and FortiGate, we find both similarities and differences. While the module names may vary, the overall process remains quite similar. It is crucial to start automating the smaller tasks first and thoroughly understand the manual process to effectively translate it into YAML code lines within an Ansible playbook. In the upcoming chapter, we will focus on creating security policies for both Palo Alto and Fortinet firewalls.

Tip

All playbooks available from the authors' GitHub page

To save time, you have the option to download the playbook from the authors' GitHub page.

URL: `https://github.com/ansnetauto/repo1`

17.8 Summary

This chapter focused on automating the creation of Palo Alto and Fortinet Firewall Administrator accounts using ansible-vault. The chapter introduced ansible-vault as a tool for encrypting sensitive information and provided a step-by-step guide on transitioning from manual account setup to automated provisioning. Readers learned how to develop a customized YAML playbook tailored for creating administrator accounts on Palo Alto and Fortinet firewalls. Through practical examples and instructions, they gained hands-on experience in crafting YAML code and incorporating ansible-vault for secure variable storage. The chapter concluded by demonstrating the execution of the YAML playbook, showcasing the efficiency of automation in streamlining the creation of Palo Alto and Fortinet Firewall Administrator accounts. This practical playbook solidified readers' understanding of ansible-vault usage, YAML playbook development, and the automation process. Overall, the chapter equipped readers with a comprehensive understanding of ansible-vault's role in securing sensitive data, the intricacies of YAML playbook development, and the practical implementation of automation for managing Palo Alto and Fortinet Firewall Administrator accounts. With this knowledge, readers are well prepared to utilize ansible-vault and harness Ansible's capabilities for efficient network administration.

## CHAPTER 18

Creating Security Policy Rules on Palo Alto and Fortinet Firewalls

This chapter aims to provide a comprehensive guide on automating the process of creating security policy rules on Palo Alto and Fortinet firewalls using YAML code and playbooks. The primary focus will be on developing a well-defined strategy and structured approach to rule creation, which is crucial for enhancing an organization's security posture. We will begin by defining what a security policy rule is and guide you through the configuration process. Throughout the chapter, we have included the complete thought processes, starting from manual security policy rule creation and extending to automated rule creation using playbooks. Each section of Ansible snippets and outputs will be thoroughly explained to ensure a clear understanding. Our objective is to share detailed information about the entire automation process, enabling you to easily apply these concepts to your network infrastructure.

© Brendan Choi and Erwin Medina 2023
B. Choi and E. Medina, *Introduction to Ansible Network Automation*,
https://doi.org/10.1007/978-1-4842-9624-0_18

18.1 Protecting the Network with Security Policies

The main responsibility of network security engineers is to maintain a strong security posture through consistent security policies using standardized configurations, thereby safeguarding the network from unauthorized access and potential security breaches. Maintaining a secure perimeter is of paramount importance in any enterprise network as it forms the first line of defense against attacks such as denial-of-service (DoS) and man-in-the-middle attacks. In segmented networks, firewalls are deployed at the borders to secure the underlying infrastructure. To close security gaps in the firewall that may serve as an entry point for attackers, the team managing the configuration must follow a well-defined strategy that translates into security policies. For example, human errors, such as setting a parameter to "any," can prove catastrophic and must be avoided. With more organizations switching to next-generation firewalls, it's important to utilize their full capabilities. One commonly overlooked aspect during the migration from a traditional firewall to the next-generation firewall is transitioning from a port-based (layer 4) inspection firewall to an application-identification-based (layer 7) inspection firewall. Every parameter in a security policy rule plays a crucial role and must be fully understood by the security engineer who is implementing the policy, as misconfigurations may have severe implications. Therefore, network security engineers must be meticulous and thorough in their approach to maintaining network security.

A security policy rule is a crucial component of all firewalls, such as Palo Alto and Fortinet firewalls that regulate incoming and outgoing traffic based on specific parameters and security policies. It serves as the heart and soul of a firewall, controlling the flow of traffic passing through it. In the firewall's operation, the rule is only applied if the incoming/outgoing session meets all the set parameters. If a match is not found, the firewall will continue to search (from top to bottom) until it reaches the catch-all-deny rule at the bottom. A security policy can be defined to block traffic from known malicious or high-risk external IPs or to allow traffic from internal networks to the outside Internet while only permitting specific applications such as SSL and web browsing. It can also be configured to allow traffic between zones and more. Ultimately, the set of rules defined by the security policy determines how the firewall manages the traffic that passes through it. Therefore, a good quality vendor firewall selection, firewall features, and well-thought-out security policy rules are critical elements of an organization's security strategy, providing visibility, control, and protection against potential threats.

18.2 Security Policy Rule Creation on Palo Alto Network Firewalls: From Manual to Automation

Before we write our playbook to create a security policy rule using an Ansible playbook, let's quickly review how we can create the rules using the standard GUI. To manually create a security policy on Palo Alto through the GUI, you can follow these steps:

Step 1: Navigate to **Policies ➤ Security ➤ Add**.

Step 2: In the resulting window, fill out the required fields, such as Name, Source, Destination, Application, Service/URL Category, and Actions, as demonstrated in Figure 18-1.

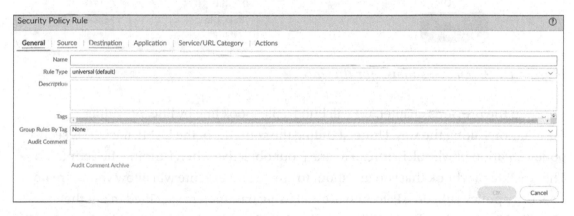

Figure 18-1. *Security Policy Rule creation*

18.3 Writing a YAML Application to Create a Security Policy Rule on a Palo Alto Network Firewall

The lab topology for this chapter is the same as in Chapter 17, and the IP addressing remains unchanged, as illustrated in Figure 18-2. Please use the same GNS3 topology for this lab.

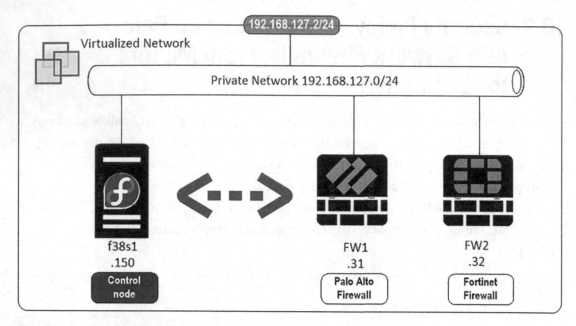

Figure 18-2. *Devices in use for this lab*

As in the previous chapter, we will build a playbook line by line, providing explanations along the way. Understanding the contents of the YAML file in this security policy creation playbook is crucial to grasp our objective when running the script. The Ansible playbook that you are about to create and execute will allow you to create a security policy rule on a Palo Alto firewall using parameters specified in another file called "security_policy.csv". The playbook excludes undefined variables from the configuration, and required parameters with undefined variables will default to preset values. You can access the complete playbook "18_create_pan_security_policy.yml" at the end of this section.

Step 1: To better manage the files used in each chapter, we will create a directory named ch18 and work in the chapter directory. As a result, we will keep all files in a single directory. Thus, the main playbook, as well as ansible.cfg and inventory files, will be created under the same directory.

```
[jdoe@f38s1 ~]$ mkdir ch18 && cd ch18
[jdoe@f38s1 ch18]$ vi ansible.cfg
[jdoe@f38s1 ch18]$ cat ansible.cfg
[defaults]
inventory=inventory
```

826

Step 2: Let's create our inventory file.

```
[jdoe@f38s1 ch18]$ vi inventory
[jdoe@f38s1 ch18]$ cat inventory
[palo]
192.168.127.31
```

Step 3: We will need to install the community.general module for us to be able to use community.general.read_csv in our playbook to read the security policy list stored in a csv file, which contains the variables to configure our security policies.

```
[jdoe@f38s1 ch18]$ ansible-galaxy collection install community.general
[…omitted for brevity]
```

Step 4: Let's now create a new playbook named "18_create_pan_security_policy.yml".

```
[jdoe@f38s1 ch18$ vi 18_create_pan_security_policy.yml
```

Here's a breakdown of the YAML file with an explanation to help you understand better.

As in all YAML files, the **three dashes** indicate the start of a new document.

```
---
```

With the use of - **name**, we can describe what this YAML file does or intends to do.

```
- name: Create Security Policy Rule from csv
```

The **hosts** line specifies the target host(s) where the playbook will be executed. In this case, the playbook will run on a Palo Alto VM with the IP address 192.168.127.31, which is defined in our inventory as a member of the group named "palo". It's important to ensure that the target host is reachable and that the appropriate authentication credentials are set up for the playbook to run successfully.

```
hosts: palo
```

The **gather_facts** module is an essential Ansible feature, as it collects information about the target host(s), such as their IP address, operating system, installed packages, and much more. By default, this module is always enabled, but in cases where you do not require information from facts, you can choose to disable it to save processor resources and speed up playbook execution. However, it's important to note that disabling gather_facts means that you will lose the opportunity to use this information as a variable, which can be useful to change the flow of your Ansible application. Therefore, before disabling gather_facts, it's important to evaluate if the facts gathered are required for your playbook execution or not. In general, if you don't need this information, disabling the gather_facts module is a good way to optimize the performance of your playbook.

```
gather_facts: false
```

The **connection: local** parameter in an Ansible playbook is a configuration setting that instructs Ansible to run the playbook locally on the machine running Ansible rather than remotely on the target host(s). This means that any tasks defined in the playbook will be executed on the Ansible control node rather than on the target hosts, which can be useful for tasks that do not require remote execution or testing purposes. By running the playbook locally, it can save network resources and speed up the execution of the playbook. However, it's important to note that this parameter should only be used when necessary and that most playbooks should be executed remotely on the target host(s) to perform the desired tasks.

```
connection: local
```

This code block defines a variable named "**provider**" that contains subparameters for the IP address, username, and password of the firewall. The IP address is dynamically set to the inventory_hostname, which refers to the hostname of the target host(s). The username and password are left blank and will be prompted later in the playbook using the vars_prompt module. This is a good practice for security as it ensures that sensitive information, such as credentials, is not stored in plain text in the playbook. By defining these variables, we can easily reuse them throughout the playbook to configure the firewall without having to hard-code the values.

```
vars:
  provider:
    ip_address: '{{ inventory_hostname }}'
    username: '{{ pan_username }}'
    password: '{{ pan_password }}'
```

The following YAML code utilizes the vars_prompt module to prompt the user running the playbook to enter a username and password for the firewall. The private flag on the password prompt indicates that the user's input should not be displayed on the screen for security reasons. These inputs will be stored as variables to be used later in the playbook when connecting to the firewall using SSH. By prompting the user for the firewall credentials, we ensure that the playbook remains secure and can only be executed by authorized users. It's important to note that these variables can be encrypted using ansible-vault in a separate file and called upon using the vars_files module in the main playbook. Additionally, if your company utilizes an enterprise password manager, you can leverage the appropriate API or integration provided by the password management system to read a password in an Ansible playbook. For now, we will make this into an interactive playbook to collect the PAN-OS username and password.

```
vars_prompt:
  - name: "pan_username"
    prompt: "login as"
    private: no

  - name: "pan_password"
    prompt: "Password"
    private: yes
```

This Ansible task uses the "community.general.read_csv" module to retrieve information from the csv file named security_policy.csv. The path to the file is specified as security_policy.csv, indicating that the file is located in the same directory as the playbook. After the csv file is read, its contents are stored as a list in the variable named policy_list. This variable can then be used throughout the playbook to configure the firewall security policy according to the parameters defined in the csv file.

```
- name: Read the csv file
  community.general.read_csv:
      path: security_policy.csv
  register: policy_list
```

This Ansible task uses the debug module to output the contents of the policy_list variable that was created earlier. The msg parameter will print the policy_list as a list. This is useful for debugging purposes, as it allows us to ensure that the csv file has been read correctly and that the information stored in policy_list is accurate. Additionally, this task can be used to verify that any modifications made to the playbook have not altered the expected output.

```
- name: display security policy list
  debug:
    msg: "{{ policy_list.list }}"
```

The following Ansible task is the core of our playbook, using the "panos_security_rule" module to create a security policy rule with parameters stored in the list named policy_list. The loop keyword is used to configure the security policy rule in each row of the list. The task creates the security policy rule with the parameters rule_name, description, source_zone, destination_zone, source_ip, source_user, destination_ip, application, service, action, and location. In this task, the "default" filter is used to provide a default value for a variable if it is not defined or if its value is empty. The "omit" keyword is used by default to instruct Ansible to omit the variable altogether if the default value is used. The commit flag is set to False, indicating that the changes made by this task will not be committed immediately. By using this task, the playbook can automate the creation of security policy rules on a Palo Alto Network Firewall based on the parameters filled in the security_policy.csv file, with flexibility for default values and the option to commit changes manually.

```
- name: Create Security Policy Rule
  paloaltonetworks.panos.panos_security_rule:
    provider: '{{ provider }}'  # Firewall connection provider
    rule_name: '{{ item.rule_name }}'  # Rule name for the security policy
    description: '{{ item.description | default(omit) }}'  # Optional
    description
    source_zone: '{{ item.source_zone | default(omit) }}'  # Source zone
    for the traffic
    destination_zone: '{{ item.destination_zone | default(omit) }}'
    # Destination zone for traffic
    source_ip: '{{ item.source_ip | default(omit) }}'  # Source IP address
    source_user: '{{ item.source_user | default(omit) }}'  # Source user
    destination_ip: '{{ item.destination_ip | default(omit) }}'
    # Destination IP address
```

```
        application: '{{ item.application | default(omit) }}'  # Application
        for the traffic
        service: '{{ item.service | default(omit) }}'  # Service for
        the traffic
        action: '{{ item.action | default(omit) }}'  # Action for the traffic
        location: '{{ item.location | default(omit) }}'  # Location of the
        security policy
        commit: 'False'  # Skip immediate commit
    loop: "{{ policy_list.list }}"  # Loop through policy_list
```

Now that we have a good understanding of how our playbook works, it is time to check the PA-VM GUI interface and execute our playbook.

Tip

The ansible-playbook command abbreviated to anp

Note: The ansible-playbook command was abbreviated in Bash shell aliases in the ~/.bashrc ($HOME/.bashrc) file.

```
[jdoe@f38s1 ~]$ vi ~/.bashrc

# .bashrc

[...omitted for brevity]

alias anp='ansible-playbook'

alias anpap='ansible-playbook --ask-become-pass'
```

18.4 Running the YAML Playbook to Create Security Policy Rules on a Palo Alto Network Firewall

Before executing the playbook, go to your PA-VM web interface and log in, then navigate to the POLICIES and check the security policies. As you can see in Figure 18-3, you can see that the security policy rules have not yet been configured on the targeted Palo Alto Network Firewall, which has an IP address of 192.168.127.31.

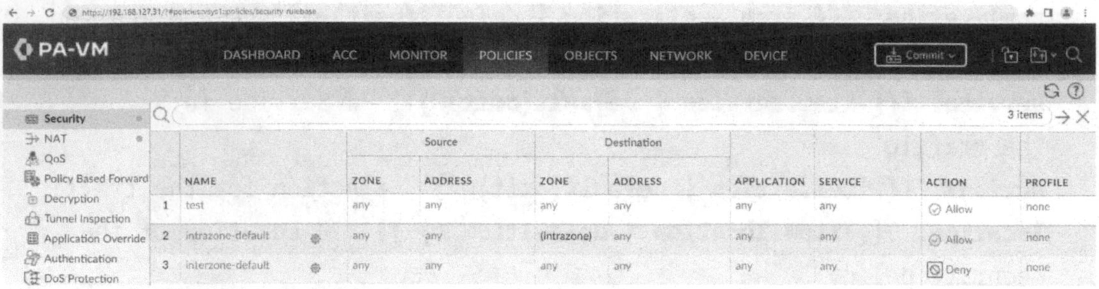

***Figure 18-3.** PA-VM security policy rule before the configuration*

Figure 18-4 shows the contents of the security_policy.csv file that we created, which includes the necessary parameters for configuring the security policy rules. The file includes columns for rule_name, description, tag_name, source_zone, source_ip, source_user, destination_ip, category, application, service, action, destination_zone, and location. Any undefined variables in the file will not be configured.

	A	B	C	D	E	F	G	H	I	J	K	L	M
1	rule_name	description	tag_name	source_zone	source_ip	source_user	destination_ip	category	application	service	action	destination_zone	location
2	Block-Outbound-Malicious-IPs			any	any	any	Spamhaus-DROP	any	any	any	deny	Internet	top
3	Block-Inbound-Malicious-IPs			Internet	Spamhaus-DROP	any	any	any	any	any	deny	any	top

***Figure 18-4.** security_policy.csv*

Note that the csv file shown in the figure needs to be uploaded to the "/home/jdoe/ch18" directory before running the playbook. The source_ip and destination_ip fields can be any object-address, object-address-group, region, or external dynamic list. For this example, we will use a custom external dynamic list named Spamhaus-DROP, which contains an IP list from `http://www.spamhaus.org/drop/drop.txt` as shown in Figure 18-5. You can add an EDL in **Objects ➤ External Dynamic List ➤ Add**.

External Dynamic Lists   ⑦

Name │ Spamhaus-DROP   │

Create List │ List Entries And Exceptions

Type │ IP List   ⌄ │

Description │ DROP (Don't Route Or Peer) and EDROP are advisory 'drop all traffic lists consisting of stolen
hijacked netblocks controlled by criminals and professional spammers'   │

Source │ http://www.spamhaus.org/drop/drop.txt   │

┌ **Server Authentication** ───

Certificate Profile │ None   ⌄ │

Check for updates │ Every five minutes   ⌄ │

(Test Source URL)   (OK)   (Cancel)

Figure 18-5. *External Dynamic List. Spamhaus-DROP*

Step 1: This is an example of running an Ansible playbook named "18_create_
pan_security_policy.yml" (refer to Figure 18-4 for an example csv file). When executed,
Ansible will prompt for the firewall username and password, which are required to
authenticate and access the device for configuration. The entered password will not
be displayed for security reasons. To confirm that the Ansible YAML script is running
successfully, you can execute the "18_create_pan_security_policy.yml" playbook.
Assuming that there are no syntax errors or typos in the playbook, you should see an
output similar to the following example. The playbook consists of three tasks that create
security policy rules based on the data in the security_policy.csv file. The output explains
each step in the playbook execution.

```
[jdoe@f38s1 ch18]$ anp 18_create_pan_security_policy.yml
login as: admin
Password: ***************
PLAY [Create Security Policy Rule from csv] *****************************

TASK [Read the csv file] ***********************************************
ok: [192.168.127.31]
```

```
TASK [Display security policy list] *************************************
ok: [192.168.127.31] => {
    "msg": [
        {
            "action": "deny",
            "application": "any",
            "category": "any",
            "description": "",
            "destination_ip": "Spamhaus-DROP",
            "destination_zone": "Internet",
            "location": "top",
            "rule_name": "Block-Outbound-Malicious-IPs",
            "service": "any",
            "source_ip": "any",
            "source_user": "any",
            "source_zone": "any",
            "tag_name": ""
        },
        {
            "action": "deny",
            "application": "any",
            "category": "any",
            "description": "",
            "destination_ip": "any",
            "destination_zone": "any",
            "location": "top",
            "rule_name": "Block-Inbound-Malicious-IPs",
            "service": "any",
            "source_ip": "Spamhaus-DROP",
            "source_user": "any",
            "source_zone": "Internet",
            "tag_name": ""
        }
    ]
}
```

```
TASK [Create Security Policy Rule] ****************************************
changed: [192.168.127.31] => (item={'rule_name': 'Block-Outbound-Malicious-
IPs', 'description': '', 'tag_name': '', 'source_zone': 'any', 'source_ip':
'any', 'source_user': 'any', 'destination_ip': 'Spamhaus-DROP', 'category':
'any', 'application': 'any', 'service': 'any', 'action': 'deny',
'destination_zone': 'Internet', 'location': 'top'})
changed: [192.168.127.31] => (item={'rule_name': 'Block-Inbound-Malicious-
IPs', 'description': '', 'tag_name': '', 'source_zone': 'Internet',
'source_ip': 'Spamhaus-DROP', 'source_user': 'any', 'destination_ip':
'any', 'category': 'any', 'application': 'any', 'service': 'any', 'action':
'deny', 'destination_zone': 'any', 'location': 'top'})

PLAY RECAP ***************************************************************
192.168.127.31              : ok=3    changed=1    unreachable=0    failed=0
skipped=0    rescued=0    ignored=0
```

The "PLAY RECAP" section in the Ansible output provides a summary of the tasks that were executed on each target host. In this example, the target host's IP address is 192.168.127.31, and the output shows that three tasks were executed on this host, all of which were successful (ok=3). Out of those three tasks, one task made changes to the system (changed=1), indicating that a new security policy rule was successfully configured, while the other task did not make any changes (changed=0). The output also indicates that there were no tasks that were unreachable, failed, or skipped (unreachable=0, failed=0, skipped=0). Finally, no tasks required being rescued or ignored (rescued=0, ignored=0). Overall, the "PLAY RECAP" section provides a quick overview of the success or failure of the tasks executed in the playbook on the target host.

Step 2: As you can see in Figure 18-6, after executing the Ansible playbook, we can confirm that the security policy rules have been successfully configured based on the parameters defined in the security_policy.csv file. This can be verified by reviewing the candidate configuration of the Palo Alto Network Firewall, where the rules should be reflected. It is worth noting that we set the "commit" parameter to "False" in each task, allowing us to review the configuration before committing the change to ensure the accuracy and completeness of the configuration.

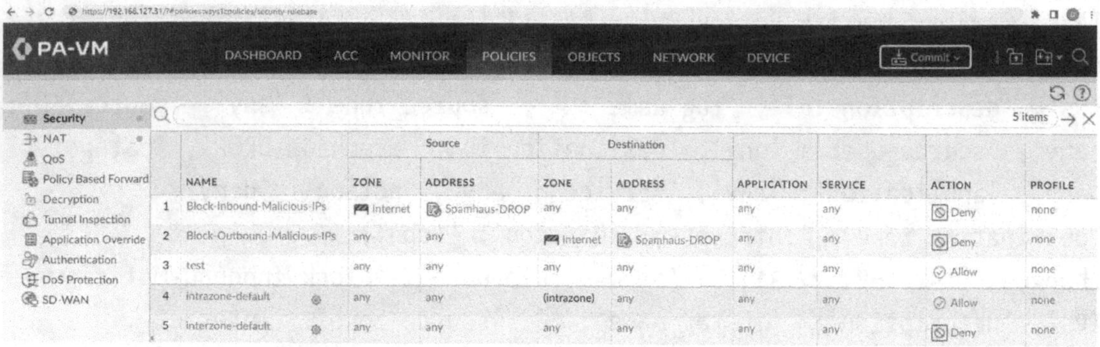

Figure 18-6. *PA-VM security policy rules after the configuration*

Step 3: Here is the completed playbook, 18_create_pan_security_policy.yml, for your reference:

```
[jdoe@f38s1 ch18]$ cat 18_create_pan_security_policy.yml
---
- name: Create Security Policy Rule from csv
  hosts: palo
  gather_facts: false
  connection: local

  vars:
    provider:
      ip_address: '{{ inventory_hostname }}'
      username: '{{ pan_username }}'
      password: '{{ pan_password }}'

  vars_prompt:
    - name: "pan_username"
      prompt: "login as"
      private: no

    - name: "pan_password"
      prompt: "Password"
      private: yes
```

```yaml
tasks:
  - name: Read the csv file
    community.general.read_csv:
      path: security_policy.csv
    register: policy_list

  - name: Display security policy list
    debug:
      msg: "{{ policy_list.list }}"
  - name: Create Security Policy Rule
    paloaltonetworks.panos.panos_security_rule:
      provider: '{{ provider }}'
      rule_name: '{{ item.rule_name }}'
      description: '{{ item.description | default(omit) }}'
      source_zone: '{{ item.source_zone | default(omit) }}'
      destination_zone: '{{ item.destination_zone | default(omit) }}'
      source_ip: '{{ item.source_ip | default(omit) }}'
      source_user: '{{ item.source_user | default(omit) }}'
      destination_ip: '{{ item.destination_ip | default(omit) }}'
      application: '{{ item.application | default(omit) }}'
      service: '{{ item.service | default(omit) }}'
      action: '{{ item.action | default(omit) }}'
      location: '{{ item.location | default(omit) }}'
      commit: 'False'
    loop: "{{ policy_list.list }}"
```

Now that you have learned how to create a firewall policy on a Palo Alto firewall, let's move on to creating a firewall policy rule on a Fortinet firewall.

18.5 Firewall Policy Rule Creation on Fortinet Firewalls: From Manual to Automation

To successfully write an Ansible playbook for a Fortinet firewall, it is essential to understand the necessary information required. This can be achieved by carefully studying the New Policy window and its information requirements. By doing so, we will be equipped to incorporate this knowledge into our Ansible playbook writing process.

Step 1: To create a security policy, go to **Policy & Objects ➤ Firewall Policy ➤ Create New**.

Step 2: In the resulting window, complete the required fields such as Name, Incoming Interface, Outgoing Interface, Source, Destination, Schedule, Service, and Action, as demonstrated in Figure 18-7.

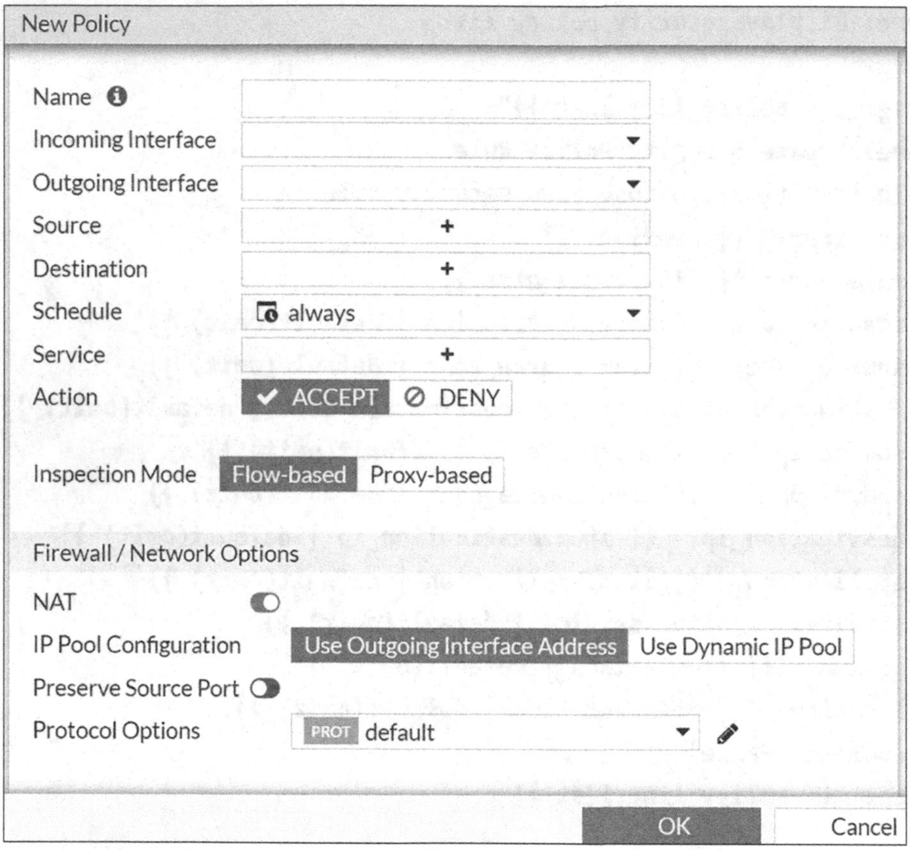

Figure 18-7.   *Security Policy Rule creation*

18.6 Writing a YAML Application to Create a Firewall Policy Rule on a Fortinet Firewall

For this exercise, you can access a complete Ansible YAML script named "18_create_forti_firewall_policy.yml". It is essential to understand the YAML file contents to grasp what we aim to achieve. The "18_create_forti_firewall_policy.yml" is an Ansible playbook that creates a security policy rule on a Fortinet firewall. Here's a brief explanation of each line of the playbook to help you understand it better.

Step 1: We already have the ansible.cfg in the directory. The only thing we need to update is the inventory and add the details of our target Fortinet firewall.

```
[jdoe@f38s1 ch18]$ vi inventory
[jdoe@f38s1 ch18]$ cat inventory
[palo]
192.168.127.31
```

```
[forti]
Forti01 ansible_host=192.168.127.32 ansible_user="admin" ansible_
password="Forti123!"
```

```
[forti:vars]
ansible_network_os=fortinet.fortios.fortios
```

Step 2: We can now create the 18_create_forti_firewall_policy.yml file. Let's go over the playbook section by section.

First, create a new playbook named 18_create_forti_firewall_policy.yml in vi or your favorite text editor.

```
[jdoe@f38s1 ch18$ vi 18_create_forti_firewall_policy.yml
```

As in all YAML files, the three dashes indicate the start of a new document.

```
---
```

With the use of - name, we can describe what this YAML file does or intends to do.

```
- name: Create Firewall Policy Rule
```

This specifies the target host(s) on which this playbook will run. In this case, it will run on a host named "palo". For this playbook, we will run it on a Fortinet VM with IP 192.168.127.32. This IP is defined in our inventory as a member of the group-name named "forti".

```
hosts: forti
```

By default, Ansible's gather_facts module is always enabled, but if you do not require information from facts, you can choose to disable this module to save processor resources and speed up playbook execution. Disabling gather_facts means that Ansible will not collect information about the target host(s), such as their IP address, operating system, installed packages, etc. It's important to note that the information collected from the gather_facts module can be useful as variables, which can be used to change the flow of your Ansible application. However, if you don't need this information, it's best to disable the gather_facts module to optimize the performance of your playbook.

```
gather_facts: false
```

The connection: httpapi parameter in an Ansible playbook is a plug-in that provides methods to connect to a Fortinet FortiOS appliance or VM via REST API.

```
connection: httpapi
```

The variables are set to be able to connect to the Fortinet firewall. As we are using a VM evaluation license, we've set the ansible_httpapi_use_ssl to "no", ansible_httpapi_validate_certs to "no", and ansible_httpapi_port to "80", which is not secure. If we have a valid license, then we set the SSL and cert checks to "yes" with the port set to "443".

```
vars:
  ansible_httpapi_use_ssl: no
  ansible_httpapi_validate_certs: no
  ansible_httpapi_port: 80
```

The Ansible task uses the "fortinet.fortios.fortios_firewall_policy" module to configure a firewall policy rule on the Fortinet firewall. The tasks create the firewall policy rule with the parameters vdom, state, name, policyid (required), action, srcaddr, srcintf, dstaddr, dstintf, service, nat, status, and schedule.

```
tasks:
- name: Configure firewall policy
```

```
fortinet.fortios.fortios_firewall_policy:
  vdom: "root"
  state: "present"
  firewall_policy:
    name: "Internal-to-Internet Rule"
    policyid: "10"
    action: "accept"
    srcaddr:
      -
        name: "Internal_Subnet"
    srcintf:
      -
        name: "port1"
    dstaddr:
      -
        name: "all"
    dstintf:
      -
        name: "port2"
    service:
      -
        name: "HTTPS"
    nat: "enable"
    status: "enable"
    schedule: "always"
```

To confirm that the Ansible playbook is running successfully, you can execute the "18_create_forti_firewall_policy.yml" playbook. Assuming that there are no syntax errors or typos in the playbook, you should see an output similar to the following example. The playbook consists of one task to create the firewall policy. The output explains each step in the playbook execution.

18.7 Running the YAML Application to Create a Firewall Policy Rule on a Fortinet Firewall

Step 1: For illustration purposes, let's first create an object address that we will use in our firewall policy. We will name it "Internal_Subnet". Go to **Policy & Objects** ➤ **Addresses** ➤ **Create New Address** as shown in Figure 18-8.

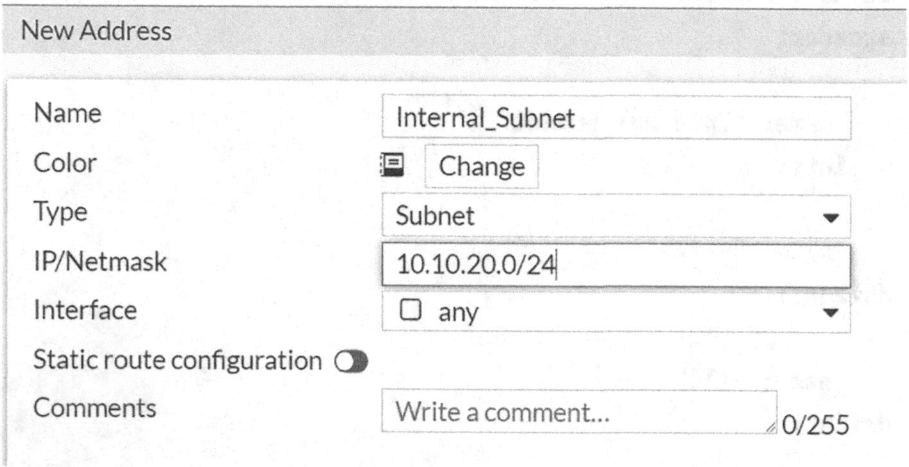

Figure 18-8. *Create an object address named Internal_Subnet.*

Before executing the playbook, as shown in Figure 18-9, the firewall policy rules have not yet been configured on the targeted Fortinet firewall, which has an IP of 192.168.127.32.

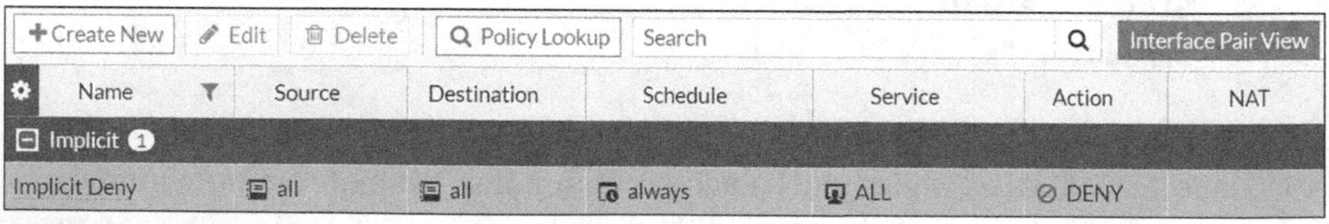

Figure 18-9. *Forti-VM firewall policy rule before the configuration*

Step 2: Once you have completed the "18_create_forti_firewall_policy.yml" playbook file in your working directory, execute your playbook.

```
[jdoe@f38s1 ch18]$ anp 18_create_forti_firewall_policy.yml

PLAY [Create Firewall Policy Rule] *************************************
```

```
TASK [Create firewall policy] *****************************************
changed: [Forti01]

PLAY RECAP ************************************************************
Forti01                   : ok=1    changed=1   unreachable=0    failed=0
skipped=0    rescued=0    ignored=0
```

The "PLAY RECAP" section in the Ansible output provides a summary of the tasks that were executed on each target host. In this example, the target host's IP address is 192.168.127.32, and the output shows that one task was executed on this host, which is successful (ok=1). The task made a change to the system (changed=1), indicating the new firewall policy rule was successfully configured. The output also indicates that there were no tasks that were unreachable, failed, or skipped (unreachable=0, failed=0, skipped=0). Finally, no tasks required being rescued or ignored (rescued=0, ignored=0). Overall, the "PLAY RECAP" section provides a quick overview of the success or failure of the tasks executed in the playbook on the target host.

Step 3: As you can see in Figure 18-10, after executing the Ansible playbook, we can confirm that the firewall policy rules have been successfully configured based on the parameters defined in the script.

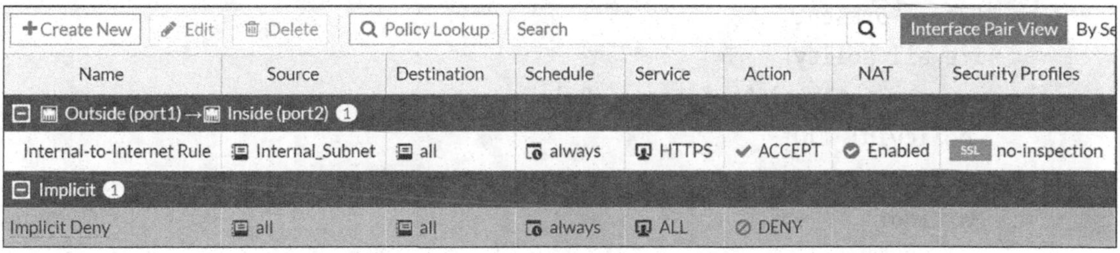

Name	Source	Destination	Schedule	Service	Action	NAT	Security Profiles
+ Create New / Edit 🗑 Delete Q Policy Lookup Search Q Interface Pair View By Se							
⊟ 🖥 Outside (port1) → 🖥 Inside (port2) ❶							
Internal-to-Internet Rule	🖥 Internal_Subnet	🖥 all	🕒 always	🔲 HTTPS	✔ ACCEPT	⊘ Enabled	SSL no-inspection
⊟ Implicit ❶							
Implicit Deny	🖥 all	🖥 all	🕒 always	🔲 ALL	⊘ DENY		

Figure 18-10. *Forti-VM firewall policy after the configuration*

Here is the completed 18_create_forti_firewall_policy.yml playbook for your reference:

18_CREATE_FORTI_FIREWALL_POLICY.YML

```yaml
---
- name: Create Firewall Policy Rule
  hosts: forti
  gather_facts: false
  connection: httpapi

  vars:
   ansible_httpapi_use_ssl: no
   ansible_httpapi_validate_certs: no
   ansible_httpapi_port: 80

  tasks:
  - name: Create firewall policy
    fortinet.fortios.fortios_firewall_policy:
      vdom: "root"
      state: "present"
      firewall_policy:
        name: "Internal-to-Internet Rule"
        policyid: "10"
        action: "accept"
        srcaddr:
          -
            name: "Internal_Subnet"
        srcintf:
          -
            name: "port1"
        dstaddr:
          -
            name: "all"
        dstintf:
          -
            name: "port2"
        service:
```

```
    -
      name: "HTTPS"
  nat: "enable"
  status: "enable"
    schedule: "always"
```

In this chapter, you have acquired knowledge on creating security policies for both Palo Alto and Fortinet firewalls using simple playbooks. From Chapters 19 to 21, our emphasis will be on the Palo Alto firewall. As we have demonstrated that the fundamental concepts and processes are similar in both vendors' firewalls, we will continue focusing exclusively on the Palo Alto firewall for the rest of the book. It's important to note that if you understand the processes for the Fortinet firewall, you can apply the same principles. In the upcoming chapter, let's explore the creation of an IPSec tunnel.

18.8 Summary

In this chapter, our focus was on automating the creation of security rules for Palo Alto and Fortinet firewalls. We highlighted the significance of effective security rule creation in safeguarding the underlying network. The chapter provided a step-by-step guideline for transitioning from manual rule creation to automated rule creation using Ansible playbooks. It included examples of automated security policy rule creations for both firewall vendors. The key takeaway from this chapter should be the process of moving away from the graphical user interface (GUI) and transitioning to writing tasks in YAML scripts. This allows for the execution of repetitive tasks through scripted applications, such as the playbooks we created in this chapter. Network automation should not be seen as an end in itself but rather as the beginning of a new journey for you and your team.

## CHAPTER 19

Creating IPSec Tunnels on Palo Alto Firewalls

This chapter aims to provide a guide on automating the creation of IPSec tunnels on Palo Alto firewalls using an Ansible playbook. We will start by exploring the practical usage of IPSec tunnels in production environments and discussing their advantages and disadvantages. Next, we will demonstrate the manual process of creating IPSec tunnels on Palo Alto firewalls, laying the groundwork for developing an Ansible playbook to automate these tasks. Throughout this chapter, we will cover the entire thought process involved in transitioning from manual configuration to an automated approach using an Ansible YAML file. Each section will include detailed explanations of the Ansible snippets and outputs, providing a step-by-step walkthrough of the automation process. Our goal is to ensure that readers have a good understanding of the actual automation process, helping them transition from manual-driven tasks to scripted applications and apply these concepts to their network infrastructure.

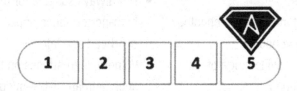

19.1 Enhancing Network Security with IPSec Tunnels

Network security engineers are responsible for managing various security devices and VPN technologies, with IPSec being one of the most commonly administered technologies. An IPSec tunnel is a security protocol that enables the establishment of a secure connection between two networks over an untrusted network, such as

© Brendan Choi and Erwin Medina 2023

B. Choi and E. Medina, *Introduction to Ansible Network Automation*,
https://doi.org/10.1007/978-1-4842-9624-0_19

the Internet. By encrypting the traffic flowing through the tunnel, IPSec ensures data confidentiality, integrity, and authentication (CIA). Numerous security appliance vendors offer IPSec tunnel services, and Palo Alto firewalls are among the most widely used products for securing enterprise networks. These firewalls incorporate VPN capabilities, including the ability to create IPSec tunnels.

By configuring IPSec tunnels on Palo Alto firewalls, organizations can establish secure connections between remote offices, partners, or cloud services, enabling users to access corporate network resources as if they were physically on-site. Additionally, IPSec tunnels contribute to preventing unauthorized network access by providing an encrypted and authenticated connection. Leveraging IPSec tunnels on Palo Alto firewalls ensures the protection of sensitive data and resources against security threats.

Before delving into the actual IPSec tunnel configuration on Palo Alto firewalls, let's take a moment to review the advantages and disadvantages of IPSec tunnels. We will examine these aspects in Table 19-1.

Table 19-1. *Advantages and disadvantages of IPSec tunnels*

Advantages of IPSec tunnels	Disadvantages of IPSec tunnels
• Provides robust security features, including data confidentiality, integrity, and authentication • Enables connectivity between various network types, such as site-to-site, remote access, and cloud-based networks • Widely adopted and standardized technology supported by multiple vendors • Protects traffic across a wide range of protocols and applications	• Requires configuration and management of IPSec endpoints on both ends of the tunnel • May introduce additional overhead and latency to traffic, depending on the encryption and authentication methods used • Not always suitable for high-bandwidth or high-performance applications due to potential overhead and latency • Vulnerable to attacks on the endpoints, such as man-in-the-middle attacks, key compromises, or configuration errors

Additionally, let's discuss other security connection methods commonly used today and compare them to IPSec tunnel connections. This comparison is briefly discussed in Table 19-2.

Table 19-2. *Other security connection methods*

Connection method	Description
SSL/TLS VPN	Offers similar security features to IPSec tunnels but operates at the application layer rather than the network layer. It may be easier to manage and configure but could have lower performance and be more susceptible to application-level attacks.
MPLS VPN	Establishes a secure and reliable network connection by utilizing a private MPLS network instead of the public Internet. Provides better performance and reliability compared to IPSec tunnels but may come with higher costs and reduced flexibility.
Direct Connect	Establishes a direct physical connection between two networks, such as a leased line or dedicated fiber connection. Offers the highest level of performance and security, but it can be expensive and challenging to manage.

Now that we have discussed the advantages and disadvantages of IPSec tunnels as well as other secure connection methods, let's delve into how a security engineer configures an IPSec tunnel on the renowned Palo Alto firewall.

Tip

Review your lab parameters to optimize your lab outcomes!

In this lab, we assume that you have followed every step specified in the complementary lab installation guide. The guide can be found at the following link, and you should refer to the installation guide titled "Ch11_Pre-task2_PaloAlto_ and_Fortinet_Firewall_Installation_on_GNS3.pdf".

https://github.com/ansnetauto/appress_ansnetauto

19.2 IPSec Tunnel Configuration on Palo Alto Firewalls

To create an IPSec tunnel on a Palo Alto firewall, a security engineer must follow several tasks sequentially to complete the required tasks:

1. Create a tunnel interface with its corresponding zone: This will be used for routing the traffic securely through the IPSec tunnel.

2. Create the phase I settings, which is the IKE crypto profile: The profile defines the encryption algorithm, hash algorithm, DH key exchange, and the key lifetime.

3. Create the phase II settings, which is the IPSec crypto profile: The profile defines the encryption algorithm, hash algorithm, perfect forward secrecy, and the key lifetime.

4. Create an IKE gateway: This gateway defines the Internet Key Exchange (IKE) parameters for establishing the phase I tunnel, such as the ikev version, local IP address and interface, peer IP address, pre-shared key, IKE crypto profile to be used, liveness check, and other options to enable/disable such as passive mode and NAT traversal.

5. Create an IPSec tunnel: This defines the parameters to be used to build the IPSec tunnel using the parameters built for both phase I and phase II. The parameters include the IPSec tunnel name, tunnel interface, IKE gateway, IPSec crypto profile, and Proxy IDs or otherwise called traffic selectors.

6. Configure static routes: If necessary, static routes may need to be configured to direct traffic through the IPSec tunnel.

While the task of creating an IPSec tunnel in Palo Alto may initially be easy and even enjoyable, it can quickly become laborious and prone to errors when manually configuring more than ten tunnels. When this task becomes repetitive and frequently occurs throughout the year, engineers may find themselves investing countless hours in IPSec tunnel creation without yielding any significant benefits for the organization or themselves. Thankfully, there are automation tools available to alleviate this burden, such as SaltStack, Ansible, Octopus Deploy, and HashiCorp Terraform. By leveraging these tools, security engineers can automate the process of creating IPSec tunnels, resulting in substantial time and effort savings.

This book focuses on Ansible, which provides a comprehensive range of modules and parameters designed to configure IPSec tunnels across multiple vendor products. Through automation, engineers can ensure the accurate establishment of IPSec tunnels and the secure flow of traffic between remote networks. This not only delivers immediate time and effort savings but also helps to secure the organization's network with standardized configurations, ultimately leading to improved operational efficiency.

19.3 Palo Alto IPSec Tunnel Creation Lab Topology

In this chapter, you only need to power on two devices in your virtual environment: the Ansible control node, f38s1 (192.168.127.150), and two Palo Alto firewalls, FW1 (192.168.127.31) and FW3 (192.168.127.33), as shown in Figure 19-1.

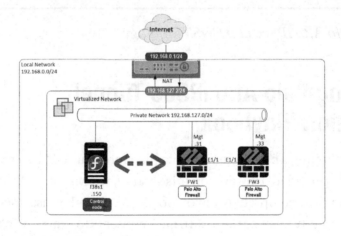

Figure 19-1. *Palo Alto IPSec lab topology*

As shown in Figure 19-2, for the lab discussed in this chapter, you will only need two Palo Alto firewalls, FW1 and FW3, connected in GNS3. Ensure that both devices are connected via Ethernet 1/1 and powered on and that you can log into the Admin pages using your preferred web browser.

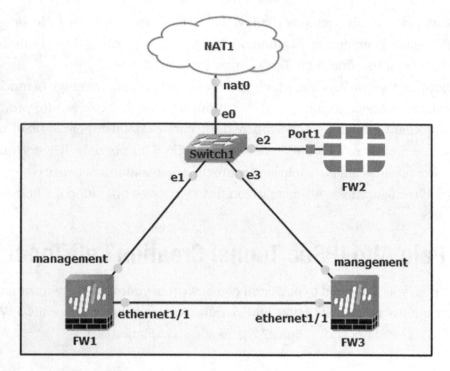

Figure 19-2. *Palo Alto IPSec Lab GNS3 topology*

19.4 Writing Palo Alto IPSec Tunnel Creation Playbook

At the end of this chapter, a completed Ansible playbook named "19_create_ipsec_tunnel.yml" will be provided. However, in this section, we will carefully examine each segment to enhance our comprehension of the playbook and its assigned tasks. It is imperative to thoroughly analyze the YAML file's contents to grasp the objectives behind writing and executing this playbook. Essentially, the primary goal of the 19_create_ipsec_tunnel.yml playbook is to establish an IPSec tunnel on a Palo Alto firewall using predefined variables.

Step 1: Again, since we are creating directories for each chapter, we aim to keep it simple by having all the components in a single directory. Therefore, we will create the main components, namely, the ansible.cfg file, the inventory file, and the playbook in the same directory.

```
[jdoe@f38s1 ~]$ mkdir ch19 && cd ch19
[jdoe@f38s1 ch19]$ vi ansible.cfg
[jdoe@f38s1 ch19]$ cat ansible.cfg
[defaults]
inventory=inventory
```

Step 2: Let's create an inventory file to include our Palo Alto firewall. We will use its IP address in our inventory to make our playbook simple.

```
[jdoe@f38s1 ch19]$ vi inventory
[jdoe@f38s1 ch19]$ cat inventory
[palo]
192.168.127.31
```

Step 3: Next, create the 19_create_ipsec_tunnel.yml playbook.

```
[jdoe@f38s1 ch19$ vi 19_create_ipsec_tunnel.yml
[jdoe@f38s1 ch19$ cat 19_create_ipsec_tunnel.yml
```

Here's an explanation of the sections in our playbook. If you're following along on your Linux Ansible Control Machine, let's assemble the playbook. It is crucial that you physically type these YAML codes into your text editor to become more acquainted with Ansible playbooks.

As in all YAML files, the three dashes indicate the start of a new document.

```
---
```

With the use of - name, we can describe what this YAML file does or intends to do.

```
- name: Create IPSec Tunne with defined variables
```

This specifies the target host(s) on which this playbook will run. In this case, it will run on a host named "palo". For this playbook, we will run it on a Palo Alto VM with IP 192.168.127.31. This IP is defined in our inventory as a member of the group-name named "palo".

```
hosts: palo
```

By default, Ansible's gather_facts module is always enabled. However, in this case, we want to specifically turn it off. To do so, add "false" next to "gather_facts:" in the playbook.

```
gather_facts: false
```

The connection: local parameter in an Ansible playbook specifies that the playbook should be executed locally on the machine running Ansible rather than remotely on the target host(s). This means that any tasks defined in the playbook will be executed on the Ansible control node rather than on the target hosts. This can be useful for tasks that do not require remote execution or for testing purposes.

```
connection: local
```

The following snippet defines a parameter named "provider" that contains subparameters for the IP address, username, and password of the firewall. The IP address is dynamically set to the inventory_hostname, which refers to the hostname of the target host(s). The username and password are left blank and will be prompted later in the playbook using the vars_prompt module. By defining these variables, we can use them throughout the playbook to configure the firewall.

```
vars:
  provider:
    ip_address: '{{ inventory_hostname }}'
    username: '{{ pan_username }}'
    password: '{{ pan_password }}'
```

This line prompts the user running the playbook to enter a username and password for the firewall. The private flag on the password prompt indicates that the user's input should not be displayed on the screen for security reasons. These inputs will be stored as variables to be used later in the playbook when connecting to the firewall using SSH.

```
vars_prompt:
  - name: "pan_username"
    prompt: "login as"
      private: no

  - name: "pan_password"
    prompt: "Password"
    private: yes
```

This Ansible task uses the "panos_tunnel" module to create the tunnel interface named "tunnel.1" with a virtual router named "default" and a zone named "VPN_Test" on a Palo Alto firewall. This tunnel interface will be used to route the traffic securely through the IPSec tunnel. The "commit" flag is set to False, which means that the changes made by this task will not be committed immediately and will stay as a candidate configuration.

```
tasks:
  - name: Create tunnel.1
    paloaltonetworks.panos.panos_tunnel:
      provider: '{{ provider }}'
      if_name: "tunnel.1"
      vr_name: 'default'
      zone_name: 'VPN_Test'
      commit: 'False'
```

This Ansible task creates an IKE (Internet Key Exchange) crypto profile named "ike-profile-test" with Diffie-Hellman group 20, SHA-512 authentication, AES-256-CBC encryption, and a lifetime of eight hours using the "panos_ike_crypto_profile" module. The task sets the specified provider and sets the name, DH group, authentication, encryption, lifetime, and commit values for the profile. The commit flag is set to False, indicating that the changes made by this task will not be committed immediately. These algorithms are the strongest we can use on a Palo Alto firewall; however, for IKE establishment, these parameters must match on both ends.

```
- name: Create IKE crypto profile
    paloaltonetworks.panos.panos_ike_crypto_profile:
      provider: '{{ provider }}'
      name: 'ike-profile-test'
      dh_group: ['group20']
      authentication: ['sha512']
      encryption: ['aes-256-cbc']
      lifetime_hours: '8'
      commit: 'False'
```

The following task creates an IPSec crypto profile on a Palo Alto firewall. The "panos_ipsec_profile" module is used to configure the profile with specific parameters such as the provider, profile name, DH group, encryption and authentication algorithms, and lifetime. The "commit" parameter is set to "False" to prevent the changes from being committed automatically. This task will create an IPSec crypto profile named "ipsec-profile-test" on the specified device. These algorithms are the strongest we can use on a Palo Alto firewall; however, for IPSec establishment, these parameters must match on both ends.

```yaml
- name: Create IPSec crypto profile
    paloaltonetworks.panos.panos_ipsec_profile:
      provider: '{{ provider }}'
      name: 'ipsec-profile-test'
      dh_group: 'group20'
      esp_authentication: ['sha512']
      esp_encryption: ['aes-256-gcm']
      lifetime_hours: '1'
      commit: 'False'
```

This YAML code is an Ansible task that creates an IKE gateway on a Palo Alto firewall. The "panos_ike_gateway" module is used to configure the gateway with specific parameters such as the provider, gateway name, version, interface, local IP address type, local IP address, peer IP address, pre-shared key, IKE crypto profile, enable/disable features like liveness check, NAT traversal, and passive mode. We will need to enable NAT traversal if a NAT device is between the VPN terminating points. The "commit" parameter is set to "False" to prevent the changes from being committed automatically. When executed, this task will create an IKE gateway named "IKEGW-TEST" on the specified Palo Alto firewall.

```yaml
- name: Create IKE Gateway
    paloaltonetworks.panos.panos_ike_gateway:
      provider: '{{ provider }}'
      name: 'IKEGW-TEST'
      version: 'ikev2'
      interface: 'ethernet1/1'
      local_ip_address_type: 'ip'
      local_ip_address: '1.1.1.1'
```

```
      enable_passive_mode: False
      enable_nat_traversal: True
      enable_liveness_check: True
      liveness_check_interval: '5'
      peer_ip_value: '3.3.3.3
      pre_shared_key: 'secretkey'
      ikev2_crypto_profile: 'ike-profile-test'
      commit: 'False'
```

This Ansible YAML code creates an IPSec tunnel on a Palo Alto firewall using the "panos_ipsec_tunnel" module. The module is configured with specific parameters, including the provider, tunnel name, tunnel interface, IKE gateway name, and IPSec crypto profile name. The "commit" parameter is set to "False" to prevent the changes from being committed automatically. When executed, this task creates an IPSec tunnel named "IPSecTunnel-Test" on the specified Palo Alto device. For troubleshooting purposes, you will be able to see the status of both phase I and phase II tunnels within the IPSec tunnels tab on the Palo Alto firewall, and you will have options to be able to restart or refresh these tunnels. For the IPSec tunnel to establish, you will need to generate interesting traffic, which will be demonstrated later in this chapter.

```
- name: Create IPSec tunnel
  paloaltonetworks.panos.panos_ipsec_tunnel:
    provider: '{{ provider }}'
    name: 'IPSecTunnel-Test'
    tunnel_interface: 'tunnel.1'
    ak_ike_gateway: 'IKEGW-TEST'
    ak_ipsec_crypto_profile: 'ipsec-profile-test
    commit: 'False'
```

This YAML code is an Ansible task that creates the Proxy IDs on the Palo Alto firewall. The "panos_ipsec_ipv4_proxyid" module is used to configure the specific parameters, including the provider, name, proxy ID name, tunnel_name, and local and remote networks to be allowed to communicate within the tunnel. The "commit" parameter is set to "False" to prevent the changes from being committed automatically. When executed, this task will create the Proxy IDs within the IPSec tunnel named

"'IPSecTunnel-Test'", which includes the local and remote subnets. The Proxy ID is also known as traffic selectors on route-based VPNs, and they will have to match on both ends of the VPN terminations to establish phase II communication.

```
- name: Add IPSec IPv4 Proxy ID
    paloaltonetworks.panos.panos_ipsec_ipv4_proxyid:
      provider: '{{ provider }}'
      name: 'Id1'
      tunnel_name: 'IPSecTunnel-Test'
      local: '10.10.10.0/24'
      remote: '10.10.30.0/24'
      commit: 'False'
```

This YAML code is an Ansible task that creates a static route on a Palo Alto firewall device. The "panos_static_route" module is used to configure the route with specific parameters such as the provider, route name, destination network, egress interface, and next-hop type. The "nexthop_type" parameter is set to "none" to indicate that the route has no next-hop IP address. The "commit" parameter is set to "False" to prevent the changes from being committed automatically. When executed, this task will create a static route named "route_10.10.30.0-24" for the destination network "10.10.30.0/24" on the specified Palo Alto device.

```
- name: Create Static route
  paloaltonetworks.panos.panos_static_route:
    provider: '{{ provider }}'
    name: 'TESTroute_10.10.30.0-24'
    destination: '10.10.30.0/24'
    interface: 'tunnel.1'
    nexthop_type: 'none'
    commit: 'False'
```

Once you have thoroughly understood the YAML playbook, you can run the 19_ create_ipsec_tunnel.yml playbook to confirm that the Ansible YAML script is running successfully. If there are no syntax errors or typos, your playbook will run successfully. If you have managed to follow along and type the playbook yourself, that's fantastic. However, if you prefer to use our playbook, you will find it in your downloaded folder named "ch19."

19.5 Running IPSec Tunnel Creation Playbook

In this section, our focus will be to check the current configuration of the PA-VM IPSec tunnel, run the playbook, and then validate the creation and functionality of our IPSec tunnel.

Step 1: Before running the playbook, log into your PA-VM web page and navigate to **Network ➤ IPSec Tunnels**. As shown in Figure 19-3, you will notice that the IPSec tunnel has not been configured yet on the target Palo Alto firewall with the IP address 192.168.127.31.

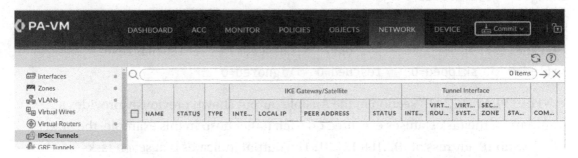

Figure 19-3. *PA-VM Network IPSec Tunnel before the configuration*

Step 2: Go to your SSH session on the Ansible Control Machine, f38s1, and execute the "19_create_ipsec_tunnel.yml" playbook. Ansible will prompt you for the firewall username and password. These credentials are necessary to authenticate and access the device for configuration. It is important to note that the entered password will not be displayed for security reasons.

```
[jdoe@f38s1 ch19]$ anp 19_create_ipsec_tunnel.yml
login as: admin
Password: ***************
PLAY [Create IPSec Tunnel with defined variables] ************************

TASK [Create tunnel.1] **************************************************
changed: [192.168.127.31]

TASK [Create IKE crypto profile] ***************************************
ok: [192.168.127.31]
TASK [Create IPSec crypto profile] ************************************
ok: [192.168.127.31]
```

```
TASK [Create IKE Gateway] ********************************************
changed: [192.168.127.31]

TASK [Create IPSec tunnel] *******************************************
changed: [192.168.127.31]

TASK [Add IPSec IPv4 Proxy ID] ***************************************
ok: [192.168.127.31]

TASK [Create Static route] *******************************************
changed: [192.168.127.31]

PLAY RECAP **********************************************************
192.168.127.31              : ok=7     changed=7     unreachable=0
failed=0     skipped=0     rescued=0     ignored=0
```

The "PLAY RECAP" section in the Ansible output shown previously provides a summary of the task statuses executed on each target host. In this example, the target host has an IP address of 192.168.127.31. The output indicates that seven tasks were executed on this host, and all of them were successful (ok=7). Out of those seven tasks, seven tasks made changes to the system (changed=7), while there were no tasks that were unreachable, failed, or skipped (unreachable=0, failed=0, skipped=0). Additionally, no tasks required rescue or were ignored (rescued=0, ignored=0).

Step 3: Now go back to the PA-VM Admin Web page; as you can see in Figure 19-4, the IPSec tunnel has been successfully configured and is now reflected in the candidate configuration of the Palo Alto firewall.

Figure 19-4. *PA-VM Network IPSec Tunnel after the configuration*

As mentioned earlier, we set each task with the "commit" parameter set to "False", enabling us to review the configuration before committing the change. Figure 19-5 visually shows this process.

OBJECT NAME	TYPE	LOCATION TYPE	LOCATION	OPERATIONS	OWNER	WILL BE COMMITTED	PREVIOUS OWNERS
IPSecTunnel-Test	IPSec Tunnel			edit	admin	Yes	admin
gateway	Others			edit	admin	Yes	admin
ike-crypto-profiles	Others			edit	admin	Yes	admin
ipsec	Others			edit	admin	Yes	admin
ipsec-crypto-profiles	Others			edit	admin	Yes	admin
tunnel	Tunnel Interface			edit	admin	Yes	admin
default	Virtual Router			edit	admin	Yes	admin
vsys1	Virtual System Import			edit	admin	Yes	admin
VPN_Test	Zone			edit	admin	Yes	admin

Change Summary — 9 items

Figure 19-5. *PA-VM Change Summary before commit*

Step 4: To showcase the IPSec tunnel's functionality, we have configured the Peer device (FW3) based on the lab preparation guide, which is another Palo Alto firewall. As mentioned earlier, the IPSec tunnel requires the generation of interesting traffic. To initiate the tunnel, SSH into FW1 and use the provided commands shown here to generate ICMP traffic on the point-to-point connection between FW1 and FW3. For this process to succeed, it is crucial that you have diligently prepared this lab and allowed ping traffic on the Ethernet 1/1 interfaces of both firewalls.

```
admin@PA-VM> ping source 1.1.1.1 host 3.3.3.3
PING 3.3.3.3 (3.3.3.3) from 1.1.1.1 : 56(84) bytes of data.
64 bytes from 3.3.3.3: icmp_seq=1 ttl=64 time=161 ms
64 bytes from 3.3.3.3: icmp_seq=2 ttl=64 time=2.14 ms
64 bytes from 3.3.3.3: icmp_seq=3 ttl=64 time=3.25 ms
64 bytes from 3.3.3.3: icmp_seq=4 ttl=64 time=2.89 ms
^C
--- 3.3.3.3 ping statistics ---
4 packets transmitted, 4 received, 0% packet loss, time 4003ms
rtt min/avg/max/mdev = 2.140/26.611/161.117/54.948 ms

admin@PA-VM> ping source 10.10.10.1 host 10.10.30.1
PING 10.10.30.1 (10.10.30.1) from 10.10.10.1 : 56(84) bytes of data.
64 bytes from 10.10.30.1: icmp_seq=2 ttl=64 time=45.4 ms
64 bytes from 10.10.30.1: icmp_seq=3 ttl=64 time=3.00 ms
64 bytes from 10.10.30.1: icmp_seq=4 ttl=64 time=3.54 ms
```

```
64 bytes from 10.10.30.1: icmp_seq=5 ttl=64 time=8.93 ms
^C
--- 10.10.30.1 ping statistics ---
4 packets transmitted, 3 received, 25% packet loss, time 5053ms
rtt min/avg/max/mdev = 3.002/8.295/45.493/12.521 ms
```

Step 5: Now check the IPSec tunnel as shown in Figure 19-6; you can see that the PA-VM's IPSec tunnel has detected the traffic and has been established. The Tunnel Info and IKE Info STATUS indicators have both turned green, indicating that the IPSec tunnel is fully functional. Additionally, the port status has also turned green, which further confirms that the IPSec tunnel has been established successfully and is operational.

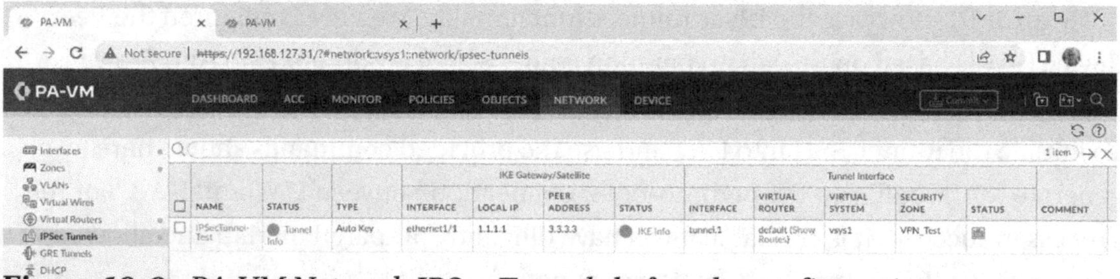

Figure 19-6. PA-VM Network IPSec Tunnels before the configuration

Now that you have completed the IPSec tunnel configuration using an Ansible playbook, it's crucial to target repetitive and time-consuming tasks, such as configuring IPSec tunnels, when considering workplace automation. These tasks are prime candidates for full automation. When initiating an automation initiative within your team or organization, it's important to start with repetitive and easily achievable tasks. By automating these tasks, engineers can free up their time to focus on more valuable work and cultivate strong client relationships. Ultimately, the work of engineers directly impacts end users and services since we serve people, not machines or computers. Despite the advent of the fourth industrial revolution and technological advancements like AI, ML, and ChatGPT, the market remains driven by human needs and desires, not machines.

Here is the completed 19_create_ipsec_tunnel.yml playbook.

19_CREATE_IPSEC_TUNNEL.YML

```yaml
---

- name: Create IPSec Tunnel with defined variables
  hosts: palo  # Targeting the Palo Alto device
  gather_facts: false  # Skipping gathering facts
  connection: local

  vars:
    provider:  # Connection parameters for the Palo Alto device
      ip_address: '{{ inventory_hostname }}'  # IP address of the device
      username: '{{ pan_username }}'  # Prompted username
      password: '{{ pan_password }}'  # Prompted password

  vars_prompt:  # Prompting for username and password
    - name: "pan_username"
      prompt: "login as"  # Prompt message for username
      private: no

    - name: "pan_password"
      prompt: "Password"  # Prompt message for password
      private: yes

  tasks:
  - name: Create tunnel.1  # Creating a tunnel
    paloaltonetworks.panos.panos_tunnel:
      provider: '{{ provider }}'
      if_name: "tunnel.1"
      vr_name: 'default'
      zone_name: 'VPN_Test'
      commit: 'False'  # Skipping immediate commit

  - name: Create IKE crypto profile  # Creating IKE crypto profile
    paloaltonetworks.panos.panos_ike_crypto_profile:
      provider: '{{ provider }}'
      name: 'ike-profile-test'
      dh_group: ['group20']
      authentication: ['sha512']
      encryption: ['aes-256-cbc']
      lifetime_hours: '8'
```

```yaml
    commit: 'False'

- name: Create IPSec crypto profile  # Creating IPSec crypto profile
  paloaltonetworks.panos.panos_ipsec_profile:
    provider: '{{ provider }}'
    name: 'ipsec-profile-test'
    dh_group: 'group20'
    esp_authentication: ['sha512']
    esp_encryption: ['aes-256-gcm']
    lifetime_hours: '1'
    commit: 'False'

- name: Create IKE Gateway  # Creating IKE gateway
  paloaltonetworks.panos.panos_ike_gateway:
    provider: '{{ provider }}'
    name: 'IKEGW-TEST'
    version: 'ikev2'
    interface: 'ethernet1/1'
    local_ip_address_type: 'ip'
    local_ip_address: '1.1.1.1'
    enable_passive_mode: False
    enable_nat_traversal: True
    enable_liveness_check: True
    liveness_check_interval: '5'
    peer_ip_value: '3.3.3.3'
    pre_shared_key: 'secretkey'
    ikev2_crypto_profile: 'ike-profile-test'
    commit: 'False'

- name: Create IPSec tunnel  # Creating IPSec tunnel
  paloaltonetworks.panos.panos_ipsec_tunnel:
    provider: '{{ provider }}'
    name: 'IPSecTunnel-Test'
    tunnel_interface: 'tunnel.1'
    ak_ike_gateway: 'IKEGW-TEST'
    ak_ipsec_crypto_profile: 'ipsec-profile-test'
    commit: 'False'

- name: Add IPSec IPv4 Proxy ID  # Adding IPSec IPv4 Proxy ID
  paloaltonetworks.panos.panos_ipsec_ipv4_proxyid:
```

```
      provider: '{{ provider }}'
      name: 'Id1'
      tunnel_name: 'IPSecTunnel-Test'
      local: '10.10.10.0/24'
      remote: '10.10.30.0/24'
      commit: 'False'

  - name: Create Static route  # Creating a static route
    paloaltonetworks.panos.panos_static_route:
      provider: '{{ provider }}'
      name: 'TESTroute_10.10.30.0-24'
      destination: '10.10.30.0/24'
      interface: 'tunnel.1'
       nexthop_type: 'none'
```

19.6 Summary

This chapter explored automating IPSec tunnel creation on Palo Alto firewalls using the Ansible playbook. We discussed the practical usage, advantages, and disadvantages of IPSec tunnels. Understanding the manual setup laid the foundation for developing an Ansible playbook to automate these tasks. We provided detailed explanations and examples of Ansible snippets, guiding readers through the automation process. Our goal was to empower readers with a comprehensive understanding of IPSec tunnel automation for their network infrastructure. Automating IPSec tunnels saves time, improves consistency, and enhances scalability. It enables faster deployment, reduces errors, and efficiently manages tunnels across multiple firewalls.

Object Addresses and Object Address Groups Creation Playbook for Palo Alto Firewall

This chapter serves as a comprehensive guide to automate the creation of object addresses and object address groups on Palo Alto firewalls using Ansible playbooks. We will delve into their usage and configuration, defining their purpose and explaining the setup process. Throughout the chapter, we will follow a step-by-step approach, starting with the manual configuration of object addresses and object address groups and gradually transitioning to an automated approach using Ansible playbooks. Each section of the playbook snippets and playbook outputs will be thoroughly explained, ensuring a clear understanding of the automation process. Our primary objective is to equip readers with a comprehensive knowledge of automation techniques, enabling them to apply these principles to their specific network infrastructure and address their unique requirements.

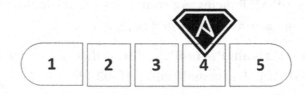

© Brendan Choi and Erwin Medina 2023
B. Choi and E. Medina, *Introduction to Ansible Network Automation*,
https://doi.org/10.1007/978-1-4842-9624-0_20

20.1 Enhancing Firewall Policies with the Use of Object Addresses and Object Address Groups

Network security engineers are responsible for changing Palo Alto firewalls' configurations, which include adds, changes, or deletions of objects on a day-to-day basis as the requests from the customers come through. For the firewall policies to be efficient, object addresses and object address groups are recommended to be used rather than static values directly on the policies. This way, it is easier to manage the objects and policies when there are changes in the existing static or dynamic entries. Requirements could be to whitelist or blacklist a range of IPs or subnets and use them in a policy for functionality or even to strengthen the rules to only allow or deny specific objects. Another example could be whitelisting of IPs or subnets to allow traffic to only the trusted IPs or subnets of third parties like AWS, O365, Azure, or even to Cloud security providers like Zscaler, Netskope, and even private internal objects, and the list could go on. Creating objects in a Palo Alto firewall is remarkably simple and easy. However, once there is the need to configure multiple objects, it becomes tedious to manually create them – more even, creating address object groups and adding members and eventually using them in the firewall's security policies, NAT policies, and the like. As we felt the agony of manually configuring multiple entries on multiple firewalls and spending the entire day and more, we decided to automate it and make it reusable, as this is a common task that we always get from the business or customer. In the end, saving time and effort means more time for other tasks with higher priority.

Moving forward, let us define what object addresses and object address groups are in a Palo Alto firewall. An object address in a Palo Alto firewall is defined to be a single IP or range of IPs, which can either be an IPv4 or IPv6. They can also be defined as an FQDN. Object addresses defined can be used in the firewall's rules within the Security, NAT, QoS, PBF, Decryption, Tunnel Inspection, Application Override, Authentication, DoS Protection, and SD-WAN Policies as a source and/or destination address. There are four types of object addresses, as enumerated here:

1. IP Netmask: This is an IPv4 or IPv6 address that can be defined as a single IP (192.168.1.1) or an IP subnet (192.168.1.0/24).

2. IP Range: This is an IPv4 or IPv6 address range defining the start and end of the IP subnet (192.168.1.1–192.168.1.254).

3. IP Wildcard Mask: This is an IPv4 address that can be defined
   as a wildcard (192.168.1.0/0.0.0.255) that can only be used in a
   security policy.

4. FQDN: This is defined as a domain name (mydomain.com).

An object address group, on the other hand, in a Palo Alto firewall is defined as a
group of one or more address objects to simplify the firewall's policies instead of adding
a list of individual address objects. Object address groups defined can be used in the
firewall's rules within the Security, NAT, QoS, PBF, Decryption, Tunnel Inspection,
Application Override, Authentication, DoS Protection, and SD-WAN Policies as a
source and/or destination address. There are two types of object address groups
enumerated here:

1. Dynamic: This is a group of object addresses that matches certain
   criteria like tags and groups them.

2. Static: This is a group of object addresses that can include
   individual object addresses and/or dynamic object
   address groups.

20.2 Object Addresses and Object Address Groups Creation on a Palo Alto Firewall

In this section, we will look at the creation of object addresses and object address groups
on a Palo Alto firewall. Open the PA-VM Admin page in your preferred web browser.

Step 1: To create an object address, go to **Objects ➤ Addresses ➤ Add**, and you'll
need to fill in the Name, Description (optional), Type, Value, and Tags (optional) as
shown in Figure 20-1.

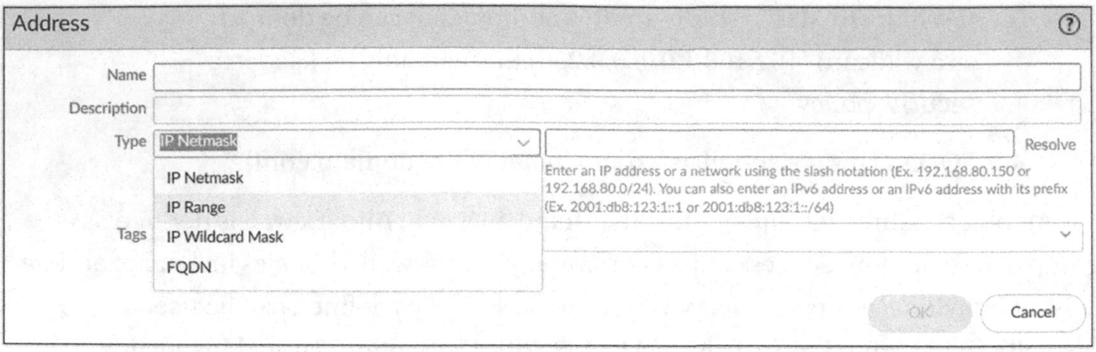

Figure 20-1. Object address creation

Step 2: To create an object address group, go to **Objects ➤ Address Groups ➤ Add**,
and you'll need to fill in the Name, Description (optional), Type (Dynamic or Static),
Addresses or match criteria, and tags (optional) as shown in Figure 20-2.

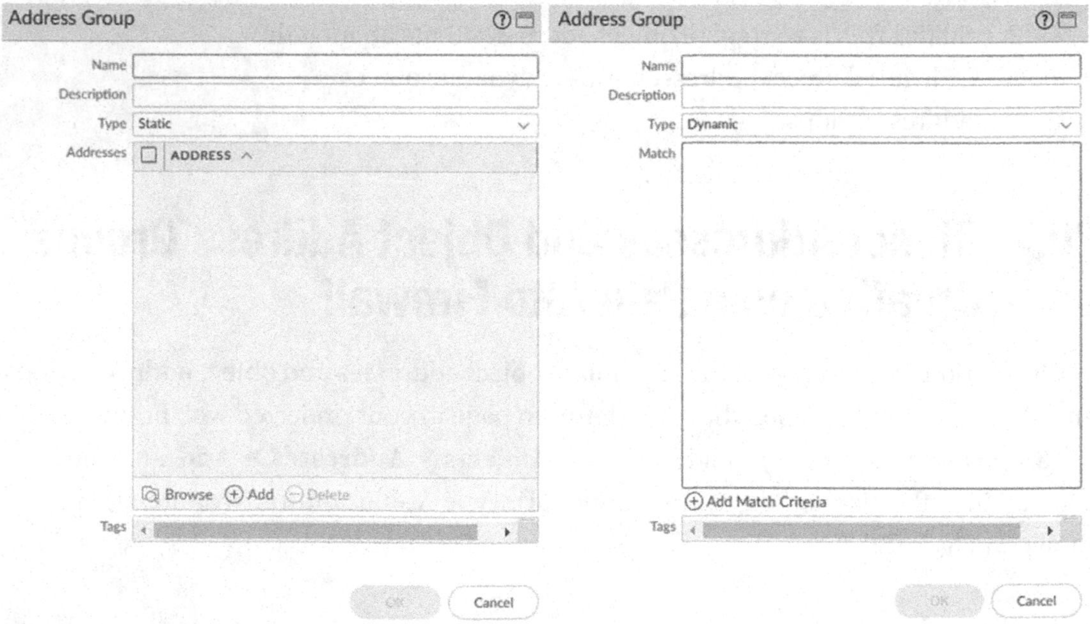

Figure 20-2. Object address group creation

20.3 Writing a Playbook to Create Object Addresses on a Palo Alto Firewall

The lab topology is the same as the last chapter; however, you will only need the
Ansible Control Machine, f38s1 (192.168.127.150), and one Palo Alto firewall, FW1
(192.168.127.31), in action. Optionally, if you want to work with two Palo Alto firewalls,
you can do so by adding the second IP address in the inventory file, but here we are only
demonstrating using a single firewall for simplicity.

Let's write a new playbook named "20_create_object_address.yml". It is important to
go over the sections of our playbook in detail to gain a better understanding of what we
are trying to achieve by writing and running this script. The playbook will create object
addresses on a Palo Alto firewall based on parameters filled with the variables defined
on a csv file named objects.csv. Undefined variables on a parameter will be omitted from
the configuration. These variables in the parameter are optional.

Step 1: As we are creating directories for every chapter, we will keep it consistent and
create a new working directory, ch20, and work from the directory. We will create a local
ansible.cfg and inventory file in the directory.

```
[jdoe@f38s1 ~]$ mkdir ch20 && cd ch20
[jdoe@f38s1 ch20]$ vi ansible.cfg
[jdoe@f38s1 ch20]$ cat ansible.cfg
[defaults]
inventory=inventory
```

Step 2: Let's quickly create an inventory file for our lab.

```
[jdoe@f38s1 ch20]$ vi inventory
[jdoe@f38s1 ch20]$ cat inventory
[palo]
192.168.127.31
```

Step 3: Let's create a new playbook named 20_create_object_address.yml.

```
[jdoe@f38s1 ch20$ vi 20_create_object_address.yml
```

Let's follow the instructions and write our playbook one line at a time.

As in all YAML files, the three dashes indicate the start of a new document.

```
---
```

With the use of - name, we can describe what this YAML file does or intends to do.

- name: Create object addresses from csv file

This specifies the target host(s) on which this playbook will run. In this case, it will run on a host named "palo". For this playbook, we will run it on a Palo Alto VM with IP 192.168.127.31. This IP is defined in our inventory as a member of the group-name named "palo".

hosts: palo

By default, Ansible's gather_facts module is enabled, but it can be disabled to save resources and improve playbook execution speed. Disabling gather_facts means that Ansible will not collect information about the target host(s) like IP address, operating system, and installed packages. While this information can be helpful as variables to modify playbook flow, disabling the module optimizes playbook performance if you don't require this data.

gather_facts: false

The "connection: local" parameter in an Ansible playbook indicates local execution on the Ansible control node instead of remote execution on target hosts. Tasks defined in the playbook are executed on the control node itself. This is beneficial for tasks that don't need remote execution or for testing purposes.

connection: local

The "provider" parameter contains subparameters for the firewall's IP address, username, and password. The IP address is dynamically set to the inventory_hostname, representing the target host(s) hostname. The username and password fields are left blank and will be prompted later in the playbook using the vars_prompt module. These variables allow us to configure the firewall throughout the playbook.

```
vars:
  provider:
    ip_address: '{{ inventory_hostname }}'
    username: '{{ pan_username }}'
    password: '{{ pan_password }}'
```

The line prompts the user for a username and password for the firewall, with the password input hidden for security (private flag). The entered values are stored as variables for later use in the playbook when establishing an SSH connection with the firewall.

```
vars_prompt:
  - name: "pan_username"
    prompt: "login as"
    private: no

  - name: "pan_password"
    prompt: "Password"
    private: yes
```

This Ansible task uses the "community.general.read_csv" module to read the csv file named objects.csv. The path is objects.csv which states that the file is locally stored where the playbook is stored. Once the csv file is read, it will store it as a list in a variable named objects_list.

```
- name: Read the csv file
  delegate_to: locahost
  community.general.read_csv:
      path: objects.csv
  register: objects_list
```

This Ansible task uses the "panos_address_object" module to create the object addresses stored in the list named objects_list with the loop keyword at the end and configure the address object in each row in the list. The task will create the object address from each row with the parameter name, value, and description in the list. As you can see, the parameter named description is defined with "default(omit)". This means that the parameter named description will not be configured if it is undefined in the list. The commit flag is set to False, indicating that the changes made by this task will not be committed immediately.

```
- name: Create object addresses from the csv file
  paloaltonetworks.panos panos_address_object:
    provider: '{{ provider }}'
    name: '{{ item.name }}'
```

```
   value: '{{ item.value }}'
   description: '{{ item.description | default(omit) }}'
   commit: False
 loop: '{{ objects_list.list }}'
```

Once you have thoroughly understood the YAML playbook, you can run the 20_
create_object_address.yml playbook to confirm that the Ansible YAML script is running
successfully. If there are no syntax errors or typos, you should see similar output to the
following example; the playbook has two tasks to create the object addresses based on
the list in the objects.csv file, and the output contains the explanation of each output.

20.4 Running the Playbook to Create Object Addresses on a Palo Alto Firewall

Before running the playbook, we can see that the object addresses have not been
configured yet on our target Palo Alto firewall with an IP address of 192.168.127.31 (see
Figure 20-3).

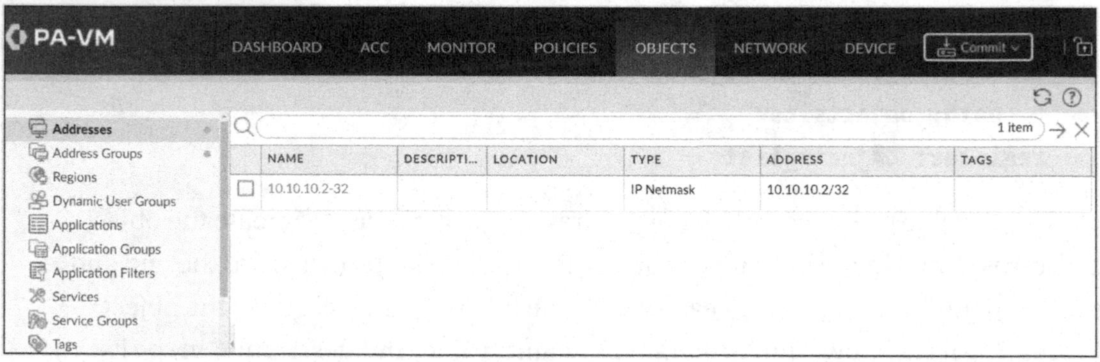

Figure 20-3. *PA-VM object addresses before executing the playbook*

Figure 20-4 shows the objects.csv file that we created, which includes the parameter
name, value, and description (optional). The description will not be configured for those
rows with an undefined value.

	A	B	C
1	name	value	description
2	test-1	1.1.1.1	testobject1
3	test-2	1.1.1.2	testobject2
4	test-3	1.1.1.3	
5	test-4	1.1.1.4	testobject4
6	test-5	1.1.1.5	testobject5
7	test-6	1.1.1.6	
8	test-7	1.1.1.7	
9	test-8	1.1.1.8	
10	test-9	1.1.1.9	
11	test-10	1.1.1.10	
12	test-11	1.1.1.11	
13	test-12	1.1.1.12	testobject12
14	test-13	1.1.1.13	testobject13
15	test-14	1.1.1.14	testobject14
16	test-15	1.1.1.15	testobject15
17	test-16	1.1.1.16	
18	test-17	1.1.1.17	
19	test-18	1.1.1.18	
20	test-19	1.1.1.19	testobject19
21	test-20	1.1.1.20	testobject20

Figure 20-4. *objects.csv*

Step 1: This is an example of running an Ansible playbook named "20_create_object_address.yml". When executed, Ansible will prompt for the firewall username and password, which are required to authenticate and access the device for configuration. The entered password will not be displayed for security reasons.

```
[jdoe@f38s1 ch20]$ anp 20_create_object_address.yml
login as: admin
Password: ***************
PLAY [Create object addresses from csv file] ****************************

TASK [Read the csv file] ***********************************************
ok: [192.168.127.31 -> locahost]
```

```
TASK [Read the csv file] *************************************************

TASK [Create object addresses from the csv file] *************************
changed: [192.168.127.31] => (item={'name': 'test-1', 'value': '1.1.1.1',
'description': 'testobject1'})
changed: [192.168.127.31] => (item={'name': 'test-2', 'value': '1.1.1.2',
'description': 'testobject2'})
changed: [192.168.127.31] => (item={'name': 'test-3', 'value': '1.1.1.3',
'description': ''})
changed: [192.168.127.31] => (item={'name': 'test-4', 'value': '1.1.1.4',
'description': 'testobject4'})
changed: [192.168.127.31] => (item={'name': 'test-5', 'value': '1.1.1.5',
'description': 'testobject5'})
changed: [192.168.127.31] => (item={'name': 'test-6', 'value': '1.1.1.6',
'description': ''})
changed: [192.168.127.31] => (item={'name': 'test-7', 'value': '1.1.1.7',
'description': ''})
changed: [192.168.127.31] => (item={'name': 'test-8', 'value': '1.1.1.8',
'description': ''})
changed: [192.168.127.31] => (item={'name': 'test-9', 'value': '1.1.1.9',
'description': ''})
changed: [192.168.127.31] => (item={'name': 'test-10', 'value': '1.1.1.10',
'description': ''})
changed: [192.168.127.31] => (item={'name': 'test-11', 'value': '1.1.1.11',
'description': ''})
changed: [192.168.127.31] => (item={'name': 'test-12', 'value': '1.1.1.12',
'description': 'testobject12'})
changed: [192.168.127.31] => (item={'name': 'test-13', 'value': '1.1.1.13',
'description': 'testobject13'})
changed: [192.168.127.31] => (item={'name': 'test-14', 'value': '1.1.1.14',
'description': 'testobject14'})
changed: [192.168.127.31] => (item={'name': 'test-15', 'value': '1.1.1.15',
'description': 'testobject15'})
changed: [192.168.127.31] => (item={'name': 'test-16', 'value': '1.1.1.16',
'description': ''})
```

```
changed: [192.168.127.31] => (item={'name': 'test-17', 'value': '1.1.1.17',
'description': ''})
changed: [192.168.127.31] => (item={'name': 'test-18', 'value': '1.1.1.18',
'description': ''})
changed: [192.168.127.31] => (item={'name': 'test-19', 'value': '1.1.1.19',
'description': 'testobject19'})
changed: [192.168.127.31] => (item={'name': 'test-20', 'value': '1.1.1.20',
'description': 'testobject20'})

PLAY RECAP ********************************************************************
192.168.127.31      : ok=2     changed=1    unreachable=0     failed=0
skipped=0     rescued=0     ignored=0
```

The "PLAY RECAP" section in the Ansible output summarizes the status of the
tasks executed on each target host. In this example, the target host's IP address is
192.168.127.31. The output shows that there were two tasks executed on this host, and
all of them were successful (ok=2). Out of those two tasks, one made changes to the
system (changed=1), while 0 tasks were unreachable, failed, or skipped (unreachable=0,
failed=0, skipped=0). Finally, no tasks required being rescued or ignored (rescued=0,
ignored=0).

Step 2: In Figure 20-5, it is evident that the object addresses have been successfully
configured as what we have defined in the objects.csv file and are now reflected in
the candidate configuration of the Palo Alto firewall. As previously mentioned, we set
each task with the "commit" parameter set to "False", which allows us to review the
configuration before committing the change.

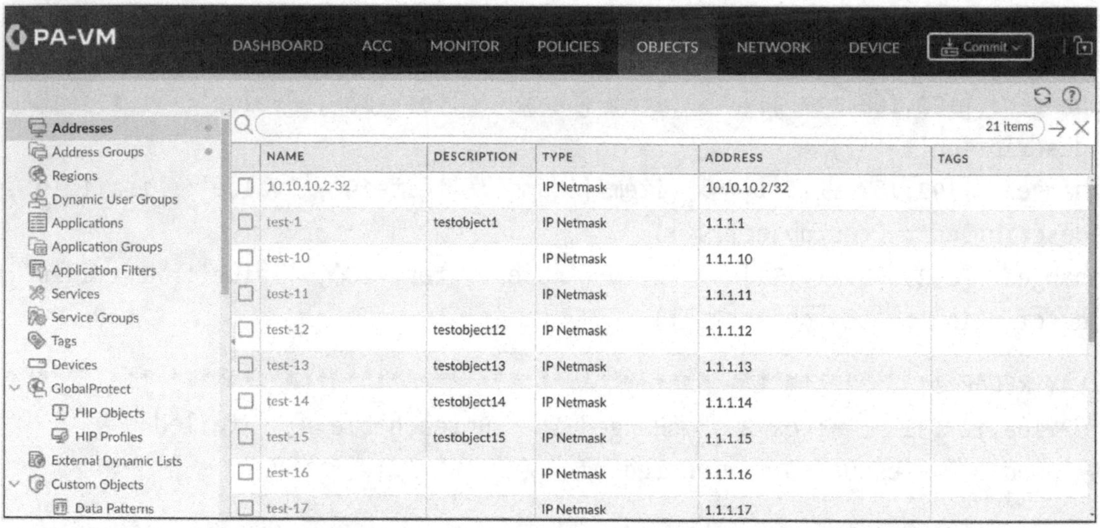

Figure 20-5. *PA-VM object addresses after executing the playbook*

Step 3: Here is the complete 20_create_object_address.yml for your reference:

```
[jdoe@f38s1 ch20]$ vi 20_create_object_address.yml
[jdoe@f38s1 ch20]$ cat 20_create_object_address.yml
---
- name: Create object addresses from csv file
  hosts: palo
  gather_facts: false
  connection: local

  vars:
    provider:
      ip_address: '{{ inventory_hostname }}'
      username: '{{ pan_username }}'
      password: '{{ pan_password }}'

  vars_prompt:
    - name: "pan_username"
      prompt: "login as"
      private: no
```

```
  - name: "pan_password"
    prompt: "Password"
    private: yes

tasks:
  - name: Read the csv file
    delegate_to: locahost
    community.general.read_csv:
      path: objects.csv
    register: objects_list

  - name: Create object addresses from the csv file
    paloaltonetworks.panos panos_address_object:
      provider: '{{ provider }}'
      name: '{{ item.name }}'
      value: '{{ item.value }}'
      description: '{{ item.description | default(omit) }}'
      commit: False
    loop: '{{ objects_list.list }}'
```

20.5 Writing a Playbook to Create Object Address Groups on a Palo Alto Firewall

In this playbook, you can find a complete Ansible YAML script named "20_create_object_address_group.yml". However, it's important to go over the contents of the YAML file in detail to gain a better understanding of what we are trying to achieve by writing and running this script. The "20_create_object_address_group.yml" is an Ansible playbook that creates a tag, object addresses with the tag defined, and, eventually, the object address group on a Palo Alto firewall. The object addresses will be created based on parameters filled with the variables defined on a csv file named objects_address. csv. Undefined variables on a parameter will be omitted from the configuration. These variables in the parameter are optional.

Here's a brief explanation of each line of the playbook.

As in all YAML files, the three dashes indicate the start of a new document.

```
---
```

With the use of - name, we can describe what this YAML file does or intends to do.

- name: Create object addresses from csv file

This specifies the target host(s) on which this playbook will run. In this case, it will run on a host named "palo". For this playbook, we will run it on a Palo Alto VM with IP 192.168.127.31. This IP is defined in our inventory as a member of the group-name named "palo".

hosts: palo

By default, Ansible's gather_facts module is always enabled, but if you do not require information from facts, you can choose to disable this module to save processor resources and speed up playbook execution. Disabling gather_facts means that Ansible will not collect information about the target host(s), such as their IP address, operating system, installed packages, etc. It's important to note that the information collected from the gather_facts module can be useful as variables, which can be used to change the flow of your Ansible playbook. However, if you don't need this information, it's best to disable the gather_facts module to optimize the performance of your playbook.

gather_facts: false

The connection: local parameter in an Ansible playbook specifies that the playbook should be executed locally on the machine running Ansible rather than remotely on the target host(s). This means that any tasks defined in the playbook will be executed on the Ansible control node rather than on the target hosts. This can be useful for tasks that do not require remote execution or for testing purposes.

connection: local

This defines a parameter named "provider" that contains subparameters for the IP address, username, and password of the firewall. The IP address is dynamically set to the inventory_hostname, which refers to the hostname of the target host(s). The username and password are left blank and will be prompted later in the playbook using the vars_ prompt module. By defining these variables, we can use them throughout the playbook to configure the firewall.

```
vars:
  provider:
    ip_address: '{{ inventory_hostname }}'
    username: '{{ pan_username }}'
    password: '{{ pan_password }}'
```

This line prompts the user running the playbook to enter a username and password for the firewall. The private flag on the password prompt indicates that the user's input should not be displayed on the screen for security reasons. These inputs will be stored as variables to be used later in the playbook when connecting to the firewall using SSH.

```
vars_prompt:
  - name: "pan_username"
    prompt: "login as"
    private: no

  - name: "pan_password"
    prompt: "Password"
    private: yes
```

This Ansible task uses the "community.general.read_csv" module to read the csv file named objects_address.csv. The path is objects_address.csv which states that the file is locally stored where the playbook is stored. Once the csv file is read, it will store it as a list in a variable named objects_address_list.

```
- name: Read the csv file
  delegate_to: locahost
  community.general.read_csv:
    path: objects_address.csv
  register: objects_address_list
```

This Ansible task uses the "panos_tag_object" module to create a tag named "test_object" with the color red. This tag will later be used to tag object addresses to be grouped. The commit flag is set to False, indicating that the changes made by this task will not be committed immediately.

```
- name: Create a tag with color
  paloaltonetworks.panos panos_tag_object:
    provider: '{{ provider }}'
```

```
    name: 'test_object'
    color: 'red'
    commit: False
```

This Ansible task uses the "panos_address_object" module to create the object addresses stored in the list named objects_address_list with the loop keyword at the end and configure the address object in each row in the list. The task will create the object address from each row with the parameter name, value, tag, and description in the list. As you can see, the parameter named description is defined with "default(omit)". This means that the parameter named description will not be configured if it is undefined in the list. The commit flag is set to False, indicating that the changes made by this task will not be committed immediately.

```
  - name: Create object address with tag
    paloaltonetworks.panos panos_address_object:
      provider: '{{ provider }}'
      name: '{{ item.name }}'
      value: '{{ item.value }}'
      tag: '{{ item.tag }}'
      description: '{{ item.description | default(omit) }}'
      commit: False
    loop: '{{ objects_address_list.list }}'
```

This Ansible task uses the "panos_address_group" module to create the address group named test_object_group. The type of the object address group is dynamic with the match criteria of test_object. All of the object addresses that were tagged with test_object that we created earlier will be a member of the object address group named "test_object_group".

```
  - name: Create object address group
    paloaltonetworks.panos panos_address_group:
      provider: '{{ provider }}'
      name: 'test_object_group'
      dynamic_value: 'test_object'
      commit: False
```

20.6 Running the Playbook to Create Object Address Groups on a Palo Alto Firewall

Before we continue with the next example in this chapter, we'll have to revert the configuration to the running configuration to clear out the candidate configuration from our previous example. Go to **Device ➤ Setup ➤ Operations ➤ Revert** to the running configuration.

Now, we can see that the object addresses and object address group have not been configured yet on our target Palo Alto firewall with an IP address of 192.168.127.31 (see Figures 20-6 and 20-7).

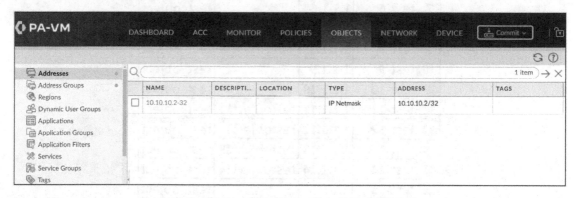

Figure 20-6. *PA-VM object addresses before executing the playbook*

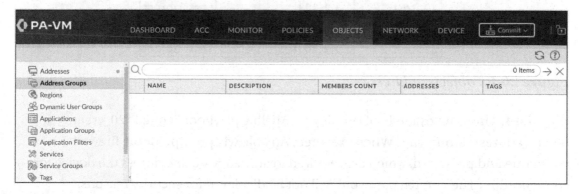

Figure 20-7. *PA-VM object address group before executing the playbook*

Figure 20-8 shows the objects_address.csv file that we created, which includes the parameter name, value and description (optional), and tag. The description will not be configured for those rows with an undefined value.

	A	B	C	D
1	name	value	description	tag
2	test-1	1.1.1.1	testobject1	test_object
3	test-2	1.1.1.2	testobject2	test_object
4	test-3	1.1.1.3	testobject3	test_object
5	test-4	1.1.1.4	testobject4	test_object
6	test-5	1.1.1.5	testobject5	test_object
7	test-6	1.1.1.6		test_object
8	test-7	1.1.1.7		test_object
9	test-8	1.1.1.8		test_object
10	test-9	1.1.1.9		test_object
11	test-10	1.1.1.10		test_object
12	test-11	1.1.1.11	testobject11	test_object
13	test-12	1.1.1.12	testobject12	test_object
14	test-13	1.1.1.13	testobject13	test_object
15	test-14	1.1.1.14	testobject14	test_object
16	test-15	1.1.1.15		test_object
17	test-16	1.1.1.16		test_object
18	test-17	1.1.1.17		test_object
19	test-18	1.1.1.18		test_object
20	test-19	1.1.1.19	testobject19	test_object
21	test-20	1.1.1.20	testobject20	test_object

Figure 20-8. *objects_address.csv*

Step 1: This is an example of running an Ansible playbook named "20_create_object_address_group.yml". When executed, Ansible will prompt for the firewall username and password, which are required to authenticate and access the device for configuration. The entered password will not be displayed for security reasons.

The "PLAY RECAP" section in the Ansible output summarizes the status of the tasks executed on each target host. In this example, the target host's IP address is 192.168.127.31. The output shows that there were four tasks executed on this host, and all of them were successful (ok=4). Out of those four tasks, three made changes to the system (changed=3), while 0 tasks were unreachable, failed, or skipped (unreachable=0, failed=0, skipped=0). Finally, no tasks required being rescued or ignored (rescued=0, ignored=0).

```
[jdoe@f38s1 ch20]$ anp 20_create_object_address_group.yml
login as: admin
Password: ***************
PLAY [Create object address group] **************************************

TASK [Read the csv file] ************************************************
ok: [192.168.127.31 -> locahost]

TASK [Create tag with color] ********************************************
changed: [192.168.127.31]
TASK [Create object address with tag] ***********************************
changed: [192.168.127.31] => (item={'name': 'test-1', 'value': '1.1.1.1',
'description': 'testobject1', 'tag': 'test_object'})
changed: [192.168.127.31] => (item={'name': 'test-2', 'value': '1.1.1.2',
'description': 'testobject2', 'tag': 'test_object'})
changed: [192.168.127.31] => (item={'name': 'test-3', 'value': '1.1.1.3',
'description': 'testobject3', 'tag': 'test_object'})
changed: [192.168.127.31] => (item={'name': 'test-4', 'value': '1.1.1.4',
'description': 'testobject4', 'tag': 'test_object'})
changed: [192.168.127.31] => (item={'name': 'test-5', 'value': '1.1.1.5',
'description': 'testobject5', 'tag': 'test_object'})
changed: [192.168.127.31] => (item={'name': 'test-6', 'value': '1.1.1.6',
'description': '', 'tag': 'test_object'})
changed: [192.168.127.31] => (item={'name': 'test-7', 'value': '1.1.1.7',
'description': '', 'tag': 'test_object'})
changed: [192.168.127.31] => (item={'name': 'test-8', 'value': '1.1.1.8',
'description': '', 'tag': 'test_object'})
changed: [192.168.127.31] => (item={'name': 'test-9', 'value': '1.1.1.9',
'description': '', 'tag': 'test_object'})
changed: [192.168.127.31] => (item={'name': 'test-10', 'value': '1.1.1.10',
'description': '', 'tag': 'test_object'})
```

```
changed: [192.168.127.31] => (item={'name': 'test-11', 'value': '1.1.1.11',
'description': 'testobject11', 'tag': 'test_object'})
changed: [192.168.127.31] => (item={'name': 'test-12', 'value': '1.1.1.12',
'description': 'testobject12', 'tag': 'test_object'})
changed: [192.168.127.31] => (item={'name': 'test-13', 'value': '1.1.1.13',
'description': 'testobject13', 'tag': 'test_object'})
changed: [192.168.127.31] => (item={'name': 'test-14', 'value': '1.1.1.14',
'description': 'testobject14', 'tag': 'test_object'})
changed: [192.168.127.31] => (item={'name': 'test-15', 'value': '1.1.1.15',
'description': '', 'tag': 'test_object'})
changed: [192.168.127.31] => (item={'name': 'test-16', 'value': '1.1.1.16',
'description': '', 'tag': 'test_object'})
changed: [192.168.127.31] => (item={'name': 'test-17', 'value': '1.1.1.17',
'description': '', 'tag': 'test_object'})
changed: [192.168.127.31] => (item={'name': 'test-18', 'value': '1.1.1.18',
'description': '', 'tag': 'test_object'})
changed: [192.168.127.31] => (item={'name': 'test-19', 'value': '1.1.1.19',
'description': 'testobject19', 'tag': 'test_object'})
changed: [192.168.127.31] => (item={'name': 'test-20', 'value': '1.1.1.20',
'description': 'testobject20', 'tag': 'test_object'})

TASK [Create object address group] ***************************************
changed: [192.168.127.31]

PLAY RECAP ***************************************************************
192.168.127.31     : ok=4    changed=3    unreachable=0    failed=0
skipped=0    rescued=0    ignored=0
```

Step 2: In Figure 20-9, it is evident that the object addresses have been successfully configured as what we have defined in the objects_address.csv file with the tag and colored red. Figure 20-10 shows the object address group created. Figure 20-11 shows the dynamic members associated with the address group and now reflected in the candidate configuration of the Palo Alto firewall. As previously mentioned, we set each task with the "commit" parameter set to "False", which allows us to review the configuration before committing the change.

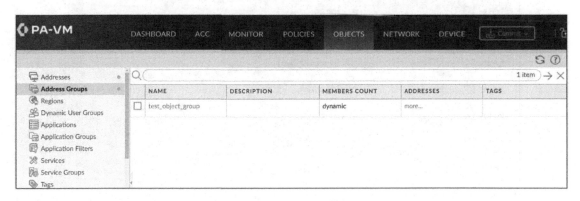

Figure 20-9. *PA-VM object addresses with tag and colored red after executing the
playbook*

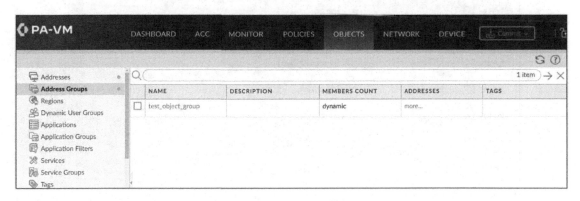

Figure 20-10. *PA-VM object address group with a dynamic member after
executing the playbook*

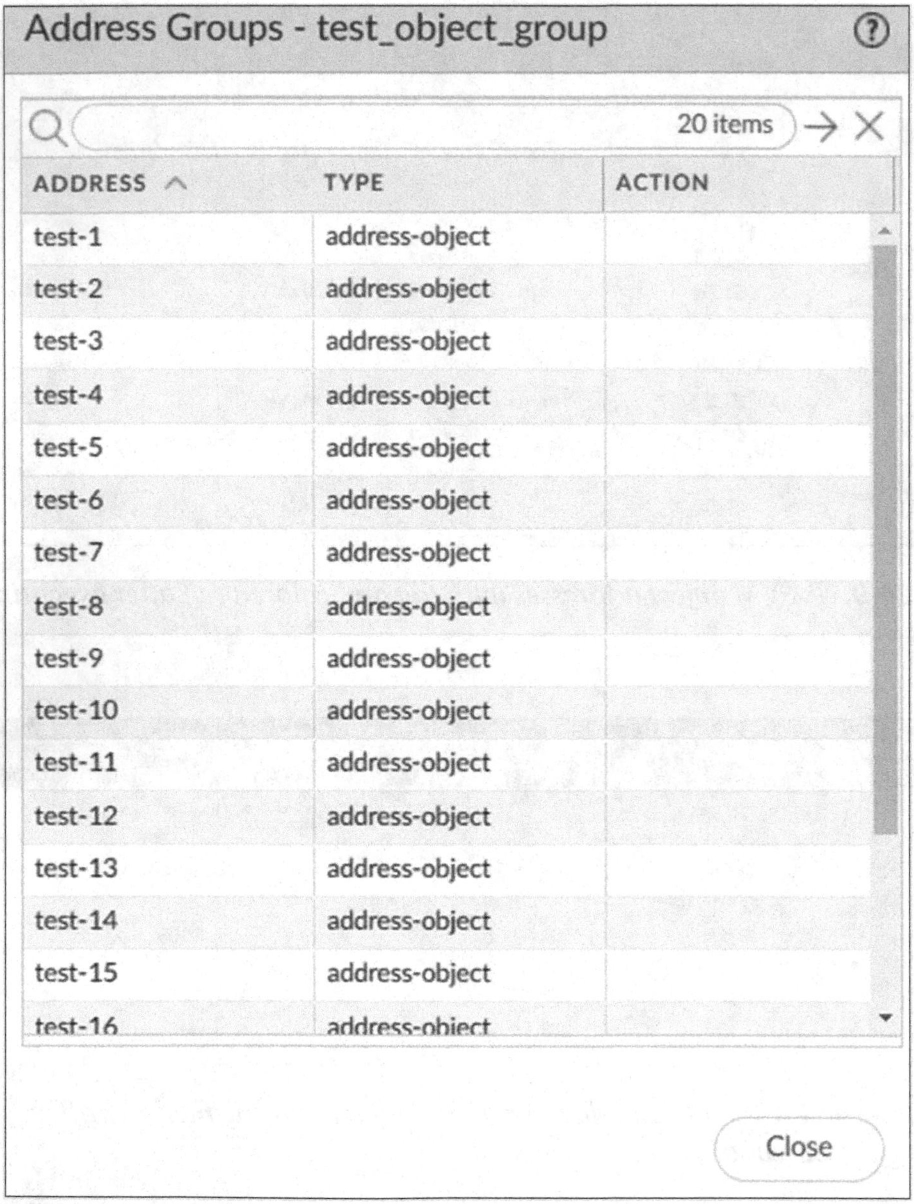

Address Groups - test_object_group   ⑦

ADDRESS ∧	TYPE	ACTION
test-1	address-object	
test-2	address-object	
test-3	address-object	
test-4	address-object	
test-5	address-object	
test-6	address-object	
test-7	address-object	
test-8	address-object	
test-9	address-object	
test-10	address-object	
test-11	address-object	
test-12	address-object	
test-13	address-object	
test-14	address-object	
test-15	address-object	
test-16	address-object	

20 items → ✕

Close

Figure 20-11. *PA-VM object addresses group dynamic members*

This chapter marks the penultimate section of the book, with only the final chapter remaining for your enjoyment. Congratulations on reaching this far and pushing yourself to the limit. From Chapters 1 to 20, we hope you have acquired valuable lessons and skill sets that are unique to this medium. Take a break, get some fresh air, and return to complete your reading with the last chapter. In the upcoming chapter, Chapter 21, we will delve into the topic of PAN-OS upgrading. It is important to note that a licensed version of PA-VM in

your environment or the actual physical PA-VM will be required for the demonstrations due
to feature restrictions imposed by the demo license. To actively follow the upgrade process,
ensure that you have a working firewall with a working license. However, if you do not have
a license, you can still follow along and envision the steps involved in upgrading a Palo
Alto firewall. Stay engaged and continue your reading with the final chapter, where we will
explore the exciting task of creating a playbook to upgrade Palo Alto's PAN-OS.

Here is the complete 20_create_object_address_group.yml file for your reference:

20_CREATE_OBJECT_ADDRESS_GROUP.YML

```
---
- name: Create object address group
  hosts: palo
  gather_facts: false
  connection: local

  vars:
    provider:
      ip_address: '{{ inventory_hostname }}'
      username: '{{ pan_username }}'
      password: '{{ pan_password }}'

  vars_prompt:
    - name: "pan_username"
      prompt: "login as"
      private: no

    - name: "pan_password"
      prompt: "Password"
      private: yes

  tasks:
   - name: read csv
     delegate_to: locahost
     community.general.read_csv:
       path: objects_address.csv
     register: objects_address_list

   - name: Create tag with color
     paloaltonetworks.panos panos_tag_object:
       provider: '{{ provider }}'
       name: 'test_object'
```

```
      color: 'red'
      commit: False

  - name: Create object address with tag
    paloaltonetworks.panos.panos_address_object:
      provider: '{{ provider }}'
      name: '{{ item.name }}'
      value: '{{ item.value }}'
      tag: '{{ item.tag }}'
      description: '{{ item.description | default(omit) }}'
      commit: False
    loop: '{{ objects_address_list.list }}'

  - name: Create object address group
    paloaltonetworks.panos panos_address_group:
      provider: '{{ provider }}'
      name: 'test_object_group'
      dynamic_value: 'test_object'
      commit: False
```

20.7 Summary

This chapter serves as a comprehensive guide, emphasizing the significance of
automation in simplifying and accelerating the creation of object addresses and
object address groups on Palo Alto firewalls. It enables network engineers to optimize
their firewall configurations and enhance security policies in an automated manner.
The chapter explores the usage and configuration of object addresses, defining their
purpose and explaining the setup process. It follows a step-by-step approach, starting
with manual configuration and gradually transitioning to automation using Ansible
playbooks. The primary objective of the chapter is to help readers move away from
mundane manual tasks and learn the steps to automate their work by translating them
into lines of YAML code. This empowers them to apply automation principles to their
specific network infrastructure and address their unique requirements. The specific
focus is on automating the creation of object addresses and object address groups on
Palo Alto firewalls. Through detailed guidance and practical examples, readers gain
the necessary skills to effectively implement automation and enhance their network
management efficiency.

CHAPTER 21

Upgrading Palo Alto Firewalls

In this concluding chapter, we delve into the crucial topic of upgrading Palo Alto's PAN-OS Firewall. For security engineers, upgrading firewalls that are actively deployed in a production environment is an essential task. Throughout this chapter, we aim to provide you with valuable insights into the PAN-OS upgrade process by exploring both manual procedures and the advantages of leveraging automated Ansible playbooks. By examining the manual upgrade process, we will gain a deeper understanding of the intricacies involved in upgrading PAN-OS firewalls. Furthermore, we will showcase the power and efficiency of utilizing Ansible playbooks to automate the upgrade process. This approach allows us to break down the various components of the upgrade into manageable snippets of YAML code, enabling a precise comprehension of the automation workflow. Ultimately, we will consolidate these code snippets into a single playbook, transforming them into a practical application. Through this chapter, you will not only acquire practical knowledge of Palo Alto's PAN-OS Firewall upgrade but will also gain hands-on experience in working with YAML codes and leveraging Ansible for automation. As we reach the end of this journey, let's seize the chance to dig deep one more time in this book.

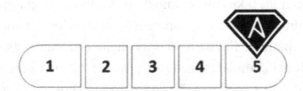

© Brendan Choi and Erwin Medina 2023
B. Choi and E. Medina, *Introduction to Ansible Network Automation*,
https://doi.org/10.1007/978-1-4842-9624-0_21

21.1 Maintaining Palo Alto Network Firewall PAN-OS to the Latest Preferred Version

Organizations invest significant time and resources in maintaining their security devices, and among them, firewalls, particularly Palo Alto firewalls, hold a crucial position at the edge of the enterprise network. In light of this, ensuring that the PAN-OS version is consistently updated becomes paramount for several compelling reasons. Of course, the foremost reason is security. Upgrading to the latest versions ensures the protection of your company's network against the most recent threats and vulnerabilities. Additionally, each upgrade incorporates bug fixes from previous versions. Furthermore, newer PAN-OS versions offer essential features that help organizations stay up to date with emerging technologies and advancements. The updates generally enhance performance as well as increase stability while minimizing disruptions caused by known bugs. However, before proceeding with a firewall upgrade, it is vital to adhere to the vendor's recommended best practices and upgrade path. This requires careful planning to achieve a successful upgrade. Compatibility between the hardware and firmware to be upgraded is a crucial consideration. Reviewing the release notes becomes essential as they provide valuable information about bug fixes and known issues, assisting us in determining the appropriate version to upgrade to. Once the target version is identified, we can begin planning the step-by-step upgrade process. Although the process may appear straightforward, it demands a significant amount of time and thorough fact-checking. Moreover, a corporate firewall upgrade often involves reboots and can impact all network services that rely on the firewall. Therefore, it is essential to ensure meticulous preparation. Seeking a peer review from colleagues and obtaining approval through the CAB (Change Approval Board) meeting are additional steps to ensure the integrity of the change. It is worth noting that, typically, the planning and preparation phase for a firewall upgrade takes more time than the actual upgrade process itself.

At the time of writing this book, the responsibility for reviewing and making decisions regarding the upgrade path still lies with security engineers, architects, and IT operations managers. However, looking ahead to the future, as AI, ML, and ChatGPT continue to advance, it is foreseeable that vendors will start to develop bots capable of replacing the engineers' decision-making processes and hence the tasks. These AI-driven bots will autonomously determine the most secure and optimal upgrade path and version for each organization. However, until that day arrives, a significant portion of the decision-making and upgrade work will continue to rest with the engineering staff themselves.

Let's quickly walk through Palo Alto's PAN-OS upgrade processes. Firstly, it is essential to create a backup of the configuration to ensure we have a copy in case of any hardware or software issues that might hinder firewall recovery. This backup can be imported into the firewall being recovered. Next, it is crucial to ensure that we have the latest content update to keep the content up to date with the new PAN-OS version we are transitioning to. To achieve this, we can use the "check now" functionality, which queries the Palo Alto updates server and retrieves the latest available versions. Subsequently, we can download and install the most recent application and threat updates. With the initial steps completed, we can proceed to the actual upgrade process. Firstly, we download the base version, which, in this case, is version 10.2.0. Then, we download and install the firmware version we are upgrading to, specifically version 10.2.4. After this, the device will reboot, and it is important to wait for the device to be ready. This can be confirmed by using the "show chassis-ready" command. Once the device is ready, we can verify if the firewall has completed the upgrade to the instructed version. By following these steps, we ensure a smooth and effective PAN-OS upgrade process.

Warning!

This chapter uses a physical firewall, Palo Alto PA-220.

In this chapter, you have the flexibility to choose between using a hardware-based and using a virtual firewall. However, it's important to note that Palo Alto imposes restrictions on PAN-OS upgrades and Dynamic Updates when using a trial license. The duration of the demo license period may vary based on Palo Alto's specific terms and conditions. For instance, the VM-Series offers a 30-day trial period in ESXi and KVM environments, but it does not include upgrade support. Therefore, to effectively follow along with this chapter, it is necessary to have a licensed version of either a hardware-based or virtual firewall.

Figure 21-1. *Palo Alto PA-220 firewall*

The initial setup process for a hardware-based Palo Alto firewall (PA-220) is identical to that of the virtual PA-VM. If you haven't already done so, I recommend following the PA-VM instructions provided in Chapter 11 to initialize your PA-VM before continuing with this chapter. This will ensure that you have a solid foundation and are familiar with the basic setup steps, which will apply to both hardware-based and virtual firewalls. Once you have completed the PA-VM initialization process, you can proceed with confidence to the next sections in this chapter.

21.2 Palo Alto Firewall PAN-OS Upgrade to Major Version: Manual Method

In this section, we will present a step-by-step manual process for the PAN-OS upgrade. However, it's important to note that **you do not need to perform this task**, as we will be developing an Ansible playbook to automate the upgrade. So **feel free to read along and familiarize yourself with the upgrade process**.

For the upgrade demonstration, we will be using a licensed physical Palo Alto firewall model PA-220, as shown in Figure 21-1. While we couldn't obtain a functional license for the virtual PA-VM firewall, it's worth mentioning that if you have a valid PA-VM firewall license, the procedures outlined here remain consistent, allowing you to follow the same steps.

Throughout this chapter, our primary focus will be on upgrading a stand-alone Palo Alto PA-220 physical firewall, adhering to the vendor's recommended procedures as documented in their best upgrading practices.

Please refer to Figure 21-2 for our test lab topology, which showcases the slight changes in IP addresses due to the introduction of a physical firewall. To provide you with a better understanding, here is the network topology of our Home Lab. The Ansible control node, identified as f38s1, is operating on the Windows host PC and connected to the natted address of 192.168.127.150. On the local network, the physical firewall named FW4 (Palo Alto PA-220) is connected to the home router/modem. We have assigned the IP address 192.168.0.31/24 to FW4. This configuration will serve as the foundation for the forthcoming steps and discussions in this chapter, aiding in your comprehension of the setup and facilitating the upgrade process.

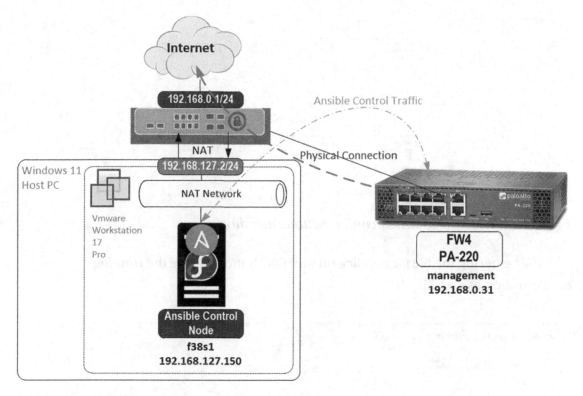

Figure 21-2. *PAN-OS Upgrade Lab Network Topology*

Step 1: First, log into PAN-OS administrator's login page at https://192.168.0.31. Let's save a backup of the running configuration. Go to **Device ➤ Setup ➤ Operations ➤ Export named configuration snapshot** and export the running-config.xml file as shown in Figures 21-3 and 21-4.

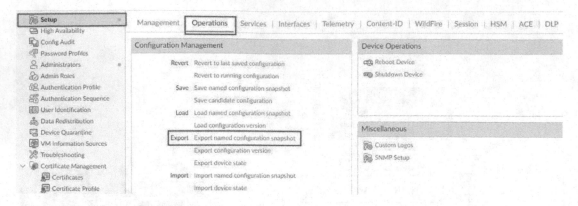

Figure 21-3. *Export named configuration snapshot*

After entering the file name, click on the "OK" button to save the running configuration as an XML file.

Figure 21-4. *Export Named Configuration running-config.xml*

Step 2: Next, we will ensure that the Palo Alto firewall is running the latest content release version. We will go to **Device ➤ Dynamic Updates** and **click Check Now** at the bottom of the page to retrieve the latest updates, as shown in Figure 21-5.

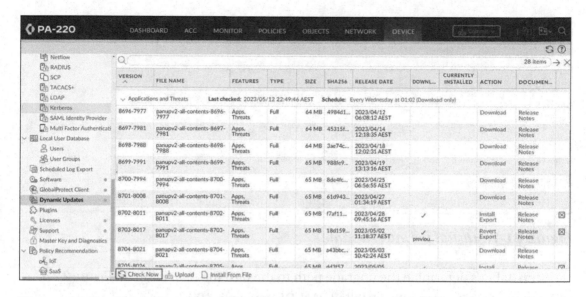

Figure 21-5. *Check Now to retrieve the latest updates*

We will then download and install the latest content update, as shown in Figures 21-6 and 21-7.

VERSION ⌃	FILE NAME	FEATURES	TYPE	SIZE	SHA256	RELEASE DATE	DOWN...	CURRENTLY INSTALLED	ACTION	DOCUME...	
⌄ Applications and Threats		**Last checked:** 2023/05/14 12:45:13 AEST			**Schedule:** Every Wednesday at 01:02 (Download only)						
8703-8017	panupv2-all-contents-8703-8017	Apps, Threats	Full	65 MB	18d15...	2023/05/02 11:18:37 AEST	✓		Install	Release Notes	☒
8704-8021	panupv2-all-contents-8704-8021	Apps, Threats	Full	65 MB	a43bb...	2023/05/03 10:42:24 AEST			Download	Release Notes	
8705-8026	panupv2-all-contents-8705-8026	Apps, Threats	Full	65 MB	dd3f5...	2023/05/05 11:13:23 AEST	✓		Install	Release Notes	☒
8706-8028	panupv2-all-contents-8706-8028	Apps, Threats	Full	65 MB	2b56c...	2023/05/09 09:52:56 AEST	✓	✓	Review Policies Review Apps	Release Notes	☒
8707-8033	panupv2-all-contents-8707-8033	Apps, Threats	Full	65 MB	95fe62...	2023/05/10 01:50:32 AEST			Download	Release Notes	
8708-8036	panupv2-all-contents-8708-8036	Apps, Threats	Full	65 MB	7738d...	2023/05/11 04:19:35 AEST			Download	Release Notes	

Figure 21-6. *Download the latest update*

VERSION ^	FILE NAME	FEATURES	TYPE	SIZE	SHA256	RELEASE DATE	DOWN...	CURRENTLY INSTALLED	ACTION	DOCUME...	
⌄ Applications and Threats		Last checked: 2023/05/14 12:46:23 AEST			Schedule:	Every Wednesday at 01:02 (Download only)					
8703-8017	panupv2-all-contents-8703-8017	Apps, Threats	Full	65 MB	18d15...	2023/05/02 11:18:37 AEST	✓		Install	Release Notes	☒
8704-8021	panupv2-all-contents-8704-8021	Apps, Threats	Full	65 MB	a43bb...	2023/05/03 10:42:24 AEST			Download	Release Notes	
8705-8026	panupv2-all-contents-8705-8026	Apps, Threats	Full	65 MB	dd3f5...	2023/05/05 11:13:23 AEST	✓		Install	Release Notes	☒
8706-8028	panupv2-all-contents-8706-8028	Apps, Threats	Full	65 MB	2b56c...	2023/05/09 09:52:56 AEST	✓	✓	Review Policies Review Apps	Release Notes	☒
8707-8033	panupv2-all-contents-8707-8033	Apps, Threats	Full	65 MB	95fe62...	2023/05/10 01:50:32 AEST			Download	Release Notes	
8708-8036	panupv2-all-contents-8708-8036	Apps, Threats	Full	65 MB	7738d...	2023/05/11 04:19:35 AEST	✓		Install Review Policies Review Apps	Release Notes	☒

Figure 21-7. *Install the latest update*

Step 3: Let's determine the upgrade path to the next major version. In Figure 21-8, you can see that the currently installed PAN-OS version is 10.1.9.

VERSION	SIZE	RELEASE DATE	AVAILABLE	CURRENTLY INSTALLED	ACTION		
10.1.9	367 MB	2023/02/05 15:26:54	Downloaded	✓	Reinstall	Release Notes	
10.1.9-h3	367 MB	2023/04/24 10:26:21			Download	Release Notes	
10.1.9-h1	367 MB	2023/03/07 08:57:10	Downloaded		Install	Release Notes	☒

Figure 21-8. *Check the current PAN-OS version*

Expand your knowledge:

Palo Alto PAN-OS Best Upgrade Practice

In PAN-OS versions prior to 10.0, the recommended upgrade path involved a two-step process. First, you would download the base version without performing the installation or rebooting. Next, you would proceed to download and install the latest preferred release of the version you intend to upgrade to. After the installation of the latest preferred release, a reboot prompt would appear. It is crucial to always consult the Palo Alto Documentation for the specific upgrade path relevant to the version you are upgrading to, as these paths may change with newer versions.

In this chapter, we will demonstrate the process of downloading the base version and subsequently downloading and installing the latest preferred version at the time of writing. This approach will be particularly beneficial for users who have yet to transition from older versions predating version 10, which are nearing their end-of-life phase. This methodology has been our standard practice before the introduction of newer versions beyond 10.0.

References:

`www.paloaltonetworks.com/services/support/end-of-life-announcements/end-of-life-summary`

`https://docs.paloaltonetworks.com/pan-os/10-1/pan-os-upgrade/upgrade-pan-os/upgrade-the-firewall-pan-os/determine-the-upgrade-path`

For this example, we will download the base version of 10.2.0, as shown in Figure 21-9.

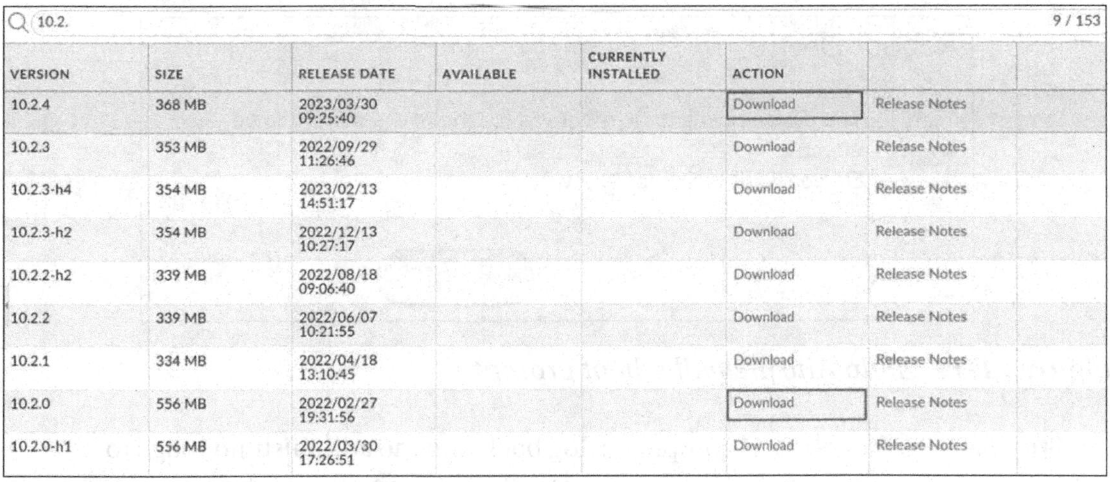

VERSION	SIZE	RELEASE DATE	AVAILABLE	CURRENTLY INSTALLED	ACTION	
10.2.4	368 MB	2023/03/30 09:25:40			Download	Release Notes
10.2.3	353 MB	2022/09/29 11:26:46			Download	Release Notes
10.2.3-h4	354 MB	2023/02/13 14:51:17			Download	Release Notes
10.2.3-h2	354 MB	2022/12/13 10:27:17			Download	Release Notes
10.2.2-h2	339 MB	2022/08/18 09:06:40			Download	Release Notes
10.2.2	339 MB	2022/06/07 10:21:55			Download	Release Notes
10.2.1	334 MB	2022/04/18 13:10:45			Download	Release Notes
10.2.0	556 MB	2022/02/27 19:31:56			Download	Release Notes
10.2.0-h1	556 MB	2022/03/30 17:26:51			Download	Release Notes

Figure 21-9. *Download base version 10.2.0*

Download and install version release 10.2.4 as shown in Figure 21-10.

VERSION	SIZE	RELEASE DATE	AVAILABLE	CURRENTLY INSTALLED	ACTION		
10.2.4	368 MB	2023/03/30 09:25:40	Downloaded		Install	Release Notes	☒
10.2.3	353 MB	2022/09/29 11:26:46			Download	Release Notes	
10.2.3-h4	354 MB	2023/02/13 14:51:17			Download	Release Notes	
10.2.3-h2	354 MB	2022/12/13 10:27:17			Download	Release Notes	
10.2.2-h2	339 MB	2022/08/18 09:06:40			Download	Release Notes	
10.2.2	339 MB	2022/06/07 10:21:55			Download	Release Notes	
10.2.1	334 MB	2022/04/18 13:10:45			Download	Release Notes	
10.2.0	556 MB	2022/02/27	Downloaded		Install	Release Notes	☒

Figure 21-10. *Install major version 10.2.4.*

Step 4: Once the installation is completed, we will be prompted with a reboot for the Palo Alto firewall to boot up with the new PAN-OS version 10.2.4, as shown in Figure 21-11. Reboot the device.

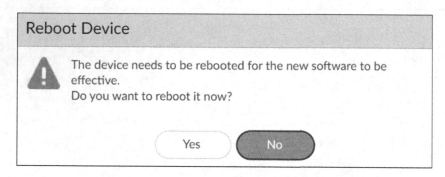

Figure 21-11. *Palo Alto firewall reboot prompt*

Step 5: Once the reboot is completed, log back into the administrator page to observe the successful boot-up of our Palo Alto firewall with the new PAN-OS version 10.2.4, as depicted in Figure 21-12.

VERSION ⌄	SIZE	RELEASE DATE	AVAILABLE	CURRENTLY INSTALLED	ACTION	
10.2.4	368 MB	2023/03/30 09:25:40	Downloaded	✓	Validate Export Reinstall	Release Notes

Figure 21-12. *Palo Alto firewall with the new PAN-OS version 10.2.4*

Having examined the manual upgrade processes from Palo Alto versions 10.1.9 to 10.2.4, let's now explore how we can transform this task into an Ansible playbook, enabling us to execute the upgrade as an automated script.

21.3 Writing a Palo Alto Firewall Upgrade Playbook: Automated Method

Now we have fully understood the PAN-OS upgrade process using Dynamic updates, let's create our basic set of files before writing our main PAN-OS upgrading playbook.

Step 1: In the same drill, we have been creating a chapter-specific working directory for each chapter, and we wanted to keep it simple and have all the components in a single directory. We will work in the ch21 directory.

Let's create the standard set of files, namely, ansible.cfg, inventory, and vars.yml files in sequence.

```
[jdoe@f38s1 ~]$ mkdir ch21 && cd ch21
[jdoe@f38s1 ch21]$ vi ansible.cfg
[jdoe@f38s1 ch21]$ cat ansible.cfg
[defaults]
inventory=inventory
```

For the last time, we will create a simple inventory file for our final lab.

```
[jdoe@f38s1 ch21]$ vi inventory
[jdoe@f38s1 ch21]$ cat inventory
[palo]
192.168.0.31
```

Let's create an unencrypted vars.yml file for now. The backup_config variable will be discussed in Section 21.4 on how it was derived.

```
[jdoe@f38s1 ch21]$ vi vars.yml
[jdoe@f38s1 ch21]$ cat vars.yml
---
provider:
  ip_address: '{{ inventory_hostname }}'
  username: admin
  password: Palo123!
```

backup_config: https://192.168.0.31/api/?
type=export&category=configuration&key=LUFRPT1mQXdpSUNwUitBMFRSY
m5DMU84cmOzUmZudmc9OGNxNOZhQitGamJtcmVPSjYyaHE2NThJZlIvaW8xcOo1
ZWFFUmloK3NDck5WWk81WVNWcmZ2OWpPQTNrcmdrcQ==

Step 2: After creating the file, let's proceed to encrypt it to secure sensitive information.

```
[jdoe@f38s1 ch21]$ ansible-vault encrypt vars.yml
New Vault password: ***************
Confirm New Vault password: ***************
Encryption successful
```

21.4 Writing a Playbook to Back Up the Running Configuration of a Palo Alto Firewall

In our first playbook, we will create a configuration backup using a combination of Ansible and Palo Alto's XML API. It is considered a best practice to back up the configuration before making any significant changes to our firewall. This allows us to recover easily in case any issues arise.

To begin, we will obtain the API key for the Palo Alto firewall, which will be used for authentication. Next, we will use the XML API syntax to export the configuration. To automate this process, we will store the XML API syntax in a vars.yml file. Then, we will use Ansible's ansible.builtin.get_url module to retrieve the configuration and store it in the specified destination directory (/home/jdoe/repo1/ch21/config_backup/). The configuration file will be named PAN01_backup_<date>_<time>.xml, incorporating the date and time of storage.

This approach ensures that we have a secure and automated backup of the configuration, providing peace of mind and enabling easy restoration if required.

Step 1: To begin the lab, create the "config_backup" directory under your working directory.

```
[jdoe@f38s1 ch21]$ mkdir config_backup
[jdoe@f38s1 ch21]$ ls config_backup
[blank directory]
```

Step 2: Let's look at the Palo Alto XML API component. To be able to use the Palo Alto XML API, we need to generate the API key from our browser as follows:

https://192.168.0.31/api/?type=keygen&user=admin&password=Palo123!

This XML file does not appear to have any style information associated with it. The document tree is shown here:

```
<response status="success">
<result>
<key> LUFRPT1mQXdpSUNwUitBMFRSYm5DMU84cm0zUmZudmc9OGNxNoZhQitGamJtcm
VPSjYyaHE2NThJZlIvaW8xcOo1ZWFFUmloK3NDck5WWk81WVNWcmZ2OWp
PQTNrcmdrcQ==</key>
</result>
</response>
```

Step 3: We will then use the XML API Url with the API key to export the running configuration. To get the XML API Url, from your browser, go to https://192.168.0.31/api. We will then be redirected to the XML API page (Figure 21-13), where we can get the XML API Url (Figure 21-14) that we will need to export the configuration.

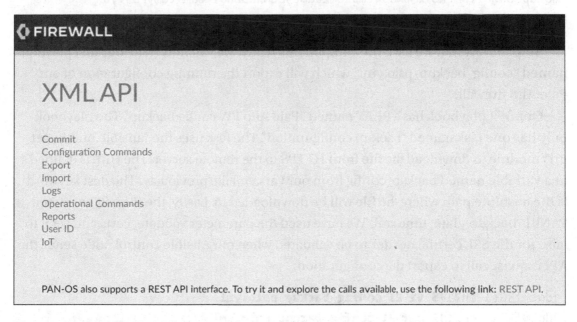

Figure 21-13. *XML API page*

Figure 21-14. *XML API Url to export the running configuration*

Step 4: Now, to extract the configuration, we will use the following syntax that includes the firewall's IP, https://192.168.0.31/api, the XML API Url, and the API key.

```
https://192.168.0.31/api/?type=export&category=configuration&key=LUFRPT
1mQXdpSUNwUitBMFRSYm5DMU84cmOzUmZudmc9OGNxNOZhQitGamJtcmVPSjYya
HE2NThJZlIvaW8xcOo1ZWFFUmlOK3NDck5WWk81WVNWcmZ2OWpPQTNrcmdrcQ==
```

Step 5: Now that we have the components ready, we will now write our first playbook named "config_backup_palo.yml", which will export the running configuration of our Palo Alto firewall.

Our first playbook has a PLAY named "Palo Alto FW config backup". The playbook only has one task named "backup configuration". The task uses the "ansible.builtin.get_url" module to download the file from HTTPS to the remote server. The URL is defined in a variable named backup_config from our vars.yml file previously. The dest keyword is the absolute path where the file will be downloaded to. Lastly, the file will be named PAN01_backup_date_time.xml. We have used the parameter validate_certs and set it to false for the SSL certificates not to be validated when our Ansible control node sends the API request call to export the configuration.

```
[jdoe@f38s1 ch21]$ vi 21_config_backup_palo.yml
[jdoe@f38s1 ch21]$ cat 21_config_backup_palo.yml
---
- name: Palo Alto FW config backup
```

```
  hosts: palo
  gather_facts: true
  connection: local
  vars_files: vars.yml

tasks:
- name: backup configuration
  ansible.builtin.get_url:
    url:  "{{ backup_config}}"
    dest: /home/jdoe/repo1/ch21/config_backup/PANO1_backup_{{ ansible_date_
    time.date }}_{{ ansible_date_time.time }}.xml
    validate_certs: false
```

21.5 Writing a Playbook Task to Update the Content (Applications and Threats) of a Palo Alto Firewall

Moving on to our second playbook, named update_content.yml, we will discuss only the tasks of the playbook for brevity. The tasks include a content check, downloading the latest content update, checking the content download status, installing the latest content update, and checking the content install status.

The first task is to request a content check for the Palo Alto firewall's application and threat update to be able to pull the updated and latest ones from the Palo Alto Networks update server. The task is named Request content check. The Ansible task uses the panos_op module to execute an operational command to the firewall. The parameter provider contains the credentials to log in to the firewall as defined in our vars.yml file. We will use an XML command by setting the parameter cmd_is_xml as true and use the XML syntax to execute the command.

Step 1: For us to be able to get the XML command, we will need to go back to the XML API page. This time, we will go to the operational commands section, as shown in Figure 21-15.

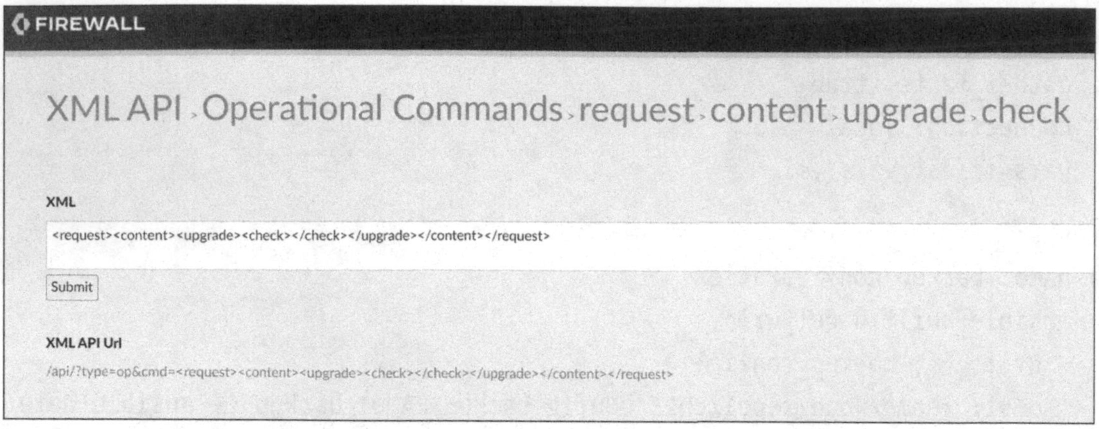

Figure 21-15. *XML API operational command*

Step 2: Now, let's begin to write the 21_update_content.yml playbook.

```
[jdoe@f38s1 ch21]$ vi 21_update_content.yml
[jdoe@f38s1 ch21]$ cat 21_update_content.yml
---
- name: App and Threat Update
  hosts: palo
  gather_facts: false
  connection: local
  vars_files: vars.yml

tasks:
 - name: Request content check
    panos_op:
      provider: '{{ provider }}'
      cmd: <request><content><upgrade><check></check></upgrade></content></
      request>
      cmd_is_xml: true
```

The second task is to download the latest content update. The task is named
Download latest content update. The Ansible task uses the panos_op module to execute
an operational command to the firewall. The parameter provider contains the credentials
to log in to the firewall as defined in our vars.yml file. We will use an XML command
by setting the parameter cmd_is_xml as true and use the XML syntax to execute the
command. We will then record the value in a new variable named download_content.

```
- name: Download the latest content update
  panos_op:
    provider: '{{ provider }}'
    cmd: <request><content><upgrade><download><latest></latest></
    download></upgrade></content></request>
    cmd_is_xml: true
    register: download_content
```

The third task is to check the content download status for it to finish before proceeding to the next task. The task is named Check content download status. The Ansible task uses the panos_op module to execute an operational command to the firewall. The command is "show jobs id <job>" where the value of the "job" will be gathered using the from_json filter and get the value of the key named "job" from the variable download_content registered in the previous task. The command will run every 60 seconds until the status is FIN (finished). The maximum retry value is set to 30, which will equate to a 30-minute task or less and will stop the playbook if it is not finished within the number of retries.

```
- name: Check content download status
  panos_op:
    provider: '{{ provider }}'
    cmd: 'show jobs id {{ (download_content.stdout | from_json).response.
    result.job }}'
  register: download_job
  until: download_job is not failed and (download_job.stdout | from_
  json).response.result.job.status == 'FIN'
  retries: 30
  delay: 60
```

For better understanding of the syntax, we will show the json output of the registered variables "download_content" and "download_job". This is for illustration purposes only, and we will not include this print output/task in our playbook.

```
[print download_content] ********************************************
ok: [192.168.0.31] => {
    "download_content.stdout": {
        "response": {
```

```
            "@code": "19",
            "@status": "success",
            "result": {
                "job": "11",
                "msg": {
                    "line": "Download job enqueued with jobid 11"
                }
            }
        }
    }
}

[print download_job] *****************************************************
ok: [192.168.0.31] => {
    "download_job.stdout": {
        "response": {
            "@status": "success",
            "result": {
                "job": {
                    "description": null,
                    "details": {
                        "line": "File successfully downloaded"
                    },
                    "id": "11",
                    "positionInQ": "0",
                    "progress": "2023/05/08 22:36:37",
                    "queued": "NO",
                    "result": "OK",
                    "status": "FIN",
                    "stoppable": "no",
                    "tdeq": "22:36:20",
                    "tenq": "2023/05/08 22:36:20",
                    "tfin": "2023/05/08 22:36:37",
                    "type": "Downld",
                    "user": null,
```

```
        "warnings": null
      }
    }
```

The fourth task is to install the latest content update, which we have downloaded in the previous task. The task is named Install the latest content update. The Ansible task uses the panos_op module to execute an operational command to the firewall. The parameter provider contains the credentials to log in to the firewall as defined in our vars.yml file. We will use an XML command by setting the parameter cmd_is_xml as true and use the XML syntax to execute the command. We will then register the value in a new variable named install_content.

```
- name: Install latest content update
  panos_op:
    provider: '{{ provider }}'
    cmd: <request><content><upgrade><install><version>latest</version></
    install></upgrade></content></request>
    cmd_is_xml: true
  register: install_content
```

Lastly, the fifth and final task of the content_update.yml playbook is to check the content install status. The task is named Check content install status. The Ansible task uses the panos_op module to execute an operational command to the firewall. The command is "show jobs id <job>" where the value of the "job" will be gathered using the from_json filter and get the value of the key named "job" from the variable install_content registered in the previous task. The command will run every 60 seconds until the status is FIN (finished). The maximum retry value is set to 30, which will equate to a 30-minute task or less and will stop the playbook if it is not finished within the number of retries.

```
  - name: Check content install status
    panos_op:
      provider: '{{ provider }}'
      cmd: 'show jobs id {{ (install_content.stdout | from_json).response.
      result.job }}'
    register: install_job
```

```
    until: install_job is not failed and (install_job.stdout | from_json).
    response.result.job.status == 'FIN'
    retries: 30
    delay: 60
```

21.6 Writing a Playbook Task to Upgrade the PAN-OS of a Palo Alto Firewall

And now, for our final playbook named update_panos.yml, we will upgrade the firmware to the next major version. The tasks include a download of the PAN-OS base version, a download of the PAN-OS desired version, installation of the PAN-OS desired version with a reboot, pause for restart checks, and checking if the device is ready.

The first task is to download the base version of the next major version. The task is named "Download PAN-OS base version". The Ansible task uses the paloaltonetworks. panos.panos_software module to download the base version. The parameter provider contains the credentials to log in to the firewall as defined in our vars.yml file. The parameter version is configured to call a variable named base_version, which we have defined in the vars section with a value of 10.2.0. The parameter install is set to false. The parameter restart is set to false as well.

```
[jdoe@f38s1 ch21]$ vi 21_update_panos.yml
[jdoe@f38s1 ch21]$ cat 21_ update_panos.yml
---
- name: PANOS Upgrade
  hosts: palo
  gather_facts: false
  connection: local
  vars_files: vars.yml

  vars:
    base_version: '10.2.0'
    desired_version: '10.2.4'

  tasks:
  - name: Download PAN-OS base version
    paloaltonetworks.panos.panos_software:
```

```
    provider: '{{ provider }}'
    version: '{{ base_version }}'
    install: false
    restart: false
```

The second task is to download the desired PAN-OS version. The task is named "Download PAN-OS desired version". The Ansible task uses the paloaltonetworks.panos. panos_software module to download the desired version. The parameter provider contains the credentials to log in to the firewall as defined in our vars.yml file. The parameter version is configured to call a variable named desired_version, which we have defined in the vars section with a value of 10.2.4. The parameter install is set to false. The parameter restart is set to false as well.

```
  - name: Download PAN-OS desired version
    paloaltonetworks.panos.panos_software:
      provider: '{{ provider }}'
      version: '{{ desired_version }}'
      install: false
      restart: false
```

The third task is to install the desired PAN-OS version. The task is named Install PAN-OS version and Reboot. The Ansible task uses the panos_software module to install the desired version. The parameter provider contains the credentials to log in to the firewall as defined in our vars.yml file. The parameter version is configured to call a variable named desired_version, which was downloaded in the previous task. This time, the parameter install is set to true, and the parameter restart is set to true as well.

```
  - name: Install PAN-OS version and Reboot
    paloaltonetworks.panos.panos_software:
      provider: '{{ provider }}'
      version: '{{ desired_version }}'
      install: true
      restart: true
```

The fourth task is to use the Ansible pause module to pause before proceeding to the next while the firewall is rebooting. You can vary the time based on how long you need for the remaining tasks to continue. The module will prompt you to continue or abort.

This module can be very helpful if you would want an interactive response in between tasks or when you need to wait within a specific time frame before proceeding with the next tasks.

```
- name: Pause for Restart Checks
  pause:
    minutes: 10
```

Finally, the last task is to check if the device is ready. The task is named Check if the device is ready. The Ansible task uses the panos_op module to execute the command show chassis-ready. The parameter provider contains the credentials to log in to the firewall as defined in our vars.yml file. The command to be executed when the Ansible control node can access the Palo Alto firewall is "show chassis-ready". The conditional statement changed_when is set to false for Ansible not to report the status as changed in the play recap as there was no change in this task. The parameter register will store the output of the command in the variable named chassis. The conditional statement is set to check that the output of the variable chassis is not failed and that the result of the show chassis-ready is yes before it stops running the task. It will run the task within 60 retries every 60 seconds.

```
- name: Check if the device is ready
  paloaltonetworks.panos.panos_op:
    provider: '{{ provider }}'
    cmd: 'show chassis-ready'
  changed_when: false
  register: chassis
  until: chassis is not failed and (chassis.stdout | from_json).response.
  result == 'yes'
  retries: 60
  delay: 60
```

21.7 Running the Playbook to Back Up the Running Configuration on a Palo Alto Firewall

We can now execute our first playbook, named "21_config_backup_palo.yml". Before running it, let's verify the contents of the /home/jdoe/repo1/ch21/config_backup directory and check for any existing files. Once we have confirmed the current files in the directory, we can proceed with running our playbook to back up the configuration and store it in the specified location. Finally, we will perform a verification step to ensure that the backup configuration has been successfully stored.

Step 1: Our first playbook, "21_config_backup_palo.yml", is to back up the running configuration. Let's check files in /home/jdoe/repo1/ch21/config_backup directory, and we can see we have a configuration backup saved on May 2.

```
[jdoe@f38s1 ch21 config_backup]$ ls -l
-rw-r--r-- 1 jdoe jdoe 50679 May  2 21:13 PAN01_backup_2023-05-02.xml
-rw-r--r-- 1 jdoe jdoe 50679 May  2 21:01 PAN01_
backup_2023-05-02_21:01:44.xml
-rw-r--r-- 1 jdoe jdoe 50679 May  2 21:16 PAN01_
backup_2023-05-02_21:16:35.xml
-rw-r--r-- 1 jdoe jdoe 50679 May  2 21:16 PAN01_
backup_2023-05-02_21:16:54.xml
```

Step 2: Now, let's run the 21_config_backup_palo.yml playbook. We will execute the playbook and query the variables from the vars.yml file to be used in the playbook with the –ask-vault-pass command to decrypt the encrypted file and grab the variables needed to execute the playbook.

The "PLAY RECAP" section in the Ansible output summarizes the status of the tasks executed on each target host. In this example, the target host's IP address is 192.168.0.31. The output shows that there are two tasks executed on this host, and it was successful (ok=2). With this task, one change made a change to the system (changed=1), while 0 tasks were unreachable, failed, or skipped (unreachable=0, failed=0, skipped=0). Finally, no tasks required being rescued or ignored (rescued=0, ignored=0).

```
[jdoe@f38s1 ch21]$ ansible-playbook --ask-vault-pass 21_config_backup_
palo.yml
Vault password:*******
PLAY [Palo Alto FW
configbackup]*********************************************
TASK [Gathering Fac
ts]********************************************************
ok: [192.168.0.31]
```

```
TASK [backup
configuration]***********************************************************
changed: [192.168.0.31]

PLAY RECAP *************************************************************
192.168.0.31                 : ok=2    changed=1    unreachable=0
failed=0    skipped=0    rescued=0    ignored=0
```

Step 3: After running the 21_config_backup_palo.yml playbook, let's check our config_backup directory. We can now see that we have a new configuration file stored dated May 12 with the specific time. The date and time were gathered from the facts of our target node.

```
[jdoe@f38s1 ch21]$ cd config_backup/
[jdoe@f38s1 ch21 config_backup]$ ls -l
total 260
-rw-r--r-- 1 jdoe jdoe 50679 May  2 21:13 PANO1_backup_2023-05-02.xml
-rw-r--r-- 1 jdoe jdoe 50679 May  2 21:01 PANO1_backup_2023-05-02_
21:01:44.xml
-rw-r--r-- 1 jdoe jdoe 50679 May  2 21:16 PANO1_backup_2023-05-02_
21:16:35.xml
-rw-r--r-- 1 jdoe jdoe 50679 May  2 21:16 PANO1_backup_2023-05-02_
21:16:54.xml
-rw-r--r-- 1 jdoe jdoe 50679 May 12 21:54 PANO1_backup_2023-05-12_
21:54:14.xml
```

21.8 Running the Playbook to Update the Application and Threats Content of a Palo Alto Firewall

Our second playbook, 21_update_content.yml, is to update the application and threat content of the Palo Alto firewall. It is recommended to update to the latest release before upgrading to the next PAN-OS version.

Step 1: Let's first check the current content update we have. As you can see, we have version 8703-8017 currently installed.

```
admin@PAN01> request content upgrade info
Version        Size    Released on Downloaded     Installed
-------------------------------------------------------------------
8696-7977      64MB 2023/04/12 06:08:12 AEST        no            no
8706-8028      65MB 2023/05/09 09:52:56 AEST        yes           no
8698-7988      64MB 2023/04/18 12:02:31 AEST        no            no
8699-7991      65MB 2023/04/19 13:13:16 AEST        yes           no
8697-7981      64MB 2023/04/14 12:18:35 AEST        no            no
8701-8008      65MB 2023/04/27 01:34:19 AEST        no            no
8705-8026      65MB 2023/05/05 11:13:23 AEST        yes           no
8704-8021      65MB 2023/05/03 10:42:24 AEST        no            no
8702-8011      65MB 2023/04/28 09:45:16 AEST        yes           no
8703-8017      65MB 2023/05/02 11:18:37 AEST        yes       current
8700-7994      65MB 2023/04/25 06:56:55 AEST        no            no
```

Step 2: Now, let's run the 21_update_content.yml playbook. We will execute the playbook and query the variables from the vars.yml file to be used in the playbook with the –ask-vault-pass command to decrypt the encrypted file and grab the variables needed to execute the playbook.

The "PLAY RECAP" section in the Ansible output summarizes the status of the tasks executed on each target host. In this example, the target host's IP address is 192.168.0.31. The output shows that there are five tasks executed on this host, and it was successful (ok=5). With this task, three changes made a change to the system (changed=3), while 0 tasks were unreachable, failed, or skipped (unreachable=0, failed=0, skipped=0). Finally, no tasks required being rescued or ignored (rescued=0, ignored=0).

```
[jdoe@f38s1 ch21]$ ansible-playbook --ask-vault-pass 21_update_content.yml
Vault password:*******
PLAY [App and Threat Update] ********************************************

TASK [Request content check] *******************************************
 changed: [192.168.0.31]

TASK [Download latest content update***********************************
changed: [192.168.0.31]

TASK [Check content download status] ***********************************
```

```
FAILED - RETRYING: Check content download status (30 retries left).
FAILED - RETRYING: Check content download status (29 retries left).
FAILED - RETRYING: Check content download status (28 retries left).
ok: [192.168.0.31]

TASK [Install latest content update] **********************************
changed: [192.168.0.31]

TASK [Check content install status] ***********************************
FAILED - RETRYING: Check content install status (30 retries left).
FAILED - RETRYING: Check content install status (29 retries left).
FAILED - RETRYING: Check content install status (28 retries left).
FAILED - RETRYING: Check content install status (27 retries left).
FAILED - RETRYING: Check content install status (26 retries left).
FAILED - RETRYING: Check content install status (25 retries left).
FAILED - RETRYING: Check content install status (24 retries left).
FAILED - RETRYING: Check content install status (23 retries left).
FAILED - RETRYING: Check content install status (22 retries left).
FAILED - RETRYING: Check content install status (21 retries left).
FAILED - RETRYING: Check content install status (20 retries left).
FAILED - RETRYING: Check content install status (19 retries left).
FAILED - RETRYING: Check content install status (18 retries left).
FAILED - RETRYING: Check content install status (17 retries left).
ok: [192.168.0.31]

PLAY RECAP ************************************************************
192.168.0.31                  : ok=5    changed=3    unreachable=0
failed=0    skipped=0    rescued=0    ignored=0
```

Step 3: Lastly, let's confirm that we have the latest content update installed. We now have version 8709-8047 as the current one, whereas we have version 8703-8017 as the previous one.

```
admin@PANO1> request content upgrade info
Version     Size    Released on Downloaded  Installed
----------------------------------------------------------------------
8707-8033   65MB 2023/05/10 01:50:32 AEST    no     no
8708-8036   65MB 2023/05/11 04:19:35 AEST    no     no
```

```
8696-7977    64MB  2023/04/12 06:08:12 AEST    no    no
8706-8028    65MB  2023/05/09 09:52:56 AEST    yes   no
8698-7988    64MB  2023/04/18 12:02:31 AEST    no    no
8699-7991    65MB  2023/04/19 13:13:16 AEST    no    no
8697-7981    64MB  2023/04/14 12:18:35 AEST    no    no
8709-8047    65MB  2023/05/12 09:25:02 AEST    yes   current
8701-8008    65MB  2023/04/27 01:34:19 AEST    no    no
8705-8026    65MB  2023/05/05 11:13:23 AEST    yes   no
8704-8021    65MB  2023/05/03 10:42:24 AEST    no    no
8702-8011    65MB  2023/04/28 09:45:16 AEST    yes   no
8703-8017    65MB  2023/05/02 11:18:37 AEST    yes   previous
8700-7994    65MB  2023/04/25 06:56:55 AEST    no    no
```

21.9 Running the Playbook to Update the PAN-OS Version of a Palo Alto Firewall

Our third and final playbook for this chapter, update_panos.yml, is to upgrade the PAN-OS version of the Palo Alto firewall from version 10.1.9 to 10.2.4.

Step 1: Now, let's check the current PAN-OS version. As you can see, we have sw-version 10.1.9.

```
admin@PANO1> show system info | match time\|sw-version
time: Sun May 14 11:30:30 2023
uptime: 0 days, 0:37:59
sw-version: 10.1.9
```

Step 2: We can now run our 21_update_panos.yml playbook. We will execute the playbook and query the variables from the vars.yml file to be used in the playbook with the –ask-vault-pass command to decrypt the encrypted file and grab the variables needed to execute the playbook. In this playbook, we have set the variable base_version as 10.2.0 and the variable desired_version as 10.2.4.

The "PLAY RECAP" section in the Ansible output summarizes the status of the tasks executed on each target host. In this example, the target host's IP address is 192.168.0.31. The output shows that there are five tasks executed on this host, and it was successful (ok=5). With this task, one change made a change to the system (changed=1), while 0 tasks were unreachable, failed, or skipped (unreachable=0, failed=0, skipped=0). Finally, no tasks required being rescued or ignored (rescued=0, ignored=0).

```
[jdoe@f38s1 ch21]$ ansible-playbook --ask-vault-pass 21_update_panos.yml
Vault password:*******
PLAY [PANOS Upgrade] ************************************************

TASK [Download PAN-OS base version] ********************************
changed: [192.168.0.31]

TASK [Download PAN-OS desired version] *****************************
changed: [192.168.0.31]

TASK [Install PAN-OS version and Reboot] ***************************
changed: [192.168.0.31]

TASK [Pause for Restart Checks] ***********************************
Pausing for 600 seconds
(ctrl+C then 'C' = continue early, ctrl+C then 'A' = abort)
ok: [192.168.0.31]

TASK [Check if device is ready] ***********************************
FAILED - RETRYING: Check if device is ready (60 retries left).
FAILED - RETRYING: Check if device is ready (59 retries left).
FAILED - RETRYING: Check if device is ready (58 retries left).
FAILED - RETRYING: Check if device is ready (57 retries left).
FAILED - RETRYING: Check if device is ready (56 retries left).
FAILED - RETRYING: Check if device is ready (55 retries left).
ok: [192.168.0.31]

PLAY RECAP *********************************************************
192.168.0.31               : ok=5    changed=1    unreachable=0
failed=0    skipped=0    rescued=0    ignored=0
```

Step 3: Since the device is ready, we can check if the firewall has booted up with the new software, which is now 10.2.4.

```
admin@PANO1> show system info | match time\|sw-version
time: Sun May 14 13:52:50 2023
uptime: 0 days, 0:40:49
sw-version: 10.2.4
```

Congratulations! You have completed the PAN-OS upgrade. In this chapter, we have covered the manual upgrade processes in detail and then transformed these tasks into scripted playbooks using YAML. By breaking down the tasks into three playbooks, we have eliminated the need for manual mouse clicks on the GUI. By understanding the procedures from end to end and mastering each step, you can now convert them into Ansible plays and tasks within your playbooks. With this knowledge, you can continue your journey into network automation using Ansible playbooks.

Here are our three playbooks for your reference:

21_CONFIG_BACKUP_PALO.YML

```yaml
---
- name: Palo Alto FW config backup
  hosts: palo
  gather_facts: true
  connection: local
  vars_files: vars.yml

  tasks:

  - name: backup configuration
    ansible.builtin.get_url:
      url:  "{{ backup_config}}"
      dest: /home/jdoe/repo1/ch21/ PANO1_backup_{{ ansible_date_time.date
      }}_{{ ansible_date_time.time }}.xml
      validate_certs: false
```

21_UPDATE_CONTENT.YML

```yaml
---
- name: App and Threat Update
```

```
    hosts: palo
    gather_facts: false
    connection: local
    vars_files: vars.yml

    tasks:
    - name: Request content check
      paloaltonetworks.panos.panos_op:
        provider: '{{ provider }}'
        cmd: <request><content><upgrade><check></check></upgrade></content>
        </request>
        cmd_is_xml: true

    - name: Download latest content update
      panos_op:
        provider: '{{ provider }}'
        cmd: <request><content><upgrade><download><latest></latest>
        </download></upgrade></content></request>
        cmd_is_xml: true
      register: download_content

    - name: Check content download status
      paloaltonetworks.panos.panos_op:
        provider: '{{ provider }}'
        cmd: 'show jobs id {{ (download_content.stdout | from_json).response.
        result.job }}'
      register: download_job
      until: download_job is not failed and (download_job.stdout | from_json).
      response.result.job.status == 'FIN'
      retries: 30
      delay: 60

    - name: Install latest content update
      paloaltonetworks.panos.panos_op:
        provider: '{{ provider }}'
        cmd: <request><content><upgrade><install><version>latest</version></
        install></upgrade></content></request>
        cmd_is_xml: true
      register: install_content
```

```yaml
- name: Check content install status
  paloaltonetworks.panos.panos_op:
    provider: '{{ provider }}'
    cmd: 'show jobs id {{ (install_content.stdout | from_json).response.
    result.job }}'
  register: install_job
  until: install_job is not failed and (install_job.stdout | from_json).
  response.result.job.status == 'FIN'
  retries: 30
  delay: 60
```

21_UPDATE_PAN-OS.YML

```yaml
---
- name: PANOS Upgrade
  hosts: palo
  gather_facts: false
  connection: local
  vars_files: vars.yml

  vars:
    base_version: '10.2.0'
    desired_version: '10.2.4'

  tasks:
  - name: Download PAN-OS base version
    paloaltonetworks.panos.panos_software:
      provider: '{{ provider }}'
      version: '{{ base_version }}'
      install: false
      restart: false

  - name: Download PAN-OS desired version
    paloaltonetworks.panos.panos_software:
      provider: '{{ provider }}'
      version: '{{ desired_version }}'
      install: false
      restart: false
    register: download_desired
```

```
  - name: Install PAN-OS version and Reboot
    paloaltonetworks.panos.panos_software:
      provider: '{{ provider }}'
      version: '{{ desired_version }}'
      install: true
      restart: true

  - name: Pause for Restart Checks
    pause:
      minutes: 10

  - name: Check if device is ready
    paloaltonetworks.panos.panos_op:
      provider: '{{ provider }}'
      cmd: 'show chassis-ready'
    changed_when: false
    register: chassis
    until: chassis is not failed and (chassis.stdout | from_json).response.
    result == 'yes'
    retries: 60
    delay: 60
```

21.10 Summary

In conclusion, this chapter has provided an exploration of upgrading Palo Alto's PAN-OS Firewall, a critical task for security engineers working with production firewalls in the real world. We have covered manual upgrade procedures and reviewed a transition to an automated upgrade approach using Ansible playbooks. If the work is mundane, repeatable, and predictable, it is a good target for Ansible automation. By breaking down the manual upgrade processes, you have gained valuable insights into the intricate aspects involved in upgrading PAN-OS firewalls. Additionally, we have demonstrated the effectiveness and efficiency of leveraging Ansible playbooks to automate the upgrade process. This approach has allowed us to break down the upgrade components into manageable YAML code snippets, facilitating an end-to-end understanding of the full automation workflow. Ultimately, we can consolidate all playbooks into a single playbook to transform it into an application, transitioning the traditional and manual processes into lines of YAML code in an Ansible playbook. Through this chapter, you have acquired not only practical knowledge of upgrading Palo Alto's PAN-OS Firewall but also gained hands-on experience in working with YAML codes, leveraging the power of Ansible automation capabilities. This knowledge equips you with the skills sought after in today's job market to successfully navigate the intricacies of firewall upgrades and harness the power of automation in your production network.

Regrettably, our book comes to a close, and we must bid our farewells. Remember, network automation is an everlasting expedition; it begins but never truly concludes. May your future network automation expeditions be filled with triumph and satisfaction!

Index

A

© Brendan Choi and Erwin Medina 2023
B. Choi and E. Medina, *Introduction to Ansible Network Automation*,
https://doi.org/10.1007/978-1-4842-9624-0

I

J

K

L

M

P

Q

R

S

Printed in the United States
by Baker & Taylor Publisher Services